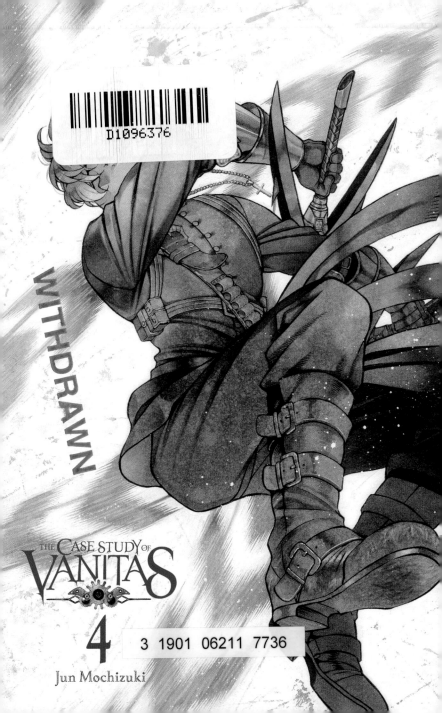

THE CASE STUDY OF
VANITAS

4

Jun Mochizuki

# THE CASE STUDY OF VANITAS 4

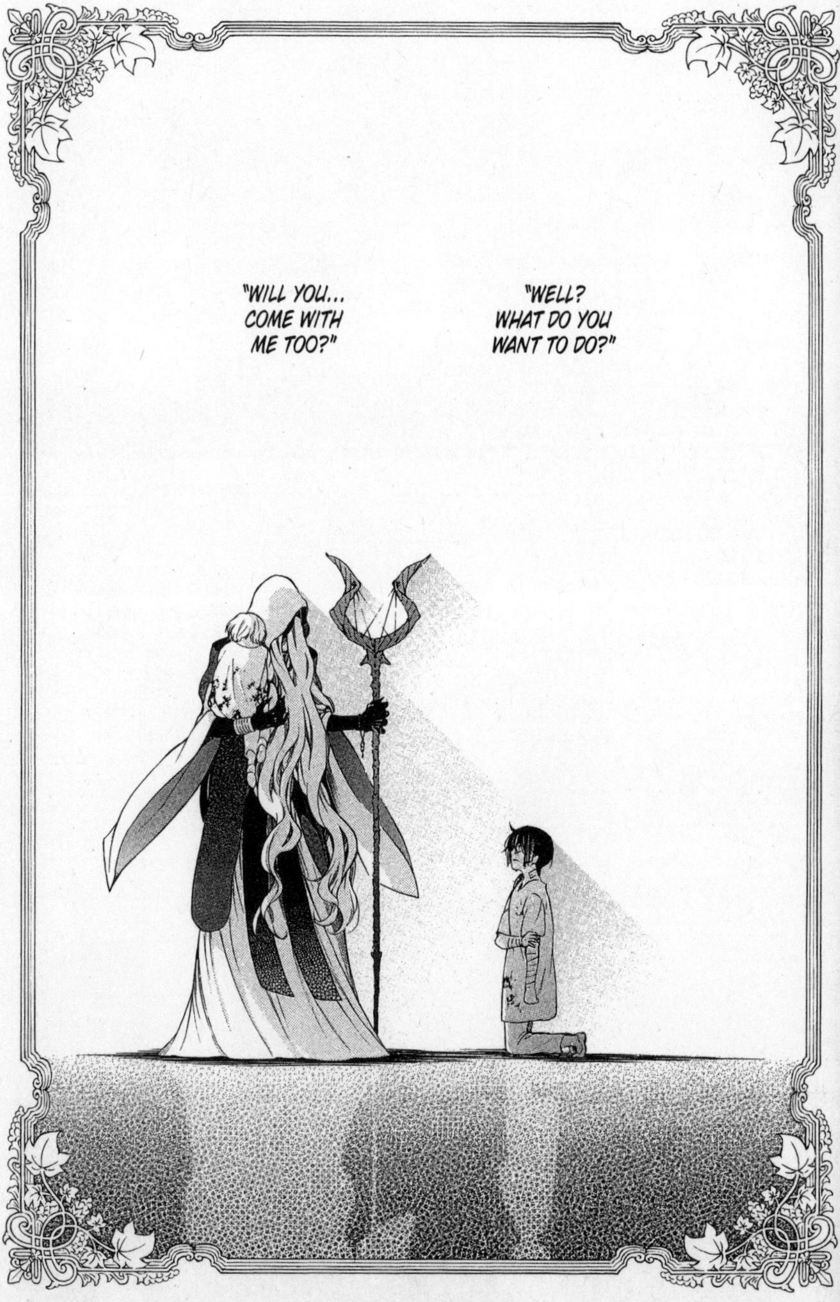
"WELL? WHAT DO YOU WANT TO DO?"
"WILL YOU... COME WITH ME TOO?"

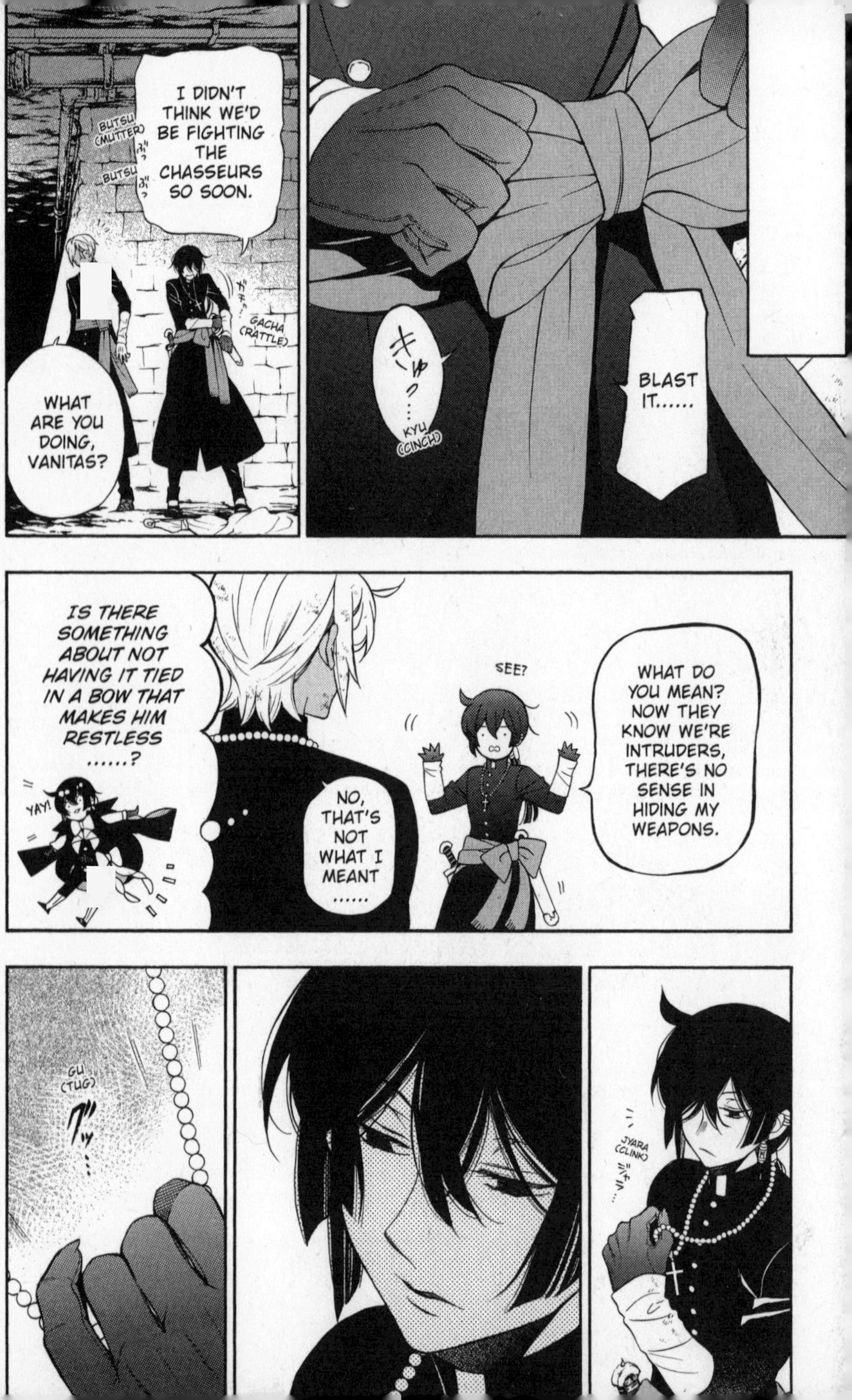

キュッ……
KYU (CINCH)
BLAST IT......
I DIDN'T THINK WE'D BE FIGHTING THE CHASSEURS SO SOON.
BUTSU (MUTTER)
BUTSU
ガチャ
GACHA (RATTLE)
WHAT ARE YOU DOING, VANITAS?
WHAT DO YOU MEAN? NOW THEY KNOW WE'RE INTRUDERS, THERE'S NO SENSE IN HIDING MY WEAPONS.
SEE?
IS THERE SOMETHING ABOUT NOT HAVING IT TIED IN A BOW THAT MAKES HIM RESTLESS ......?
NO, THAT'S NOT WHAT I MEANT ......
YAY!
JYARA (CLINK)
GU (TUG)

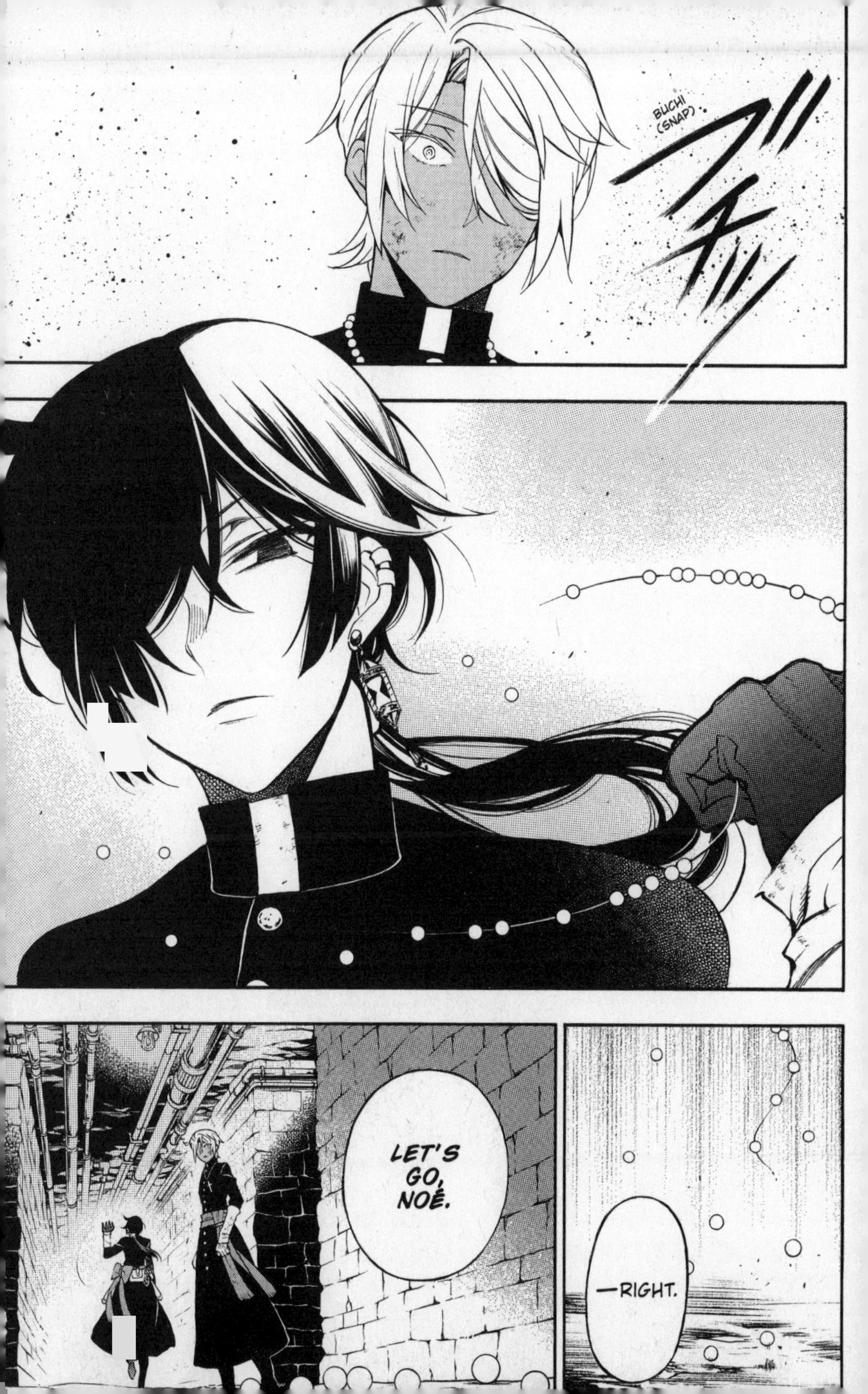
BUCHI (SNAP)
LET'S GO, NOÉ.
—RIGHT.

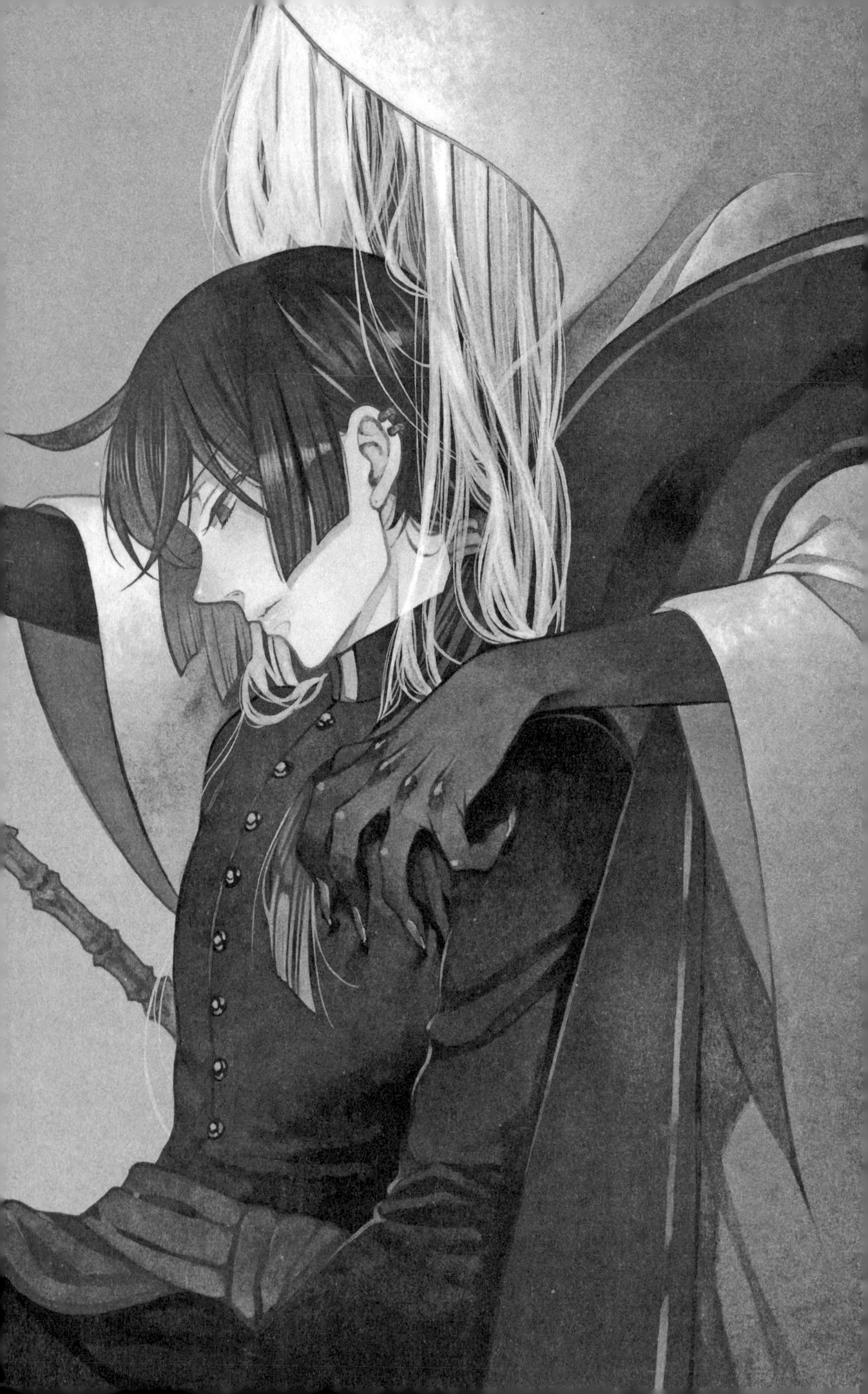

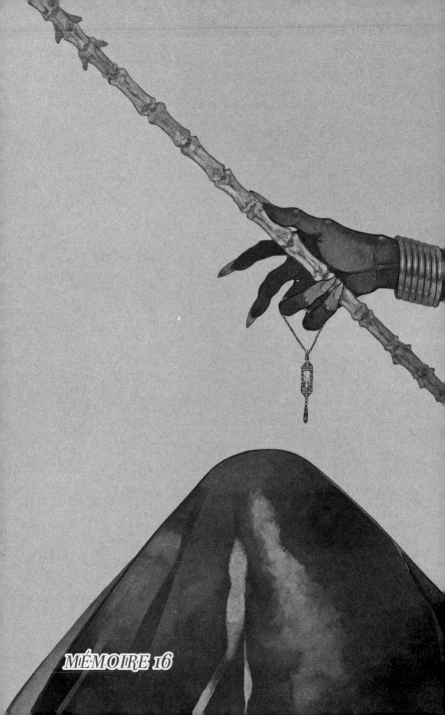

MÉMOIRE 16

Les Mémoires de Vanitas

# THE CASE STUDY OF
# VANITAS

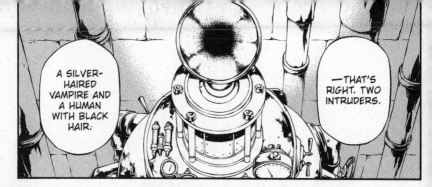

—THAT'S RIGHT. TWO INTRUDERS.
A SILVER-HAIRED VAMPIRE AND A HUMAN WITH BLACK HAIR.
THEY'VE STOLEN CLOTHES FROM CLERGY-MEN.
THE VAMPIRE IS A FORMIDABLE FOE. BE CAREFUL.
AND...
...MAKE SURE YOU TAKE THE HUMAN ALIVE.
WHAT-EVER YOU DO, DON'T KILL HIM.
WHEW...
TO THINK I'D HAVE TROUBLE WITH A COUPLE OF INTRUDERS...
OLIVIER'S GOING TO BE MAD AT ME LATER.

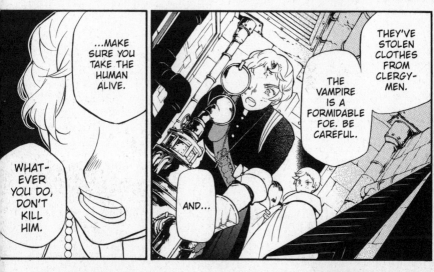

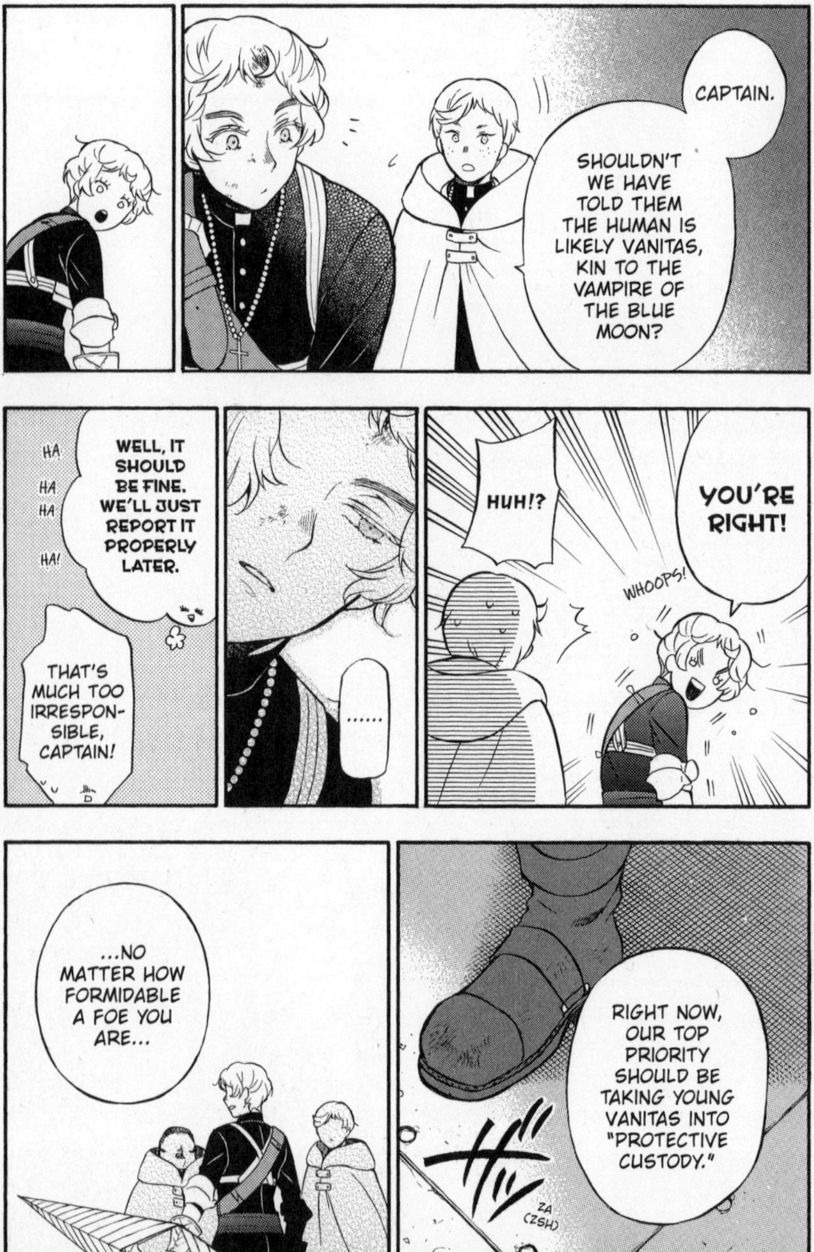
CAPTAIN.
SHOULDN'T WE HAVE TOLD THEM THE HUMAN IS LIKELY VANITAS, KIN TO THE VAMPIRE OF THE BLUE MOON?
YOU'RE RIGHT!
HUH!?
WHOOPS!
......
HA HA HA HA!
WELL, IT SHOULD BE FINE. WE'LL JUST REPORT IT PROPERLY LATER.
THAT'S MUCH TOO IRRESPON-SIBLE, CAPTAIN!
RIGHT NOW, OUR TOP PRIORITY SHOULD BE TAKING YOUNG VANITAS INTO "PROTECTIVE CUSTODY."
ZA (ZSH)
...NO MATTER HOW FORMIDABLE A FOE YOU ARE...

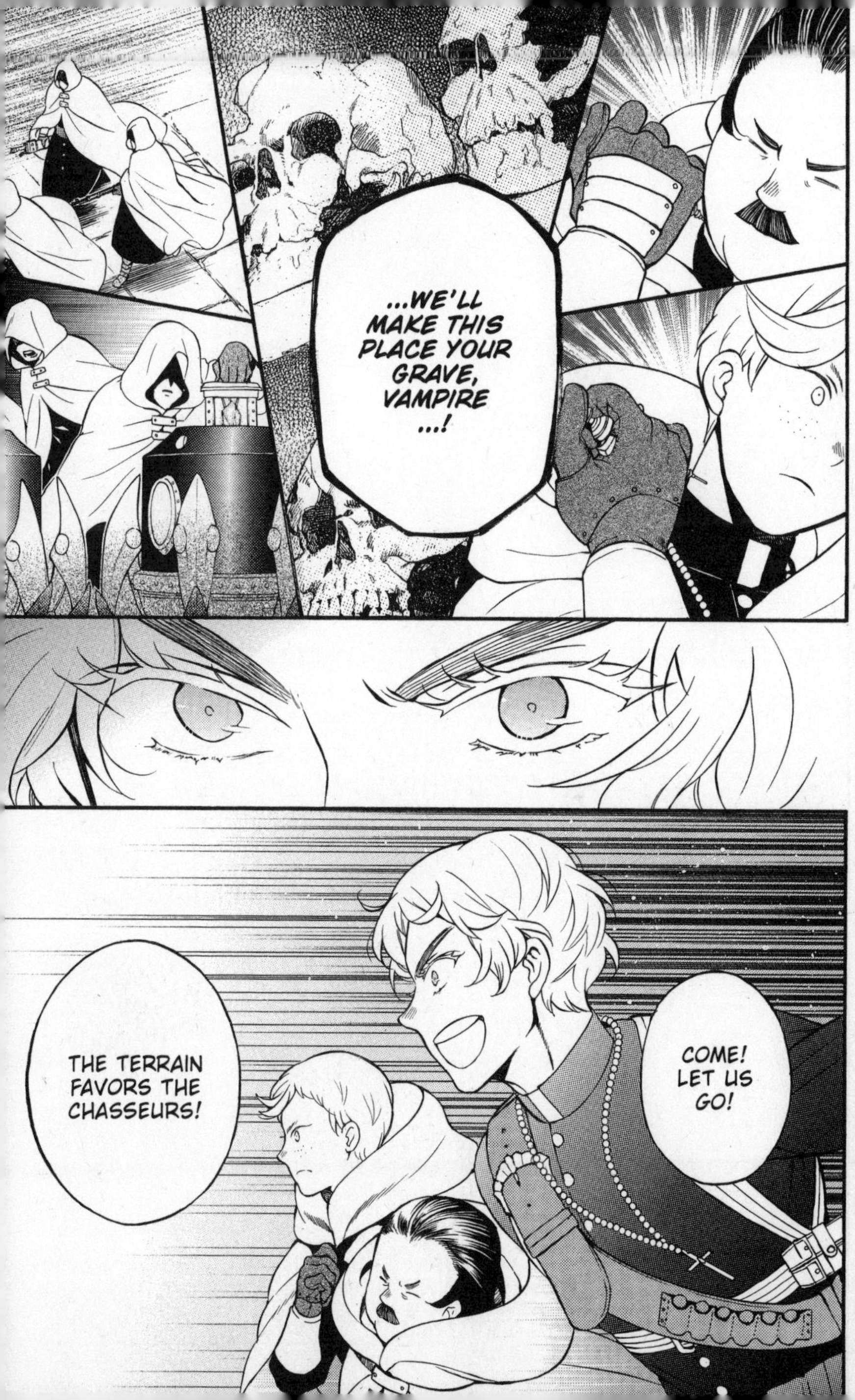
...WE'LL MAKE THIS PLACE YOUR GRAVE, VAMPIRE ...!
COME! LET US GO!
THE TERRAIN FAVORS THE CHASSEURS!

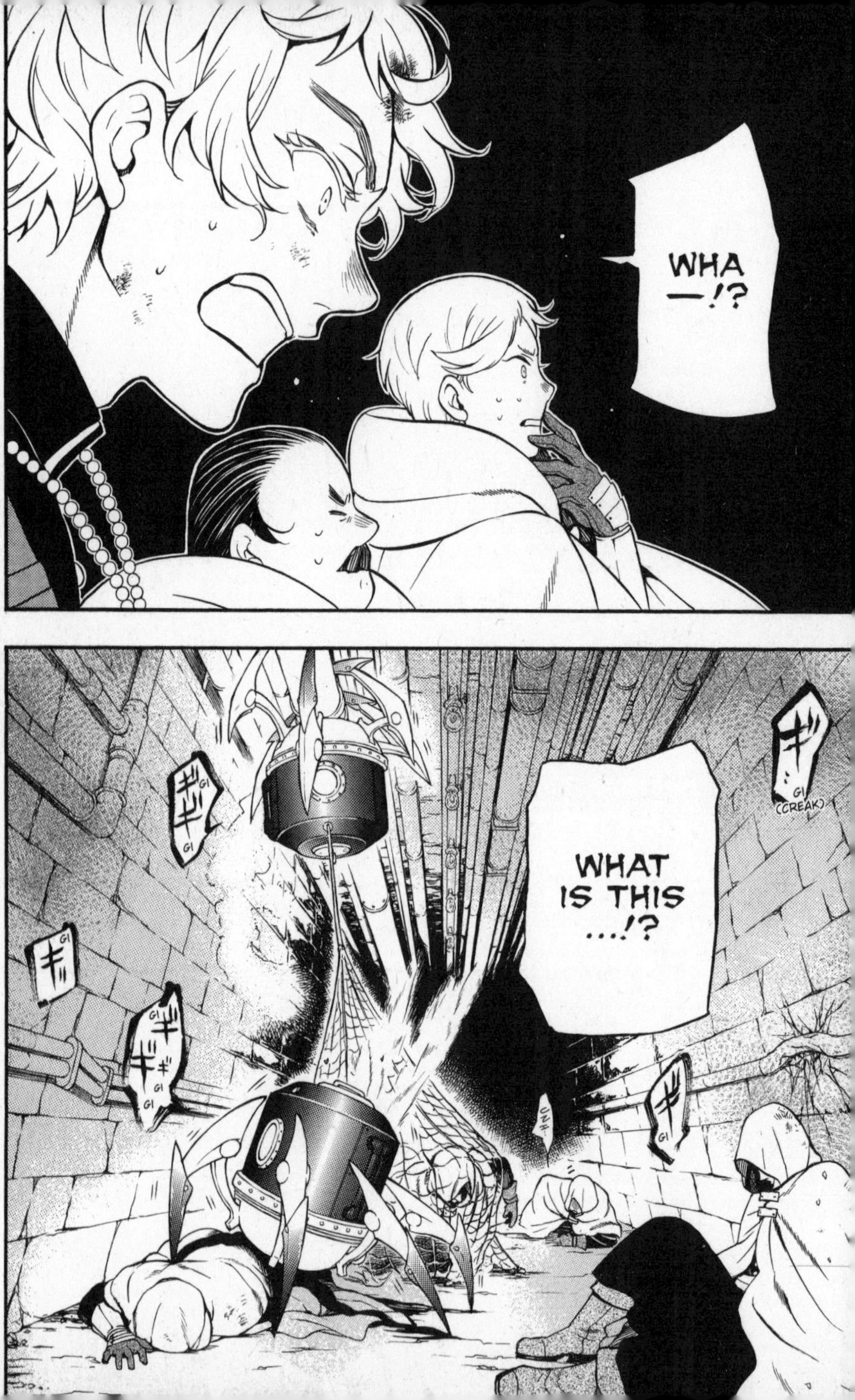
WHA—!?
ギ
GI
(CREAK)
WHAT IS THIS ....!?
ギギ
GI
GI
ギ
GI
ギギ
GI
GI
GI
ギ
GI

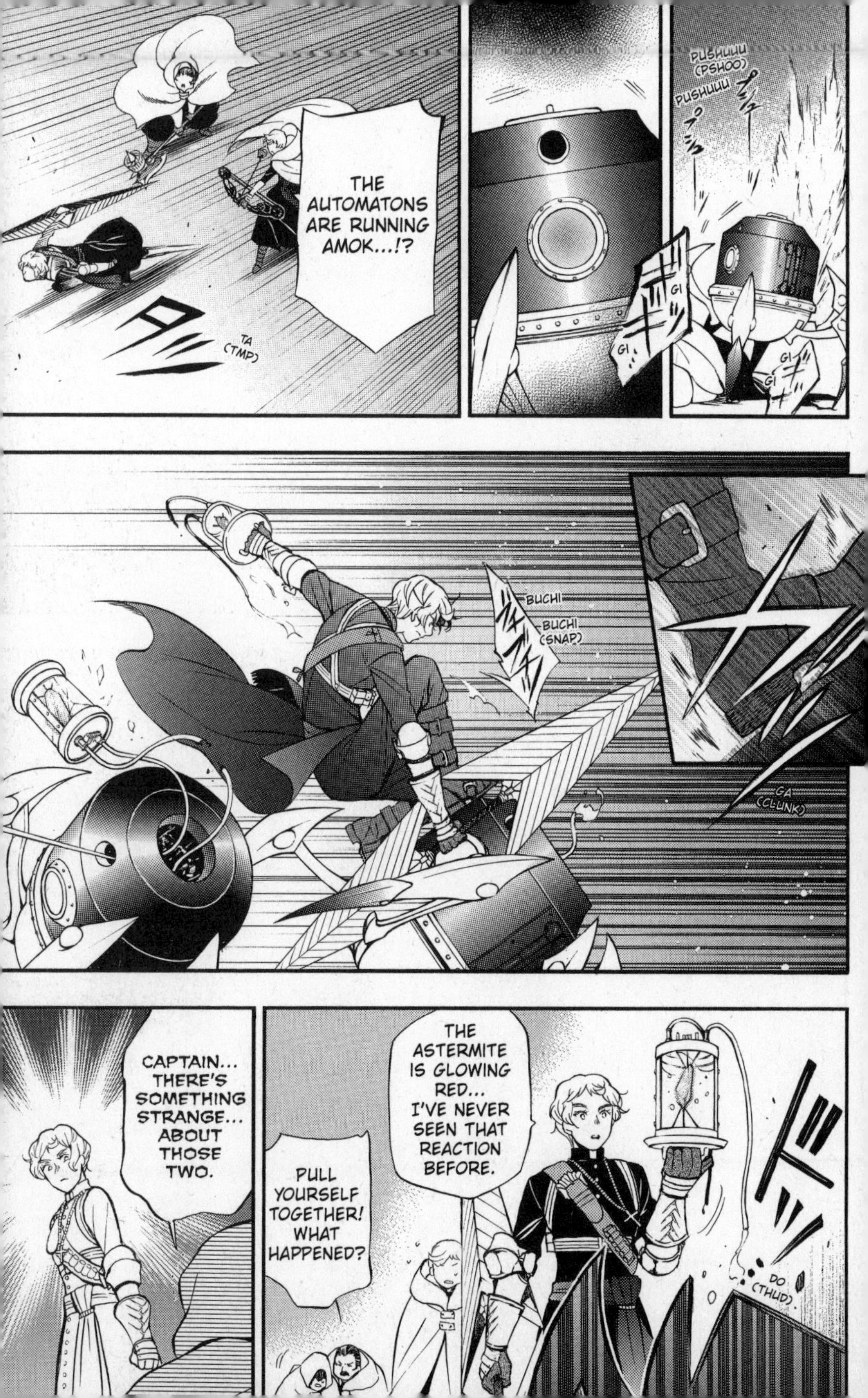
PUSHUUU (PSHOO)
PUSHUUU
GI
GI
GI
GI
THE AUTOMATONS ARE RUNNING AMOK...!?
TA (TMP)
GA (CLUNK)
BUCHI
BUCHI (SNAP)
THE ASTERMITE IS GLOWING RED... I'VE NEVER SEEN THAT REACTION BEFORE.
DO (THUD)
PULL YOURSELF TOGETHER! WHAT HAPPENED?
CAPTAIN... THERE'S SOMETHING STRANGE... ABOUT THOSE TWO.

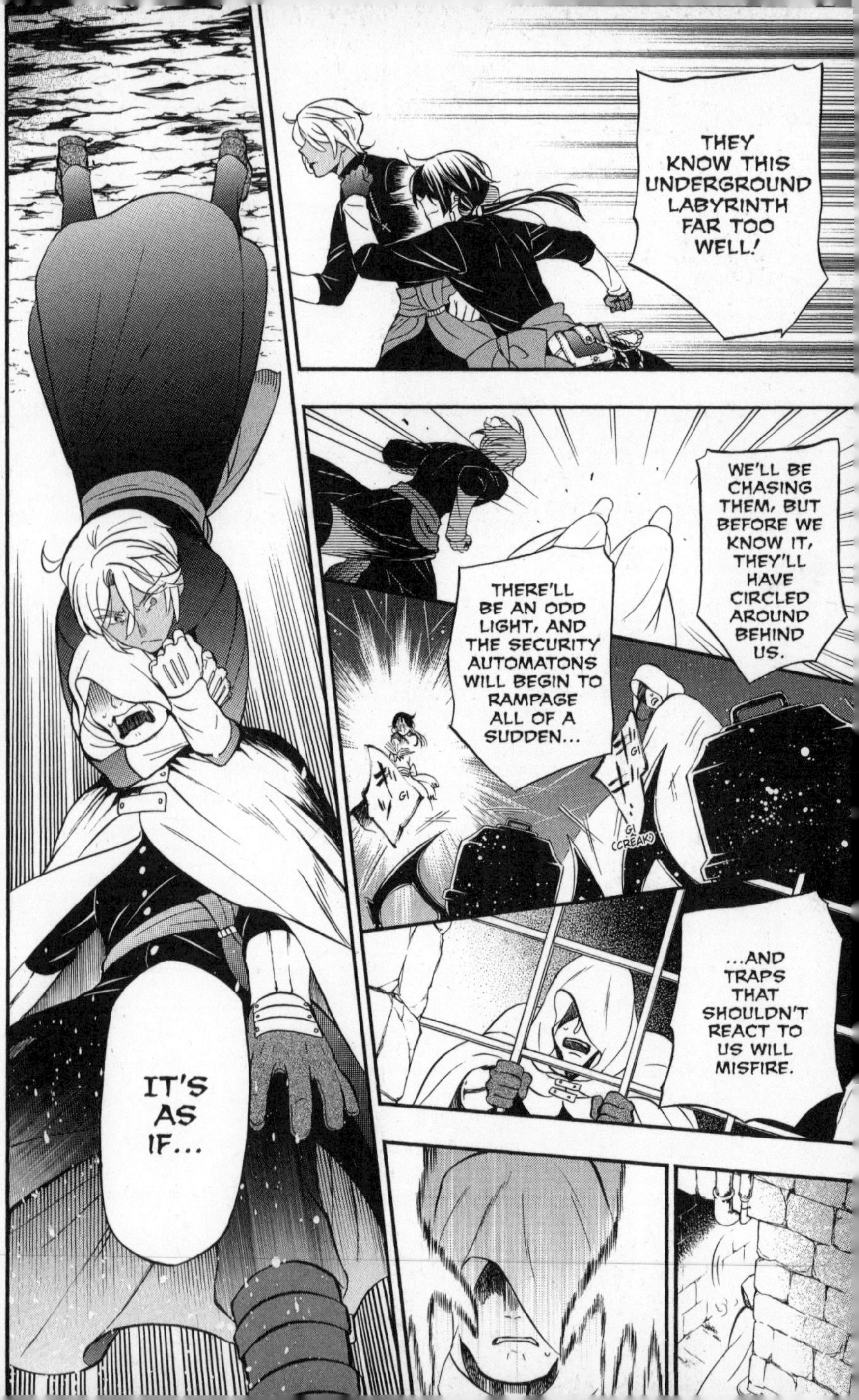
THEY KNOW THIS UNDERGROUND LABYRINTH FAR TOO WELL!
WE'LL BE CHASING THEM, BUT BEFORE WE KNOW IT, THEY'LL HAVE CIRCLED AROUND BEHIND US.
THERE'LL BE AN ODD LIGHT, AND THE SECURITY AUTOMATONS WILL BEGIN TO RAMPAGE ALL OF A SUDDEN...
GI
GI
GI (CREAK)
...AND TRAPS THAT SHOULDN'T REACT TO US WILL MISFIRE.
IT'S AS IF...

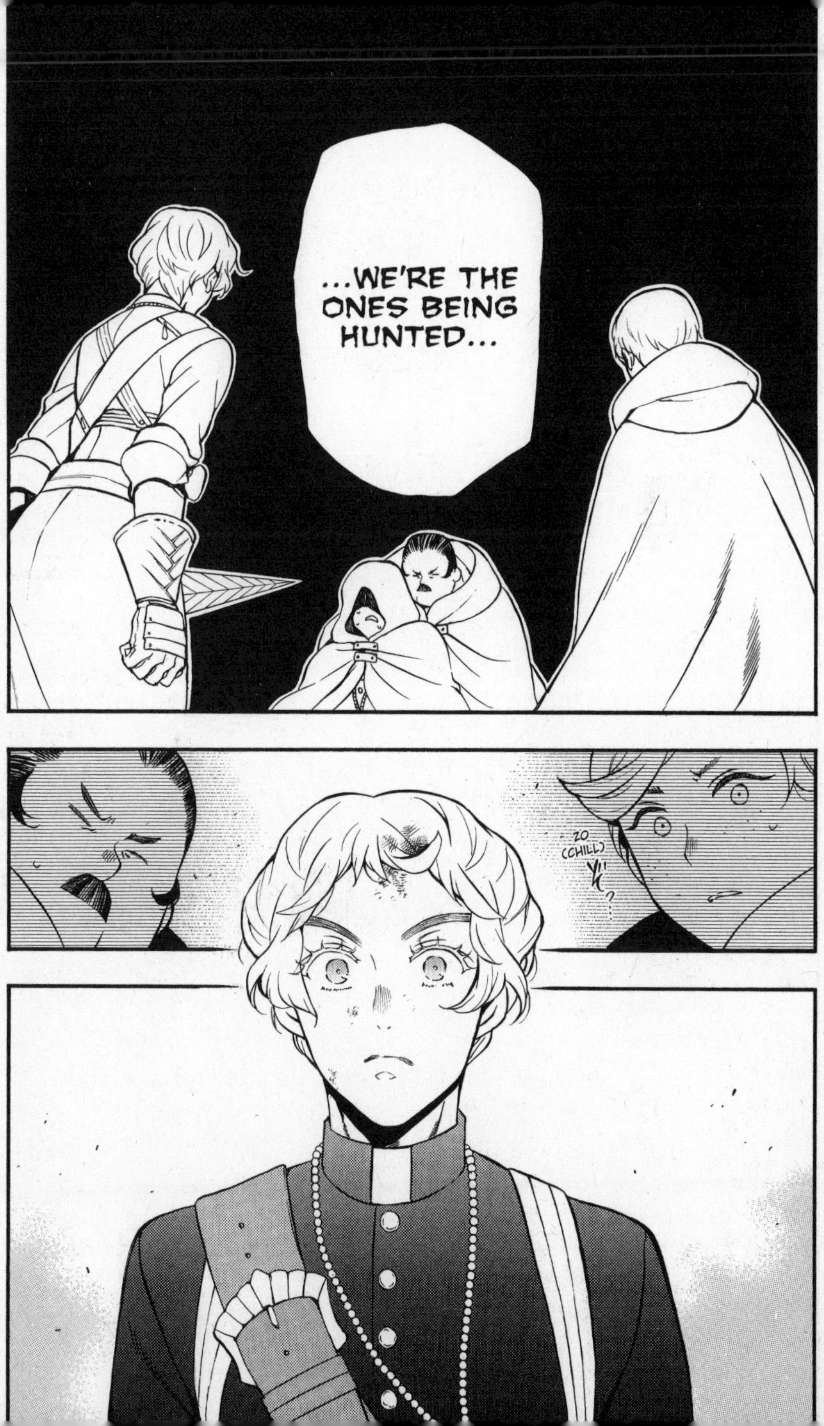
...WE'RE THE ONES BEING HUNTED...
ZO
(CHILL)

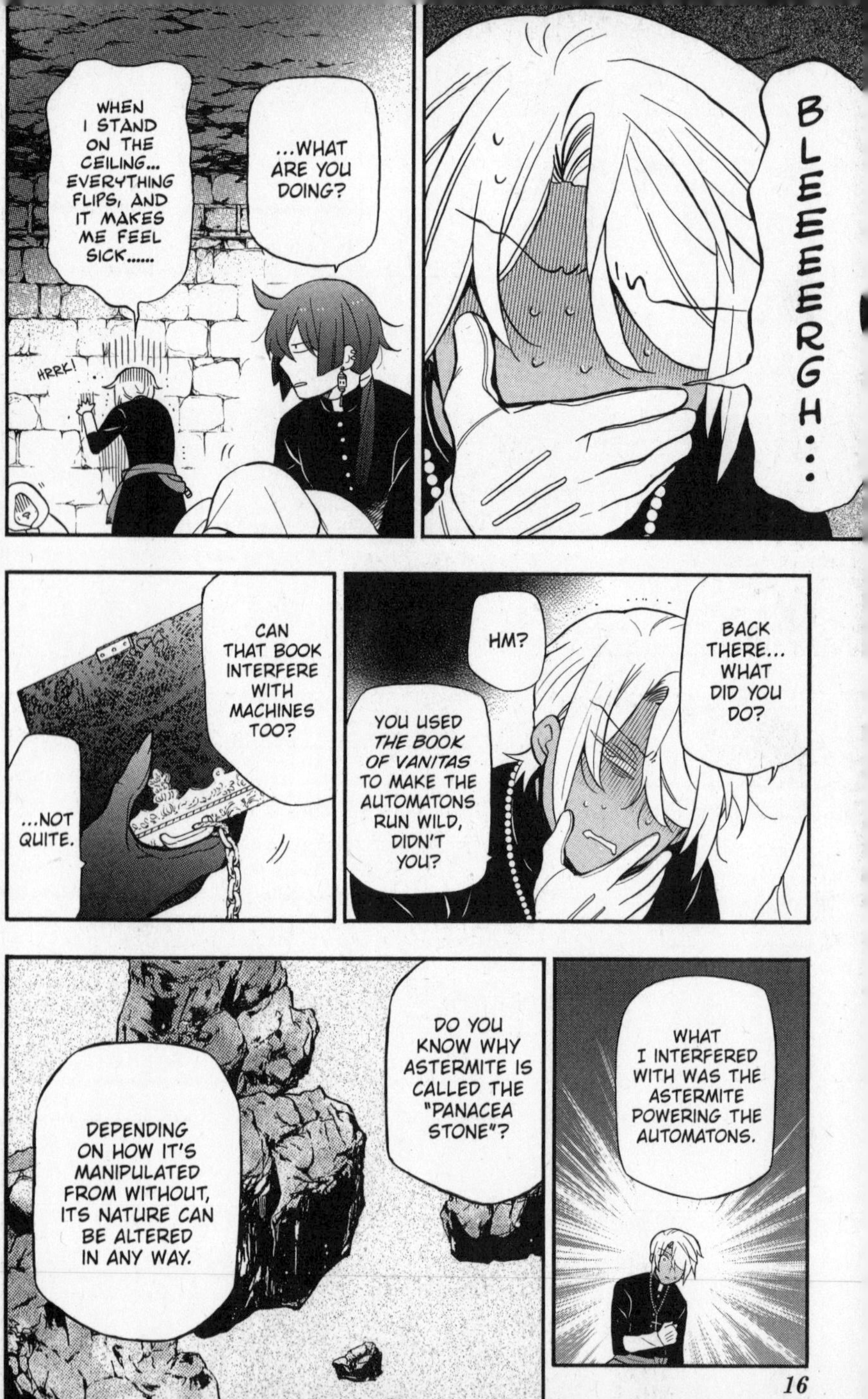
BLEEEERGH...
...WHAT ARE YOU DOING?
WHEN I STAND ON THE CEILING... EVERYTHING FLIPS, AND IT MAKES ME FEEL SICK......
HRRK!
BACK THERE... WHAT DID YOU DO?
HM?
YOU USED *THE BOOK OF VANITAS* TO MAKE THE AUTOMATONS RUN WILD, DIDN'T YOU?
CAN THAT BOOK INTERFERE WITH MACHINES TOO?
...NOT QUITE.
WHAT I INTERFERED WITH WAS THE ASTERMITE POWERING THE AUTOMATONS.
DO YOU KNOW WHY ASTERMITE IS CALLED THE "PANACEA STONE"?
DEPENDING ON HOW IT'S MANIPULATED FROM WITHOUT, ITS NATURE CAN BE ALTERED IN ANY WAY.

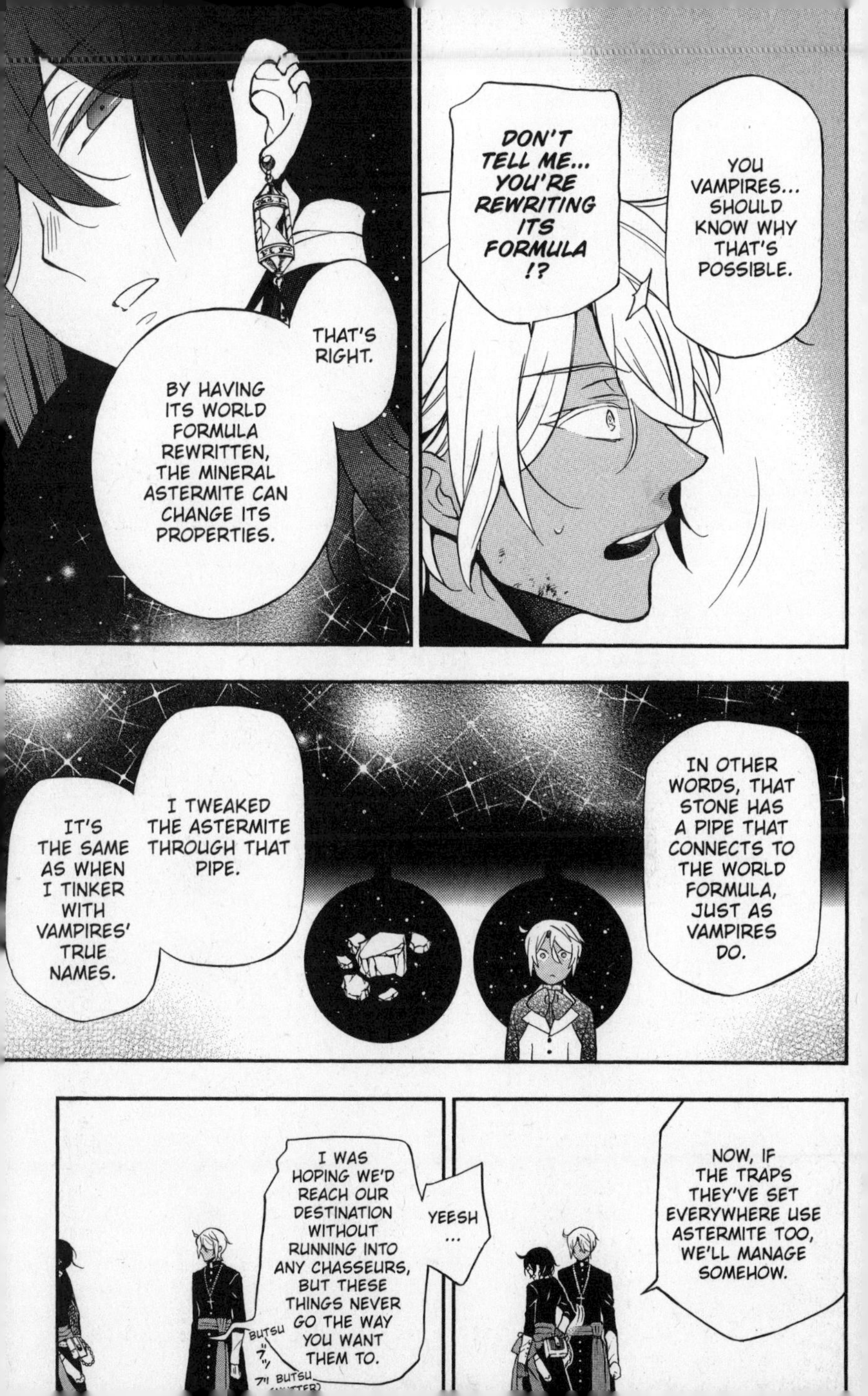

YOU VAMPIRES... SHOULD KNOW WHY THAT'S POSSIBLE.
DON'T TELL ME... YOU'RE REWRITING ITS FORMULA!?
THAT'S RIGHT.
BY HAVING ITS WORLD FORMULA REWRITTEN, THE MINERAL ASTERMITE CAN CHANGE ITS PROPERTIES.
IN OTHER WORDS, THAT STONE HAS A PIPE THAT CONNECTS TO THE WORLD FORMULA, JUST AS VAMPIRES DO.
I TWEAKED THE ASTERMITE THROUGH THAT PIPE.
IT'S THE SAME AS WHEN I TINKER WITH VAMPIRES' TRUE NAMES.
NOW, IF THE TRAPS THEY'VE SET EVERYWHERE USE ASTERMITE TOO, WE'LL MANAGE SOMEHOW.
YEESH...
I WAS HOPING WE'D REACH OUR DESTINATION WITHOUT RUNNING INTO ANY CHASSEURS, BUT THESE THINGS NEVER GO THE WAY YOU WANT THEM TO.
BUTSU
BUTSU

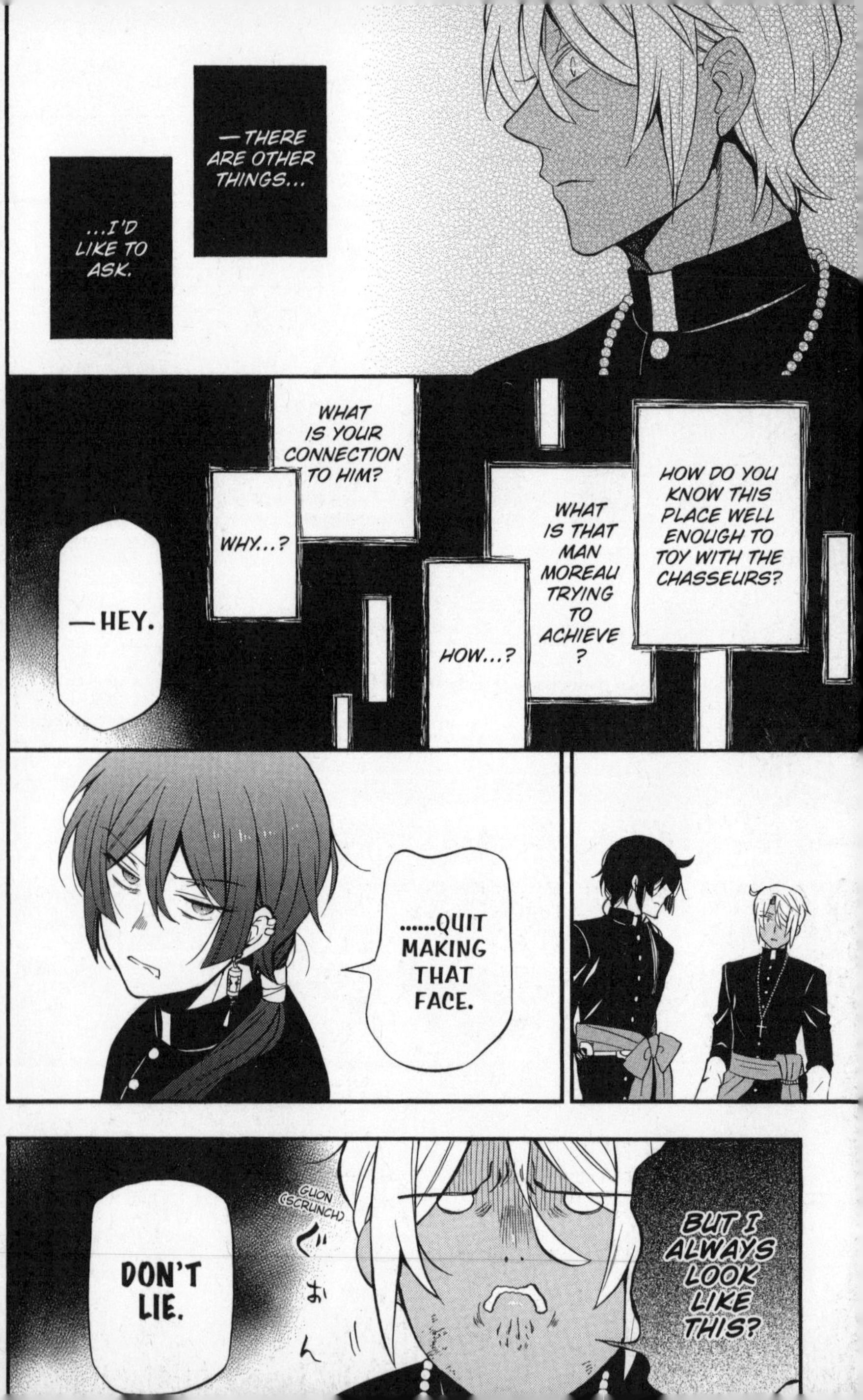
—THERE ARE OTHER THINGS...
...I'D LIKE TO ASK.
HOW DO YOU KNOW THIS PLACE WELL ENOUGH TO TOY WITH THE CHASSEURS?
WHAT IS THAT MAN MOREAU TRYING TO ACHIEVE?
HOW...?
WHAT IS YOUR CONNECTION TO HIM?
WHY...?
—HEY.
......QUIT MAKING THAT FACE.
BUT I ALWAYS LOOK LIKE THIS?
GUON (SCRUNCH)
ぐおん
DON'T LIE.

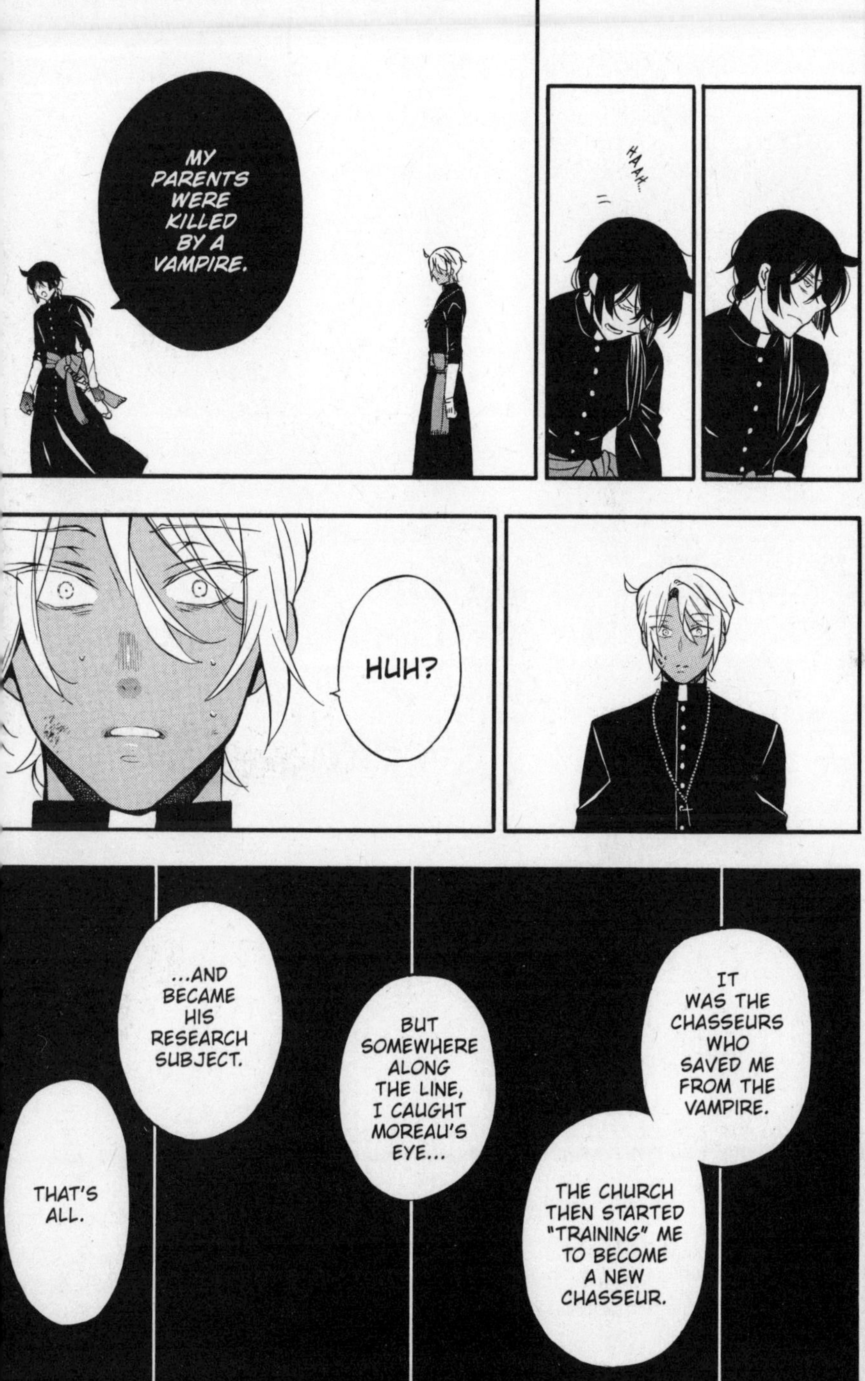
HAAA...
MY PARENTS WERE KILLED BY A VAMPIRE.
HUH?
IT WAS THE CHASSEURS WHO SAVED ME FROM THE VAMPIRE.
THE CHURCH THEN STARTED "TRAINING" ME TO BECOME A NEW CHASSEUR.
BUT SOMEWHERE ALONG THE LINE, I CAUGHT MOREAU'S EYE...
...AND BECAME HIS RESEARCH SUBJECT.
THAT'S ALL.

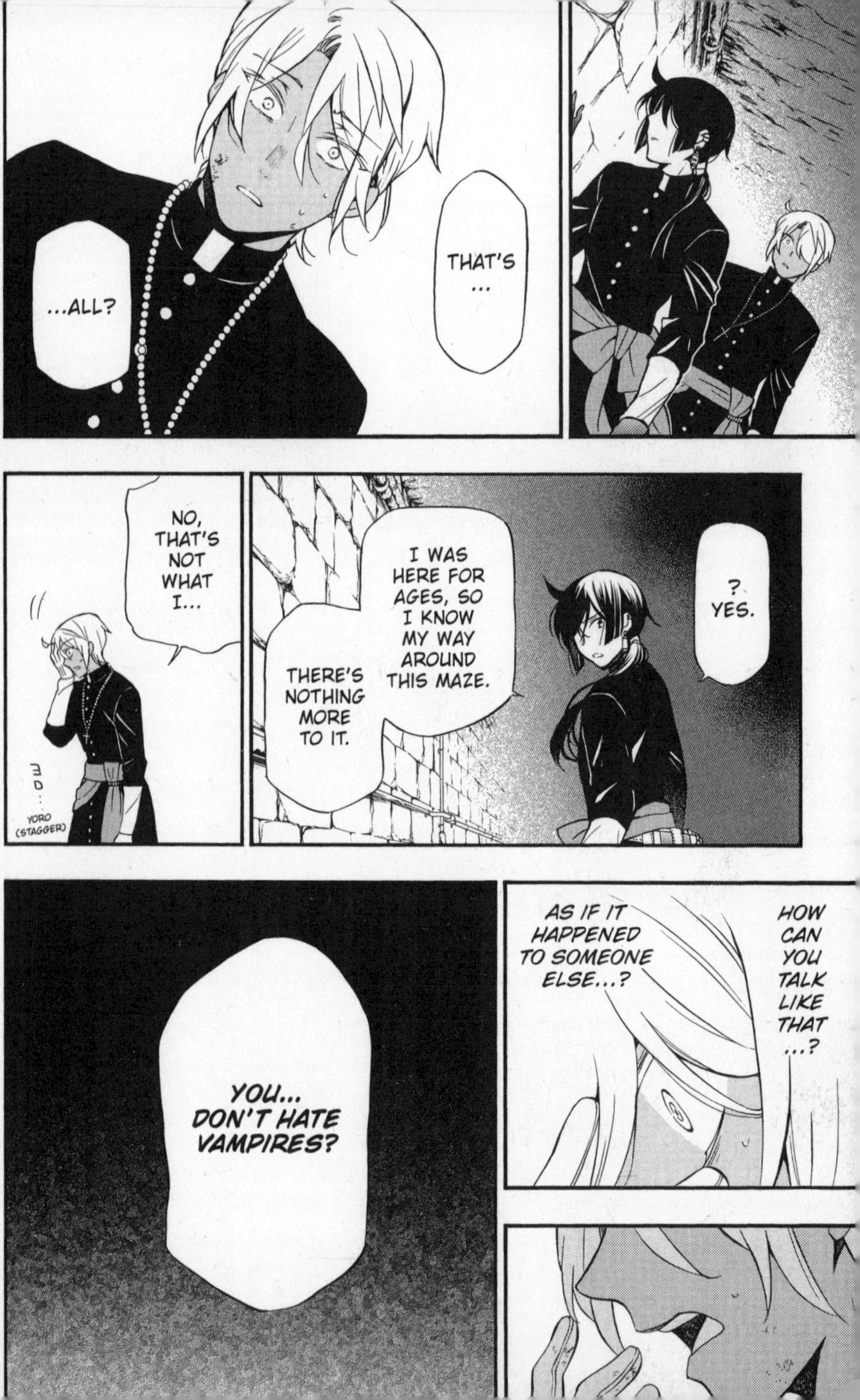
THAT'S ...
...ALL?
? YES.
I WAS HERE FOR AGES, SO I KNOW MY WAY AROUND THIS MAZE.
THERE'S NOTHING MORE TO IT.
NO, THAT'S NOT WHAT I...
YORO (STAGGER)
HOW CAN YOU TALK LIKE THAT...?
AS IF IT HAPPENED TO SOMEONE ELSE...?
YOU... DON'T HATE VAMPIRES?

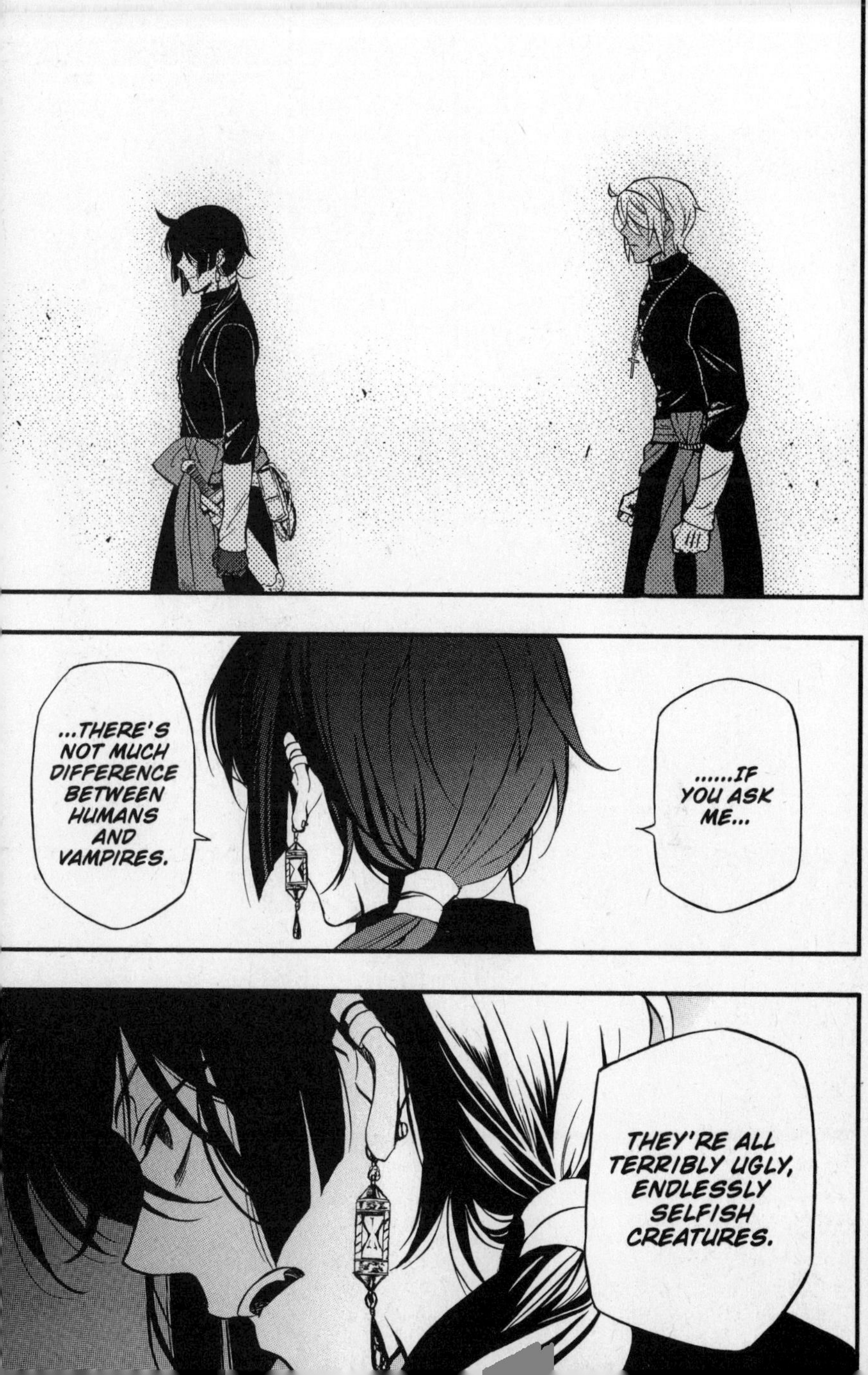
......IF YOU ASK ME...
...THERE'S NOT MUCH DIFFERENCE BETWEEN HUMANS AND VAMPIRES.
THEY'RE ALL TERRIBLY UGLY, ENDLESSLY SELFISH CREATURES.

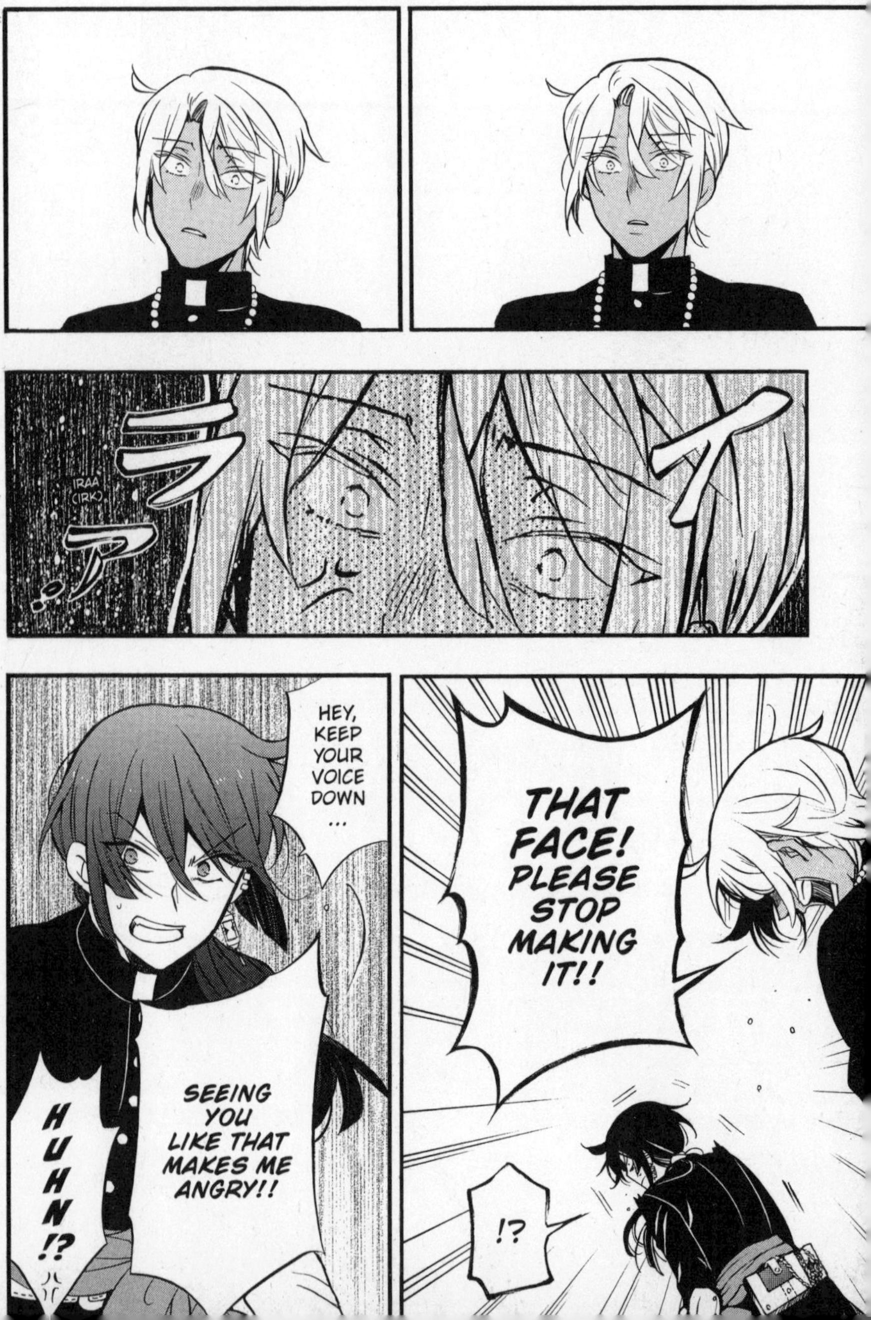
IRAA (IRK)
THAT FACE! PLEASE STOP MAKING IT!!
!?
HEY, KEEP YOUR VOICE DOWN ...
SEEING YOU LIKE THAT MAKES ME ANGRY!!
HUHN!?

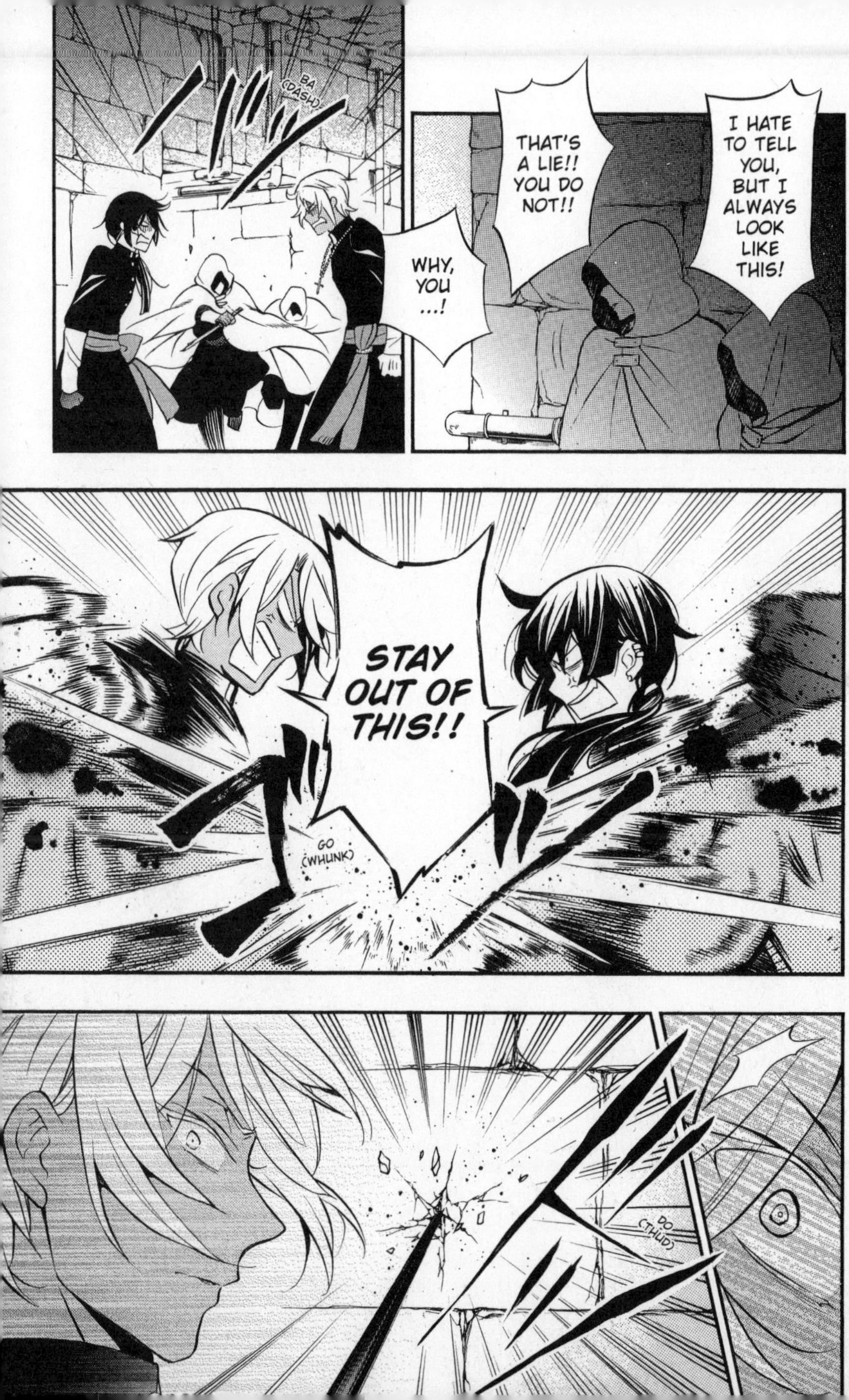
I HATE TO TELL YOU, BUT I ALWAYS LOOK LIKE THIS!
THAT'S A LIE!! YOU DO NOT!!
WHY, YOU ...!
BA (DASH)
STAY OUT OF THIS!!
GO (WHUNK)
DO (THUD)

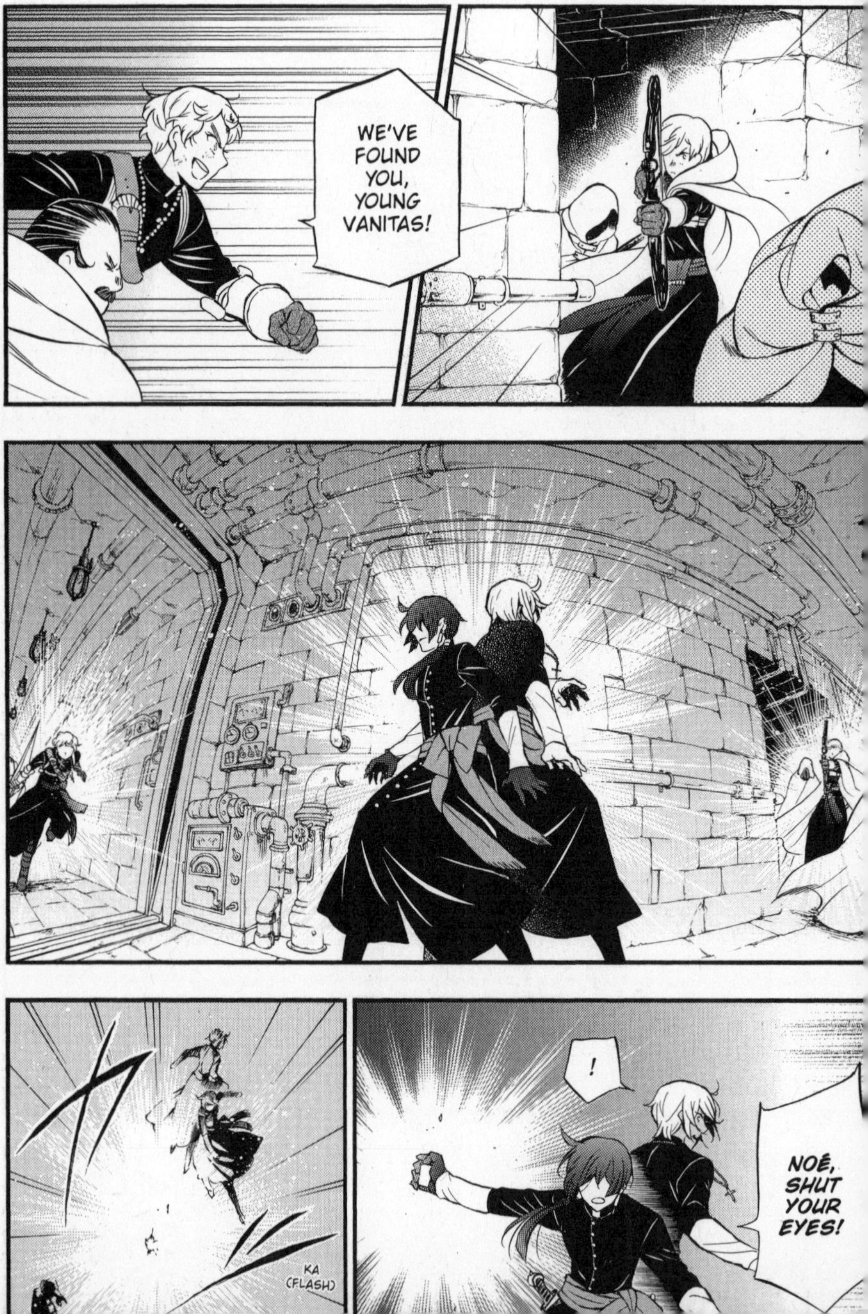
WE'VE FOUND YOU, YOUNG VANITAS!
!
NOÉ, SHUT YOUR EYES!
KA (FLASH)

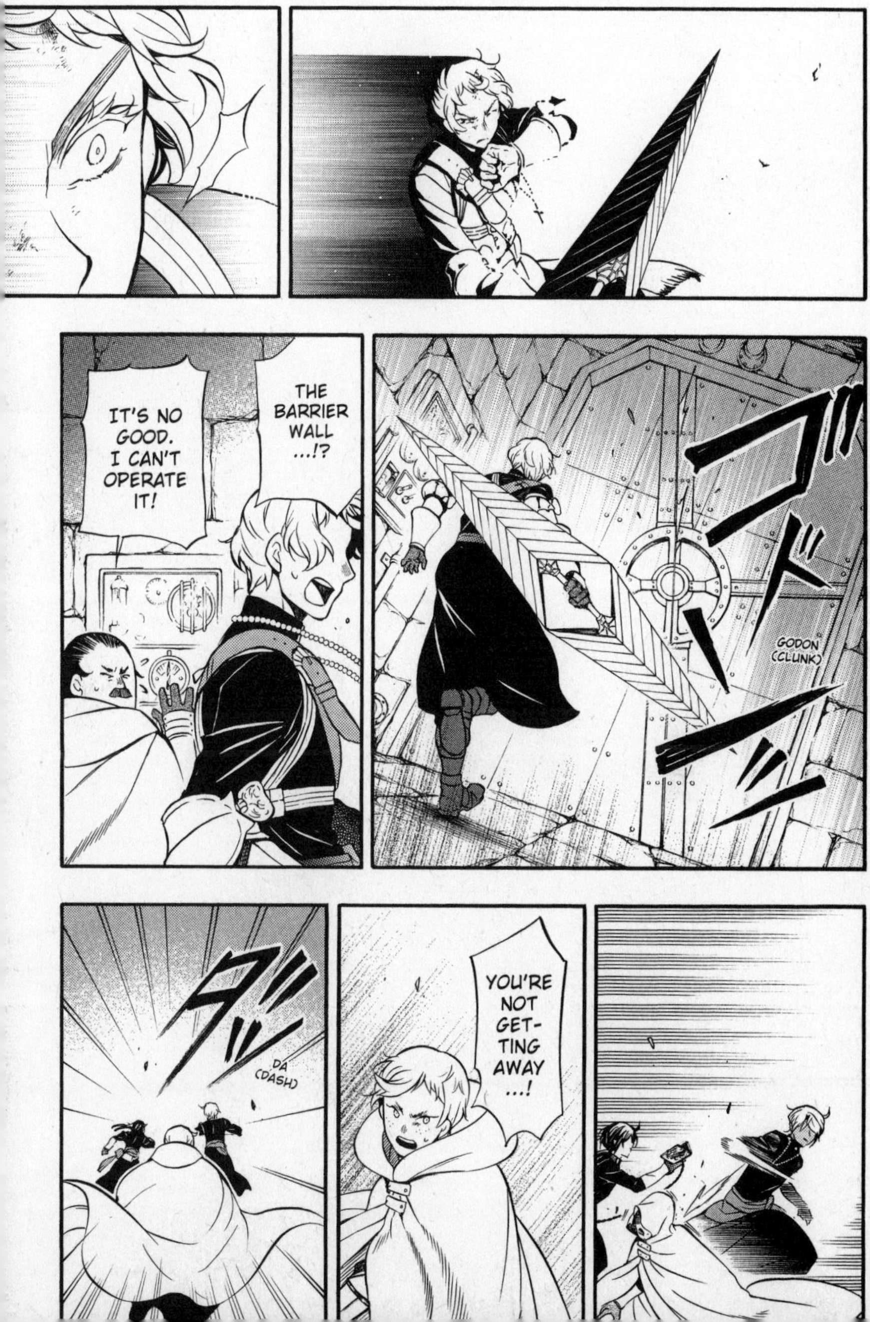
GODON (CLUNK)
THE BARRIER WALL ...!?
IT'S NO GOOD. I CAN'T OPERATE IT!
YOU'RE NOT GET-TING AWAY ...!
DA (DASH)

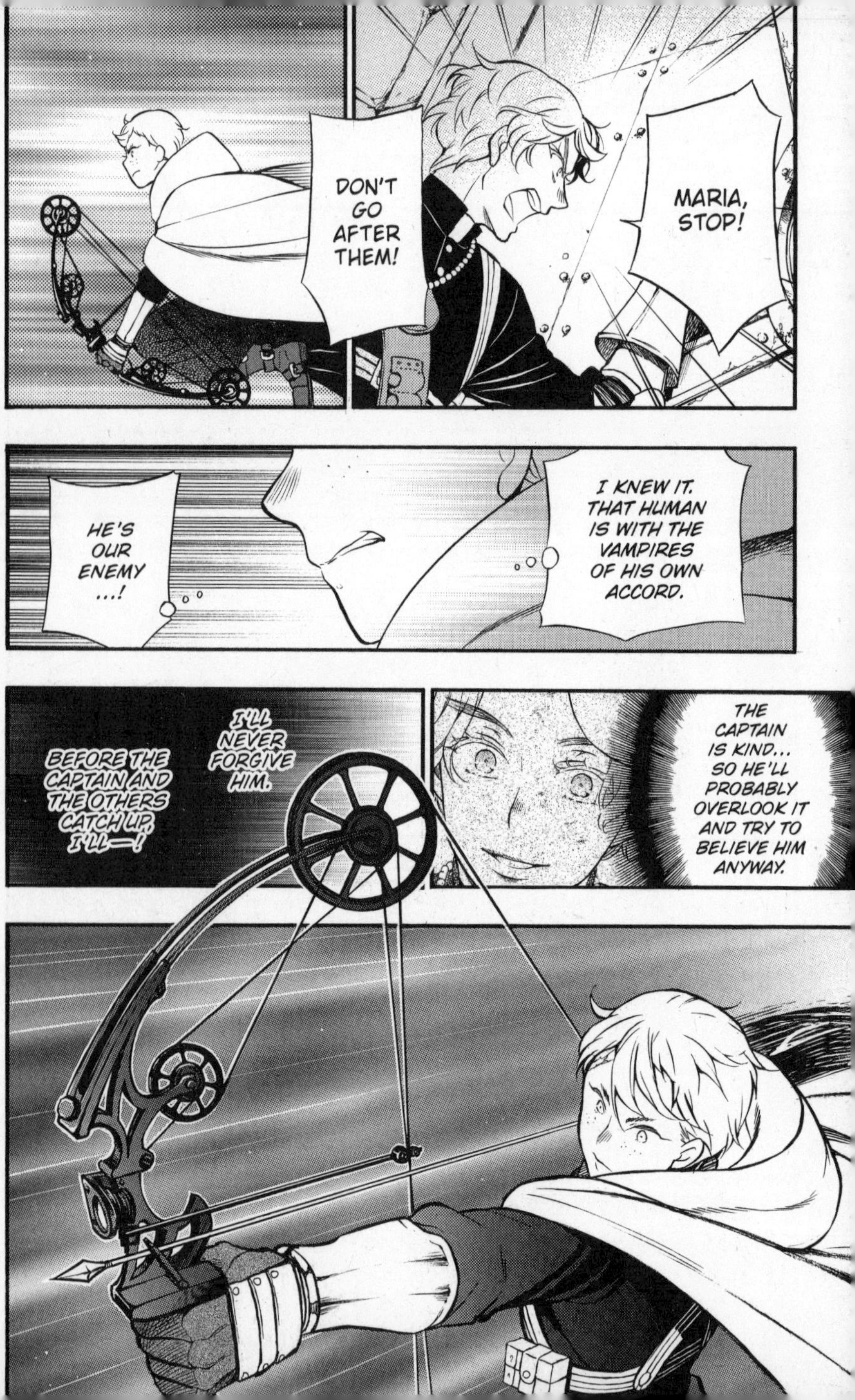
MARIA, STOP!
DON'T GO AFTER THEM!
I KNEW IT. THAT HUMAN IS WITH THE VAMPIRES OF HIS OWN ACCORD.
HE'S OUR ENEMY ...!
THE CAPTAIN IS KIND... SO HE'LL PROBABLY OVERLOOK IT AND TRY TO BELIEVE HIM ANYWAY.
I'LL NEVER FORGIVE HIM.
BEFORE THE CAPTAIN AND THE OTHERS CATCH UP, I'LL—!

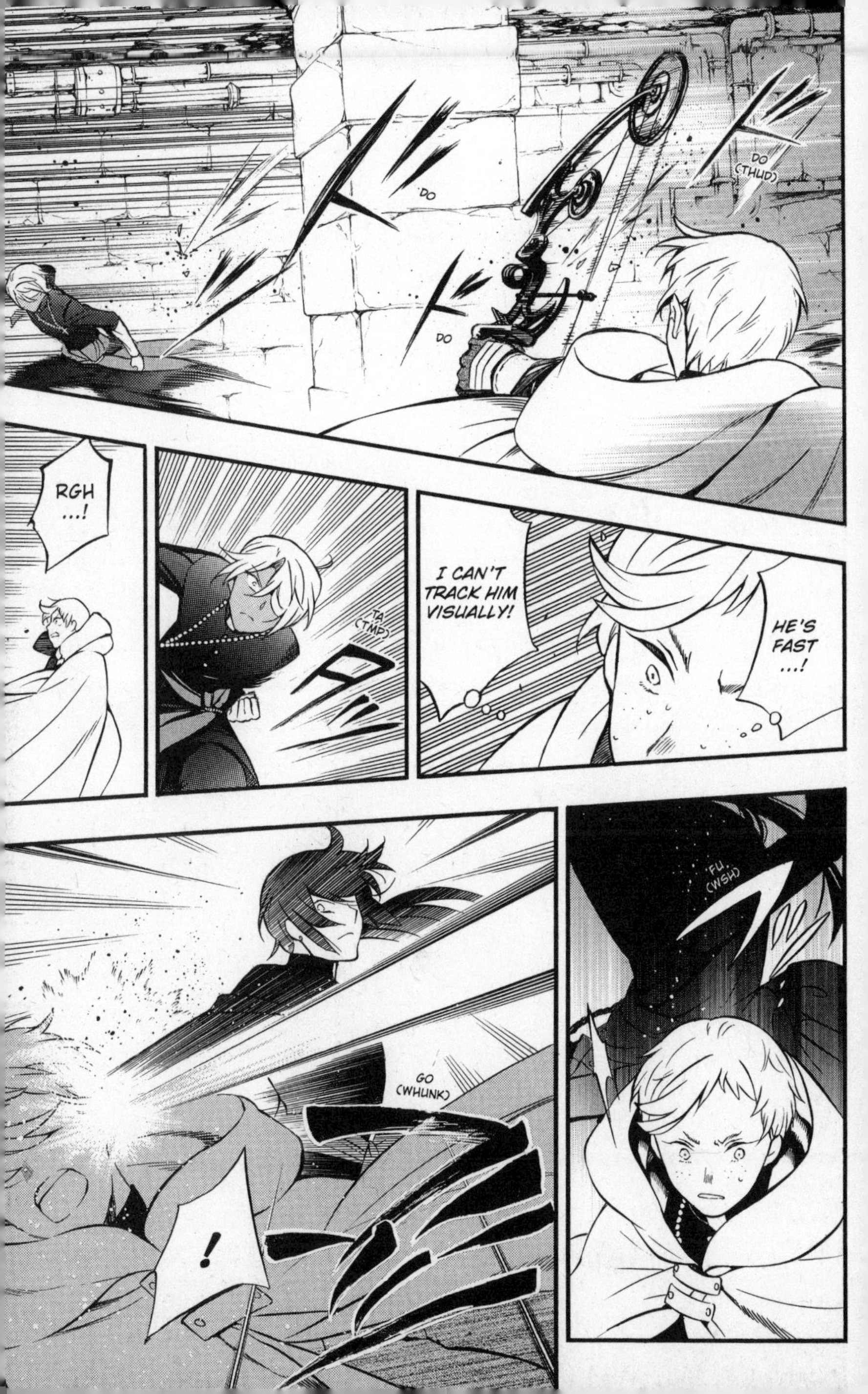
DO (THUD)
DO
DO
HE'S FAST...!
I CAN'T TRACK HIM VISUALLY!
TA (TMP)
RGH...!
FU (WSH)
GO (WHUNK)
!

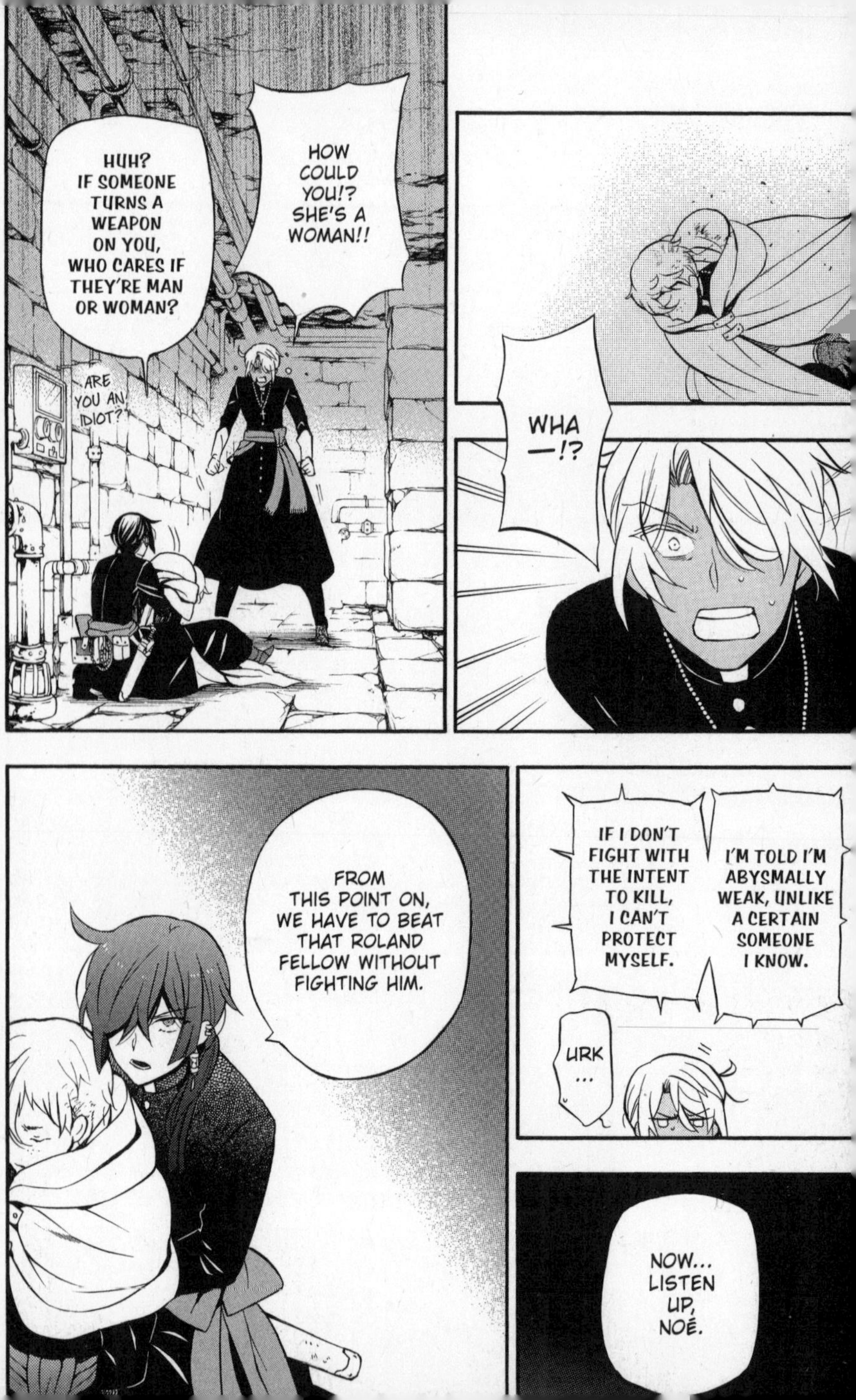

WHA—!?
HOW COULD YOU!? SHE'S A WOMAN!!
HUH? IF SOMEONE TURNS A WEAPON ON YOU, WHO CARES IF THEY'RE MAN OR WOMAN?
ARE YOU AN IDIOT?
I'M TOLD I'M ABYSMALLY WEAK, UNLIKE A CERTAIN SOMEONE I KNOW.
IF I DON'T FIGHT WITH THE INTENT TO KILL, I CAN'T PROTECT MYSELF.
URK...
NOW... LISTEN UP, NOÉ.
FROM THIS POINT ON, WE HAVE TO BEAT THAT ROLAND FELLOW WITHOUT FIGHTING HIM.

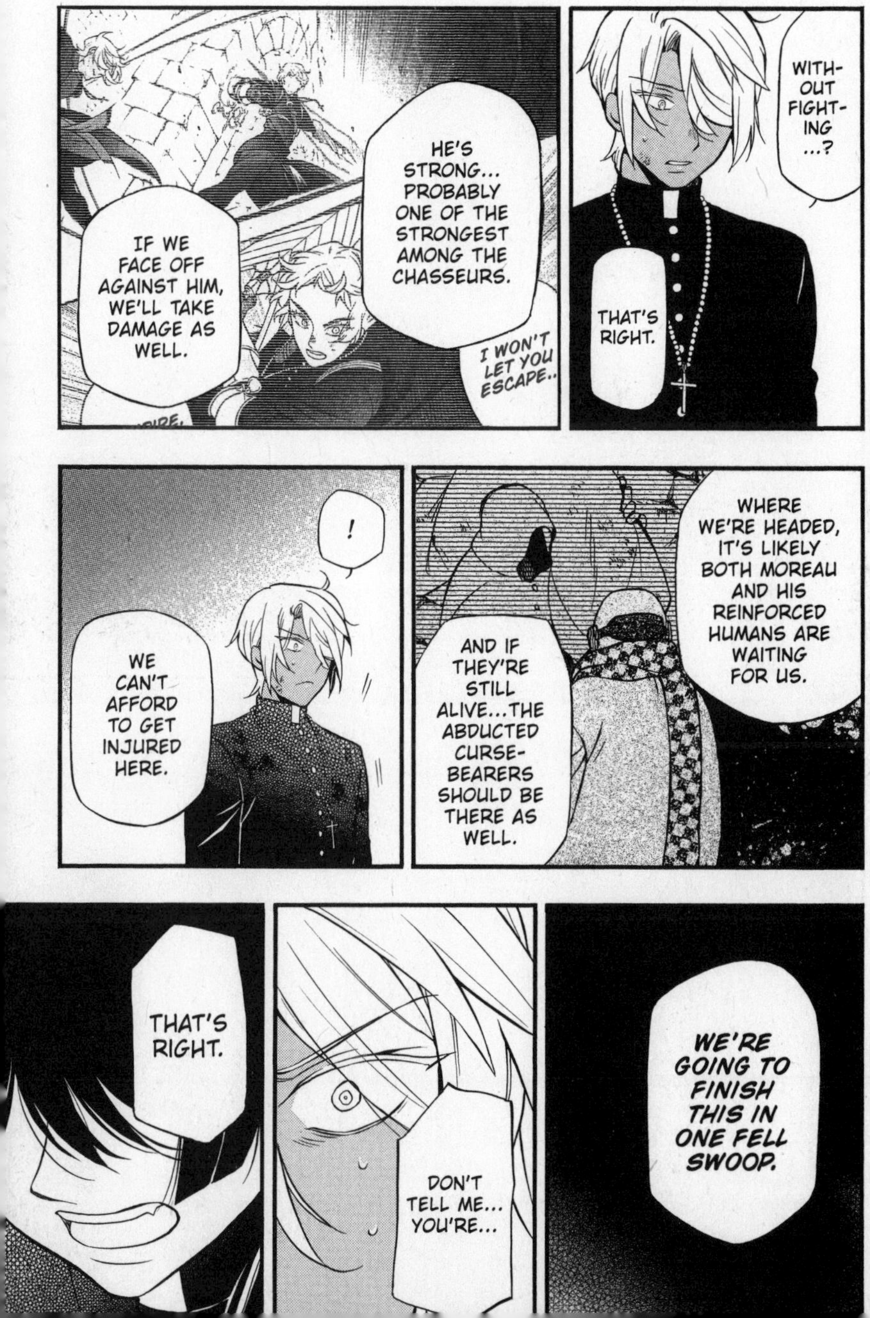
WITHOUT FIGHTING...?
THAT'S RIGHT.
HE'S STRONG... PROBABLY ONE OF THE STRONGEST AMONG THE CHASSEURS.
IF WE FACE OFF AGAINST HIM, WE'LL TAKE DAMAGE AS WELL.
I WON'T LET YOU ESCAPE..
WHERE WE'RE HEADED, IT'S LIKELY BOTH MOREAU AND HIS REINFORCED HUMANS ARE WAITING FOR US.
AND IF THEY'RE STILL ALIVE...THE ABDUCTED CURSE-BEARERS SHOULD BE THERE AS WELL.
!
WE CAN'T AFFORD TO GET INJURED HERE.
WE'RE GOING TO FINISH THIS IN ONE FELL SWOOP.
DON'T TELL ME... YOU'RE...
THAT'S RIGHT.

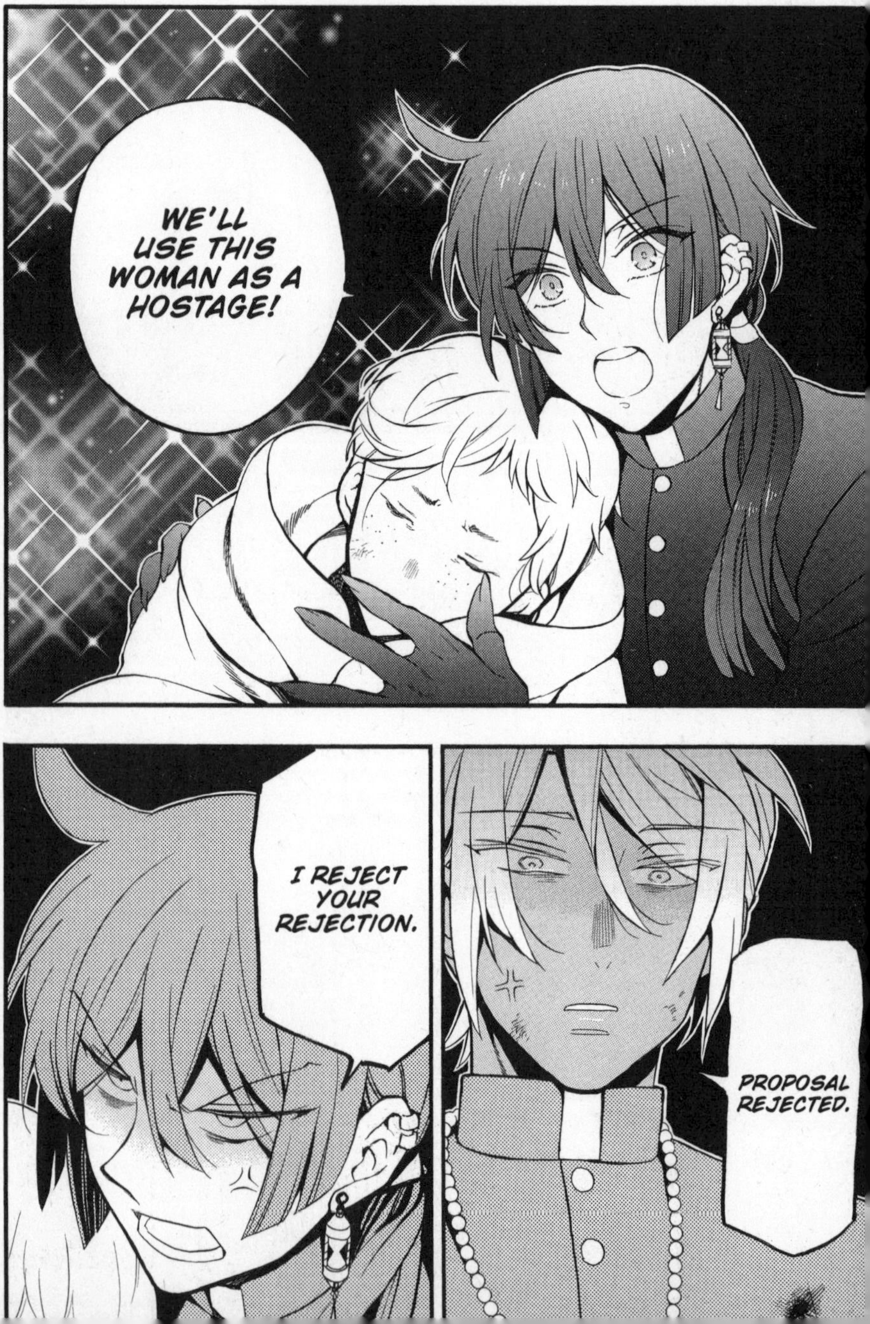
WE'LL USE THIS WOMAN AS A HOSTAGE!
PROPOSAL REJECTED.
I REJECT YOUR REJECTION.

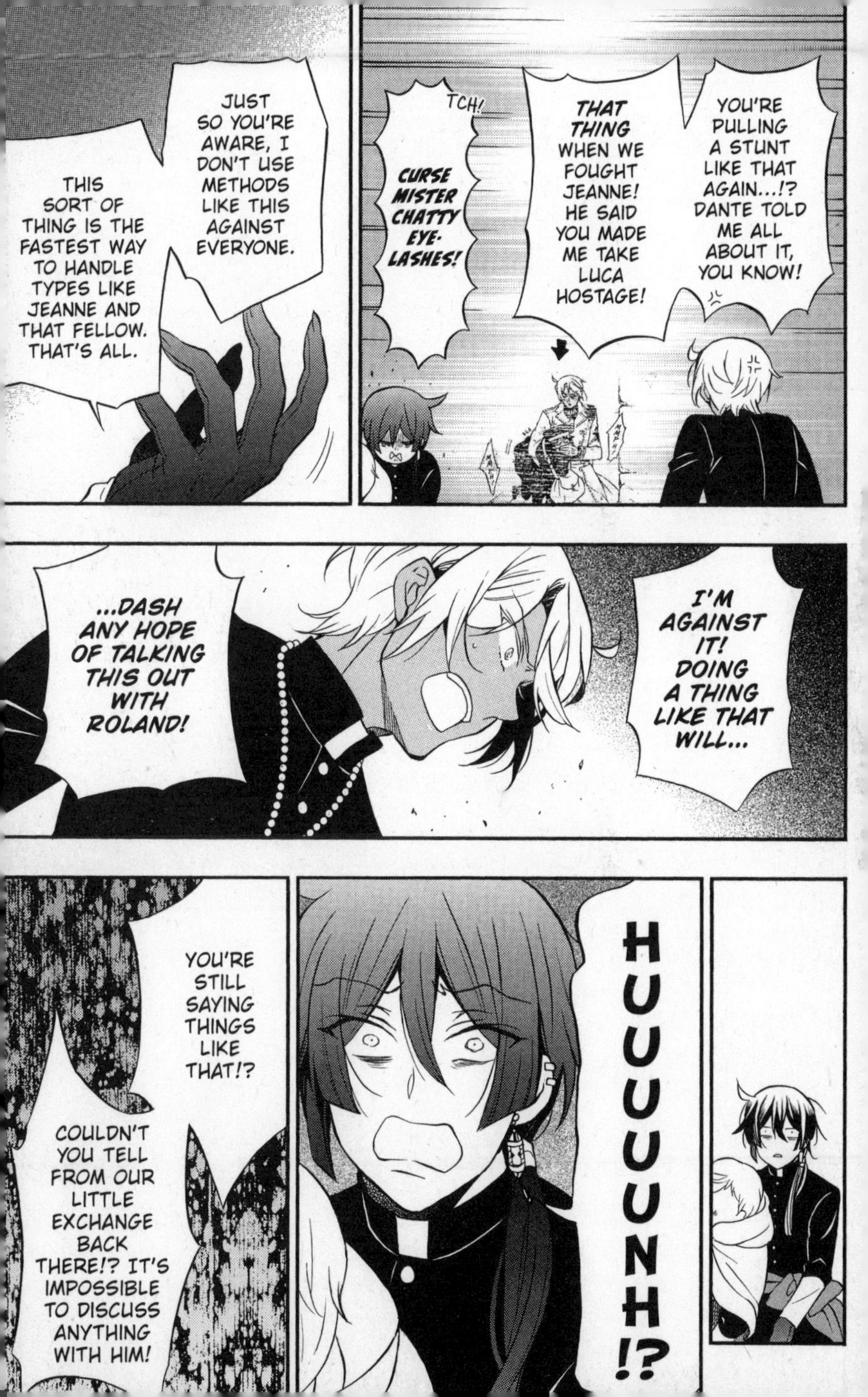
YOU'RE PULLING A STUNT LIKE THAT AGAIN...!? DANTE TOLD ME ALL ABOUT IT, YOU KNOW!
THAT THING WHEN WE FOUGHT JEANNE! HE SAID YOU MADE ME TAKE LUCA HOSTAGE!
TCH!
CURSE MISTER CHATTY EYE-LASHES!
JUST SO YOU'RE AWARE, I DON'T USE METHODS LIKE THIS AGAINST EVERYONE.
THIS SORT OF THING IS THE FASTEST WAY TO HANDLE TYPES LIKE JEANNE AND THAT FELLOW. THAT'S ALL.
I'M AGAINST IT! DOING A THING LIKE THAT WILL...
...DASH ANY HOPE OF TALKING THIS OUT WITH ROLAND!
HUUUUUNH!?
YOU'RE STILL SAYING THINGS LIKE THAT!?
COULDN'T YOU TELL FROM OUR LITTLE EXCHANGE BACK THERE!? IT'S IMPOSSIBLE TO DISCUSS ANYTHING WITH HIM!

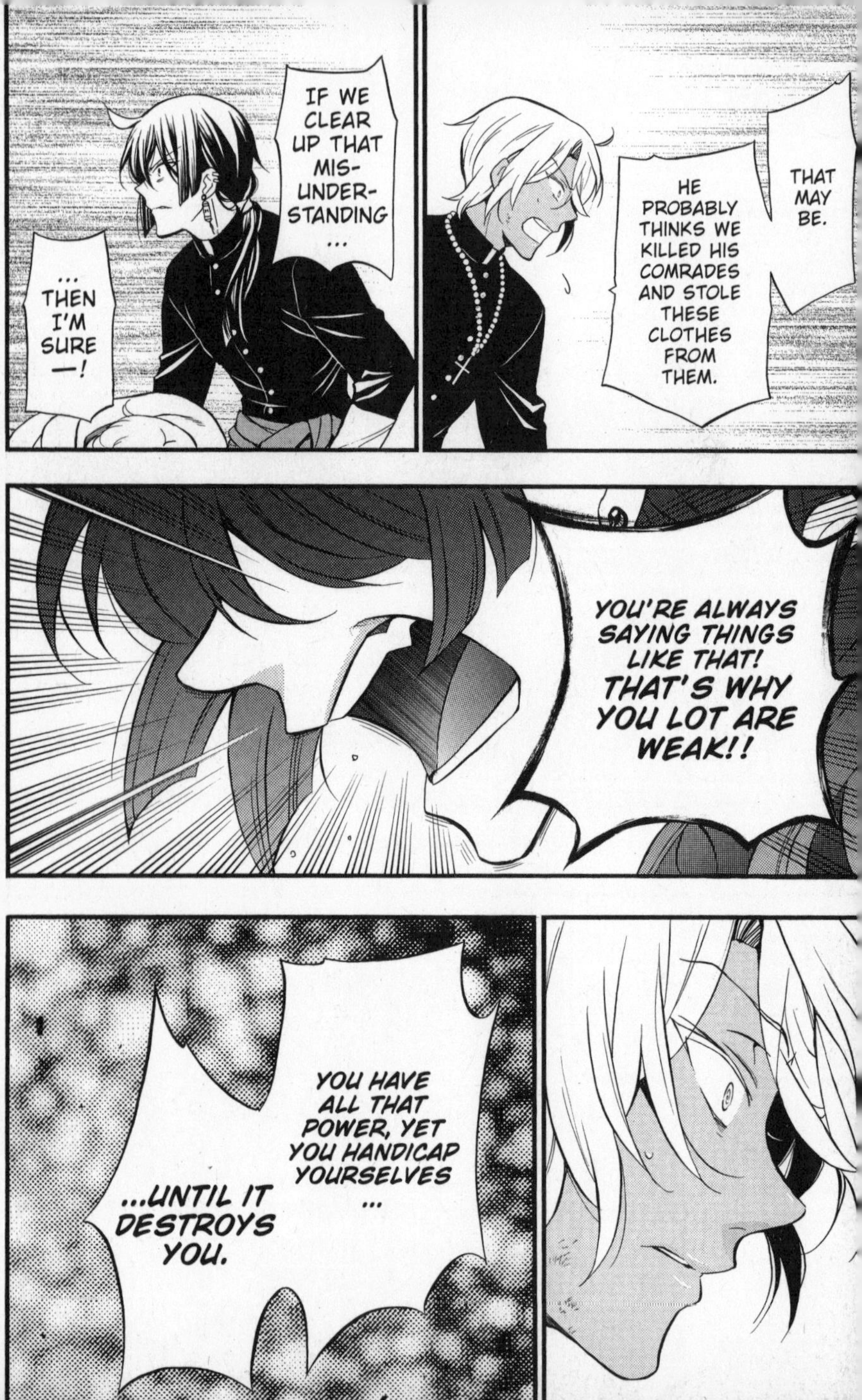
THAT MAY BE.
HE PROBABLY THINKS WE KILLED HIS COMRADES AND STOLE THESE CLOTHES FROM THEM.
IF WE CLEAR UP THAT MIS-UNDER-STANDING...
...THEN I'M SURE—!
YOU'RE ALWAYS SAYING THINGS LIKE THAT! THAT'S WHY YOU LOT ARE WEAK!!
YOU HAVE ALL THAT POWER, YET YOU HANDICAP YOURSELVES...
...UNTIL IT DESTROYS YOU.

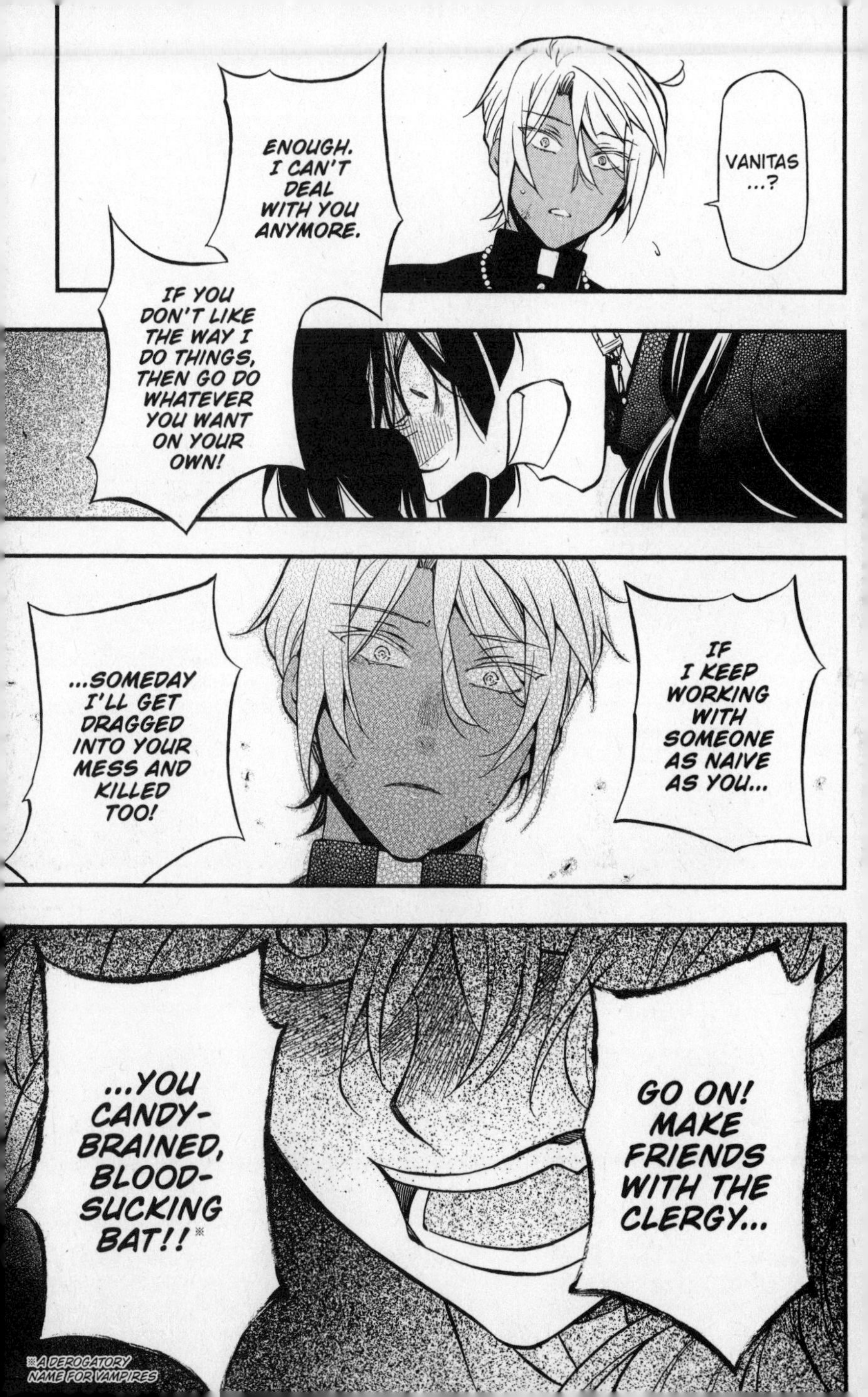
VANITAS ...?
ENOUGH. I CAN'T DEAL WITH YOU ANYMORE.
IF YOU DON'T LIKE THE WAY I DO THINGS, THEN GO DO WHATEVER YOU WANT ON YOUR OWN!
IF I KEEP WORKING WITH SOMEONE AS NAIVE AS YOU...
...SOMEDAY I'LL GET DRAGGED INTO YOUR MESS AND KILLED TOO!
GO ON! MAKE FRIENDS WITH THE CLERGY...
...YOU CANDY-BRAINED, BLOOD-SUCKING BAT!!※
※A DEROGATORY NAME FOR VAMPIRES

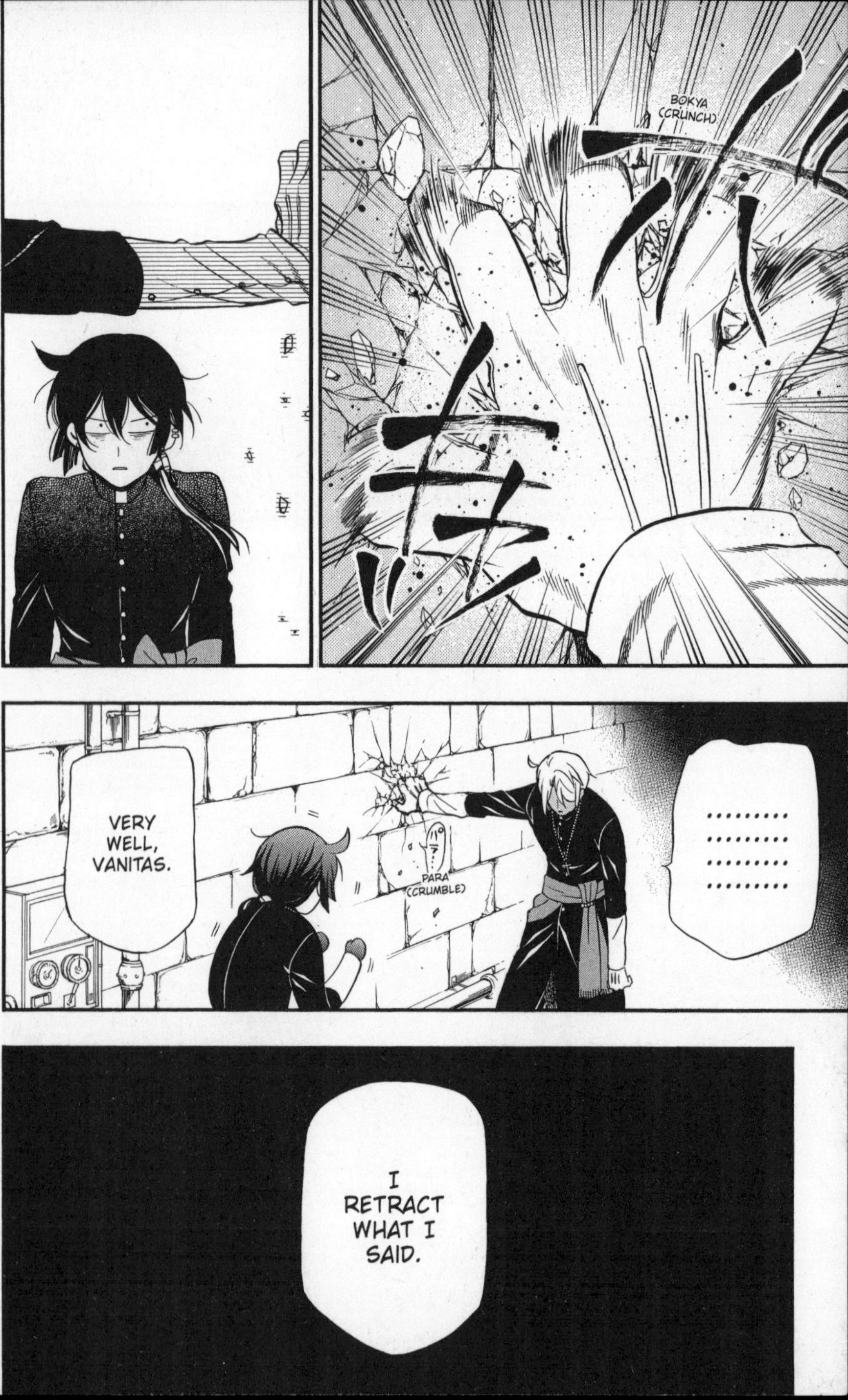
BOKYA (CRUNCH)
PARA (CRUMBLE)
VERY WELL, VANITAS.
........
........
........
........
I RETRACT WHAT I SAID.

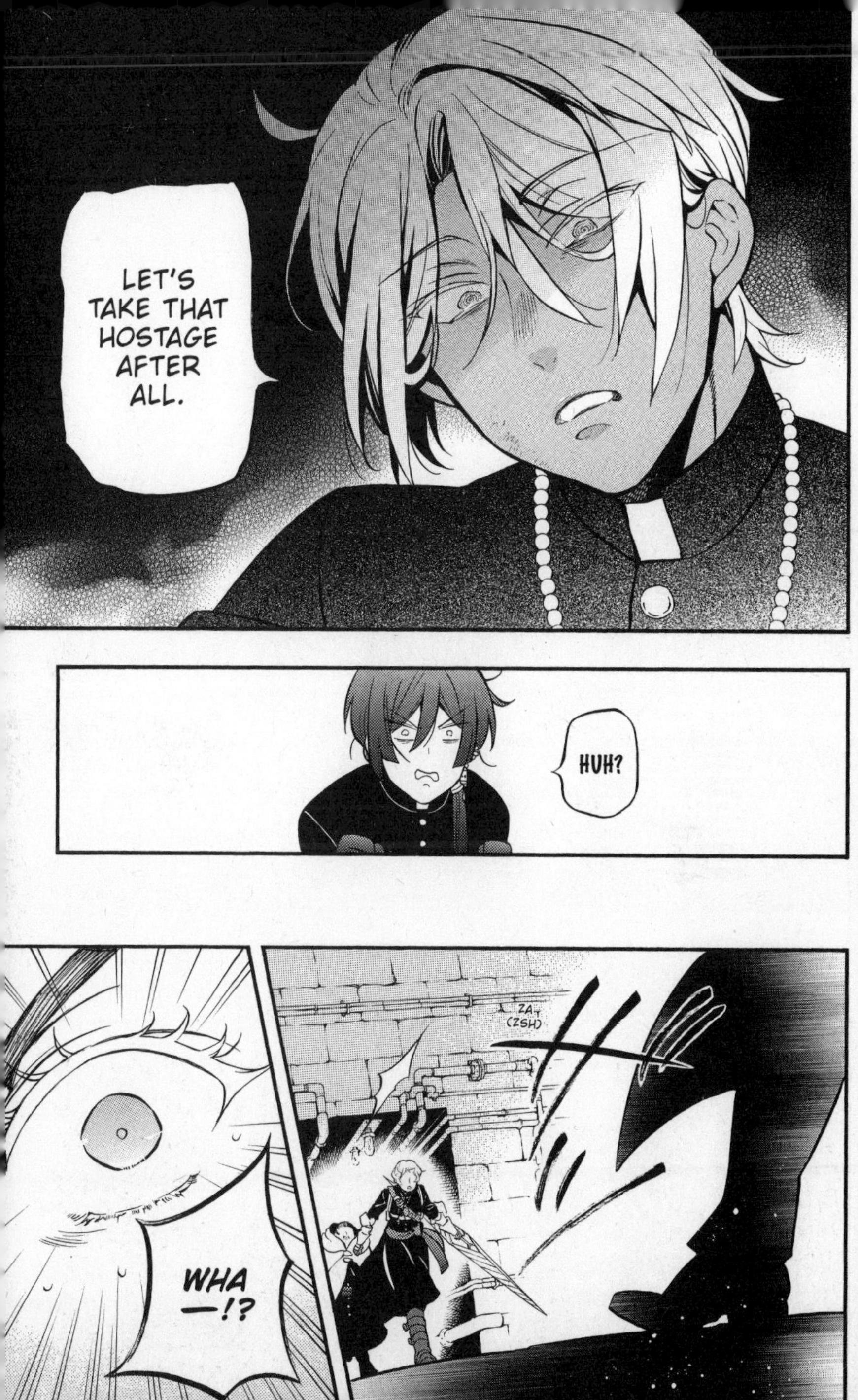
LET'S TAKE THAT HOSTAGE AFTER ALL.
HUH?
ZA (ZSH)
WHA—!?

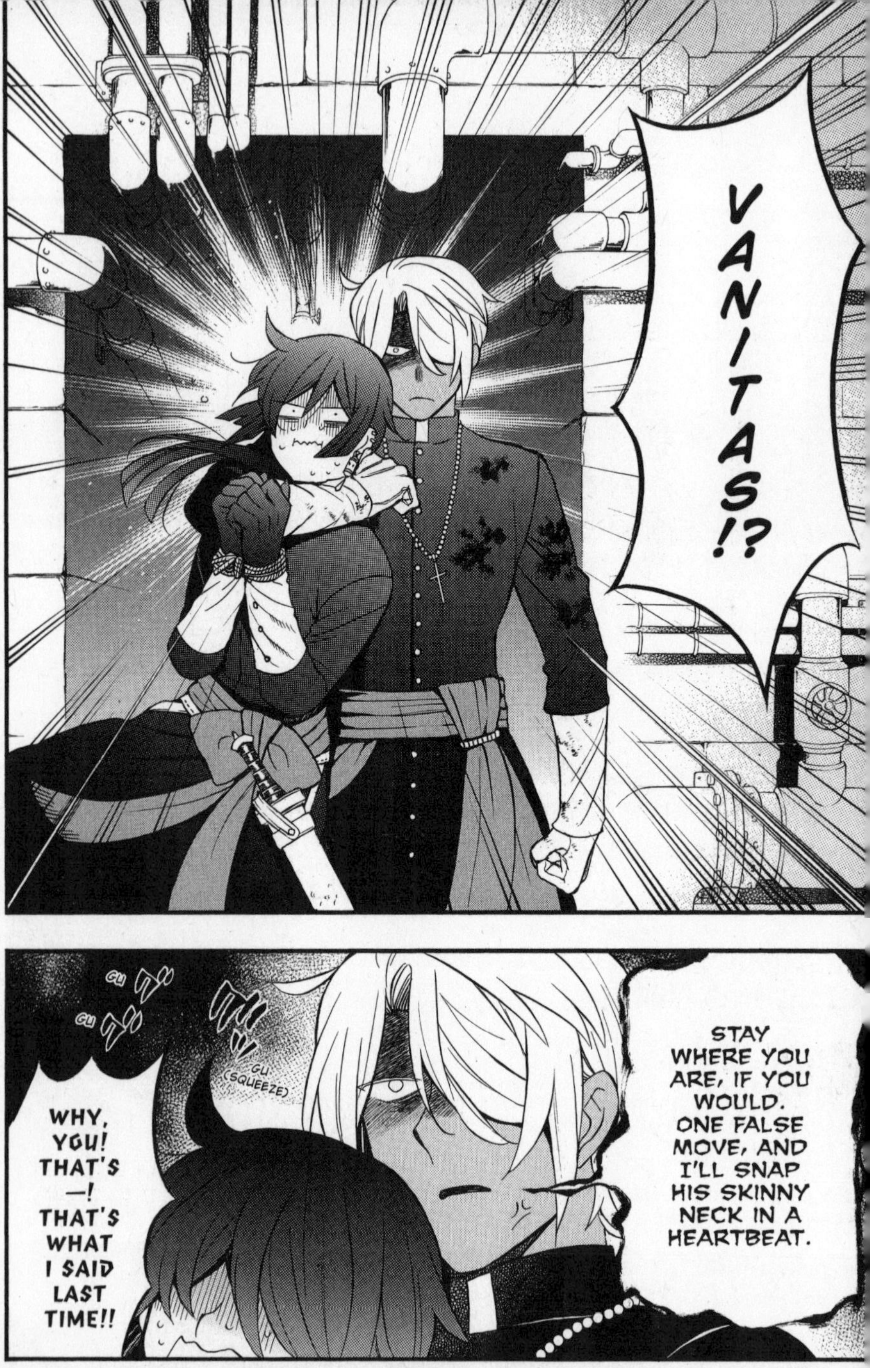
VANITAS!?
STAY WHERE YOU ARE, IF YOU WOULD. ONE FALSE MOVE, AND I'LL SNAP HIS SKINNY NECK IN A HEARTBEAT.
GU (SQUEEZE)
GU
GU
WHY, YOU! THAT'S—! THAT'S WHAT I SAID LAST TIME!!

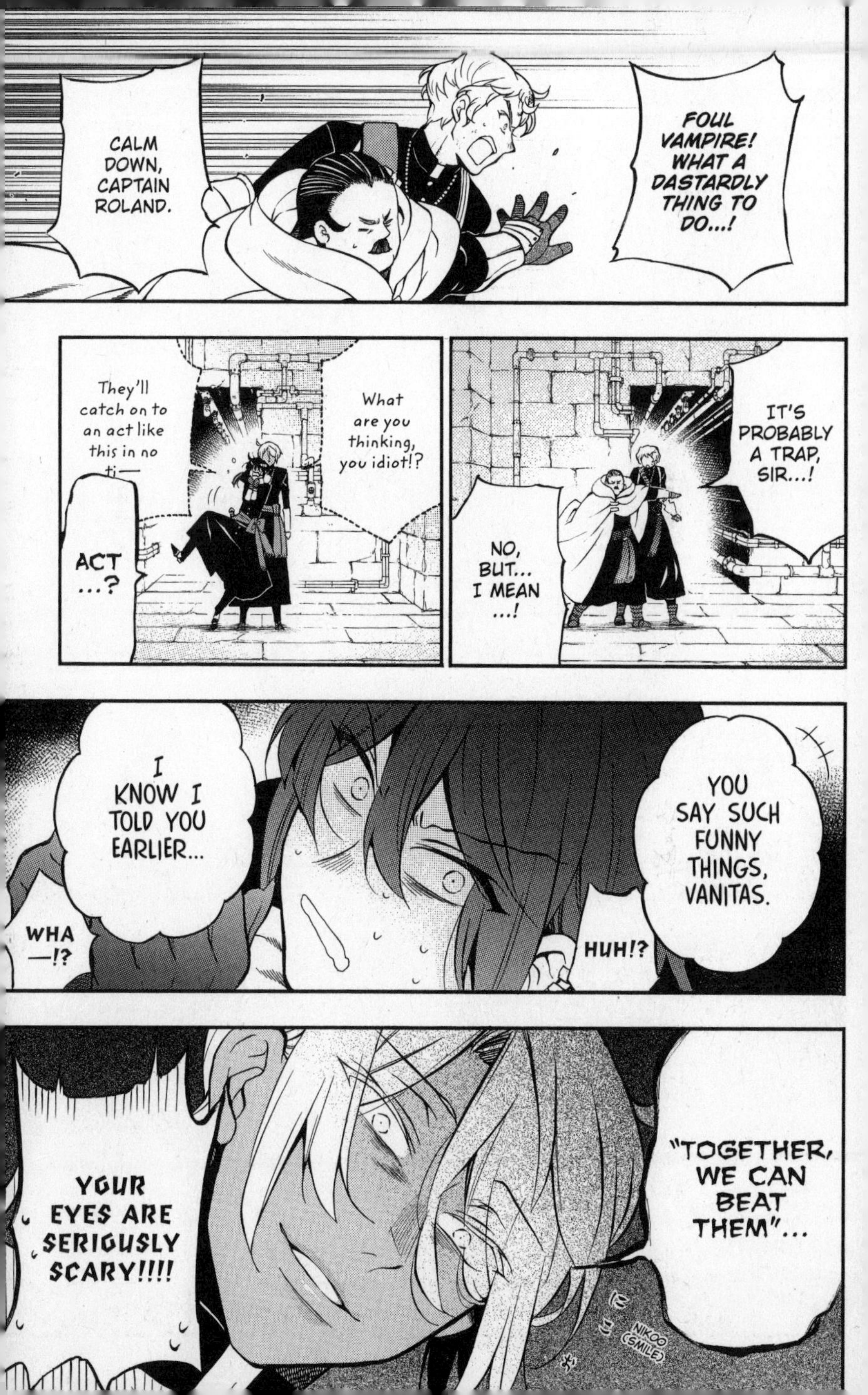
FOUL VAMPIRE! WHAT A DASTARDLY THING TO DO...!
CALM DOWN, CAPTAIN ROLAND.
IT'S PROBABLY A TRAP, SIR...!
NO, BUT... I MEAN...!
What are you thinking, you idiot!?
They'll catch on to an act like this in no ti—
ACT...?
YOU SAY SUCH FUNNY THINGS, VANITAS.
HUH!?
I KNOW I TOLD YOU EARLIER...
WHA—!?
"TOGETHER, WE CAN BEAT THEM"...
NIKOO (SMILE)
YOUR EYES ARE SERIOUSLY SCARY!!!!

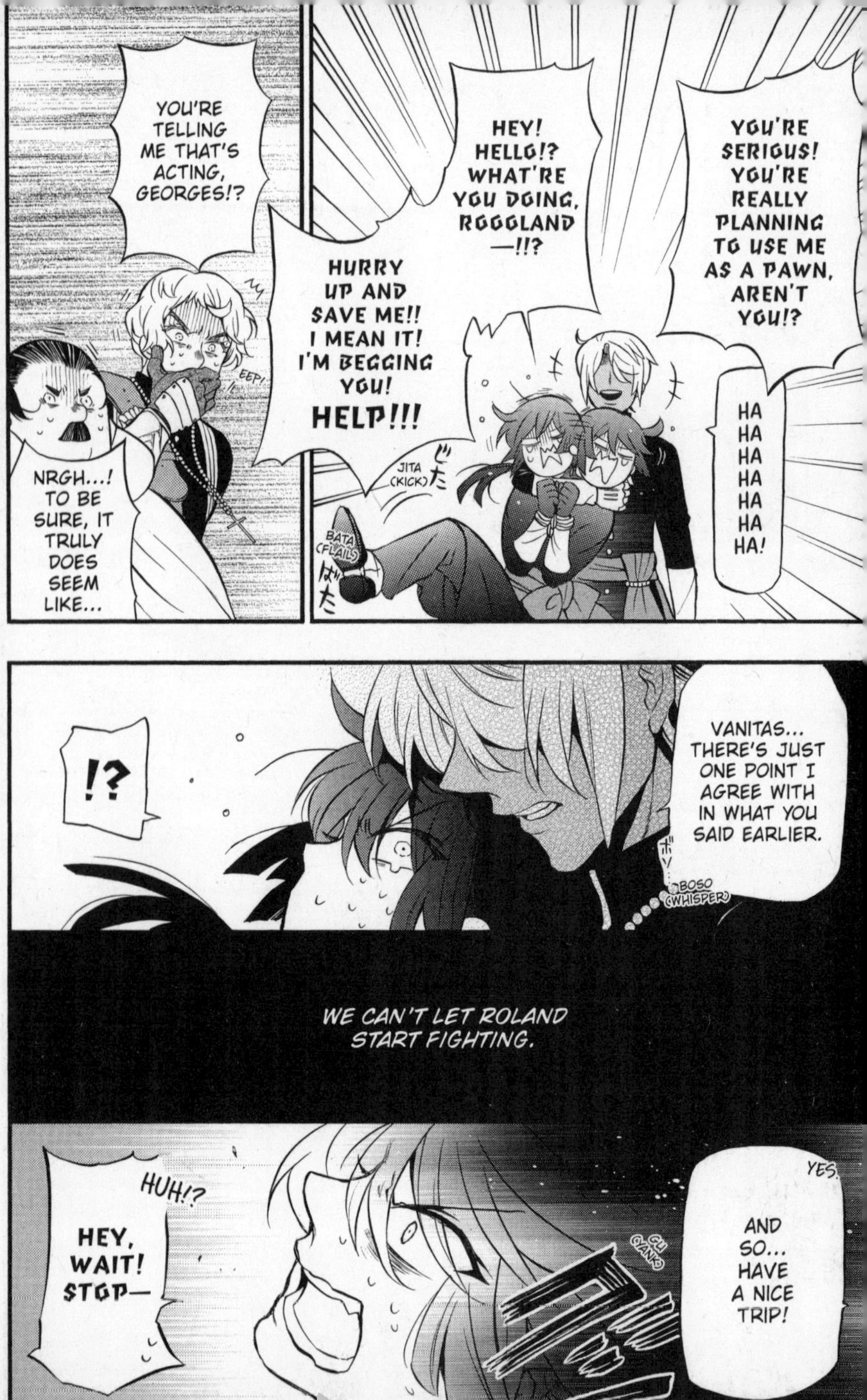
YOU'RE SERIOUS! YOU'RE REALLY PLANNING TO USE ME AS A PAWN, AREN'T YOU!?
HEY! HELLO!? WHAT'RE YOU DOING, ROOOLAND—!!?
HA HA HA HA HA HA HA!
HURRY UP AND SAVE ME!! I MEAN IT! I'M BEGGING YOU! HELP!!!
JITA (KICK)
BATA (FLAIL)
YOU'RE TELLING ME THAT'S ACTING, GEORGES!?
EEP!
NRGH...! TO BE SURE, IT TRULY DOES SEEM LIKE...
VANITAS... THERE'S JUST ONE POINT I AGREE WITH IN WHAT YOU SAID EARLIER.
BOSO (WHISPER)
!?
WE CAN'T LET ROLAND START FIGHTING.
YES.
AND SO... HAVE A NICE TRIP!
GU (YANK)
HUH!?
HEY, WAIT! STOP—

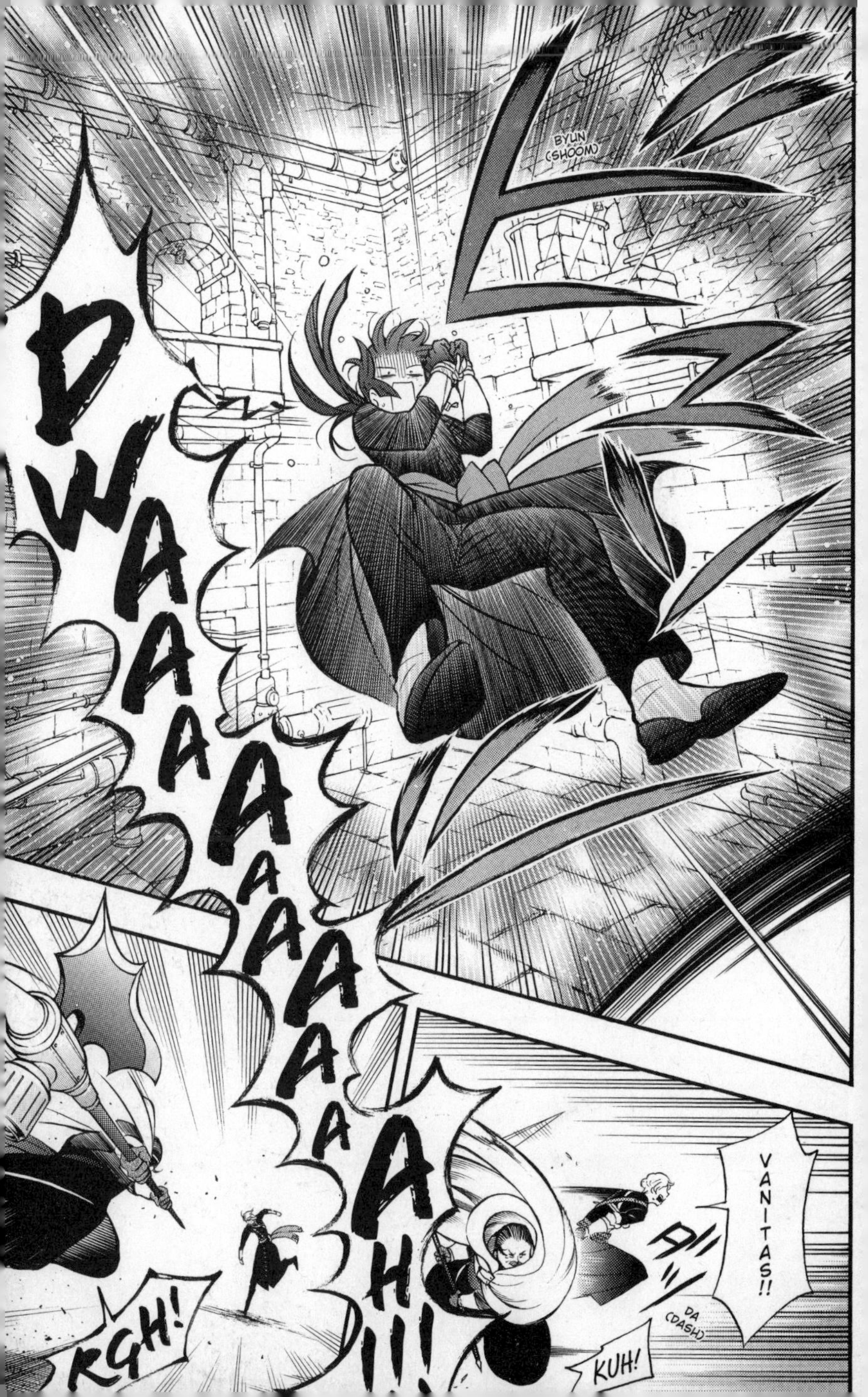
BYUN
(SHOOM)
DWAAAAAAAAAAAAAH!!
VANITAS!!
DA
(DASH)
KUH!
RGH!

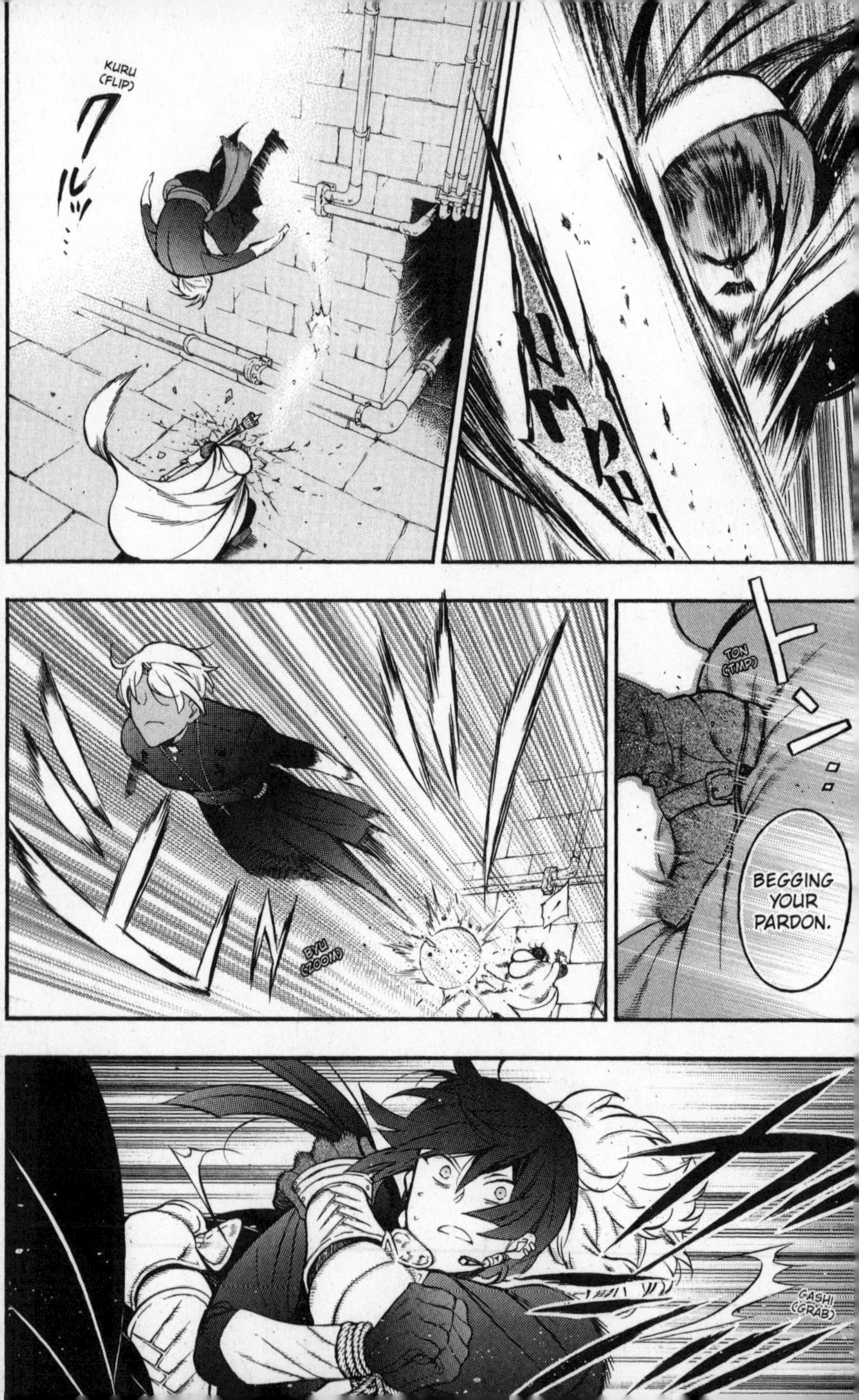

KURU (FLIP)
TON (TMP)
BEGGING YOUR PARDON.
BYU (ZOOM)
GASHI (GRAB)

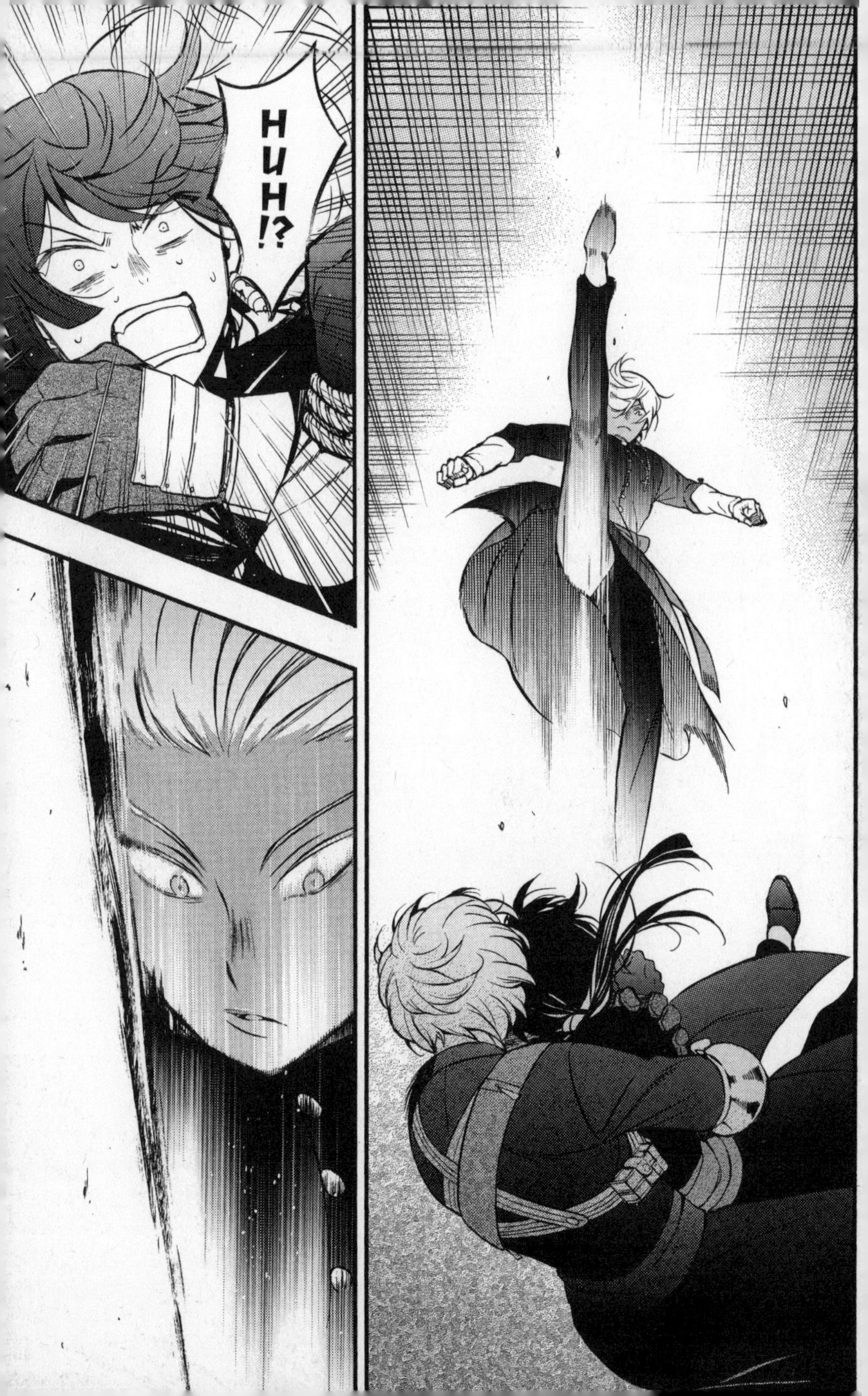
HUH!?

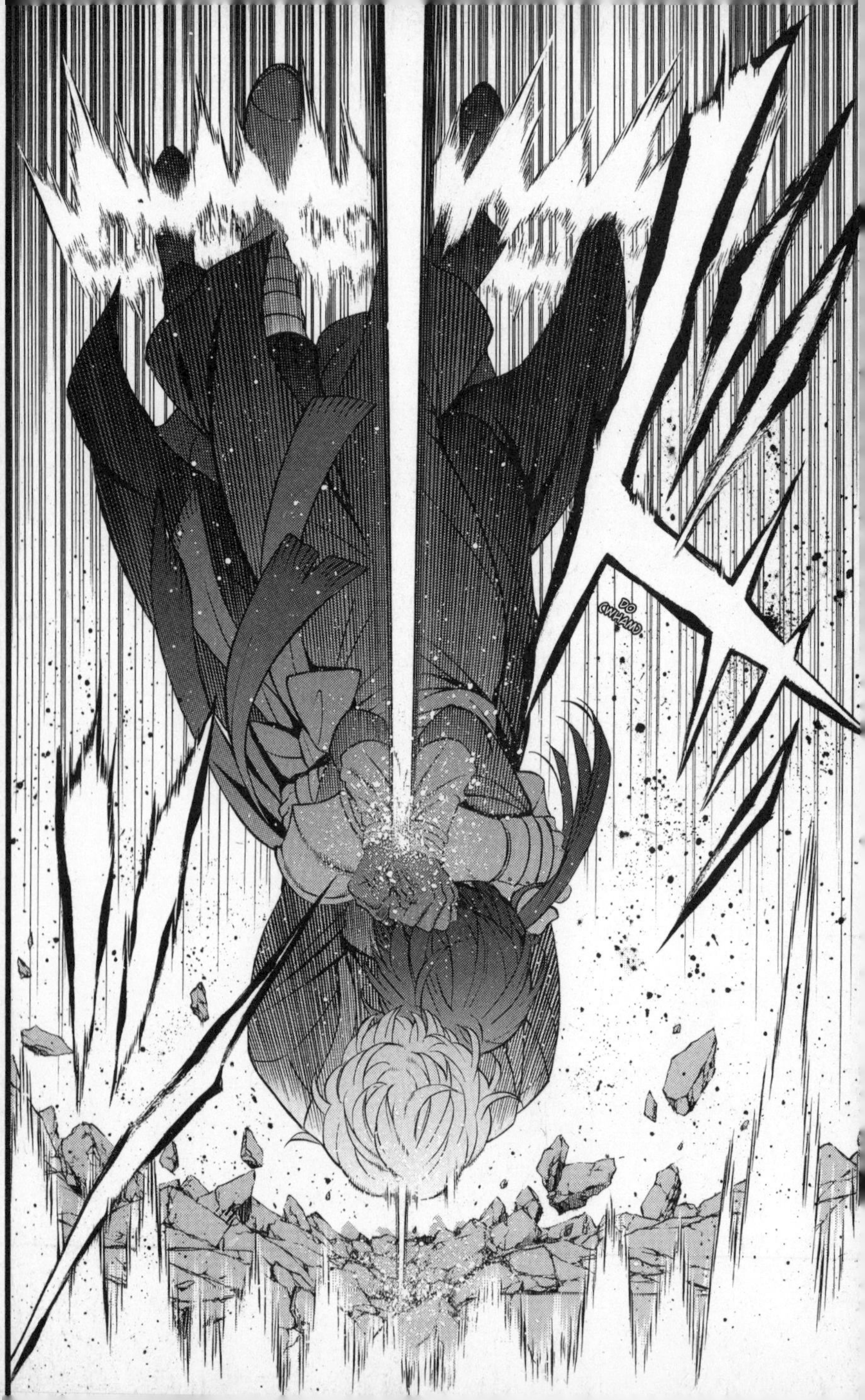
DO (WHAM)

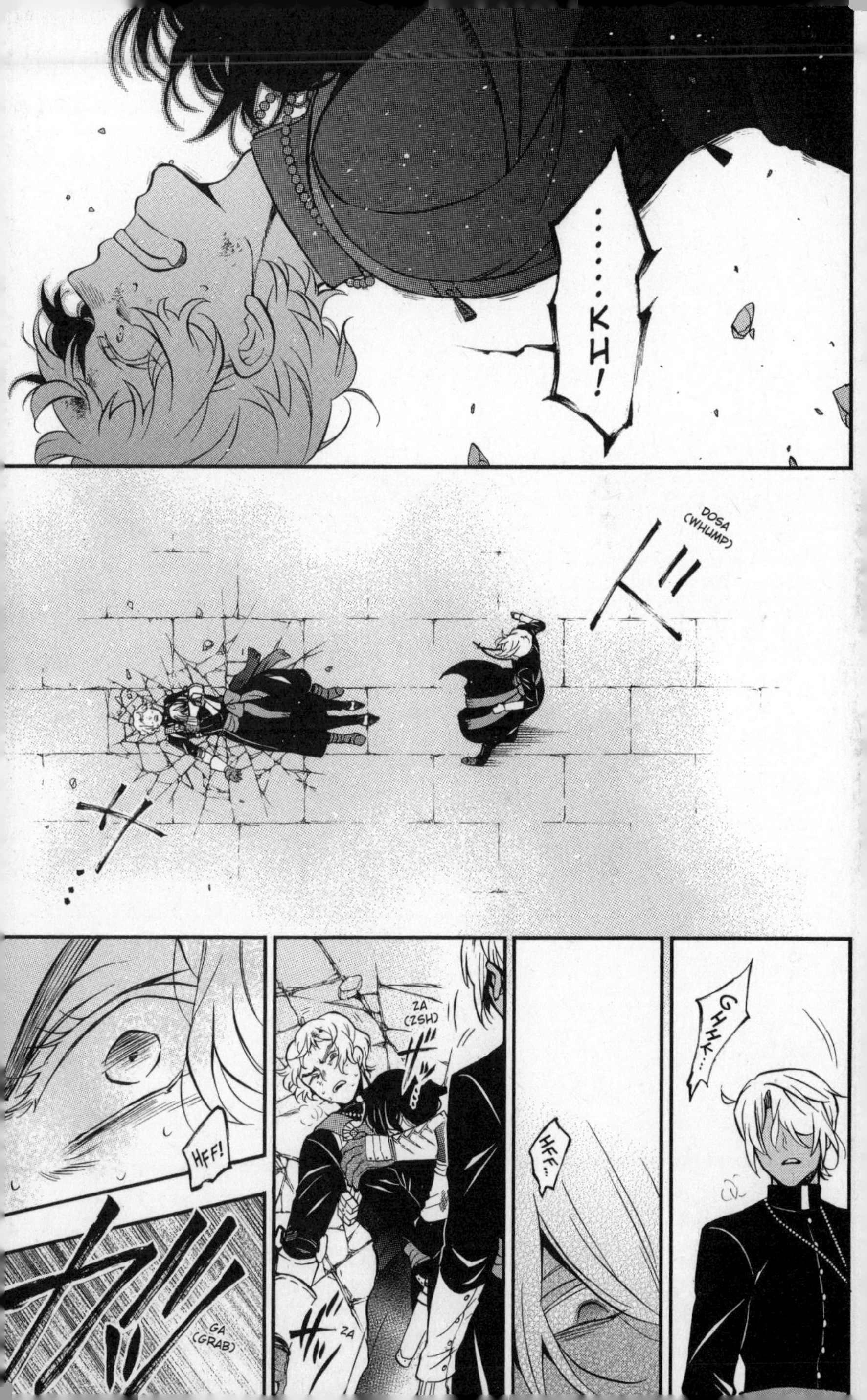
......KH!
DOSA (WHUMP)
GHHK...
HFF...
ZA (ZSH)
ZA
HFF!
GA (GRAB)

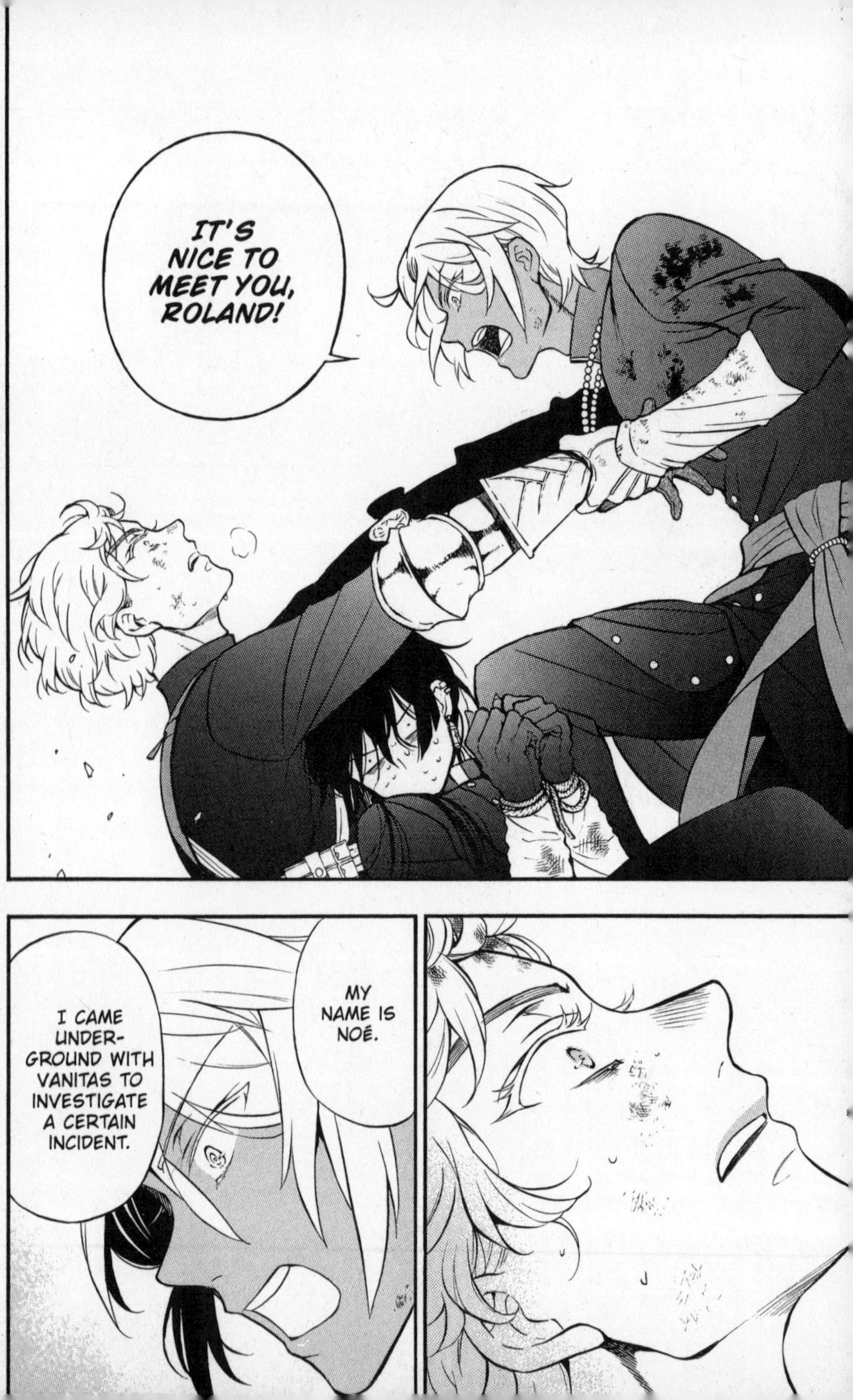
IT'S NICE TO MEET YOU, ROLAND!
MY NAME IS NOÉ.
I CAME UNDER-GROUND WITH VANITAS TO INVESTIGATE A CERTAIN INCIDENT.

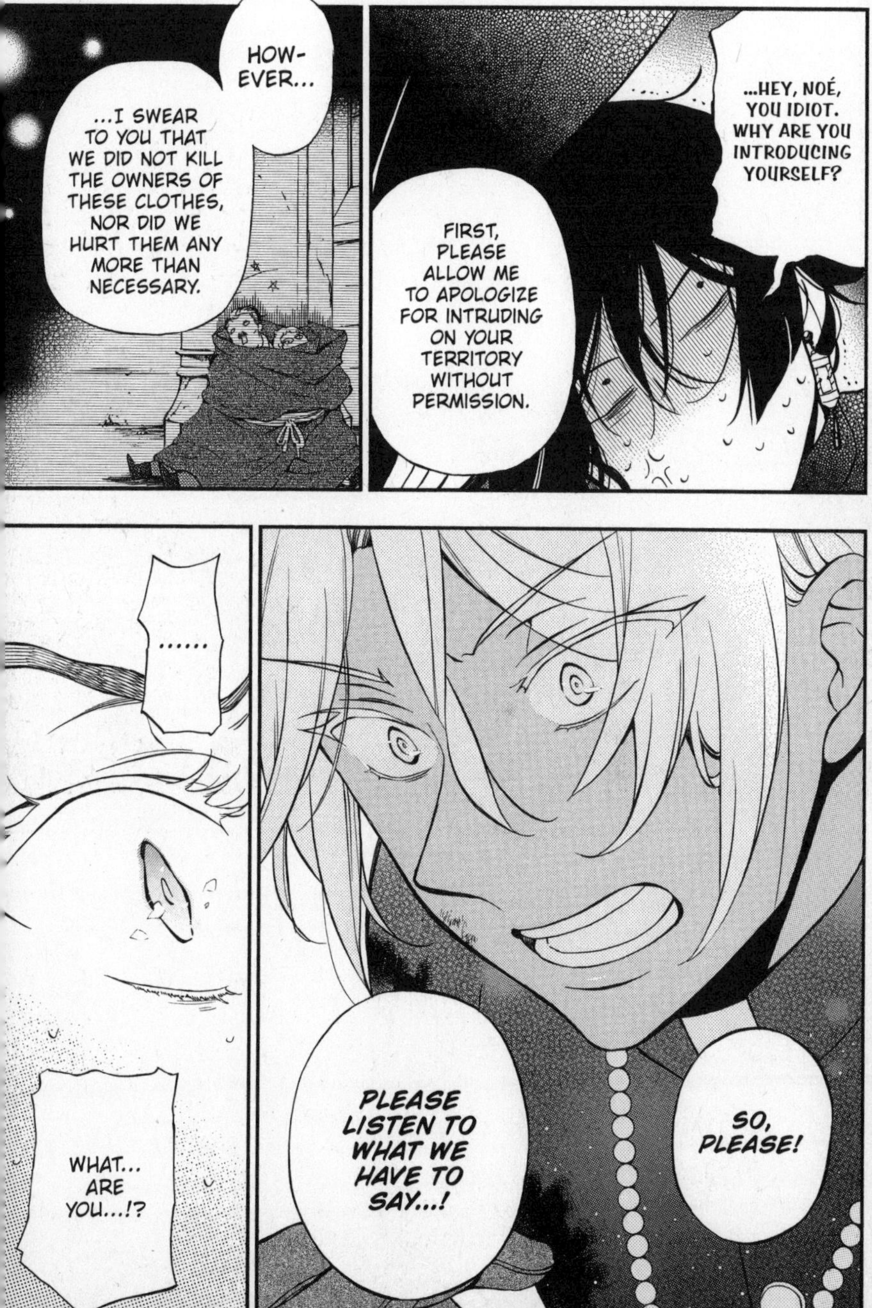
...HEY, NOÉ, YOU IDIOT. WHY ARE YOU INTRODUCING YOURSELF?
FIRST, PLEASE ALLOW ME TO APOLOGIZE FOR INTRUDING ON YOUR TERRITORY WITHOUT PERMISSION.
HOW-EVER...
...I SWEAR TO YOU THAT WE DID NOT KILL THE OWNERS OF THESE CLOTHES, NOR DID WE HURT THEM ANY MORE THAN NECESSARY.
SO, PLEASE!
PLEASE LISTEN TO WHAT WE HAVE TO SAY...!
......
WHAT... ARE YOU...!?

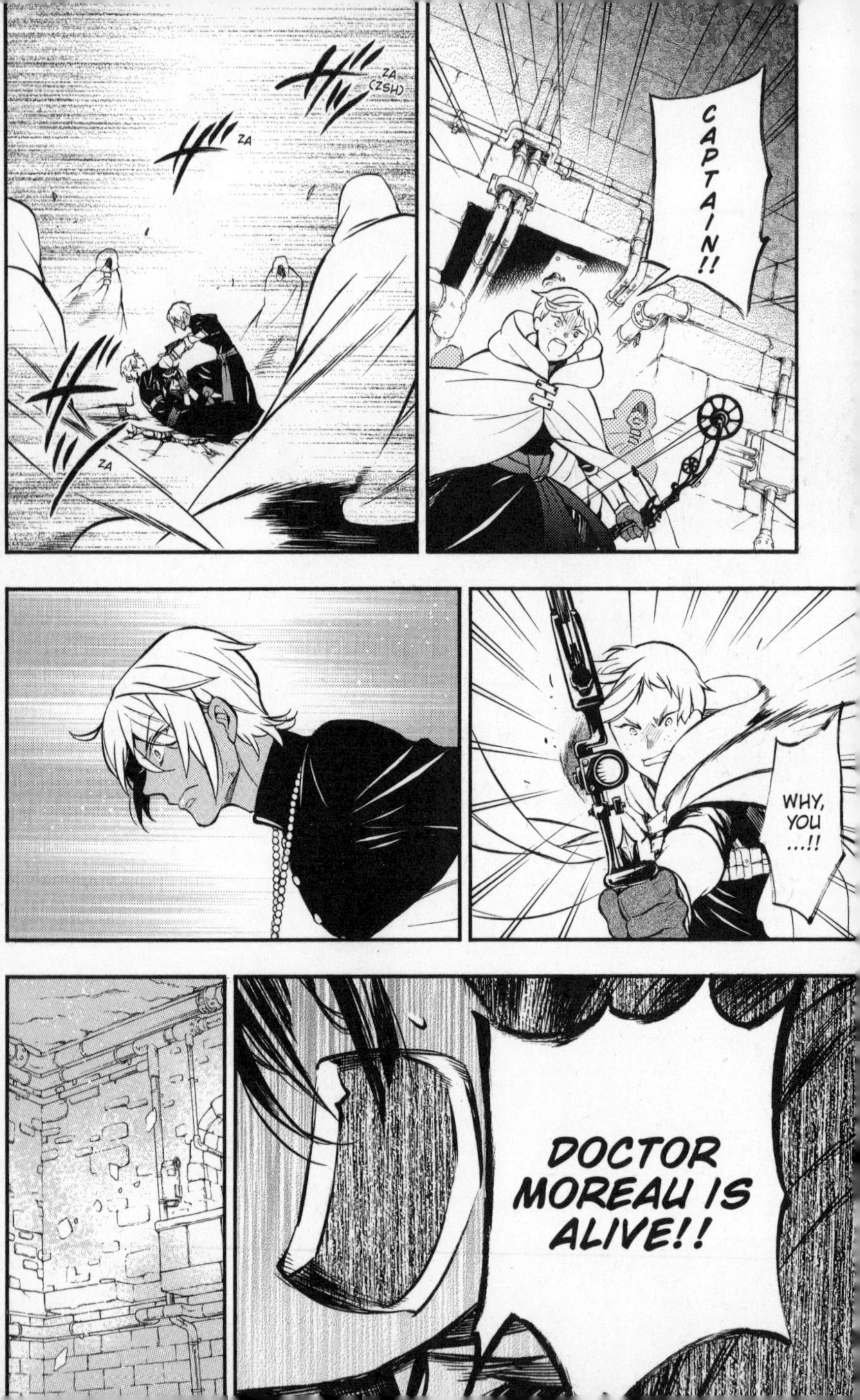
CAPTAIN!!
ZA (ZSH)
ZA
ZA
WHY, YOU ...!!
DOCTOR MOREAU IS ALIVE!!

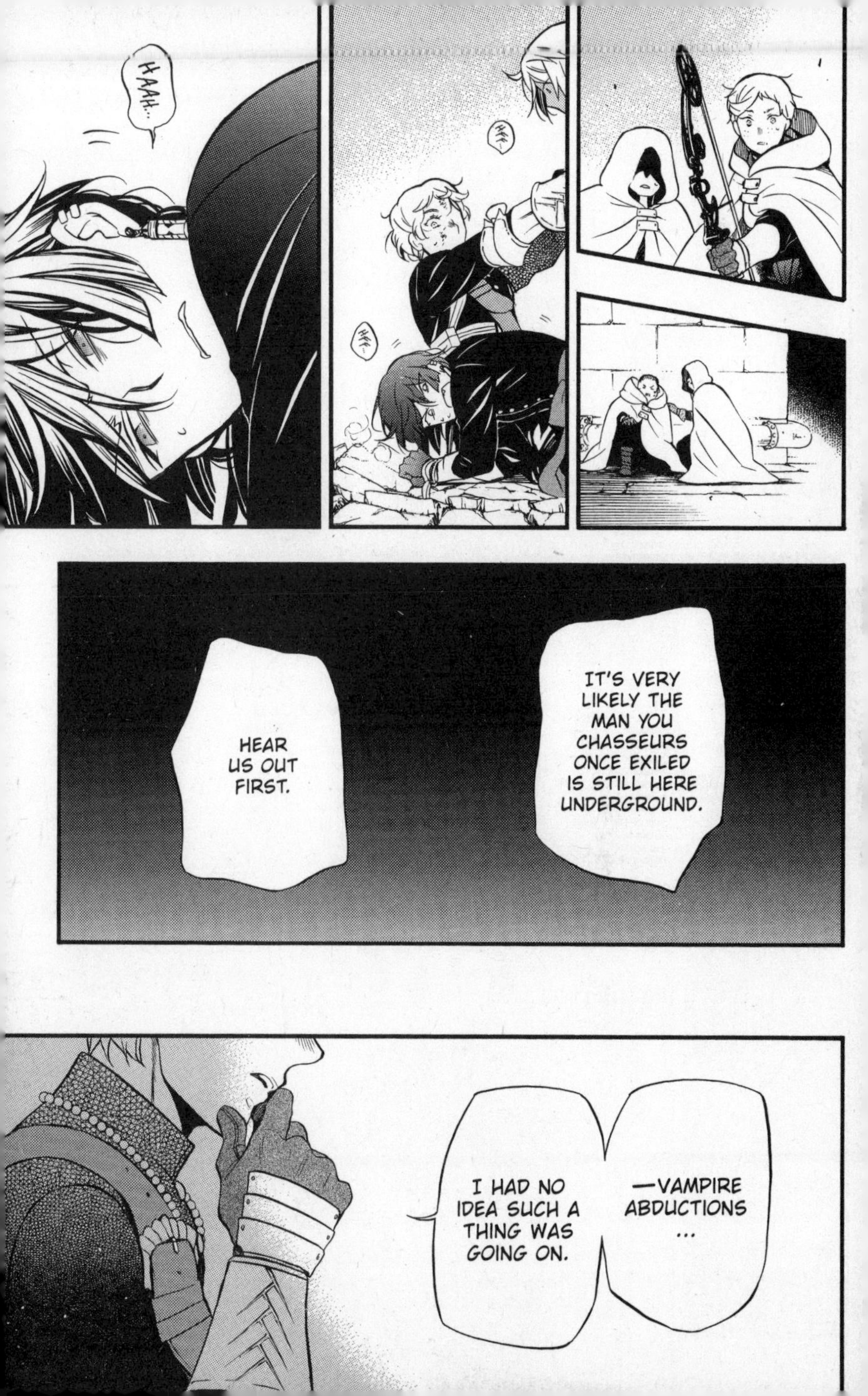
HAAAH...
IT'S VERY LIKELY THE MAN YOU CHASSEURS ONCE EXILED IS STILL HERE UNDERGROUND.
HEAR US OUT FIRST.
—VAMPIRE ABDUCTIONS ...
I HAD NO IDEA SUCH A THING WAS GOING ON.

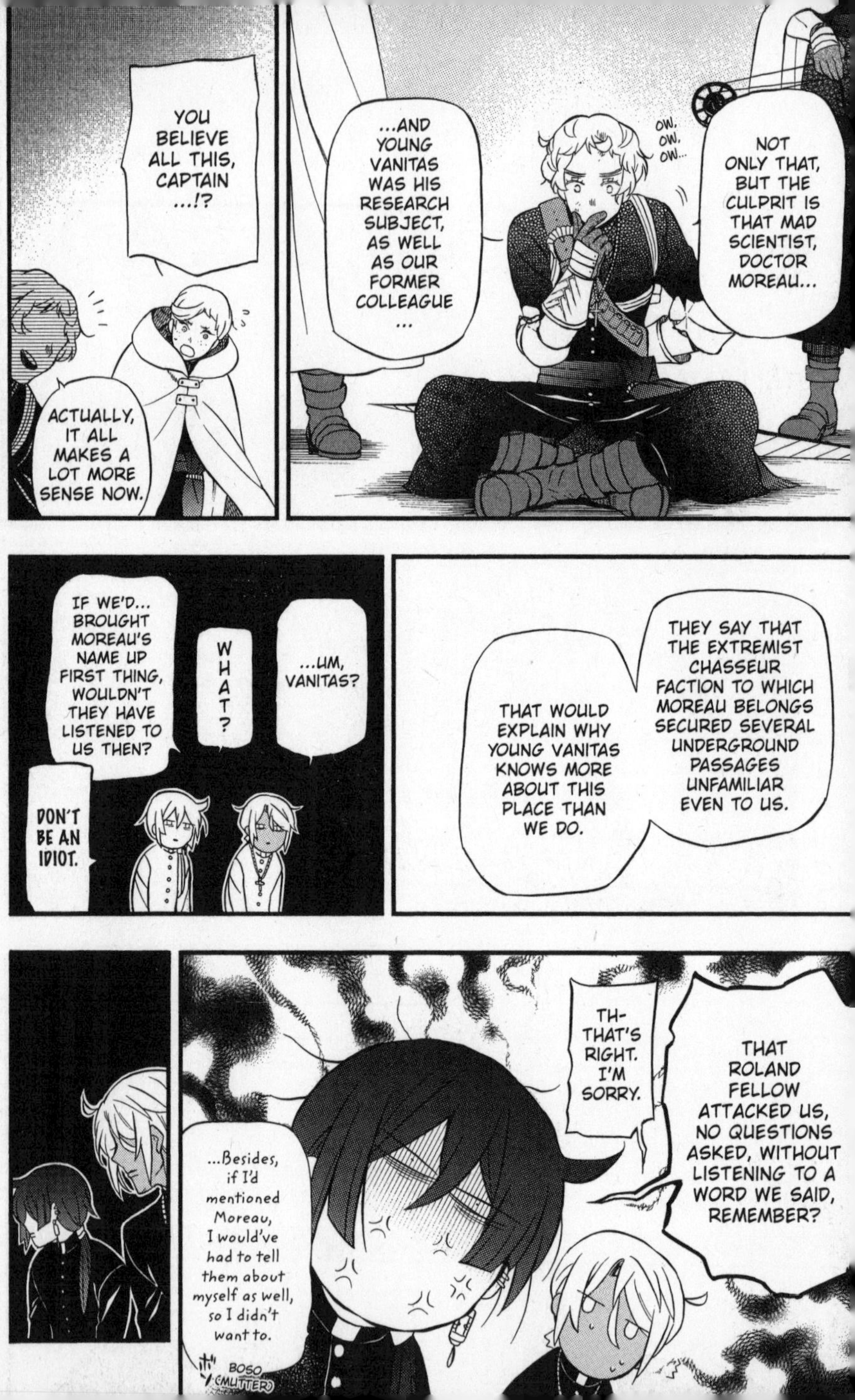
NOT ONLY THAT, BUT THE CULPRIT IS THAT MAD SCIENTIST, DOCTOR MOREAU...
OW, OW, OW...
...AND YOUNG VANITAS WAS HIS RESEARCH SUBJECT, AS WELL AS OUR FORMER COLLEAGUE...
YOU BELIEVE ALL THIS, CAPTAIN...!?
ACTUALLY, IT ALL MAKES A LOT MORE SENSE NOW.
THEY SAY THAT THE EXTREMIST CHASSEUR FACTION TO WHICH MOREAU BELONGS SECURED SEVERAL UNDERGROUND PASSAGES UNFAMILIAR EVEN TO US.
THAT WOULD EXPLAIN WHY YOUNG VANITAS KNOWS MORE ABOUT THIS PLACE THAN WE DO.
...UM, VANITAS?
WHAT?
IF WE'D... BROUGHT MOREAU'S NAME UP FIRST THING, WOULDN'T THEY HAVE LISTENED TO US THEN?
DON'T BE AN IDIOT.
THAT ROLAND FELLOW ATTACKED US, NO QUESTIONS ASKED, WITHOUT LISTENING TO A WORD WE SAID, REMEMBER?
TH-THAT'S RIGHT. I'M SORRY.
...Besides, if I'd mentioned Moreau, I would've had to tell them about myself as well, so I didn't want to.
BOSO (MUTTER)

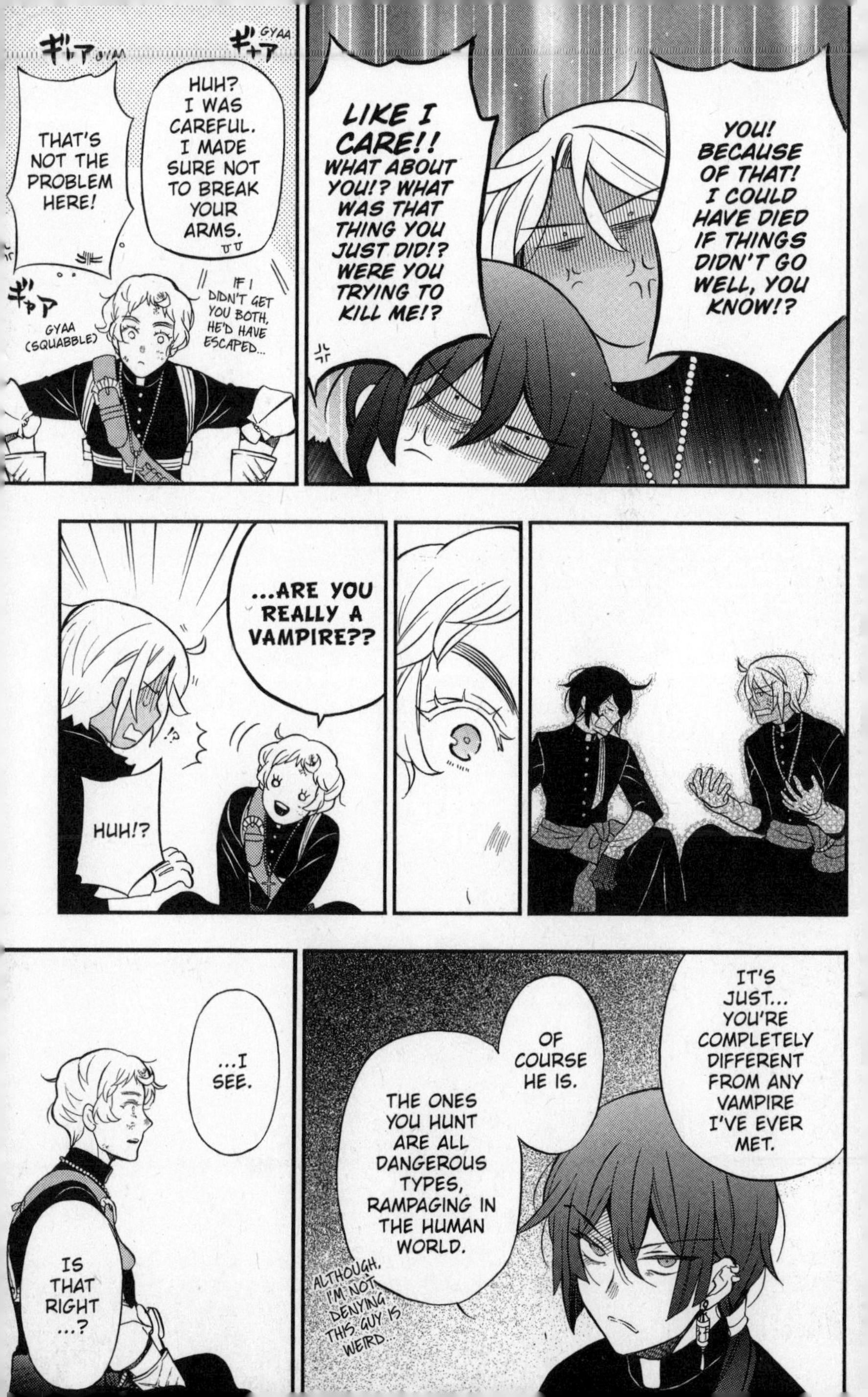
YOU! BECAUSE OF THAT! I COULD HAVE DIED IF THINGS DIDN'T GO WELL, YOU KNOW!?
LIKE I CARE!! WHAT ABOUT YOU!? WHAT WAS THAT THING YOU JUST DID!? WERE YOU TRYING TO KILL ME!?
ギャア GYAA
ギャア GYAA
HUH? I WAS CAREFUL. I MADE SURE NOT TO BREAK YOUR ARMS.
THAT'S NOT THE PROBLEM HERE!
ギャア GYAA (SQUABBLE)
IF I DIDN'T GET YOU BOTH, HE'D HAVE ESCAPED...
...ARE YOU REALLY A VAMPIRE??
HUH!?
IT'S JUST... YOU'RE COMPLETELY DIFFERENT FROM ANY VAMPIRE I'VE EVER MET.
OF COURSE HE IS.
THE ONES YOU HUNT ARE ALL DANGEROUS TYPES, RAMPAGING IN THE HUMAN WORLD.
ALTHOUGH, I'M NOT DENYING THIS GUY IS WEIRD...
...I SEE.
IS THAT RIGHT...?

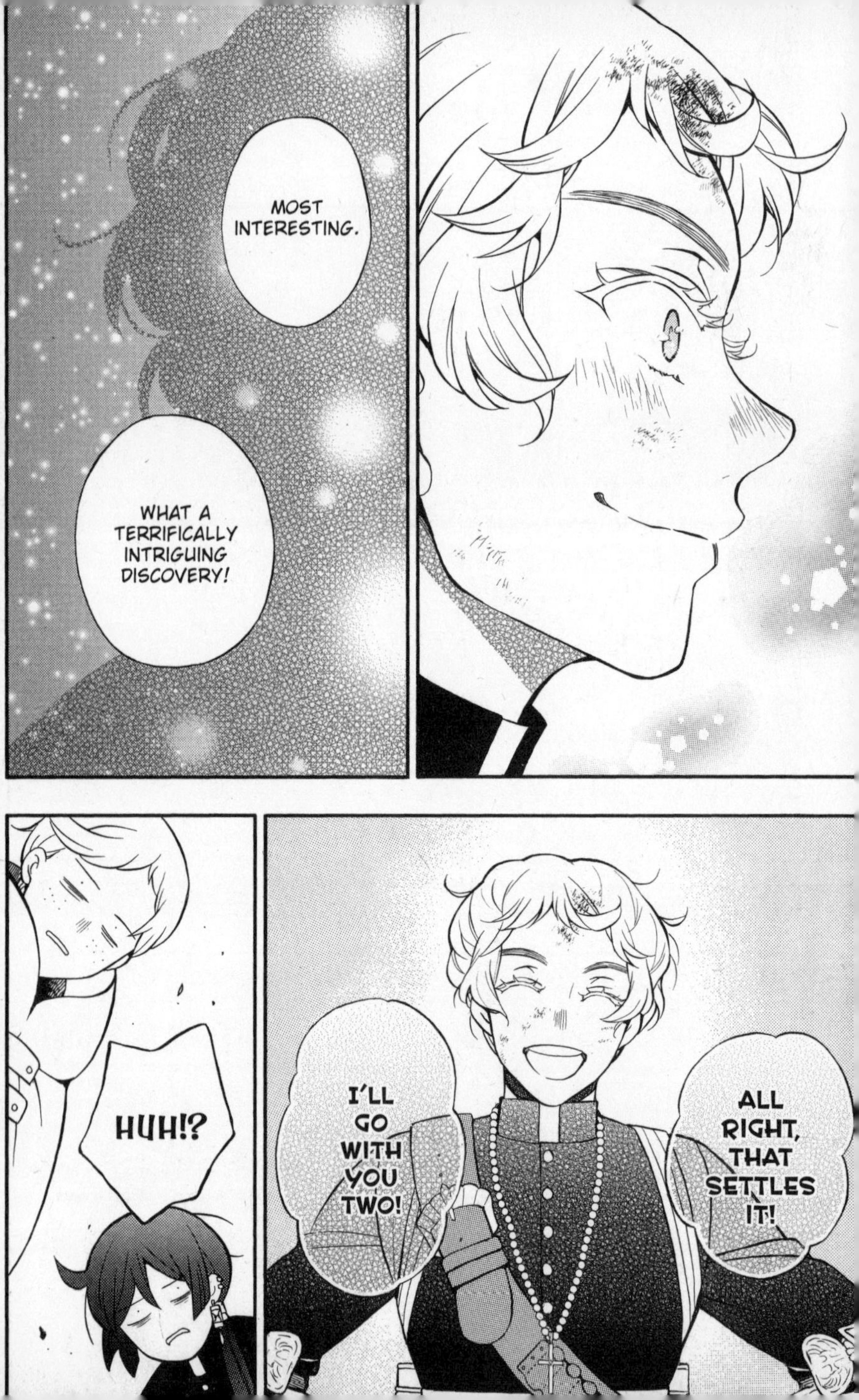
MOST INTERESTING.
WHAT A TERRIFICALLY INTRIGUING DISCOVERY!
ALL RIGHT, THAT SETTLES IT!
I'LL GO WITH YOU TWO!
HUH!?

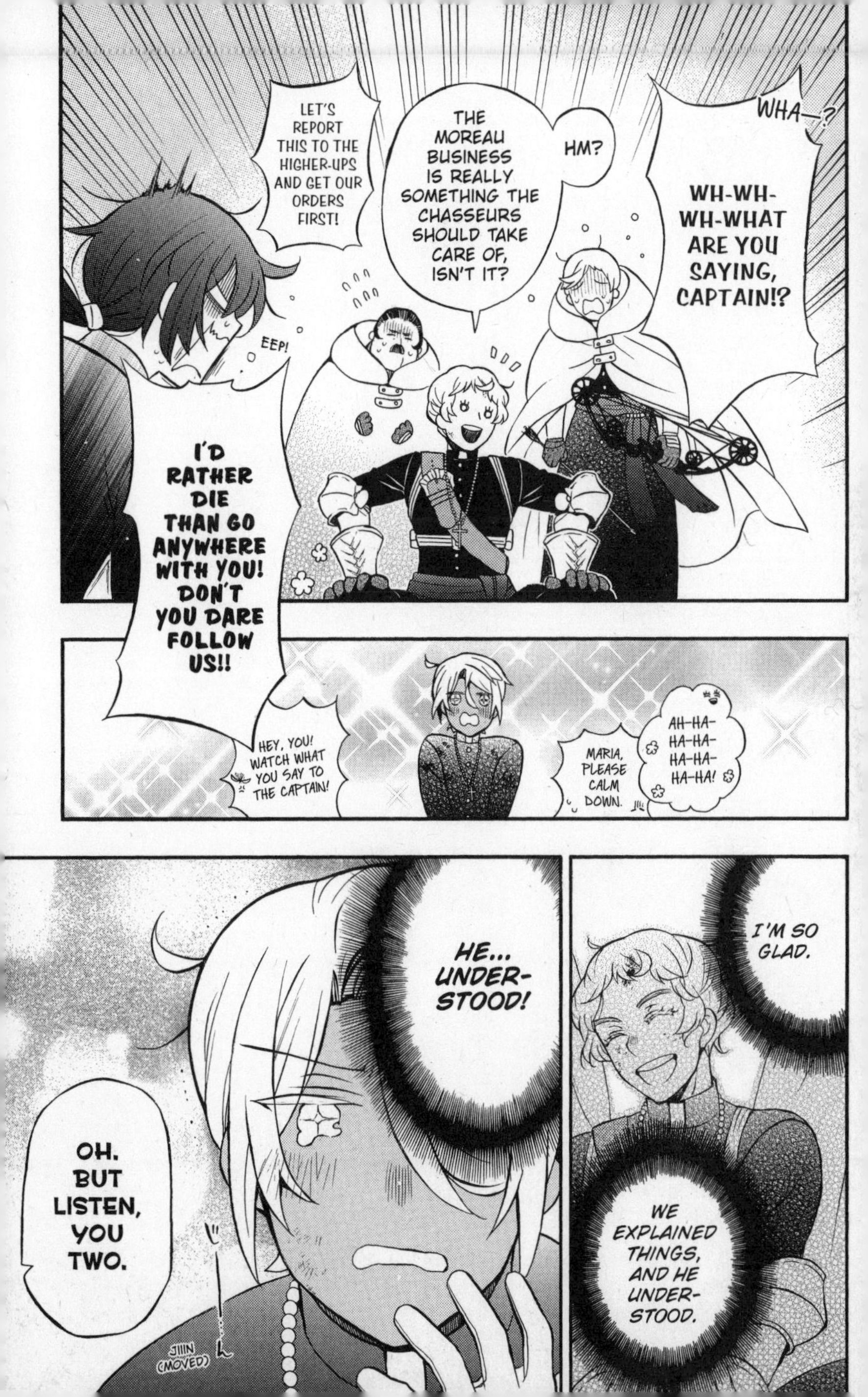
WHA—?
WH-WH-WH-WHAT ARE YOU SAYING, CAPTAIN!?
HM?
THE MOREAU BUSINESS IS REALLY SOMETHING THE CHASSEURS SHOULD TAKE CARE OF, ISN'T IT?
LET'S REPORT THIS TO THE HIGHER-UPS AND GET OUR ORDERS FIRST!
EEP!
I'D RATHER DIE THAN GO ANYWHERE WITH YOU! DON'T YOU DARE FOLLOW US!!
AH-HA-HA-HA-HA-HA-HA-HA!
MARIA, PLEASE CALM DOWN.
HEY, YOU! WATCH WHAT YOU SAY TO THE CAPTAIN!
I'M SO GLAD.
WE EXPLAINED THINGS, AND HE UNDERSTOOD.
HE... UNDERSTOOD!
OH. BUT LISTEN, YOU TWO.
JIIN (MOVED)

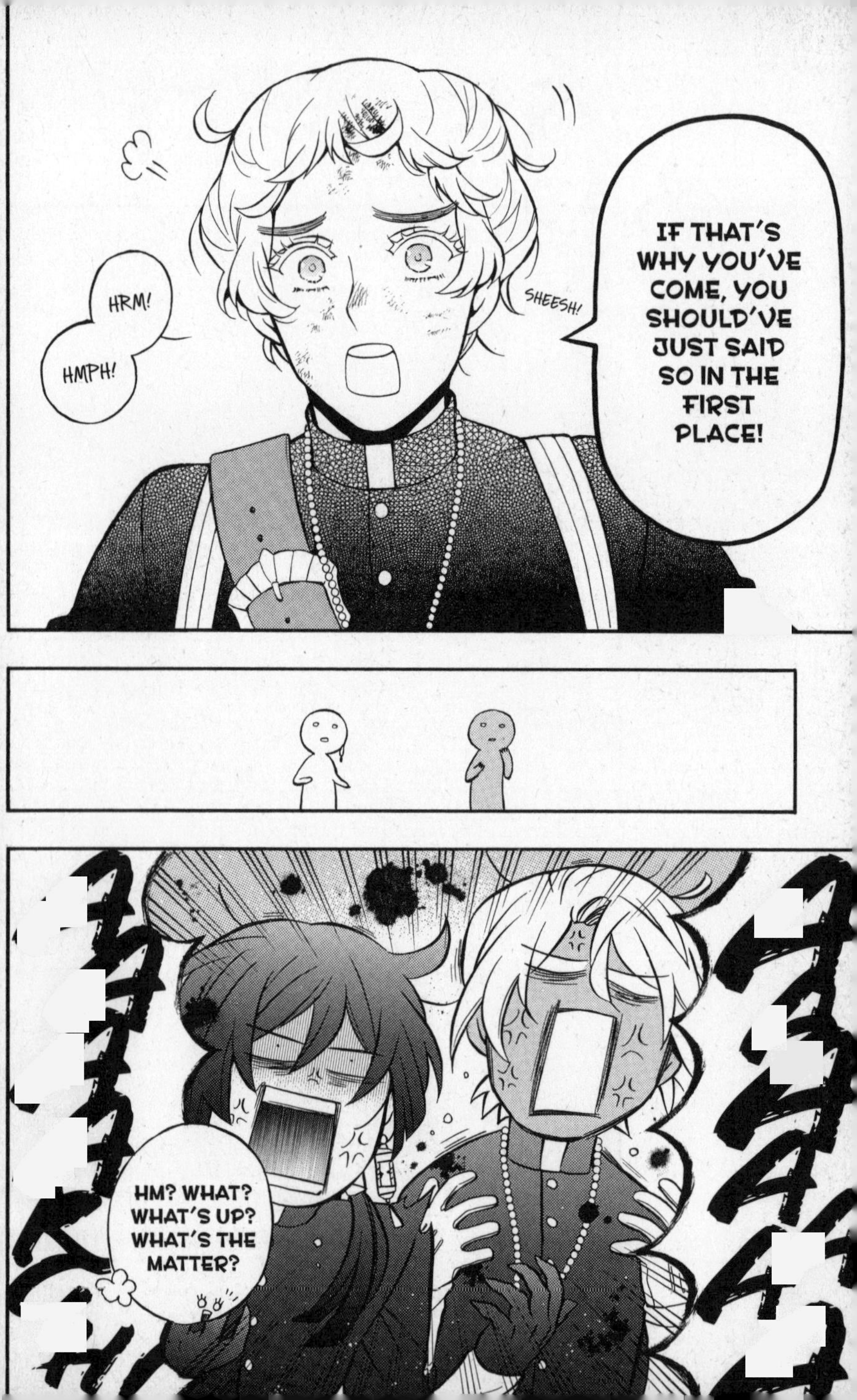
IF THAT'S WHY YOU'VE COME, YOU SHOULD'VE JUST SAID SO IN THE FIRST PLACE!
SHEESH!
HRM!
HMPH!
HM? WHAT? WHAT'S UP? WHAT'S THE MATTER?

*Mémoire 16 Galopp* AT THE END OF THE RIOT

*Les Mémoires de Vanitas*

SHE USES HER BANGS TO HIDE AN OLD SCAR ON HER FOREHEAD.

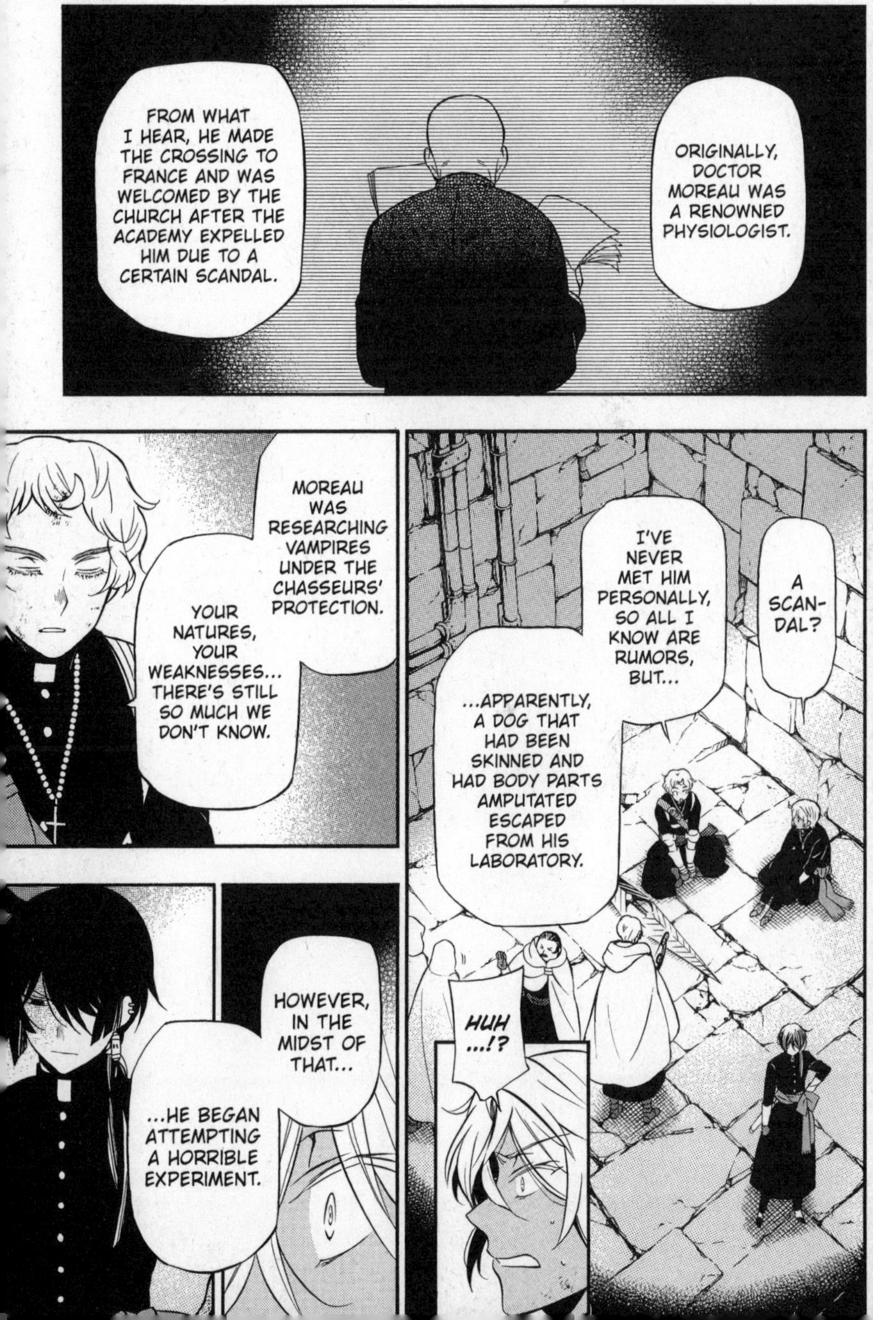
ORIGINALLY, DOCTOR MOREAU WAS A RENOWNED PHYSIOLOGIST.
FROM WHAT I HEAR, HE MADE THE CROSSING TO FRANCE AND WAS WELCOMED BY THE CHURCH AFTER THE ACADEMY EXPELLED HIM DUE TO A CERTAIN SCANDAL.
A SCAN-DAL?
I'VE NEVER MET HIM PERSONALLY, SO ALL I KNOW ARE RUMORS, BUT...
...APPARENTLY, A DOG THAT HAD BEEN SKINNED AND HAD BODY PARTS AMPUTATED ESCAPED FROM HIS LABORATORY.
HUH ...!?
MOREAU WAS RESEARCHING VAMPIRES UNDER THE CHASSEURS' PROTECTION.
YOUR NATURES, YOUR WEAKNESSES... THERE'S STILL SO MUCH WE DON'T KNOW.
HOWEVER, IN THE MIDST OF THAT...
...HE BEGAN ATTEMPTING A HORRIBLE EXPERIMENT.

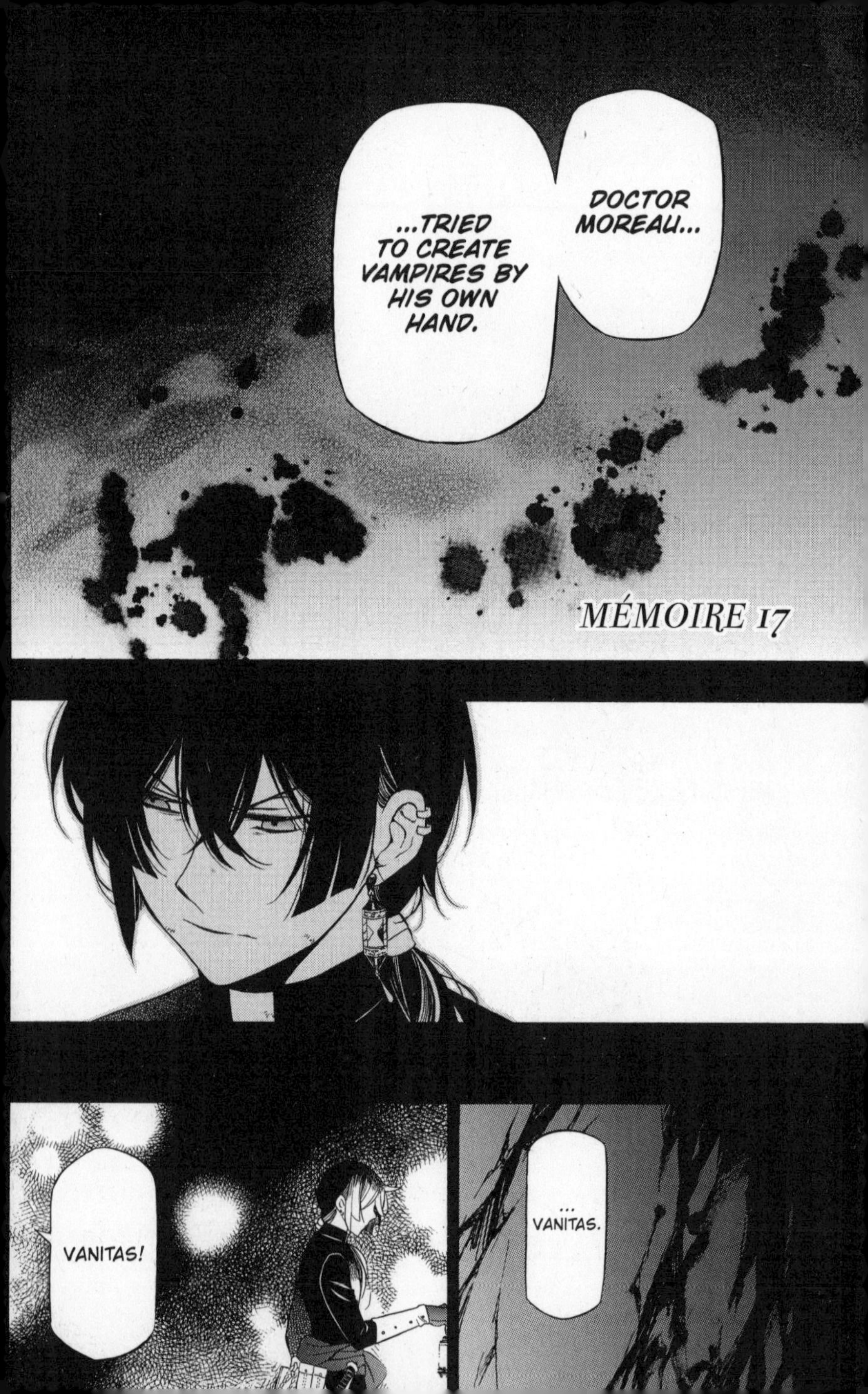
DOCTOR MOREAU...
...TRIED TO CREATE VAMPIRES BY HIS OWN HAND.
MÉMOIRE 17
...VANITAS.
VANITAS!

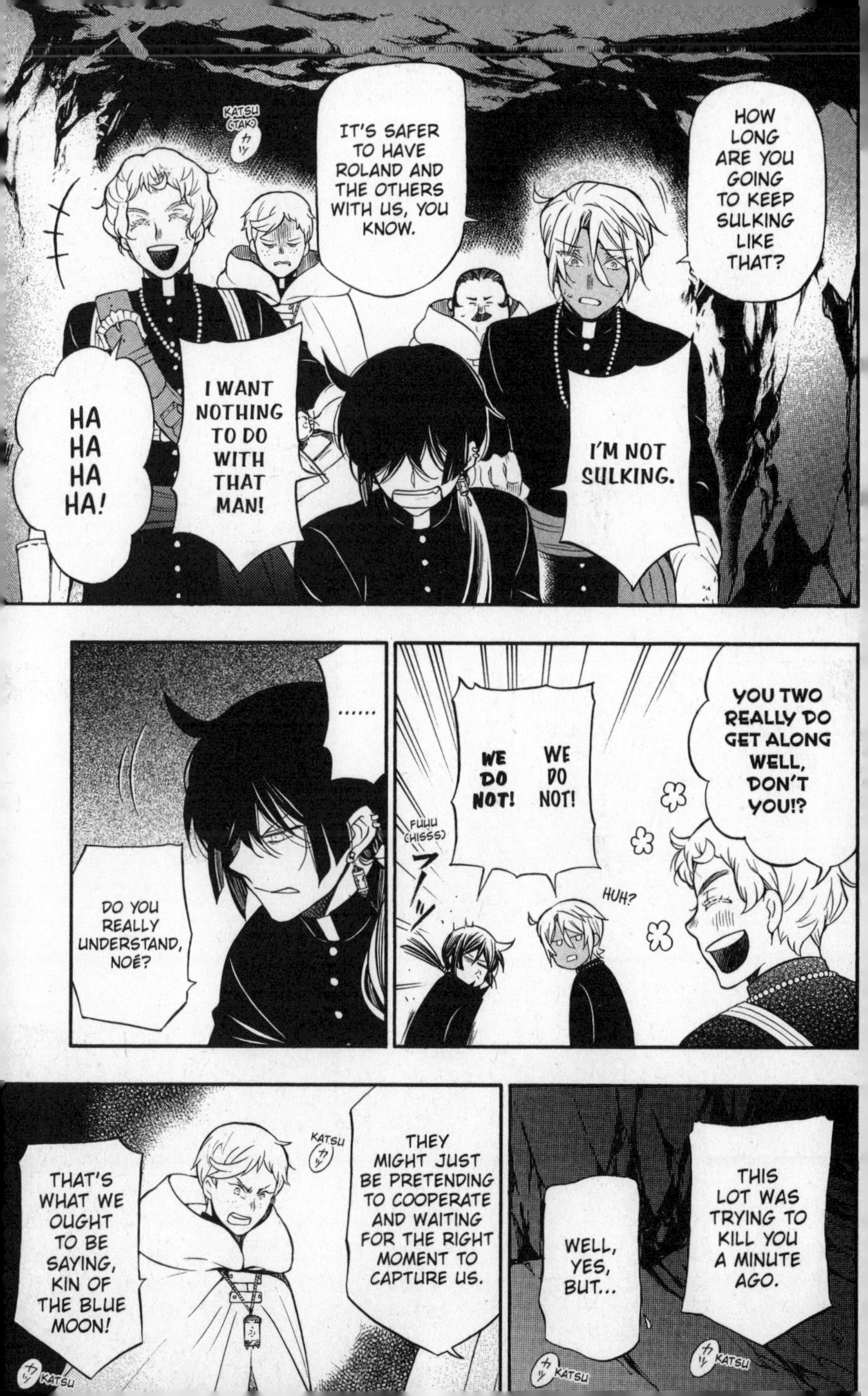

HOW LONG ARE YOU GOING TO KEEP SULKING LIKE THAT?
IT'S SAFER TO HAVE ROLAND AND THE OTHERS WITH US, YOU KNOW.
KATSU (TAK)
I'M NOT SULKING.
I WANT NOTHING TO DO WITH THAT MAN!
HA HA HA HA!
YOU TWO REALLY DO GET ALONG WELL, DON'T YOU!?
WE DO NOT!
WE DO NOT!
FUUU (HISSS)
HUH?
......
DO YOU REALLY UNDERSTAND, NOÉ?
THIS LOT WAS TRYING TO KILL YOU A MINUTE AGO.
WELL, YES, BUT...
KATSU
KATSU
THEY MIGHT JUST BE PRETENDING TO COOPERATE AND WAITING FOR THE RIGHT MOMENT TO CAPTURE US.
KATSU
THAT'S WHAT WE OUGHT TO BE SAYING, KIN OF THE BLUE MOON!
KATSU

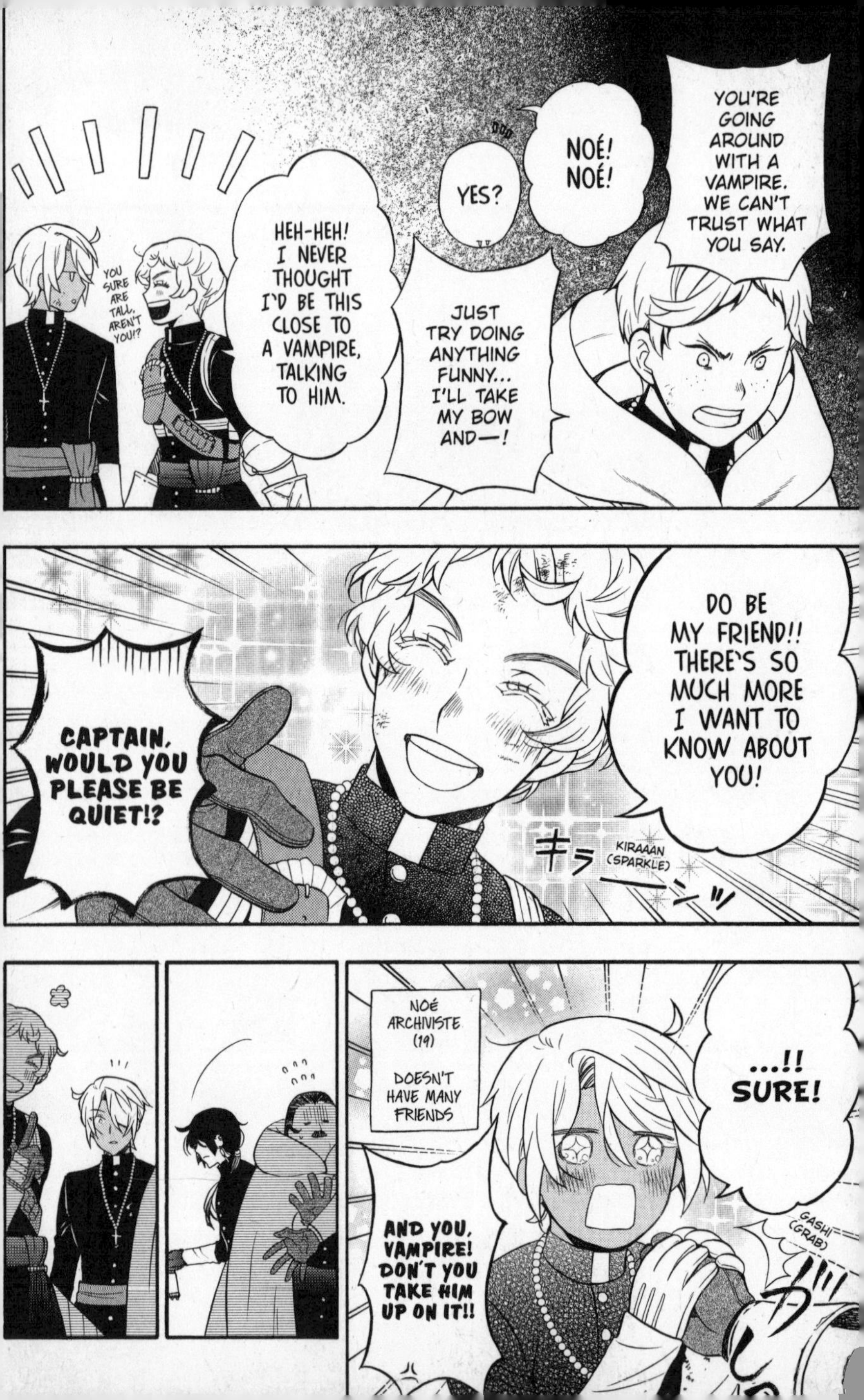
YOU'RE GOING AROUND WITH A VAMPIRE. WE CAN'T TRUST WHAT YOU SAY.
NOÉ! NOÉ!
YES?
JUST TRY DOING ANYTHING FUNNY... I'LL TAKE MY BOW AND—!
HEH-HEH! I NEVER THOUGHT I'D BE THIS CLOSE TO A VAMPIRE, TALKING TO HIM.
YOU SURE ARE TALL, AREN'T YOU!?
DO BE MY FRIEND!! THERE'S SO MUCH MORE I WANT TO KNOW ABOUT YOU!
KIRAAAN (SPARKLE)
CAPTAIN, WOULD YOU PLEASE BE QUIET!?
...!! SURE!
GASHI (GRAB)
NOÉ ARCHIVISTE (19)
DOESN'T HAVE MANY FRIENDS
AND YOU, VAMPIRE! DON'T YOU TAKE HIM UP ON IT!!

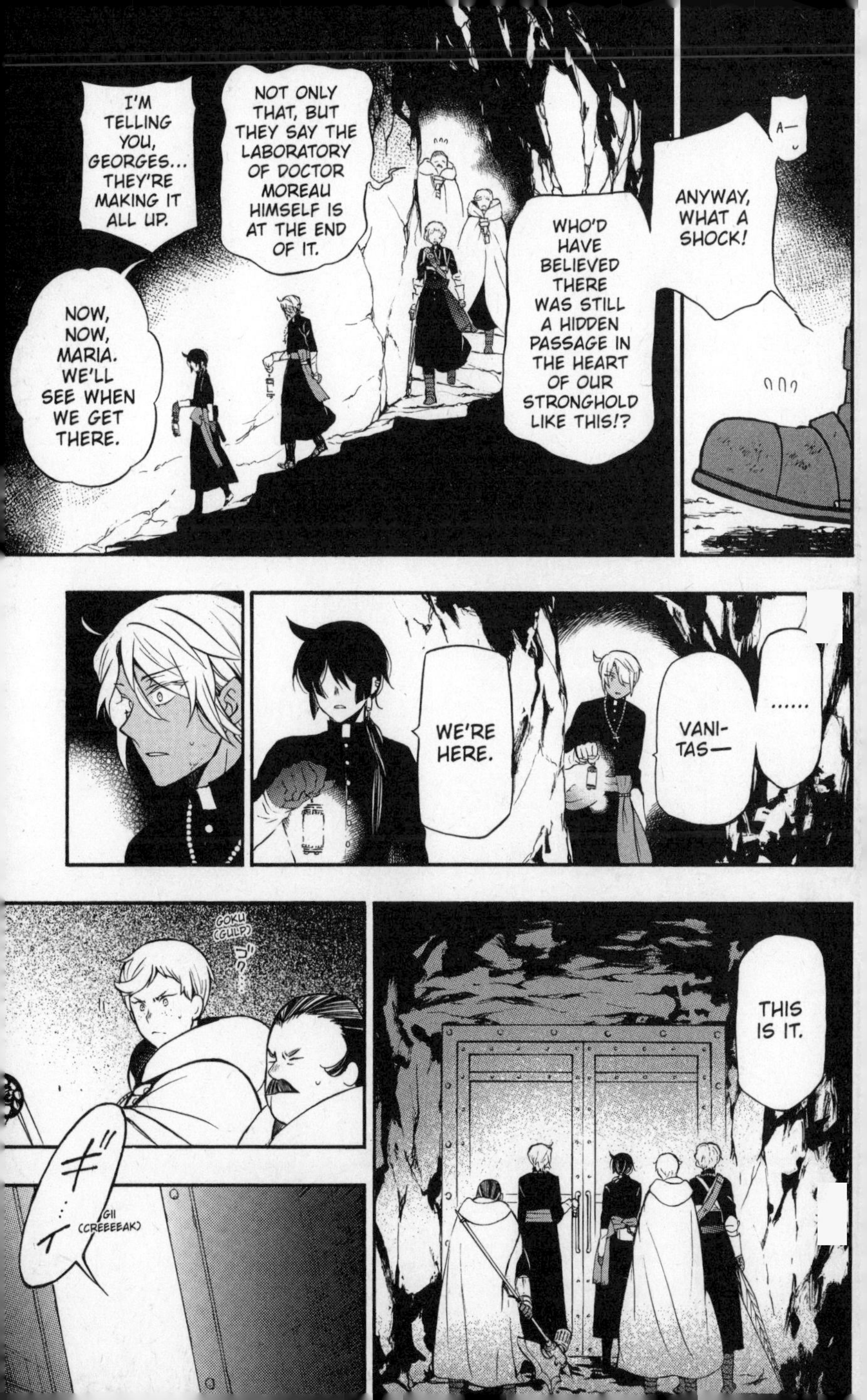
A—
ANYWAY, WHAT A SHOCK!
WHO'D HAVE BELIEVED THERE WAS STILL A HIDDEN PASSAGE IN THE HEART OF OUR STRONGHOLD LIKE THIS!?
NOT ONLY THAT, BUT THEY SAY THE LABORATORY OF DOCTOR MOREAU HIMSELF IS AT THE END OF IT.
I'M TELLING YOU, GEORGES... THEY'RE MAKING IT ALL UP.
NOW, NOW, MARIA. WE'LL SEE WHEN WE GET THERE.
......
VANI-TAS—
WE'RE HERE.
THIS IS IT.
GOKU (GULP)
GII (CREEEEAK)

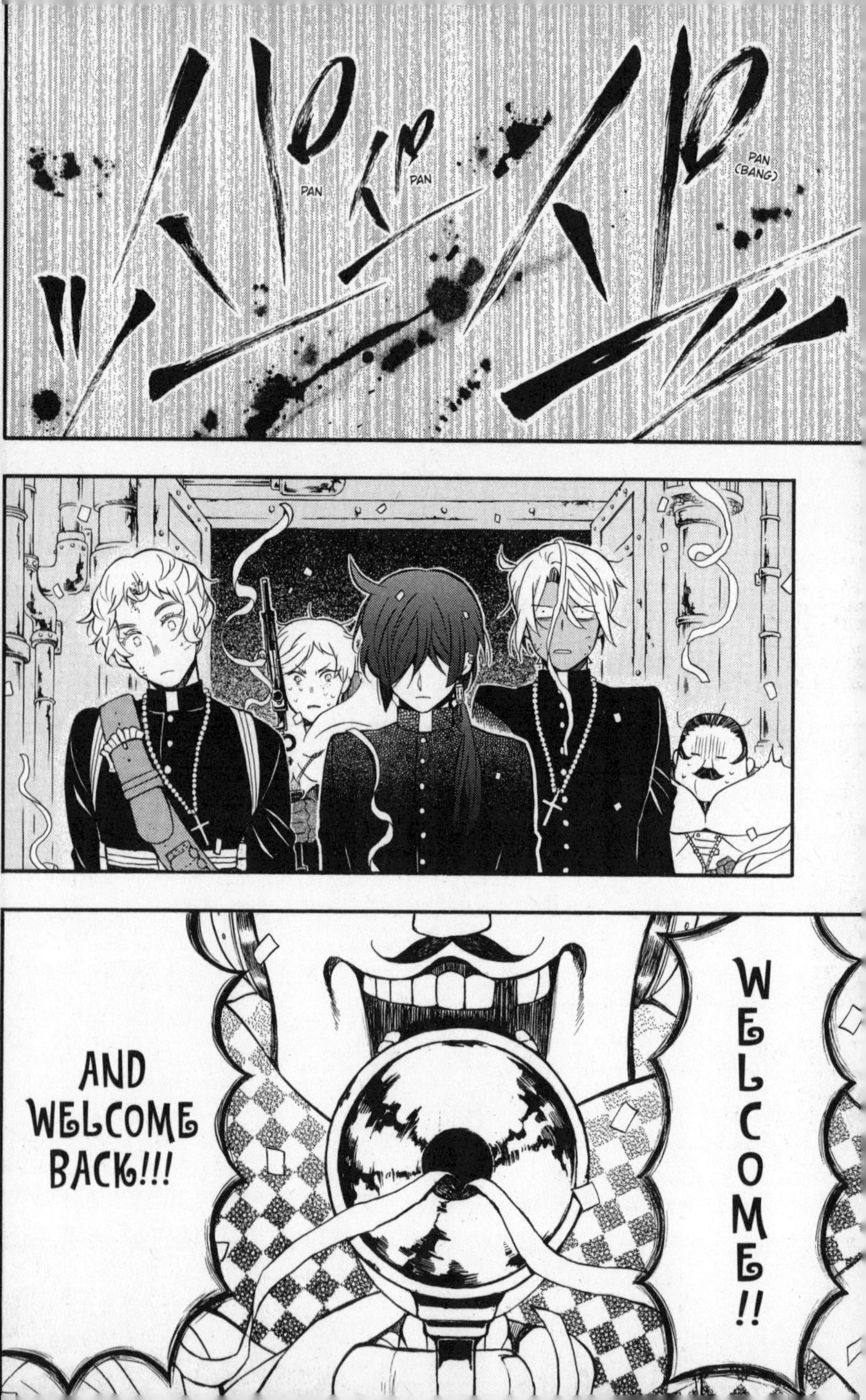
PAN
(BANG)
PAN
PAN
WELCOME!!
AND WELCOME BACK!!!

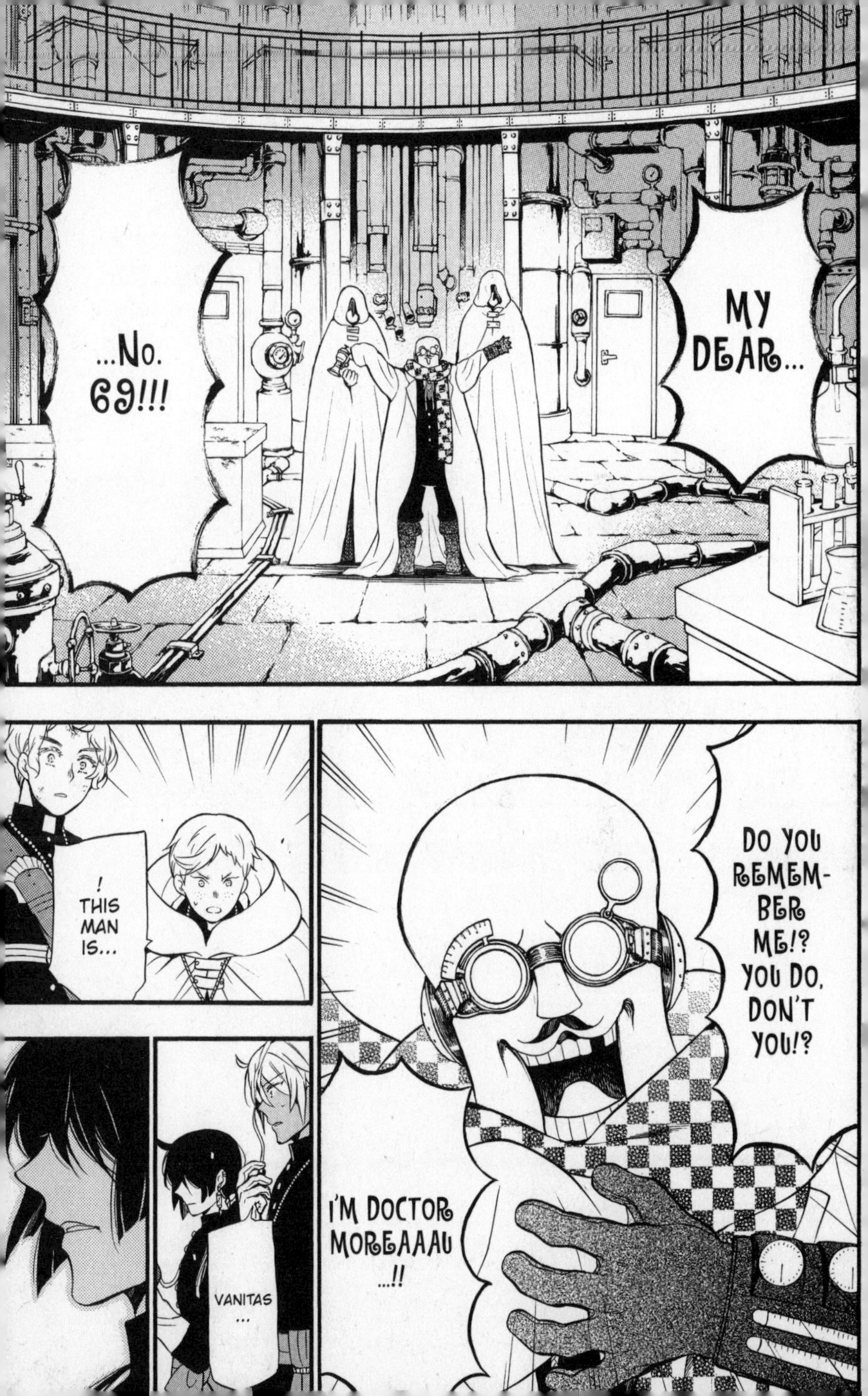
MY DEAR...
...No. 69!!!
DO YOU REMEM-BER ME!? YOU DO, DON'T YOU!?
I'M DOCTOR MOREAAAU ...!!
! THIS MAN IS...
VANITAS ...

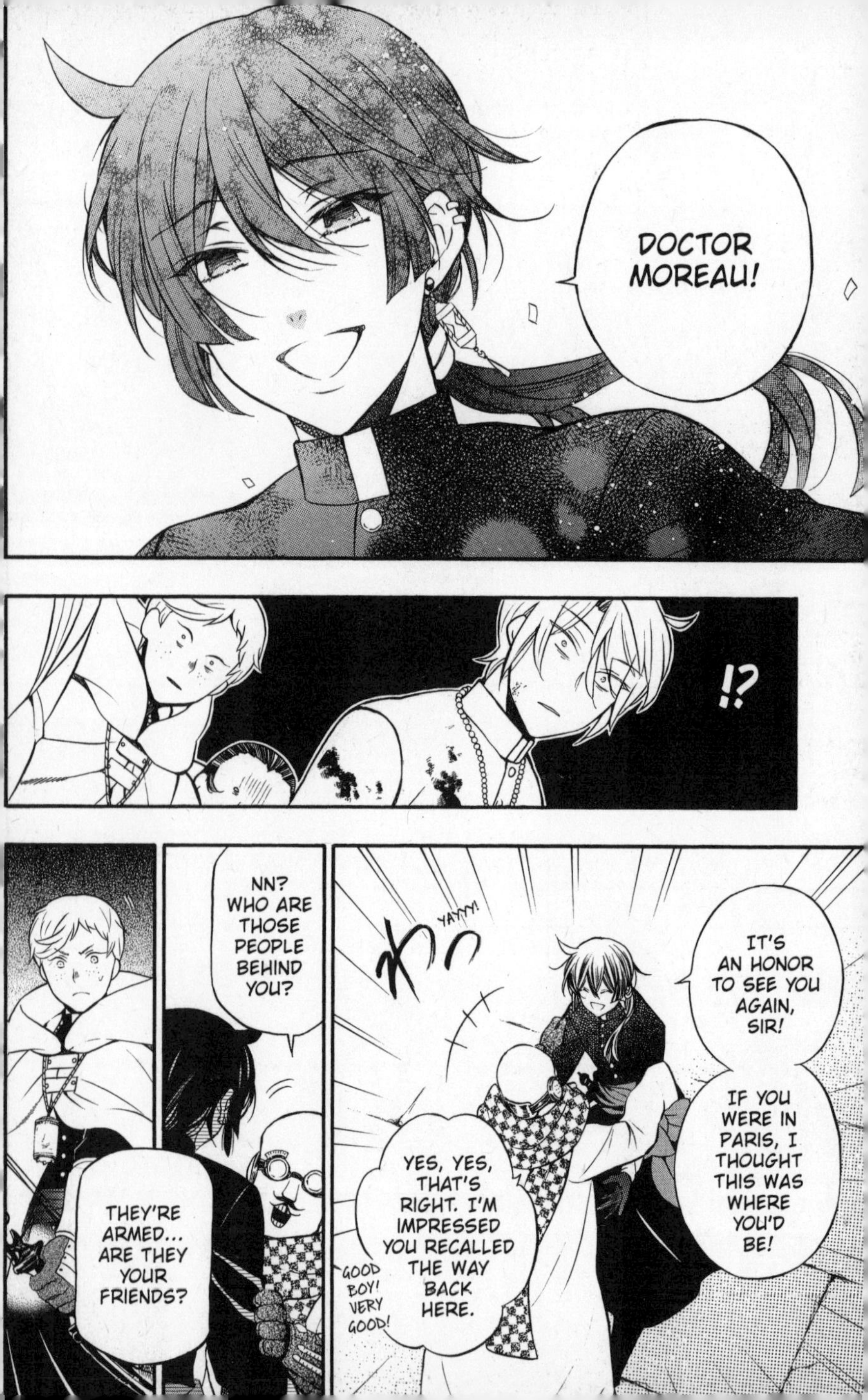
DOCTOR MOREAU!
!?
IT'S AN HONOR TO SEE YOU AGAIN, SIR!
IF YOU WERE IN PARIS, I THOUGHT THIS WAS WHERE YOU'D BE!
YAYYY!
YES, YES, THAT'S RIGHT. I'M IMPRESSED YOU RECALLED THE WAY BACK HERE.
GOOD BOY! VERY GOOD!
NN? WHO ARE THOSE PEOPLE BEHIND YOU?
THEY'RE ARMED... ARE THEY YOUR FRIENDS?

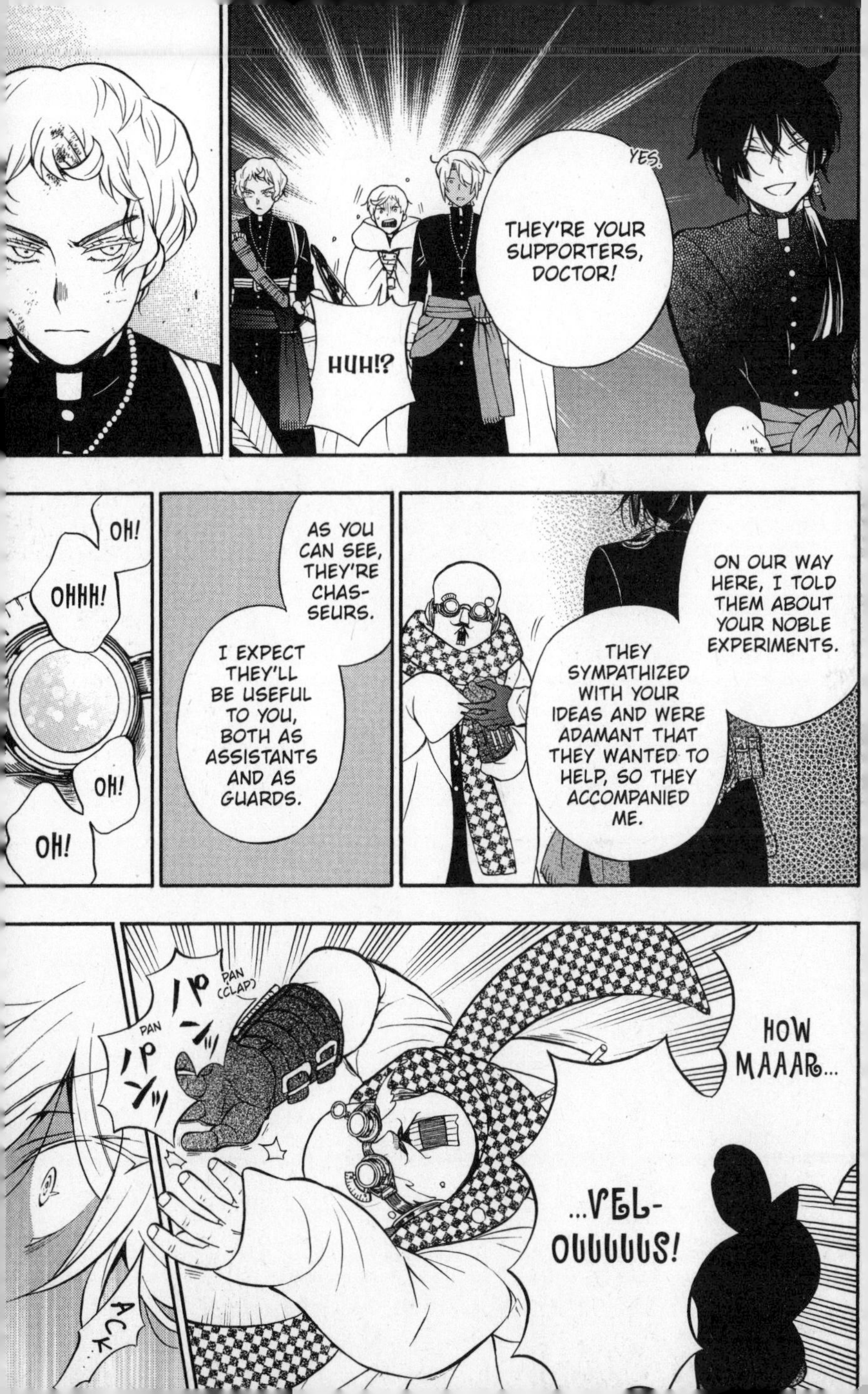
YES.
THEY'RE YOUR SUPPORTERS, DOCTOR!
HUH!?
ON OUR WAY HERE, I TOLD THEM ABOUT YOUR NOBLE EXPERIMENTS.
THEY SYMPATHIZED WITH YOUR IDEAS AND WERE ADAMANT THAT THEY WANTED TO HELP, SO THEY ACCOMPANIED ME.
AS YOU CAN SEE, THEY'RE CHASSEURS.
I EXPECT THEY'LL BE USEFUL TO YOU, BOTH AS ASSISTANTS AND AS GUARDS.
OH!
OHHH!
OH!
OH!
HOW MAAAR...
...VEL-OUUUUUS!
パンッ PAN (CLAP)
パンッ PAN
ACK

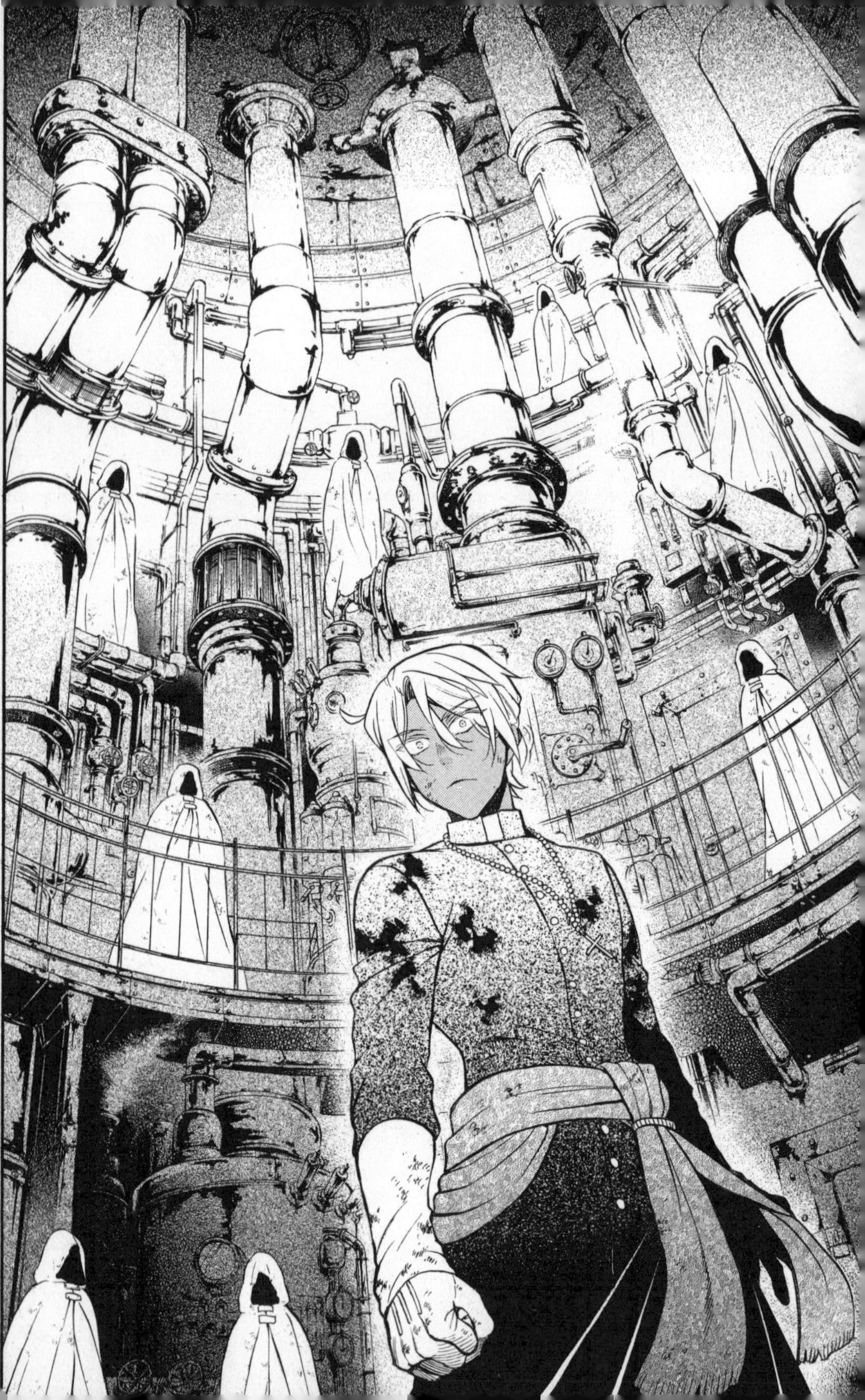

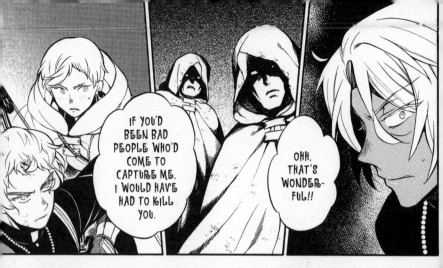

OHH, THAT'S WONDER-FUL!!
IF YOU'D BEEN BAD PEOPLE WHO'D COME TO CAPTURE ME, I WOULD HAVE HAD TO KILL YOU.
COME, COME, EVERYONE! HURRY UP!
PAN (CLAP)
PAN
PREPARE TO ENTERTAIN OUR GUESTS!!
KACHA (CLATTER)
KACHA

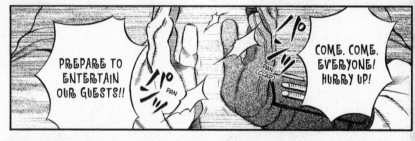

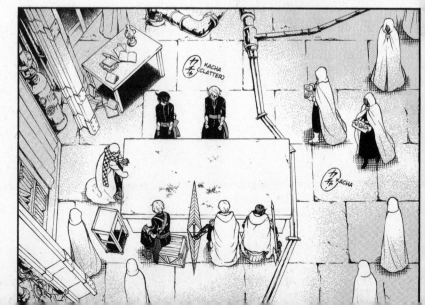

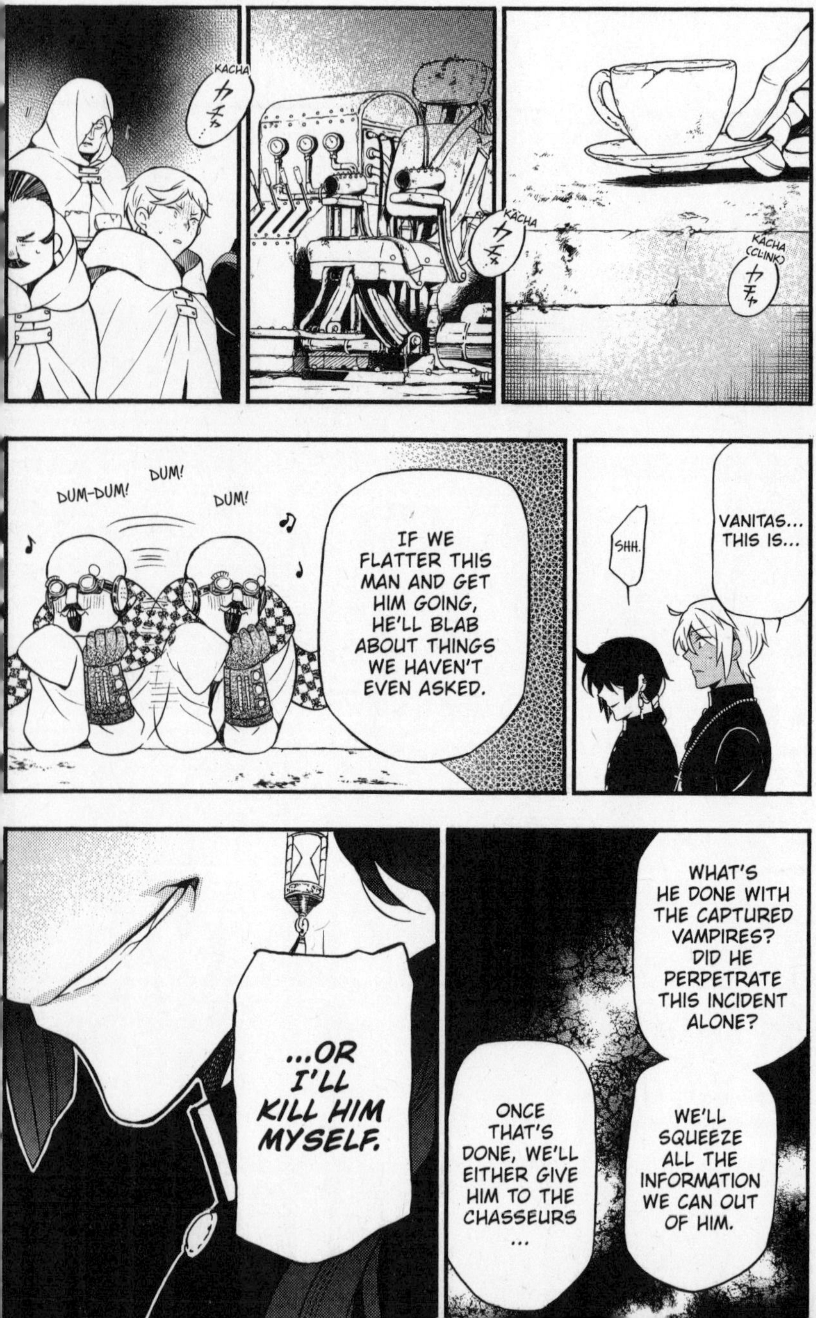
KACHA (CLINK)
カチャ
KACHA
カチャ
KACHA
カチャ…
VANITAS... THIS IS...
SHH.
IF WE FLATTER THIS MAN AND GET HIM GOING, HE'LL BLAB ABOUT THINGS WE HAVEN'T EVEN ASKED.
DUM!
DUM!
DUM-DUM!
WHAT'S HE DONE WITH THE CAPTURED VAMPIRES? DID HE PERPETRATE THIS INCIDENT ALONE?
WE'LL SQUEEZE ALL THE INFORMATION WE CAN OUT OF HIM.
ONCE THAT'S DONE, WE'LL EITHER GIVE HIM TO THE CHASSEURS...
...OR I'LL KILL HIM MYSELF.

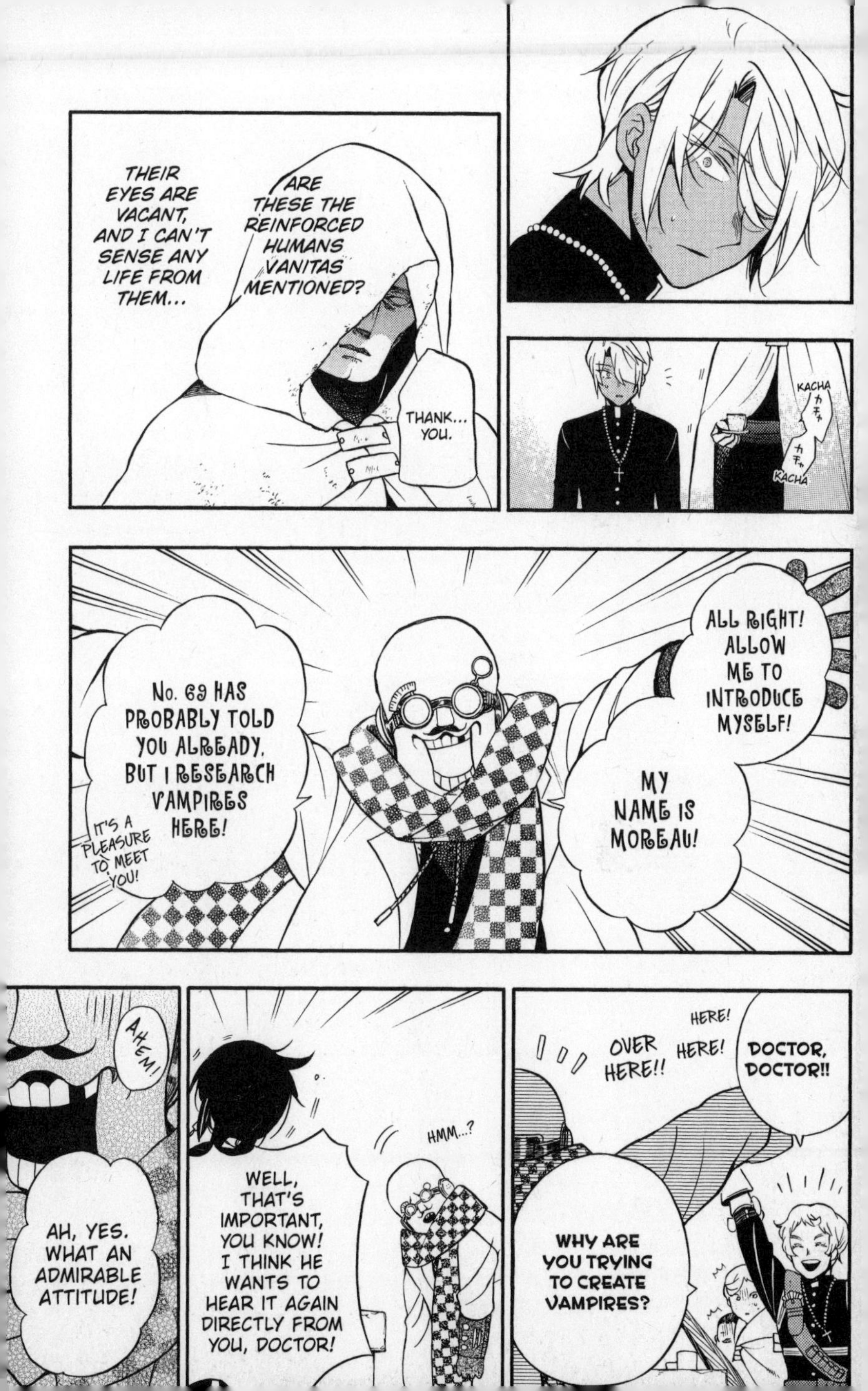
KACHA
KACHA
ARE THESE THE REINFORCED HUMANS VANITAS MENTIONED?
THEIR EYES ARE VACANT, AND I CAN'T SENSE ANY LIFE FROM THEM...
THANK... YOU.
ALL RIGHT! ALLOW ME TO INTRODUCE MYSELF!
MY NAME IS MOREAU!
No. 69 HAS PROBABLY TOLD YOU ALREADY, BUT I RESEARCH VAMPIRES HERE!
IT'S A PLEASURE TO MEET YOU!
DOCTOR, DOCTOR!!
HERE!
HERE!
OVER HERE!!
WHY ARE YOU TRYING TO CREATE VAMPIRES?
HMM...?
WELL, THAT'S IMPORTANT, YOU KNOW! I THINK HE WANTS TO HEAR IT AGAIN DIRECTLY FROM YOU, DOCTOR!
AHEM!
AH, YES. WHAT AN ADMIRABLE ATTITUDE!

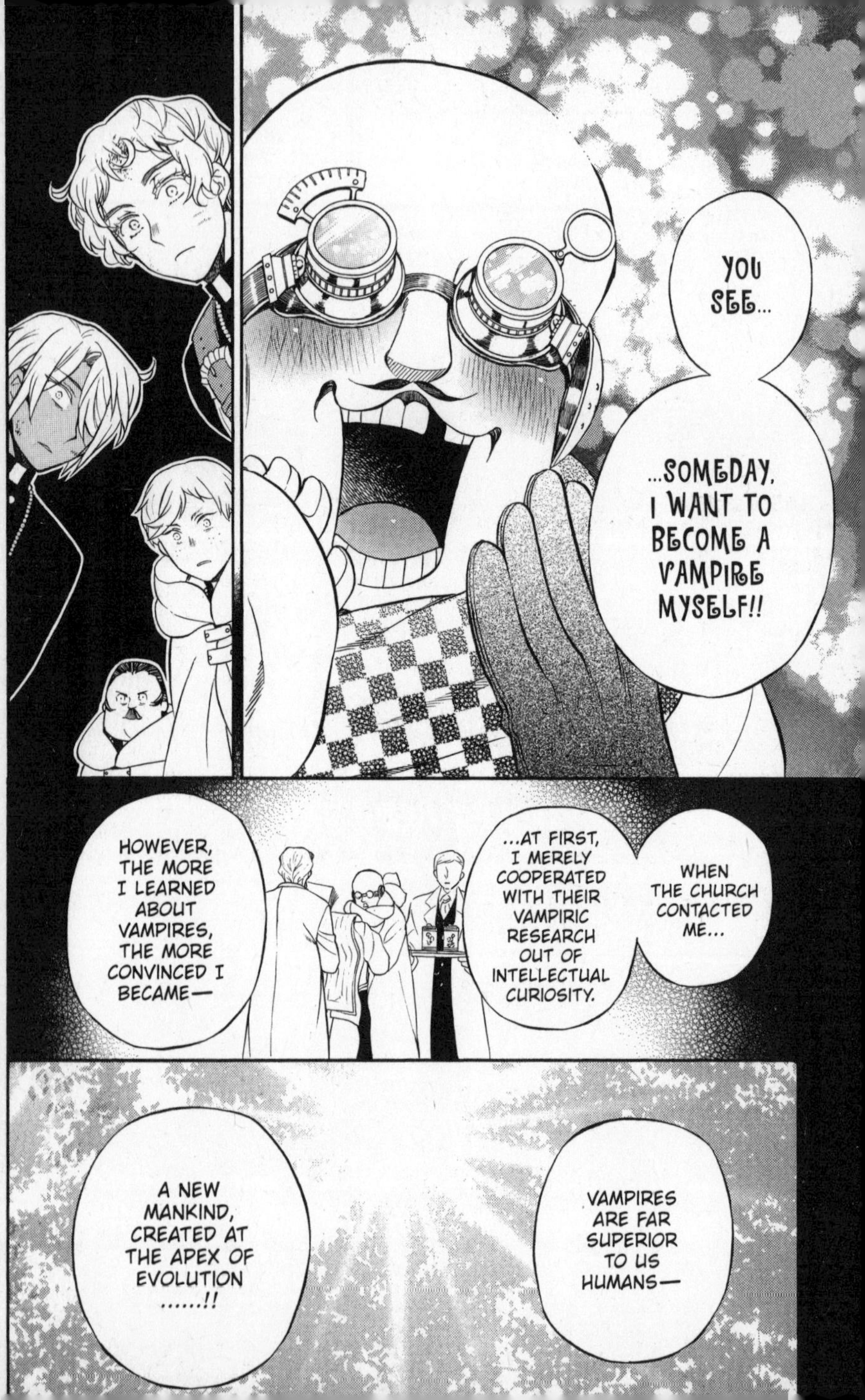
YOU SEE...
...SOMEDAY, I WANT TO BECOME A VAMPIRE MYSELF!!
WHEN THE CHURCH CONTACTED ME...
...AT FIRST, I MERELY COOPERATED WITH THEIR VAMPIRIC RESEARCH OUT OF INTELLECTUAL CURIOSITY.
HOWEVER, THE MORE I LEARNED ABOUT VAMPIRES, THE MORE CONVINCED I BECAME—
VAMPIRES ARE FAR SUPERIOR TO US HUMANS—
A NEW MANKIND, CREATED AT THE APEX OF EVOLUTION ......!!

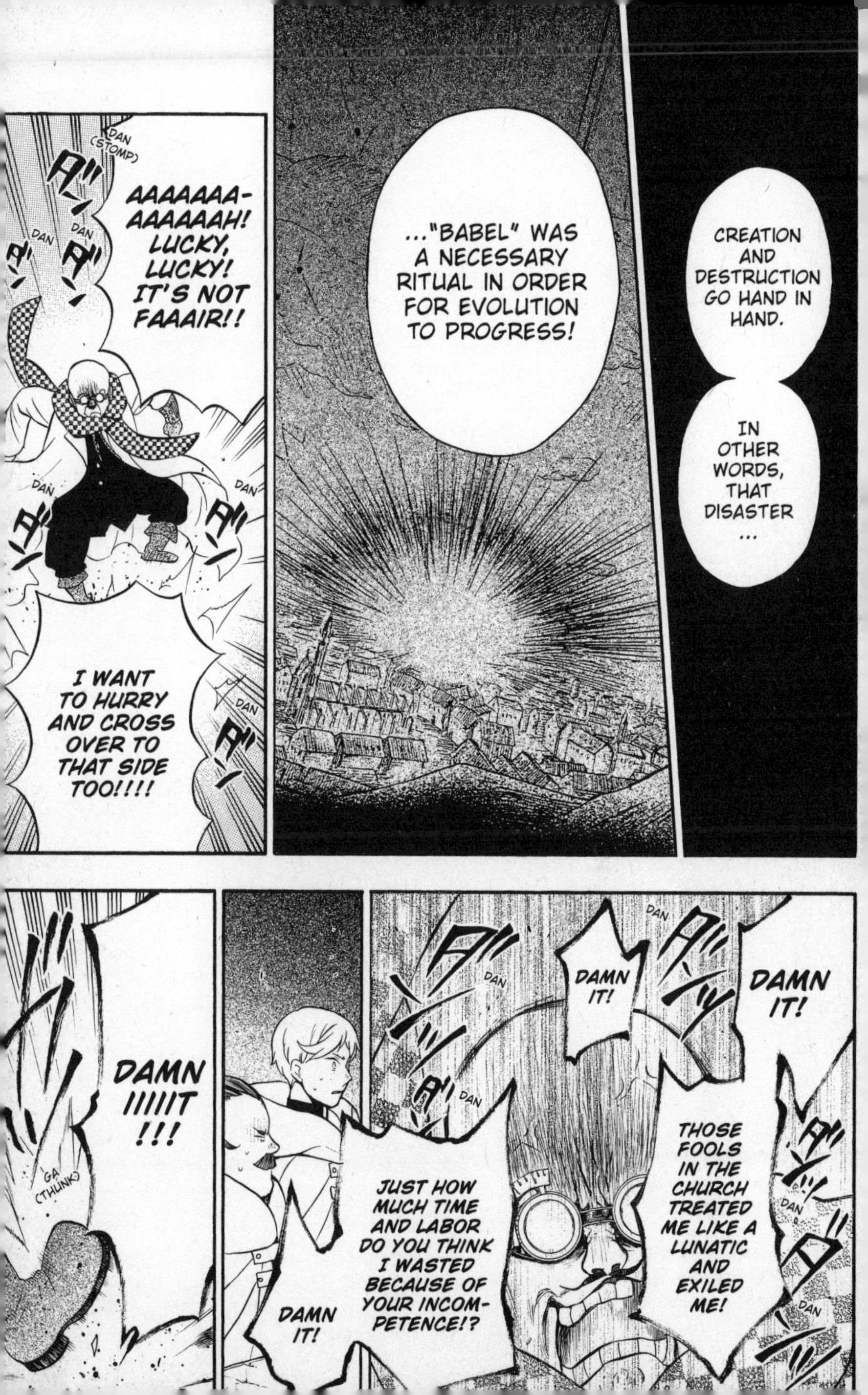
CREATION AND DESTRUCTION GO HAND IN HAND.
IN OTHER WORDS, THAT DISASTER ...
..."BABEL" WAS A NECESSARY RITUAL IN ORDER FOR EVOLUTION TO PROGRESS!
DAN (STOMP)
AAAAAAA-AAAAAAH! LUCKY, LUCKY! IT'S NOT FAAAIR!!
DAN
DAN
DAN
DAN
DAN
I WANT TO HURRY AND CROSS OVER TO THAT SIDE TOO!!!!
DAN
DAMN IT!
DAN
DAMN IT!
DAN
THOSE FOOLS IN THE CHURCH TREATED ME LIKE A LUNATIC AND EXILED ME!
DAN
DAN
DAN
JUST HOW MUCH TIME AND LABOR DO YOU THINK I WASTED BECAUSE OF YOUR INCOMPETENCE!?
DAMN IT!
DAMN IIIIIIT!!!
GA (THUNK)

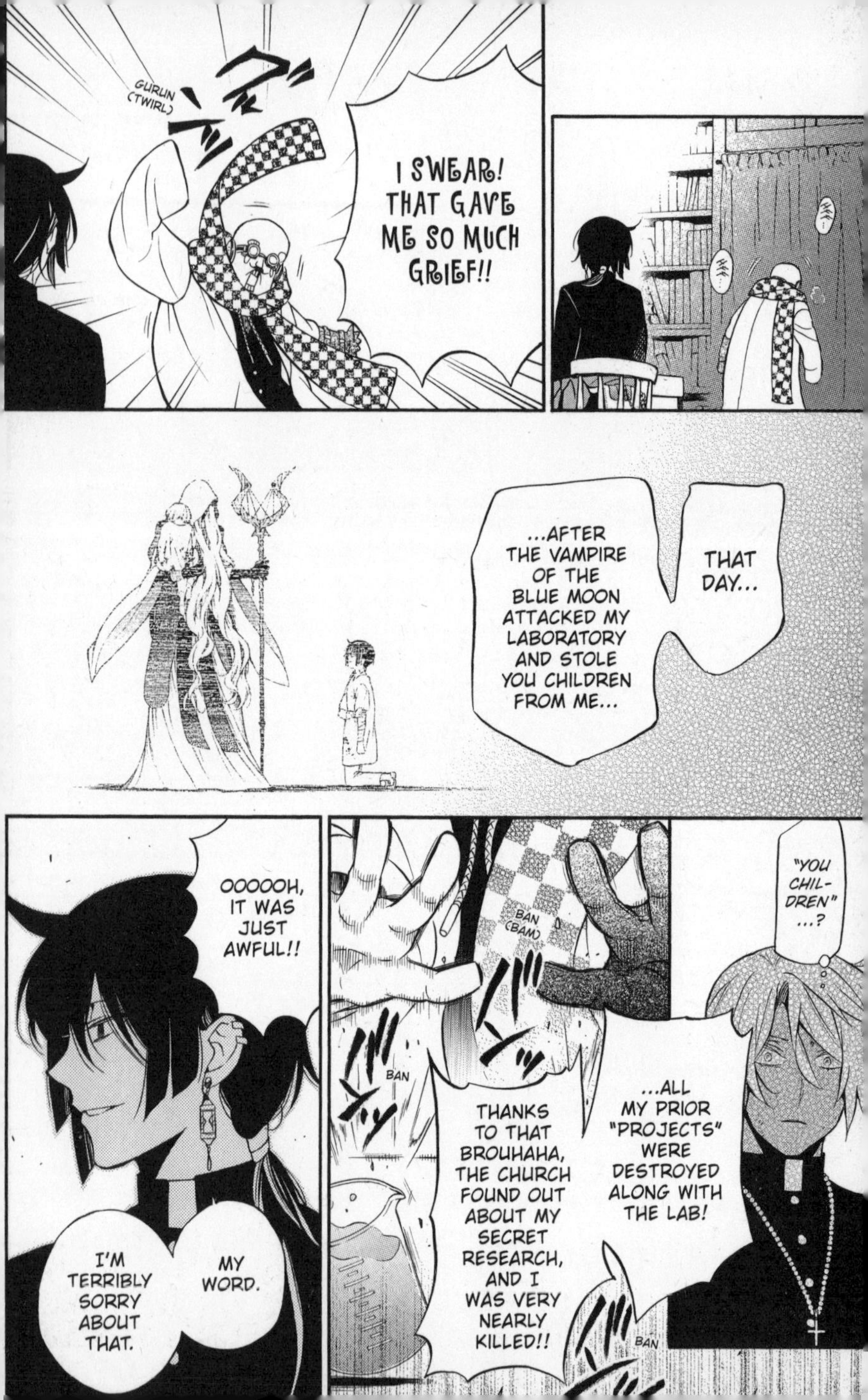
GURUN (TWIRL)
I SWEAR! THAT GAVE ME SO MUCH GRIEF!!
THAT DAY...
...AFTER THE VAMPIRE OF THE BLUE MOON ATTACKED MY LABORATORY AND STOLE YOU CHILDREN FROM ME...
"YOU CHILDREN"...?
BAN (BAM)
BAN
THANKS TO THAT BROUHAHA, THE CHURCH FOUND OUT ABOUT MY SECRET RESEARCH, AND I WAS VERY NEARLY KILLED!!
...ALL MY PRIOR "PROJECTS" WERE DESTROYED ALONG WITH THE LAB!
BAN
OOOOOH, IT WAS JUST AWFUL!!
MY WORD.
I'M TERRIBLY SORRY ABOUT THAT.

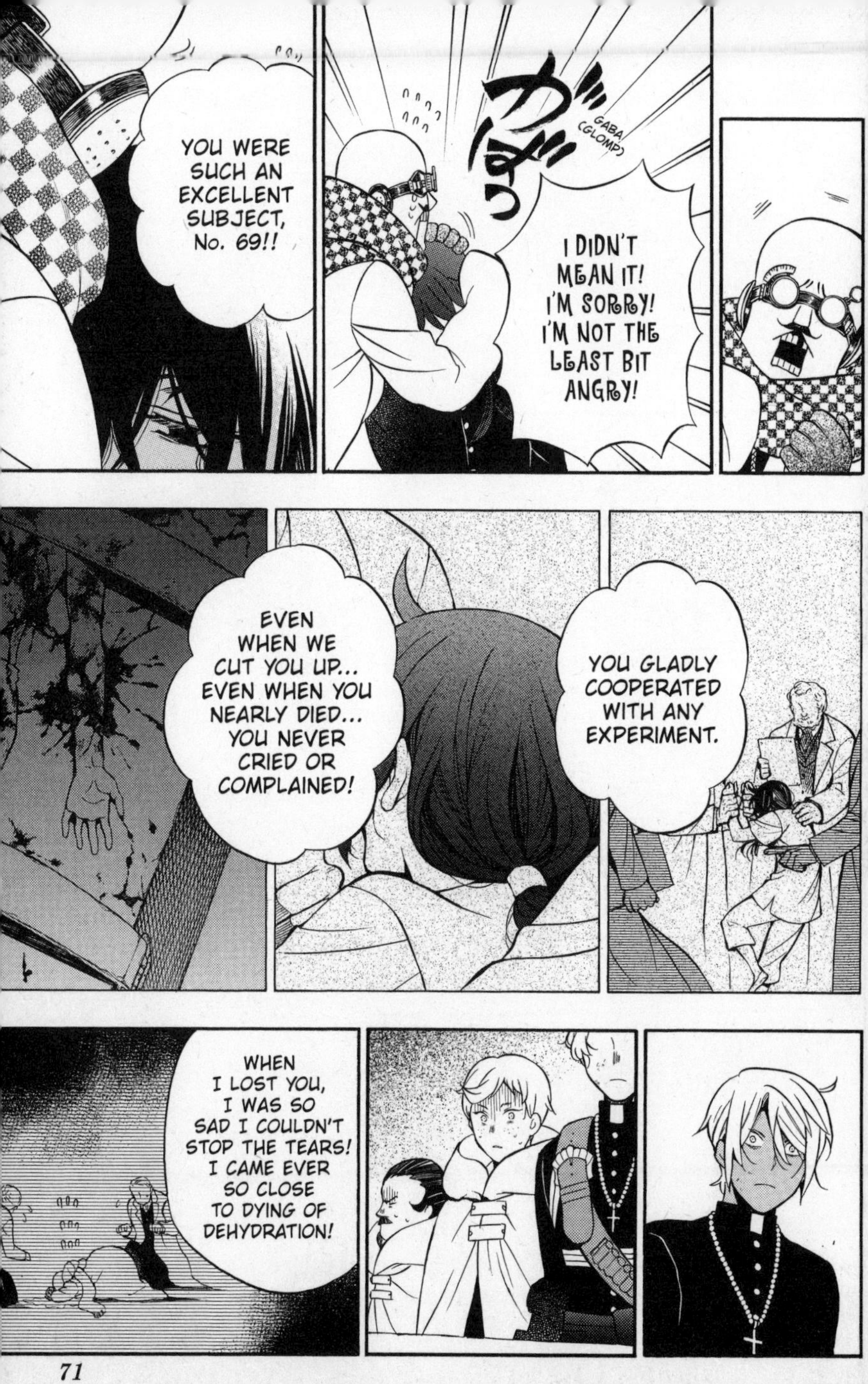
GABA (GLOMP)
I DIDN'T MEAN IT! I'M SORRY! I'M NOT THE LEAST BIT ANGRY!
YOU WERE SUCH AN EXCELLENT SUBJECT, No. 69!!
YOU GLADLY COOPERATED WITH ANY EXPERIMENT.
EVEN WHEN WE CUT YOU UP... EVEN WHEN YOU NEARLY DIED... YOU NEVER CRIED OR COMPLAINED!
WHEN I LOST YOU, I WAS SO SAD I COULDN'T STOP THE TEARS! I CAME EVER SO CLOSE TO DYING OF DEHYDRATION!

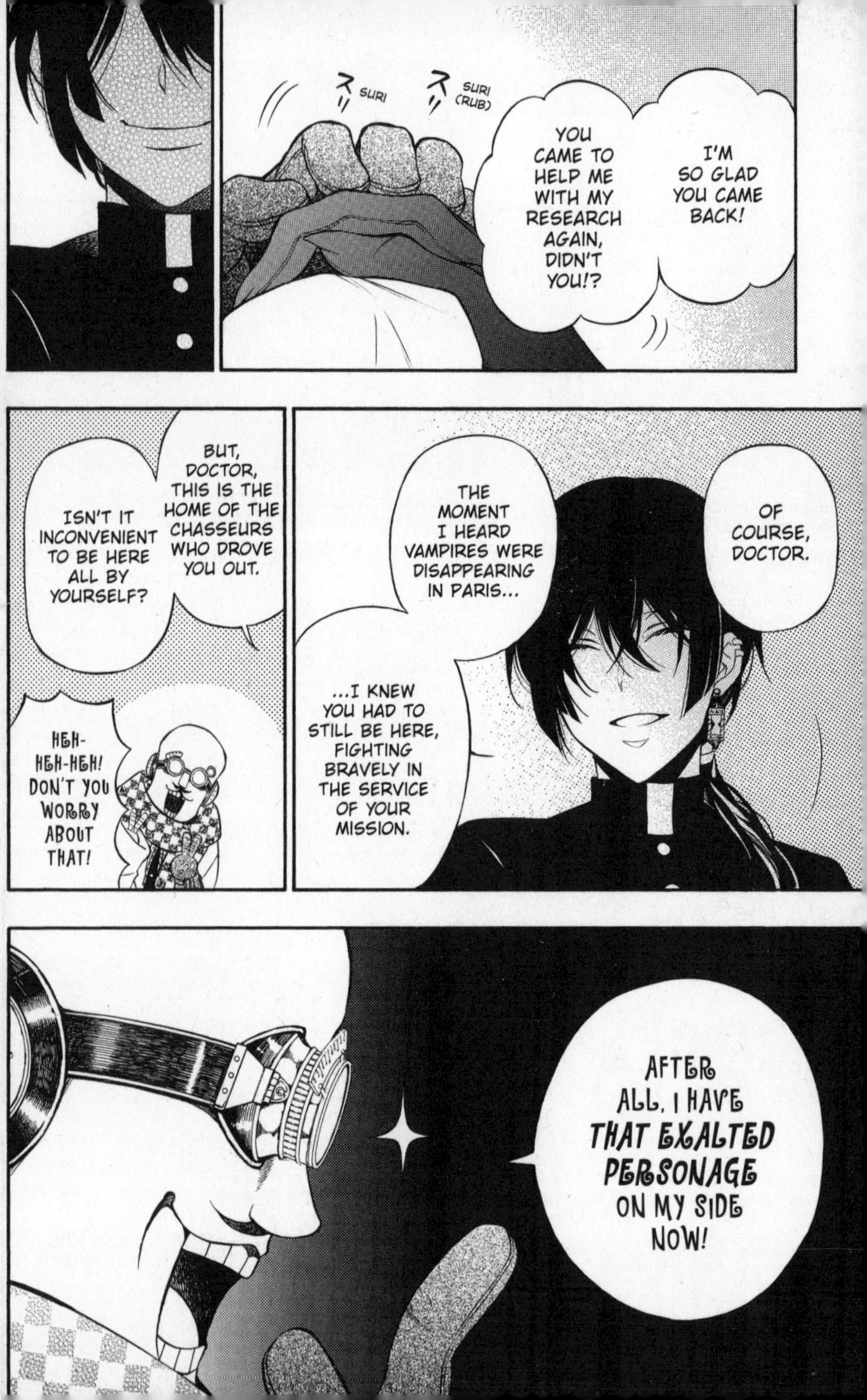
SURI (RUB)
SURI
I'M SO GLAD YOU CAME BACK!
YOU CAME TO HELP ME WITH MY RESEARCH AGAIN, DIDN'T YOU!?
OF COURSE, DOCTOR.
THE MOMENT I HEARD VAMPIRES WERE DISAPPEARING IN PARIS...
...I KNEW YOU HAD TO STILL BE HERE, FIGHTING BRAVELY IN THE SERVICE OF YOUR MISSION.
BUT, DOCTOR, THIS IS THE HOME OF THE CHASSEURS WHO DROVE YOU OUT.
ISN'T IT INCONVENIENT TO BE HERE ALL BY YOURSELF?
HEH-HEH-HEH! DON'T YOU WORRY ABOUT THAT!
AFTER ALL, I HAVE **THAT EXALTED PERSONAGE** ON MY SIDE NOW!

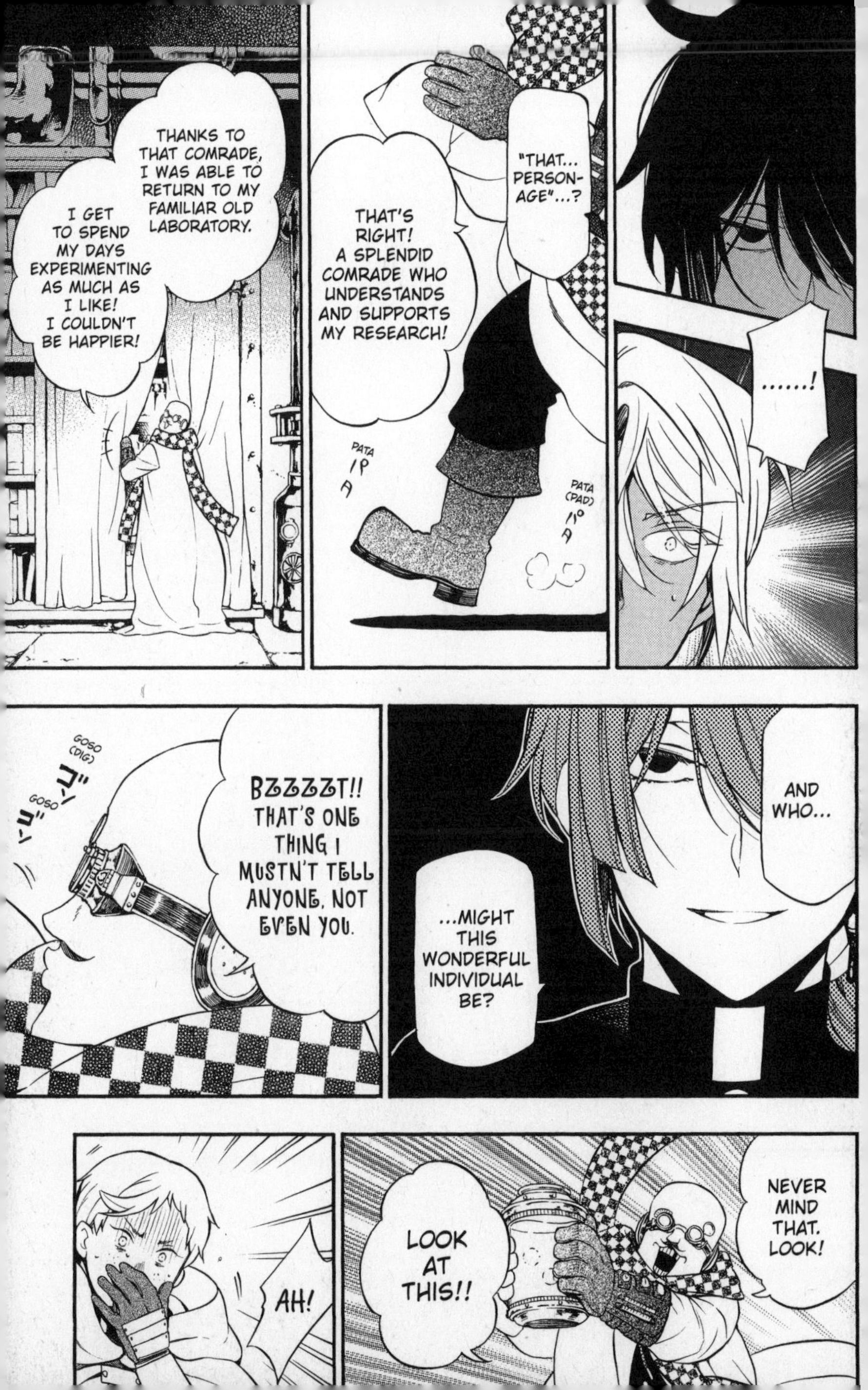
"THAT... PERSONAGE"...?
......!
THAT'S RIGHT! A SPLENDID COMRADE WHO UNDERSTANDS AND SUPPORTS MY RESEARCH!
PATA
PATA (PAD)
THANKS TO THAT COMRADE, I WAS ABLE TO RETURN TO MY FAMILIAR OLD LABORATORY.
I GET TO SPEND MY DAYS EXPERIMENTING AS MUCH AS I LIKE! I COULDN'T BE HAPPIER!
AND WHO...
...MIGHT THIS WONDERFUL INDIVIDUAL BE?
BZZZZT!! THAT'S ONE THING I MUSTN'T TELL ANYONE, NOT EVEN YOU.
GOSO (DIG)
GOSO
NEVER MIND THAT. LOOK!
LOOK AT THIS!!
AH!

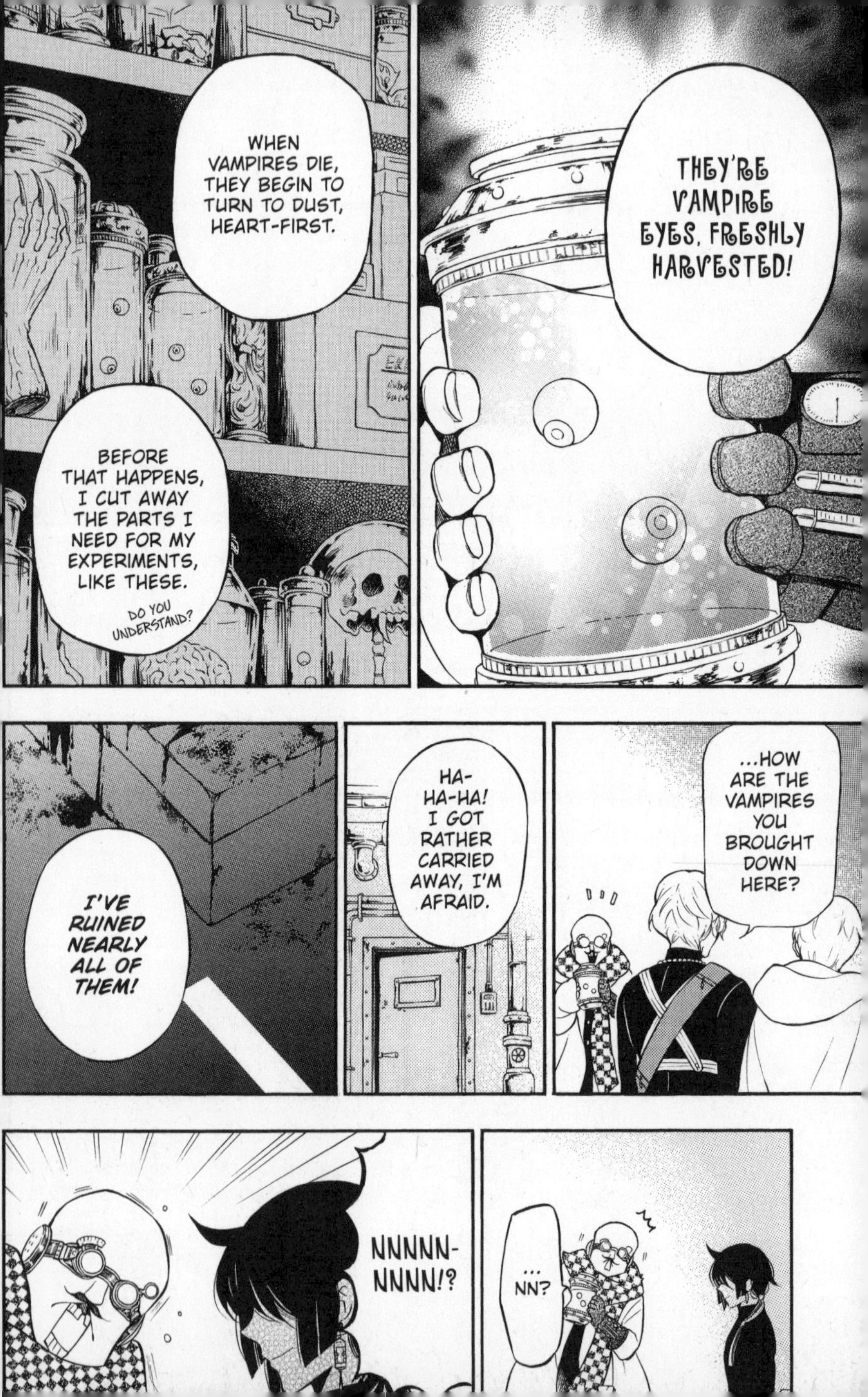
THEY'RE VAMPIRE EYES, FRESHLY HARVESTED!
WHEN VAMPIRES DIE, THEY BEGIN TO TURN TO DUST, HEART-FIRST.
BEFORE THAT HAPPENS, I CUT AWAY THE PARTS I NEED FOR MY EXPERIMENTS, LIKE THESE.
DO YOU UNDERSTAND?
...HOW ARE THE VAMPIRES YOU BROUGHT DOWN HERE?
HA-HA-HA! I GOT RATHER CARRIED AWAY, I'M AFRAID.
I'VE RUINED NEARLY ALL OF THEM!
...NN?
NNNNN-NNNN!?

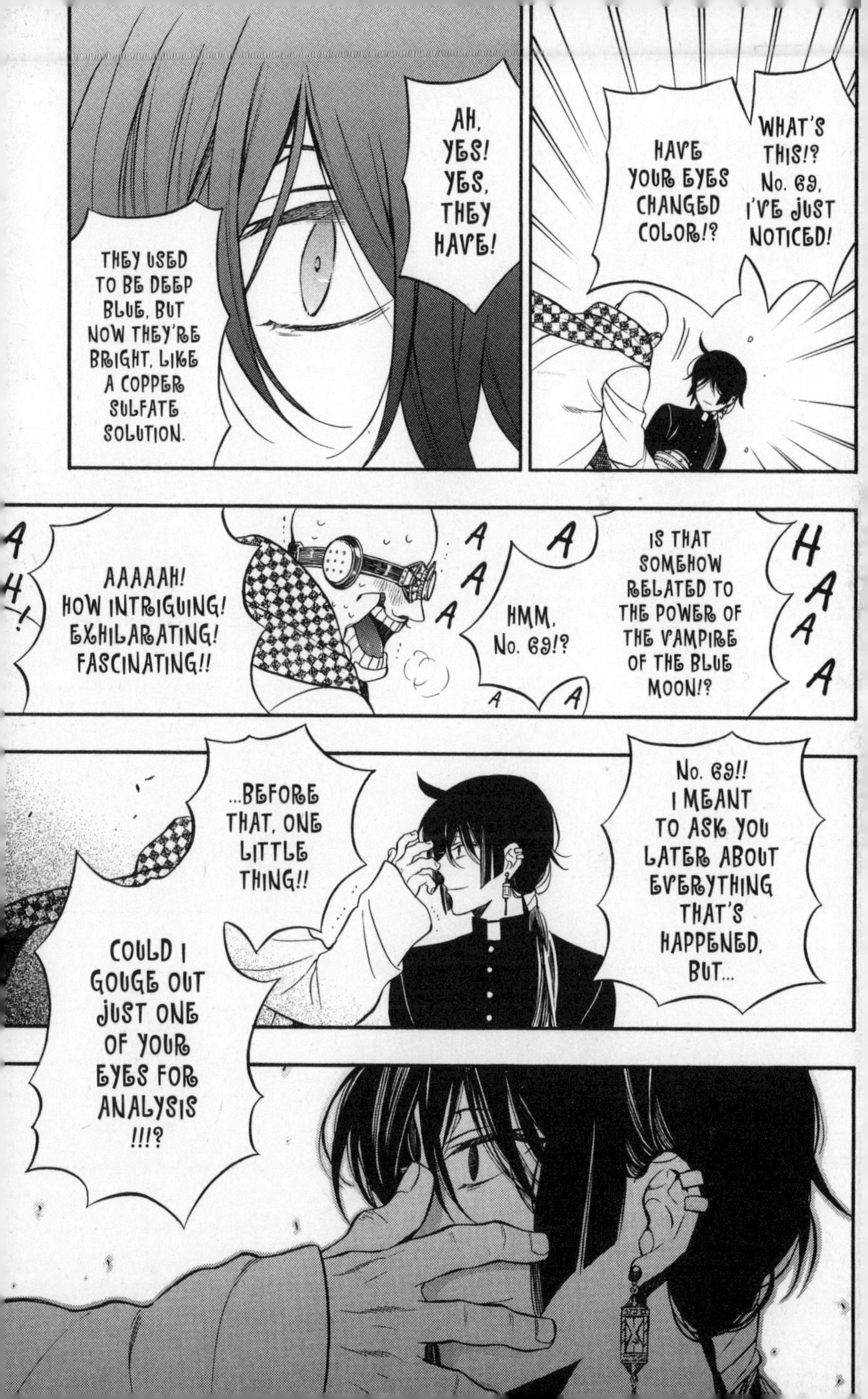
WHAT'S THIS!? No. 69, I'VE JUST NOTICED!
HAVE YOUR EYES CHANGED COLOR!?
AH, YES! YES, THEY HAVE!
THEY USED TO BE DEEP BLUE, BUT NOW THEY'RE BRIGHT, LIKE A COPPER SULFATE SOLUTION.
HAAAA
IS THAT SOMEHOW RELATED TO THE POWER OF THE VAMPIRE OF THE BLUE MOON!?
HMM, No. 69!?
AAAAAA
AAAAAH! HOW INTRIGUING! EXHILARATING! FASCINATING!!
AH!
No. 69!! I MEANT TO ASK YOU LATER ABOUT EVERYTHING THAT'S HAPPENED, BUT...
...BEFORE THAT, ONE LITTLE THING!!
COULD I GOUGE OUT JUST ONE OF YOUR EYES FOR ANALYSIS!!!?

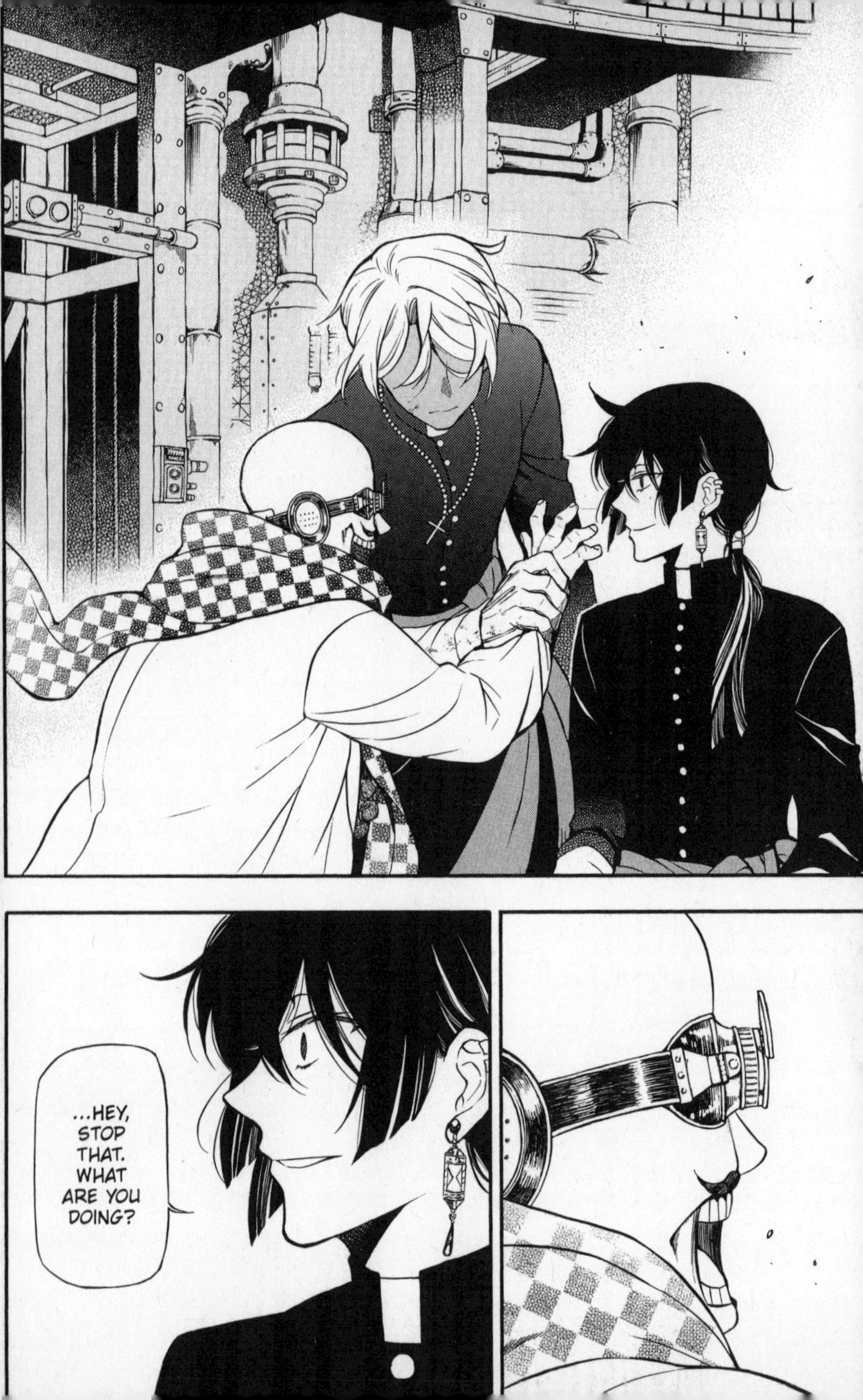
...HEY, STOP THAT. WHAT ARE YOU DOING?

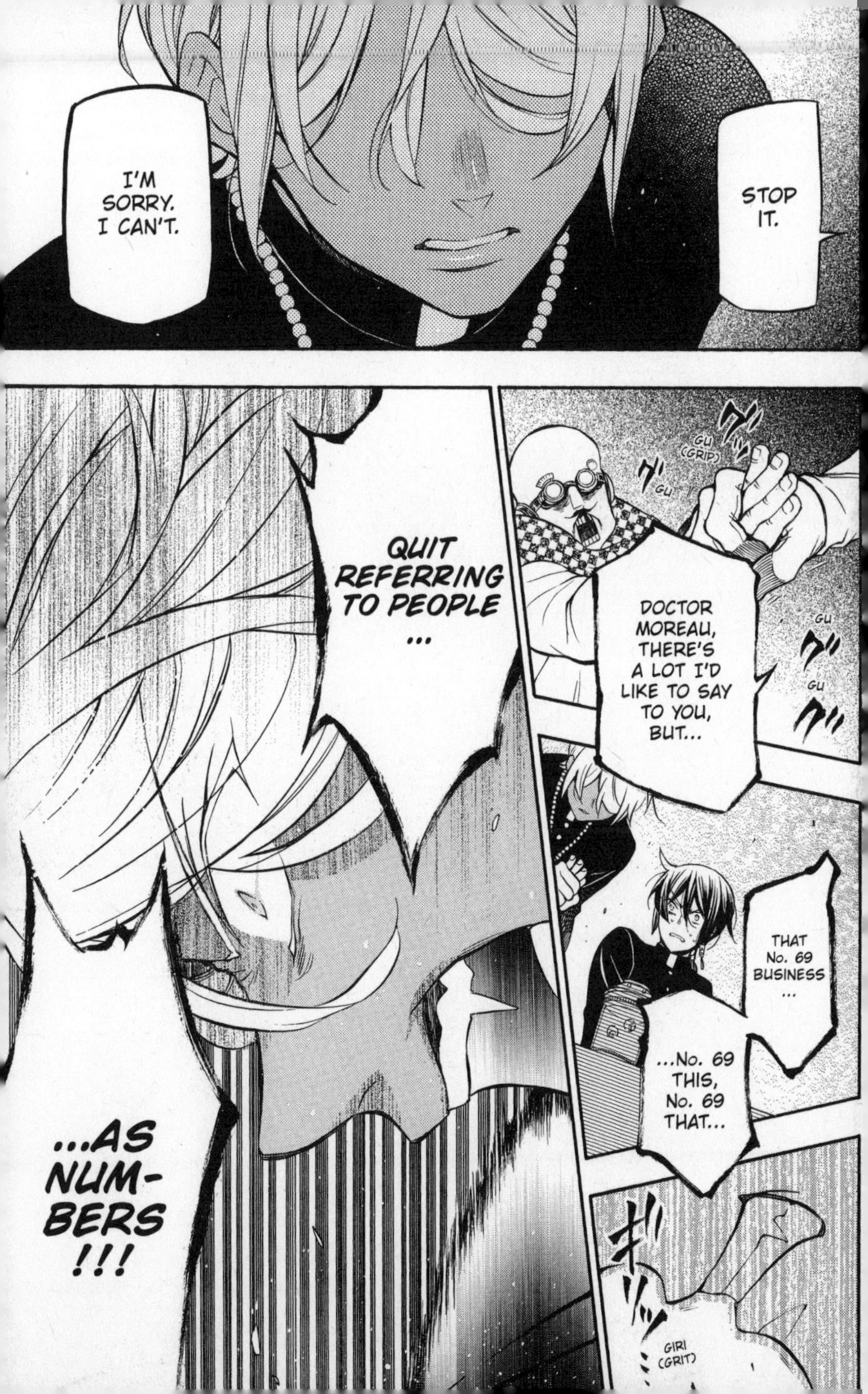
STOP IT.
I'M SORRY. I CAN'T.
GU (GRIP)
GU
DOCTOR MOREAU, THERE'S A LOT I'D LIKE TO SAY TO YOU, BUT...
GU
GU
THAT No. 69 BUSINESS ...
...No. 69 THIS, No. 69 THAT...
GIRI (GRIT)
QUIT REFERRING TO PEOPLE ...
...AS NUM-BERS!!!

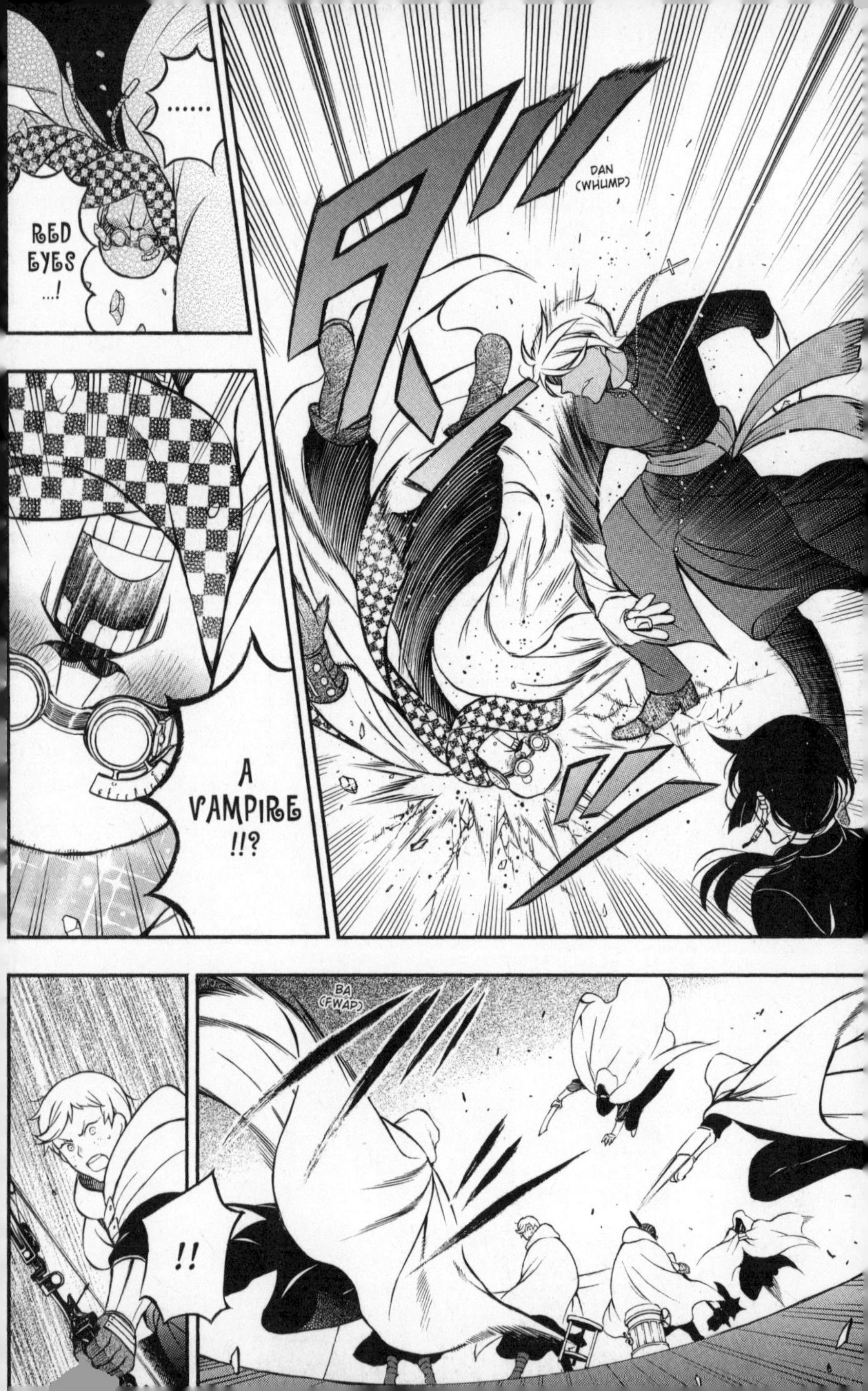
DAN (WHUMP)
......
RED EYES ...!
A VAMPIRE !!?
BA (FWAP)
!!

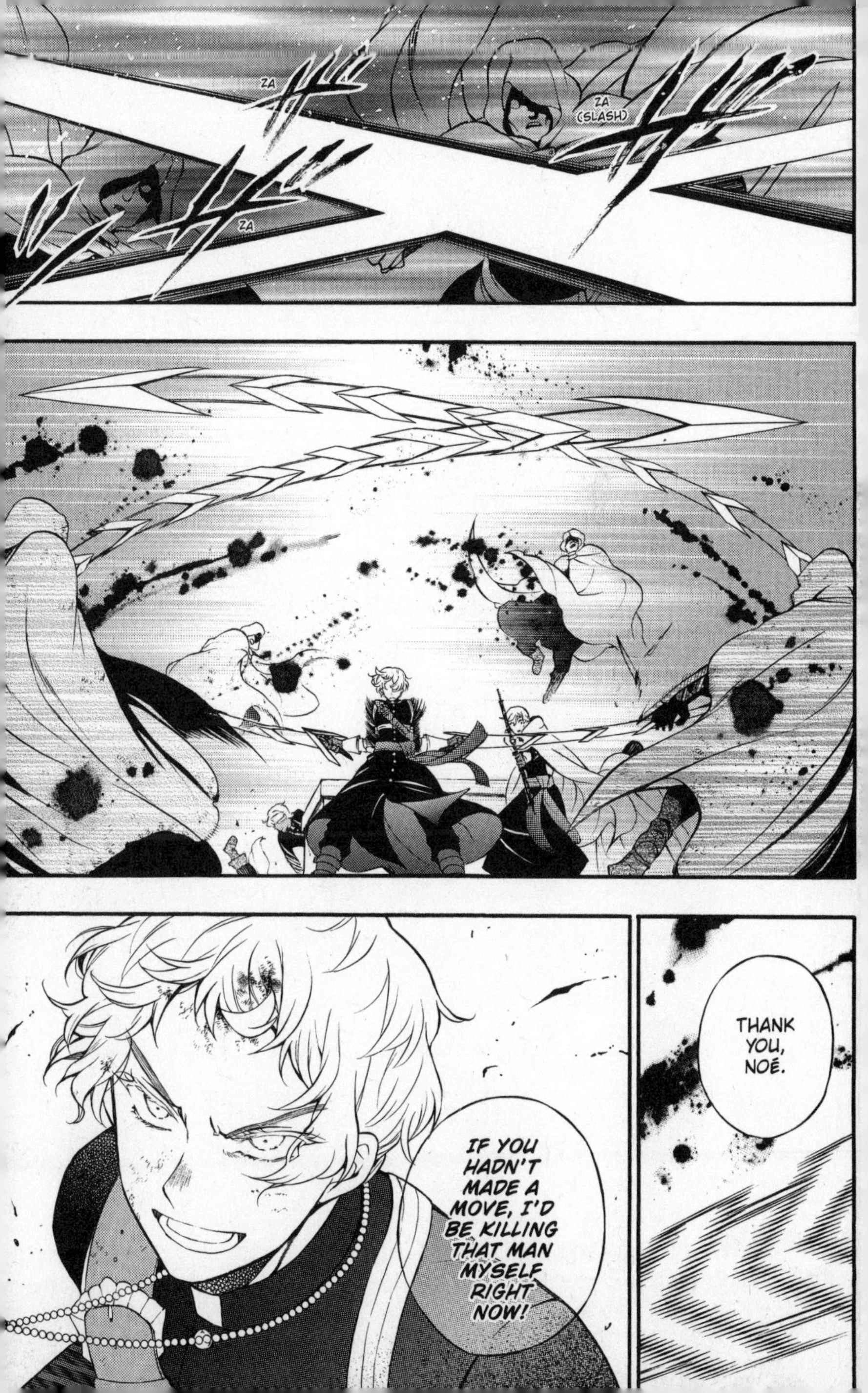
ZA (SLASH)
ZA
ZA
THANK YOU, NOÉ.
IF YOU HADN'T MADE A MOVE, I'D BE KILLING THAT MAN MYSELF RIGHT NOW!

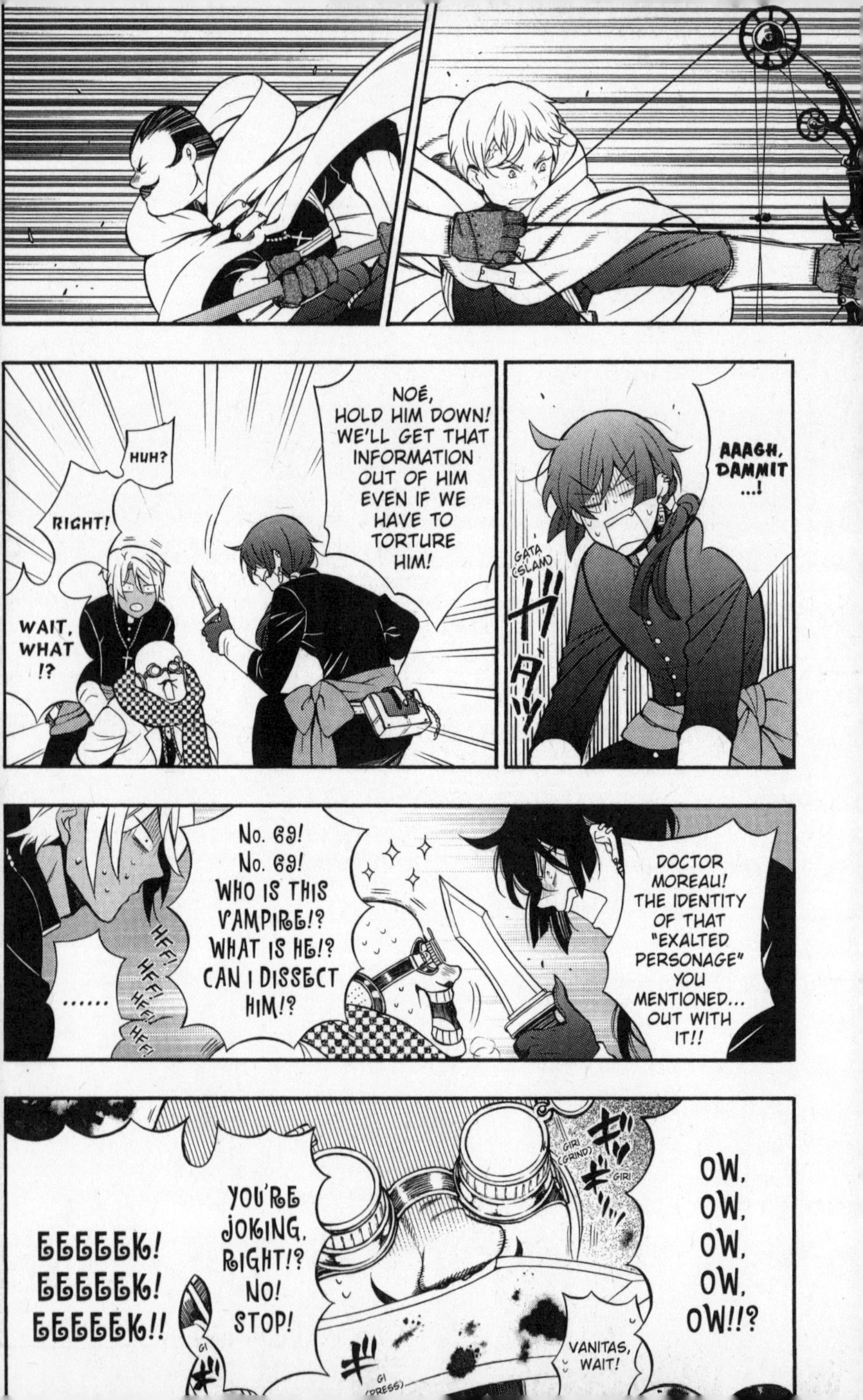
AAAGH, DAMMIT ...!
GATA (SLAM)
NOÉ, HOLD HIM DOWN! WE'LL GET THAT INFORMATION OUT OF HIM EVEN IF WE HAVE TO TORTURE HIM!
HUH?
RIGHT!
WAIT, WHAT !?
DOCTOR MOREAU! THE IDENTITY OF THAT "EXALTED PERSONAGE" YOU MENTIONED... OUT WITH IT!!
No. 69! No. 69! WHO IS THIS VAMPIRE!? WHAT IS HE!? CAN I DISSECT HIM!?
HFF! HFF! HFF! HFF!
......
OW, OW, OW, OW, OW, OW!!?
GIRI (GRIND)
GIRI
VANITAS, WAIT!
YOU'RE JOKING, RIGHT!? NO! STOP!
EEEEEK! EEEEEK! EEEEEK!!
GI (PRESS)
GI

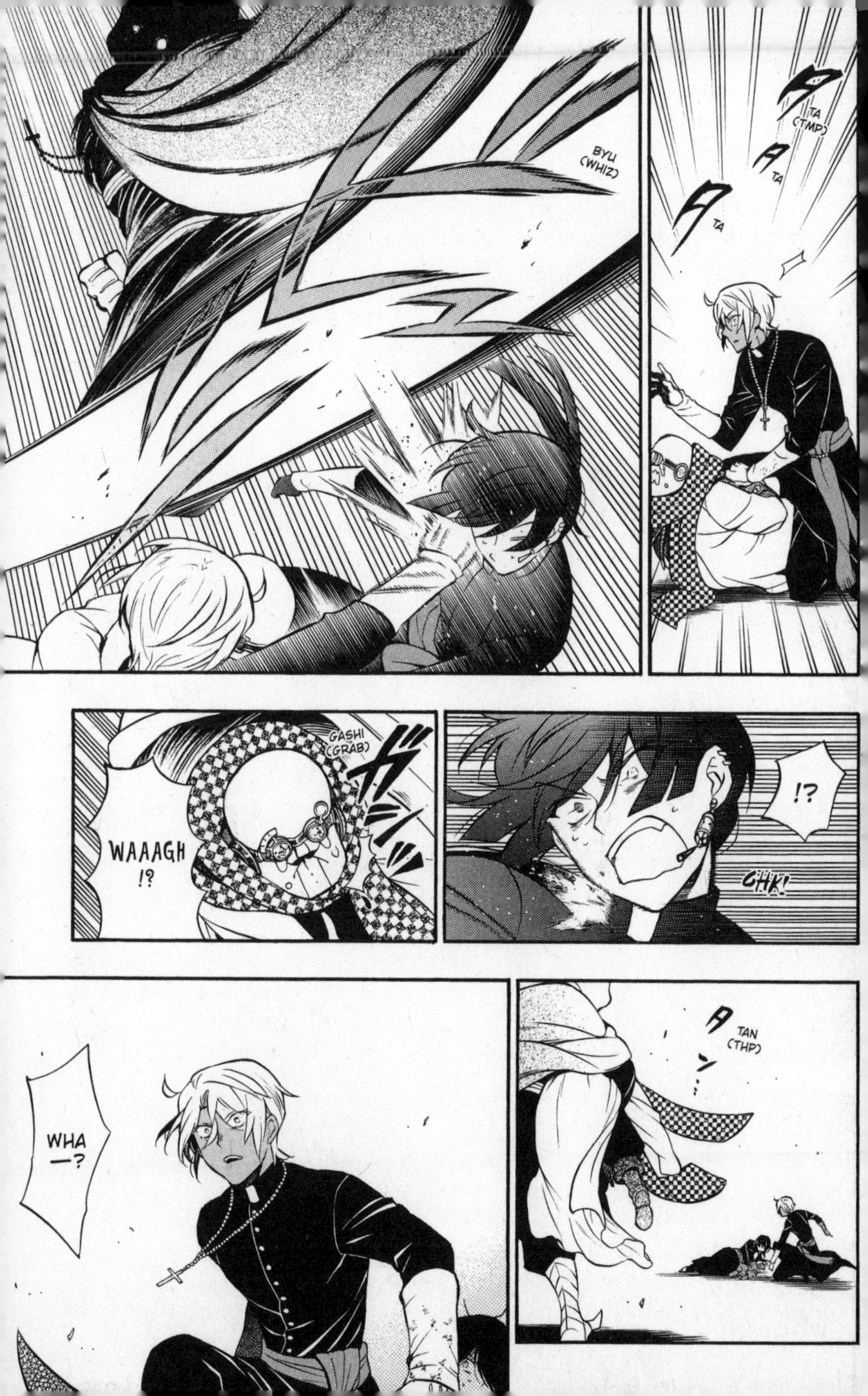
TA (TMP)
TA
TA
BYU (WHIZ)
!?
CHK!
GASHI (GRAB)
WAAAGH !?
TAN (THP)
WHA —?

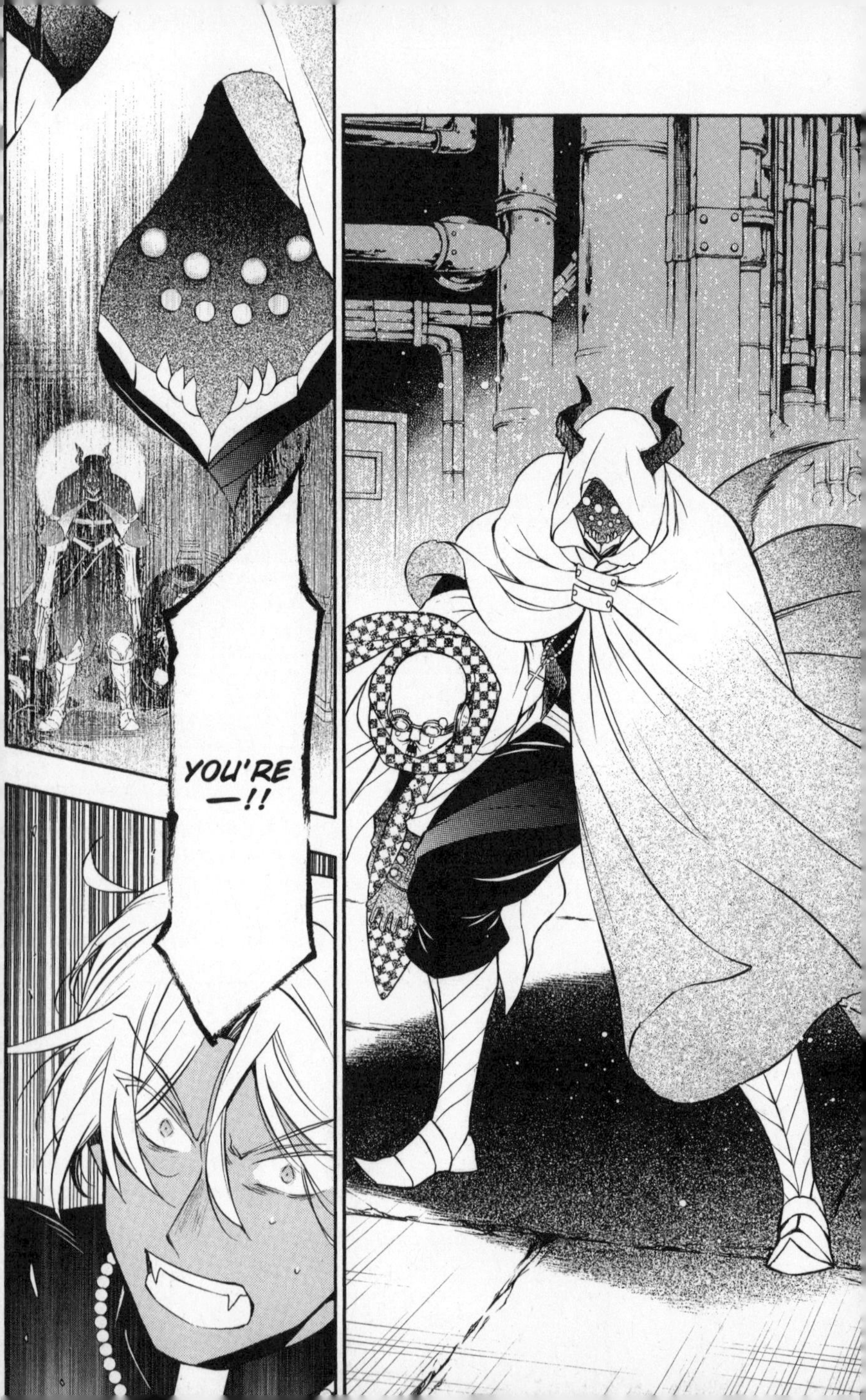
YOU'RE
—!!

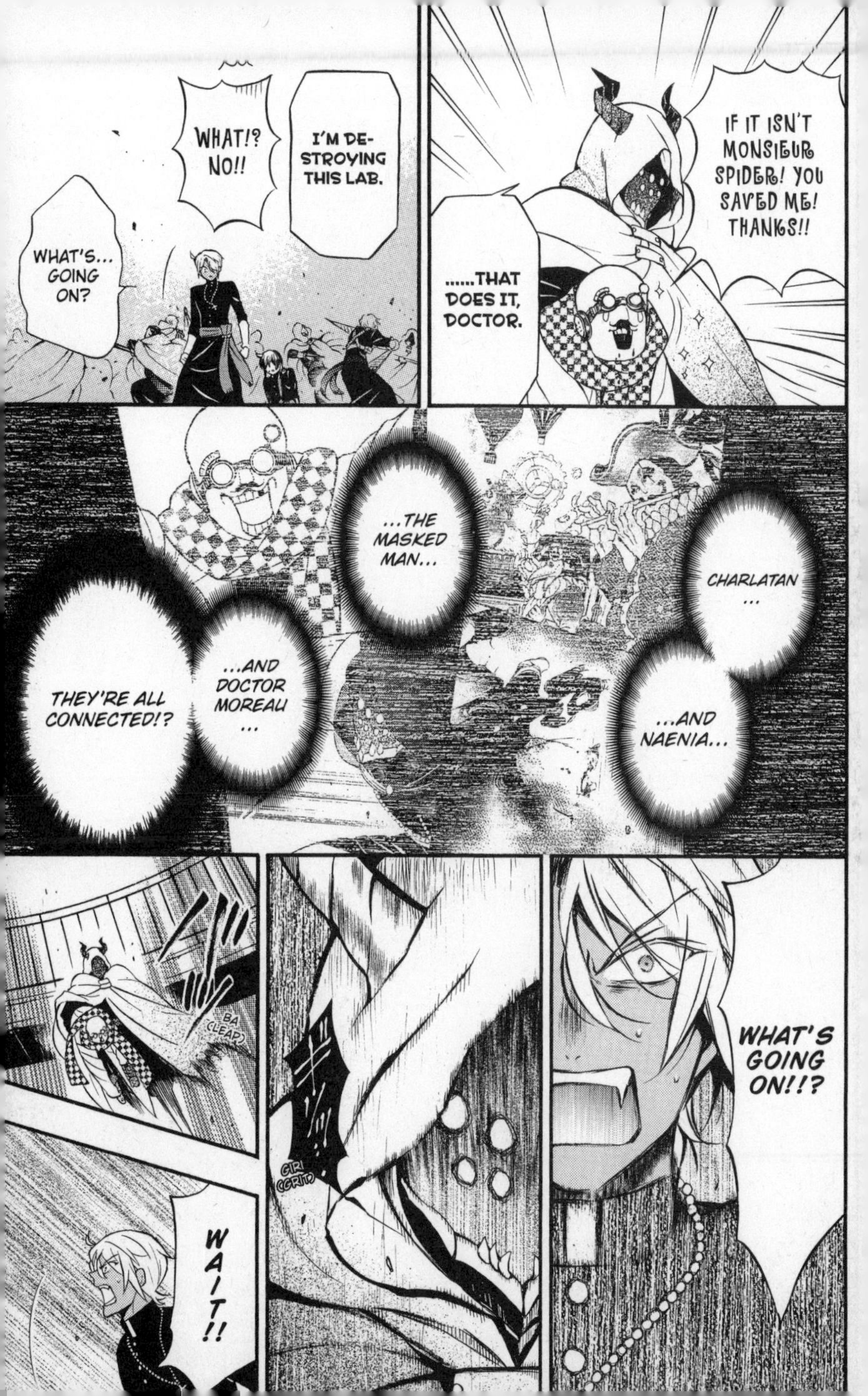
IF IT ISN'T MONSIEUR SPIDER! YOU SAVED ME! THANKS!!
......THAT DOES IT, DOCTOR.
I'M DE-STROYING THIS LAB.
WHAT!? NO!!
WHAT'S... GOING ON?
CHARLATAN ...
...AND NAENIA...
...THE MASKED MAN...
...AND DOCTOR MOREAU ...
THEY'RE ALL CONNECTED!?
WHAT'S GOING ON!!?
GIRI (GRIT)
BA (LEAP)
WAIT!!

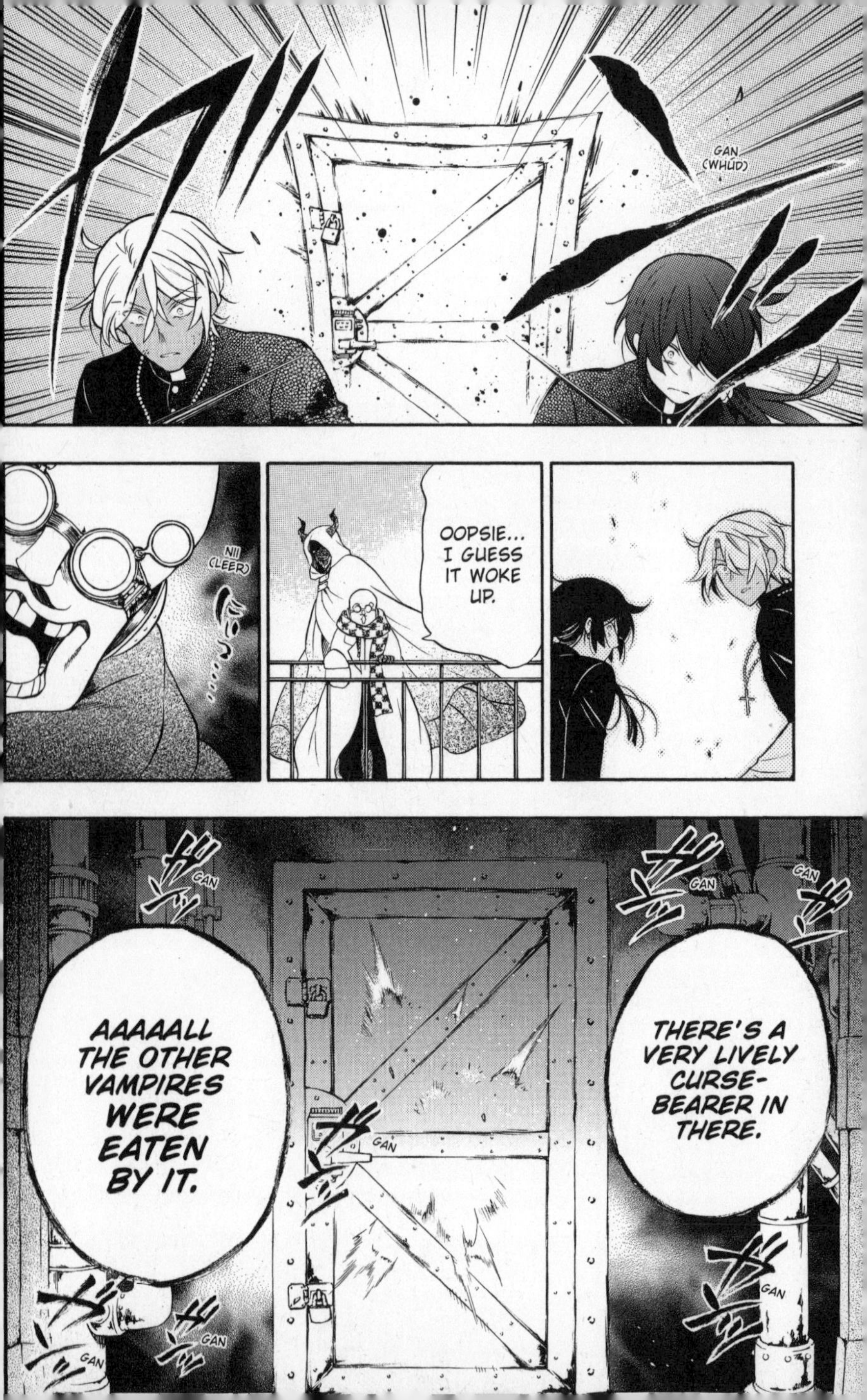
GAN (WHUD)
OOPSIE... I GUESS IT WOKE UP.
NII (LEER)
GAN
GAN
GAN
THERE'S A VERY LIVELY CURSE-BEARER IN THERE.
AAAAALL THE OTHER VAMPIRES WERE EATEN BY IT.
GAN
GAN
GAN
GAN
GAN

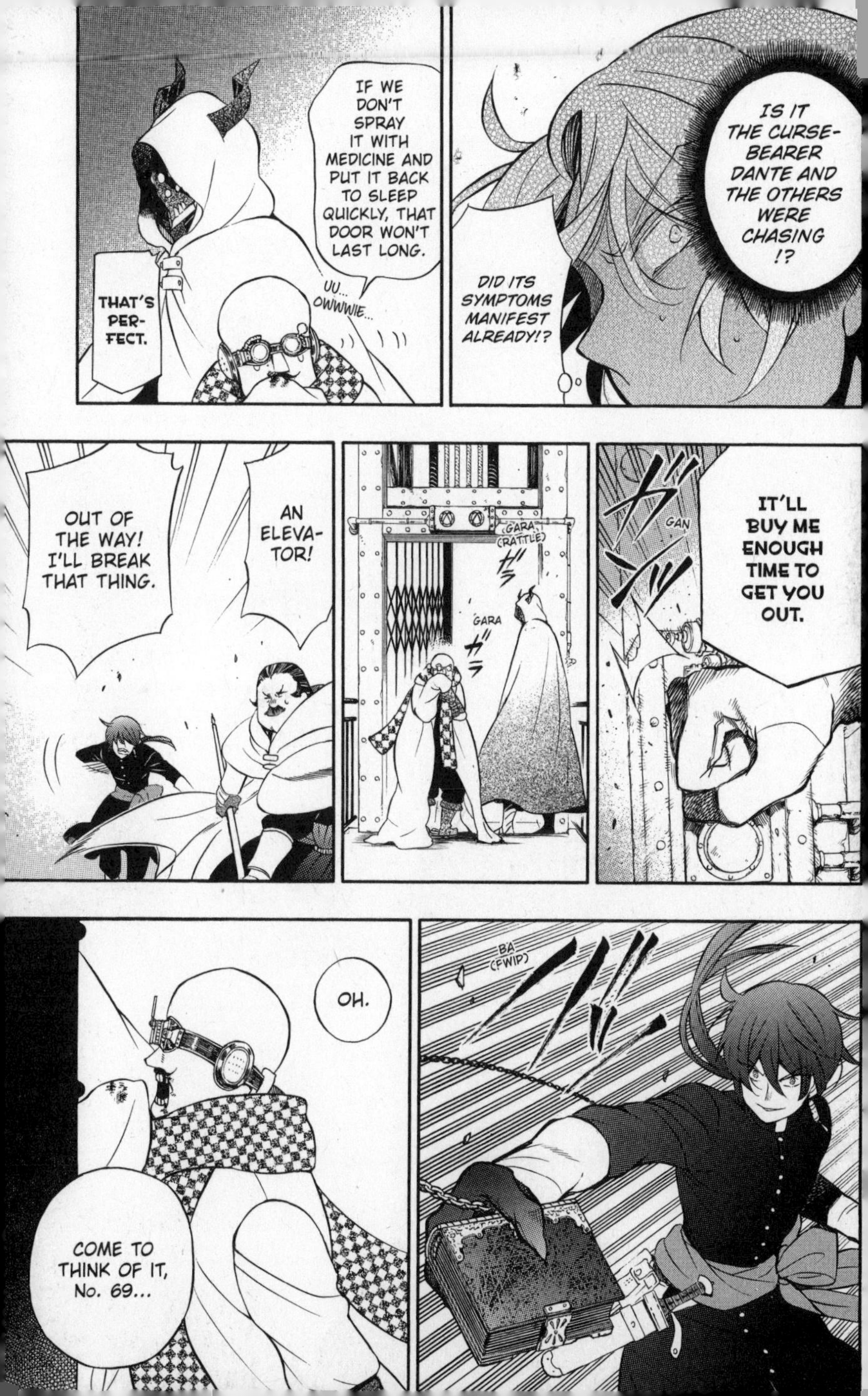
IS IT THE CURSE-BEARER DANTE AND THE OTHERS WERE CHASING !?
DID ITS SYMPTOMS MANIFEST ALREADY!?
IF WE DON'T SPRAY IT WITH MEDICINE AND PUT IT BACK TO SLEEP QUICKLY, THAT DOOR WON'T LAST LONG.
UU... OWWWIE...
THAT'S PER-FECT.
GAN
IT'LL BUY ME ENOUGH TIME TO GET YOU OUT.
GARA (RATTLE)
GARA
AN ELEVA-TOR!
OUT OF THE WAY! I'LL BREAK THAT THING.
BA (FWIP)
OH.
COME TO THINK OF IT, No. 69...

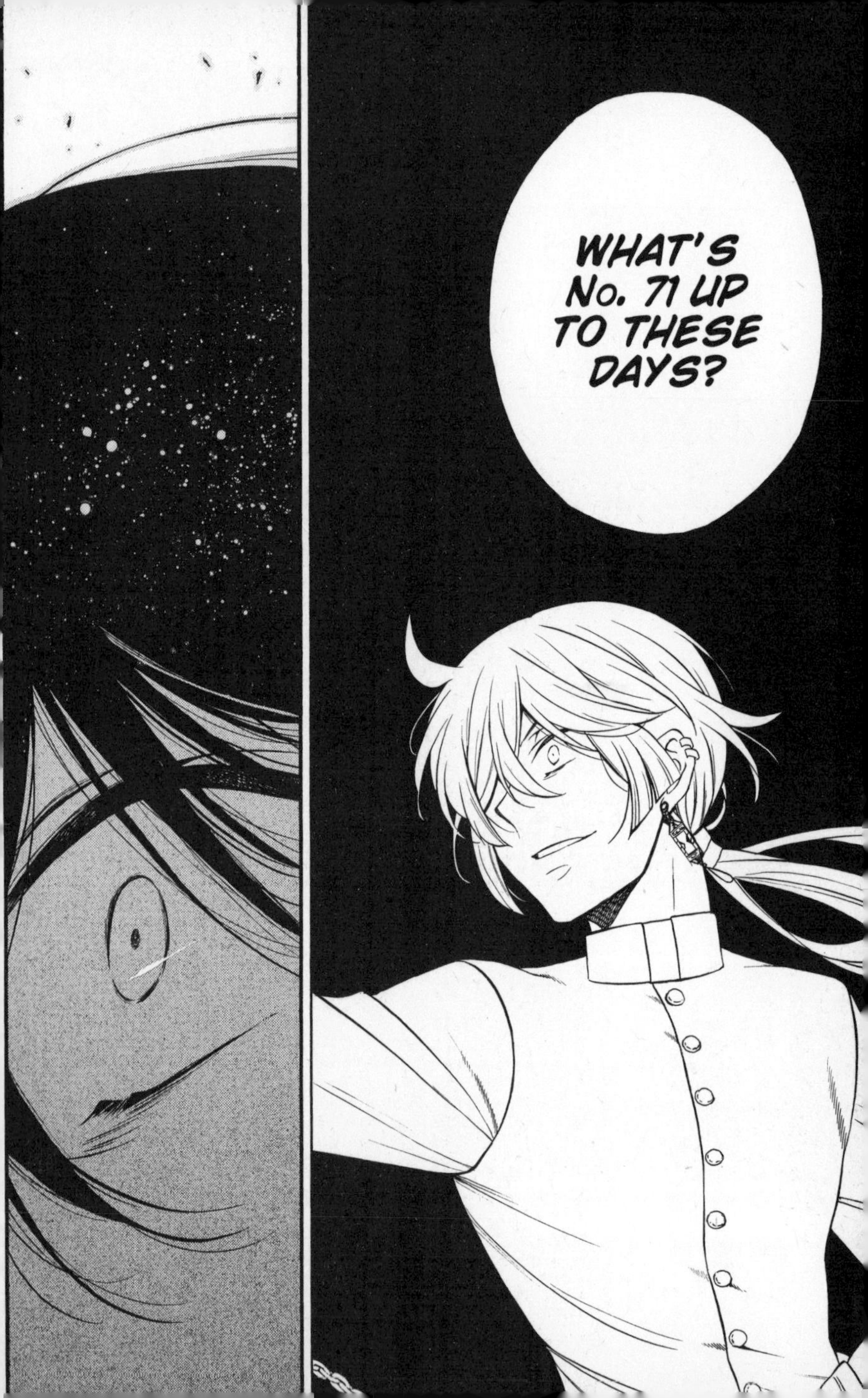
WHAT'S No. 71 UP TO THESE DAYS?

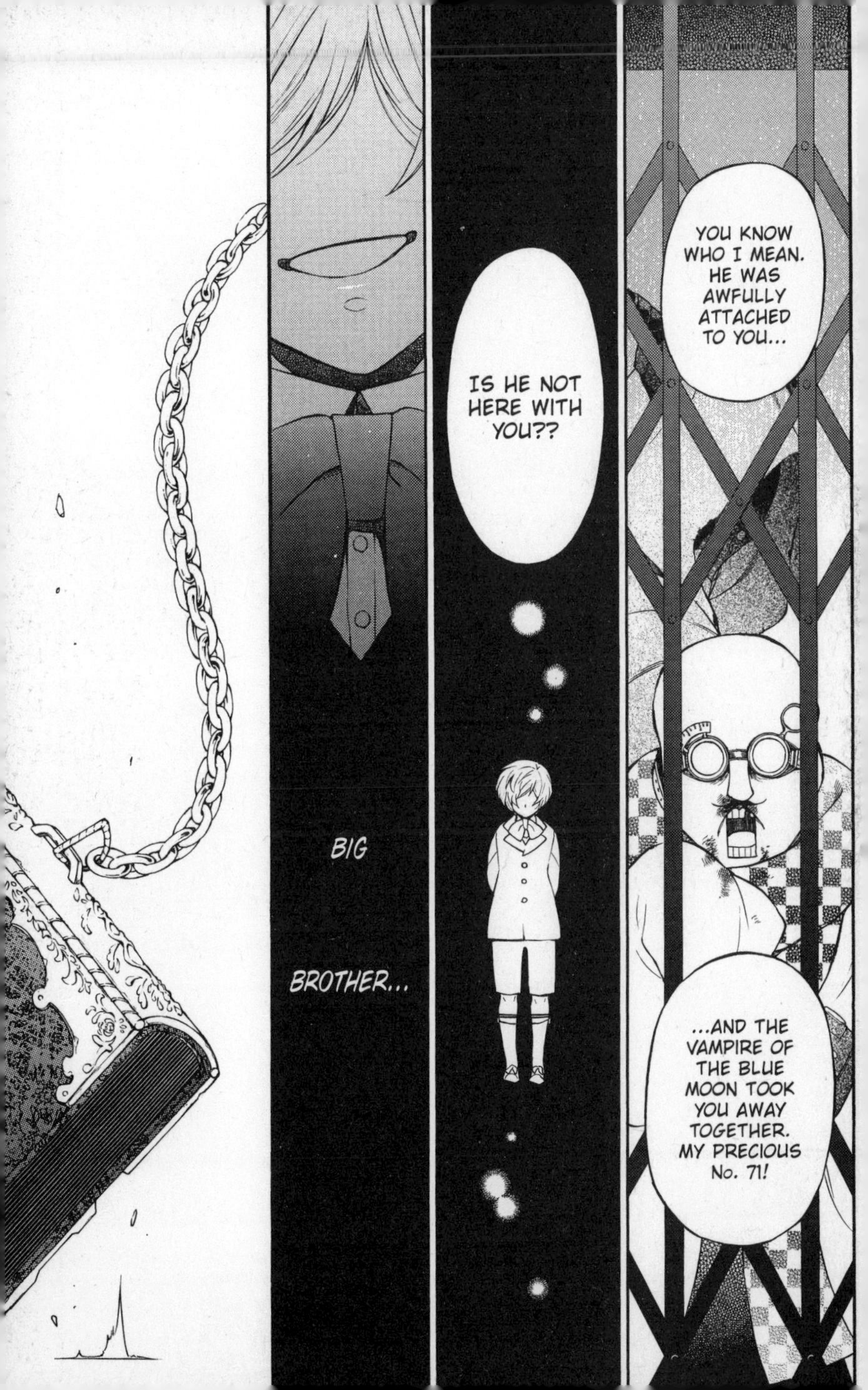
YOU KNOW WHO I MEAN. HE WAS AWFULLY ATTACHED TO YOU...
...AND THE VAMPIRE OF THE BLUE MOON TOOK YOU AWAY TOGETHER. MY PRECIOUS No. 71!
IS HE NOT HERE WITH YOU??
BIG
BROTHER...

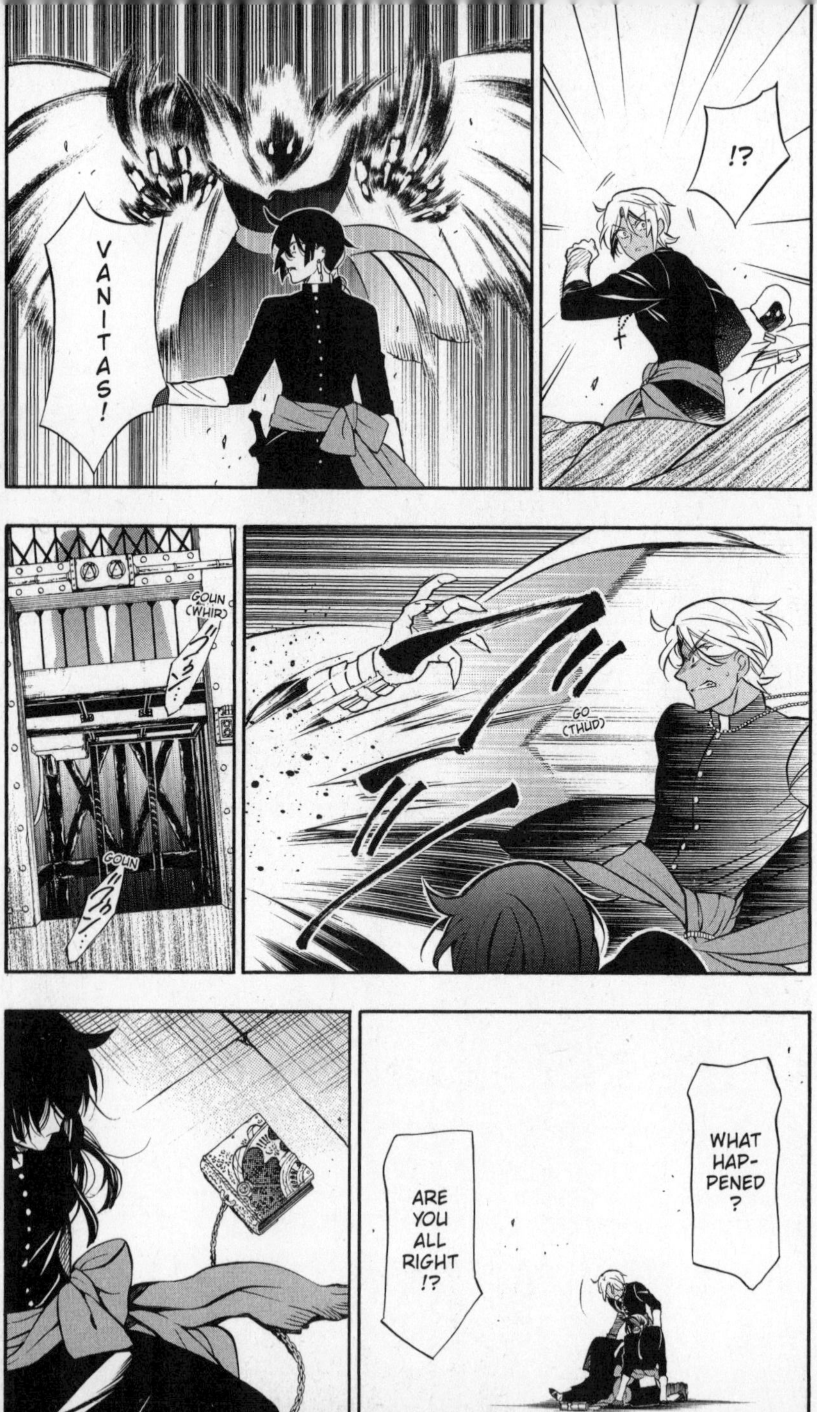
!?
VANITAS!
GO (THUD)
GOUN (WHIR)
GOUN
WHAT HAPPENED?
ARE YOU ALL RIGHT!?

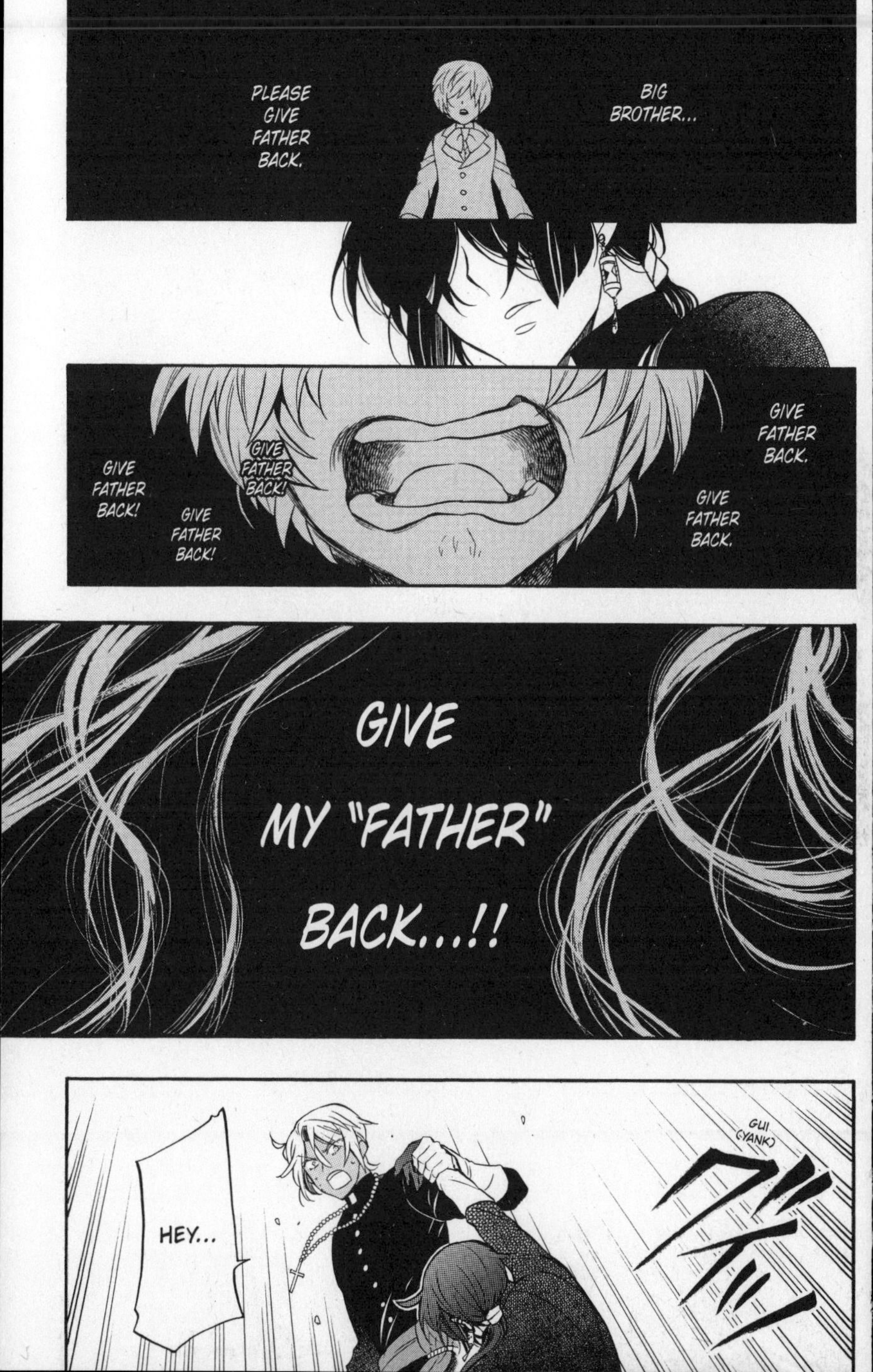

BIG BROTHER...
PLEASE GIVE FATHER BACK.
GIVE FATHER BACK.
GIVE FATHER BACK.
GIVE FATHER BACK!
GIVE FATHER BACK!
GIVE FATHER BACK!
GIVE MY "FATHER" BACK...!!
GUI (YANK)
HEY...

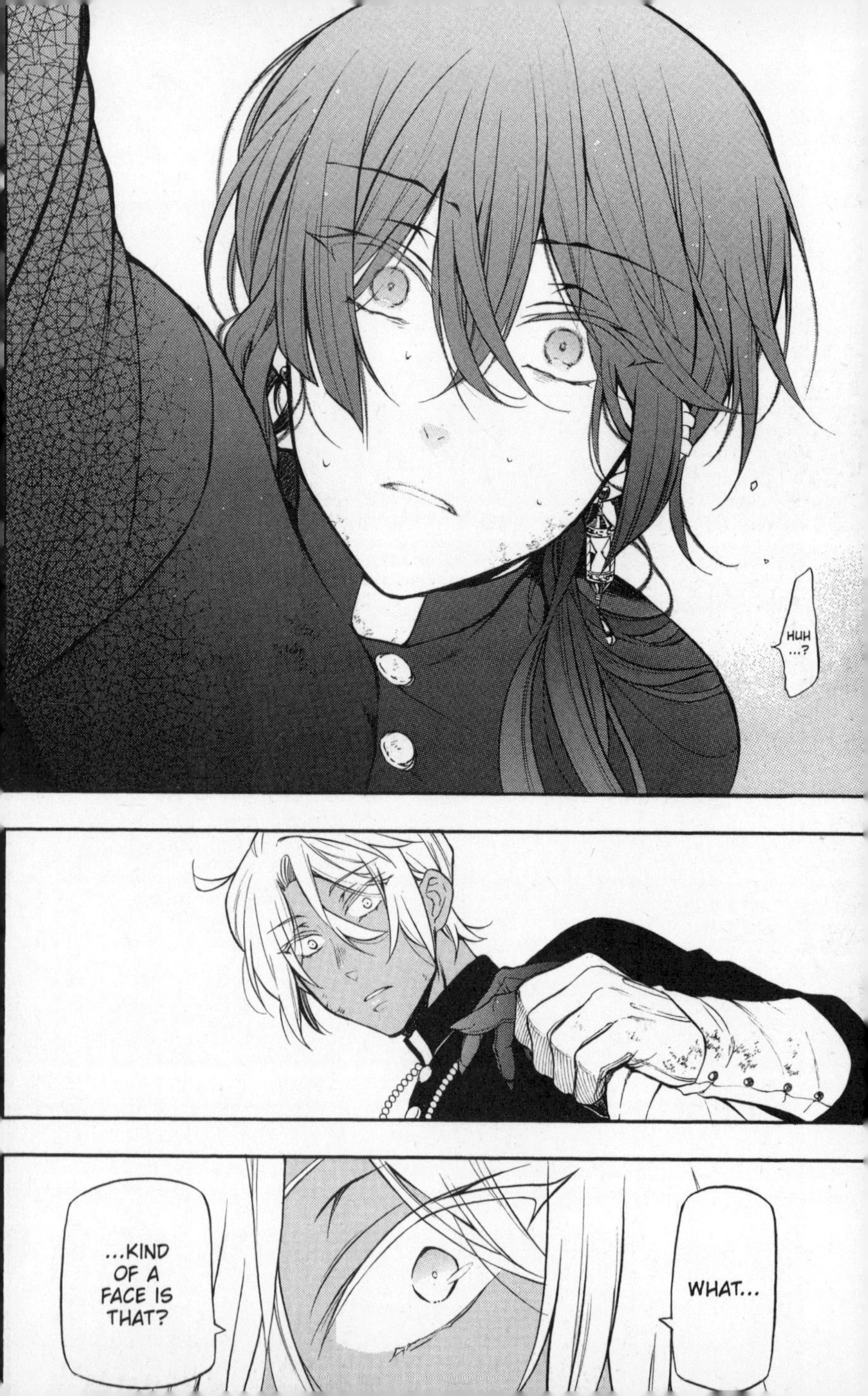

HUH ...?
WHAT...
...KIND OF A FACE IS THAT?

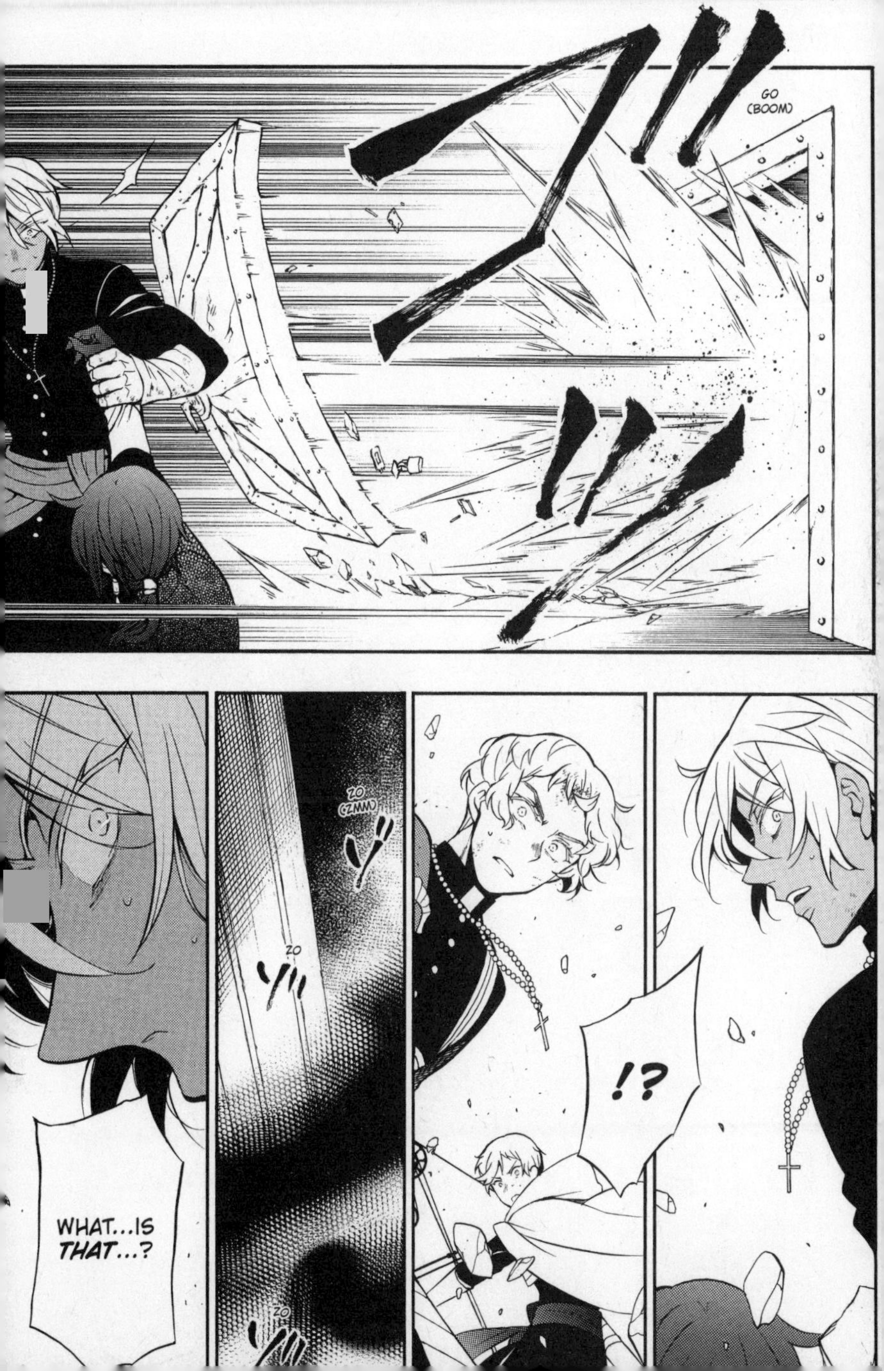

GO (BOOM)
!?
ZO (ZMM)
ZO
ZO
WHAT...IS *THAT*...?

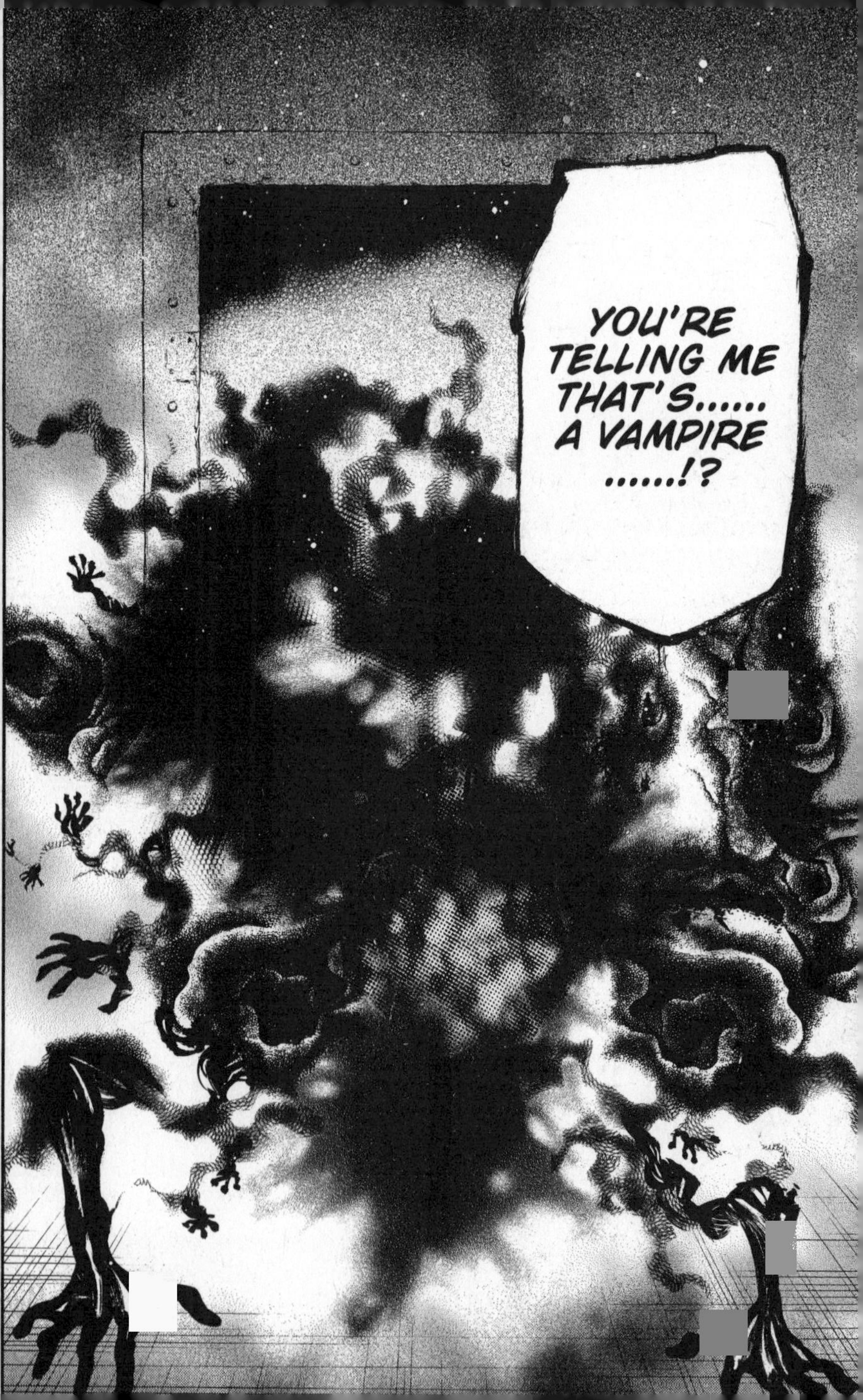
YOU'RE TELLING ME THAT'S...... A VAMPIRE ......!?

# Mémoire 17 Cicatrice No. 69

*Les Mémoires de Vanitas*

THE CASE STUDY OF VANITAS

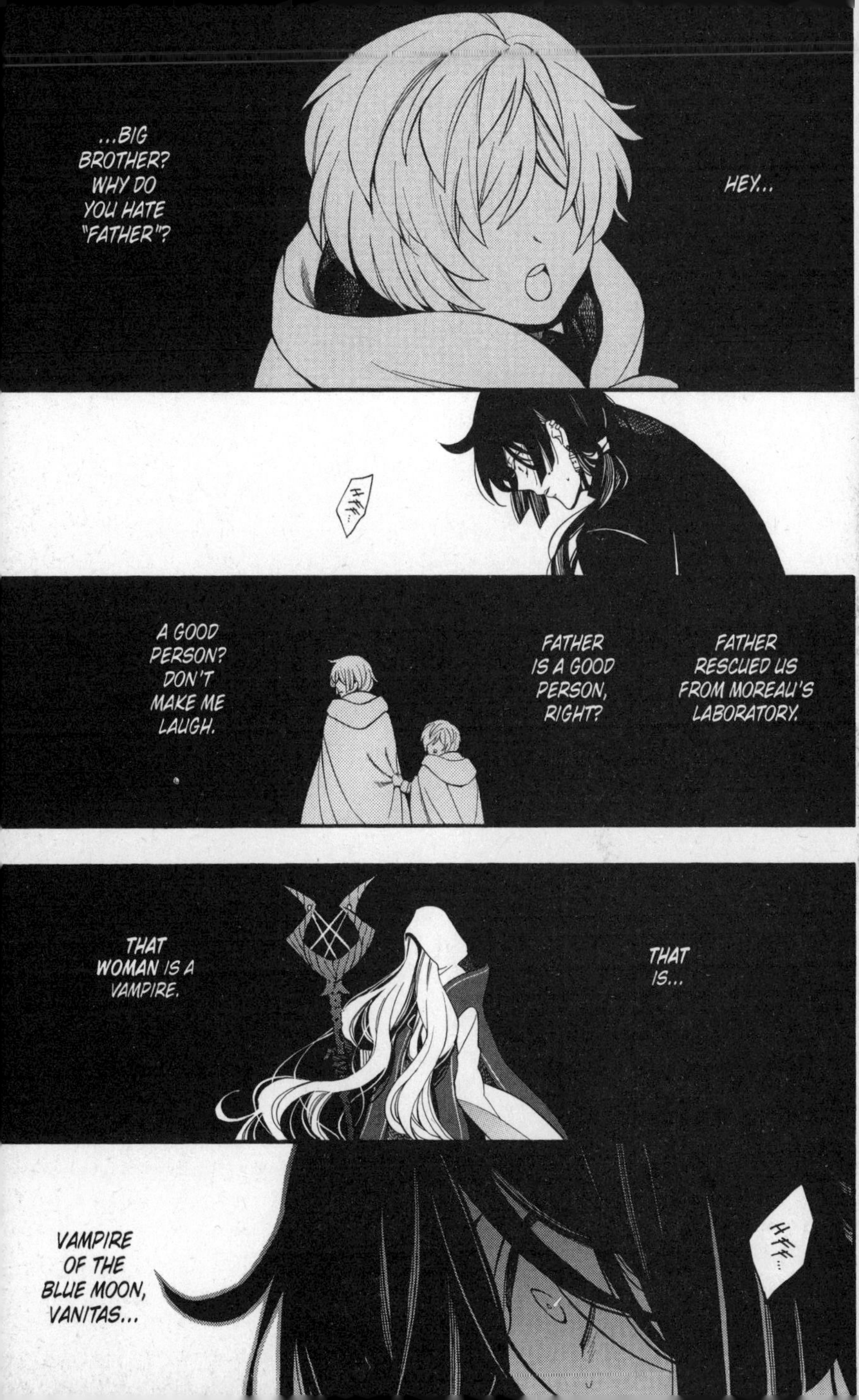
HEY...
...BIG BROTHER? WHY DO YOU HATE "FATHER"?
HFF...
FATHER RESCUED US FROM MOREAU'S LABORATORY.
FATHER IS A GOOD PERSON, RIGHT?
A GOOD PERSON? DON'T MAKE ME LAUGH.
THAT IS...
THAT WOMAN IS A VAMPIRE.
HFF...
VAMPIRE OF THE BLUE MOON, VANITAS...

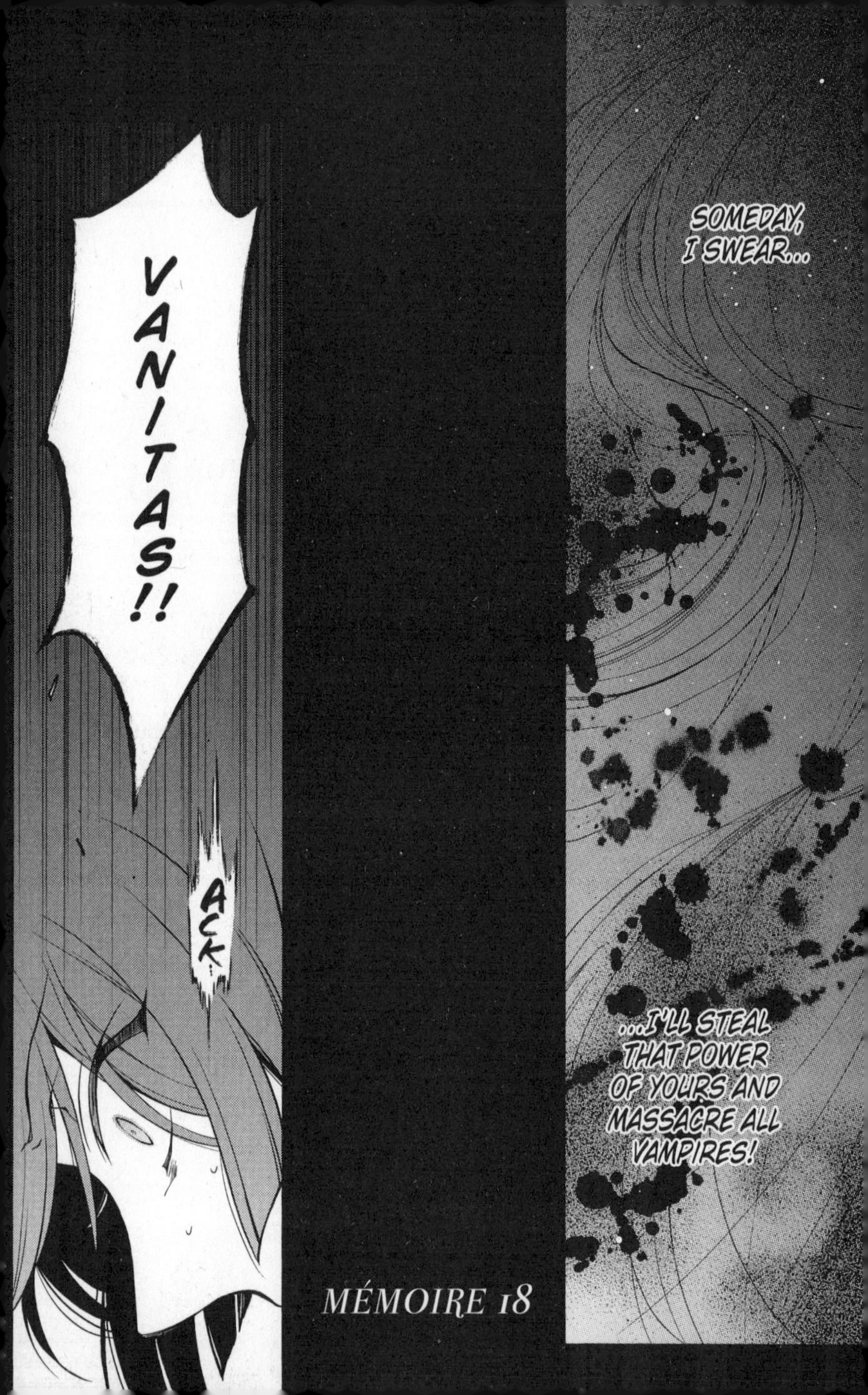
SOMEDAY, I SWEAR...
...I'LL STEAL THAT POWER OF YOURS AND MASSACRE ALL VAMPIRES!
MÉMOIRE 18
VANITAS!!
ACK...

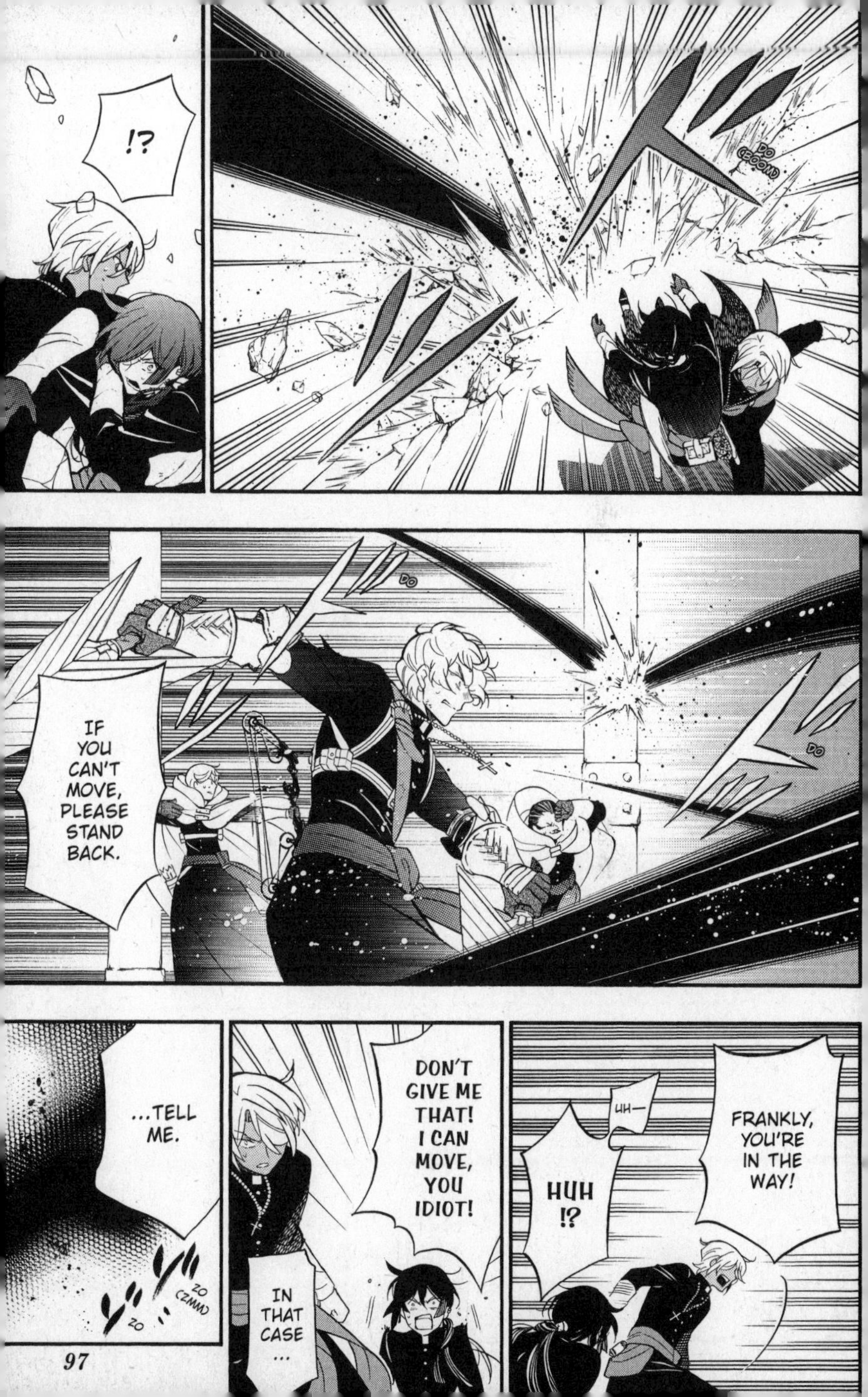
DO
(DOOM)
!?
DO
DO
IF YOU CAN'T MOVE, PLEASE STAND BACK.
FRANKLY, YOU'RE IN THE WAY!
UH—
HUH !?
DON'T GIVE ME THAT! I CAN MOVE, YOU IDIOT!
IN THAT CASE...
...TELL ME.
ZO
(ZMMM)
ZO

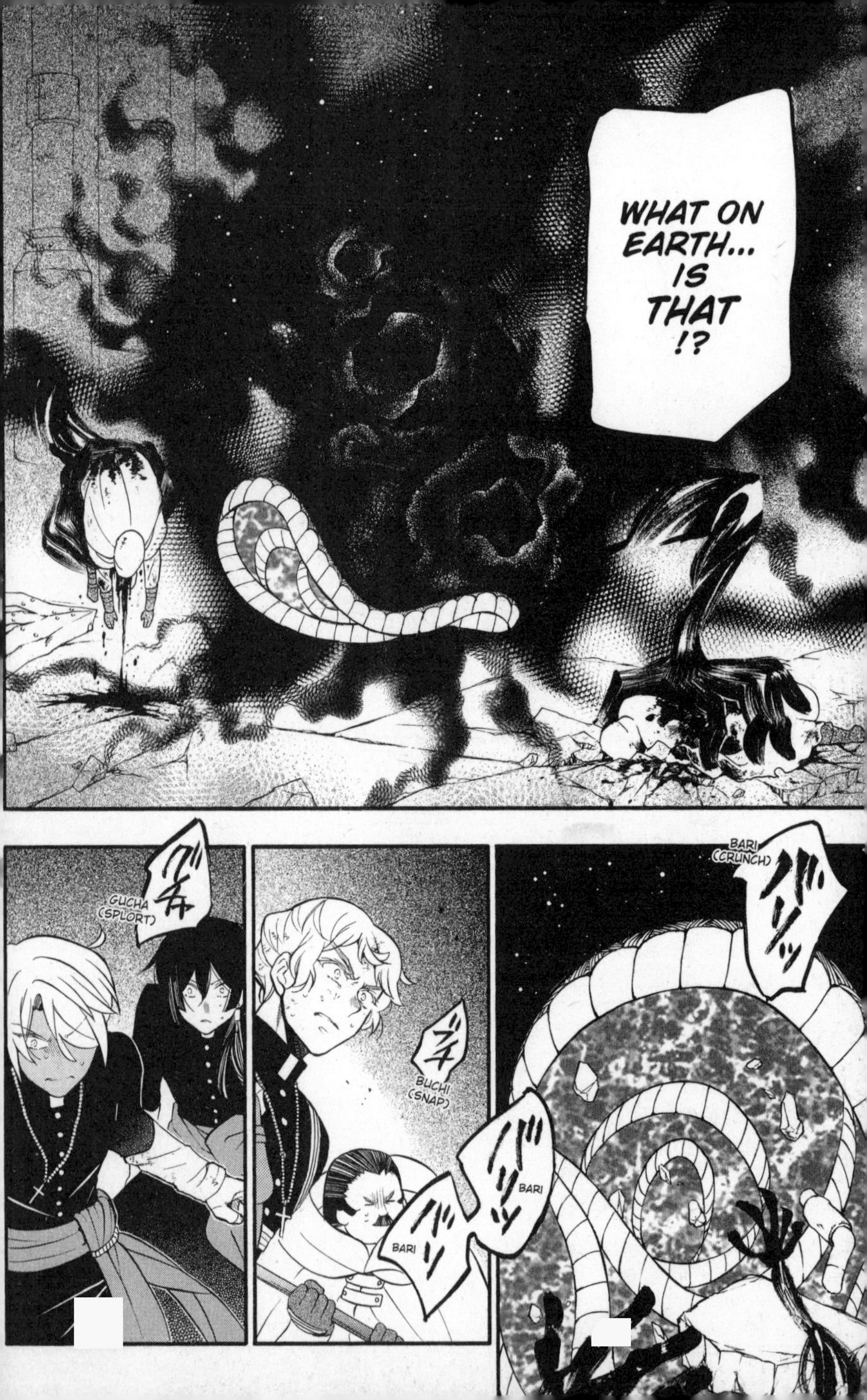
WHAT ON EARTH... IS THAT!?
BARI (CRUNCH)
BUCHI (SNAP)
BARI
BARI
GUCHA (SPLORT)

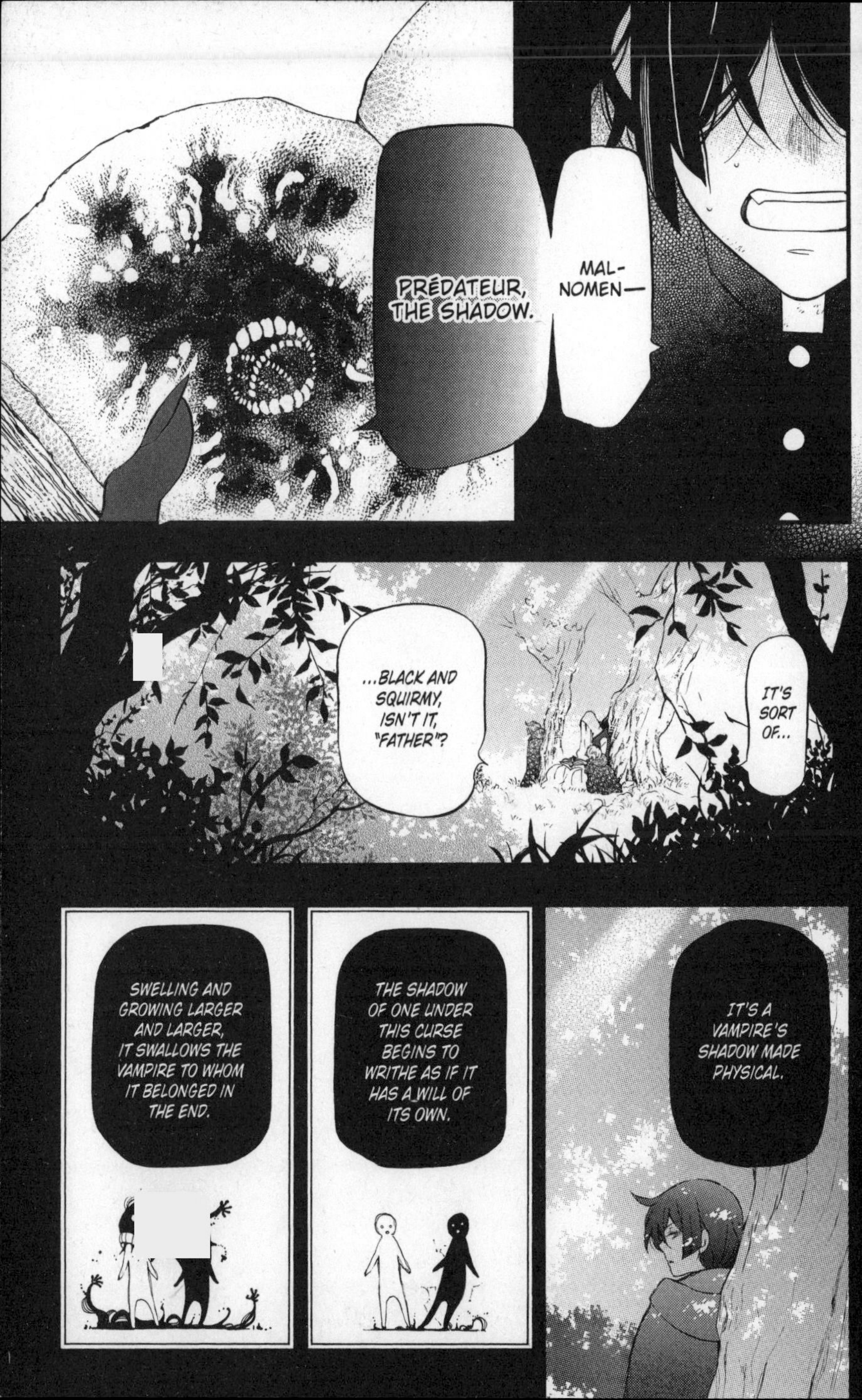
MAL-
NOMEN—
PRÉDATEUR,
THE SHADOW.
IT'S SORT OF...
...BLACK AND SQUIRMY, ISN'T IT, "FATHER"?
IT'S A VAMPIRE'S SHADOW MADE PHYSICAL.
THE SHADOW OF ONE UNDER THIS CURSE BEGINS TO WRITHE AS IF IT HAS A WILL OF ITS OWN.
SWELLING AND GROWING LARGER AND LARGER, IT SWALLOWS THE VAMPIRE TO WHOM IT BELONGED IN THE END.

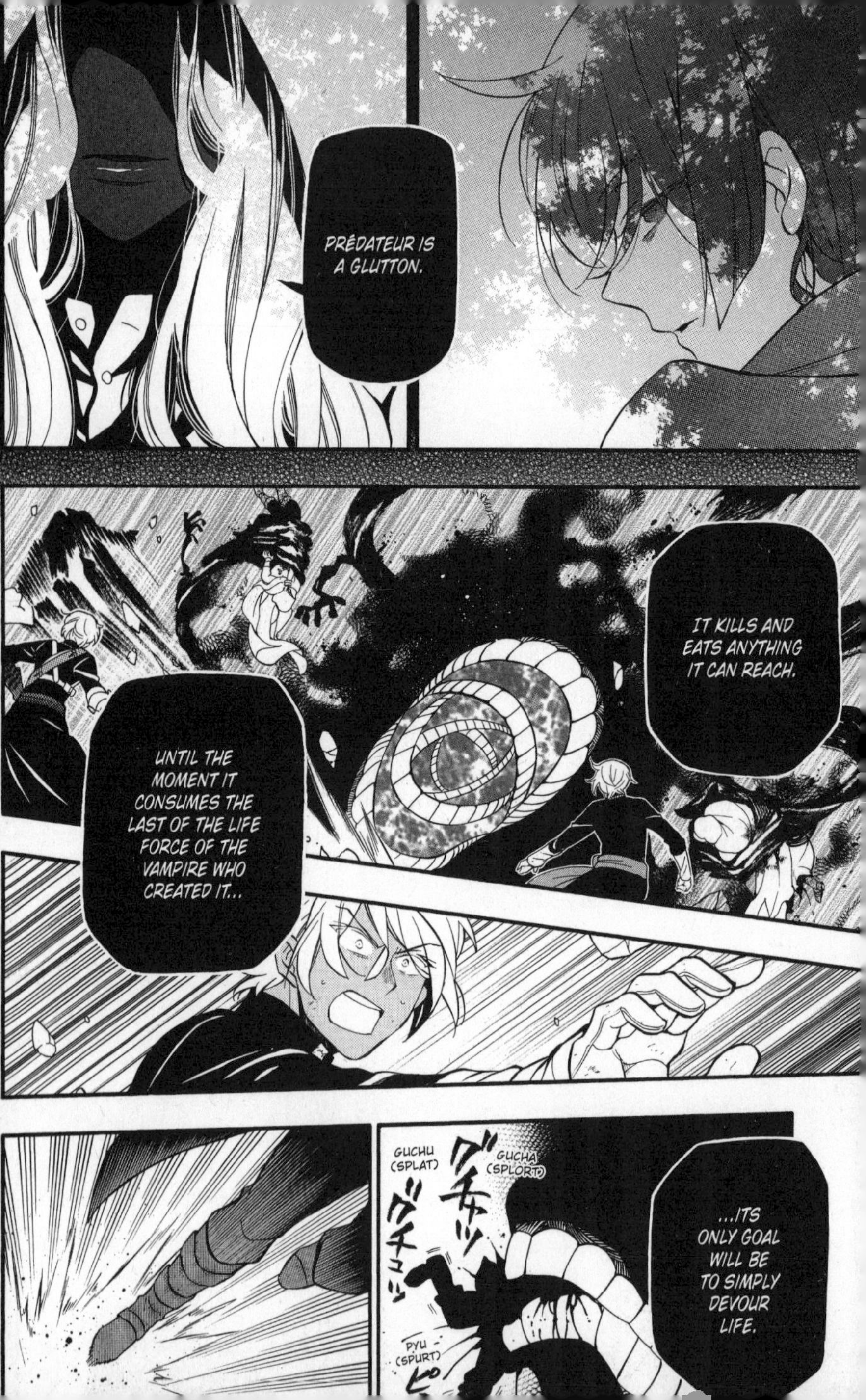
PRÉDATEUR IS A GLUTTON.
IT KILLS AND EATS ANYTHING IT CAN REACH.
UNTIL THE MOMENT IT CONSUMES THE LAST OF THE LIFE FORCE OF THE VAMPIRE WHO CREATED IT...
GUCHA (SPLORT)
GUCHU (SPLAT)
...ITS ONLY GOAL WILL BE TO SIMPLY DEVOUR LIFE.
PYU (SPURT)

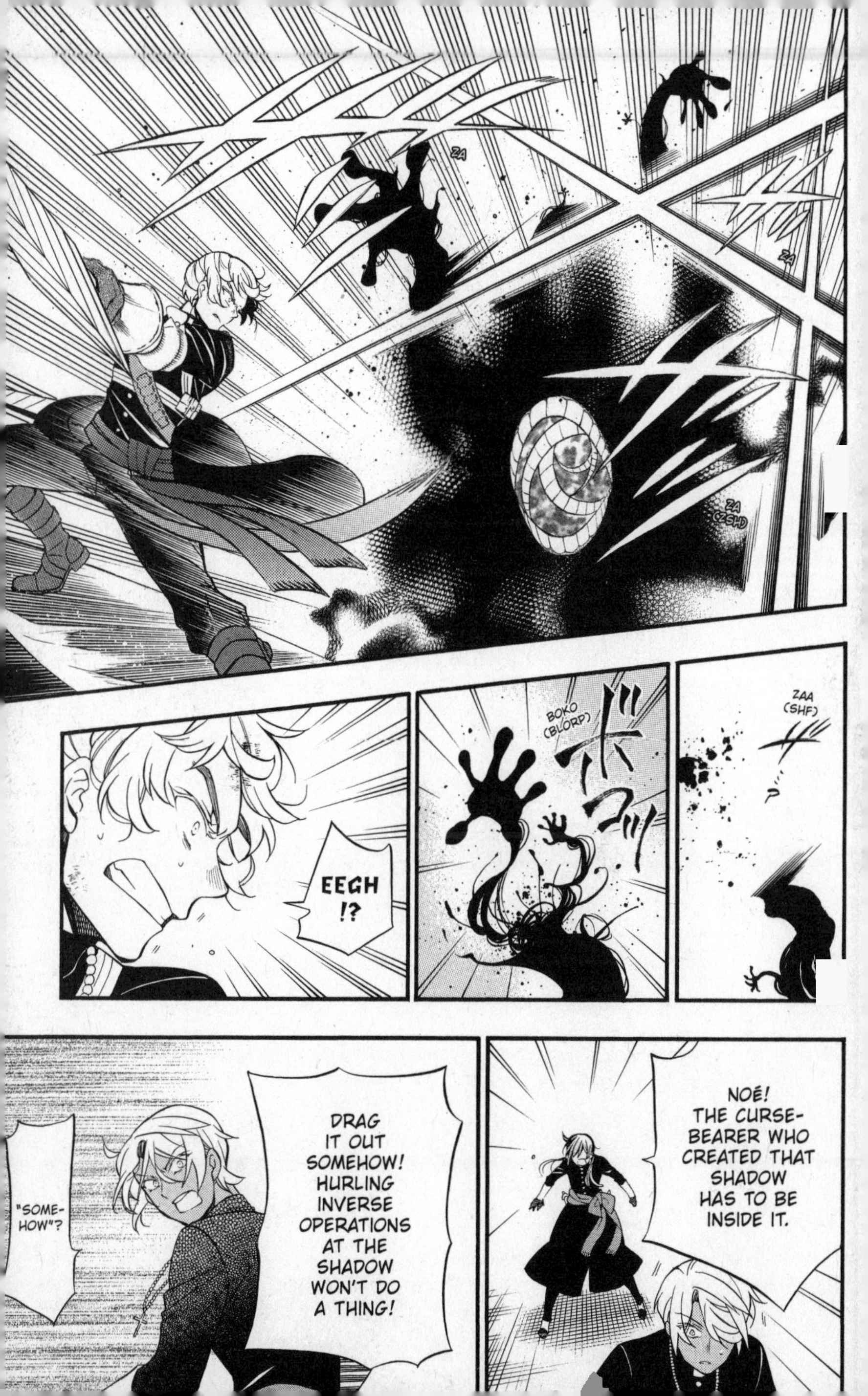
ZA
ZA
ZA (ZSHD)
ZAA (SHF)
BOKO (BLORP)
EEGH !?
NOÉ! THE CURSE-BEARER WHO CREATED THAT SHADOW HAS TO BE INSIDE IT.
DRAG IT OUT SOMEHOW! HURLING INVERSE OPERATIONS AT THE SHADOW WON'T DO A THING!
"SOME-HOW"?

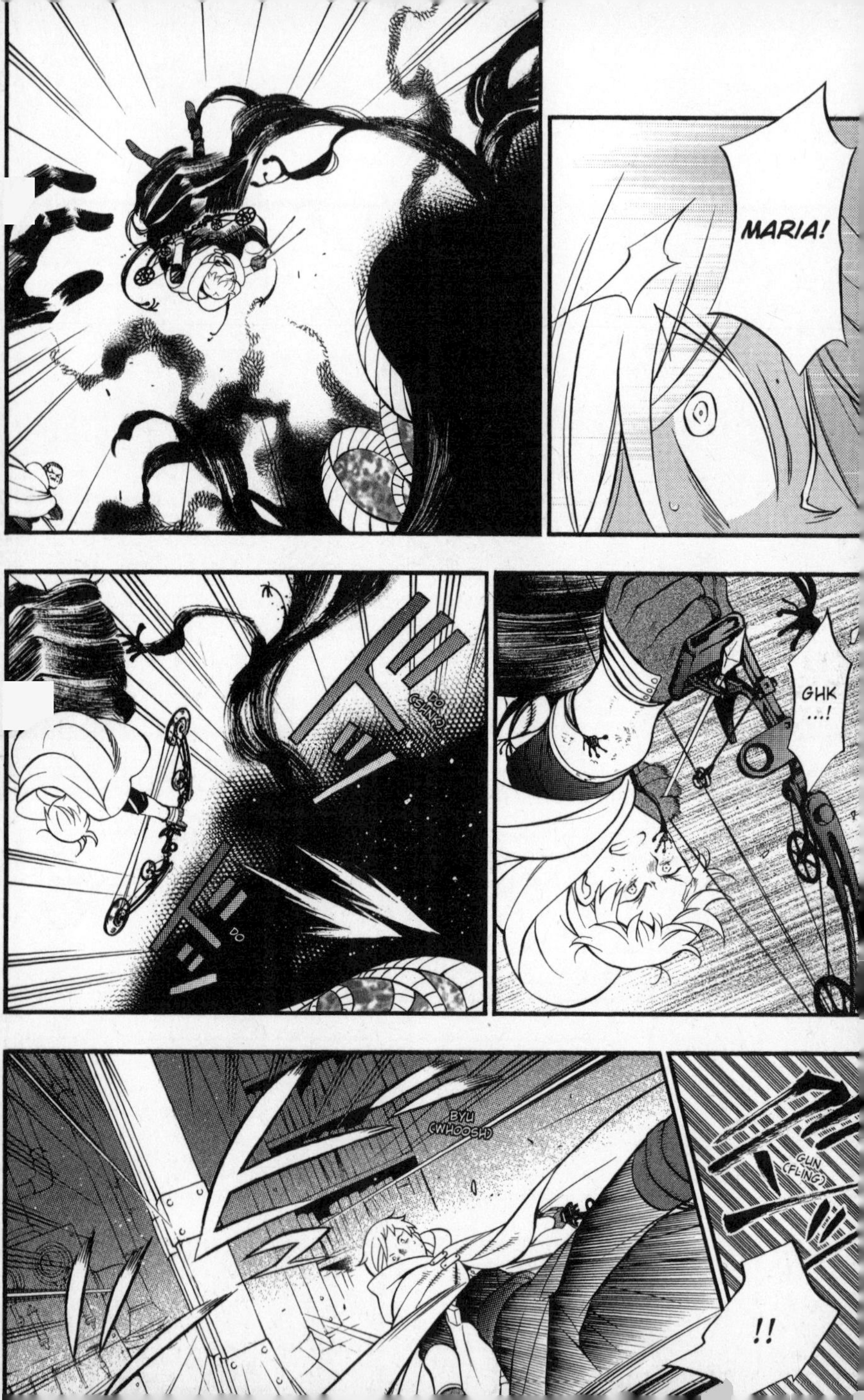
MARIA!
GHK ...!
DO (SHNK)
DO
GUN (FLING)
!!
BYU (WHOOSH)

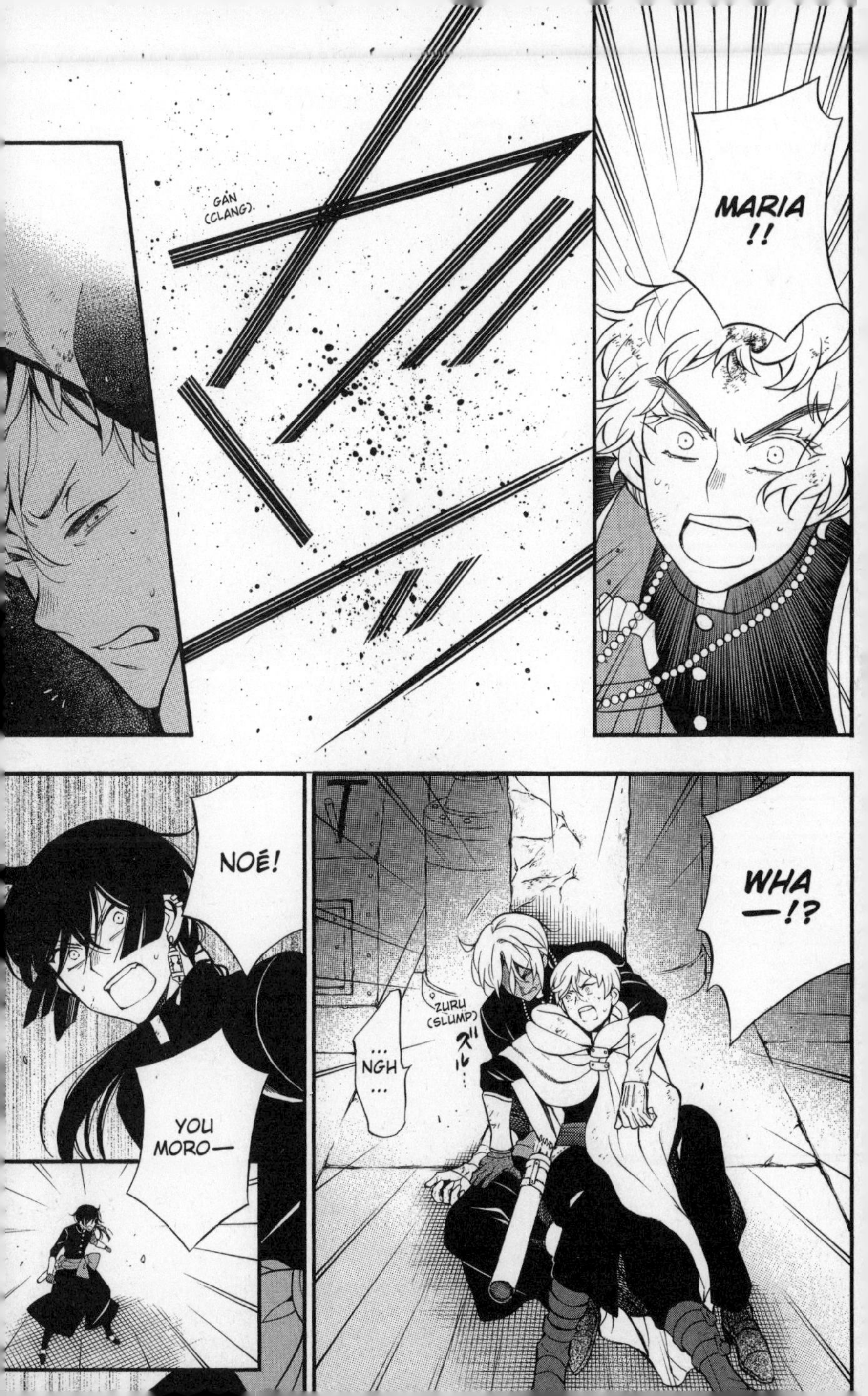
MARIA !!
GAN (CLANG).
WHA—!?
ZURU (SLUMP)
ズル…
...NGH...
NOÉ!
YOU MORO—

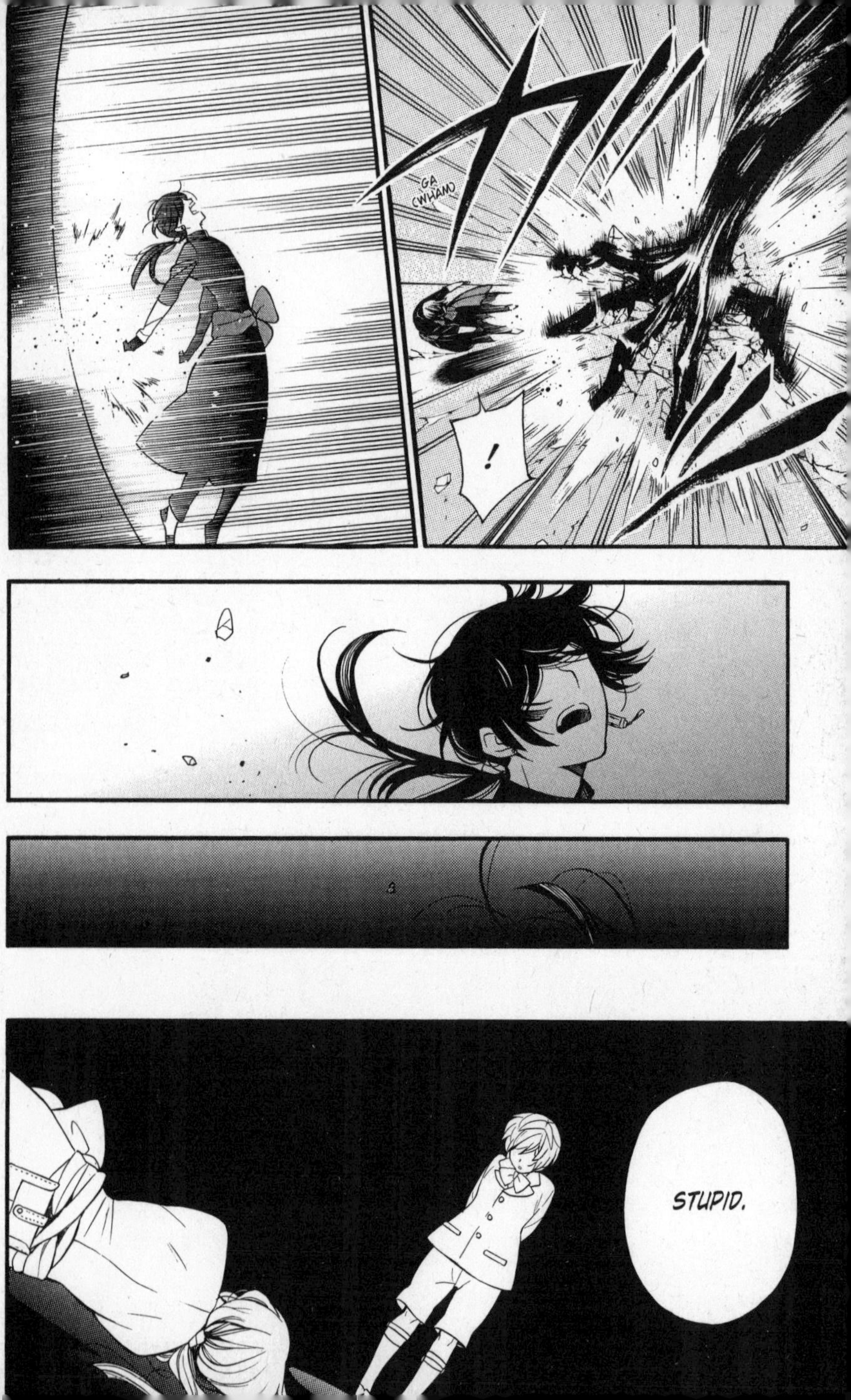
GA
(WHAM)
!
STUPID.

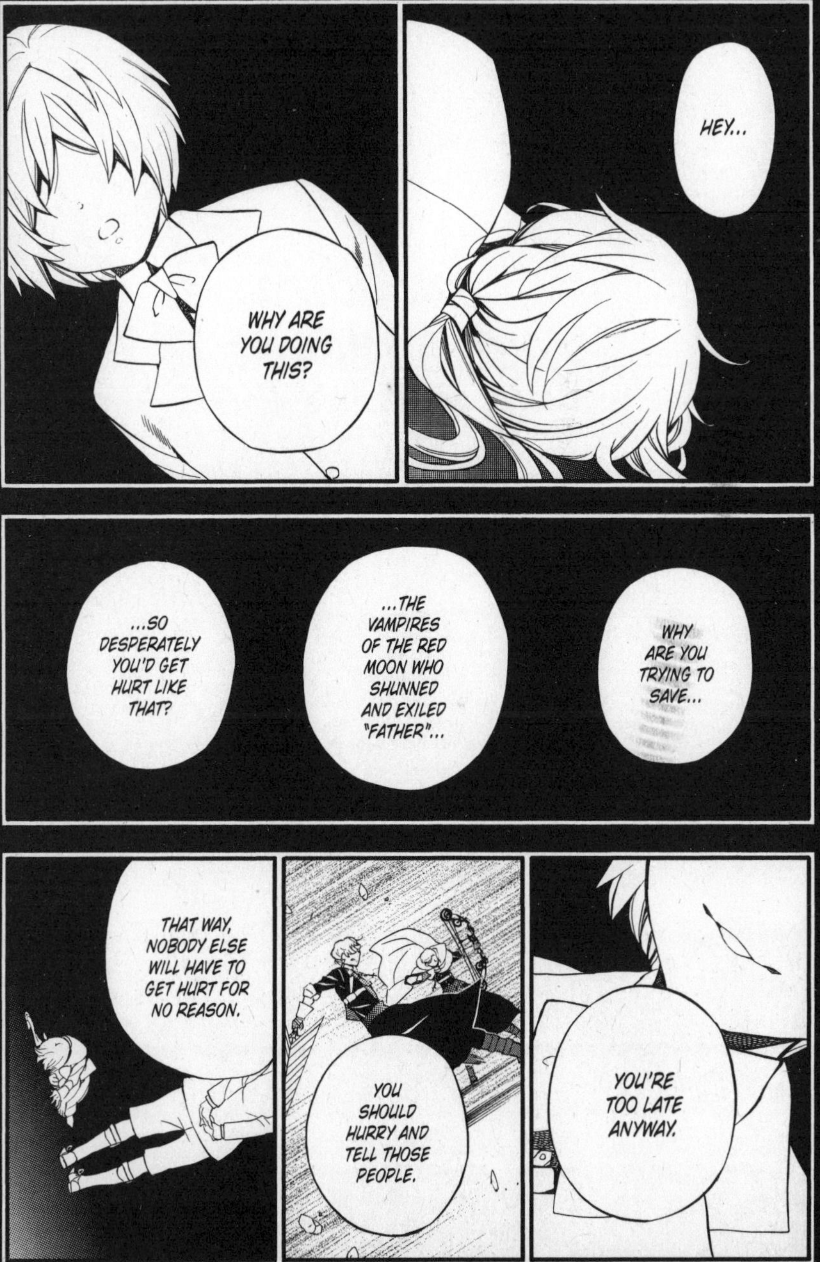
HEY...
WHY ARE YOU DOING THIS?
WHY ARE YOU TRYING TO SAVE...
...THE VAMPIRES OF THE RED MOON WHO SHUNNED AND EXILED "FATHER"...
...SO DESPERATELY YOU'D GET HURT LIKE THAT?
YOU'RE TOO LATE ANYWAY.
YOU SHOULD HURRY AND TELL THOSE PEOPLE.
THAT WAY, NOBODY ELSE WILL HAVE TO GET HURT FOR NO REASON.

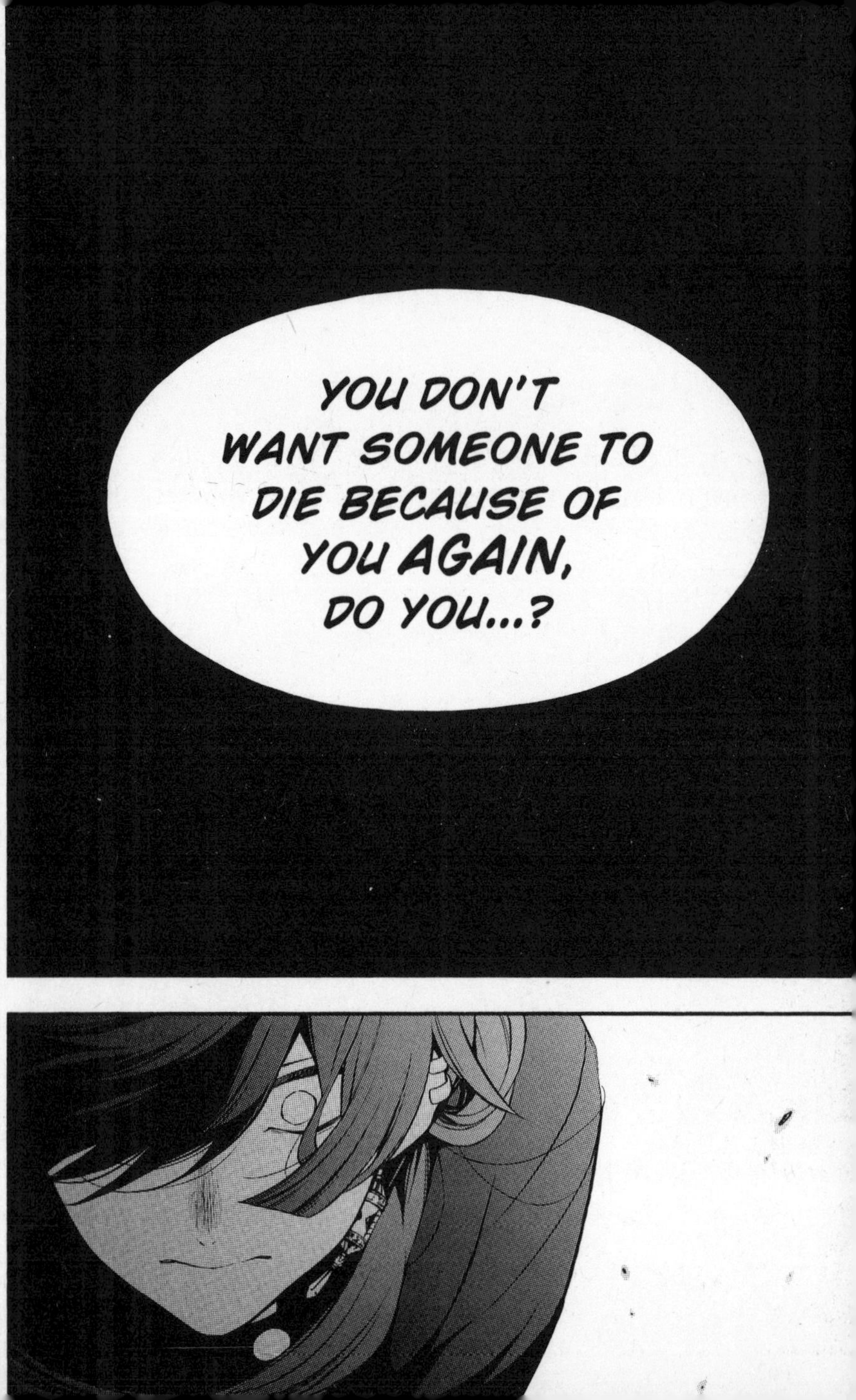
YOU DON'T WANT SOMEONE TO DIE BECAUSE OF YOU AGAIN, DO YOU...?

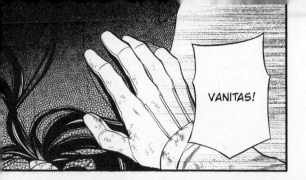

VANITAS!

...

UGH...

ZU (DRAG)

PULL
YOURSELF
TOGETHER,
VANITAS!

DO

DO
(THUNK)

DOGA
(THUD)

BICHA
(SPLAT)

BICHA

GAN
(CLANG)

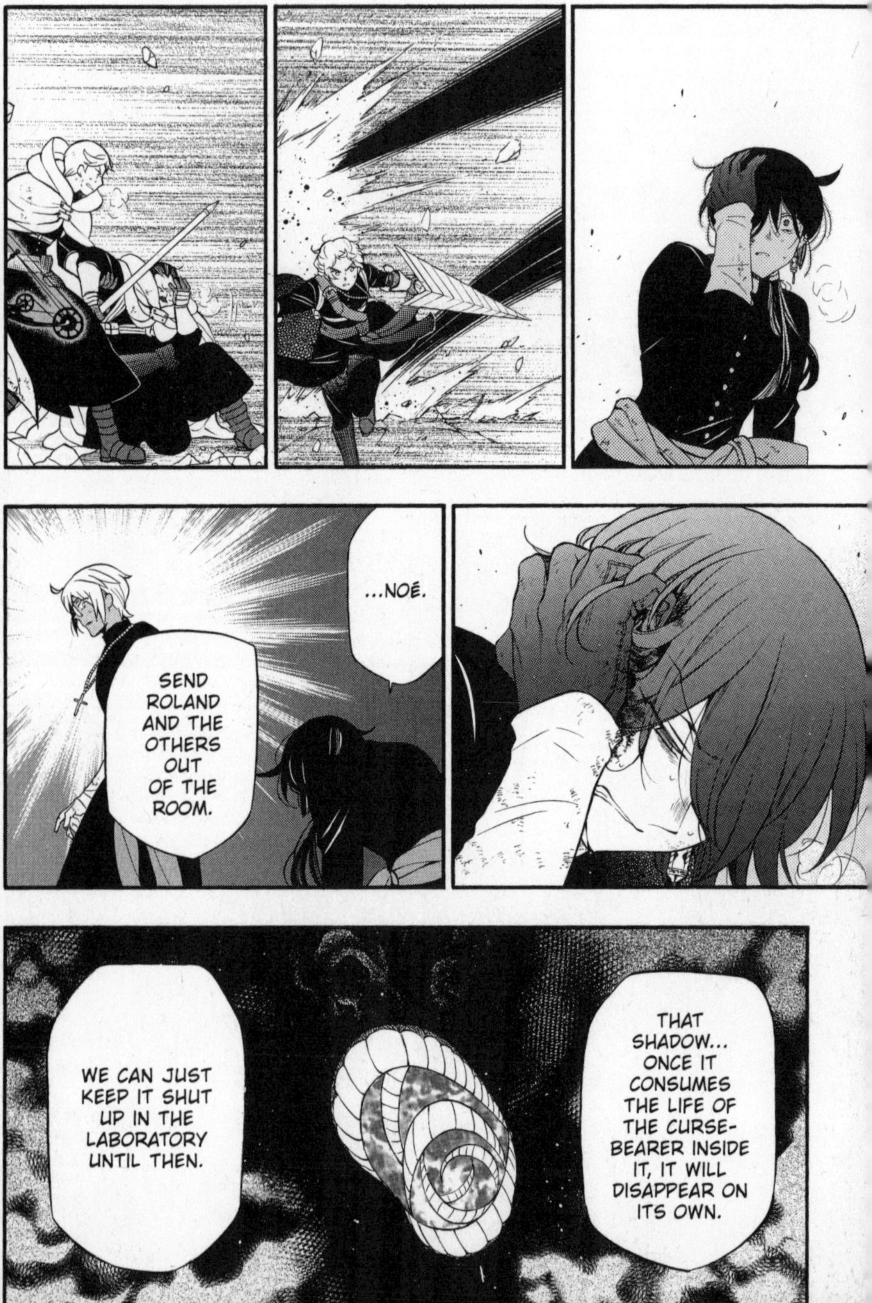
...NOÉ.
SEND ROLAND AND THE OTHERS OUT OF THE ROOM.
THAT SHADOW... ONCE IT CONSUMES THE LIFE OF THE CURSE-BEARER INSIDE IT, IT WILL DISAPPEAR ON ITS OWN.
WE CAN JUST KEEP IT SHUT UP IN THE LABORATORY UNTIL THEN.

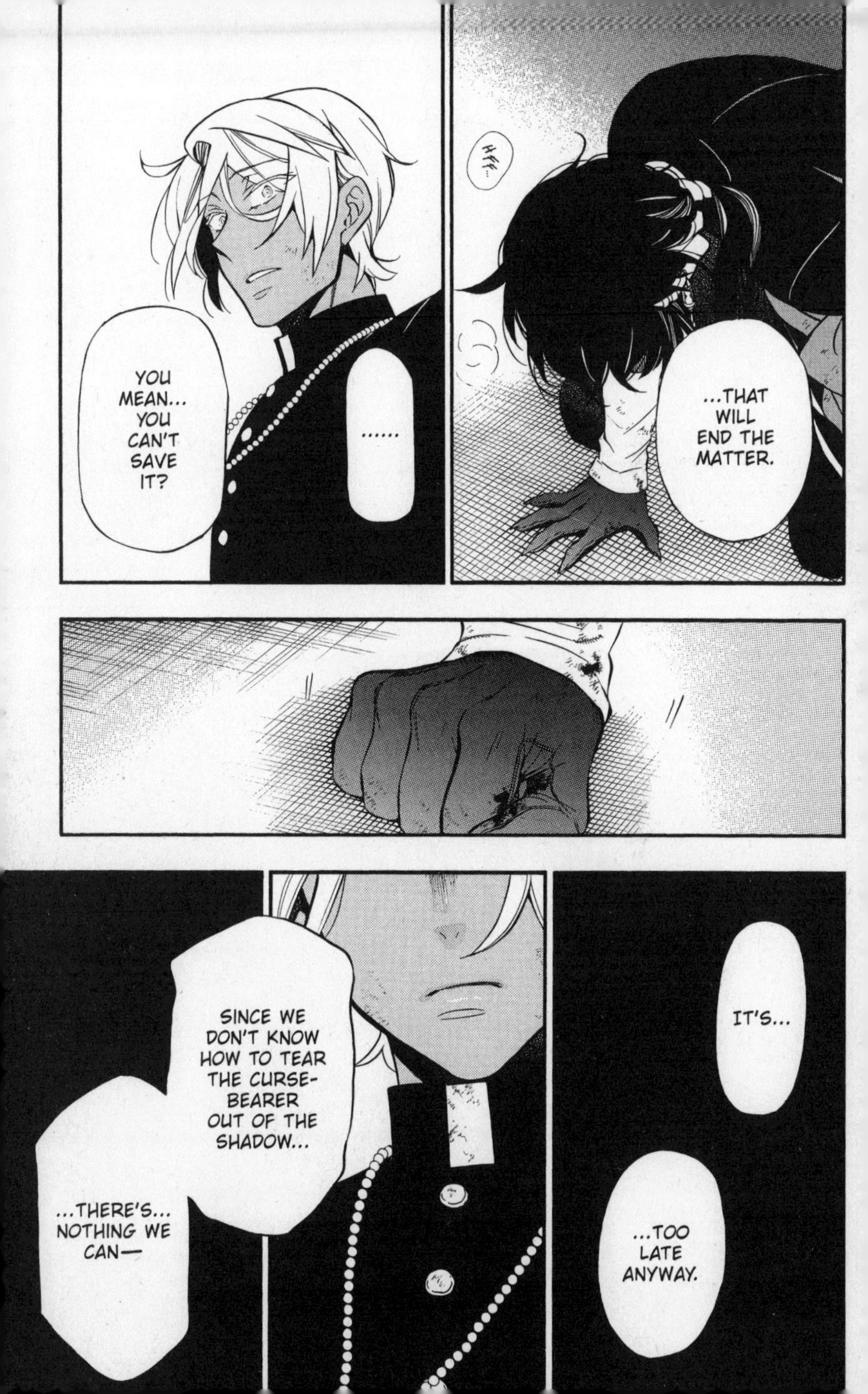
HFF...
...THAT WILL END THE MATTER.
......
YOU MEAN... YOU CAN'T SAVE IT?
IT'S...
...TOO LATE ANYWAY.
SINCE WE DON'T KNOW HOW TO TEAR THE CURSE-BEARER OUT OF THE SHADOW...
...THERE'S... NOTHING WE CAN—

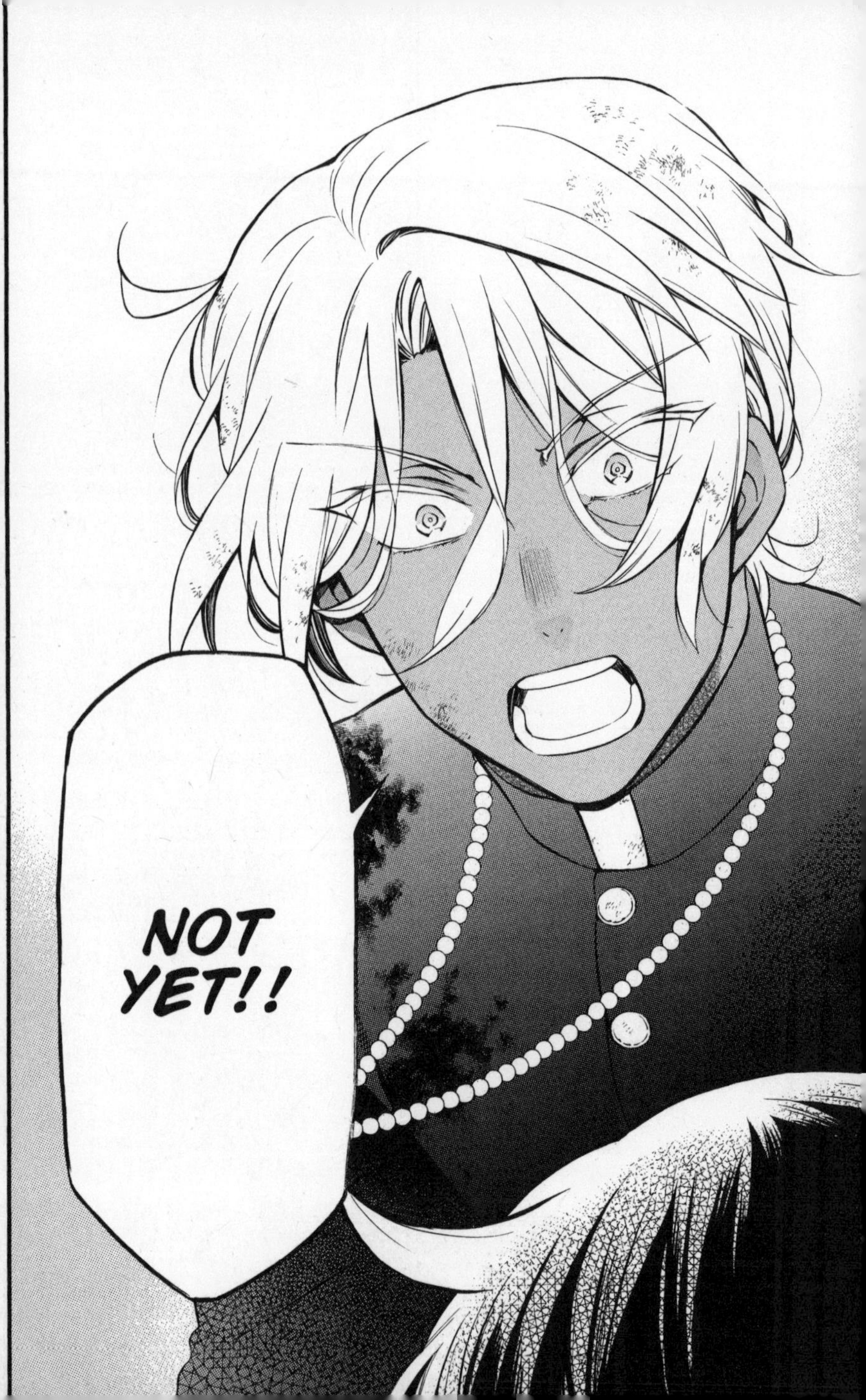
NOT YET!!

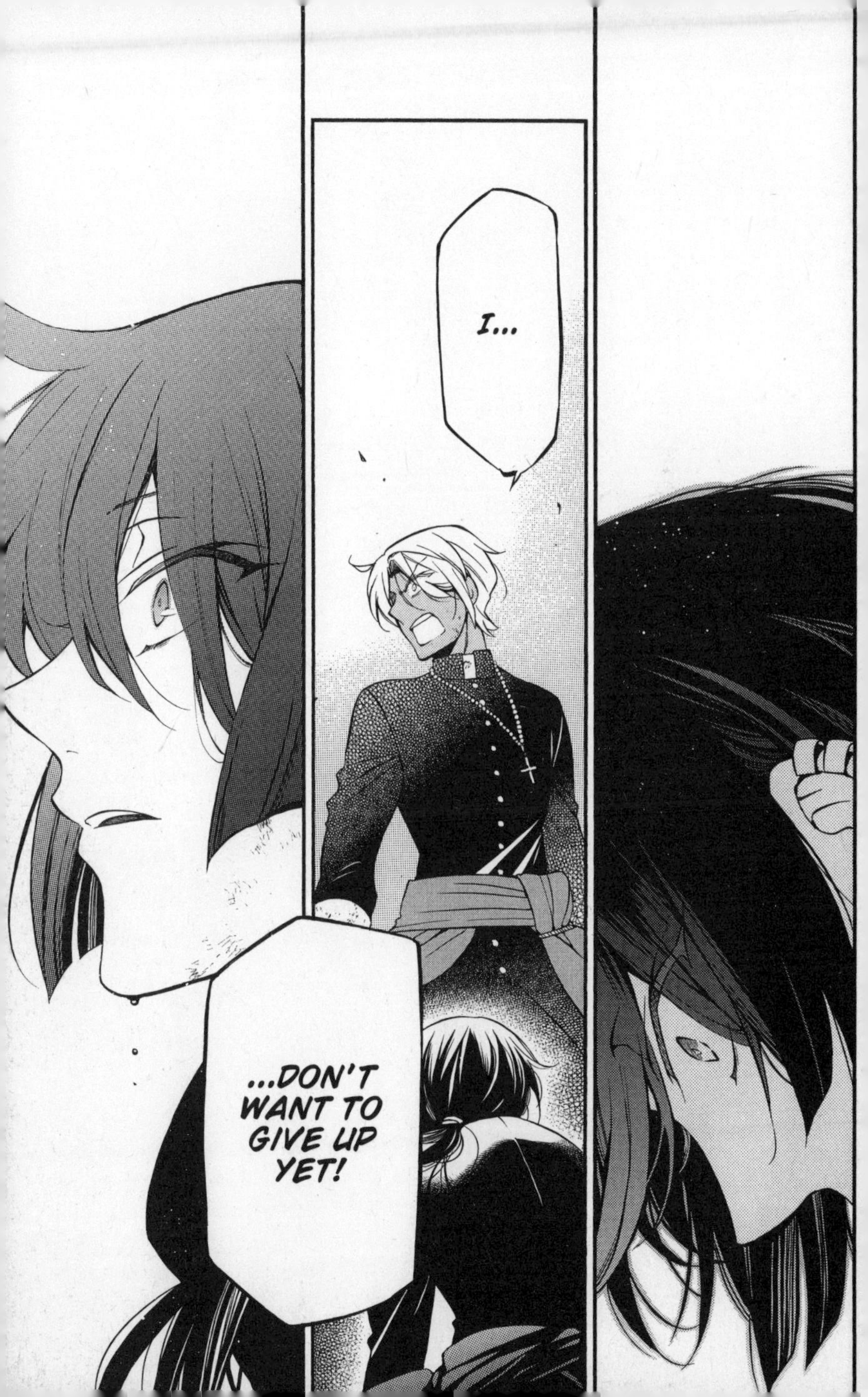
I...
...DON'T WANT TO GIVE UP YET!

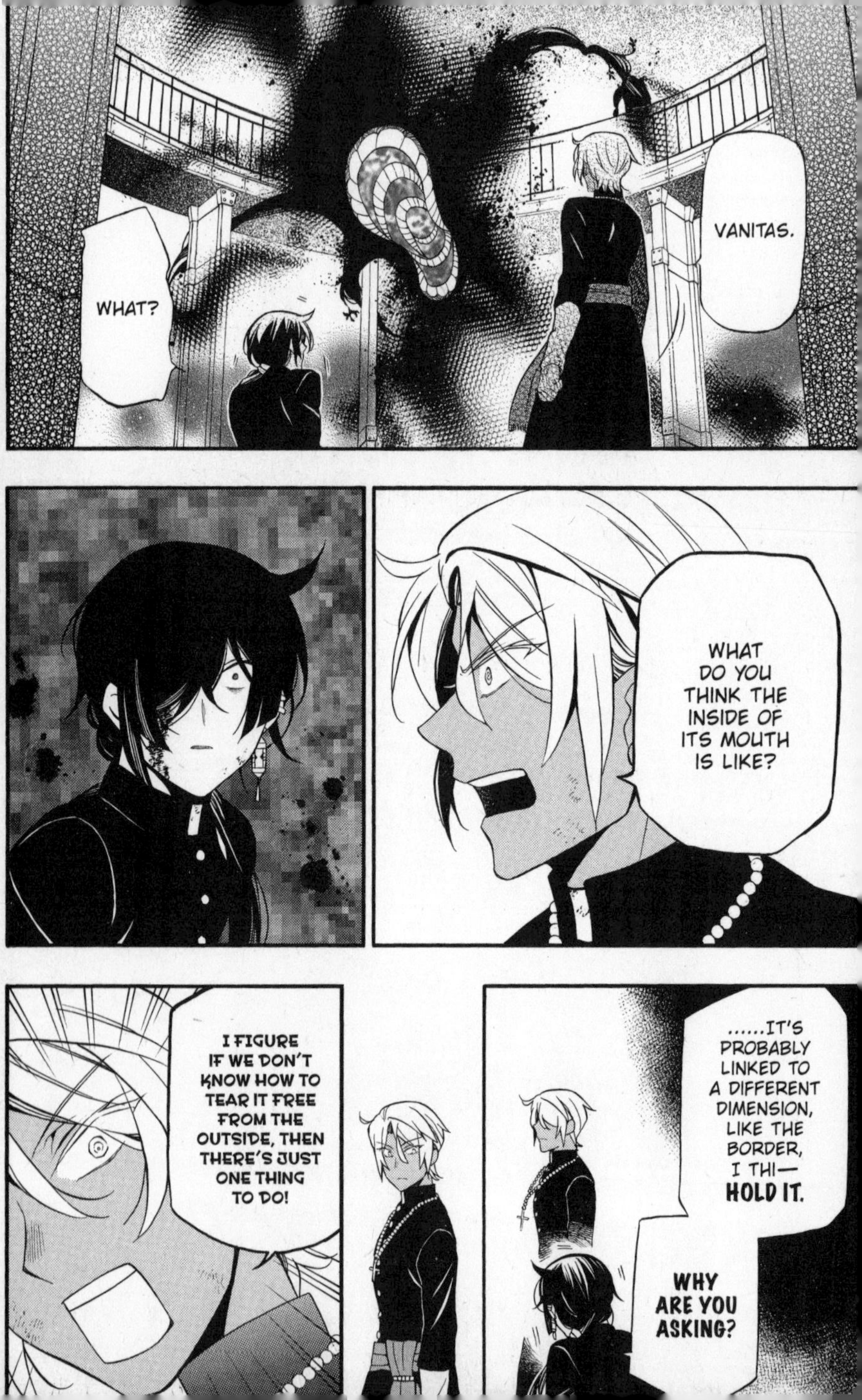
VANITAS.
WHAT?
WHAT DO YOU THINK THE INSIDE OF ITS MOUTH IS LIKE?
......IT'S PROBABLY LINKED TO A DIFFERENT DIMENSION, LIKE THE BORDER, I THI—
HOLD IT.
WHY ARE YOU ASKING?
I FIGURE IF WE DON'T KNOW HOW TO TEAR IT FREE FROM THE OUTSIDE, THEN THERE'S JUST ONE THING TO DO!

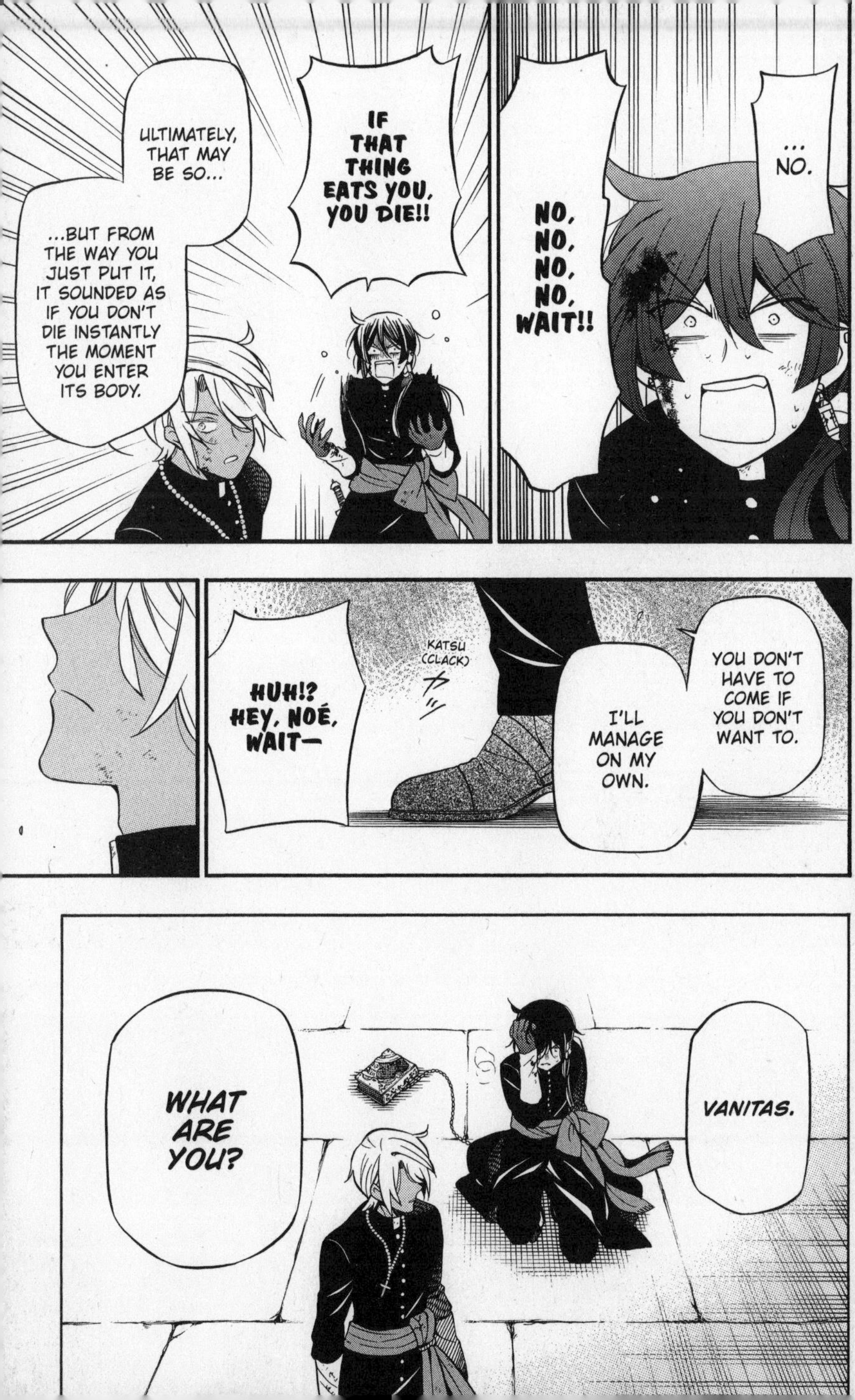
...NO.
NO, NO, NO, NO, WAIT!!
IF THAT THING EATS YOU, YOU DIE!!
ULTIMATELY, THAT MAY BE SO...
...BUT FROM THE WAY YOU JUST PUT IT, IT SOUNDED AS IF YOU DON'T DIE INSTANTLY THE MOMENT YOU ENTER ITS BODY.
YOU DON'T HAVE TO COME IF YOU DON'T WANT TO.
I'LL MANAGE ON MY OWN.
KATSU (CLACK)
HUH!? HEY, NOÉ, WAIT—
VANITAS.
WHAT ARE YOU?

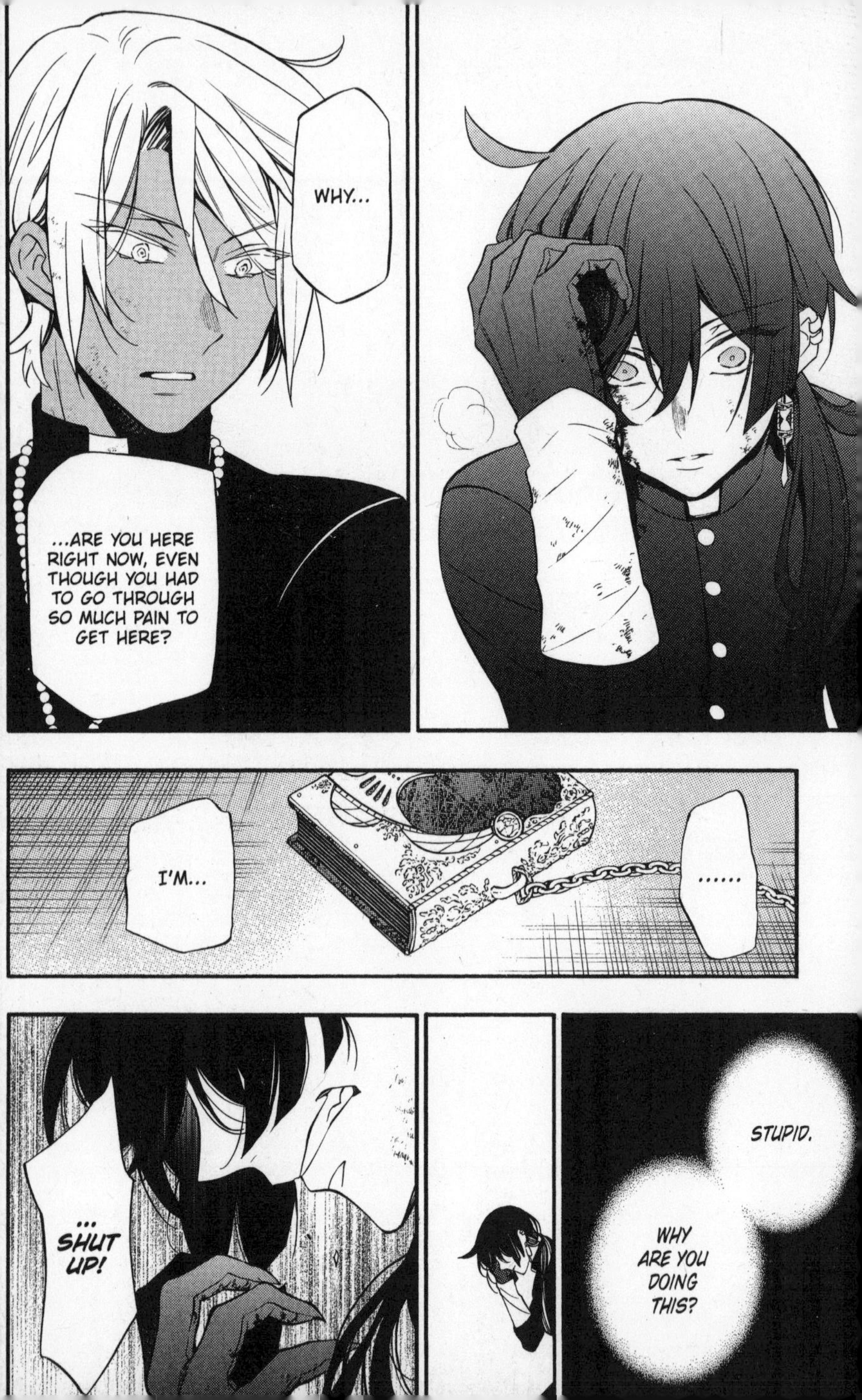
WHY...
...ARE YOU HERE RIGHT NOW, EVEN THOUGH YOU HAD TO GO THROUGH SO MUCH PAIN TO GET HERE?
......
I'M...
STUPID.
WHY ARE YOU DOING THIS?
... SHUT UP!

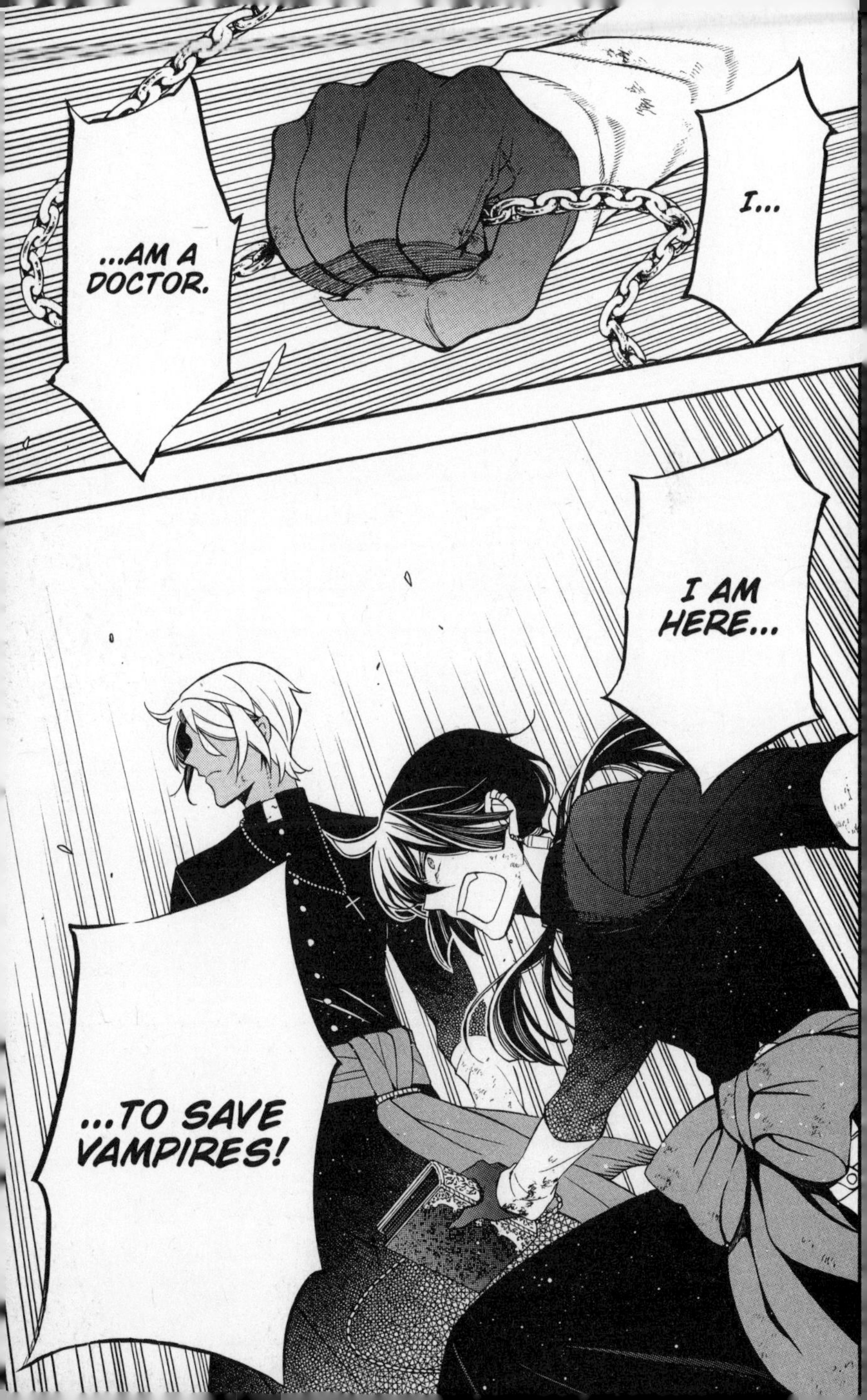
I...
...AM A DOCTOR.
I AM HERE...
...TO SAVE VAMPIRES!

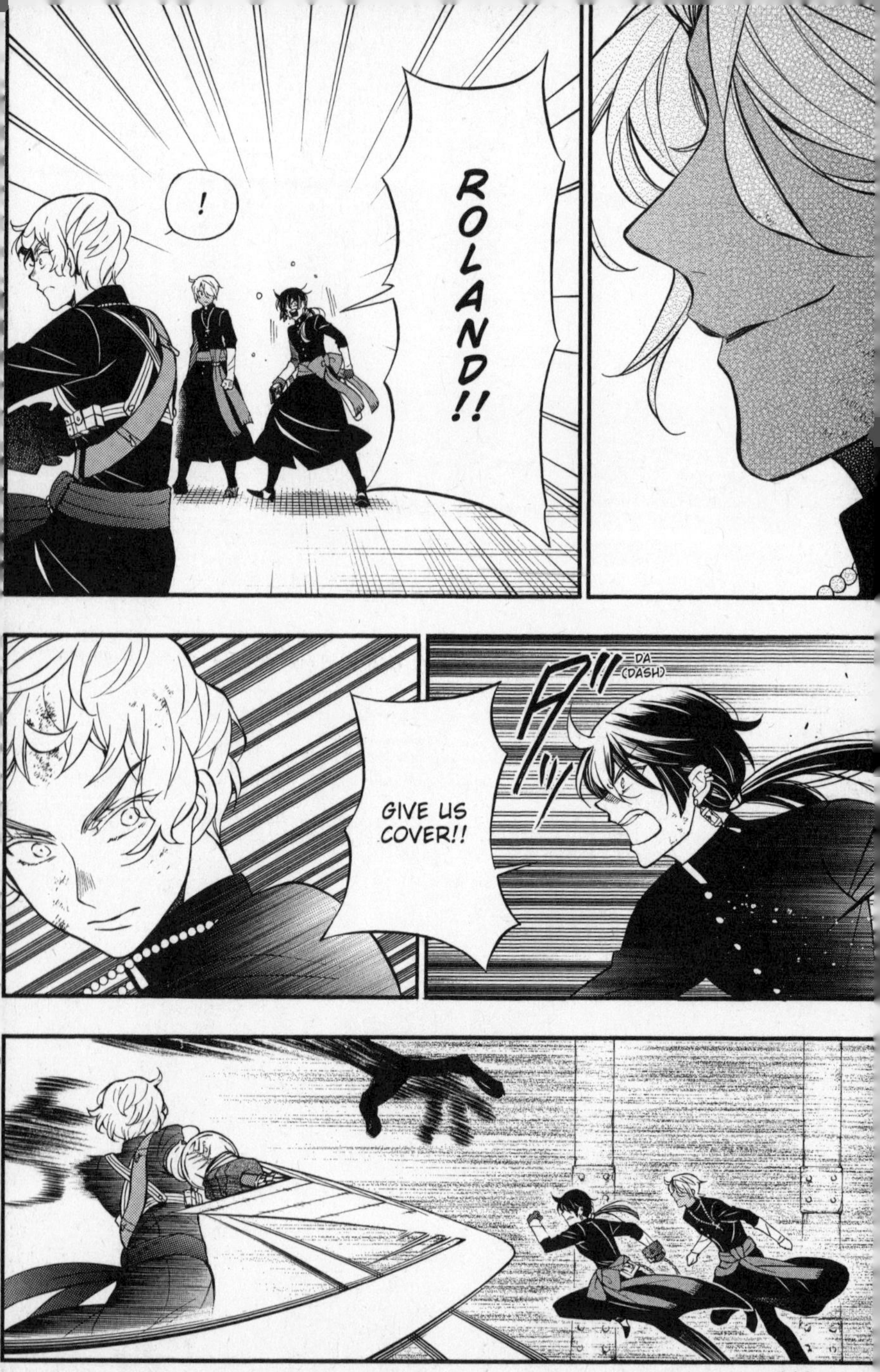
ROLAND!!
!
DA (DASH)
GIVE US COVER!!

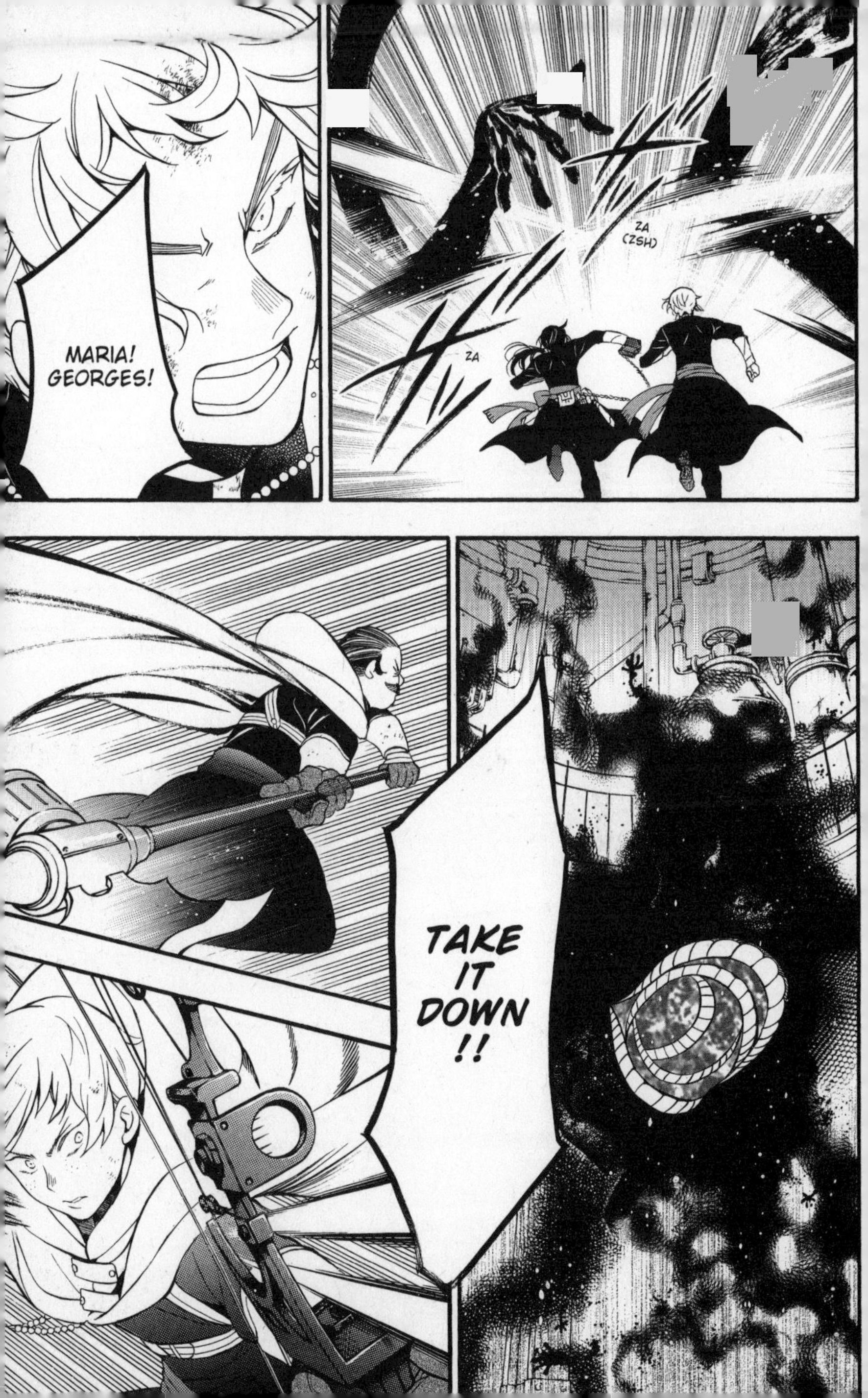
ZA (ZSH)
ZA
MARIA! GEORGES!
TAKE IT DOWN!!

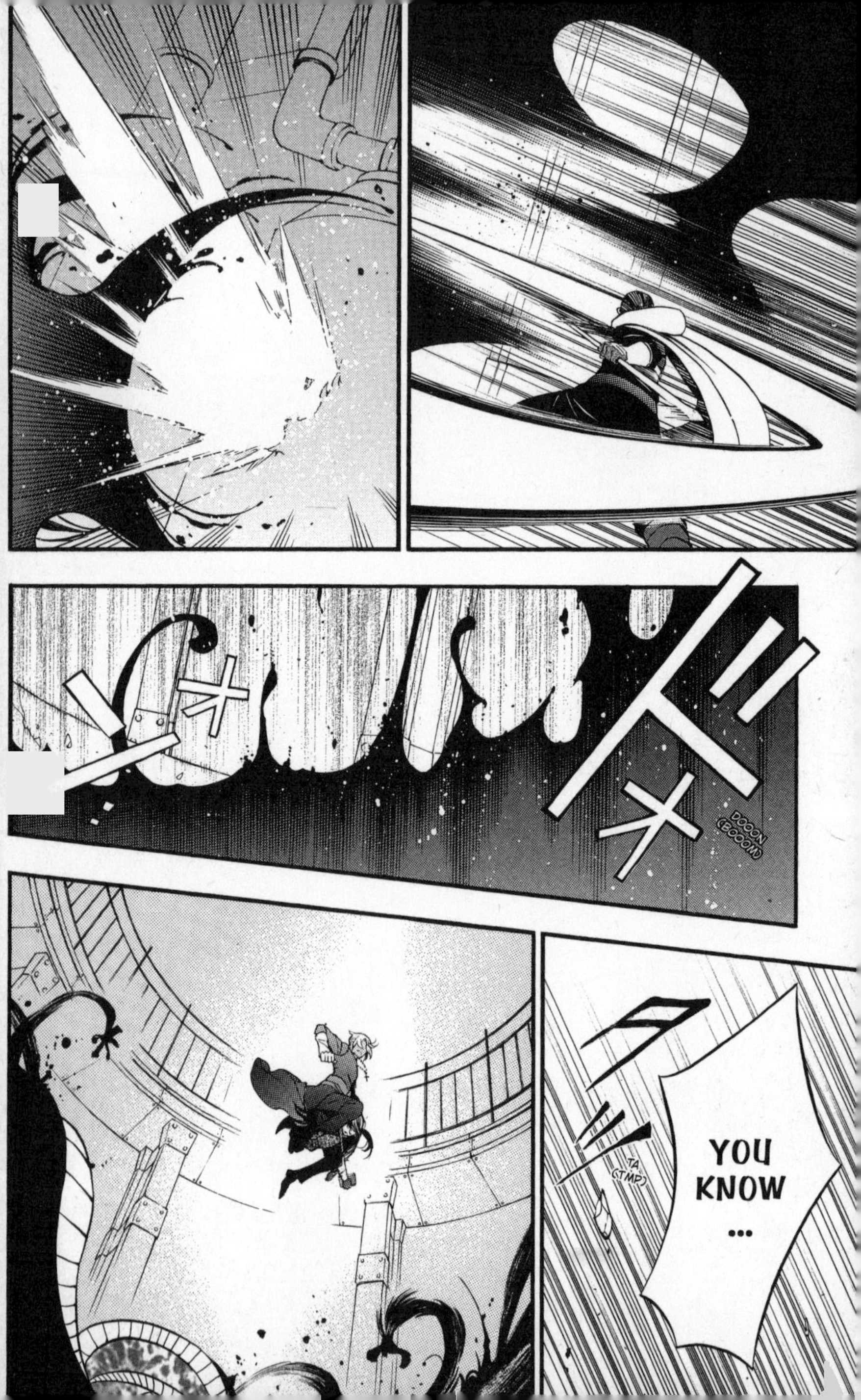
DOOON
(BOOOM)
TA
(TMP)
YOU KNOW ...

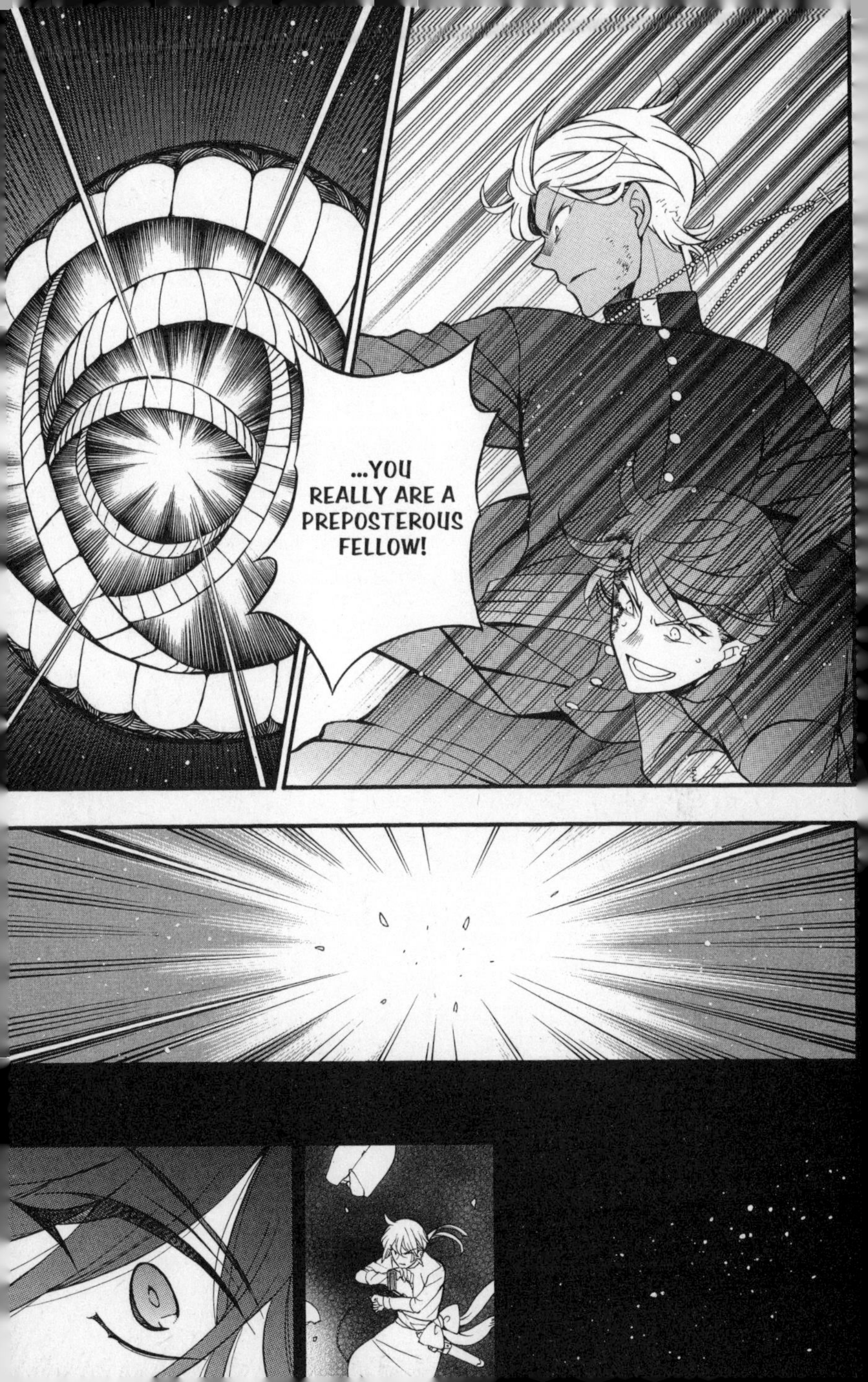
...YOU REALLY ARE A PREPOSTEROUS FELLOW!

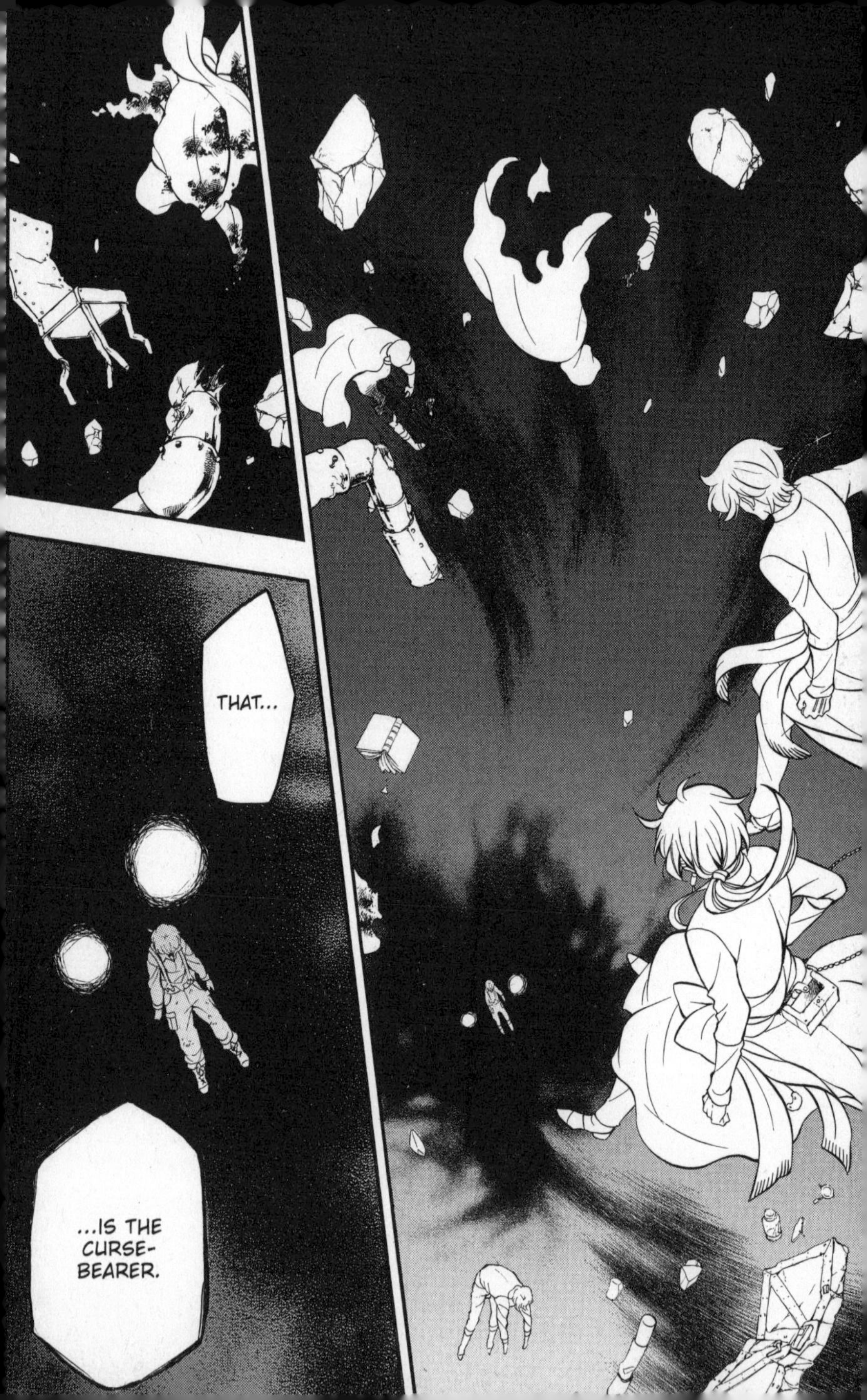
THAT...
...IS THE CURSE-BEARER.

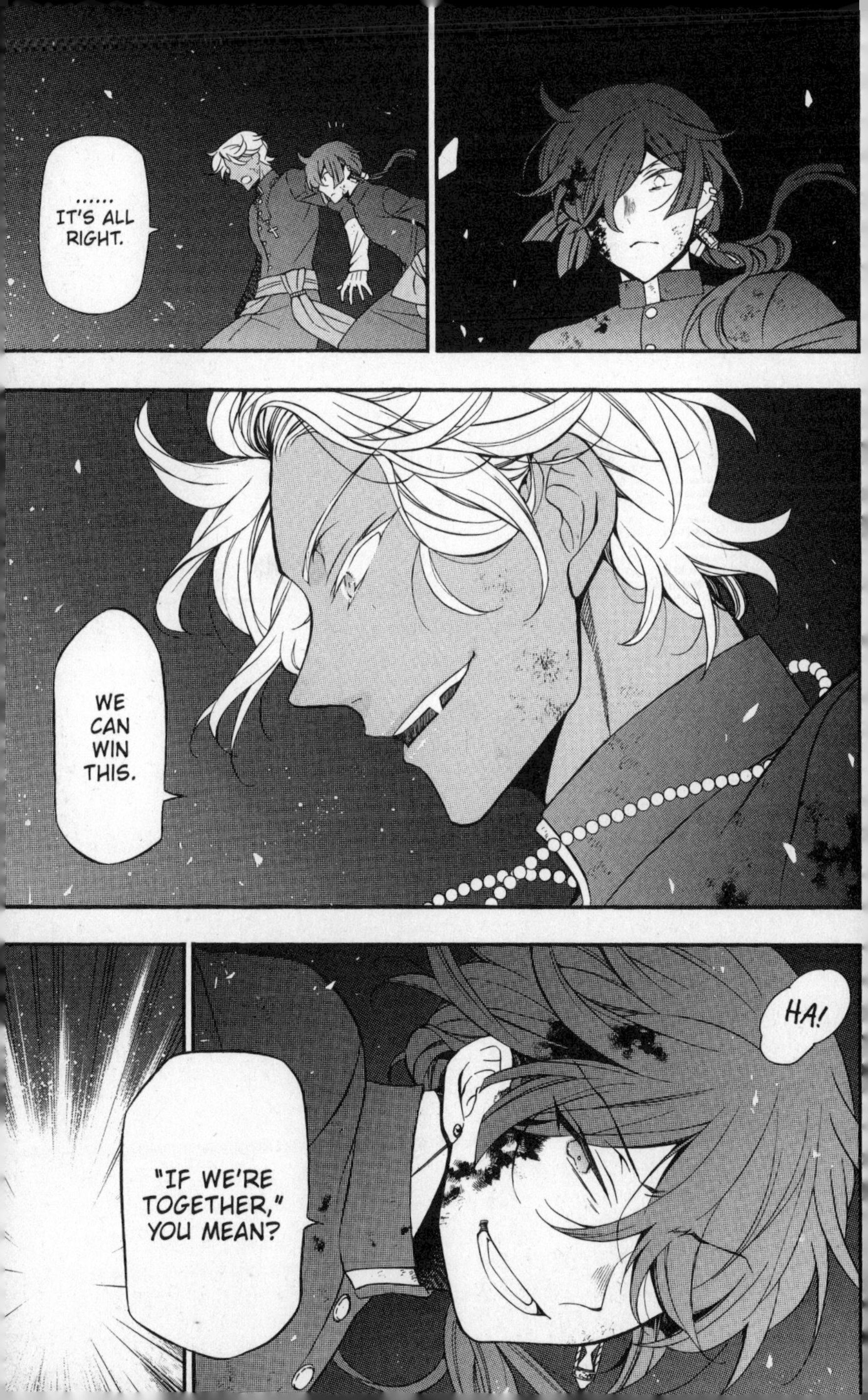
...... IT'S ALL RIGHT.
WE CAN WIN THIS.
HA!
"IF WE'RE TOGETHER," YOU MEAN?

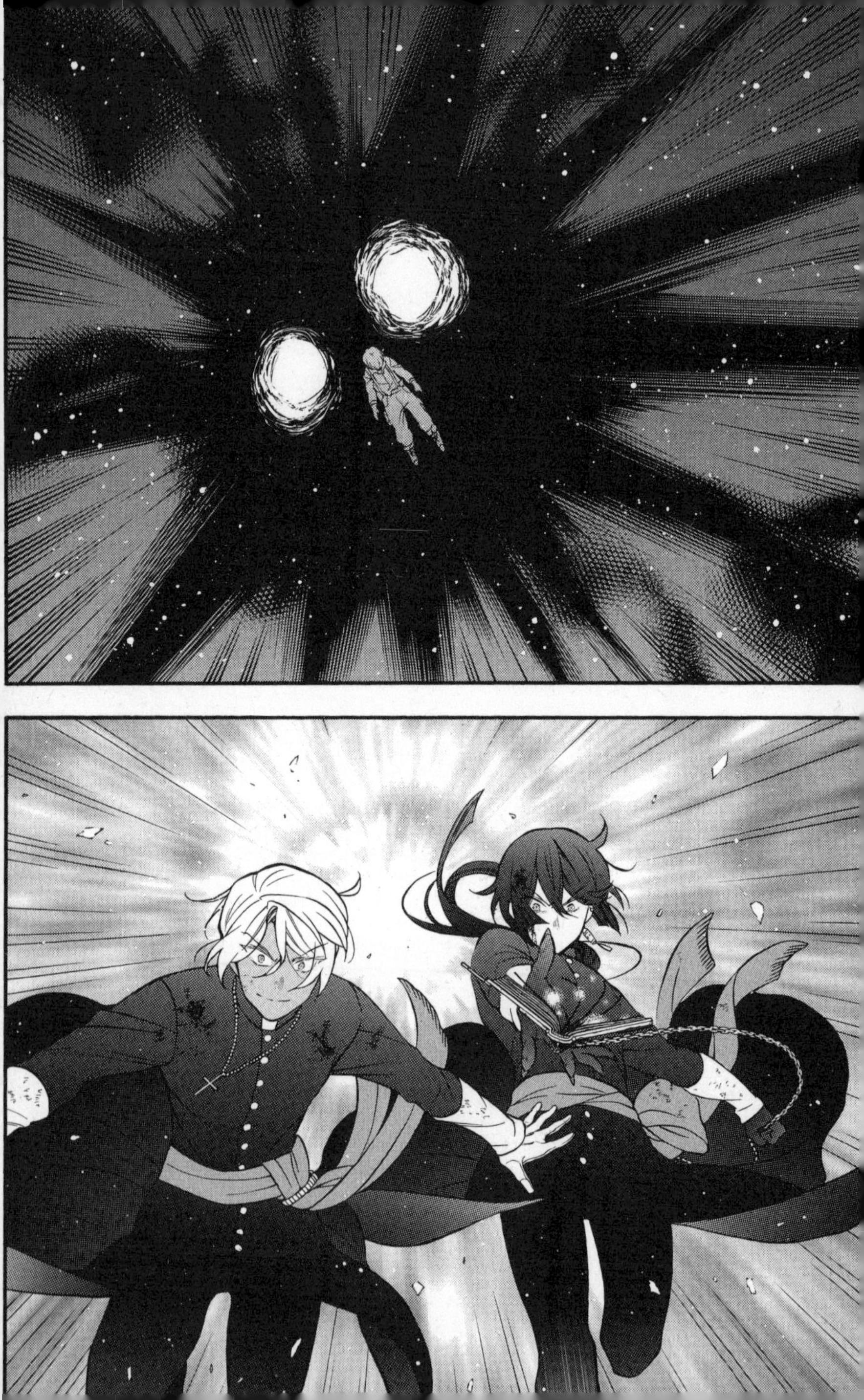

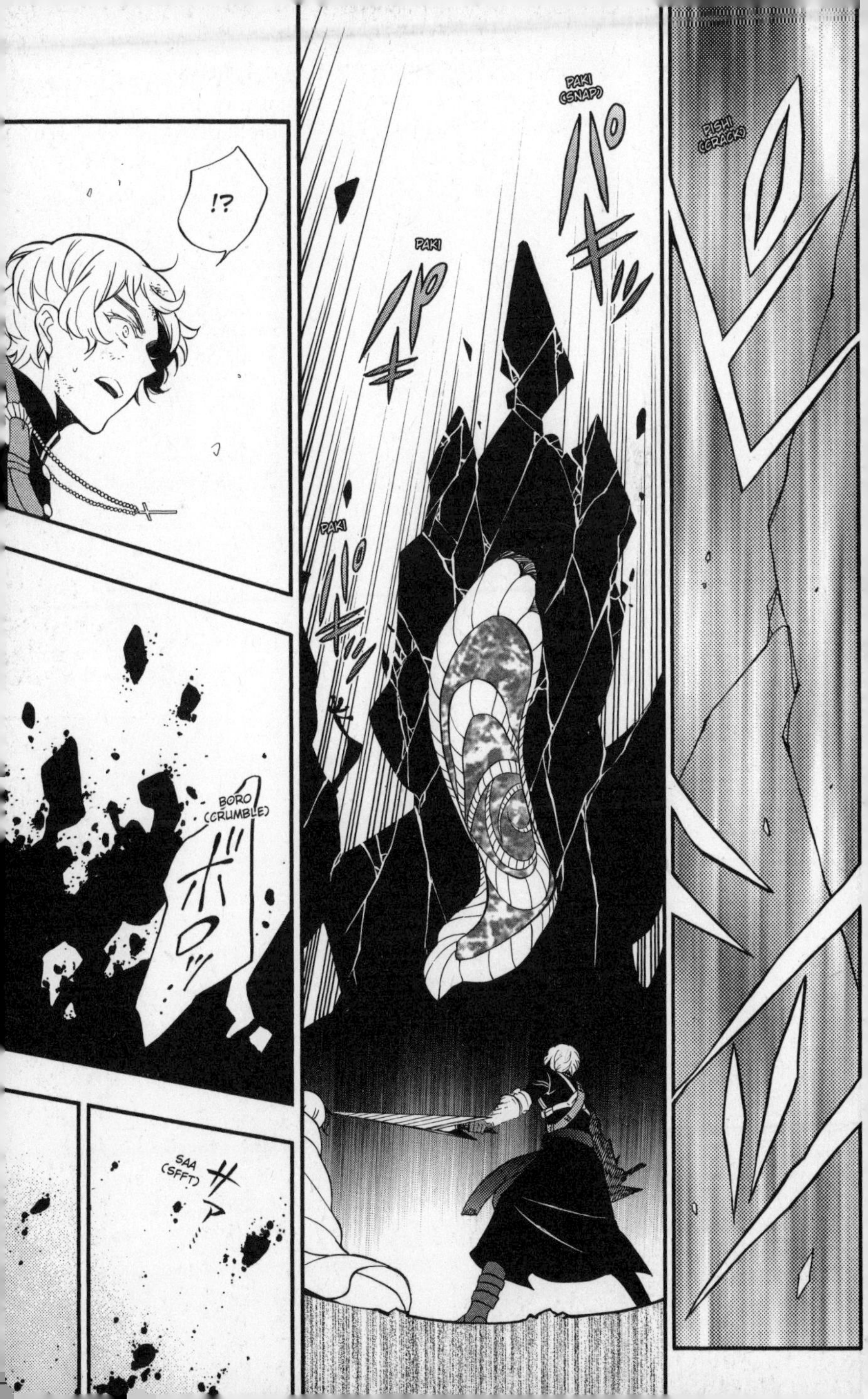
PISHI (CRACK)
PAKI (SNAP)
PAKI
PAKI
!?
BORO (CRUMBLE)
SAA (SFFT)

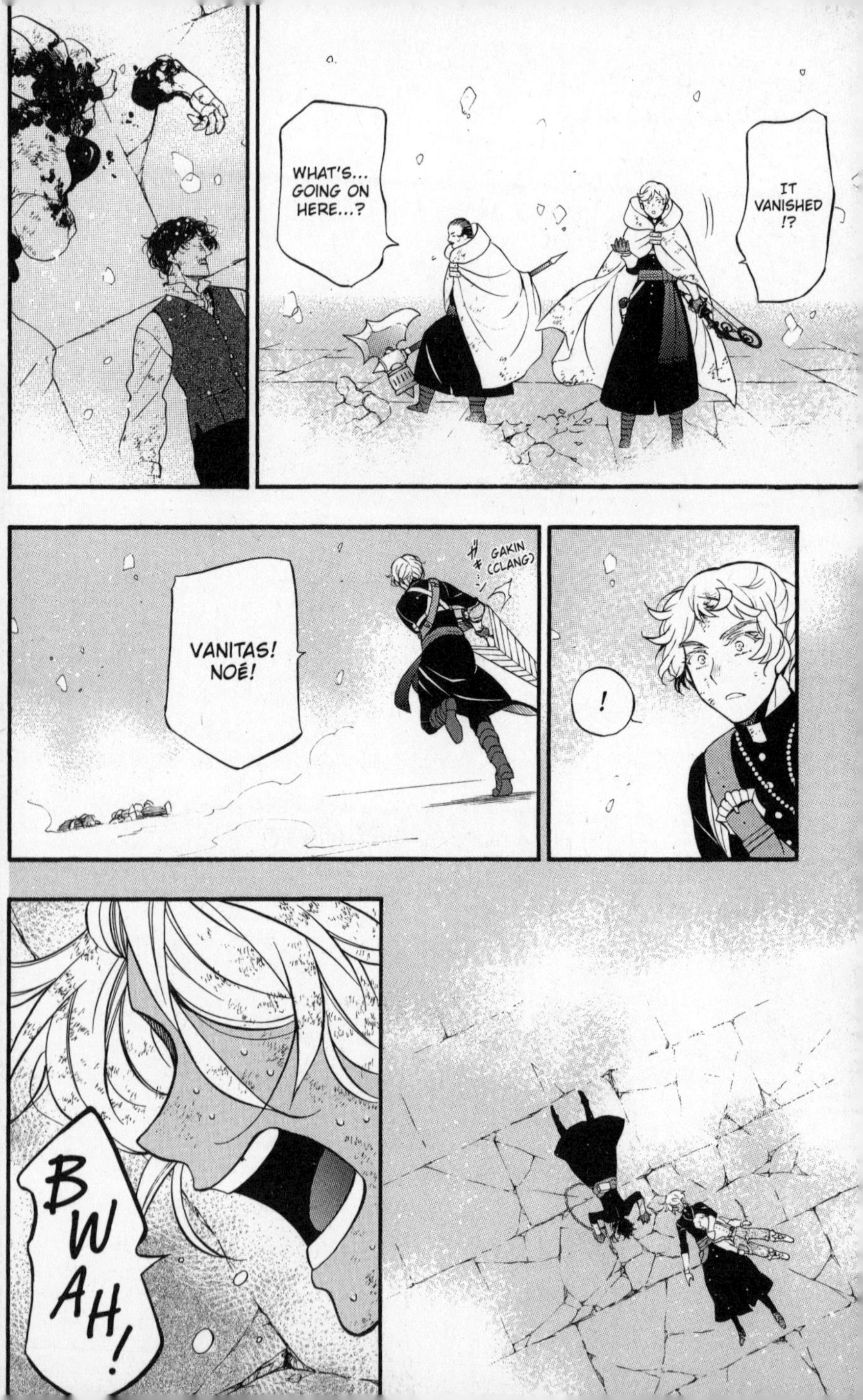

IT VANISHED!?
WHAT'S... GOING ON HERE...?
!
GAKIN (CLANG)
VANITAS! NOÉ!
BWAH!

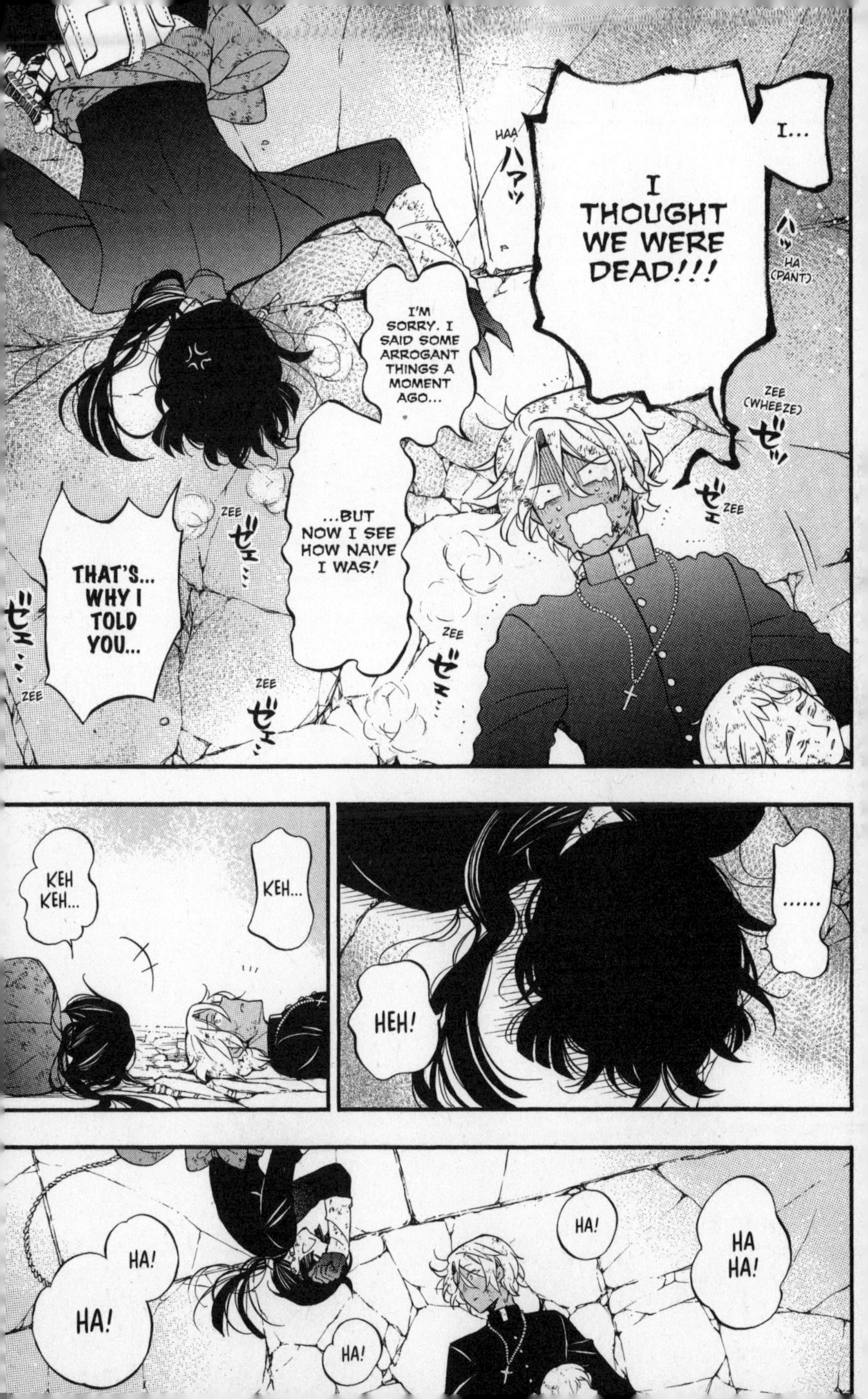
I...
HA ハッ (PANT)
I THOUGHT WE WERE DEAD!!!
HAA ハアッ
ZEE ゼッ (WHEEZE)
ZEE ゼェ
I'M SORRY. I SAID SOME ARROGANT THINGS A MOMENT AGO...
...BUT NOW I SEE HOW NAIVE I WAS!
ZEE ゼェ
ZEE ゼェ
ZEE ゼェ
THAT'S... WHY I TOLD YOU...
ZEE ゼェ
......
HEH!
KEH...
KEH KEH...
HA HA!
HA!
HA!
HA!
HA!

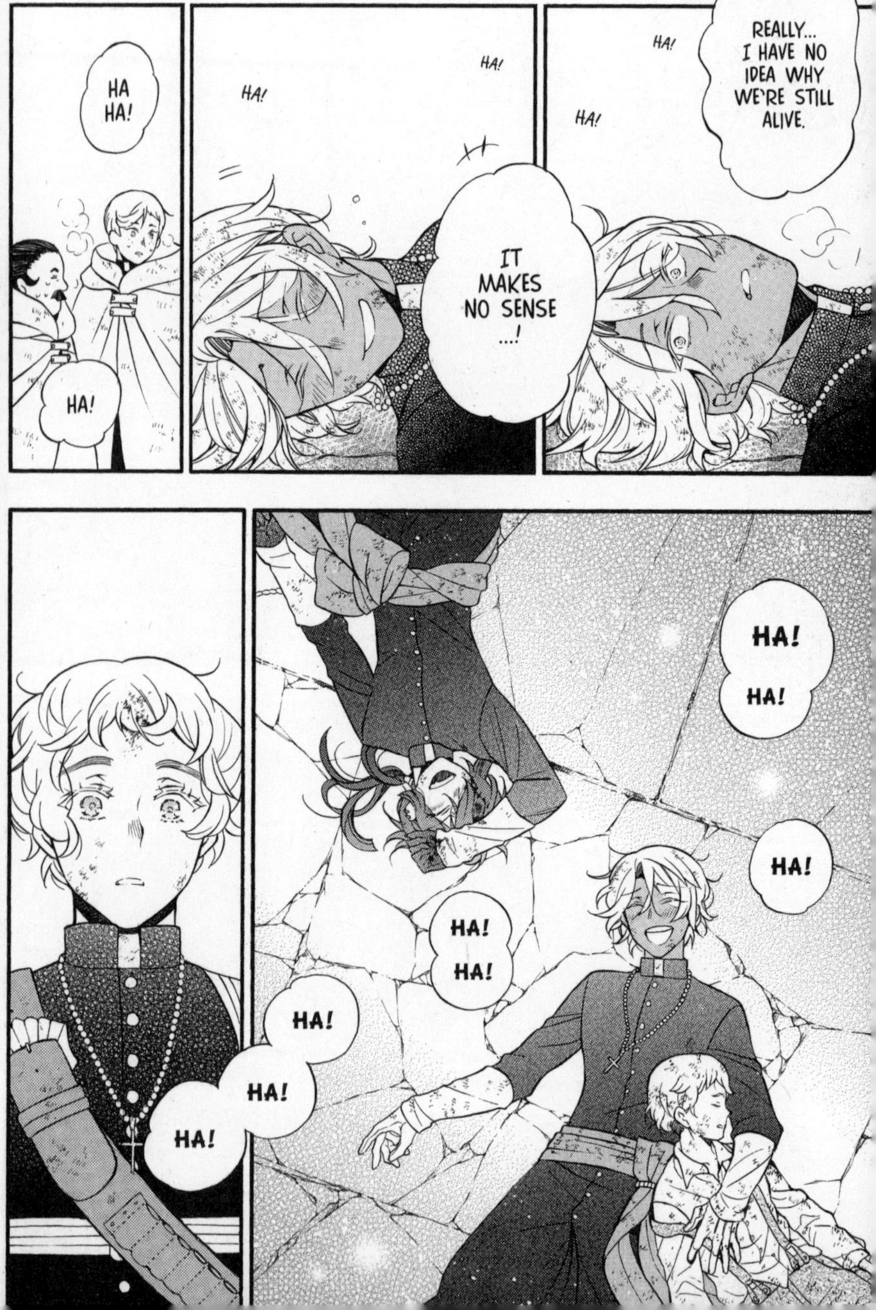
REALLY... I HAVE NO IDEA WHY WE'RE STILL ALIVE.
HA!
HA!
HA!
HA!
IT MAKES NO SENSE ...!
HA HA!
HA!
HA!
HA!
HA!
HA!
HA!
HA!
HA!
HA!

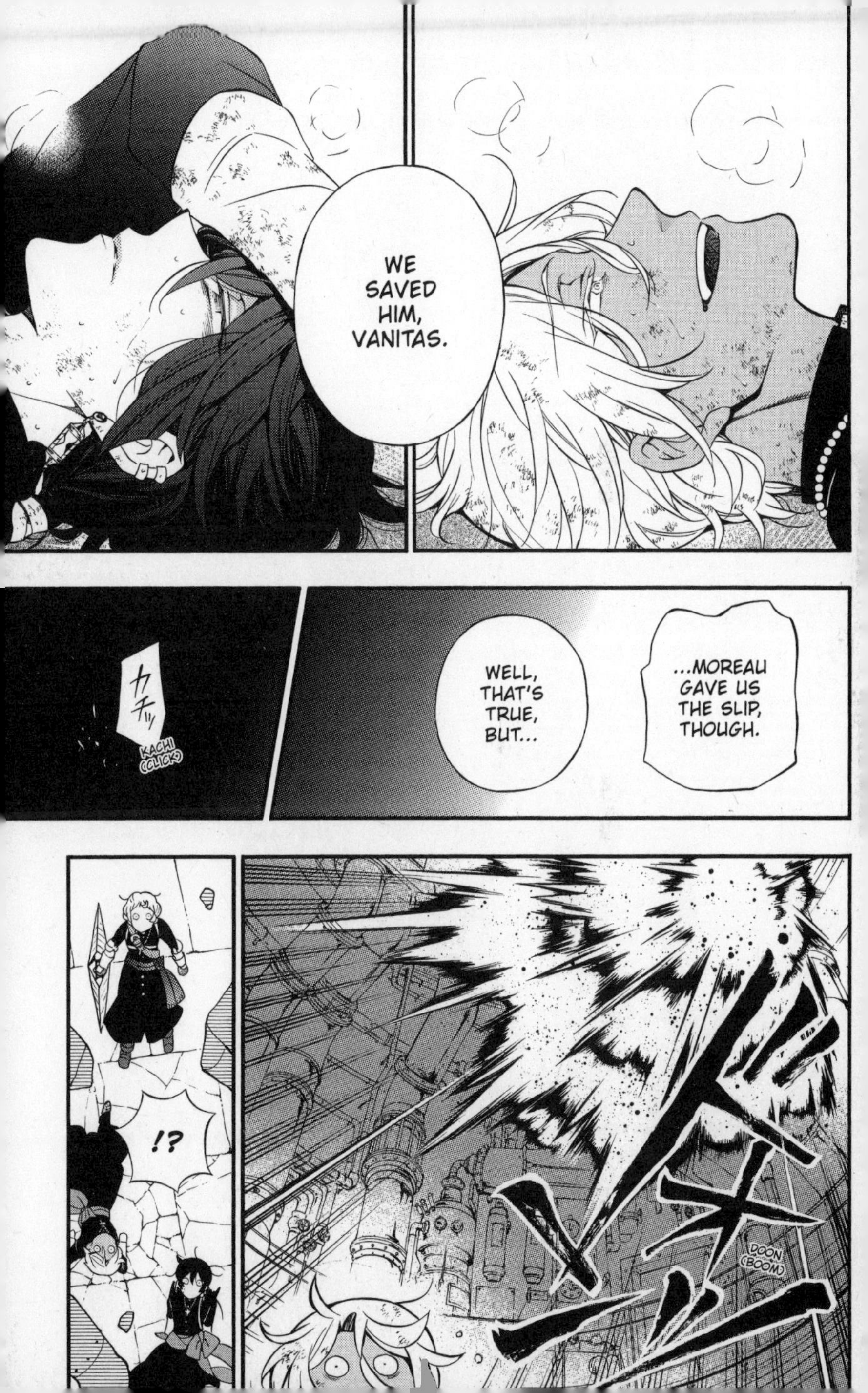
WE SAVED HIM, VANITAS.
WELL, THAT'S TRUE, BUT...
...MOREAU GAVE US THE SLIP, THOUGH.
カチッ
KACHI (CLICK)
DOON (BOOM)
!?

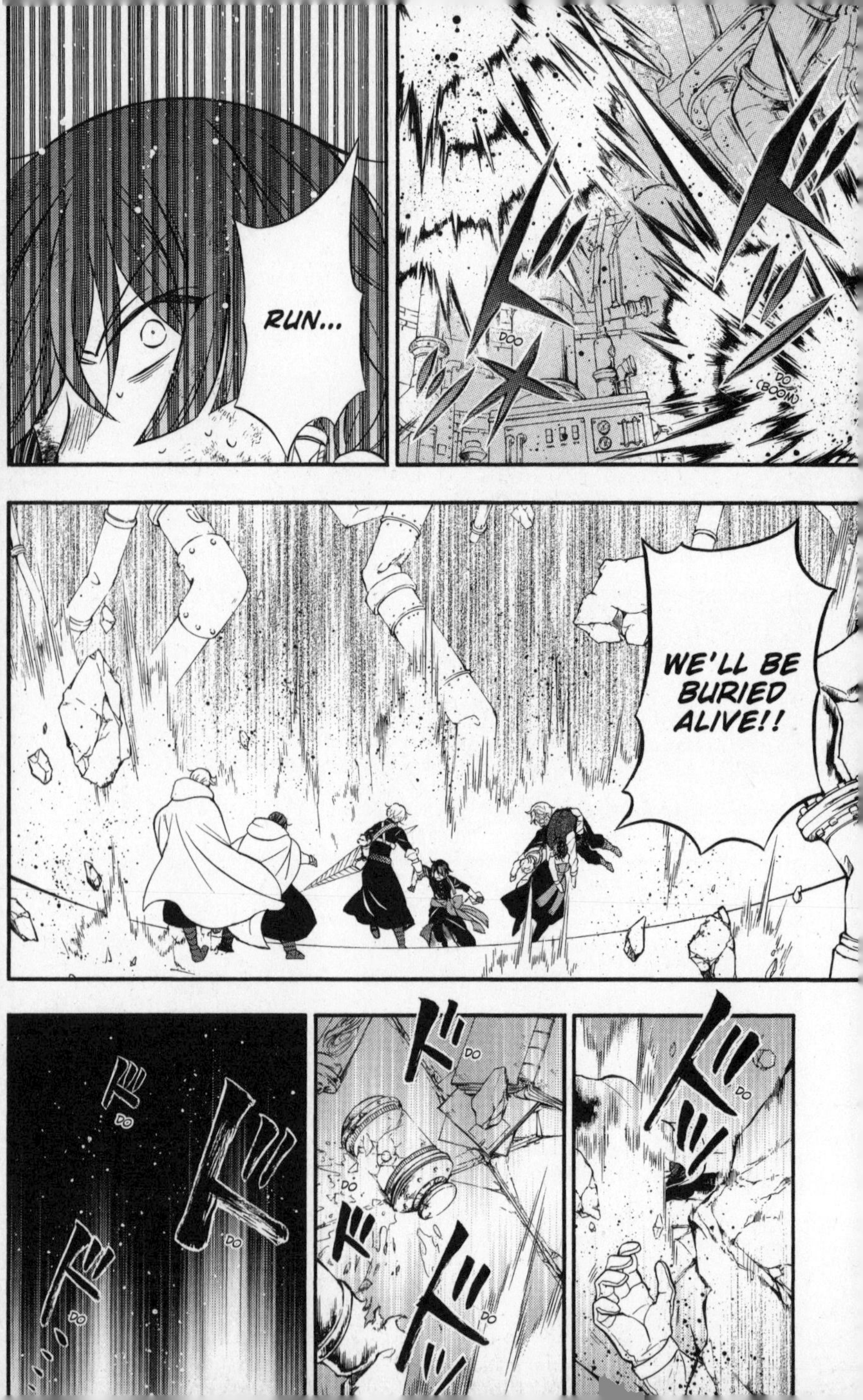
DOO
DO (BOOM)
RUN...
WE'LL BE BURIED ALIVE!!
DO
DO
DO
DO
DO
DO
DO

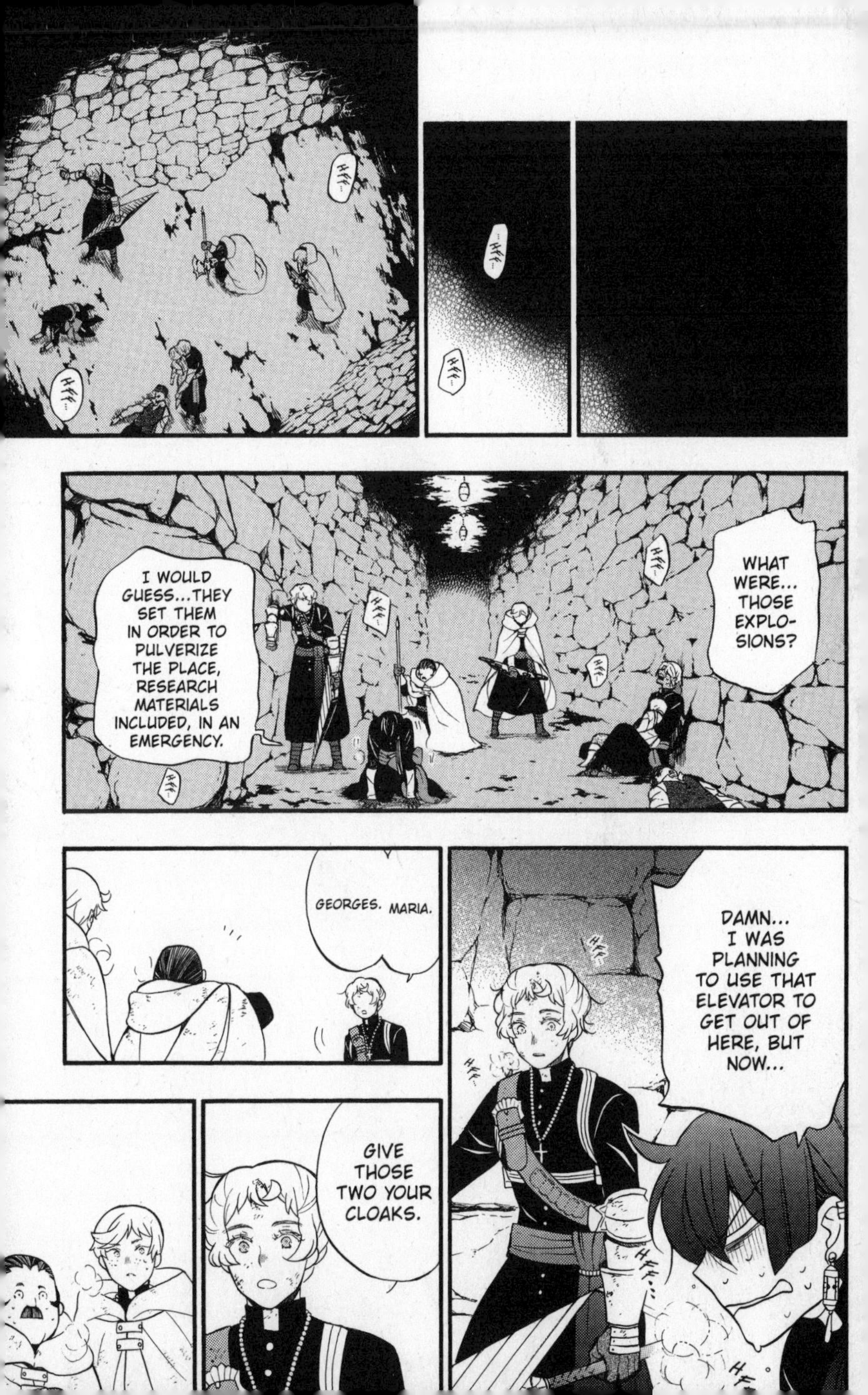

...HFF...
HFF...
HFF...
HFF...
WHAT WERE... THOSE EXPLOSIONS?
I WOULD GUESS...THEY SET THEM IN ORDER TO PULVERIZE THE PLACE, RESEARCH MATERIALS INCLUDED, IN AN EMERGENCY.
DAMN... I WAS PLANNING TO USE THAT ELEVATOR TO GET OUT OF HERE, BUT NOW...
GEORGES. MARIA.
GIVE THOSE TWO YOUR CLOAKS.

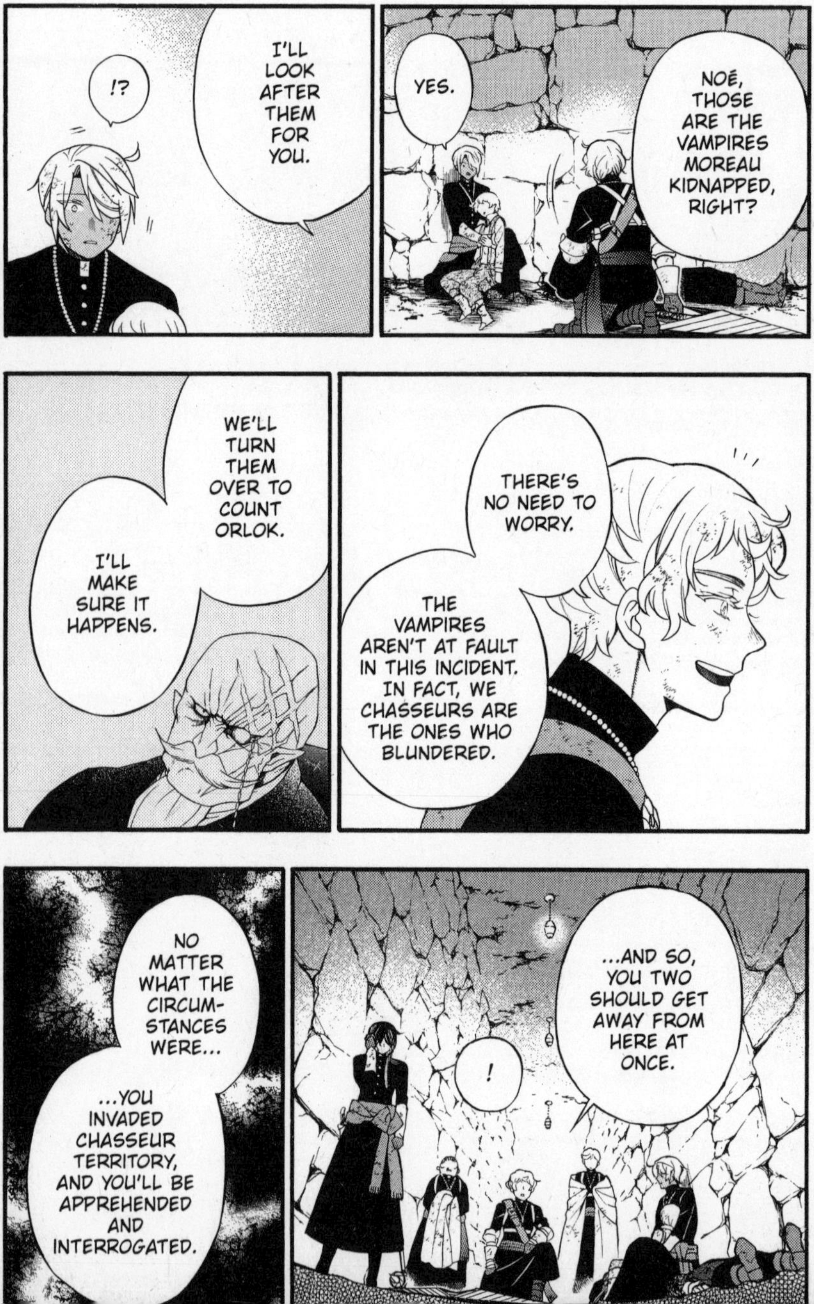
NOÉ, THOSE ARE THE VAMPIRES MOREAU KIDNAPPED, RIGHT?
YES.
I'LL LOOK AFTER THEM FOR YOU.
!?
THERE'S NO NEED TO WORRY.
THE VAMPIRES AREN'T AT FAULT IN THIS INCIDENT. IN FACT, WE CHASSEURS ARE THE ONES WHO BLUNDERED.
WE'LL TURN THEM OVER TO COUNT ORLOK.
I'LL MAKE SURE IT HAPPENS.
...AND SO, YOU TWO SHOULD GET AWAY FROM HERE AT ONCE.
!
NO MATTER WHAT THE CIRCUM-STANCES WERE...
...YOU INVADED CHASSEUR TERRITORY, AND YOU'LL BE APPREHENDED AND INTERROGATED.

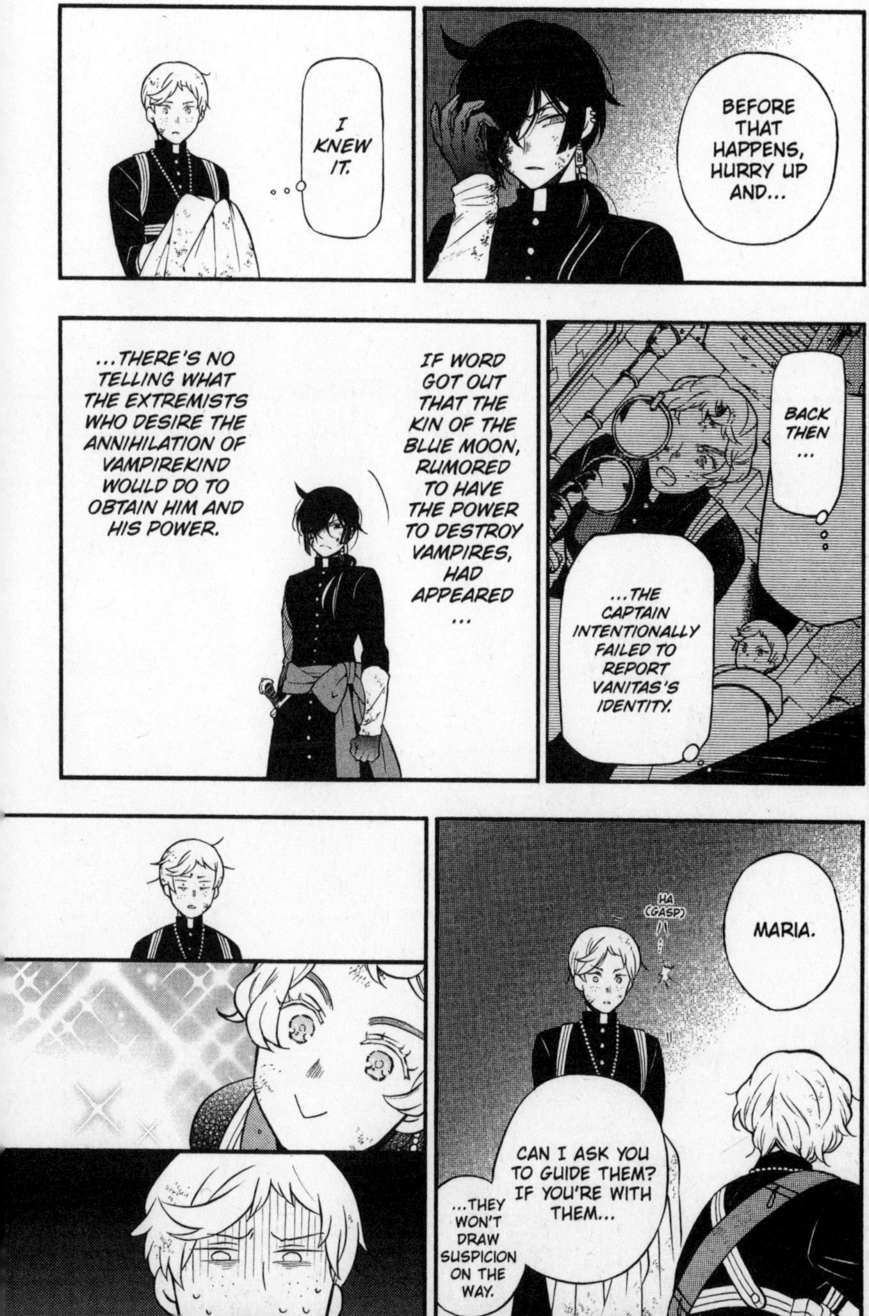
BEFORE THAT HAPPENS, HURRY UP AND...
I KNEW IT.
BACK THEN...
...THE CAPTAIN INTENTIONALLY FAILED TO REPORT VANITAS'S IDENTITY.
IF WORD GOT OUT THAT THE KIN OF THE BLUE MOON, RUMORED TO HAVE THE POWER TO DESTROY VAMPIRES, HAD APPEARED...
...THERE'S NO TELLING WHAT THE EXTREMISTS WHO DESIRE THE ANNIHILATION OF VAMPIREKIND WOULD DO TO OBTAIN HIM AND HIS POWER.
MARIA.
HA (GASP)
CAN I ASK YOU TO GUIDE THEM? IF YOU'RE WITH THEM...
...THEY WON'T DRAW SUSPICION ON THE WAY.

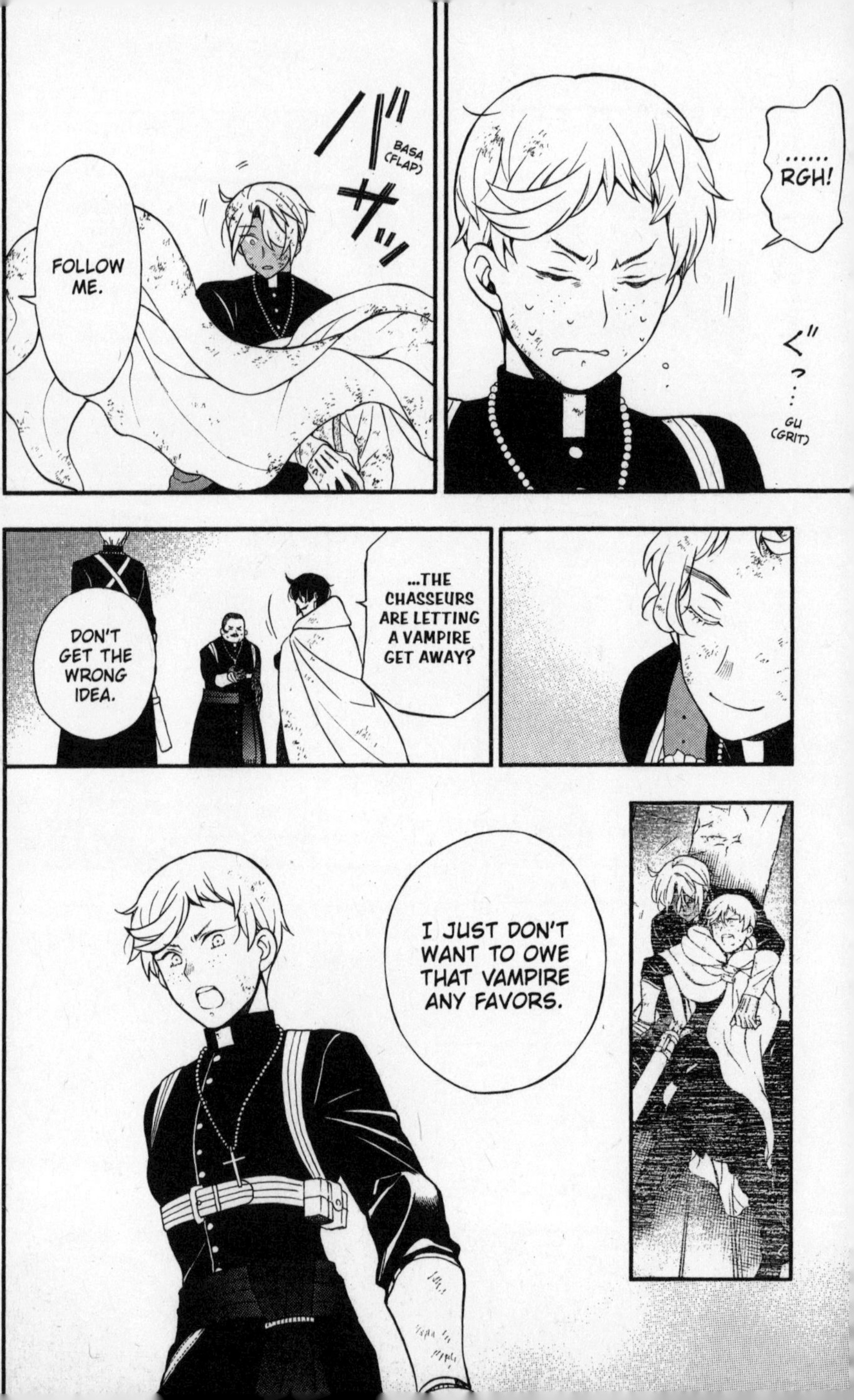
......RGH!
ぐっ
GU (GRIT)
バサッ
BASA (FLAP)
FOLLOW ME.
...THE CHASSEURS ARE LETTING A VAMPIRE GET AWAY?
DON'T GET THE WRONG IDEA.
I JUST DON'T WANT TO OWE THAT VAMPIRE ANY FAVORS.

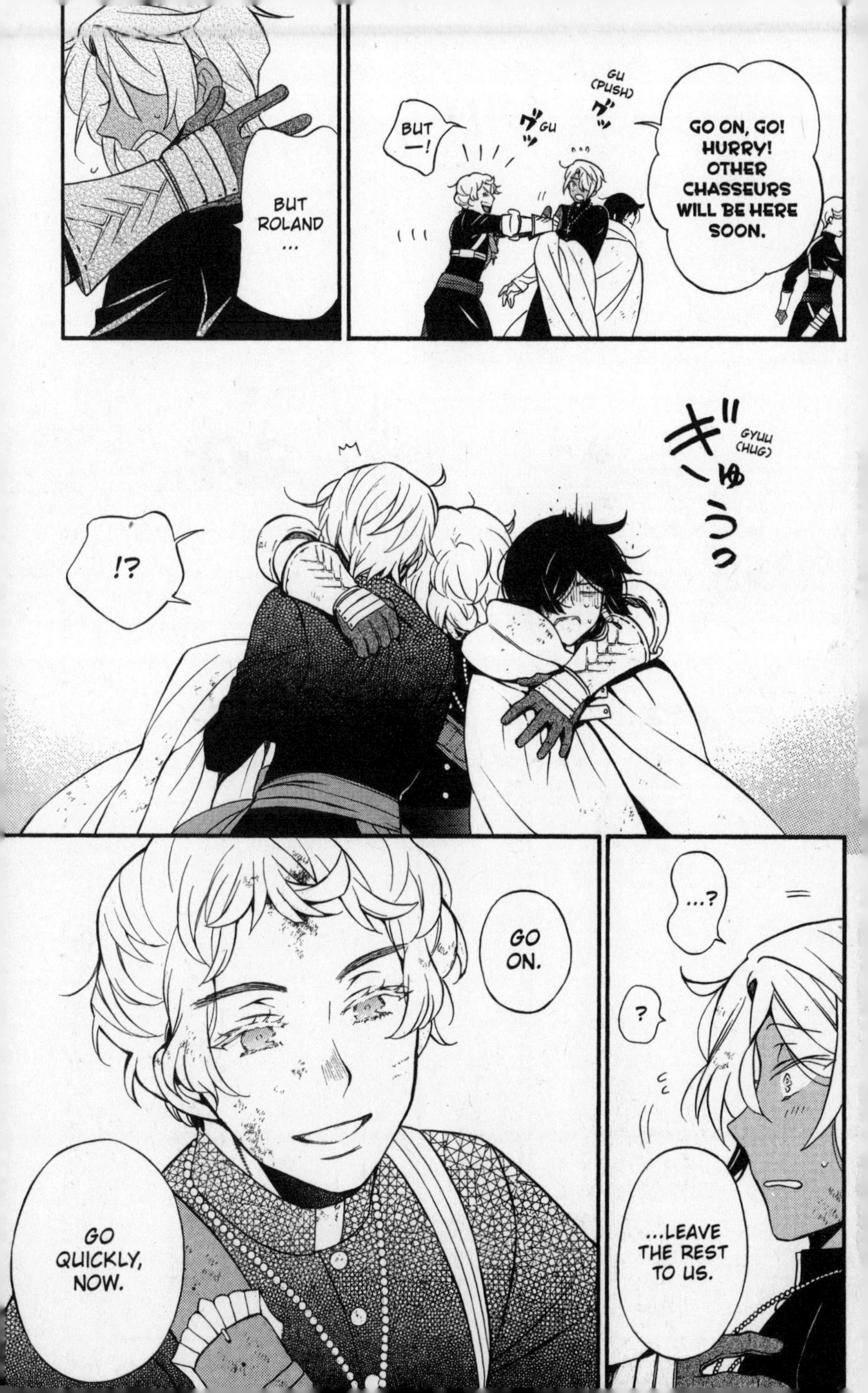
GO ON, GO! HURRY! OTHER CHASSEURS WILL BE HERE SOON.
GU (PUSH)
GU
BUT—!
BUT ROLAND ...
GYUU (HUG)
!?
...?
?
...LEAVE THE REST TO US.
GO ON.
GO QUICKLY, NOW.

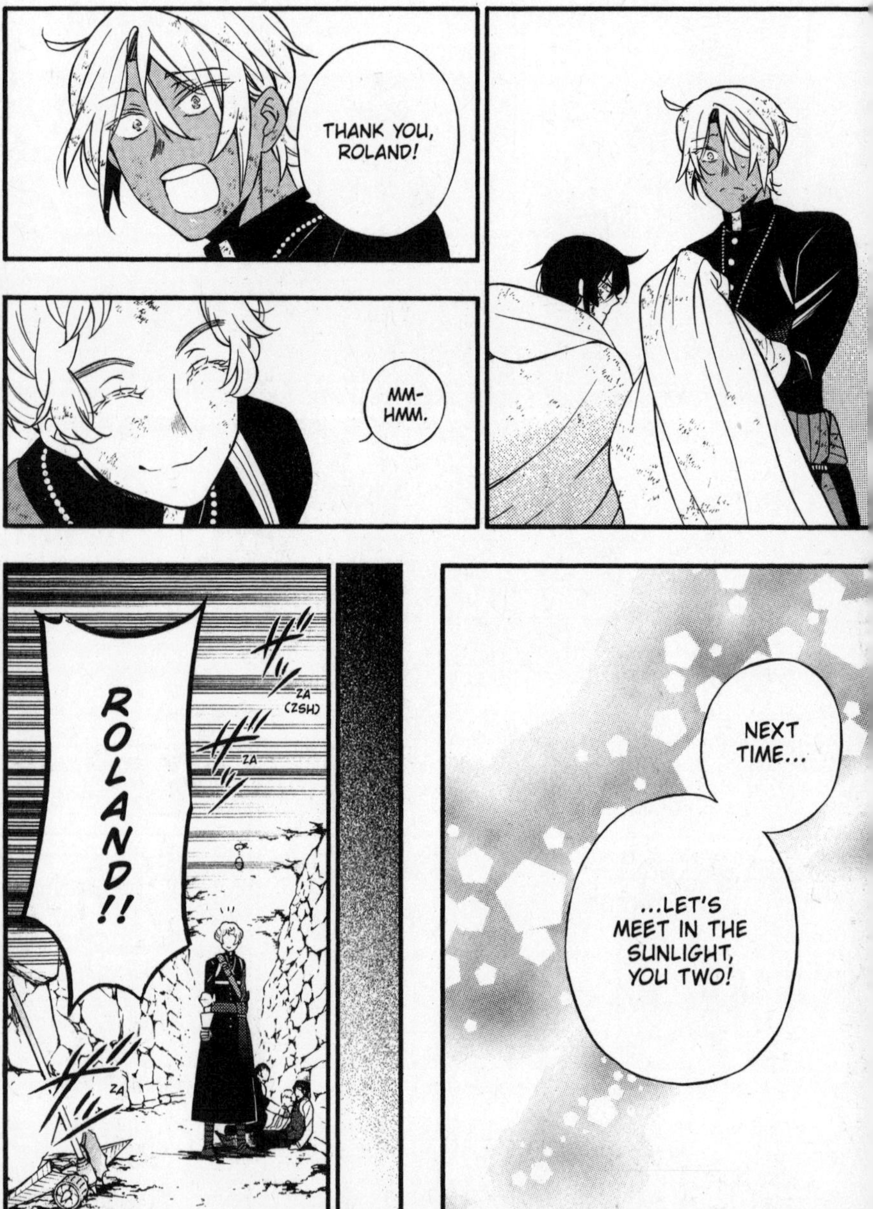
THANK YOU, ROLAND!
MM-HMM.
NEXT TIME...
...LET'S MEET IN THE SUNLIGHT, YOU TWO!
ROLAND!!
ZA (ZSH)
ZA
ZA

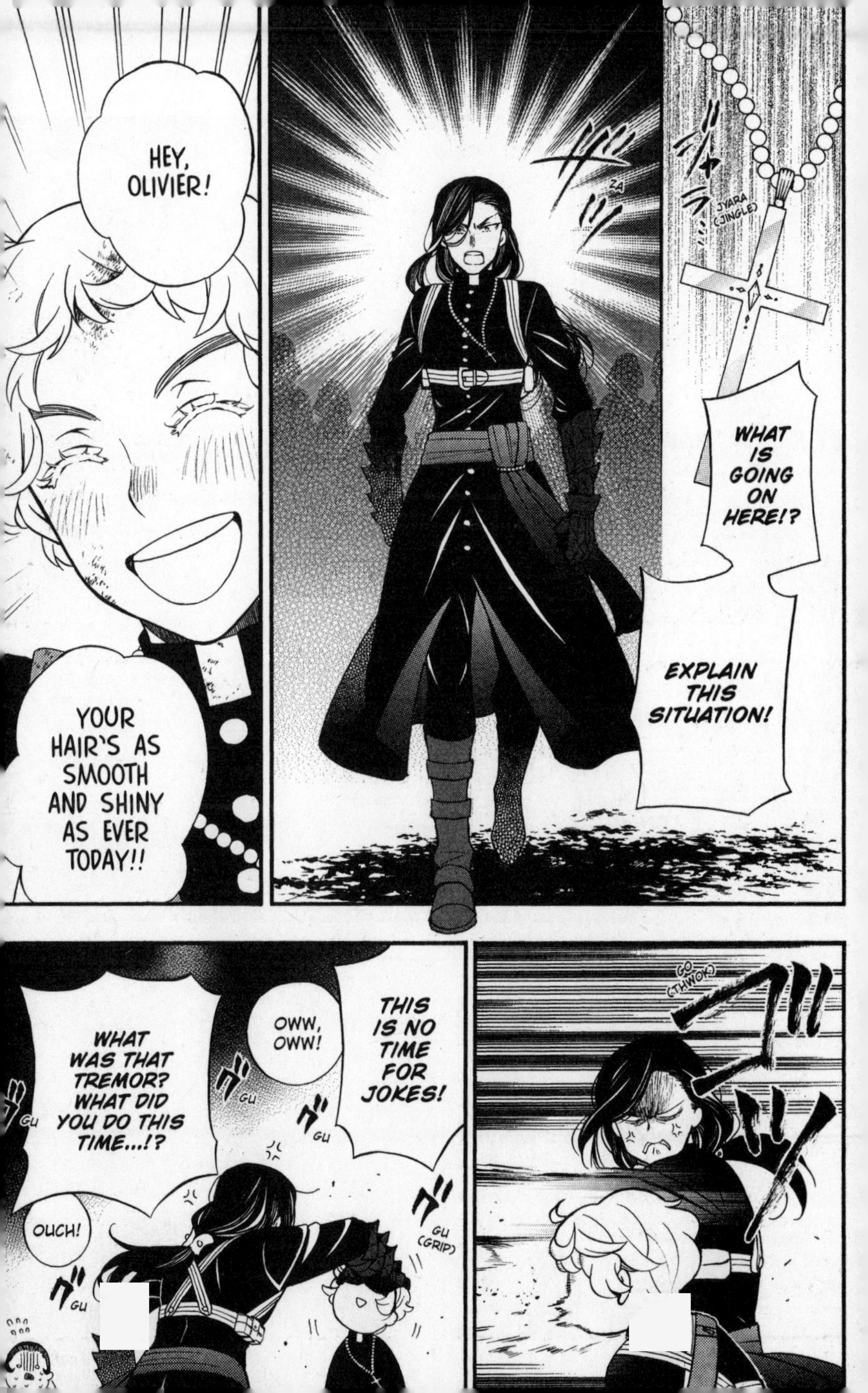
JYARA (JINGLE)
WHAT IS GOING ON HERE!?
ZA
EXPLAIN THIS SITUATION!
HEY, OLIVIER!
YOUR HAIR'S AS SMOOTH AND SHINY AS EVER TODAY!!
GO (THWOK)
THIS IS NO TIME FOR JOKES!
OWW, OWW!
WHAT WAS THAT TREMOR? WHAT DID YOU DO THIS TIME...!?
GU
GU
GU
GU (GRIP)
OUCH!
GU

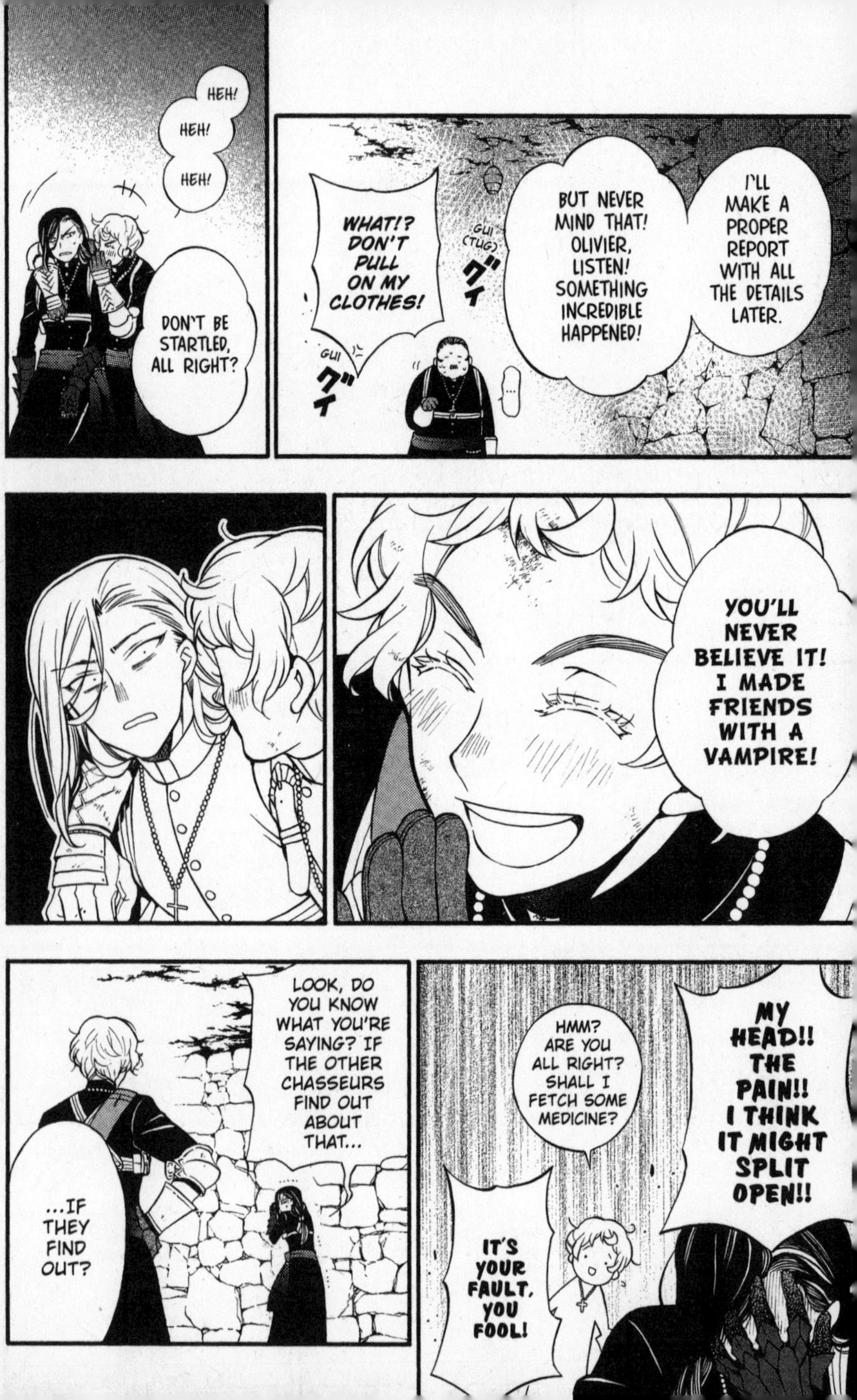
I'LL MAKE A PROPER REPORT WITH ALL THE DETAILS LATER.
BUT NEVER MIND THAT! OLIVIER, LISTEN! SOMETHING INCREDIBLE HAPPENED!
GUI (TUG) グイ
WHAT!? DON'T PULL ON MY CLOTHES!
GUI グイ
...
HEH!
HEH!
HEH!
DON'T BE STARTLED, ALL RIGHT?
YOU'LL NEVER BELIEVE IT! I MADE FRIENDS WITH A VAMPIRE!
MY HEAD!! THE PAIN!! I THINK IT MIGHT SPLIT OPEN!!
HMM? ARE YOU ALL RIGHT? SHALL I FETCH SOME MEDICINE?
IT'S YOUR FAULT, YOU FOOL!
LOOK, DO YOU KNOW WHAT YOU'RE SAYING? IF THE OTHER CHASSEURS FIND OUT ABOUT THAT...
...IF THEY FIND OUT?

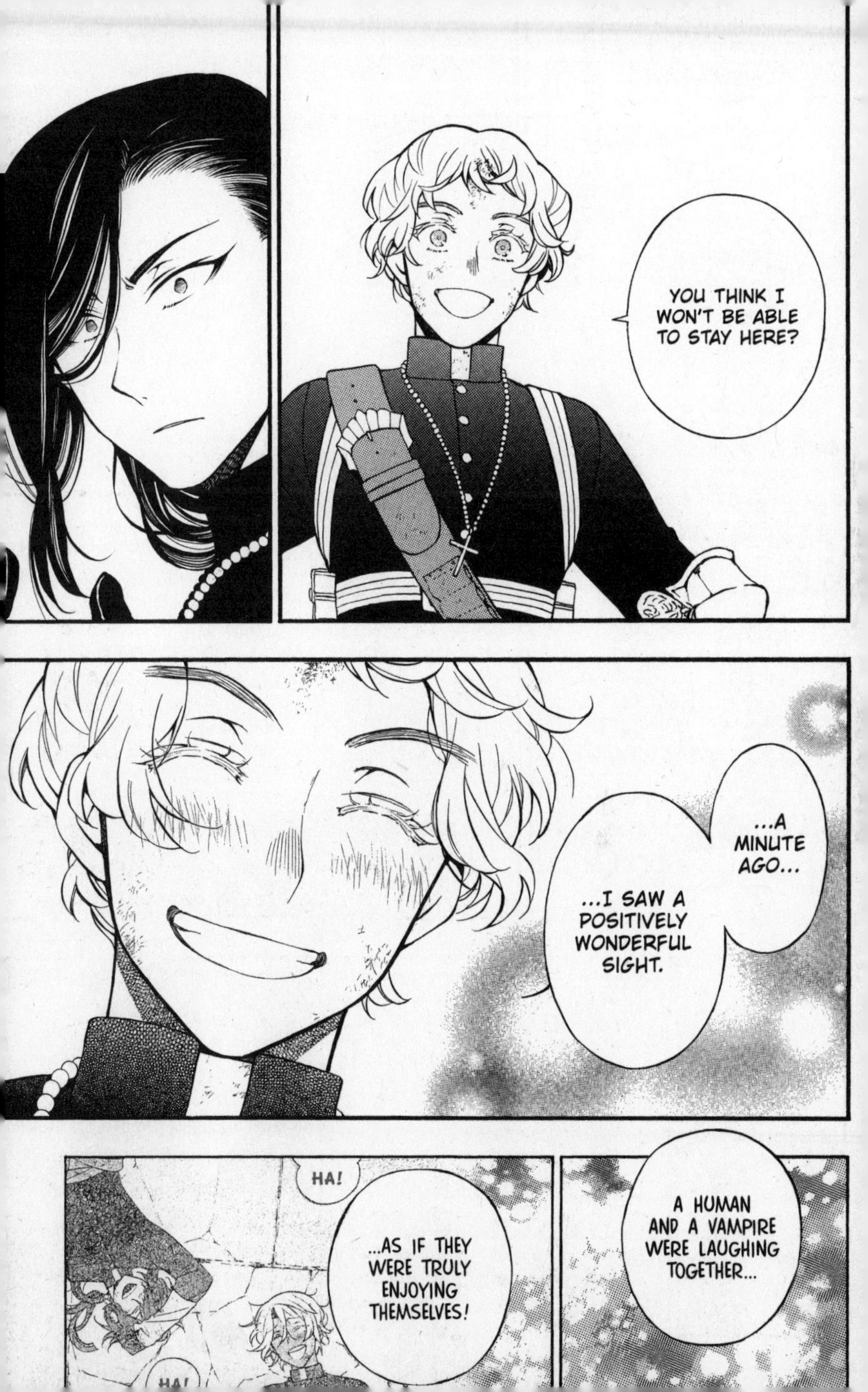
YOU THINK I WON'T BE ABLE TO STAY HERE?
...A MINUTE AGO...
...I SAW A POSITIVELY WONDERFUL SIGHT.
A HUMAN AND A VAMPIRE WERE LAUGHING TOGETHER...
HA!
...AS IF THEY WERE TRULY ENJOYING THEMSELVES!
HA!

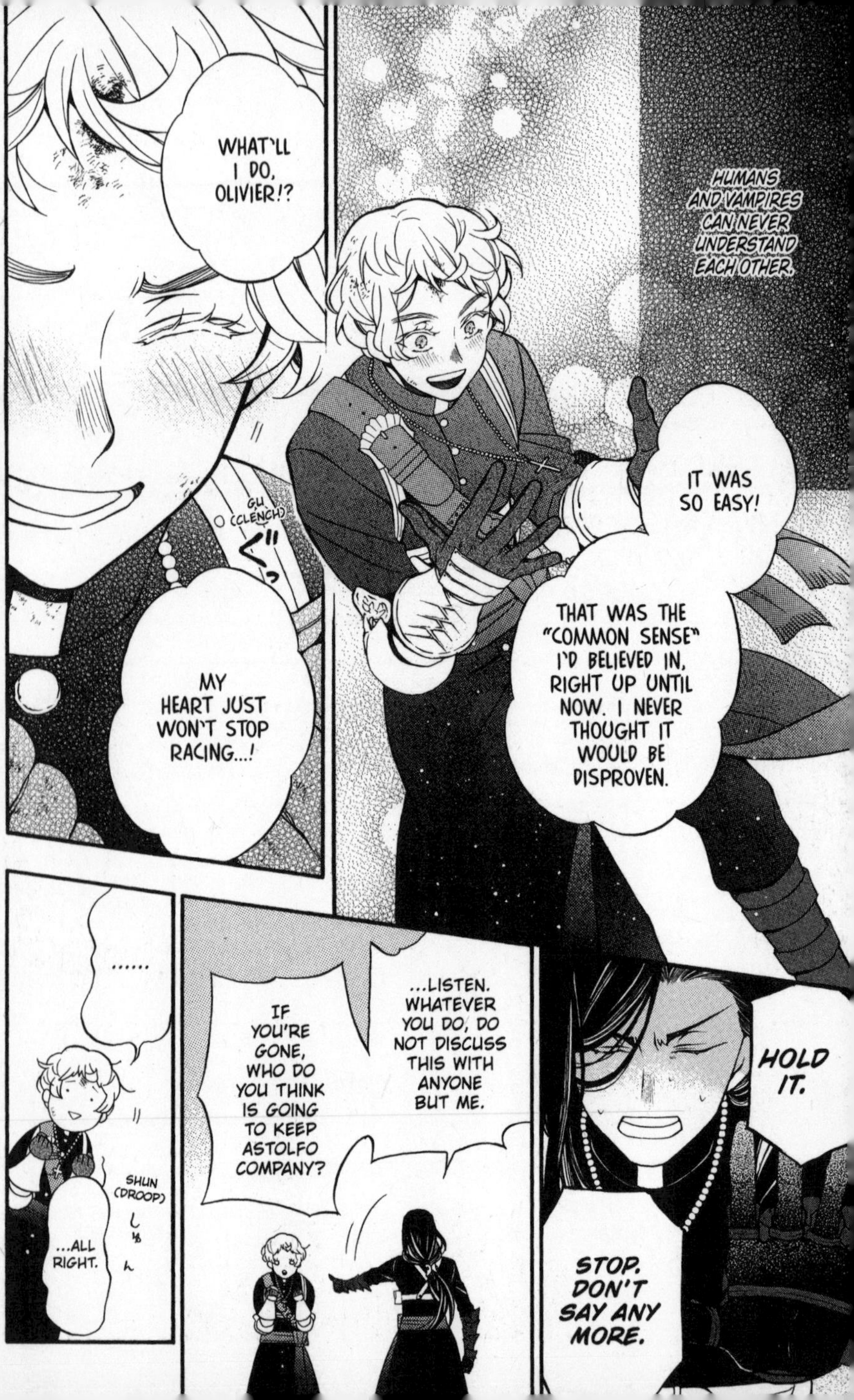
HUMANS AND VAMPIRES CAN NEVER UNDERSTAND EACH OTHER.
IT WAS SO EASY!
THAT WAS THE "COMMON SENSE" I'D BELIEVED IN, RIGHT UP UNTIL NOW. I NEVER THOUGHT IT WOULD BE DISPROVEN.
WHAT'LL I DO, OLIVIER!?
GU (CLENCH)
MY HEART JUST WON'T STOP RACING...!
HOLD IT.
STOP. DON'T SAY ANY MORE.
...LISTEN. WHATEVER YOU DO, DO NOT DISCUSS THIS WITH ANYONE BUT ME.
IF YOU'RE GONE, WHO DO YOU THINK IS GOING TO KEEP ASTOLFO COMPANY?
......
SHUN (DROOP)
...ALL RIGHT.

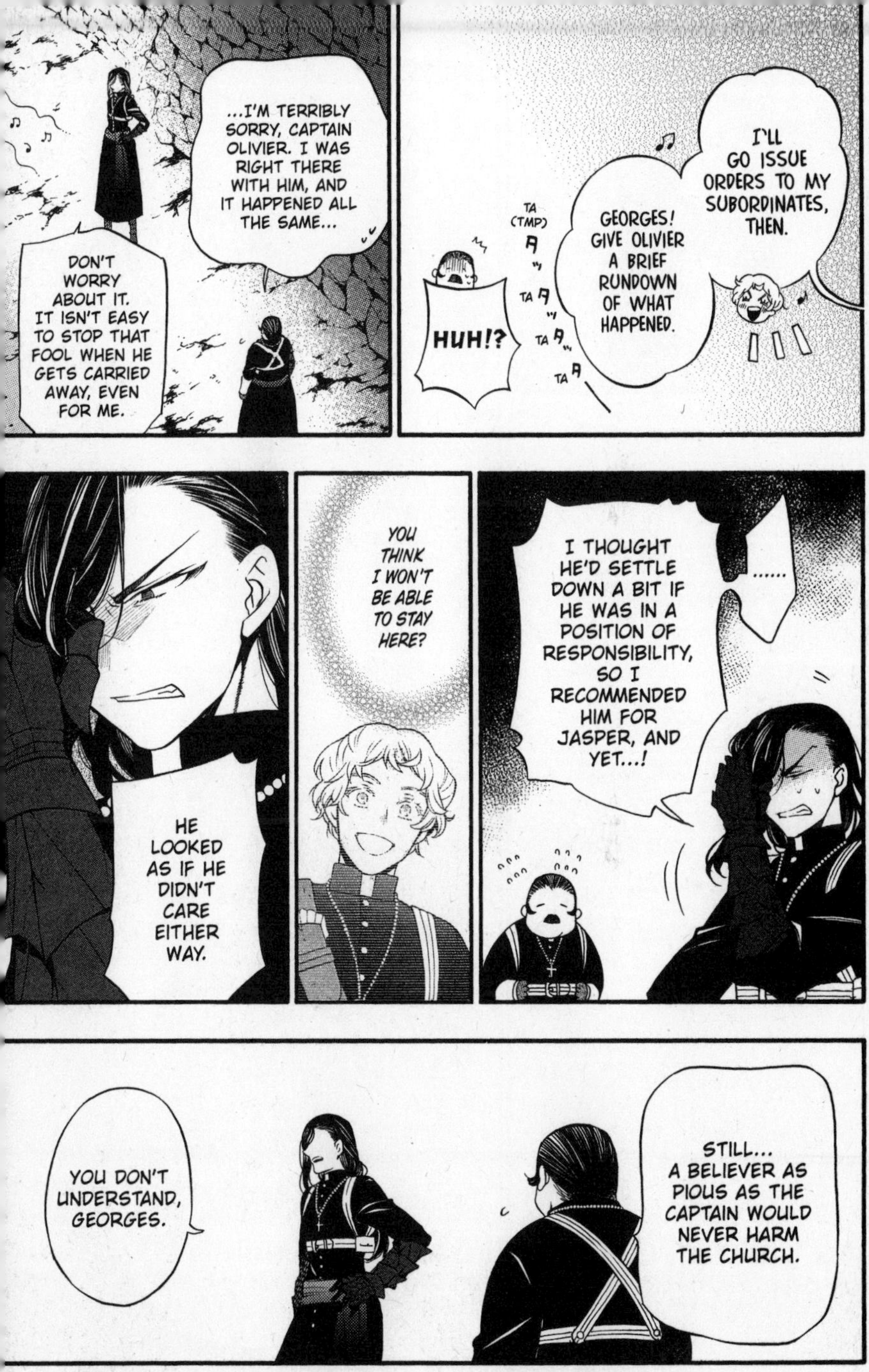
I'LL GO ISSUE ORDERS TO MY SUBORDINATES, THEN.
GEORGES! GIVE OLIVIER A BRIEF RUNDOWN OF WHAT HAPPENED.
TA (TMP)
TA
TA
TA
HUH!?
...I'M TERRIBLY SORRY, CAPTAIN OLIVIER. I WAS RIGHT THERE WITH HIM, AND IT HAPPENED ALL THE SAME...
DON'T WORRY ABOUT IT. IT ISN'T EASY TO STOP THAT FOOL WHEN HE GETS CARRIED AWAY, EVEN FOR ME.
I THOUGHT HE'D SETTLE DOWN A BIT IF HE WAS IN A POSITION OF RESPONSIBILITY, SO I RECOMMENDED HIM FOR JASPER, AND YET...!
......
YOU THINK I WON'T BE ABLE TO STAY HERE?
HE LOOKED AS IF HE DIDN'T CARE EITHER WAY.
STILL... A BELIEVER AS PIOUS AS THE CAPTAIN WOULD NEVER HARM THE CHURCH.
YOU DON'T UNDERSTAND, GEORGES.

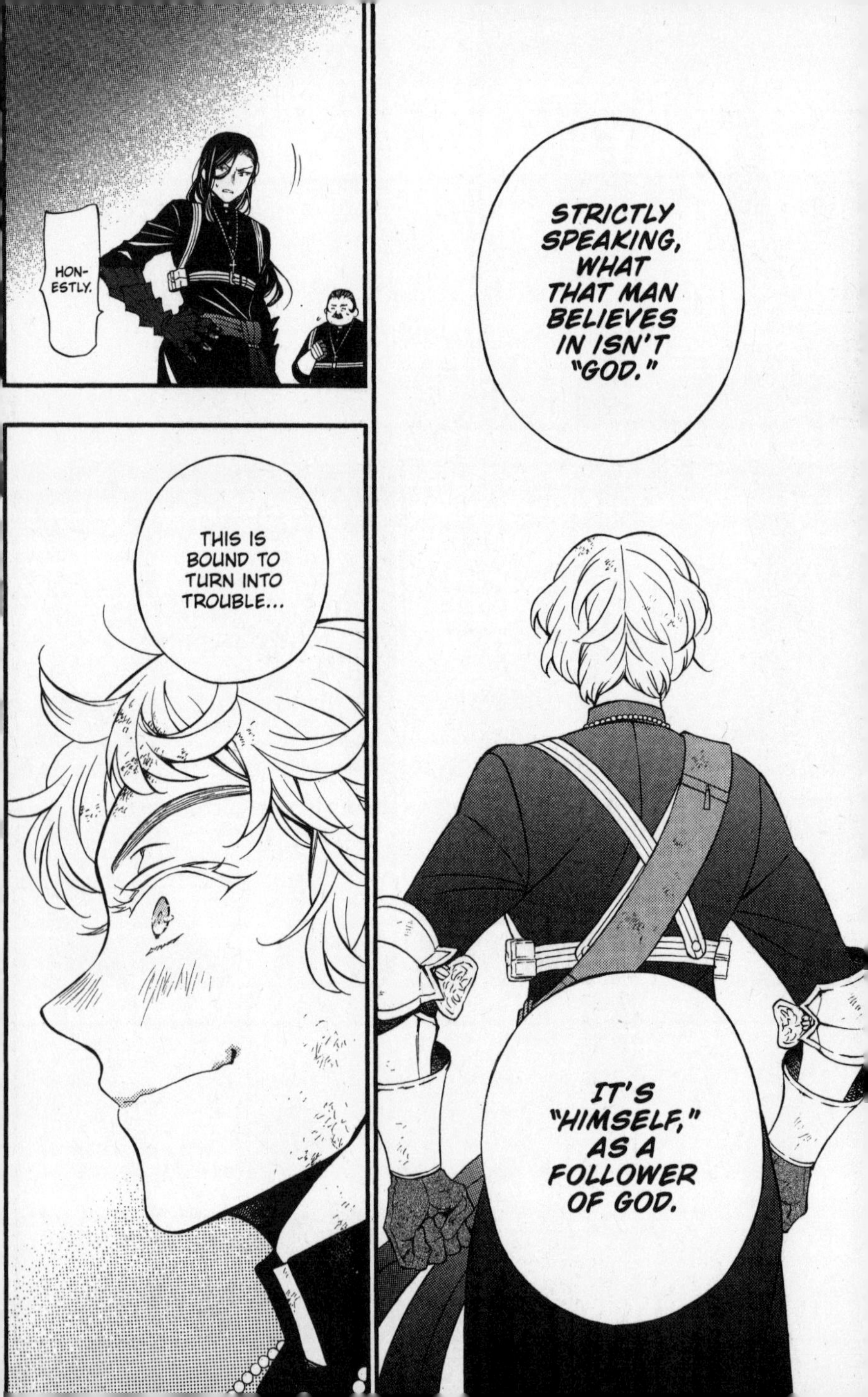
STRICTLY SPEAKING, WHAT THAT MAN BELIEVES IN ISN'T "GOD."
IT'S "HIMSELF," AS A FOLLOWER OF GOD.
HON-ESTLY.
THIS IS BOUND TO TURN INTO TROUBLE...

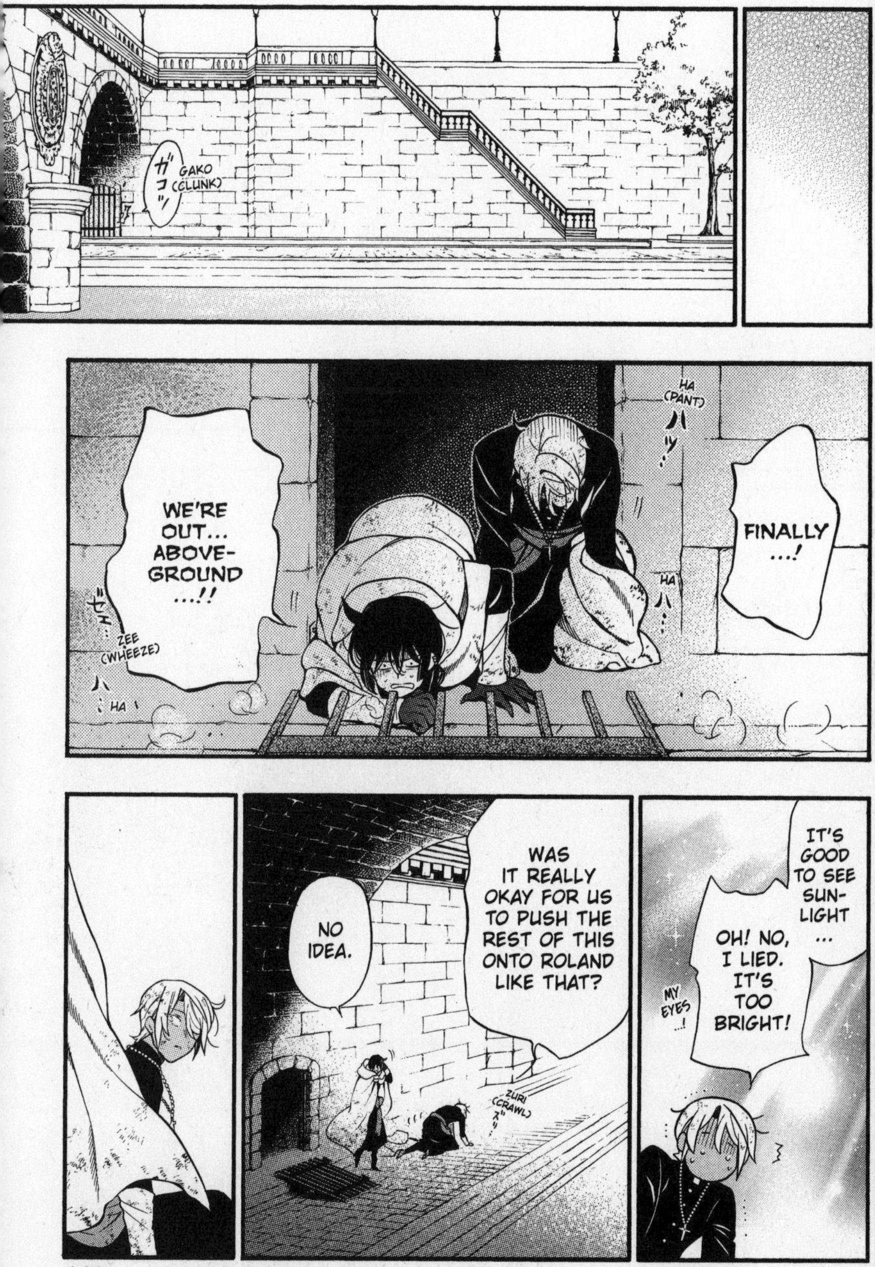
GAKO (CLUNK)
HA (PANT)
FINALLY ...!
HA
WE'RE OUT... ABOVE-GROUND ...!!
ZEE (WHEEZE)
HA
IT'S GOOD TO SEE SUN-LIGHT ...
OH! NO, I LIED. IT'S TOO BRIGHT!
MY EYES ...!
WAS IT REALLY OKAY FOR US TO PUSH THE REST OF THIS ONTO ROLAND LIKE THAT?
NO IDEA.
ZURI (CRAWL)

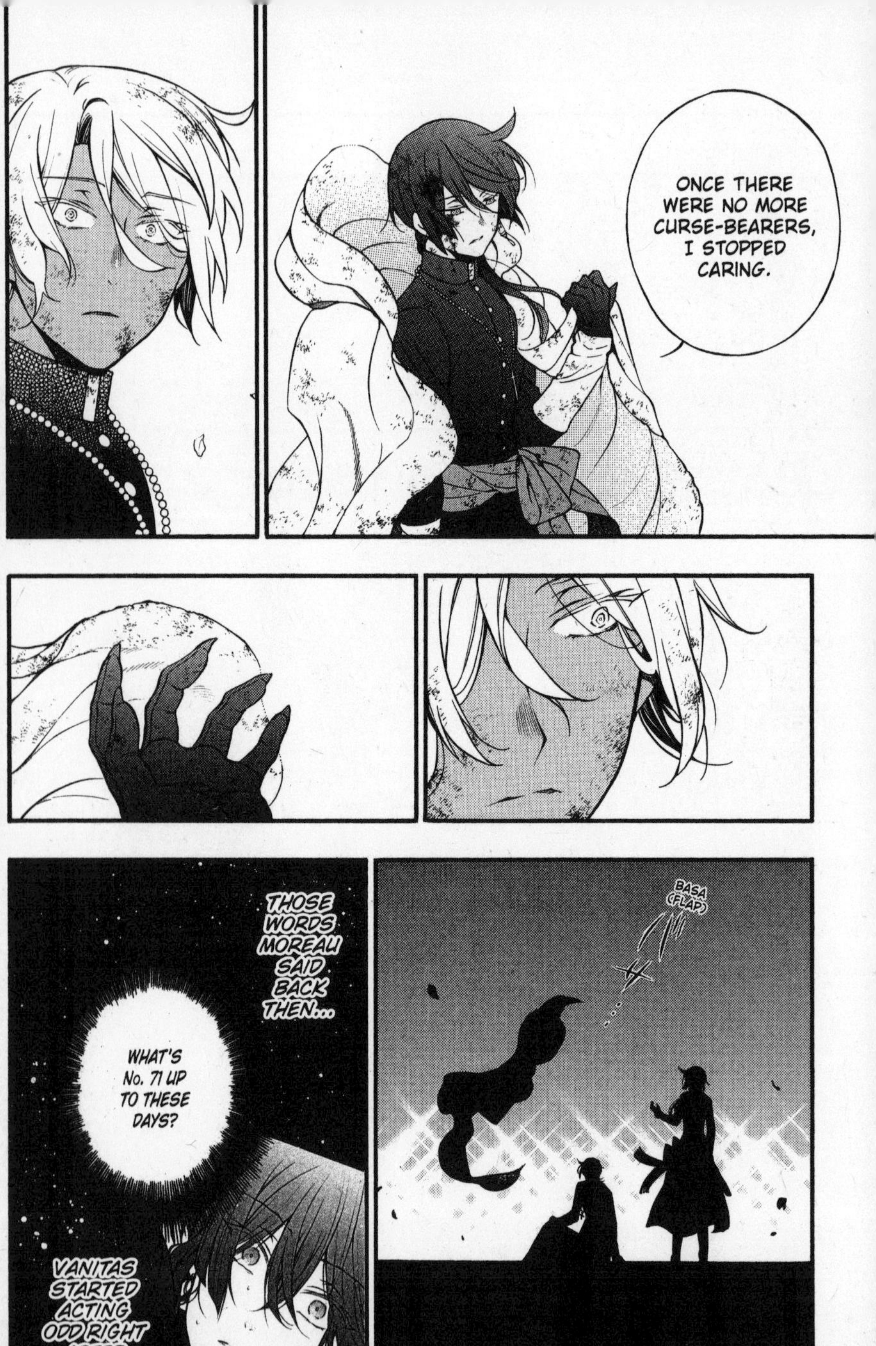
ONCE THERE WERE NO MORE CURSE-BEARERS, I STOPPED CARING.
BASA (FLAP)
THOSE WORDS MOREAU SAID BACK THEN...
WHAT'S No. 71 UP TO THESE DAYS?
VANITAS STARTED ACTING ODD RIGHT AFTER THAT.

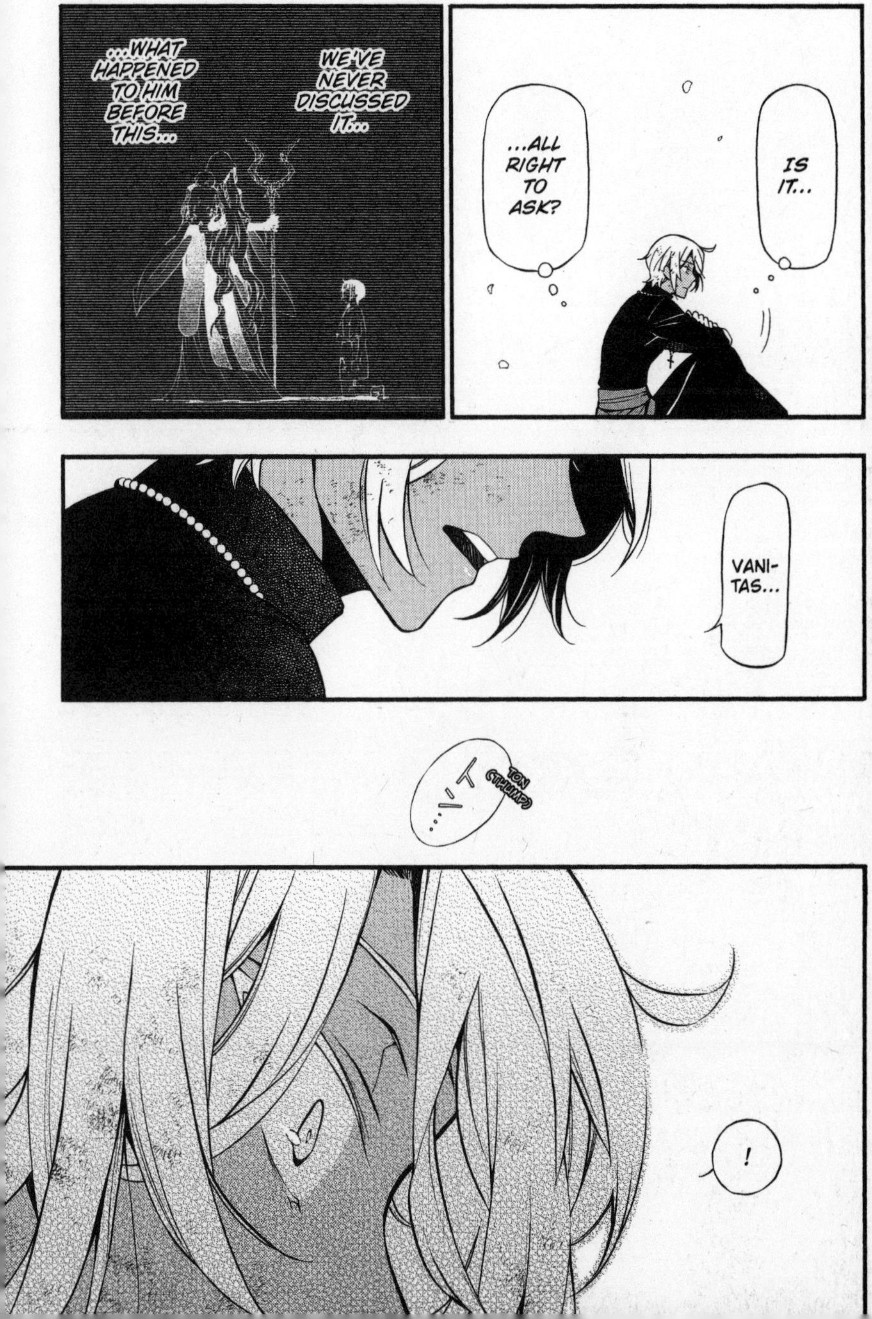
IS IT...
...ALL RIGHT TO ASK?
WE'VE NEVER DISCUSSED IT...
...WHAT HAPPENED TO HIM BEFORE THIS...
VANITAS...
TON (THUMP)
!

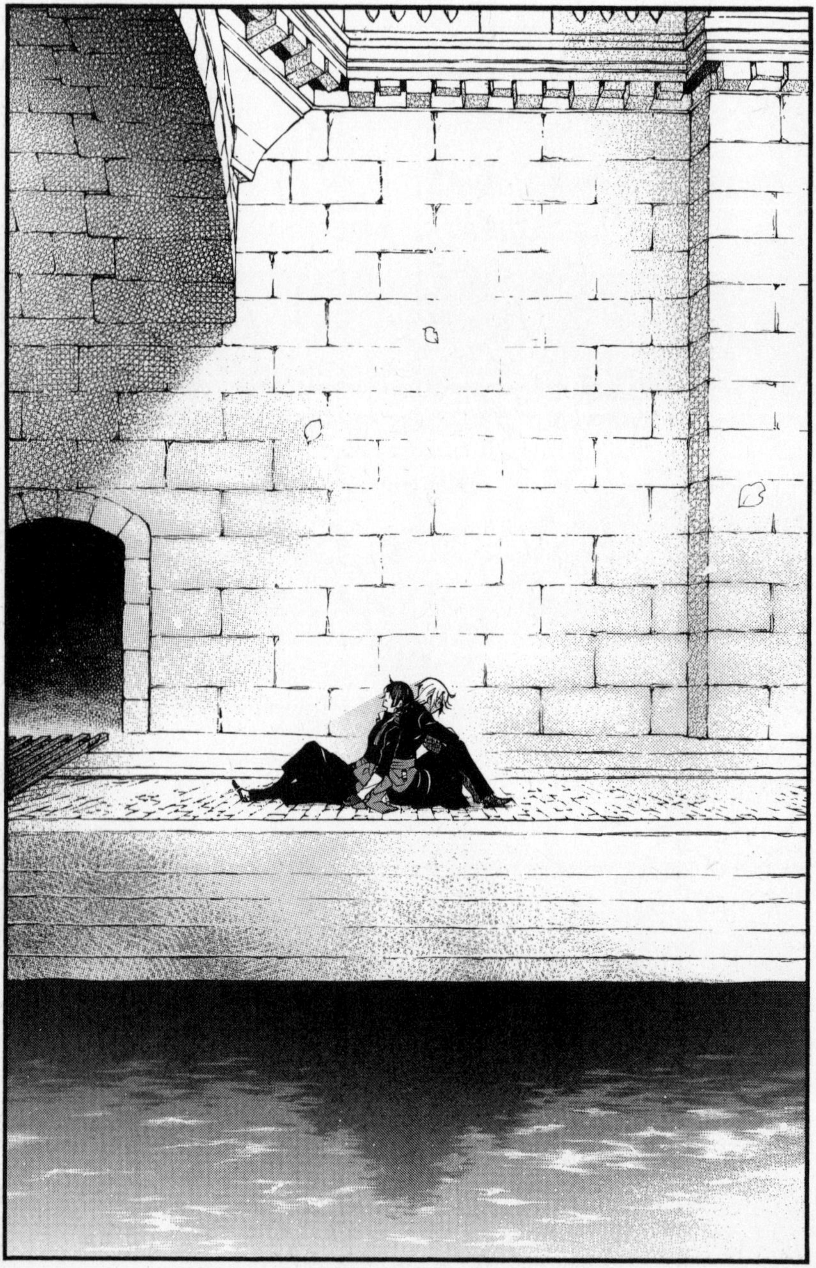

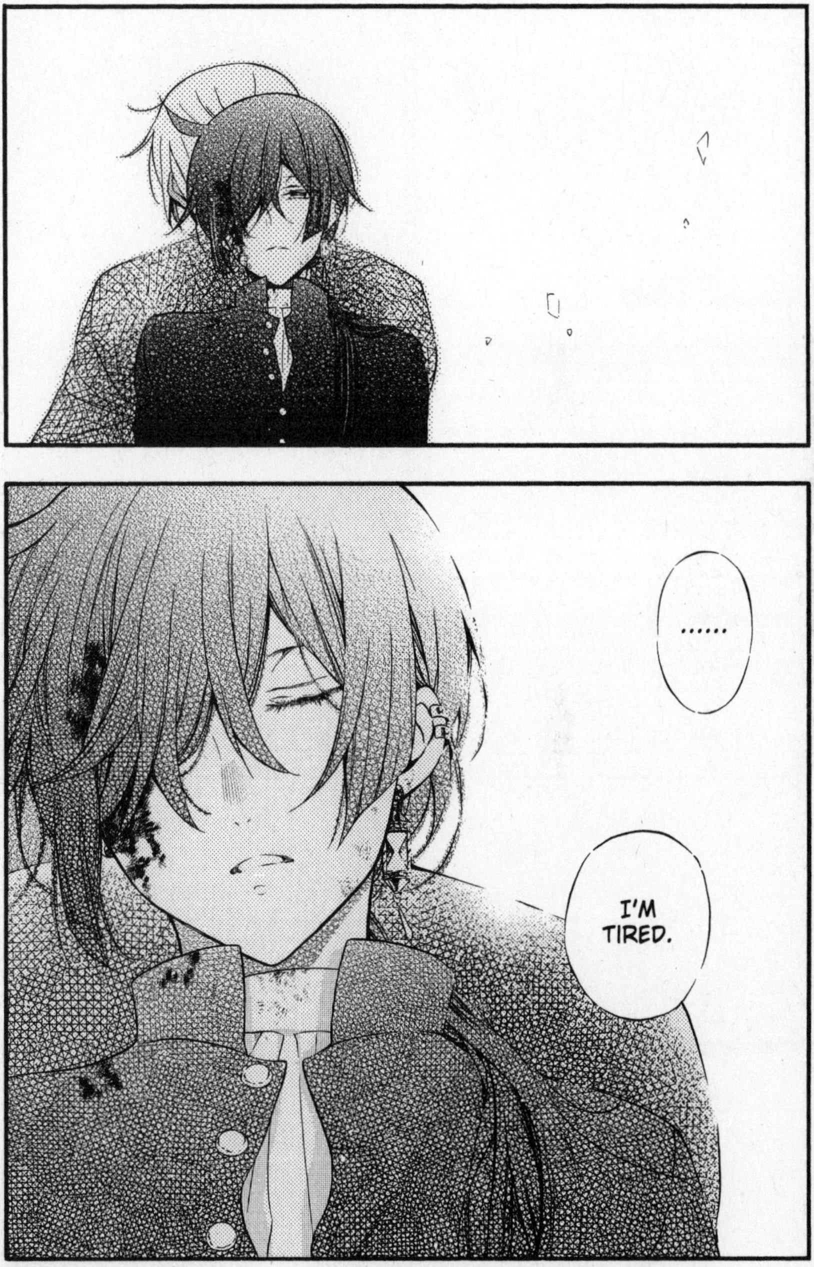
......
I'M TIRED.

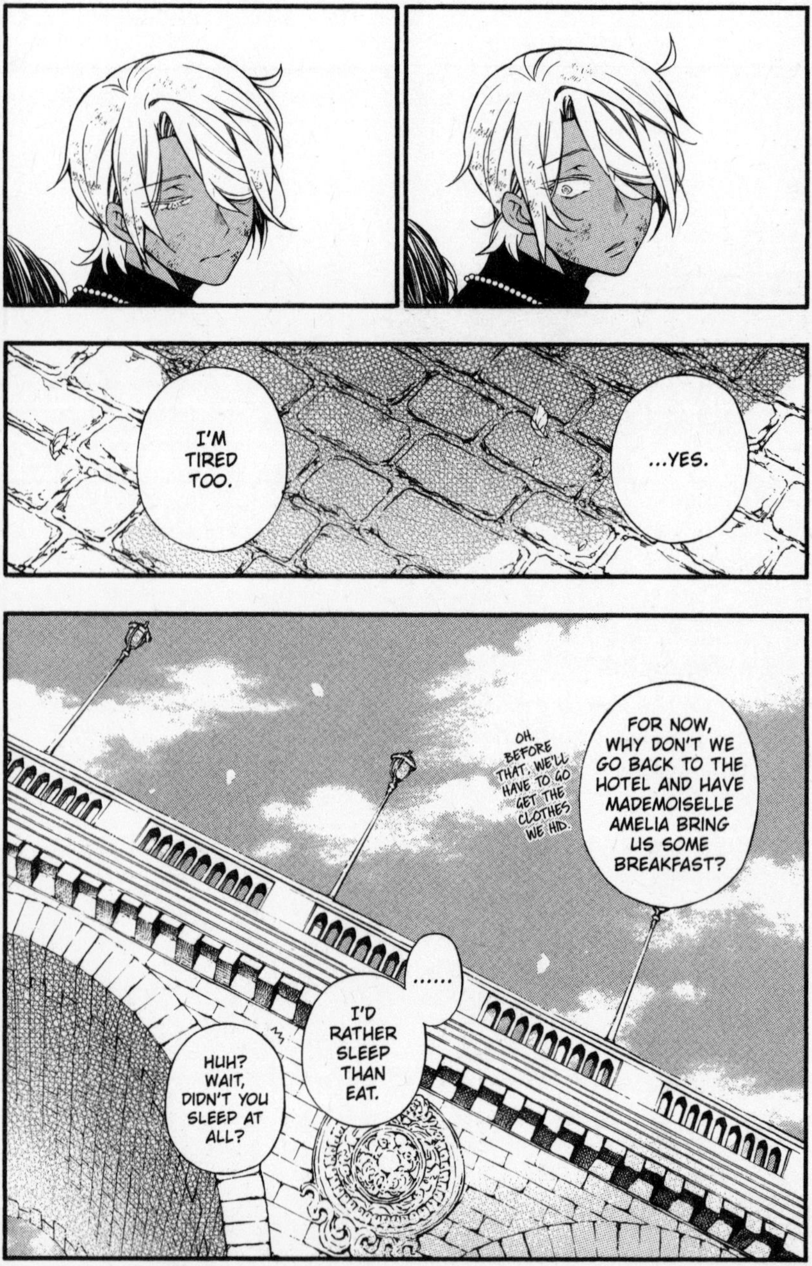
...YES.
I'M TIRED TOO.
FOR NOW, WHY DON'T WE GO BACK TO THE HOTEL AND HAVE MADEMOISELLE AMELIA BRING US SOME BREAKFAST?
OH, BEFORE THAT, WE'LL HAVE TO GO GET THE CLOTHES WE HID.
......
I'D RATHER SLEEP THAN EAT.
HUH? WAIT, DIDN'T YOU SLEEP AT ALL?

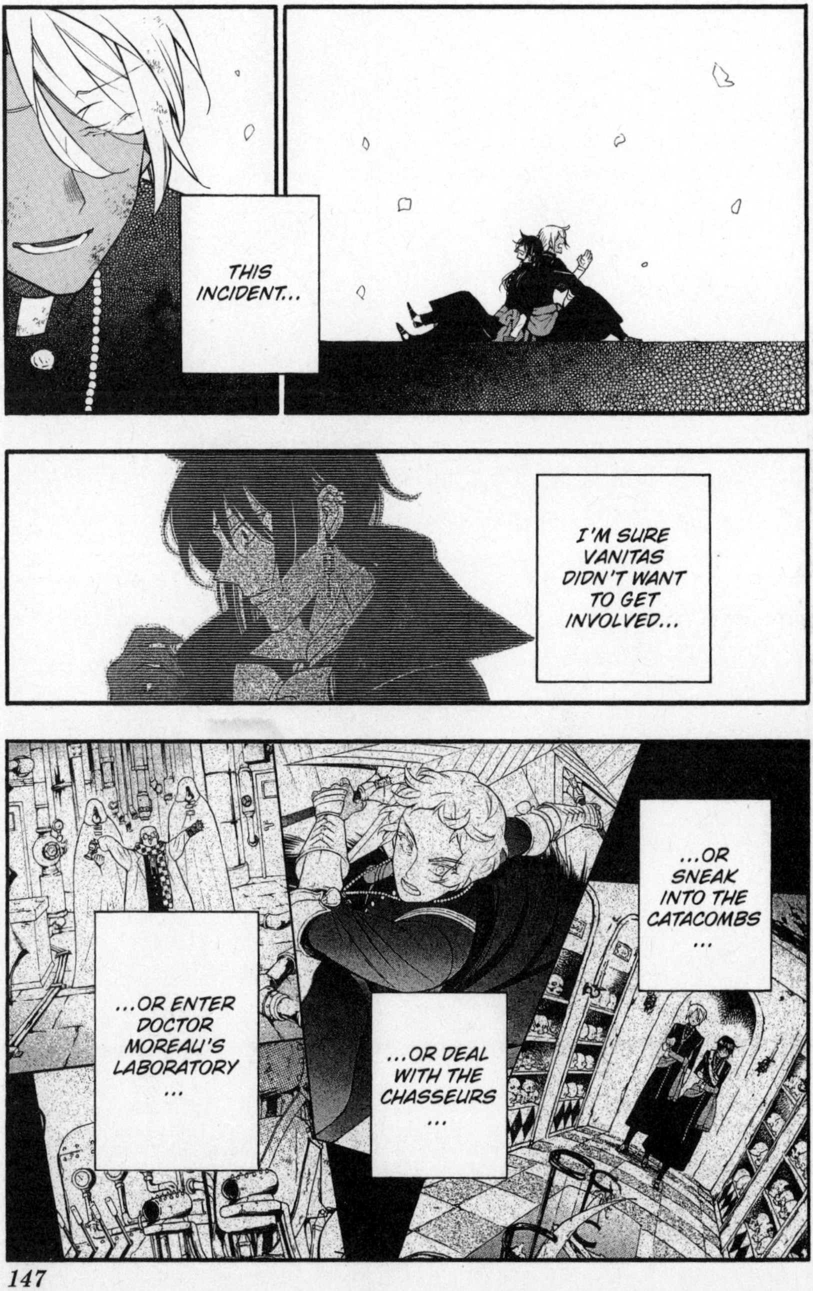
THIS INCIDENT...
I'M SURE VANITAS DIDN'T WANT TO GET INVOLVED...
...OR SNEAK INTO THE CATACOMBS ...
...OR DEAL WITH THE CHASSEURS ...
...OR ENTER DOCTOR MOREAU'S LABORATORY ...

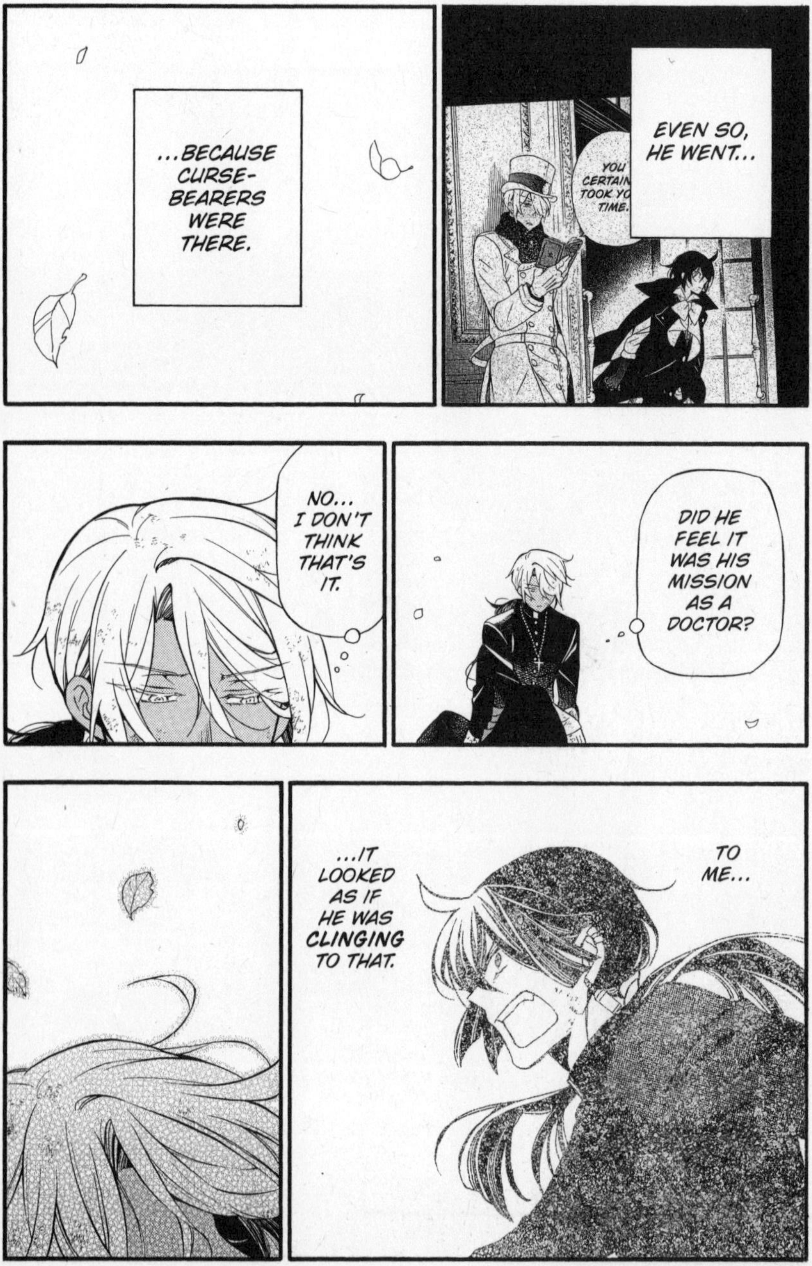
EVEN SO, HE WENT...
YOU CERTAIN TOOK YO TIME.
...BECAUSE CURSE-BEARERS WERE THERE.
DID HE FEEL IT WAS HIS MISSION AS A DOCTOR?
NO... I DON'T THINK THAT'S IT.
TO ME...
...IT LOOKED AS IF HE WAS CLINGING TO THAT.

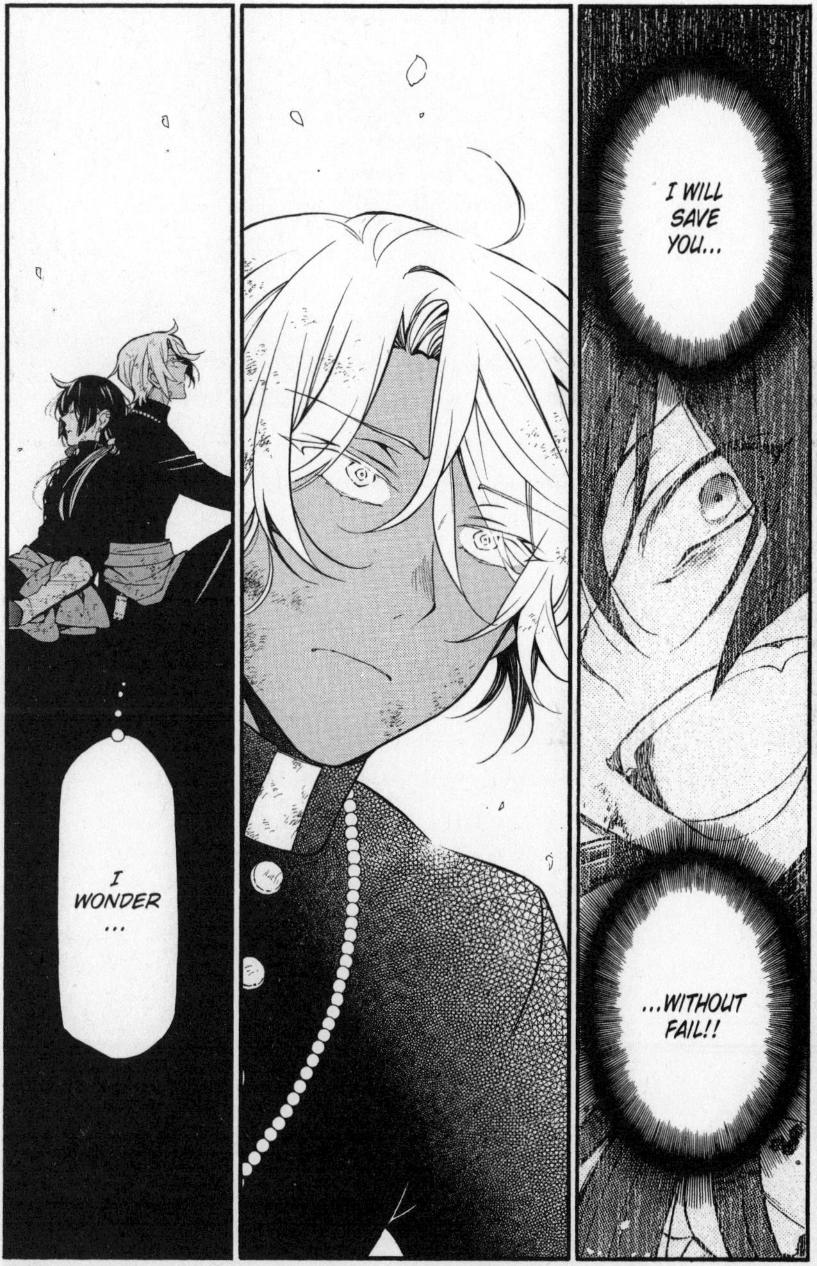
I WILL SAVE YOU...
...WITHOUT FAIL!!
I WONDER ...

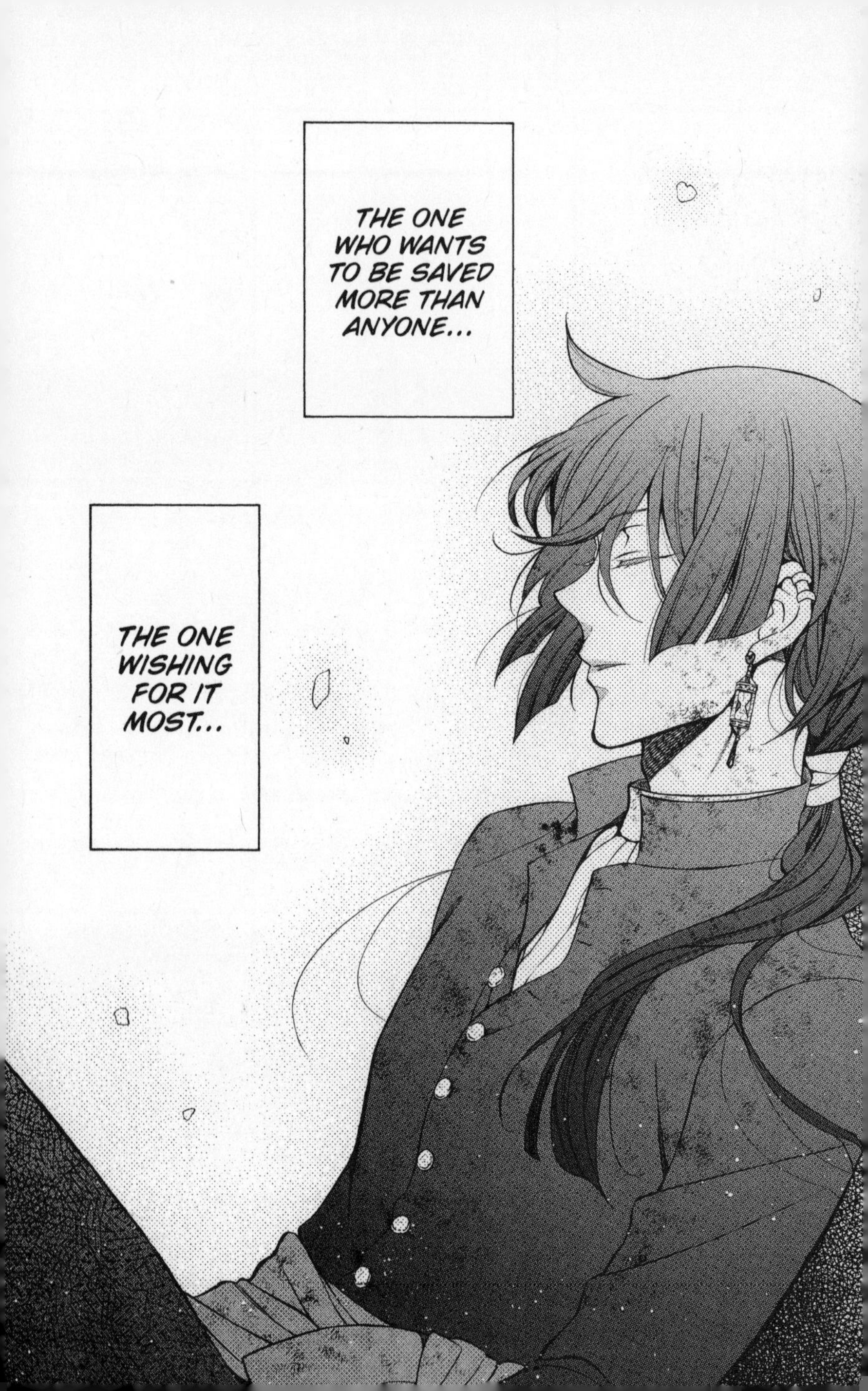
THE ONE WHO WANTS TO BE SAVED MORE THAN ANYONE...
THE ONE WISHING FOR IT MOST...

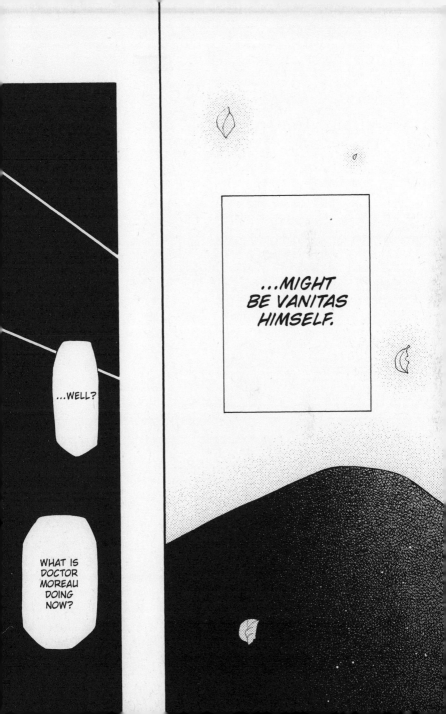

...MIGHT
BE VANITAS
HIMSELF.

...WELL?

WHAT IS
DOCTOR
MOREAU
DOING
NOW?

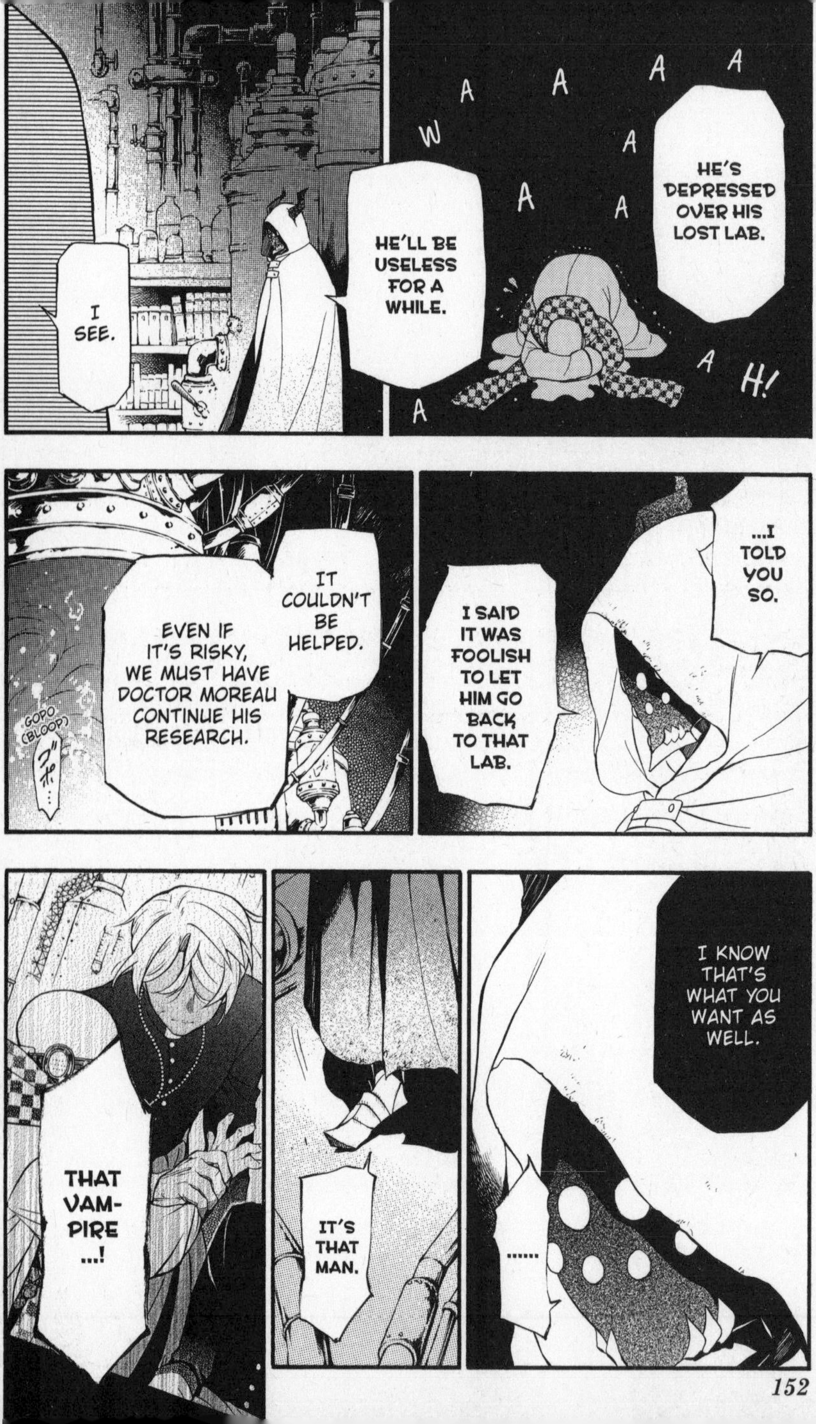
WAAAAAAAAAH!
HE'S DEPRESSED OVER HIS LOST LAB.
HE'LL BE USELESS FOR A WHILE.
I SEE.
...I TOLD YOU SO.
I SAID IT WAS FOOLISH TO LET HIM GO BACK TO THAT LAB.
IT COULDN'T BE HELPED.
EVEN IF IT'S RISKY, WE MUST HAVE DOCTOR MOREAU CONTINUE HIS RESEARCH.
GOPO (BLOOP)
ゴポ…
I KNOW THAT'S WHAT YOU WANT AS WELL.
......
IT'S THAT MAN.
THAT VAMPIRE...!

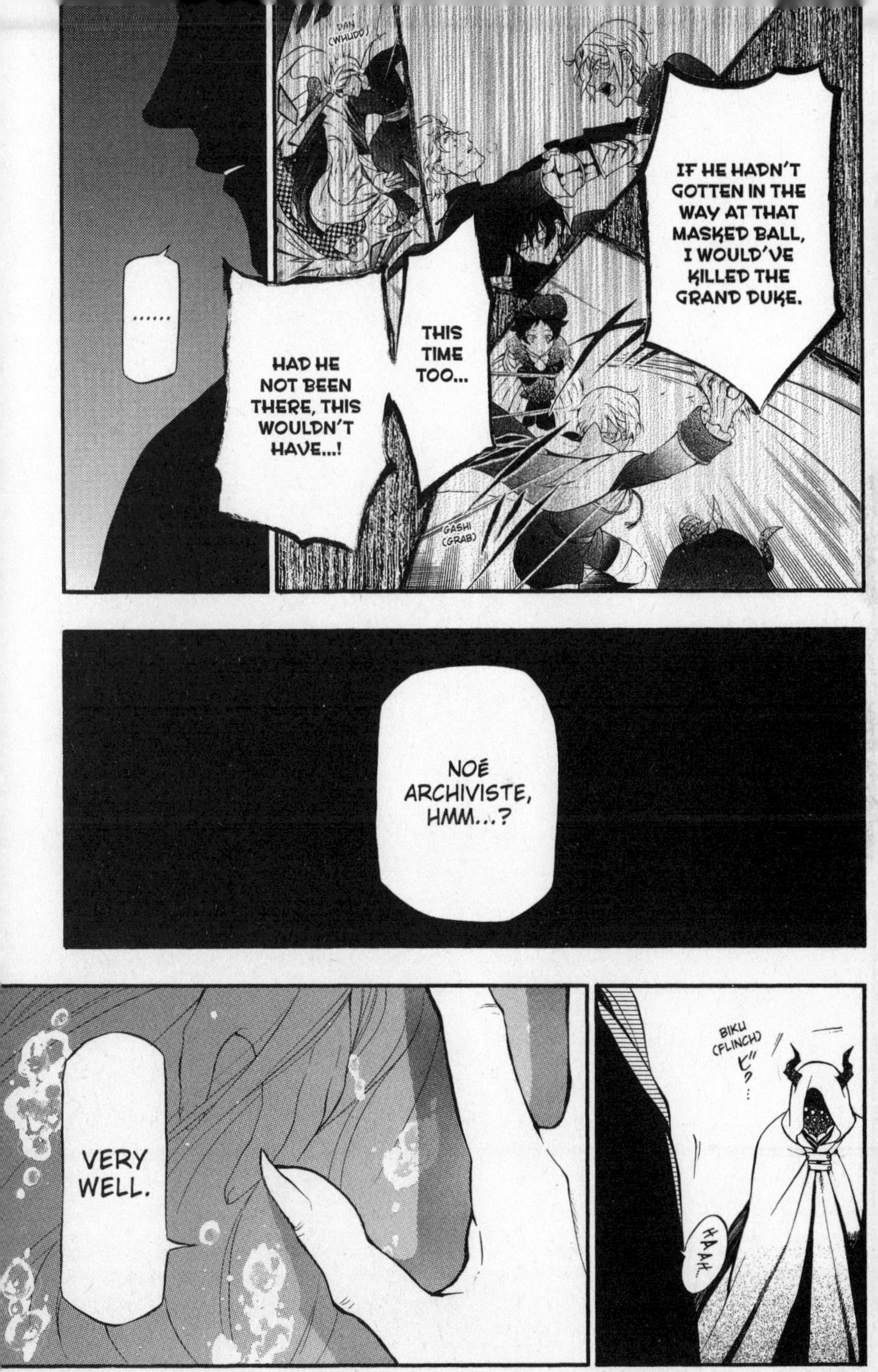
IF HE HADN'T GOTTEN IN THE WAY AT THAT MASKED BALL, I WOULD'VE KILLED THE GRAND DUKE.
THIS TIME TOO...
HAD HE NOT BEEN THERE, THIS WOULDN'T HAVE...!
DAN (WHUD)
GASHI (GRAB)
......
NOÉ ARCHIVISTE, HMM...?
BIKU (FLINCH)
ビク…
HAAK...
VERY WELL.

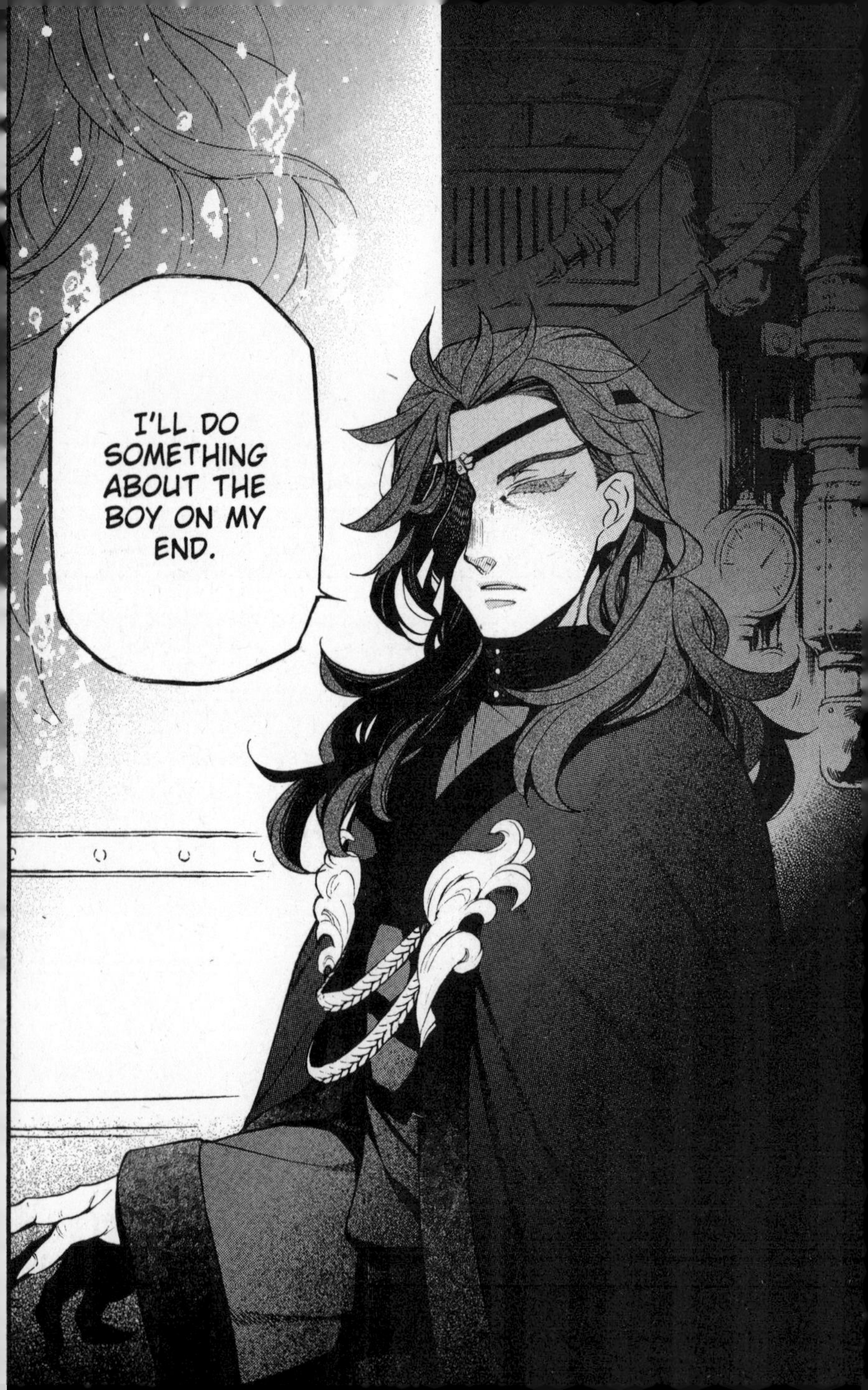
I'LL DO SOMETHING ABOUT THE BOY ON MY END.

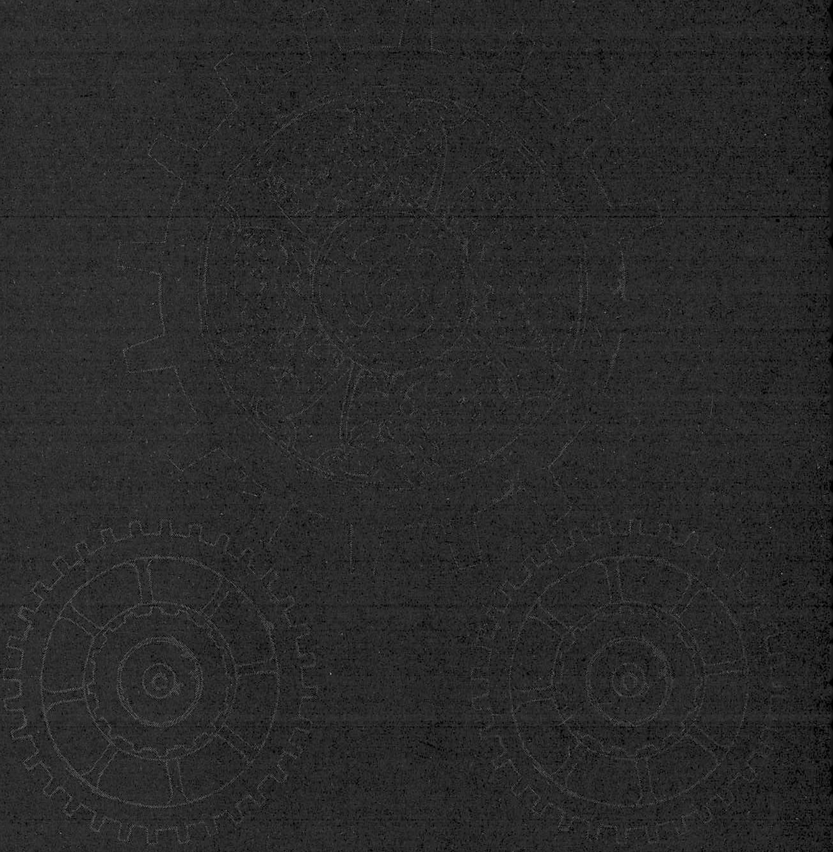

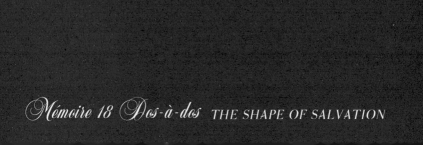

# *Mémoire 18 Dos-à-dos* THE SHAPE OF SALVATION

*Les Mémoires de Vanitas*

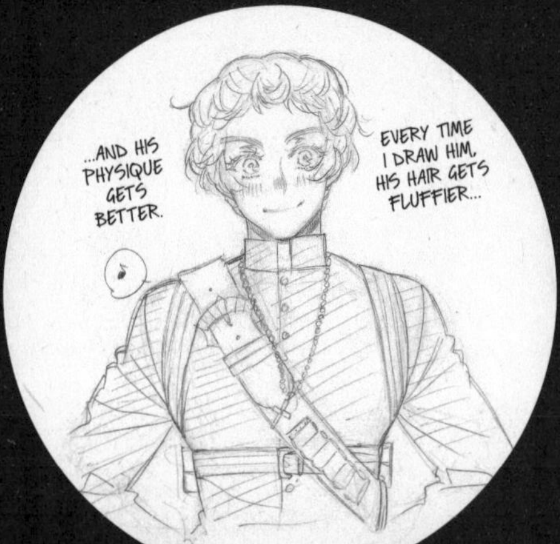
EVERY TIME I DRAW HIM, HIS HAIR GETS FLUFFIER...
...AND HIS PHYSIQUE GETS BETTER.

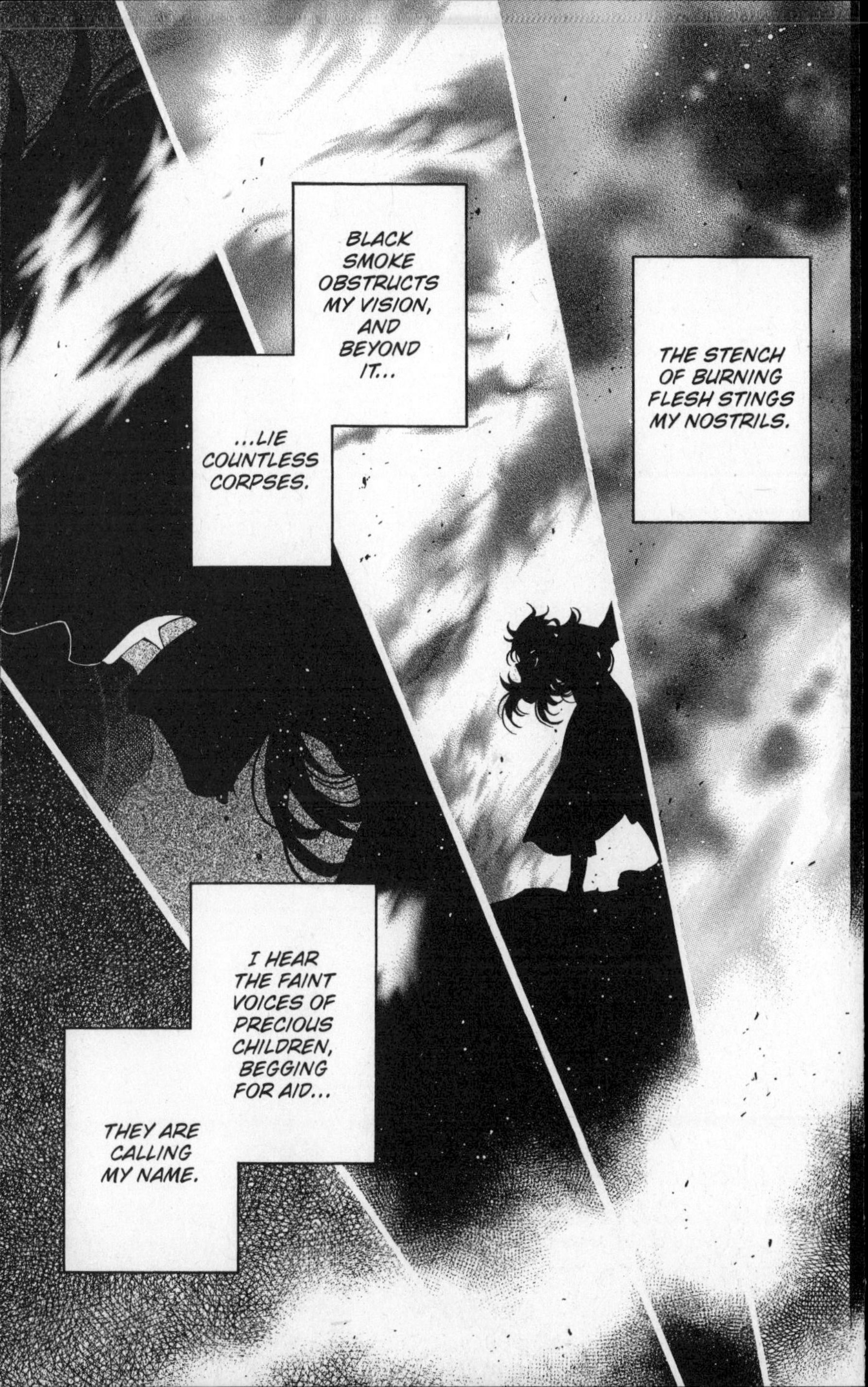
THE STENCH OF BURNING FLESH STINGS MY NOSTRILS.
BLACK SMOKE OBSTRUCTS MY VISION, AND BEYOND IT...
...LIE COUNTLESS CORPSES.
I HEAR THE FAINT VOICES OF PRECIOUS CHILDREN, BEGGING FOR AID...
THEY ARE CALLING MY NAME.

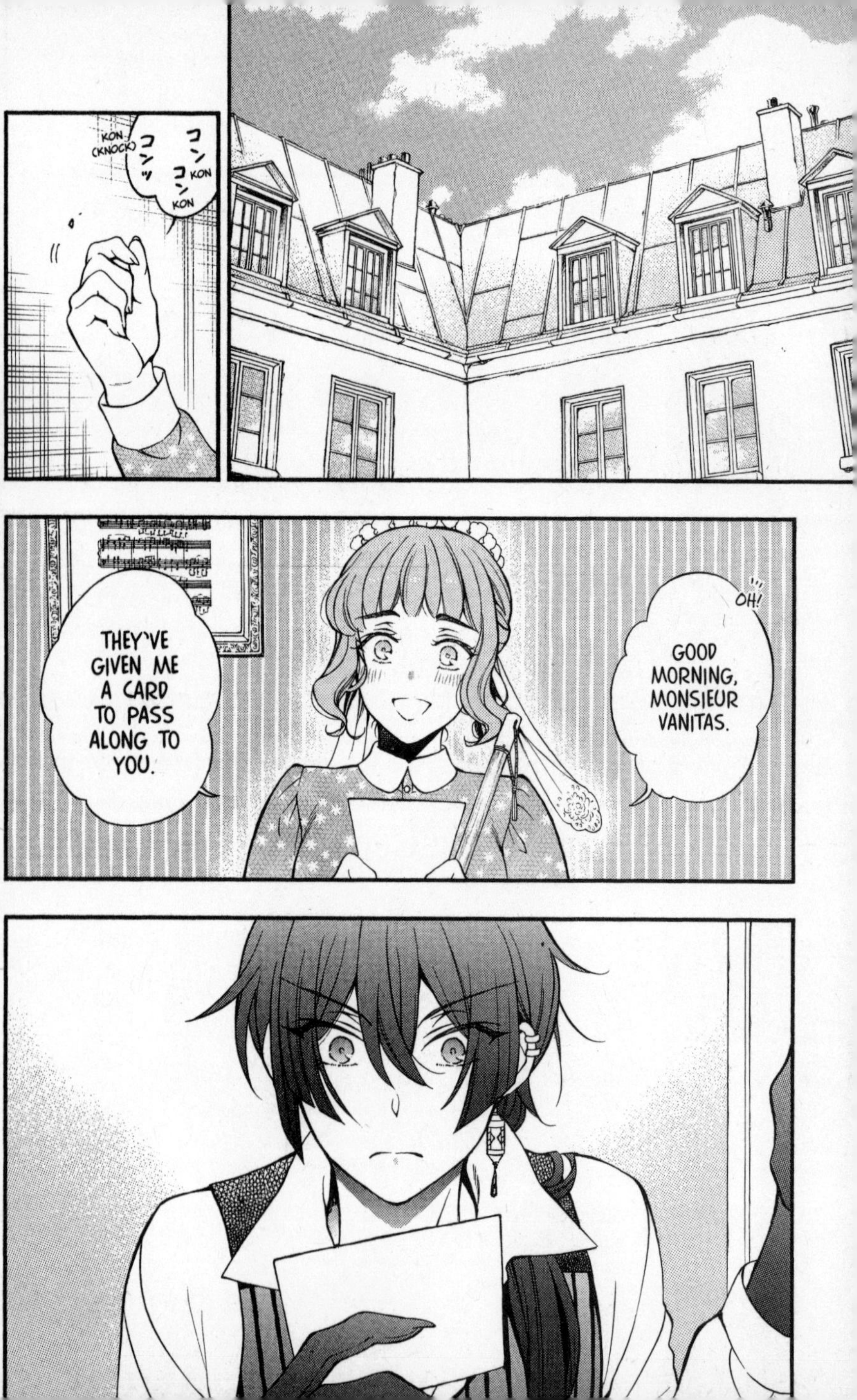
コン KON
コン KON
コンッ KON (KNOCK)
OH!
GOOD MORNING, MONSIEUR VANITAS.
THEY'VE GIVEN ME A CARD TO PASS ALONG TO YOU.

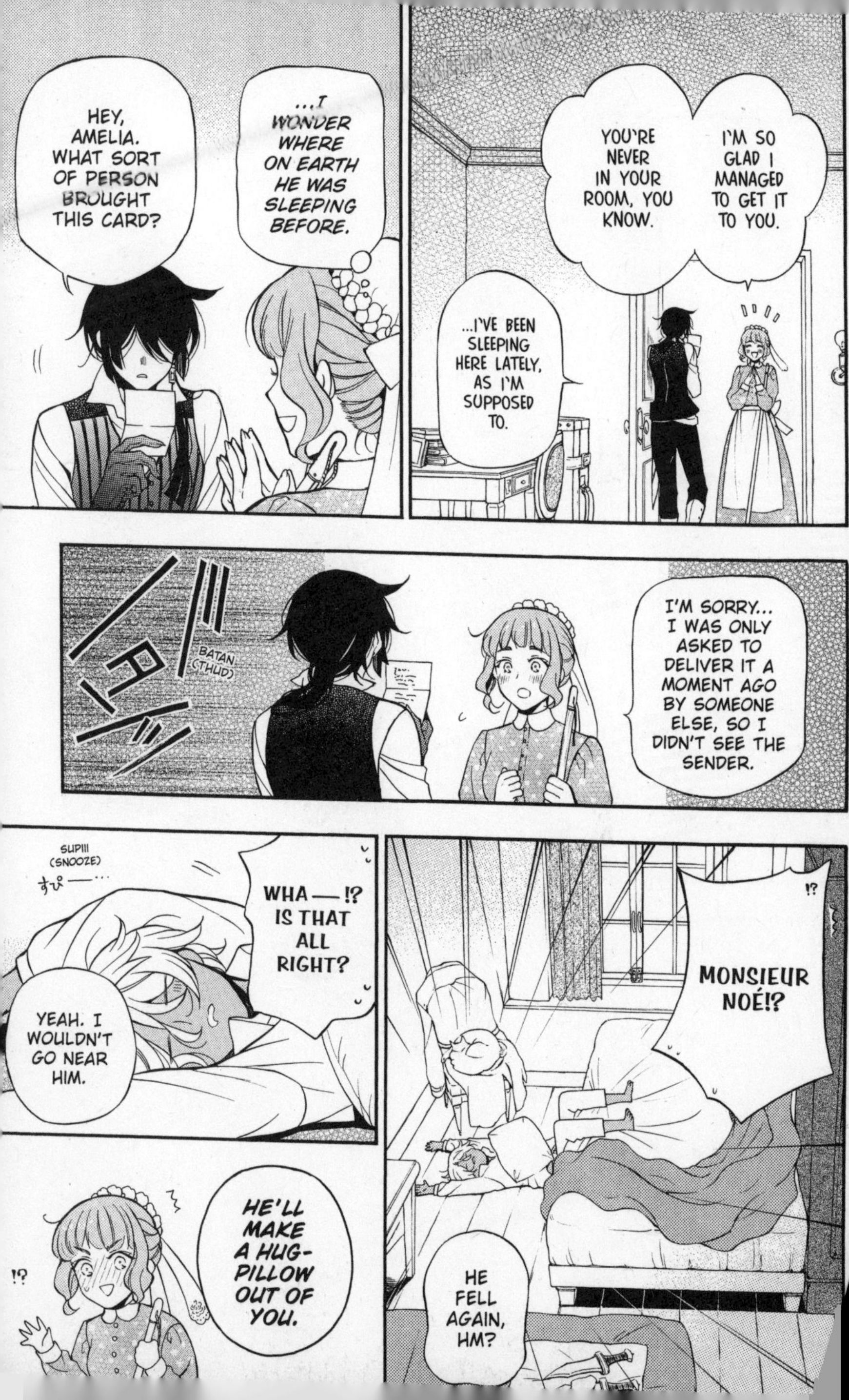
I'M SO GLAD I MANAGED TO GET IT TO YOU.
YOU'RE NEVER IN YOUR ROOM, YOU KNOW.
...I'VE BEEN SLEEPING HERE LATELY, AS I'M SUPPOSED TO.
...I WONDER WHERE ON EARTH HE WAS SLEEPING BEFORE.
HEY, AMELIA. WHAT SORT OF PERSON BROUGHT THIS CARD?
I'M SORRY... I WAS ONLY ASKED TO DELIVER IT A MOMENT AGO BY SOMEONE ELSE, SO I DIDN'T SEE THE SENDER.
BATAN (THUD)
!?
MONSIEUR NOÉ!?
HE FELL AGAIN, HM?
SUPIII (SNOOZE)
すぴー…
WHA—!? IS THAT ALL RIGHT?
YEAH. I WOULDN'T GO NEAR HIM.
HE'LL MAKE A HUG-PILLOW OUT OF YOU.
!?

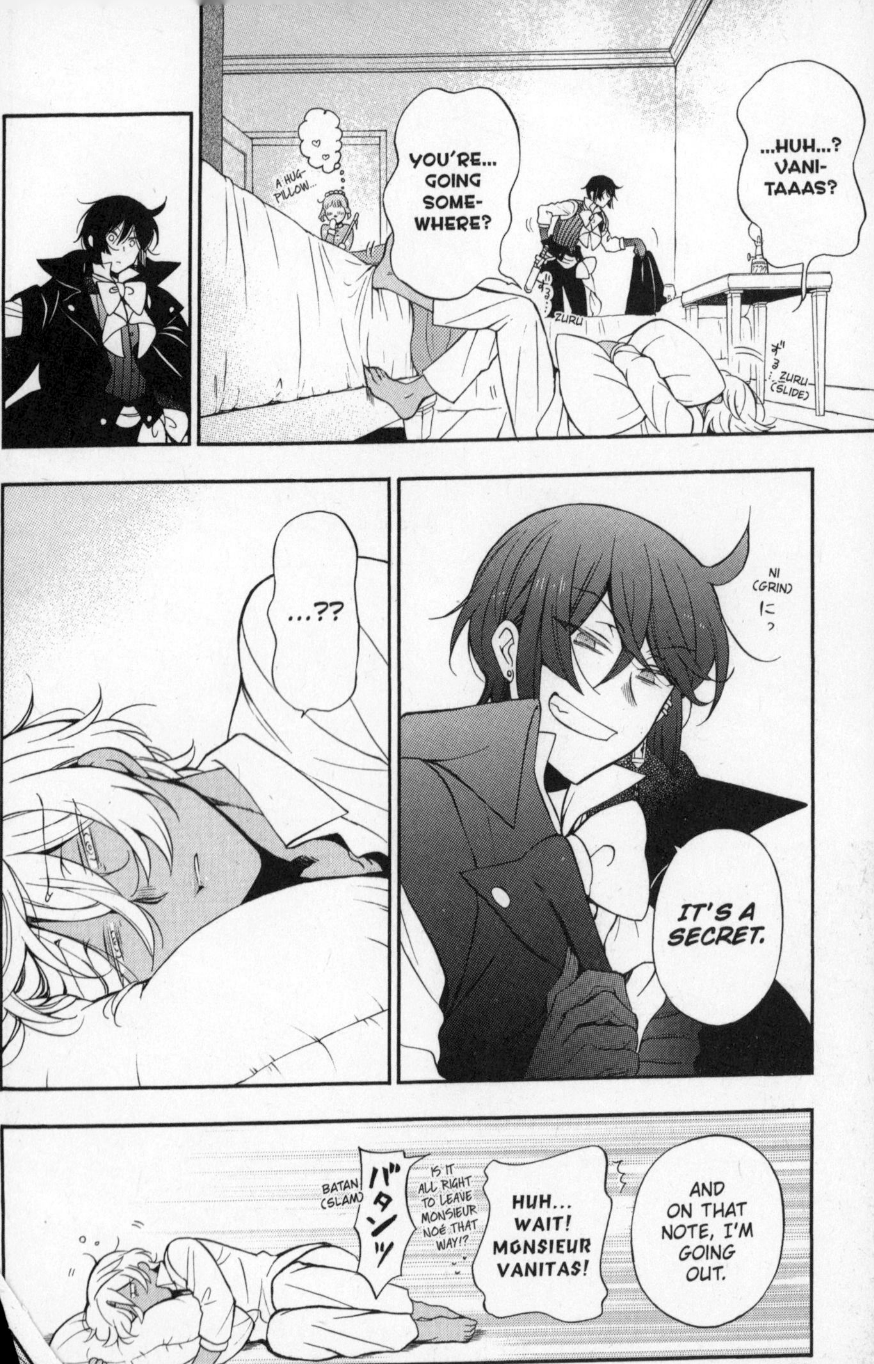
...HUH...? VANI-TAAAS?
YOU'RE... GOING SOME-WHERE?
A HUG-PILLOW...
ずる... ZURU
ずる... ZURU (SLIDE)
NI (GRIN) にっ
IT'S A SECRET.
...??
AND ON THAT NOTE, I'M GOING OUT.
HUH... WAIT! MONSIEUR VANITAS!
IS IT ALL RIGHT TO LEAVE MONSIEUR NOÉ THAT WAY!?
バタンッ
BATAN (SLAM)

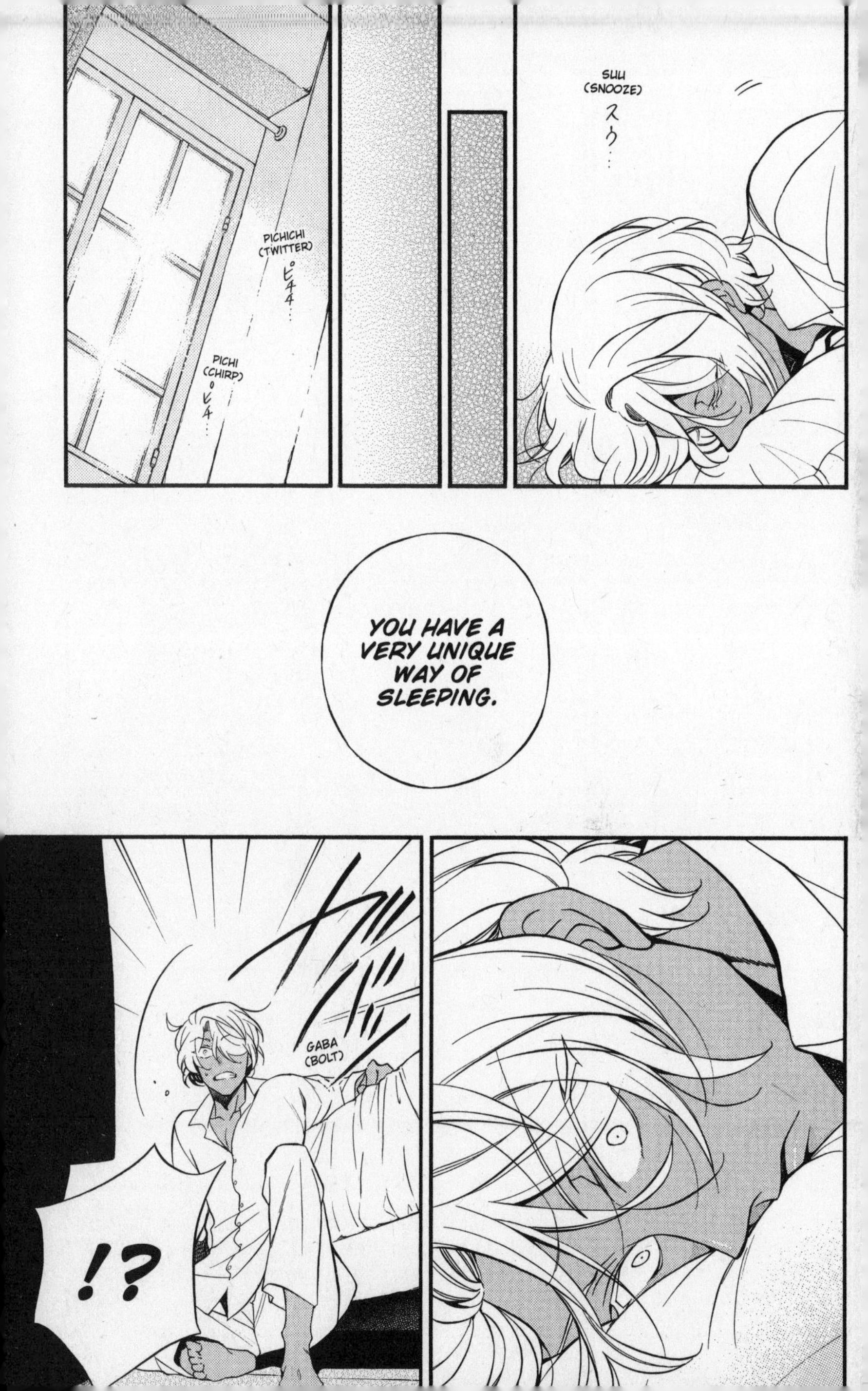
SUU (SNOOZE)
スゥ…
PICHICHI (TWITTER)
ピチチ…
PICHI (CHIRP)
ピチ…
YOU HAVE A VERY UNIQUE WAY OF SLEEPING.
GABA (BOLT)
!?

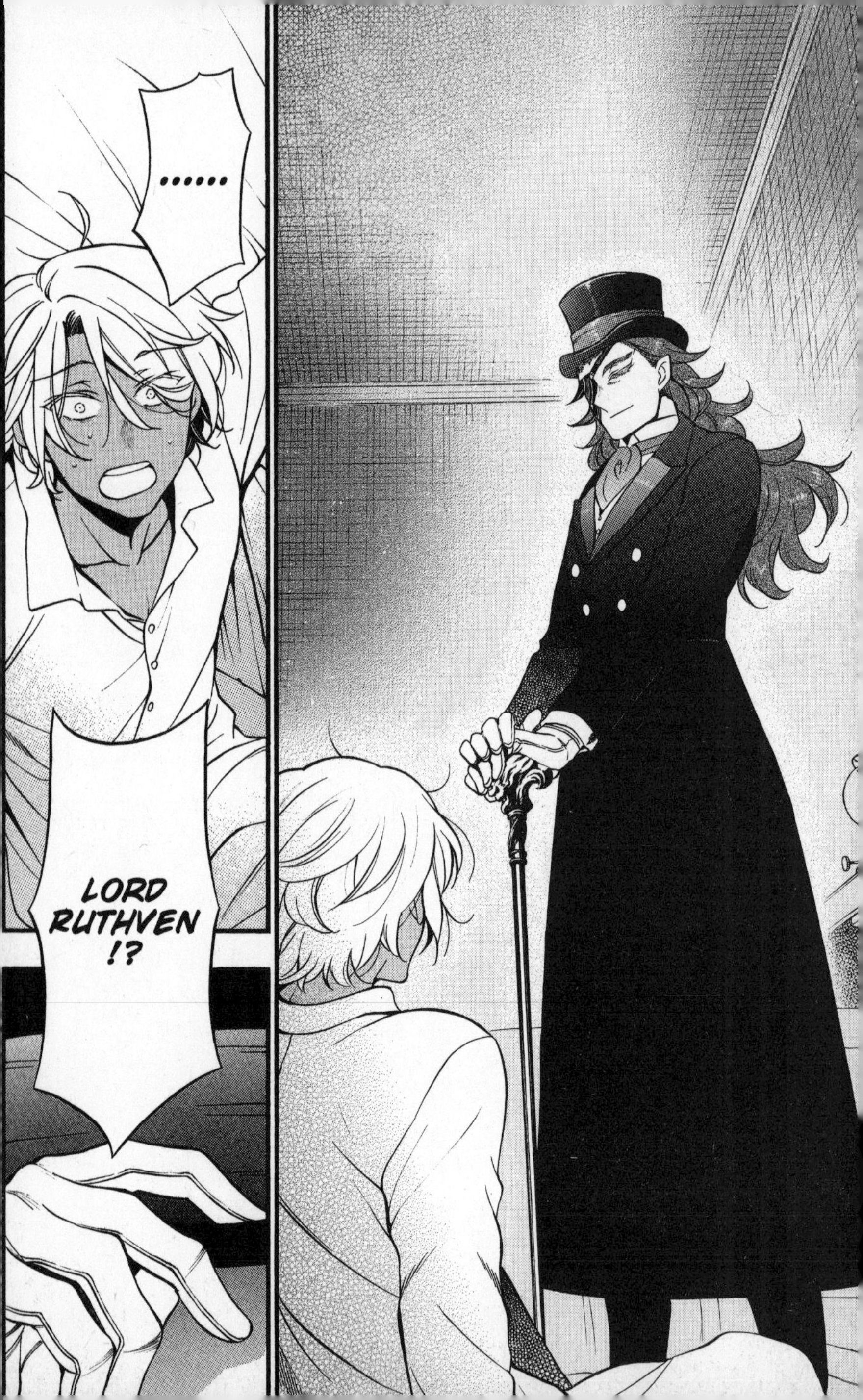
......
LORD RUTHVEN !?

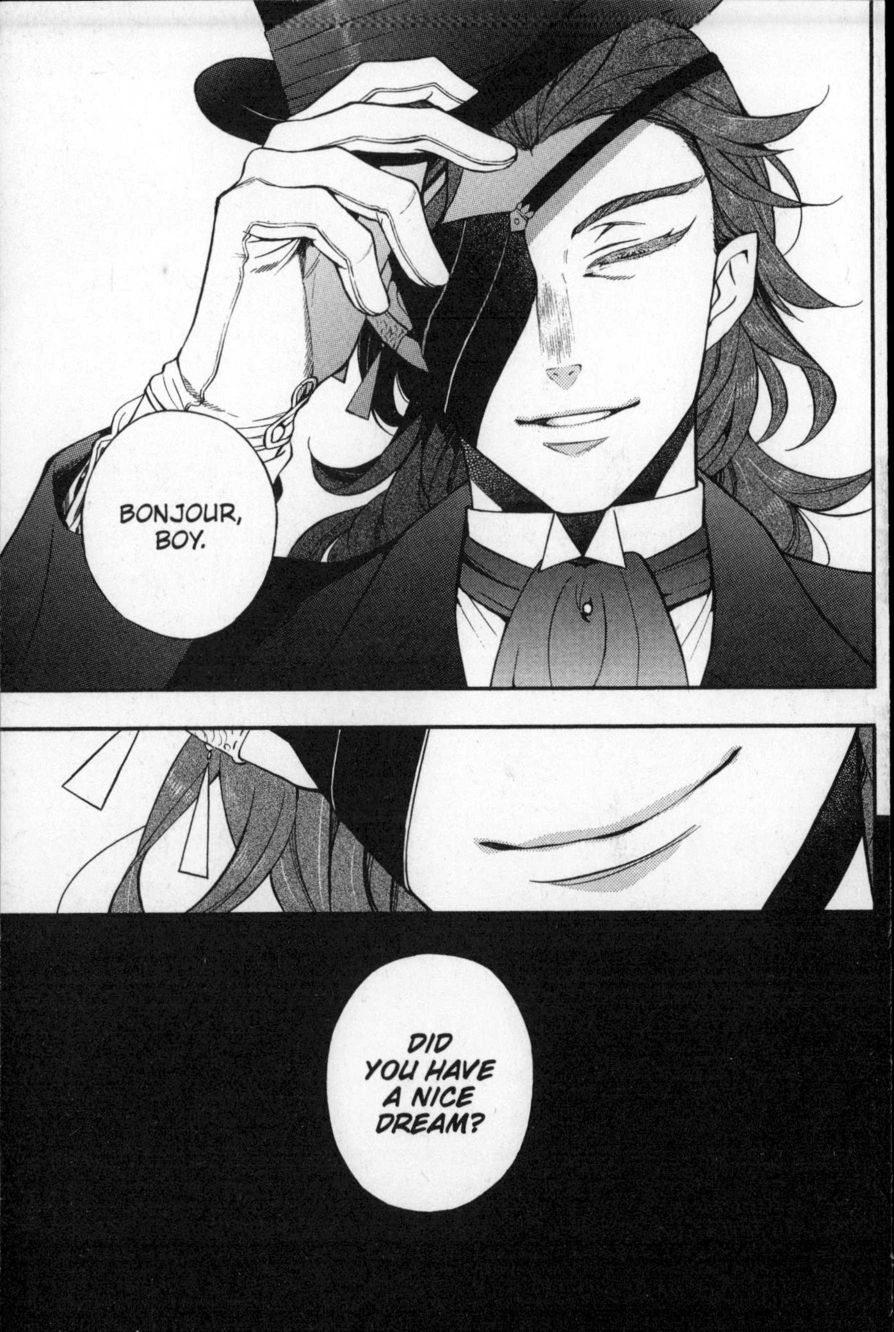
BONJOUR, BOY.
DID YOU HAVE A NICE DREAM?

# MÉMOIRE 19

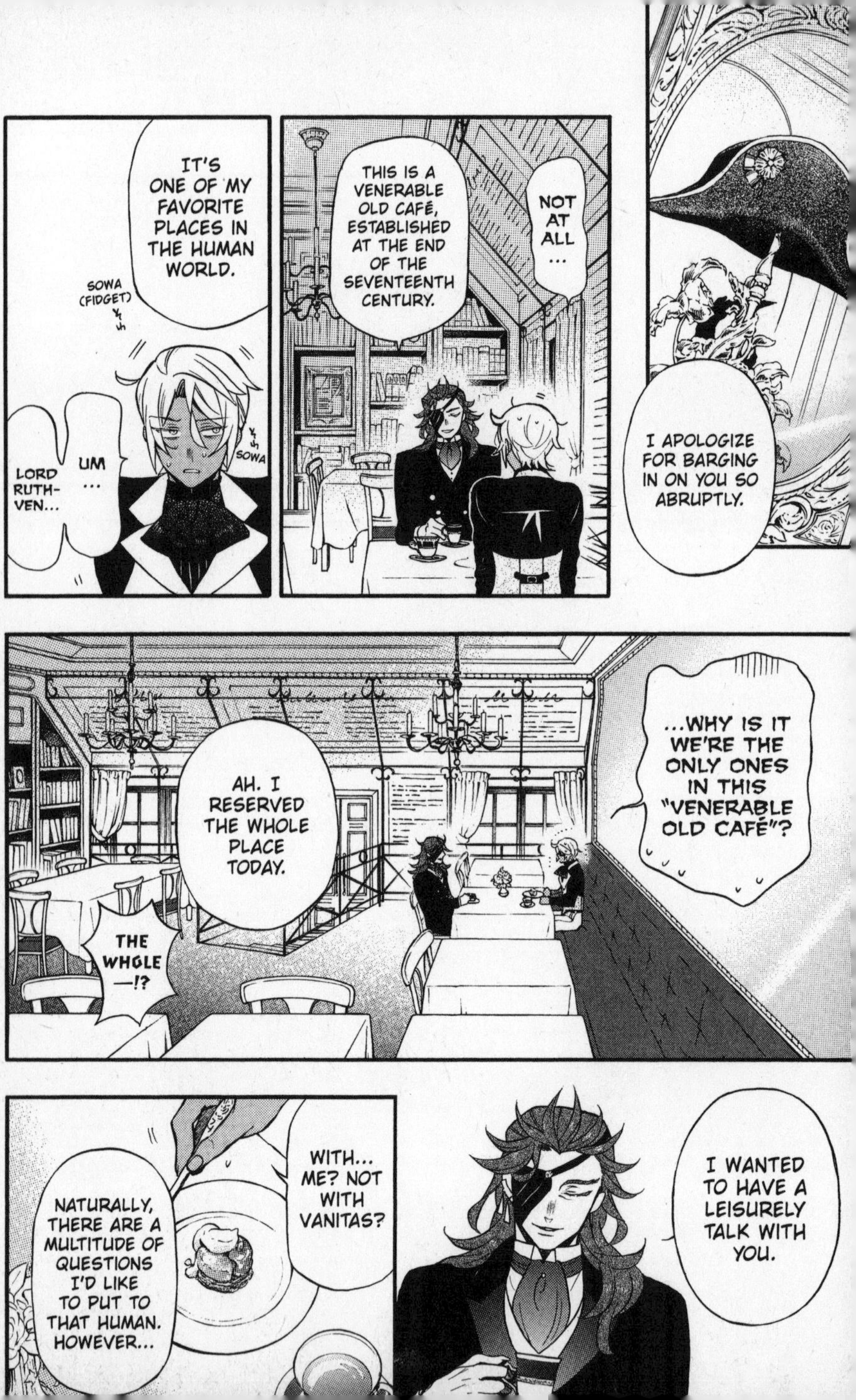
I APOLOGIZE FOR BARGING IN ON YOU SO ABRUPTLY.
NOT AT ALL...
THIS IS A VENERABLE OLD CAFÉ, ESTABLISHED AT THE END OF THE SEVENTEENTH CENTURY.
IT'S ONE OF MY FAVORITE PLACES IN THE HUMAN WORLD.
SOWA (FIDGET)
SOWA
UM...
LORD RUTHVEN...
...WHY IS IT WE'RE THE ONLY ONES IN THIS "VENERABLE OLD CAFÉ"?
AH. I RESERVED THE WHOLE PLACE TODAY.
THE WHOLE—!?
I WANTED TO HAVE A LEISURELY TALK WITH YOU.
WITH... ME? NOT WITH VANITAS?
NATURALLY, THERE ARE A MULTITUDE OF QUESTIONS I'D LIKE TO PUT TO THAT HUMAN. HOWEVER...

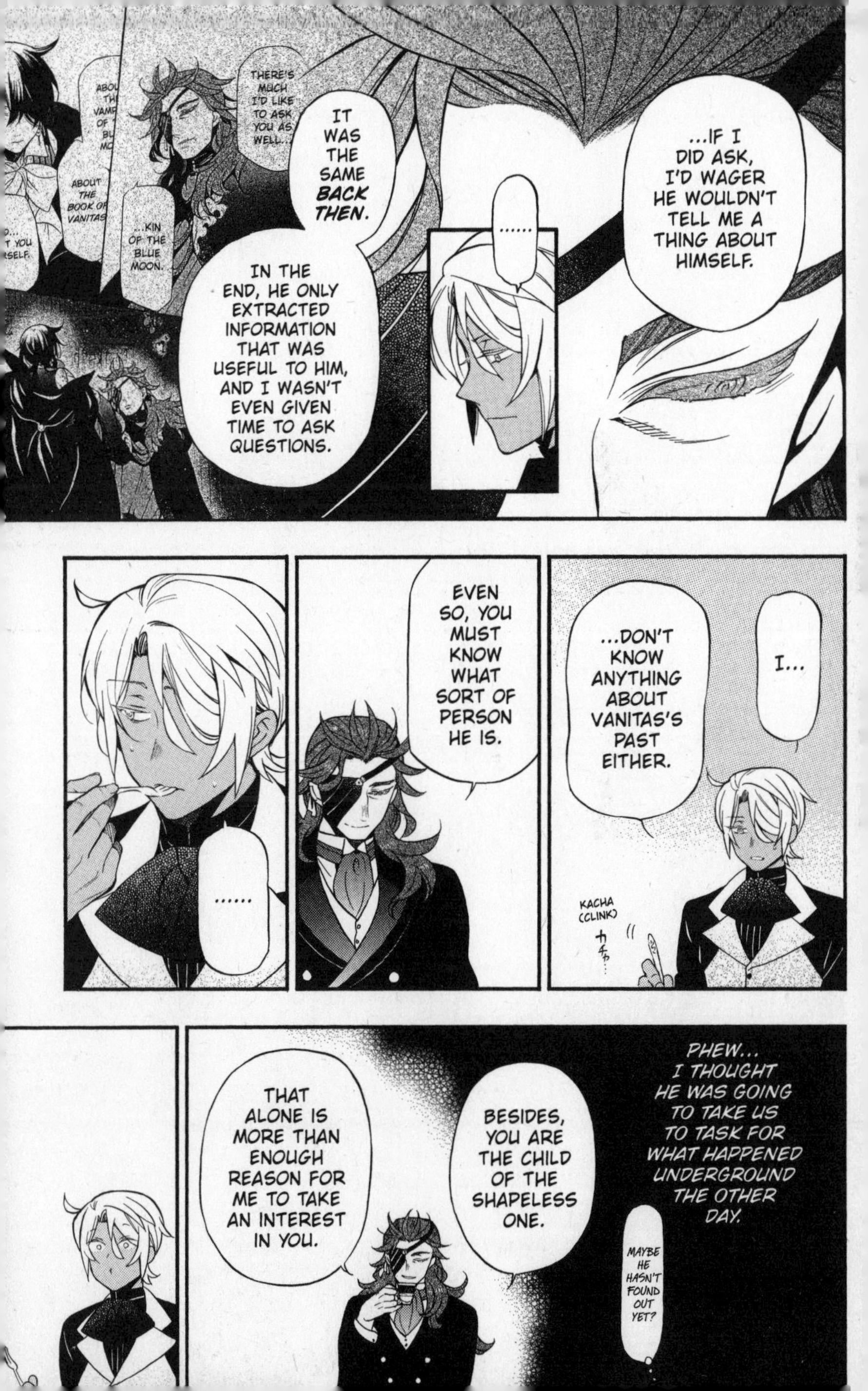
...IF I DID ASK, I'D WAGER HE WOULDN'T TELL ME A THING ABOUT HIMSELF.
......
IT WAS THE SAME **BACK THEN**.
THERE'S MUCH I'D LIKE TO ASK YOU AS WELL...
...KIN OF THE BLUE MOON.
ABOUT THE BOOK OF VANITAS
IN THE END, HE ONLY EXTRACTED INFORMATION THAT WAS USEFUL TO HIM, AND I WASN'T EVEN GIVEN TIME TO ASK QUESTIONS.
I...
...DON'T KNOW ANYTHING ABOUT VANITAS'S PAST EITHER.
KACHA (CLINK)
EVEN SO, YOU MUST KNOW WHAT SORT OF PERSON HE IS.
......
*PHEW... I THOUGHT HE WAS GOING TO TAKE US TO TASK FOR WHAT HAPPENED UNDERGROUND THE OTHER DAY.*
MAYBE HE HASN'T FOUND OUT YET?
BESIDES, YOU ARE THE CHILD OF THE SHAPELESS ONE.
THAT ALONE IS MORE THAN ENOUGH REASON FOR ME TO TAKE AN INTEREST IN YOU.

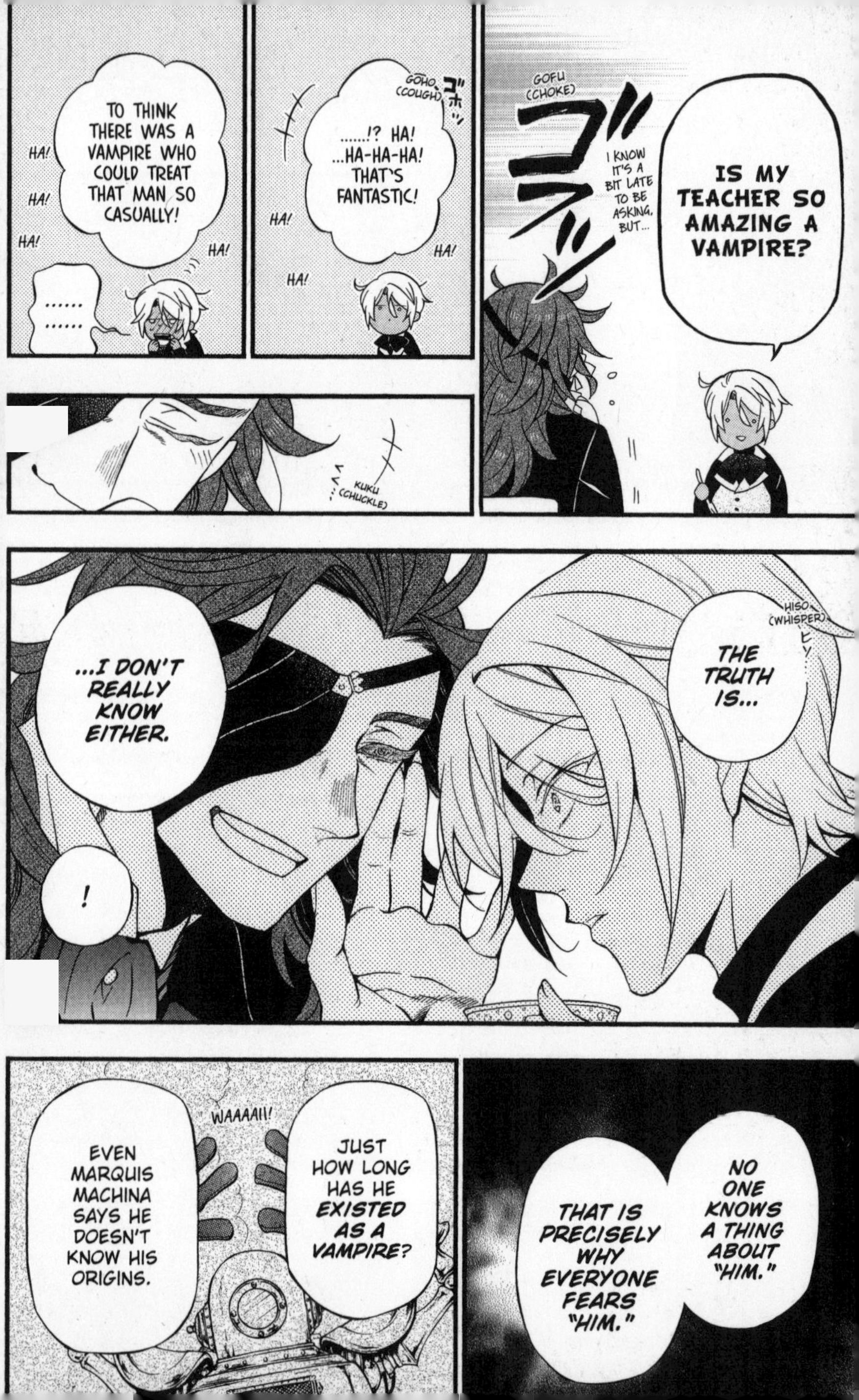
I KNOW IT'S A BIT LATE TO BE ASKING, BUT...
IS MY TEACHER SO AMAZING A VAMPIRE?
GOFU (CHOKE)
GOHO (COUGH)
......!? HA! ...HA-HA-HA! THAT'S FANTASTIC!
HA!
HA!
HA!
TO THINK THERE WAS A VAMPIRE WHO COULD TREAT THAT MAN SO CASUALLY!
HA!
HA!
HA!
HA!
...... ......
KUKU (CHUCKLE)
HISO (WHISPER)
THE TRUTH IS...
...I DON'T REALLY KNOW EITHER.
!
NO ONE KNOWS A THING ABOUT "HIM."
THAT IS PRECISELY WHY EVERYONE FEARS "HIM."
WAAAAII!
JUST HOW LONG HAS HE EXISTED AS A VAMPIRE?
EVEN MARQUIS MACHINA SAYS HE DOESN'T KNOW HIS ORIGINS.

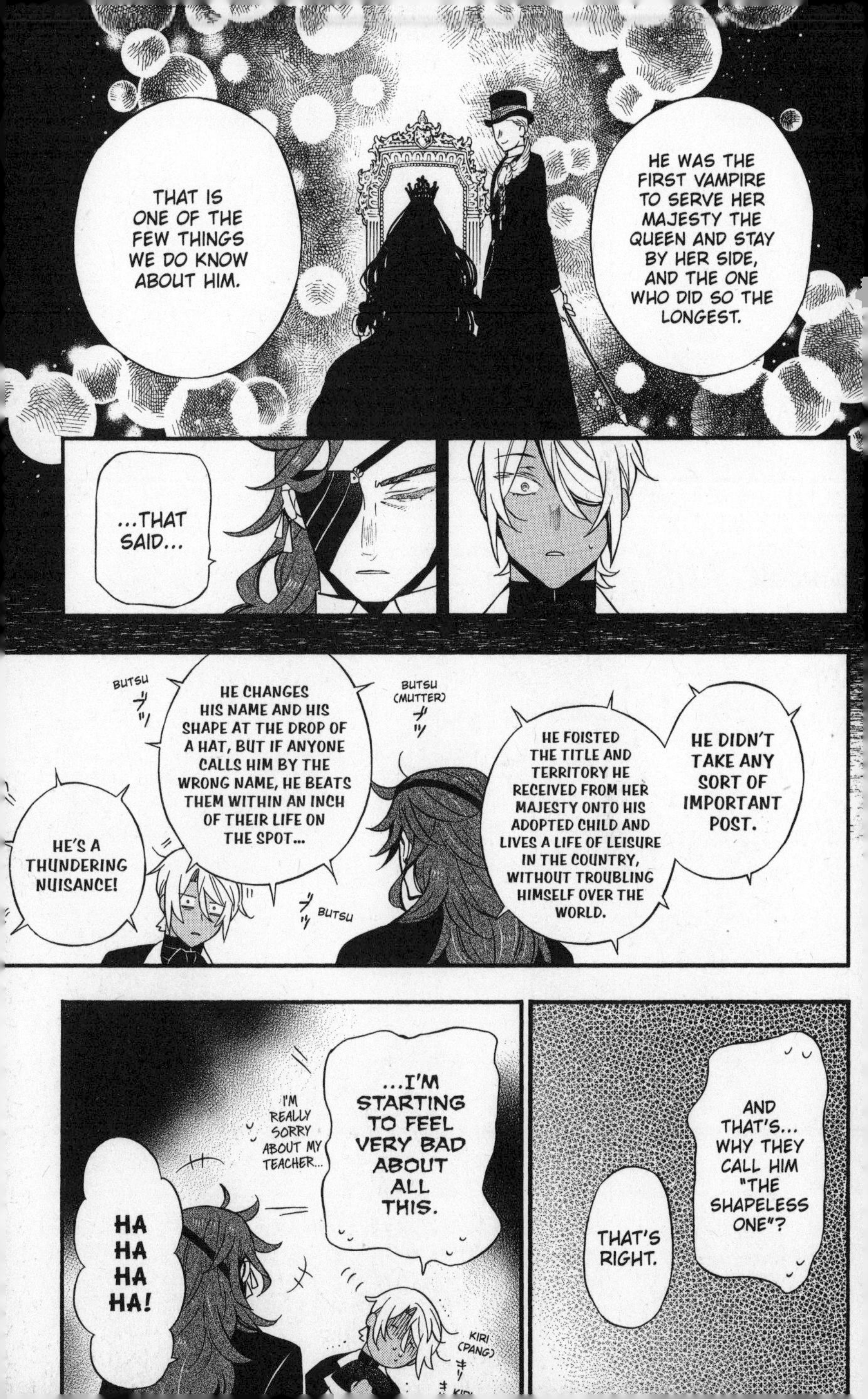
HE WAS THE FIRST VAMPIRE TO SERVE HER MAJESTY THE QUEEN AND STAY BY HER SIDE, AND THE ONE WHO DID SO THE LONGEST.
THAT IS ONE OF THE FEW THINGS WE DO KNOW ABOUT HIM.
...THAT SAID...
HE DIDN'T TAKE ANY SORT OF IMPORTANT POST.
HE FOISTED THE TITLE AND TERRITORY HE RECEIVED FROM HER MAJESTY ONTO HIS ADOPTED CHILD AND LIVES A LIFE OF LEISURE IN THE COUNTRY, WITHOUT TROUBLING HIMSELF OVER THE WORLD.
BUTSU (MUTTER)
HE CHANGES HIS NAME AND HIS SHAPE AT THE DROP OF A HAT, BUT IF ANYONE CALLS HIM BY THE WRONG NAME, HE BEATS THEM WITHIN AN INCH OF THEIR LIFE ON THE SPOT...
BUTSU
BUTSU
HE'S A THUNDERING NUISANCE!
AND THAT'S... WHY THEY CALL HIM "THE SHAPELESS ONE"?
THAT'S RIGHT.
...I'M STARTING TO FEEL VERY BAD ABOUT ALL THIS.
I'M REALLY SORRY ABOUT MY TEACHER...
HA HA HA HA!
KIRI (PANG)

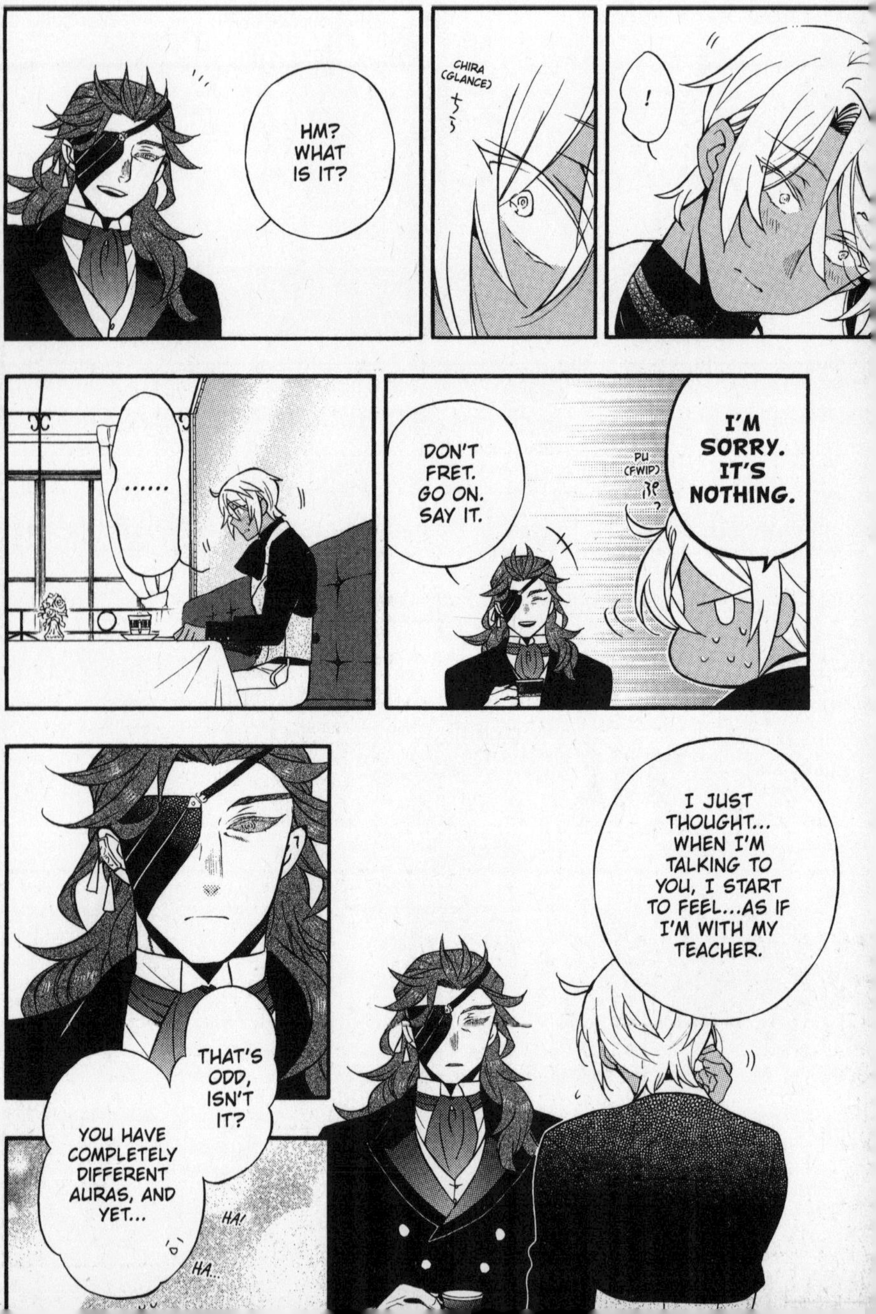
!
CHIRA (GLANCE)
HM? WHAT IS IT?
I'M SORRY. IT'S NOTHING.
PU (FWIP)
DON'T FRET. GO ON. SAY IT.
......
I JUST THOUGHT... WHEN I'M TALKING TO YOU, I START TO FEEL...AS IF I'M WITH MY TEACHER.
THAT'S ODD, ISN'T IT?
YOU HAVE COMPLETELY DIFFERENT AURAS, AND YET...
HA!
HA...

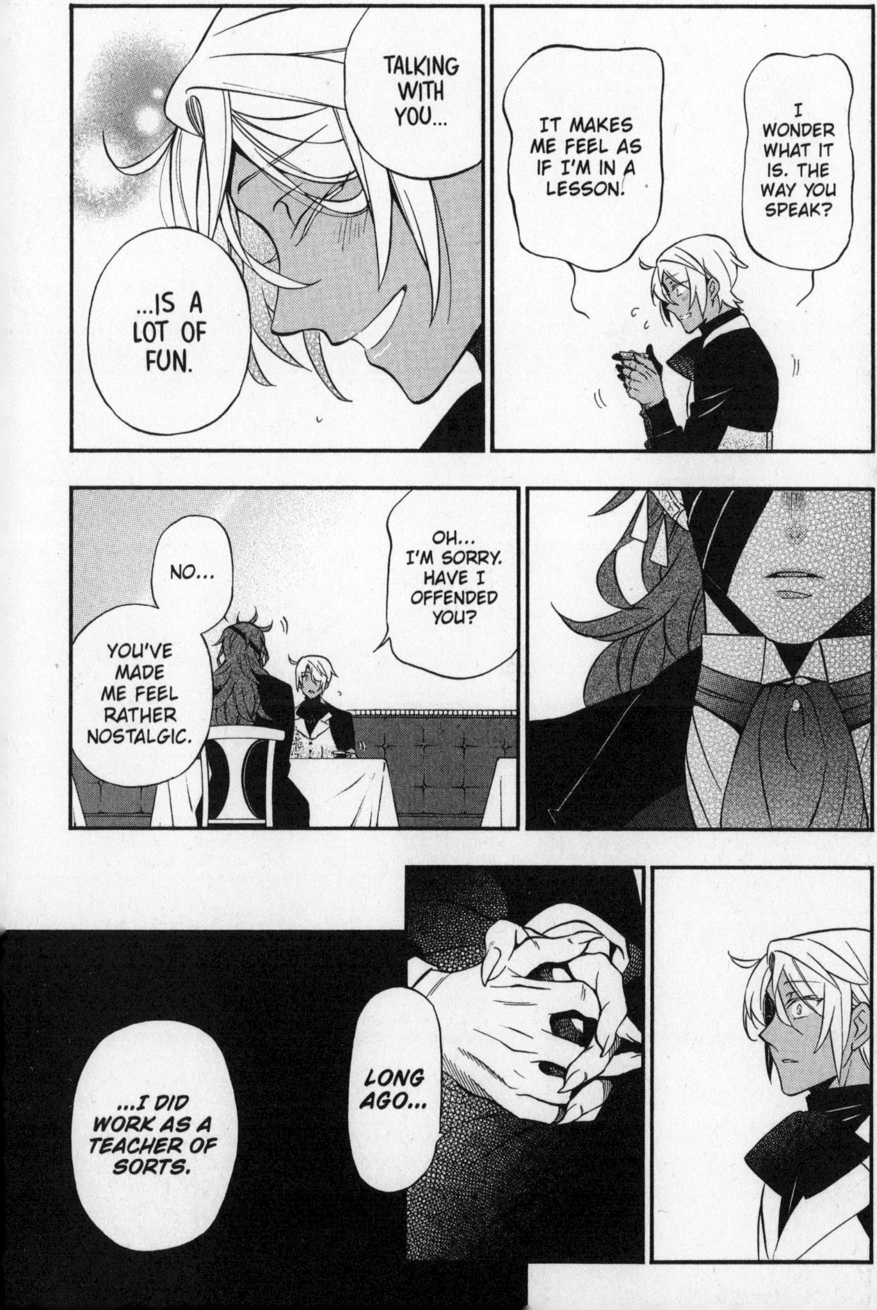
I WONDER WHAT IT IS. THE WAY YOU SPEAK?
IT MAKES ME FEEL AS IF I'M IN A LESSON.
TALKING WITH YOU...
...IS A LOT OF FUN.
OH... I'M SORRY. HAVE I OFFENDED YOU?
NO...
YOU'VE MADE ME FEEL RATHER NOSTALGIC.
LONG AGO...
...I DID WORK AS A TEACHER OF SORTS.

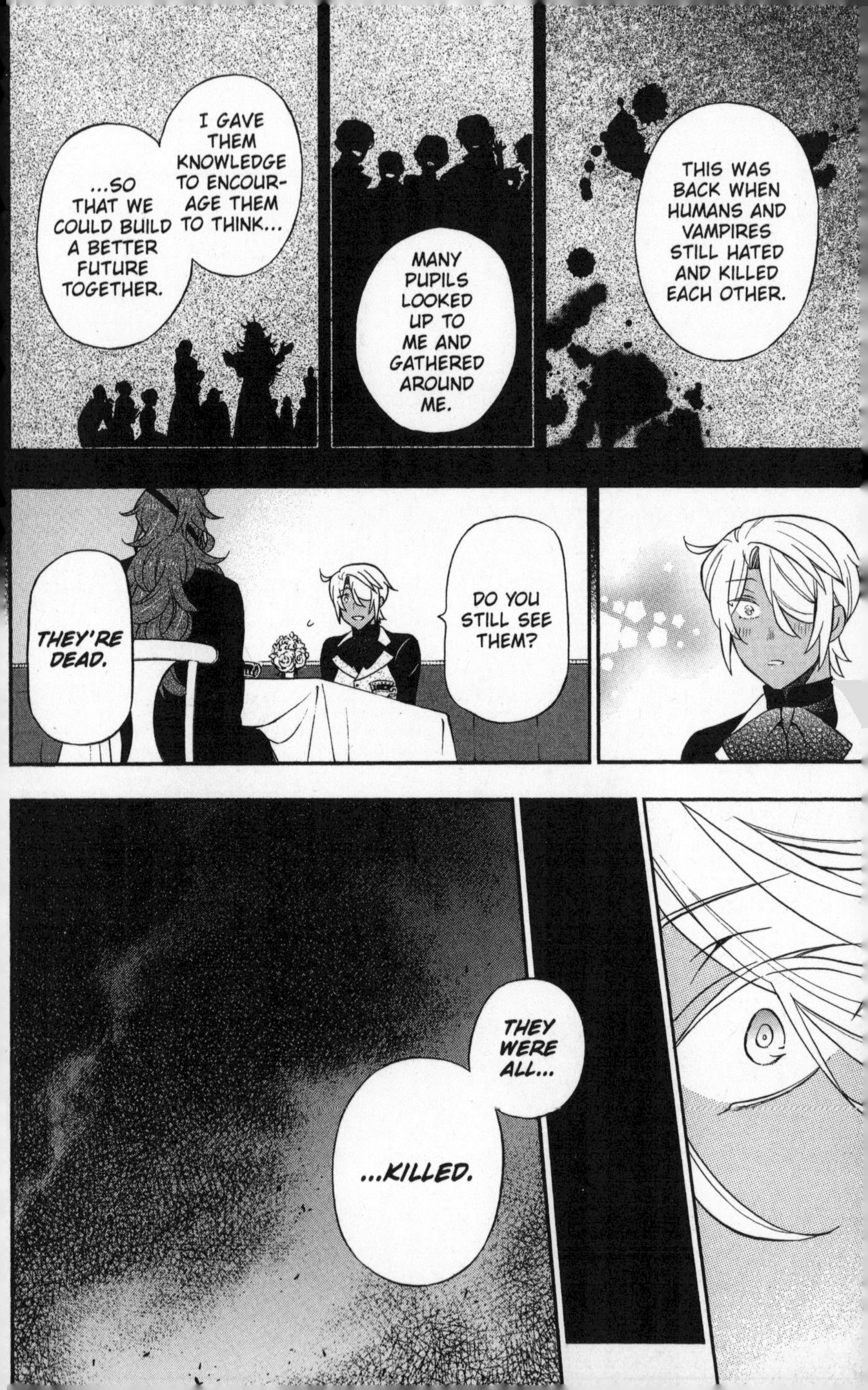
THIS WAS BACK WHEN HUMANS AND VAMPIRES STILL HATED AND KILLED EACH OTHER.
MANY PUPILS LOOKED UP TO ME AND GATHERED AROUND ME.
I GAVE THEM KNOWLEDGE TO ENCOURAGE THEM TO THINK...
...SO THAT WE COULD BUILD A BETTER FUTURE TOGETHER.
DO YOU STILL SEE THEM?
THEY'RE DEAD.
THEY WERE ALL...
...KILLED.

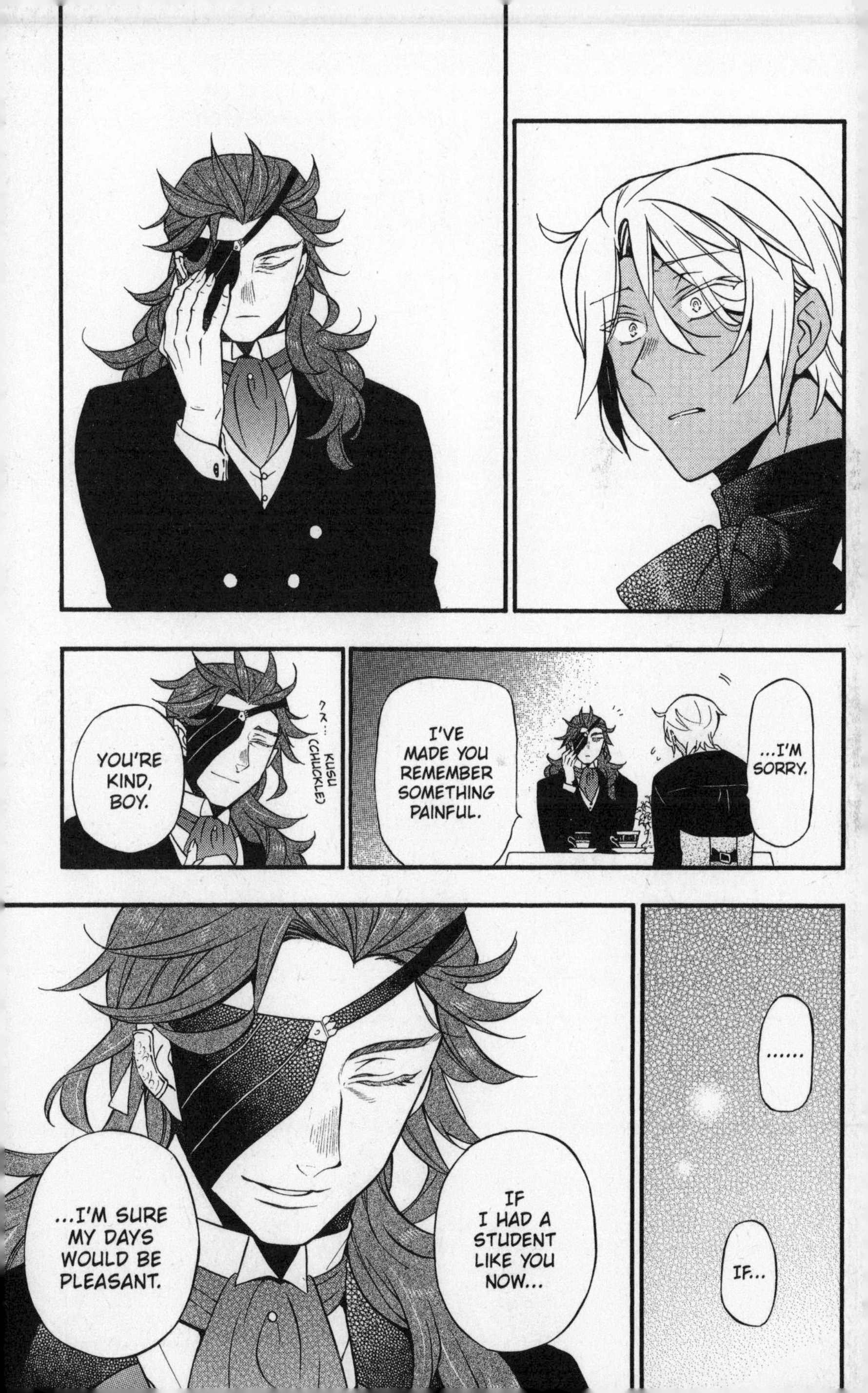
...I'M SORRY.
I'VE MADE YOU REMEMBER SOMETHING PAINFUL.
KUSU (CHUCKLE)
YOU'RE KIND, BOY.
......
IF...
IF I HAD A STUDENT LIKE YOU NOW...
...I'M SURE MY DAYS WOULD BE PLEASANT.

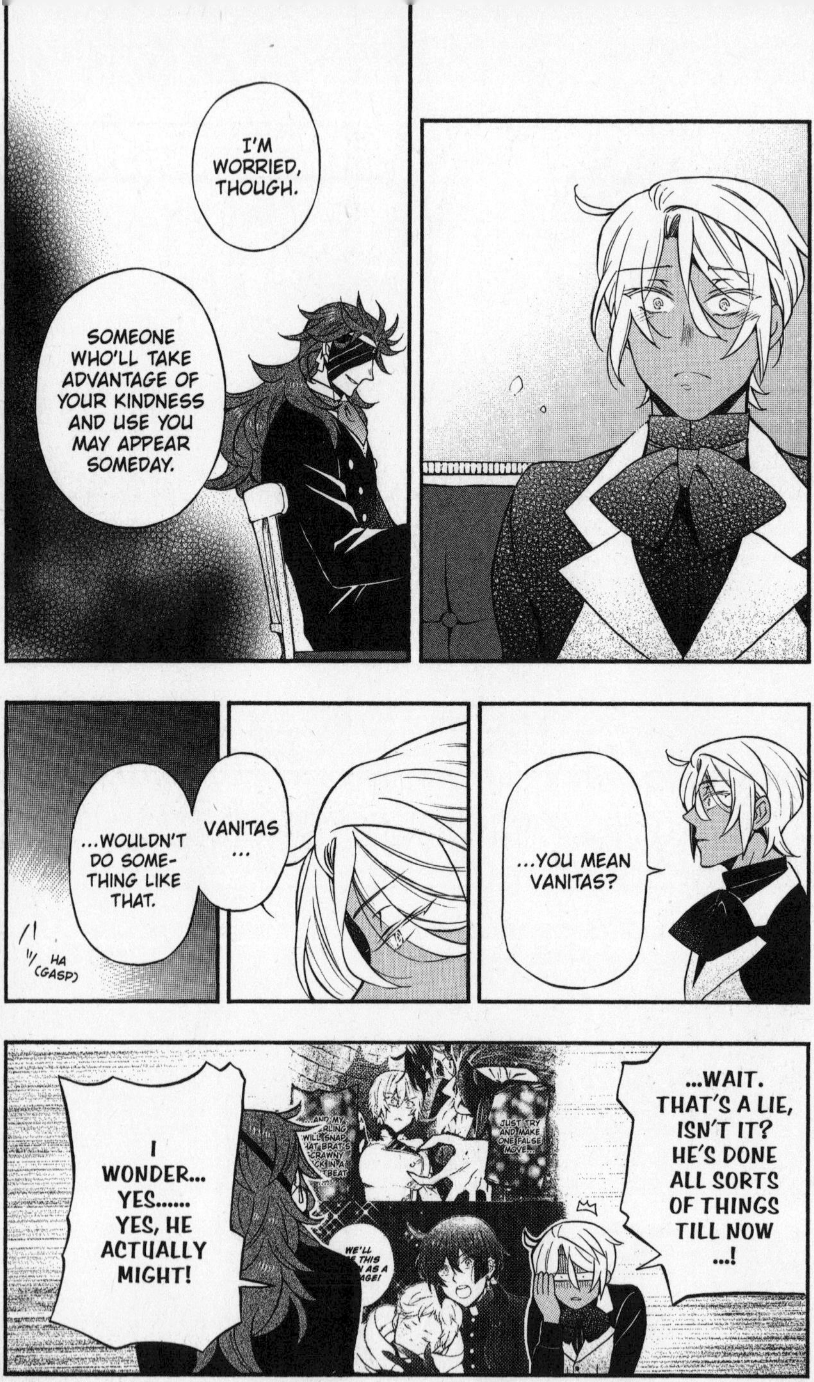
I'M WORRIED, THOUGH.
SOMEONE WHO'LL TAKE ADVANTAGE OF YOUR KINDNESS AND USE YOU MAY APPEAR SOMEDAY.
...YOU MEAN VANITAS?
VANITAS ...
...WOULDN'T DO SOME-THING LIKE THAT.
HA (GASP)
...WAIT. THAT'S A LIE, ISN'T IT? HE'S DONE ALL SORTS OF THINGS TILL NOW ...!
JUST TRY AND MAKE ONE FALSE MOVE...
I WONDER... YES...... YES, HE ACTUALLY MIGHT!

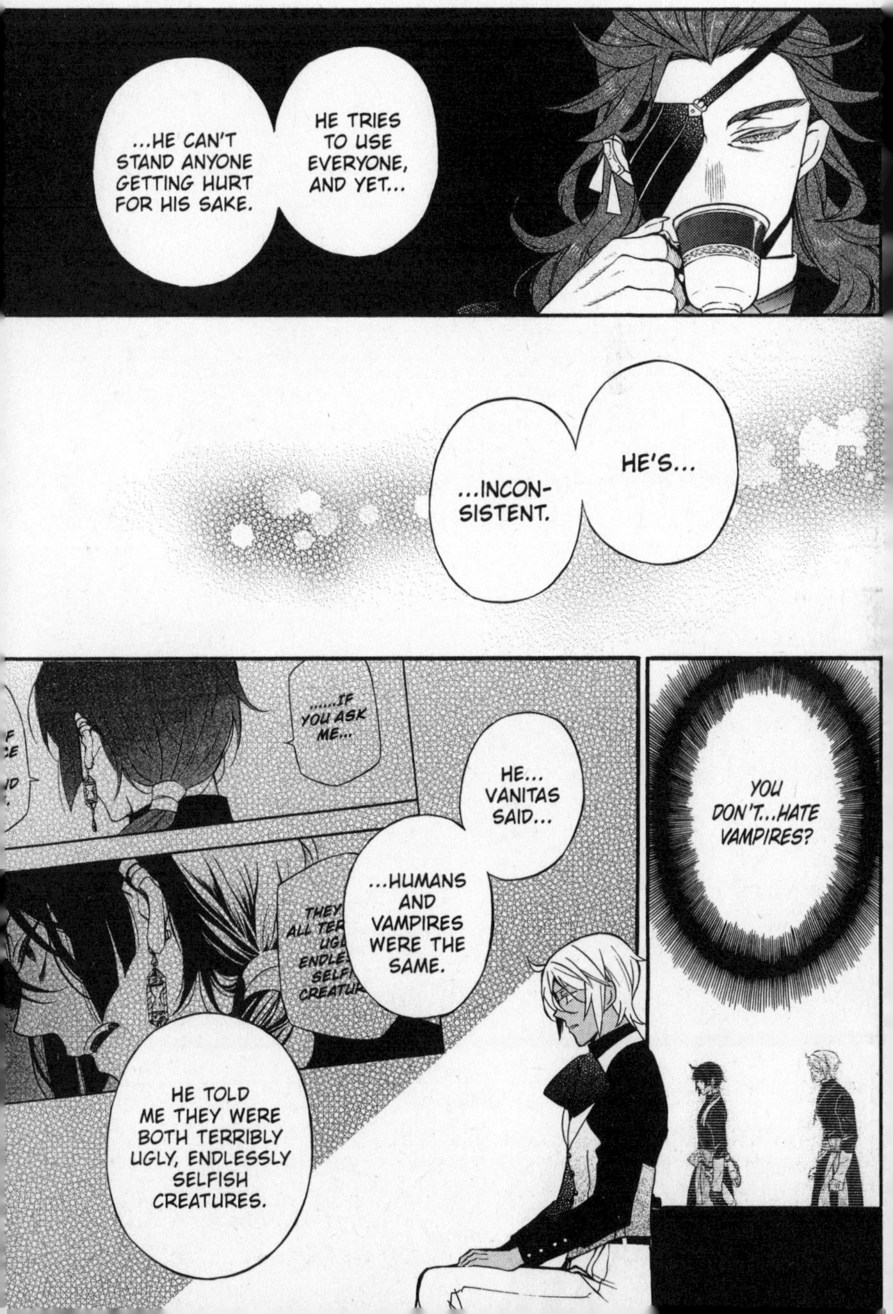
HE TRIES TO USE EVERYONE, AND YET...
...HE CAN'T STAND ANYONE GETTING HURT FOR HIS SAKE.
HE'S...
...INCON-SISTENT.
YOU DON'T...HATE VAMPIRES?
......IF YOU ASK ME...
HE... VANITAS SAID...
...HUMANS AND VAMPIRES WERE THE SAME.
HE TOLD ME THEY WERE BOTH TERRIBLY UGLY, ENDLESSLY SELFISH CREATURES.

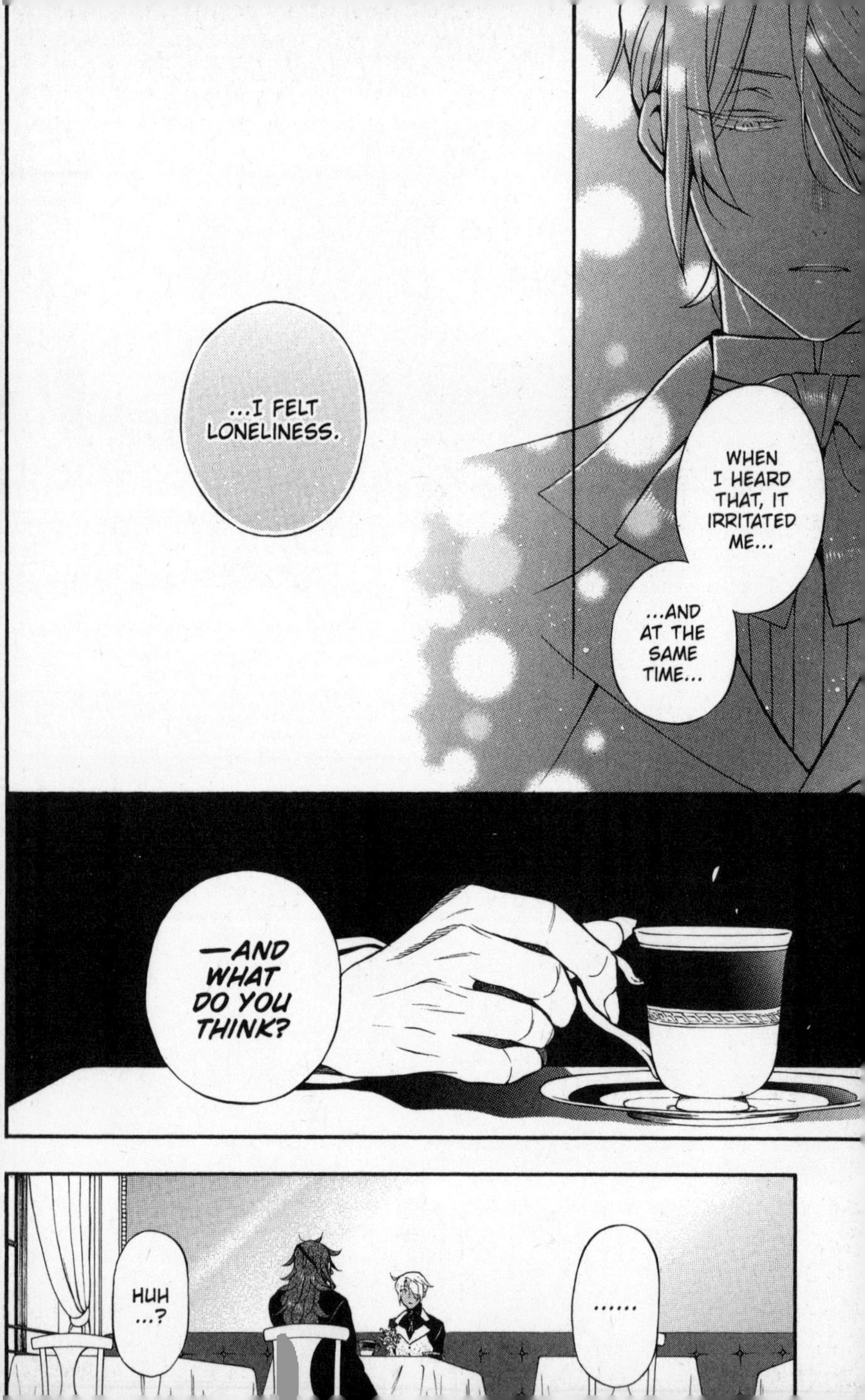
WHEN I HEARD THAT, IT IRRITATED ME...
...AND AT THE SAME TIME...
...I FELT LONELINESS.
—AND WHAT DO YOU THINK?
......
HUH ...?

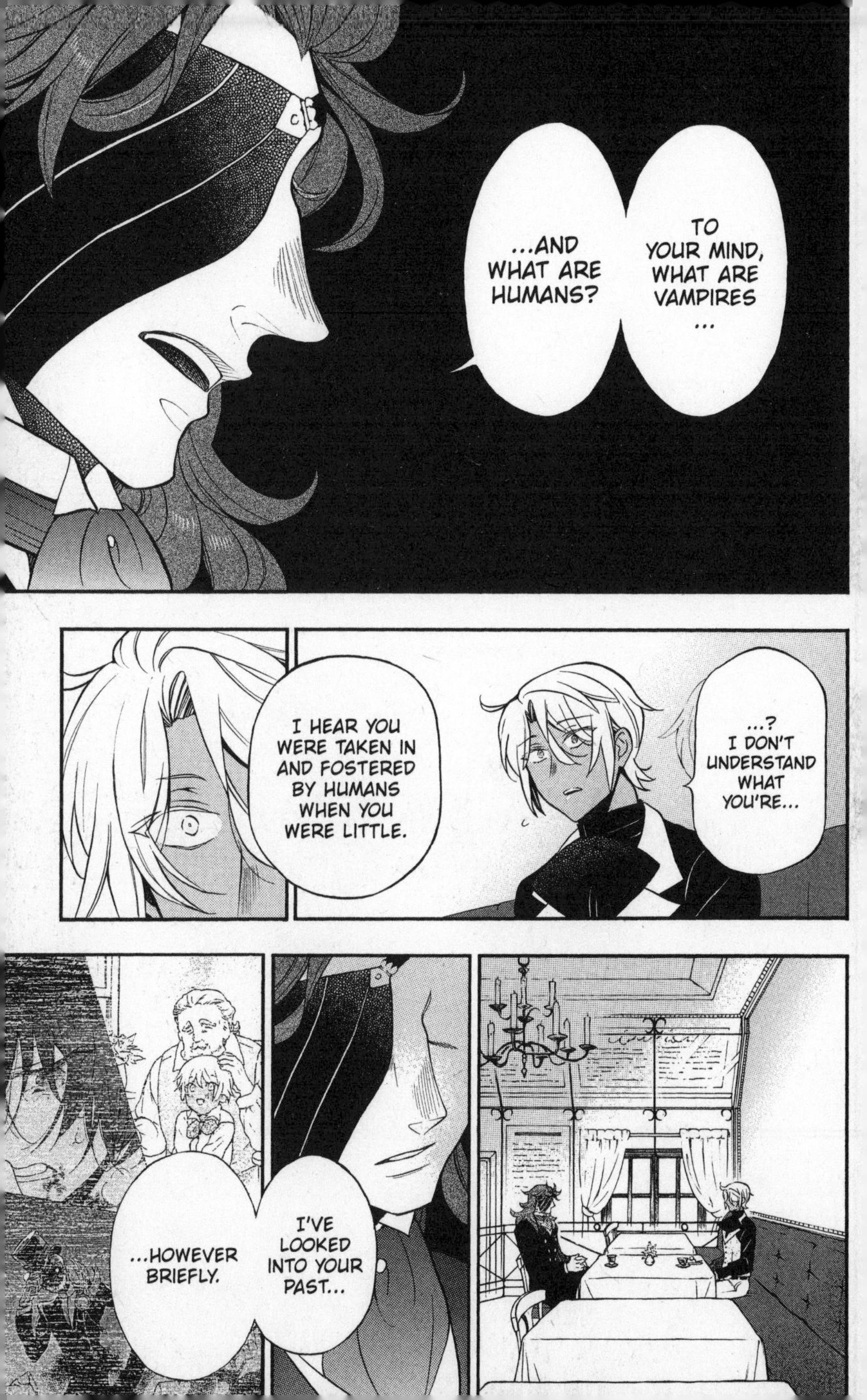
TO YOUR MIND, WHAT ARE VAMPIRES...
...AND WHAT ARE HUMANS?
...? I DON'T UNDERSTAND WHAT YOU'RE...
I HEAR YOU WERE TAKEN IN AND FOSTERED BY HUMANS WHEN YOU WERE LITTLE.
I'VE LOOKED INTO YOUR PAST...
...HOWEVER BRIEFLY.

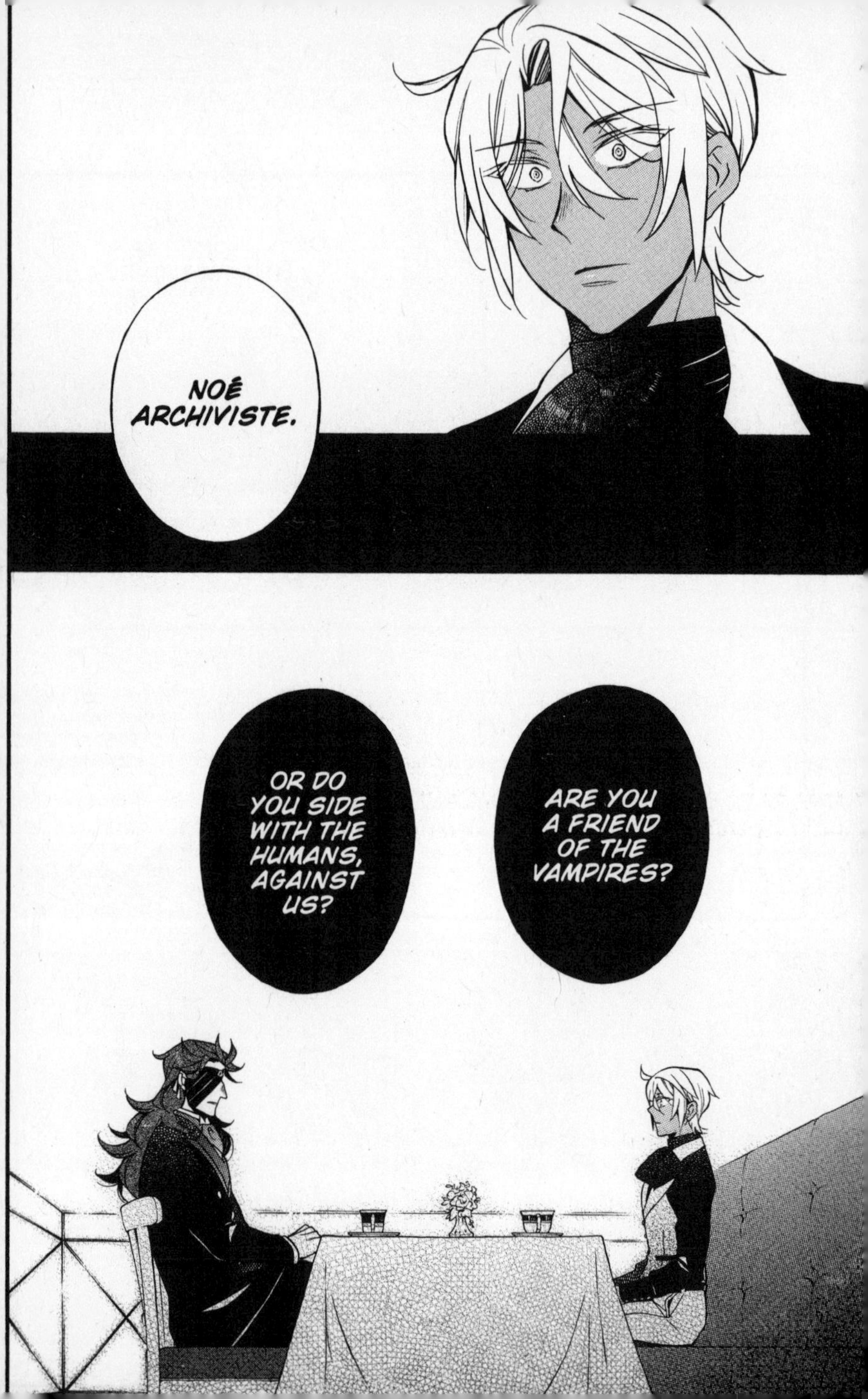
NOÉ ARCHIVISTE.
ARE YOU A FRIEND OF THE VAMPIRES?
OR DO YOU SIDE WITH THE HUMANS, AGAINST US?

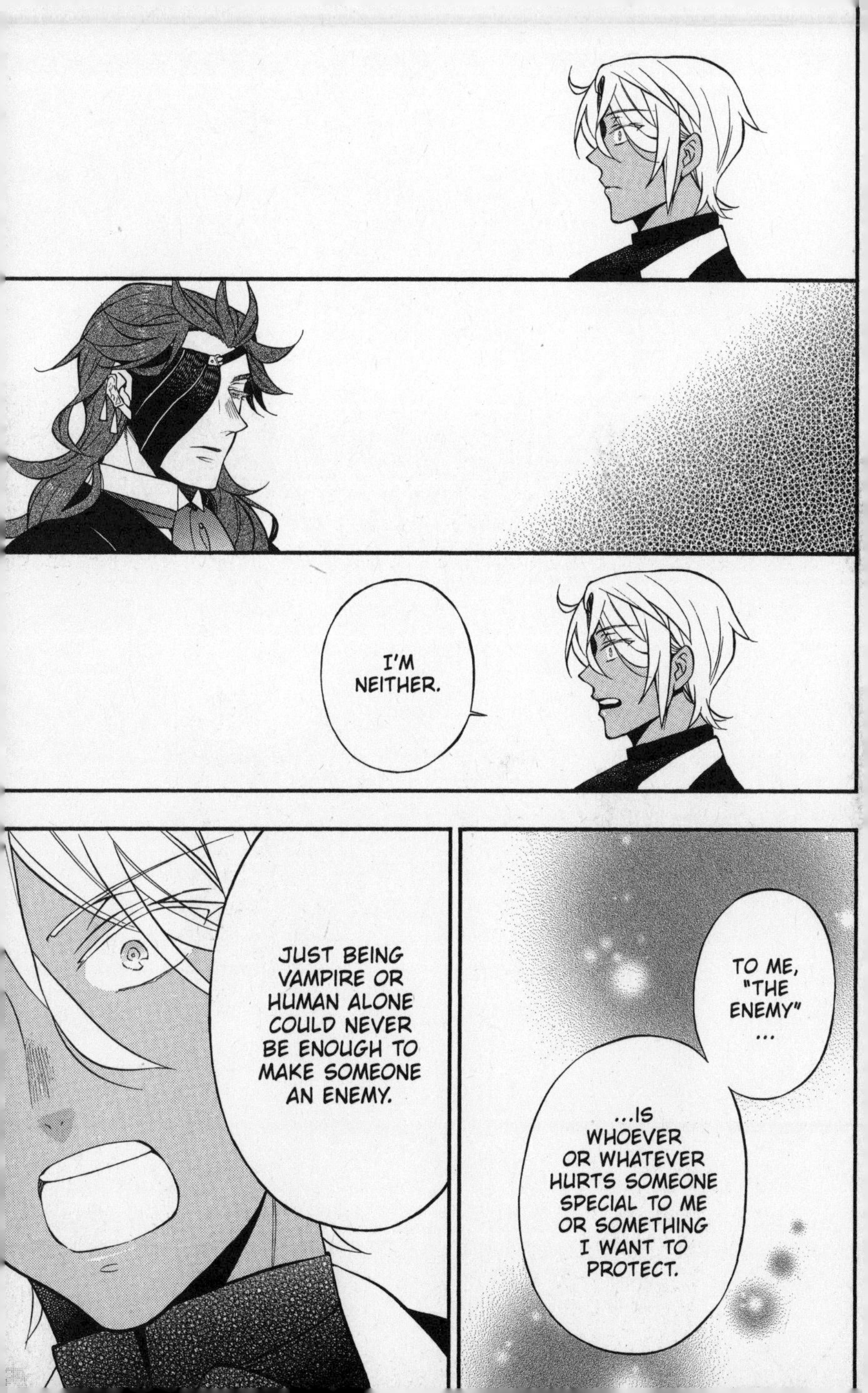
I'M NEITHER.
TO ME, "THE ENEMY"...
...IS WHOEVER OR WHATEVER HURTS SOMEONE SPECIAL TO ME OR SOMETHING I WANT TO PROTECT.
JUST BEING VAMPIRE OR HUMAN ALONE COULD NEVER BE ENOUGH TO MAKE SOMEONE AN ENEMY.

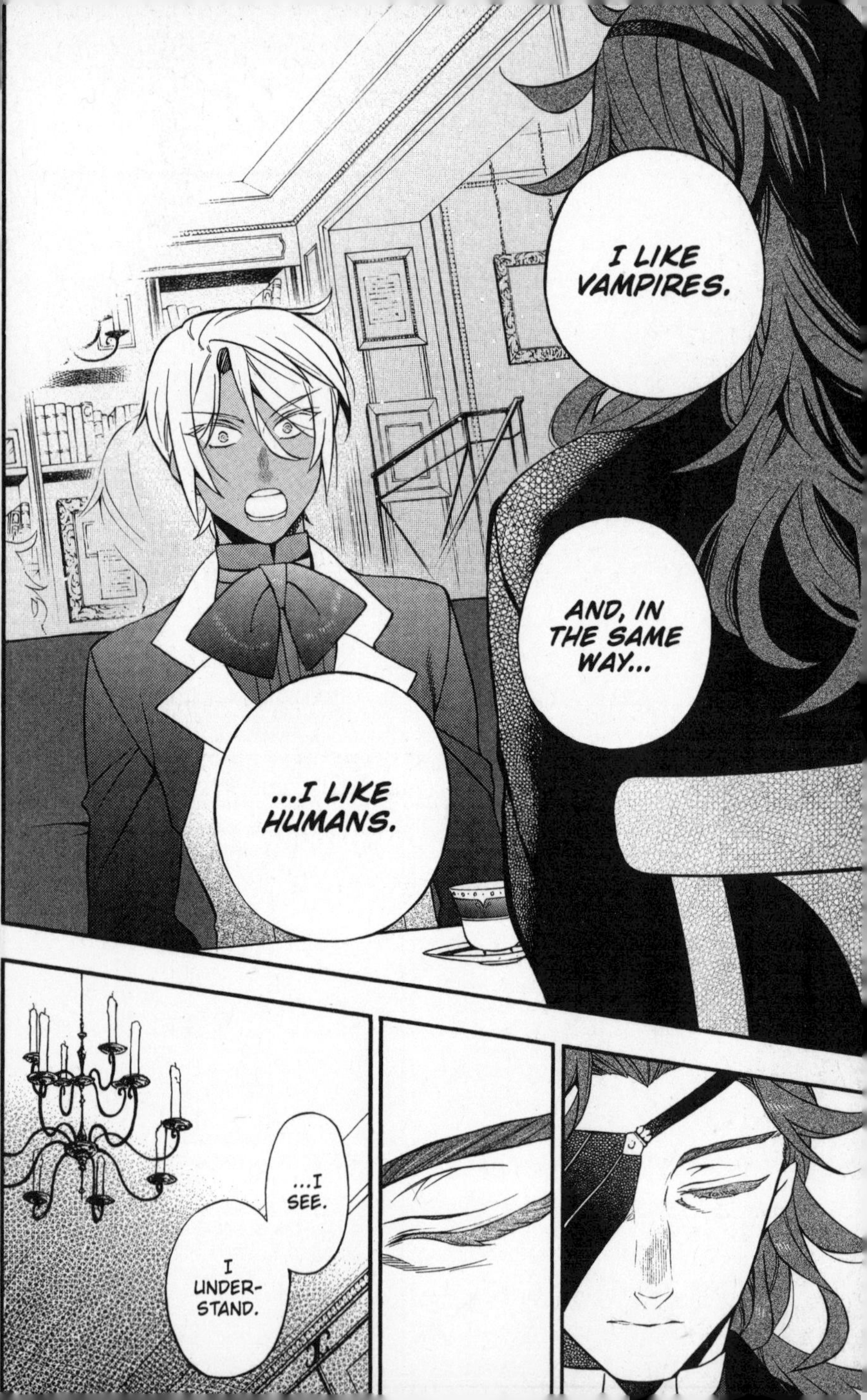
I LIKE VAMPIRES.
AND, IN THE SAME WAY...
...I LIKE HUMANS.
...I SEE.
I UNDER-STAND.

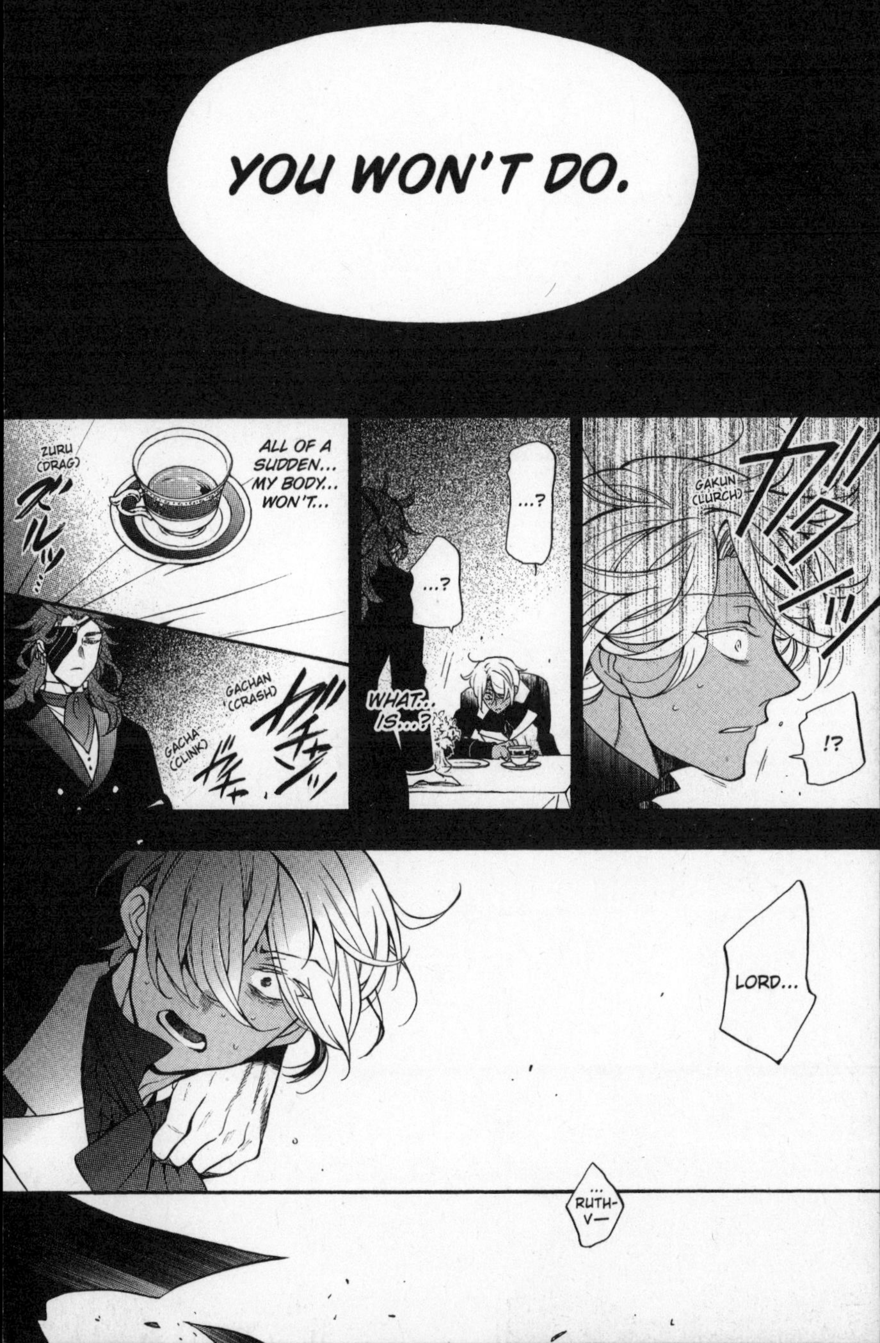
YOU WON'T DO.
GAKUN (LURCH)
!?
...?
...?
WHAT... IS...?
ALL OF A SUDDEN... MY BODY... WON'T...
ZURU (DRAG)
GACHAN (CRASH)
GACHA (CLINK)
LORD...
... RUTH-V—

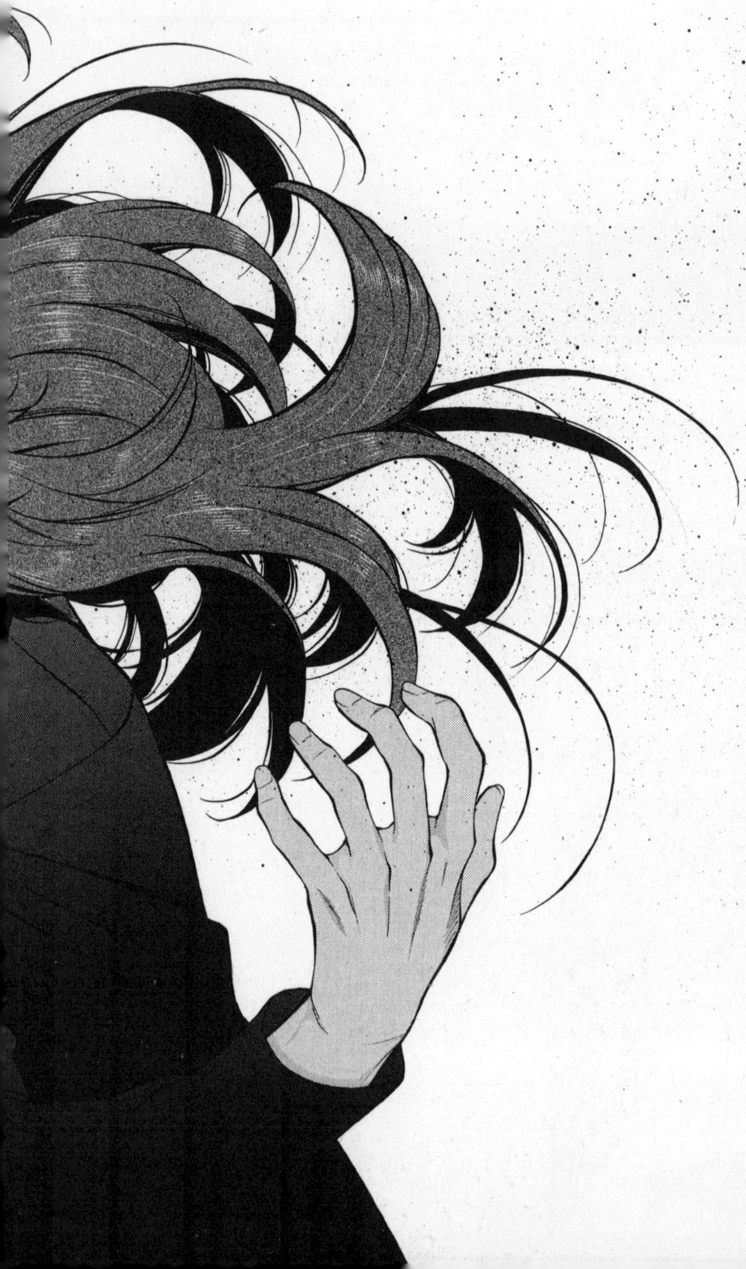

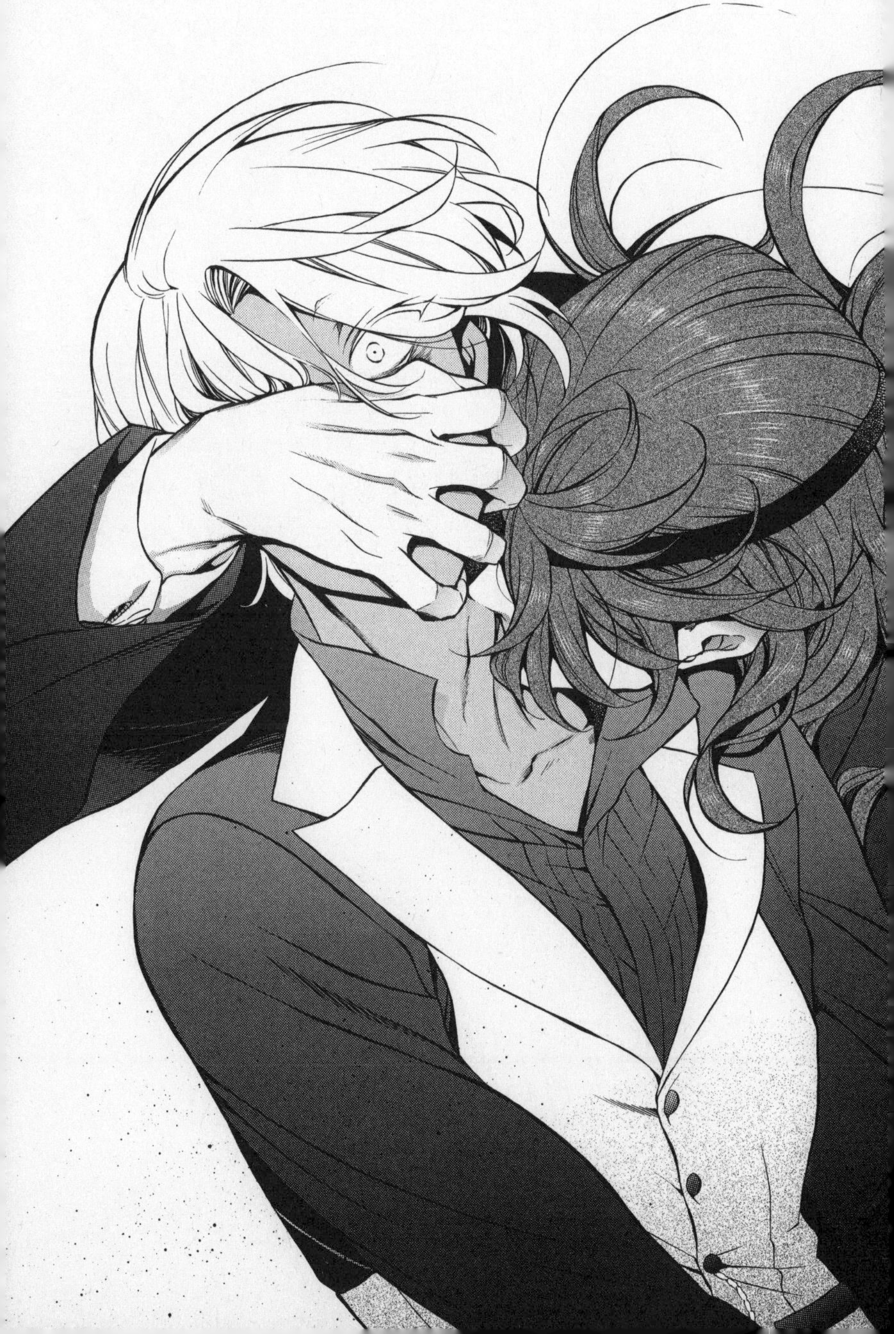

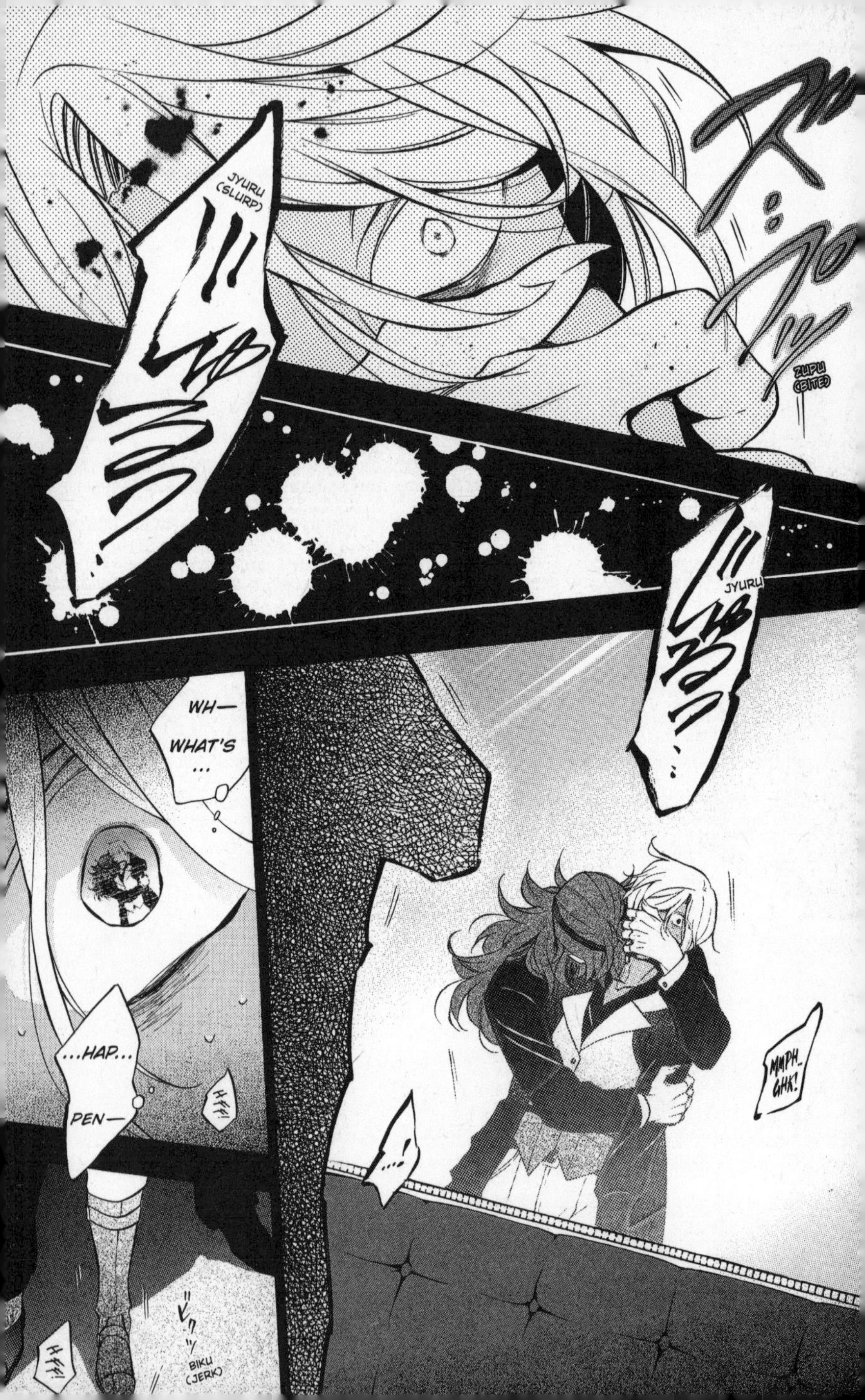
ZUPU (BITE)
JYURU (SLURP)
JYURU
MMPH... GHK!
...!
WH— WHAT'S ...
...HAP... PEN—
HFF!
BIKU (JERK)
HFF!

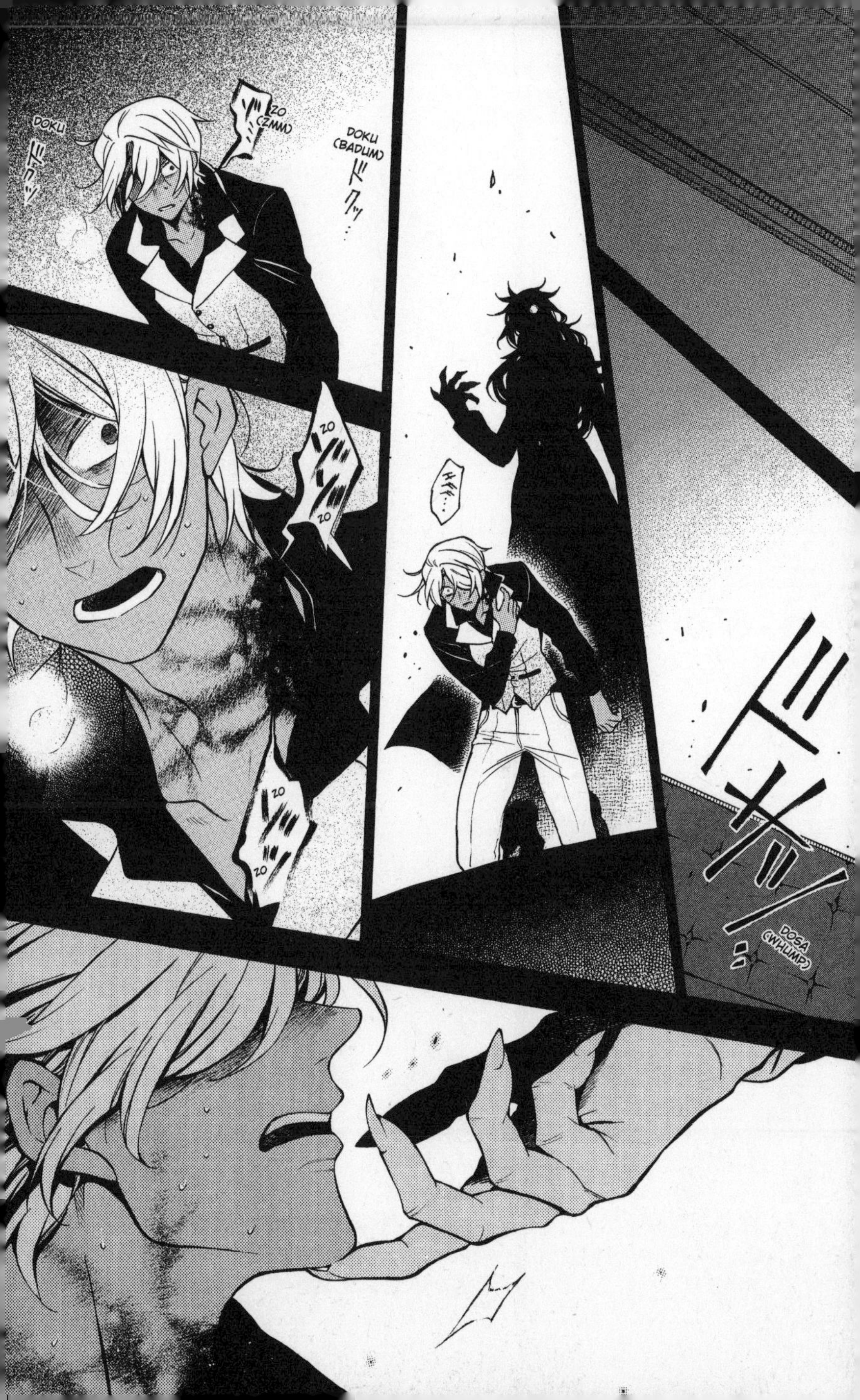
DOSA (WHUMP)
DOKU (BADUM)
ZO (ZMM)
DOKU
ZO
ZO
ZO
ZO

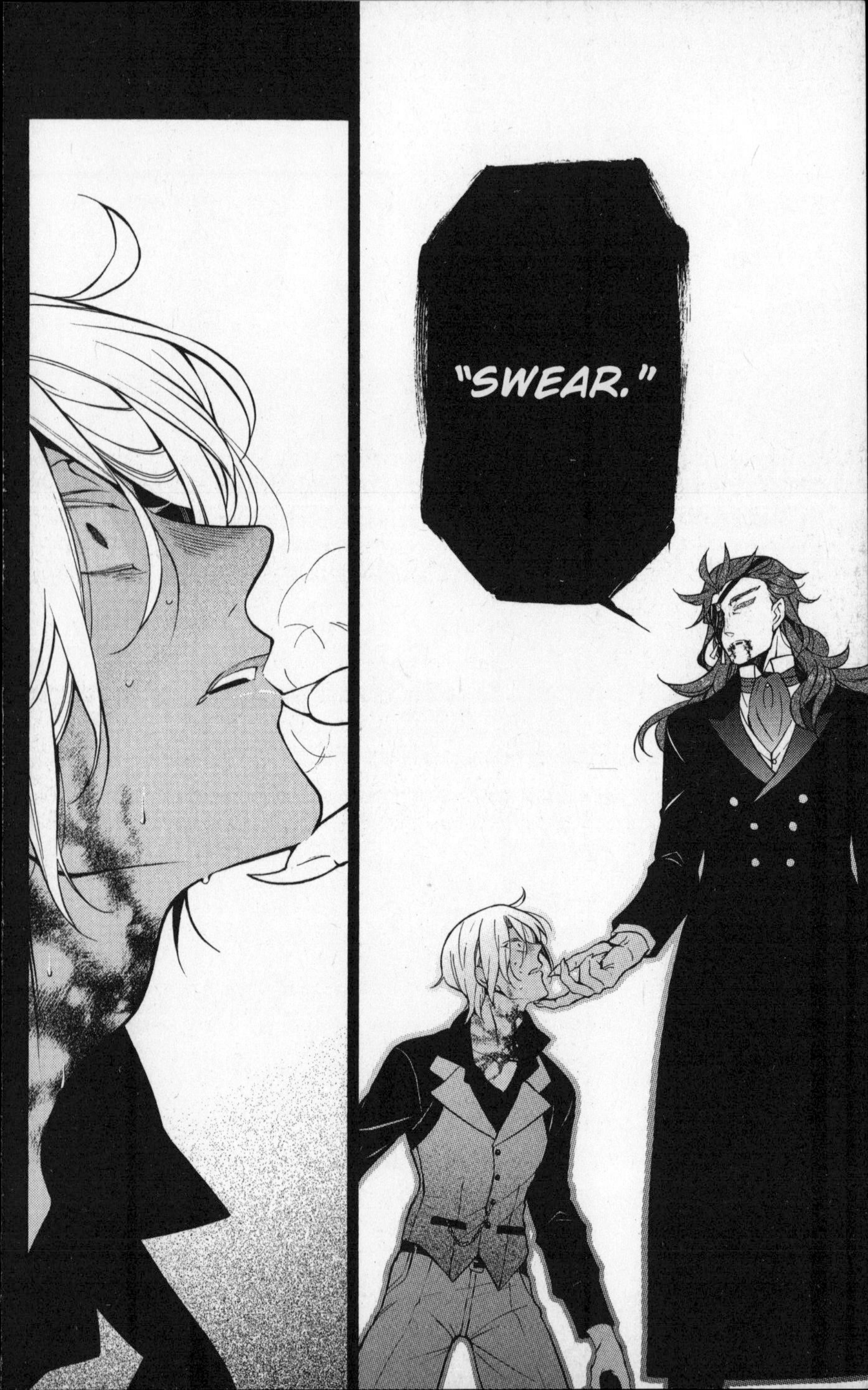
"SWEAR."

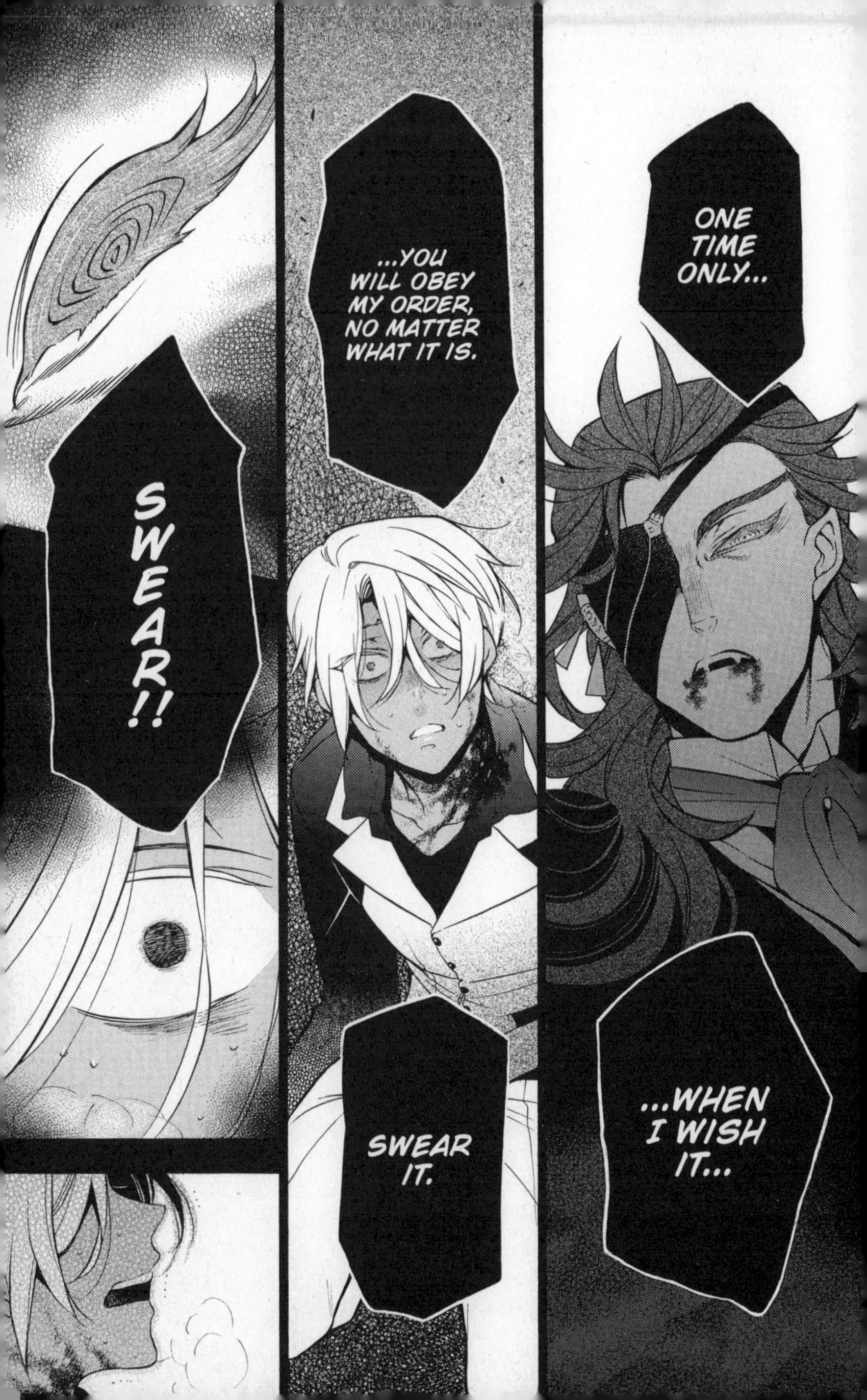
ONE TIME ONLY...
...WHEN I WISH IT...
...YOU WILL OBEY MY ORDER, NO MATTER WHAT IT IS.
SWEAR IT.
SWEAR!!

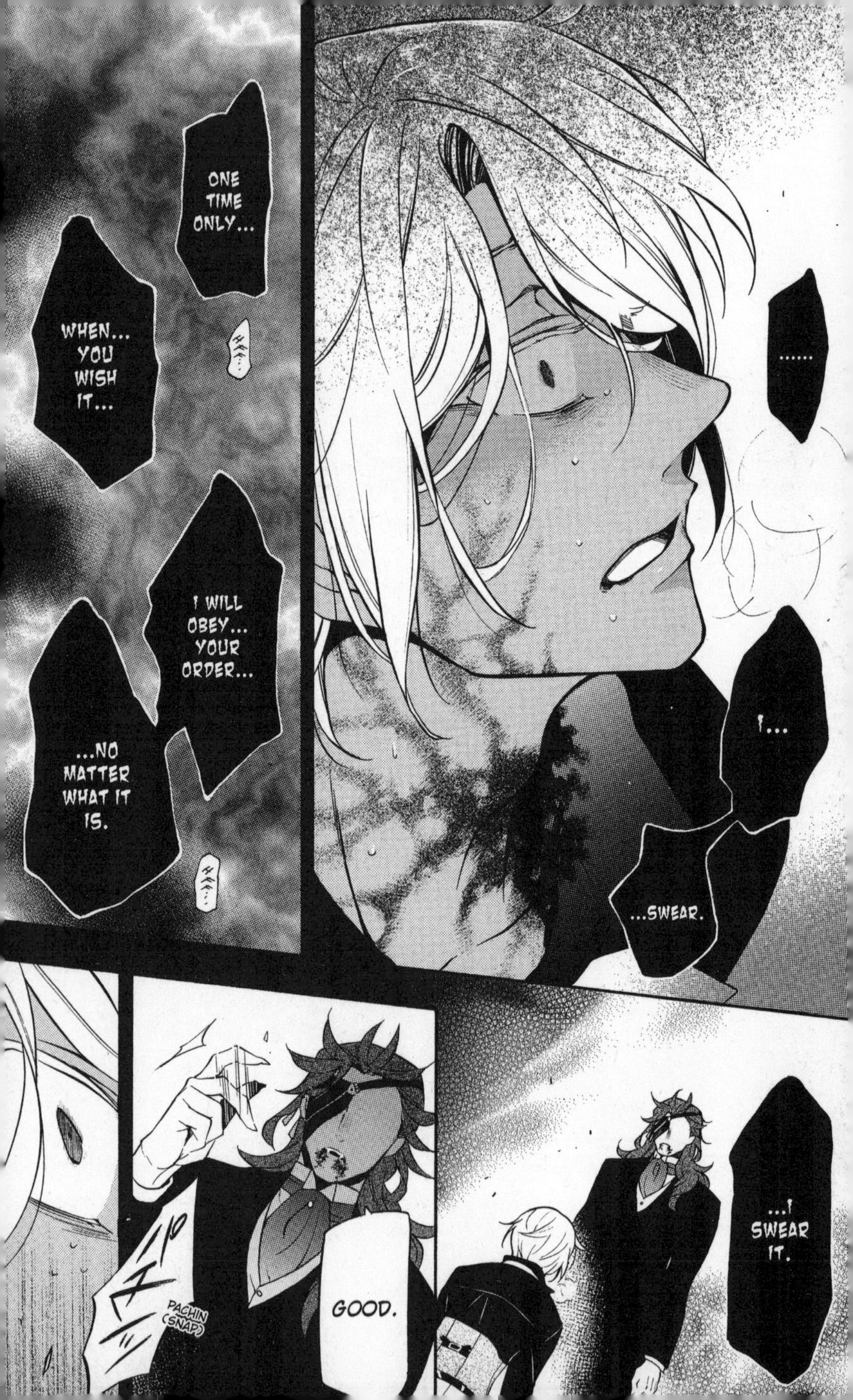
......
I...
...SWEAR.
ONE TIME ONLY...
WHEN... YOU WISH IT...
I WILL OBEY... YOUR ORDER...
...NO MATTER WHAT IT IS.
...I SWEAR IT.
GOOD.
PACHIN (SNAP)

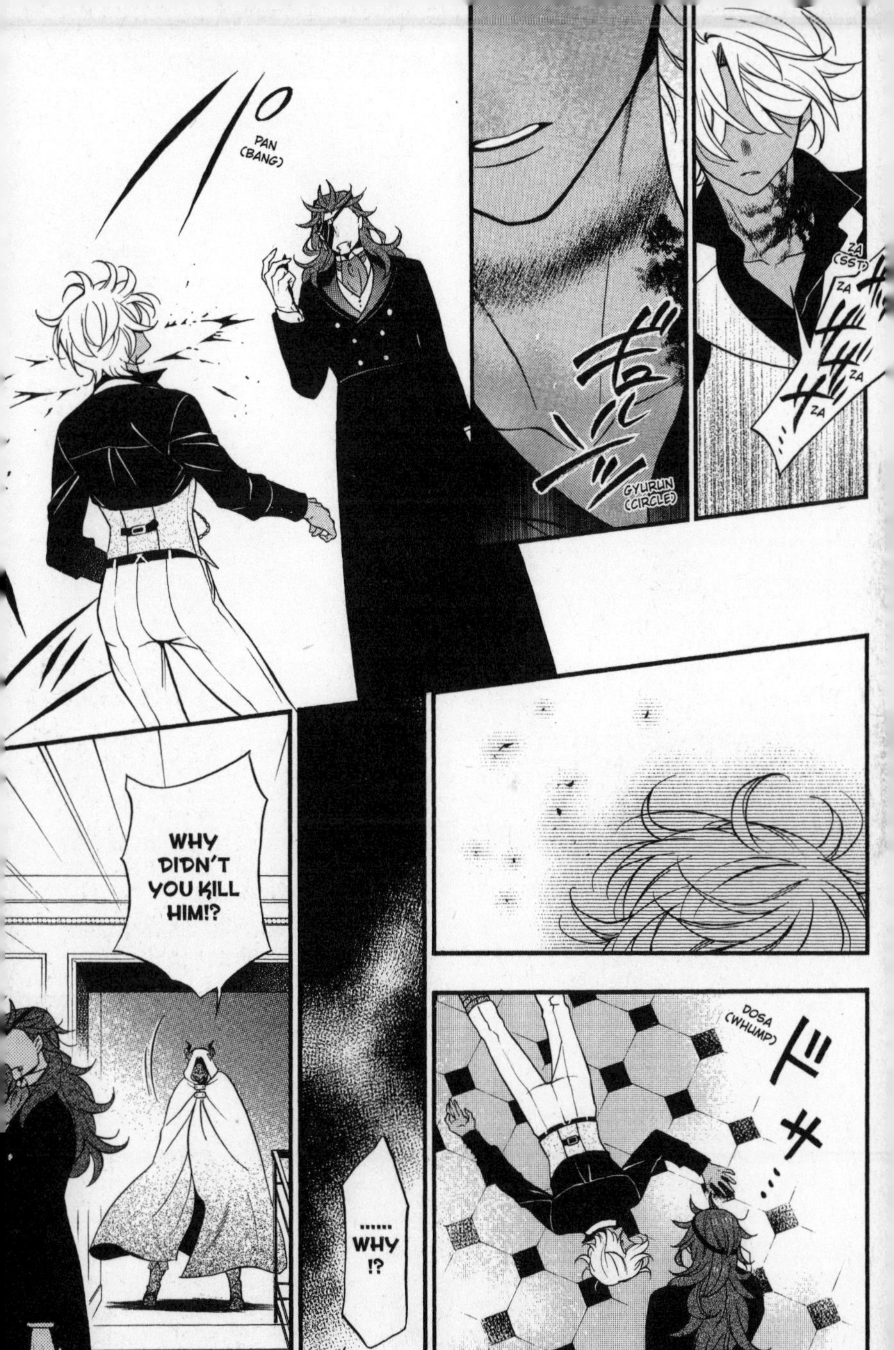
ZA (SST)
ZA
ZA
ZA
GYURUN (CIRCLE)
PAN (BANG)
DOSA (WHUMP)
......WHY !?
KATSU (CLACK)
WHY DIDN'T YOU KILL HIM!?

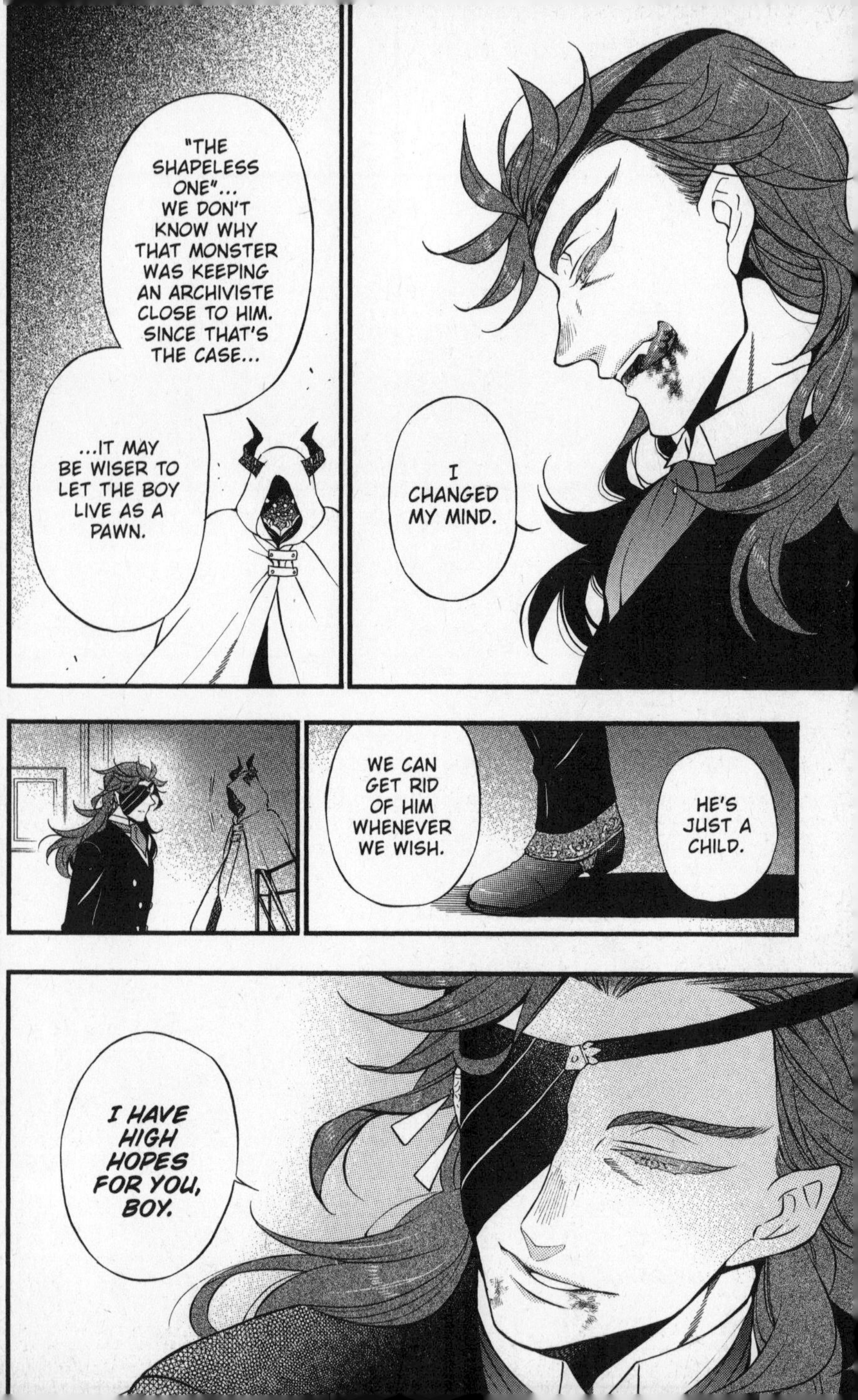
I CHANGED MY MIND.
"THE SHAPELESS ONE"... WE DON'T KNOW WHY THAT MONSTER WAS KEEPING AN ARCHIVISTE CLOSE TO HIM. SINCE THAT'S THE CASE...
...IT MAY BE WISER TO LET THE BOY LIVE AS A PAWN.
HE'S JUST A CHILD.
WE CAN GET RID OF HIM WHENEVER WE WISH.
I HAVE HIGH HOPES FOR YOU, BOY.

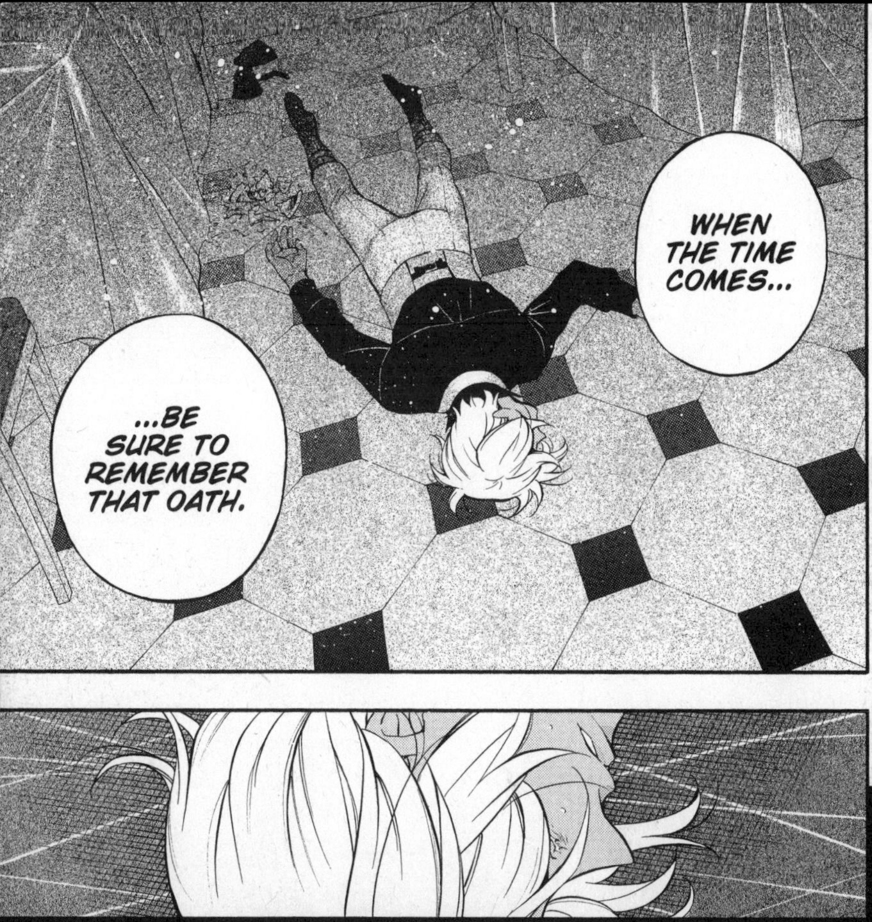
WHEN THE TIME COMES...
...BE SURE TO REMEMBER THAT OATH.

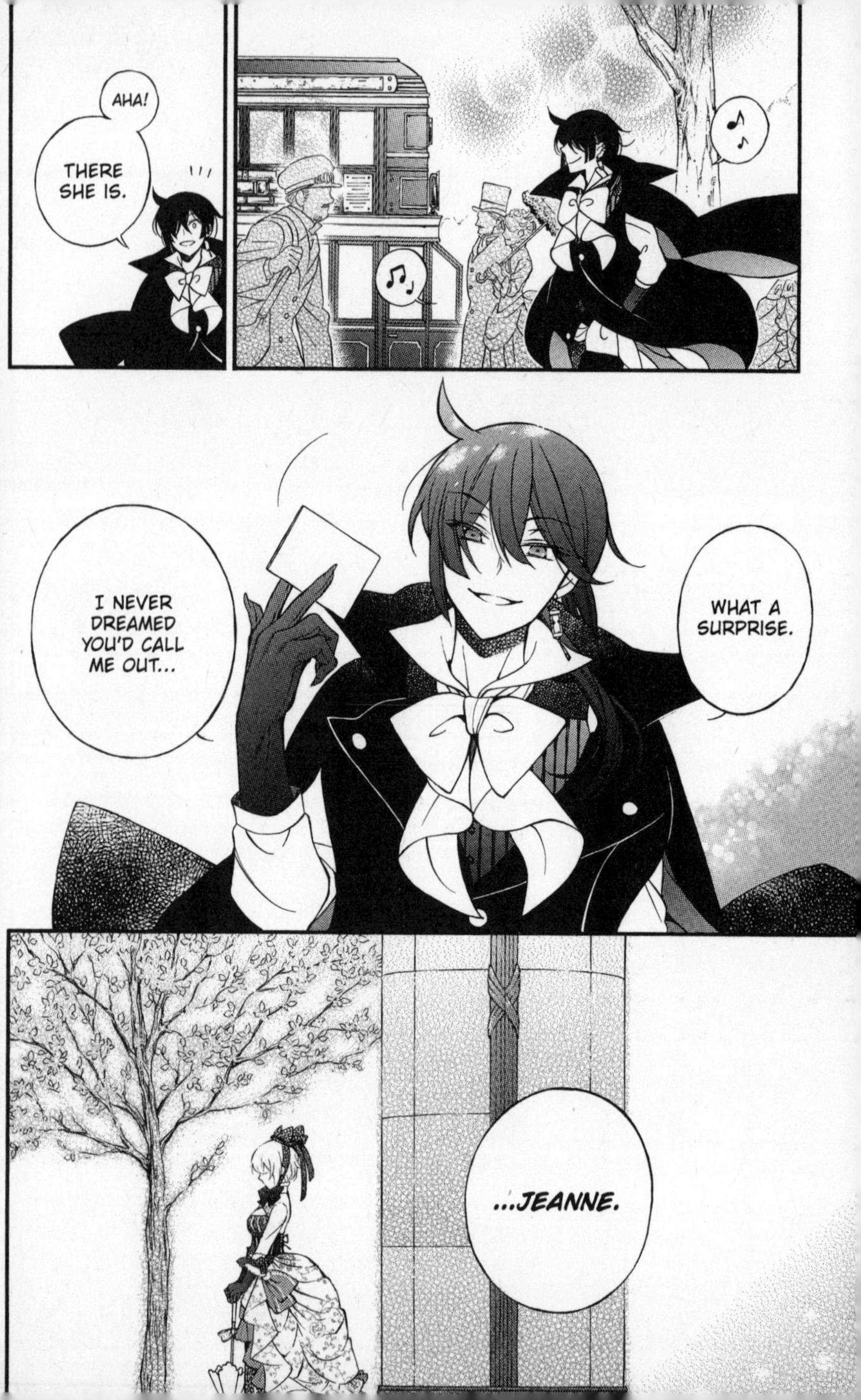
AHA!
THERE SHE IS.
WHAT A SURPRISE.
I NEVER DREAMED YOU'D CALL ME OUT...
...JEANNE.

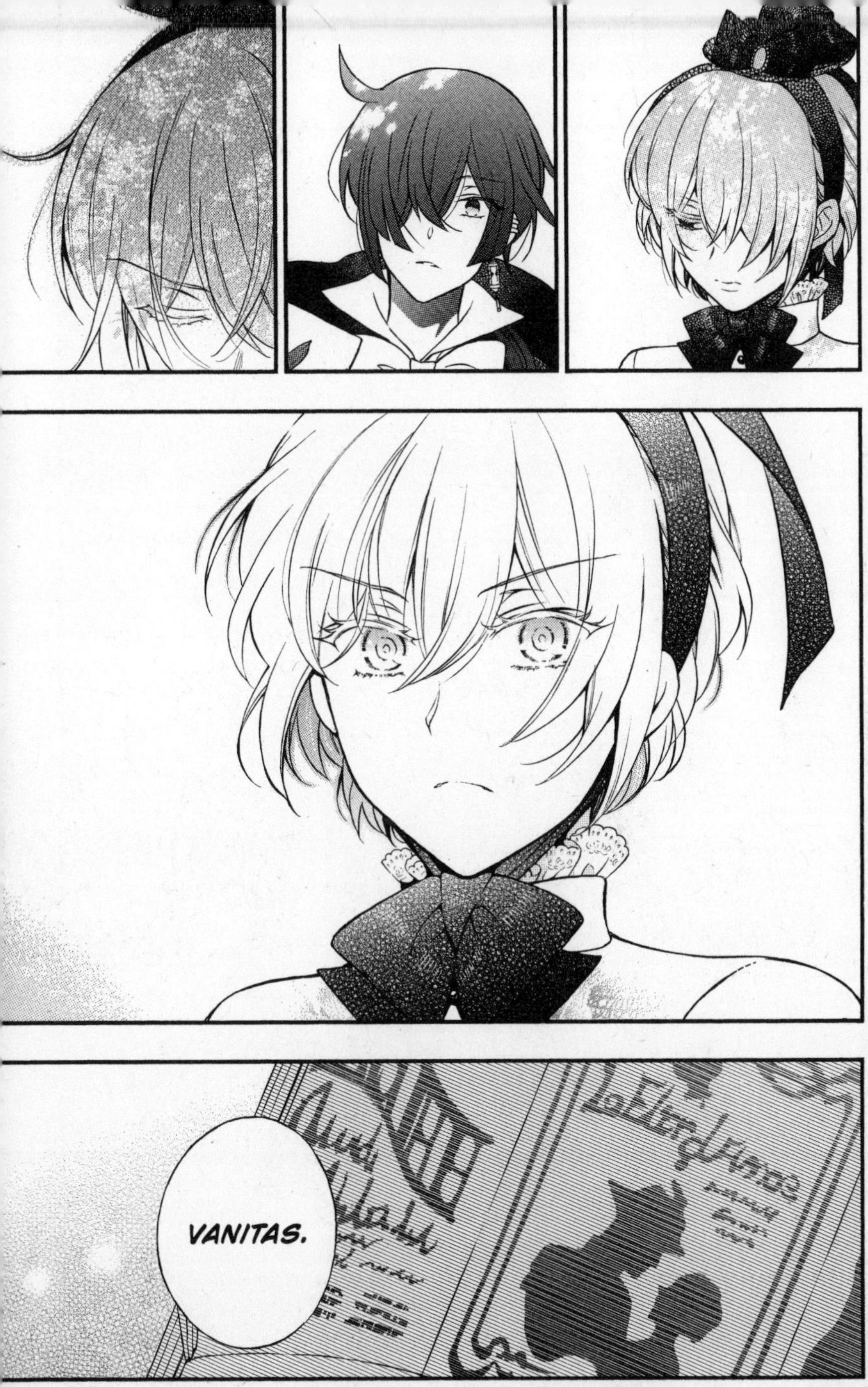
VANITAS.

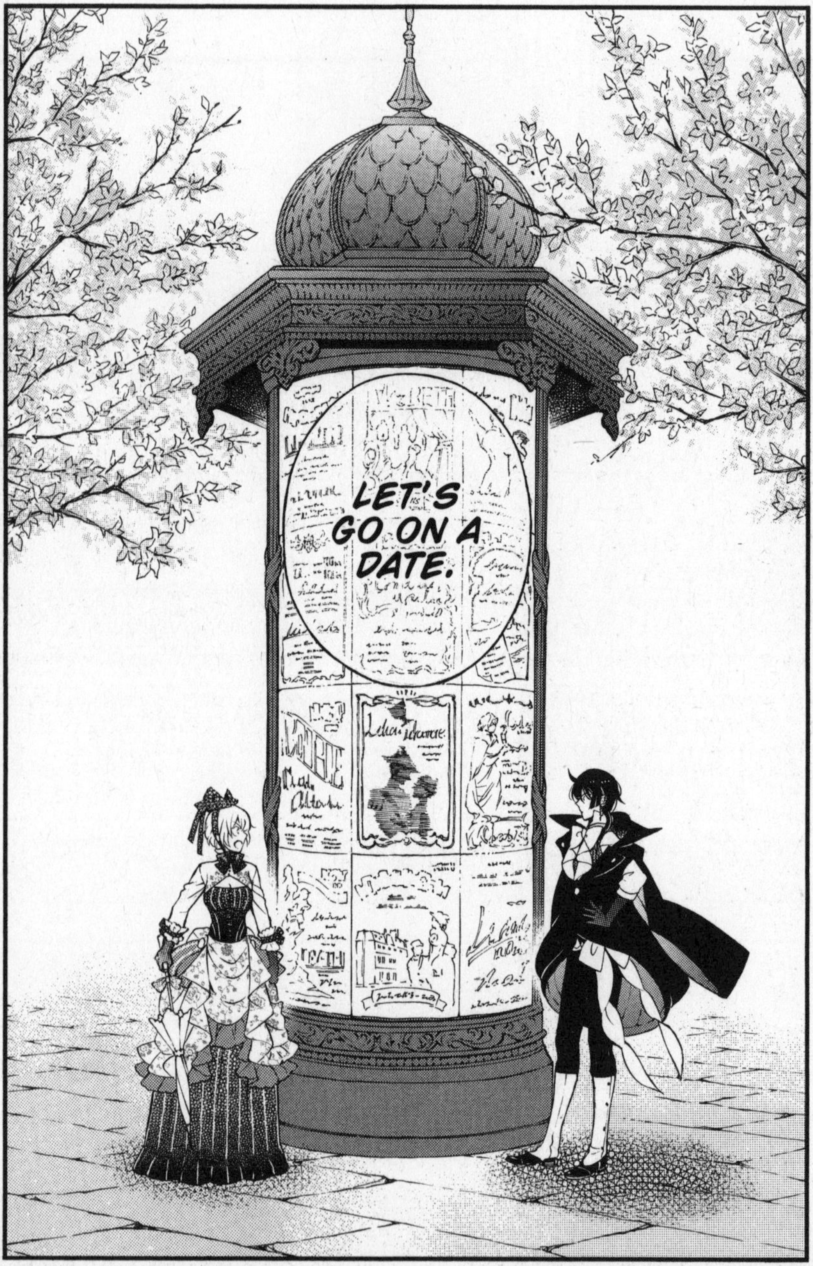
LET'S GO ON A DATE.

Mémoire 19 *Serment* SPELLBOUND

*Les Mémoires de Vanitas*

# THE CASE STUDY OF
# VANITAS

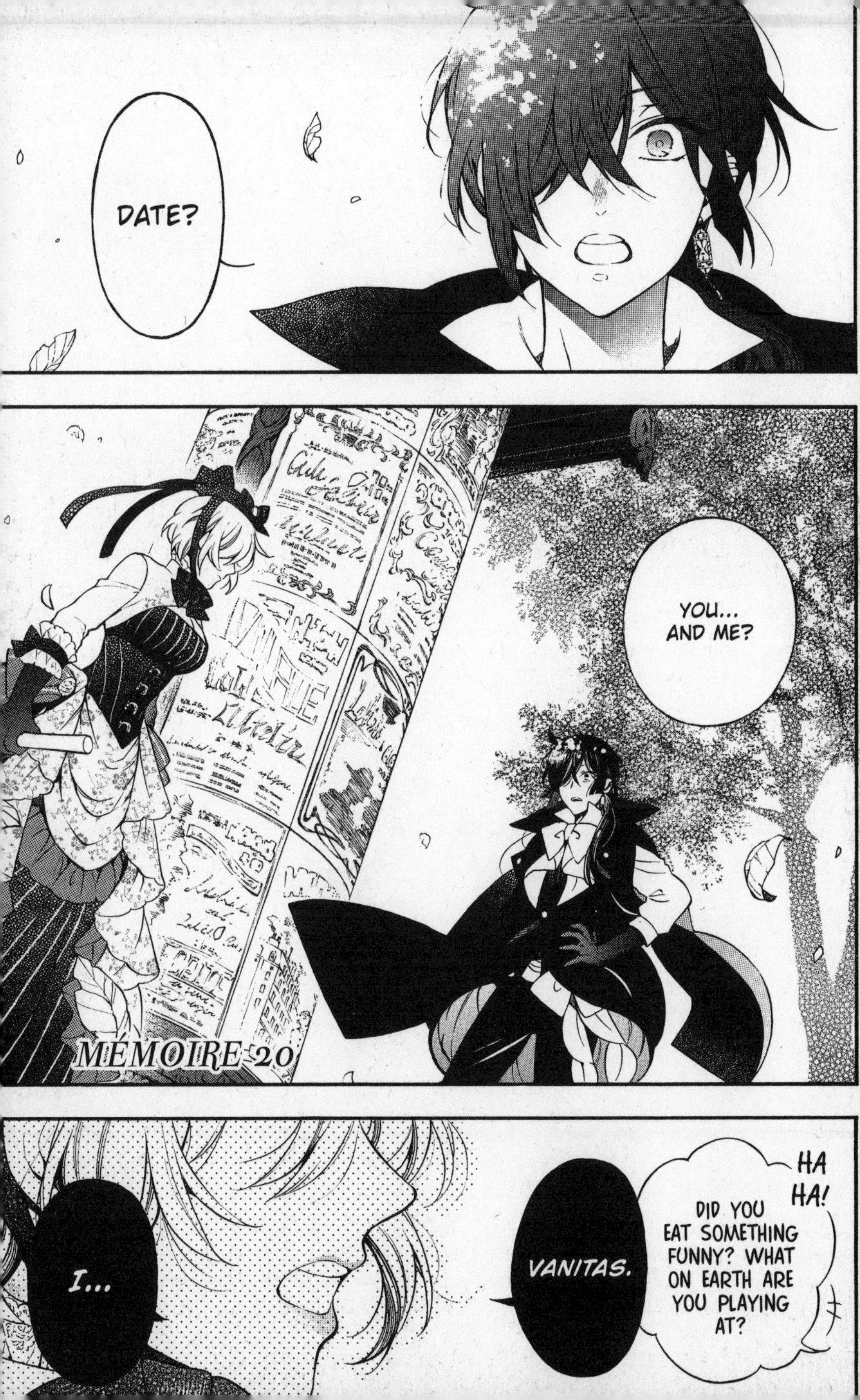
DATE?
YOU... AND ME?
MÉMOIRE 20
HA HA!
DID YOU EAT SOMETHING FUNNY? WHAT ON EARTH ARE YOU PLAYING AT?
VANITAS.
I...

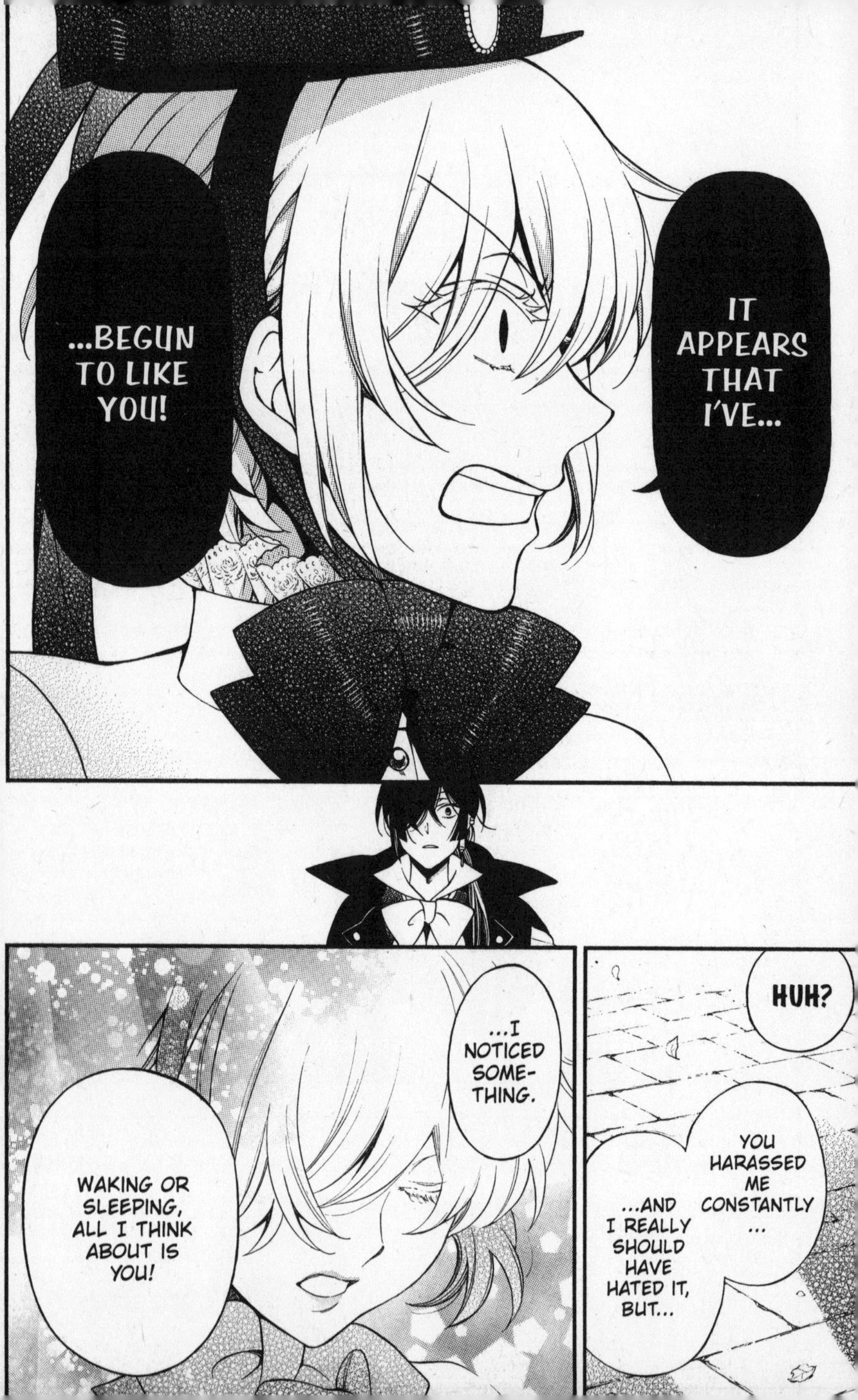
IT APPEARS THAT I'VE...
...BEGUN TO LIKE YOU!
HUH?
YOU HARASSED ME CONSTANTLY ...
...AND I REALLY SHOULD HAVE HATED IT, BUT...
...I NOTICED SOME-THING.
WAKING OR SLEEPING, ALL I THINK ABOUT IS YOU!

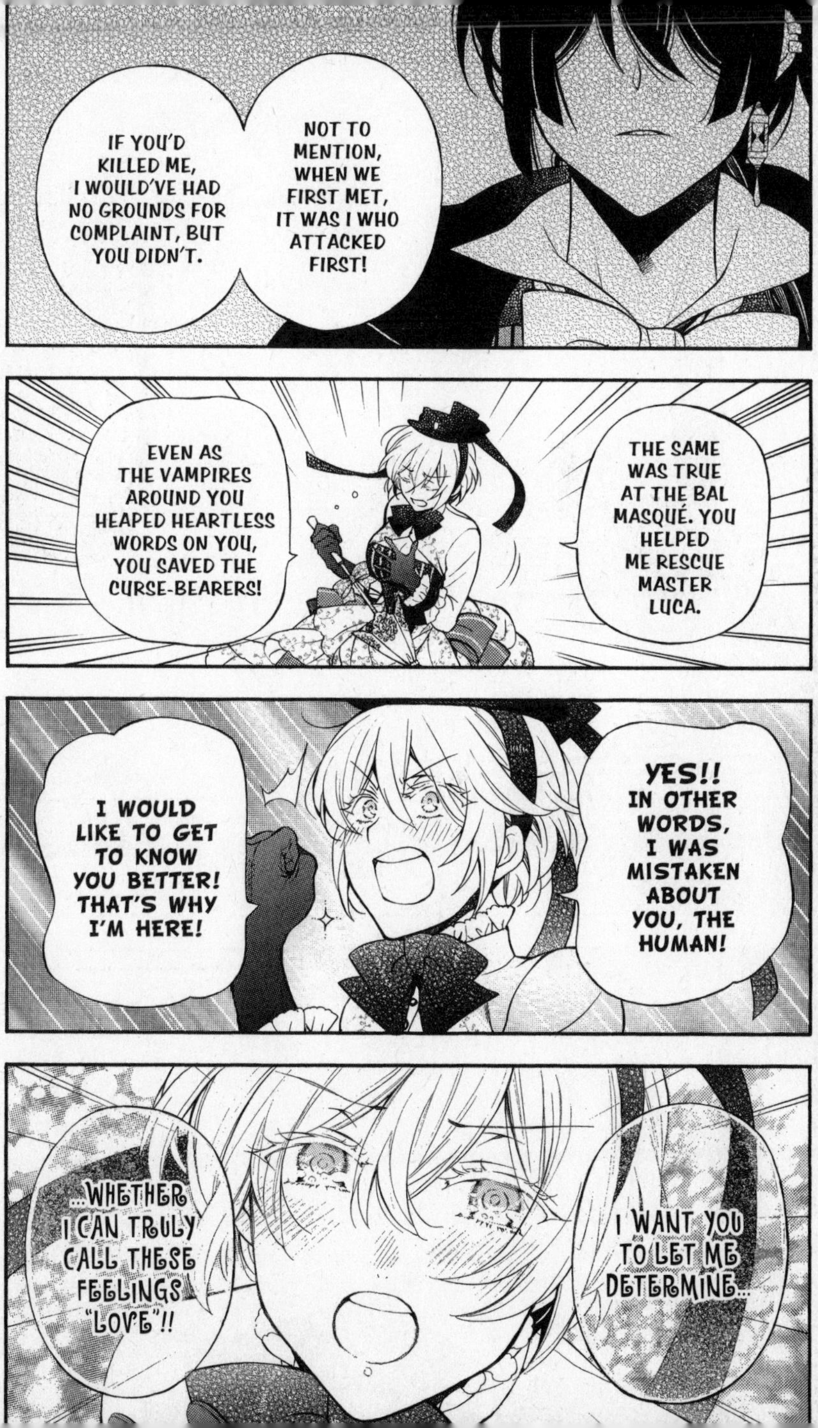
NOT TO MENTION, WHEN WE FIRST MET, IT WAS I WHO ATTACKED FIRST!
IF YOU'D KILLED ME, I WOULD'VE HAD NO GROUNDS FOR COMPLAINT, BUT YOU DIDN'T.
THE SAME WAS TRUE AT THE BAL MASQUÉ. YOU HELPED ME RESCUE MASTER LUCA.
EVEN AS THE VAMPIRES AROUND YOU HEAPED HEARTLESS WORDS ON YOU, YOU SAVED THE CURSE-BEARERS!
YES!! IN OTHER WORDS, I WAS MISTAKEN ABOUT YOU, THE HUMAN!
I WOULD LIKE TO GET TO KNOW YOU BETTER! THAT'S WHY I'M HERE!
I WANT YOU TO LET ME DETERMINE...
...WHETHER I CAN TRULY CALL THESE FEELINGS "LOVE"!!

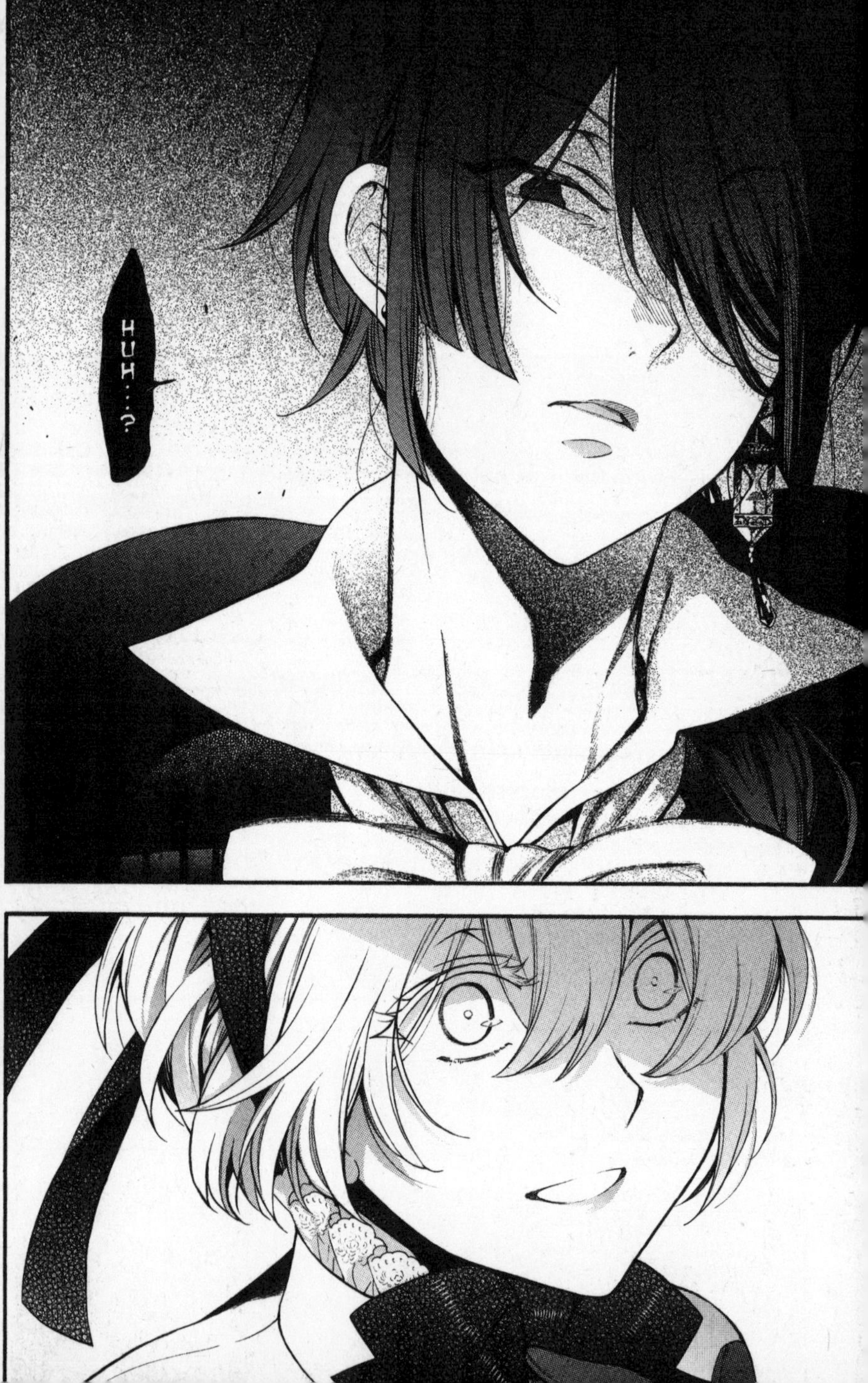
HUH...?

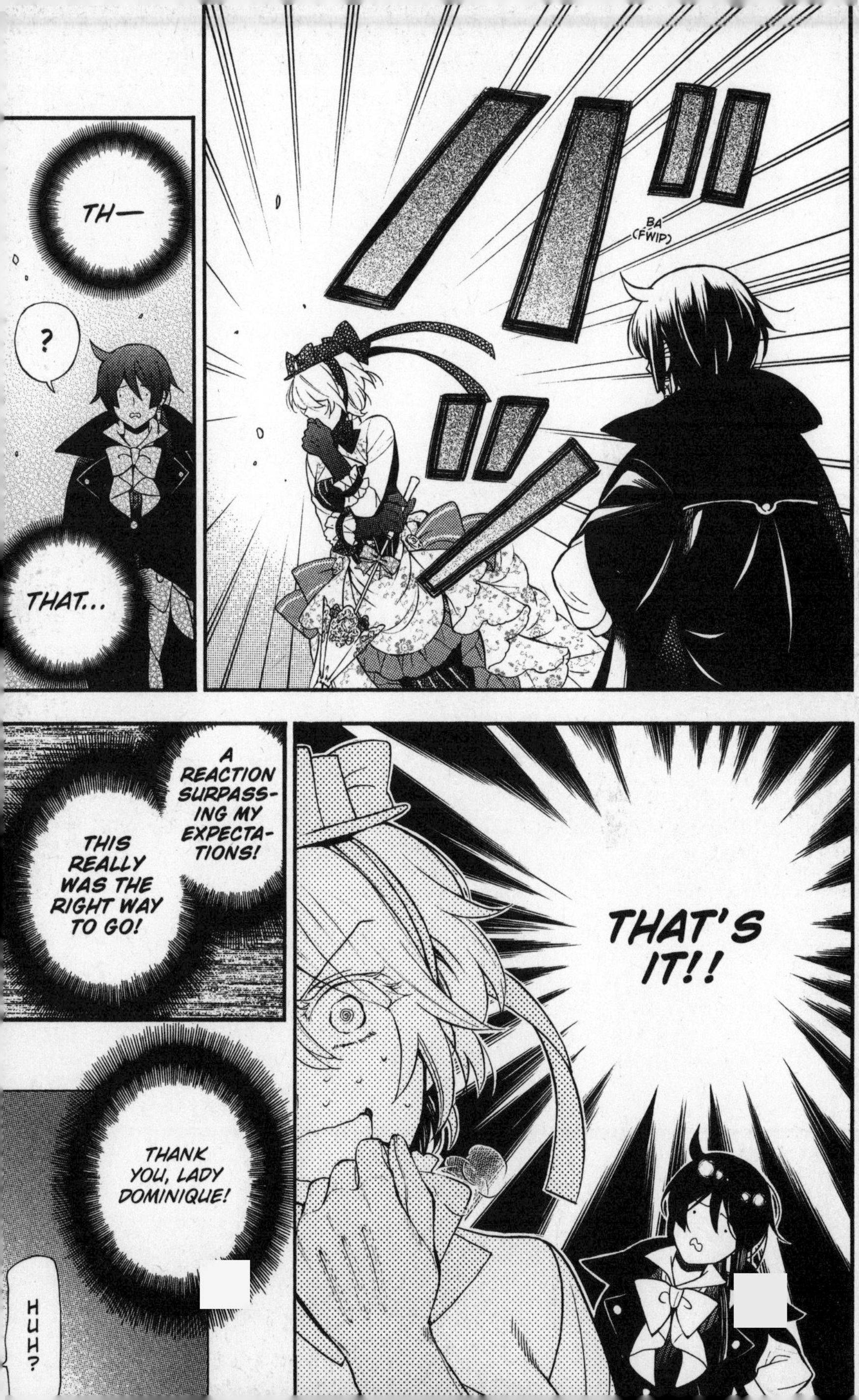
BA (FWIP)
TH—
?
THAT...
THAT'S IT!!
A REACTION SURPASSING MY EXPECTATIONS!
THIS REALLY WAS THE RIGHT WAY TO GO!
THANK YOU, LADY DOMINIQUE!
HUH?

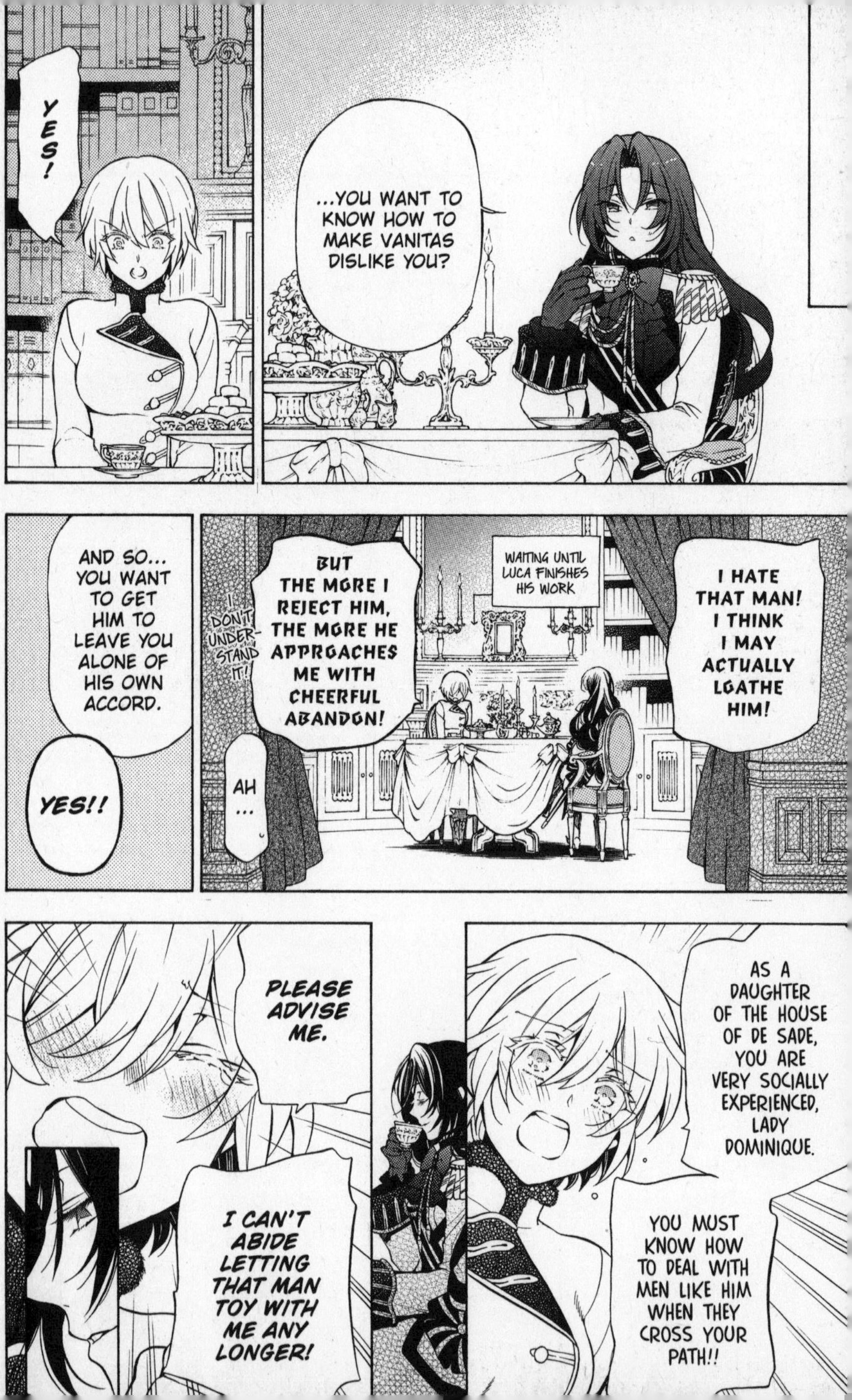
...YOU WANT TO KNOW HOW TO MAKE VANITAS DISLIKE YOU?
YES!
WAITING UNTIL LUCA FINISHES HIS WORK
I HATE THAT MAN! I THINK I MAY ACTUALLY LOATHE HIM!
BUT THE MORE I REJECT HIM, THE MORE HE APPROACHES ME WITH CHEERFUL ABANDON!
I DON'T UNDERSTAND IT!
AH...
AND SO... YOU WANT TO GET HIM TO LEAVE YOU ALONE OF HIS OWN ACCORD.
YES!!
AS A DAUGHTER OF THE HOUSE OF DE SADE, YOU ARE VERY SOCIALLY EXPERIENCED, LADY DOMINIQUE.
YOU MUST KNOW HOW TO DEAL WITH MEN LIKE HIM WHEN THEY CROSS YOUR PATH!!
PLEASE ADVISE ME.
I CAN'T ABIDE LETTING THAT MAN TOY WITH ME ANY LONGER!

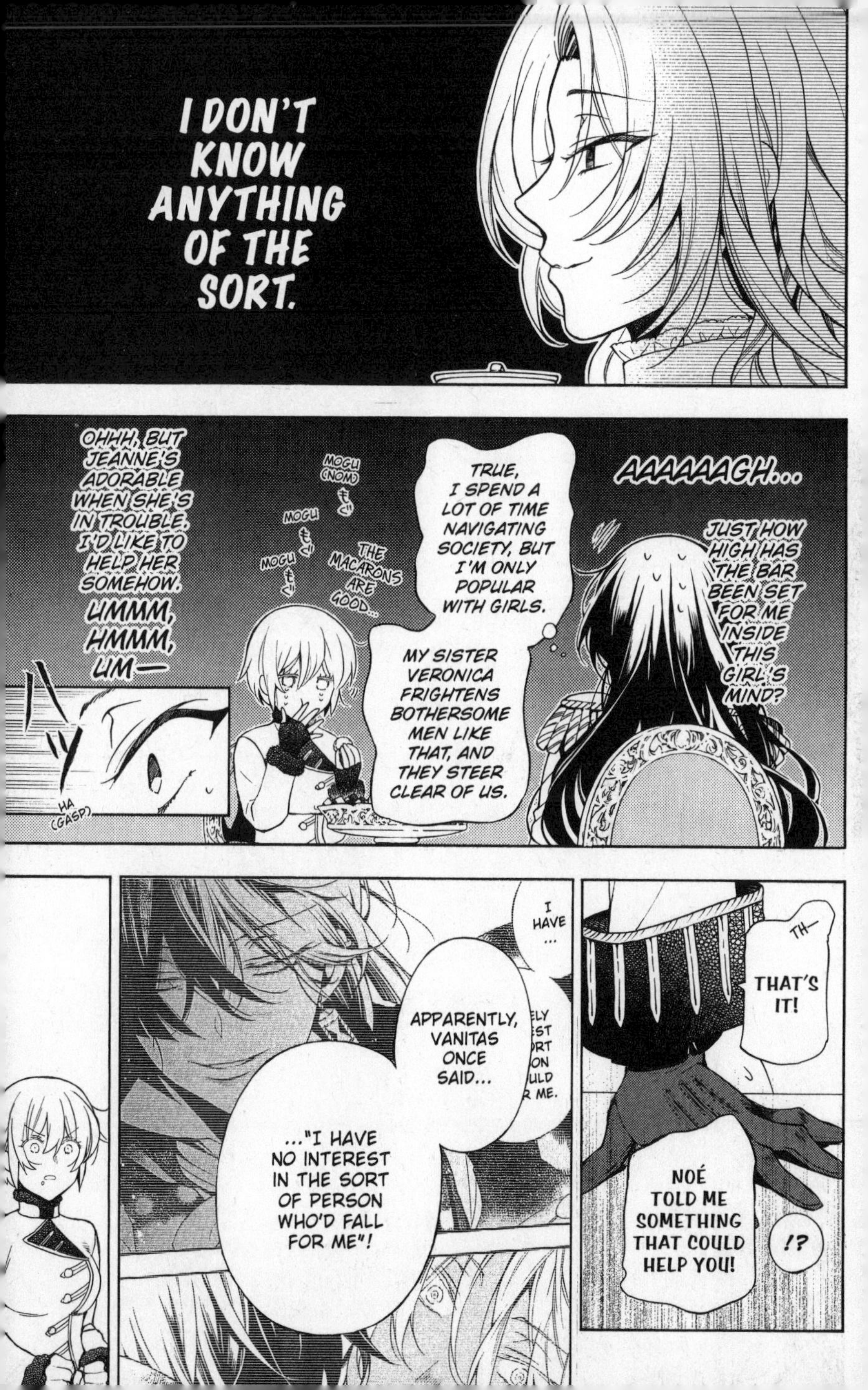
I DON'T KNOW ANYTHING OF THE SORT.
AAAAAAGH...
JUST HOW HIGH HAS THE BAR BEEN SET FOR ME INSIDE THIS GIRL'S MIND?
TRUE, I SPEND A LOT OF TIME NAVIGATING SOCIETY, BUT I'M ONLY POPULAR WITH GIRLS.
MY SISTER VERONICA FRIGHTENS BOTHERSOME MEN LIKE THAT, AND THEY STEER CLEAR OF US.
THE MACARONS ARE GOOD...
MOGU (NOM)
MOGU
MOGU
OHHH, BUT JEANNE'S ADORABLE WHEN SHE'S IN TROUBLE. I'D LIKE TO HELP HER SOMEHOW.
UMMM, HMMM, UM—
HA (GASP)
TH—
THAT'S IT!
NOÉ TOLD ME SOMETHING THAT COULD HELP YOU!
!?
I HAVE ...
APPARENTLY, VANITAS ONCE SAID...
..."I HAVE NO INTEREST IN THE SORT OF PERSON WHO'D FALL FOR ME"!

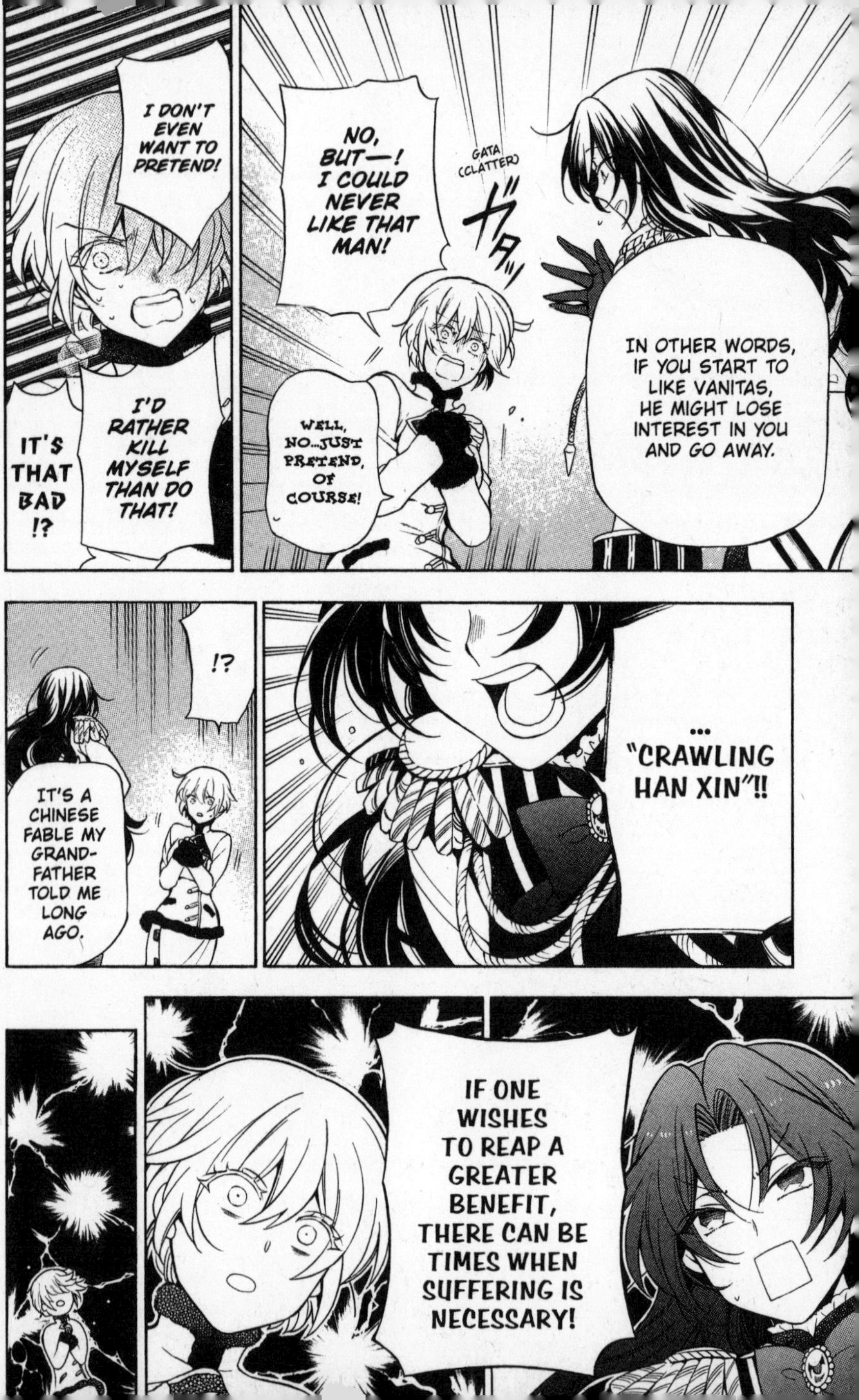
IN OTHER WORDS, IF YOU START TO LIKE VANITAS, HE MIGHT LOSE INTEREST IN YOU AND GO AWAY.
GATA (CLATTER)
NO, BUT—! I COULD NEVER LIKE THAT MAN!
WELL, NO...JUST PRETEND, OF COURSE!
I DON'T EVEN WANT TO PRETEND!
I'D RATHER KILL MYSELF THAN DO THAT!
IT'S THAT BAD!?
... "CRAWLING HAN XIN"!!
!?
IT'S A CHINESE FABLE MY GRAND-FATHER TOLD ME LONG AGO.
IF ONE WISHES TO REAP A GREATER BENEFIT, THERE CAN BE TIMES WHEN SUFFERING IS NECESSARY!

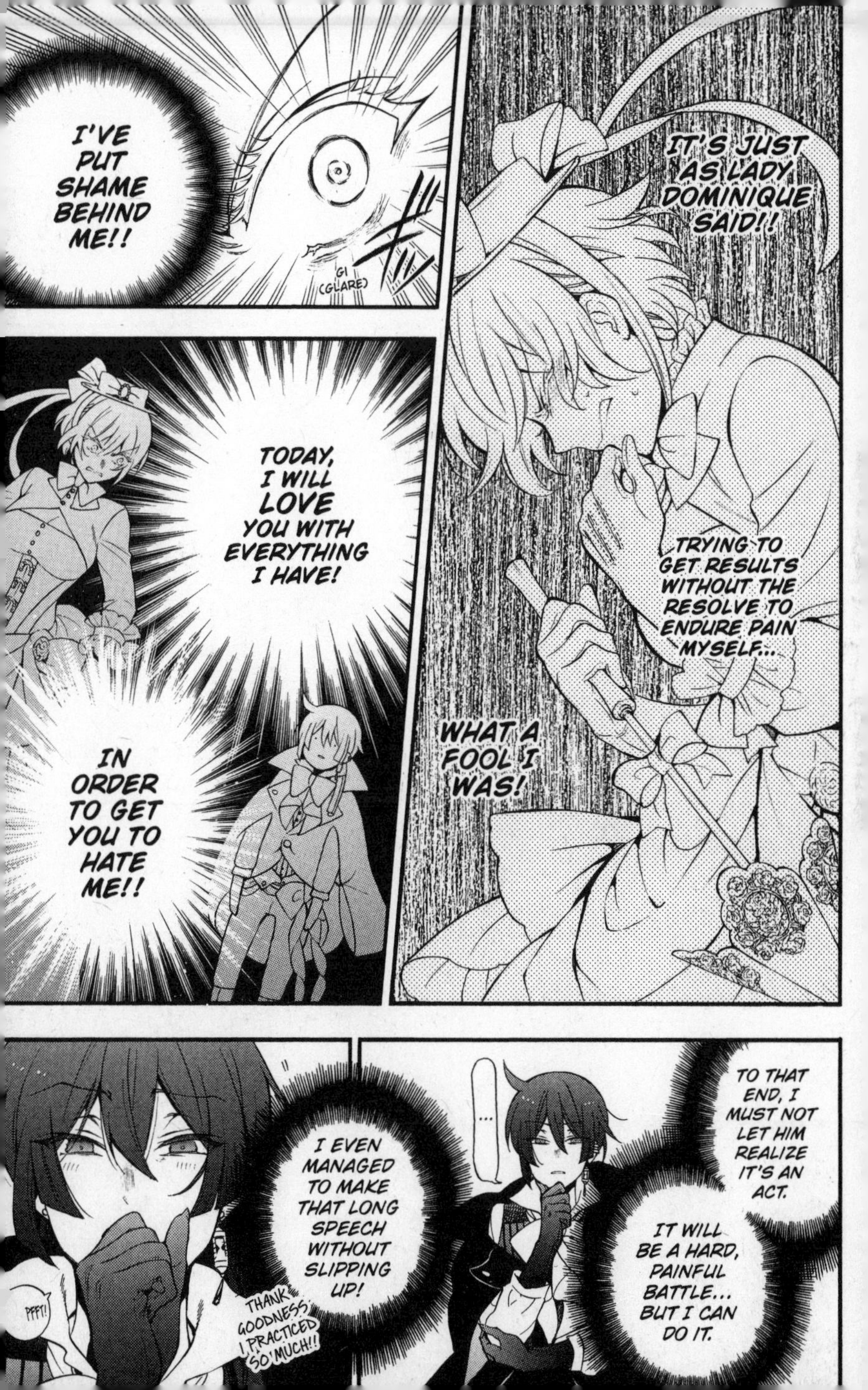
IT'S JUST AS LADY DOMINIQUE SAID!!
TRYING TO GET RESULTS WITHOUT THE RESOLVE TO ENDURE PAIN MYSELF...
WHAT A FOOL I WAS!
I'VE PUT SHAME BEHIND ME!!
GI (GLARE)
TODAY, I WILL LOVE YOU WITH EVERYTHING I HAVE!
IN ORDER TO GET YOU TO HATE ME!!
...
TO THAT END, I MUST NOT LET HIM REALIZE IT'S AN ACT.
IT WILL BE A HARD, PAINFUL BATTLE... BUT I CAN DO IT.
I EVEN MANAGED TO MAKE THAT LONG SPEECH WITHOUT SLIPPING UP!
THANK GOODNESS I PRACTICED SO MUCH!!
PFFT!

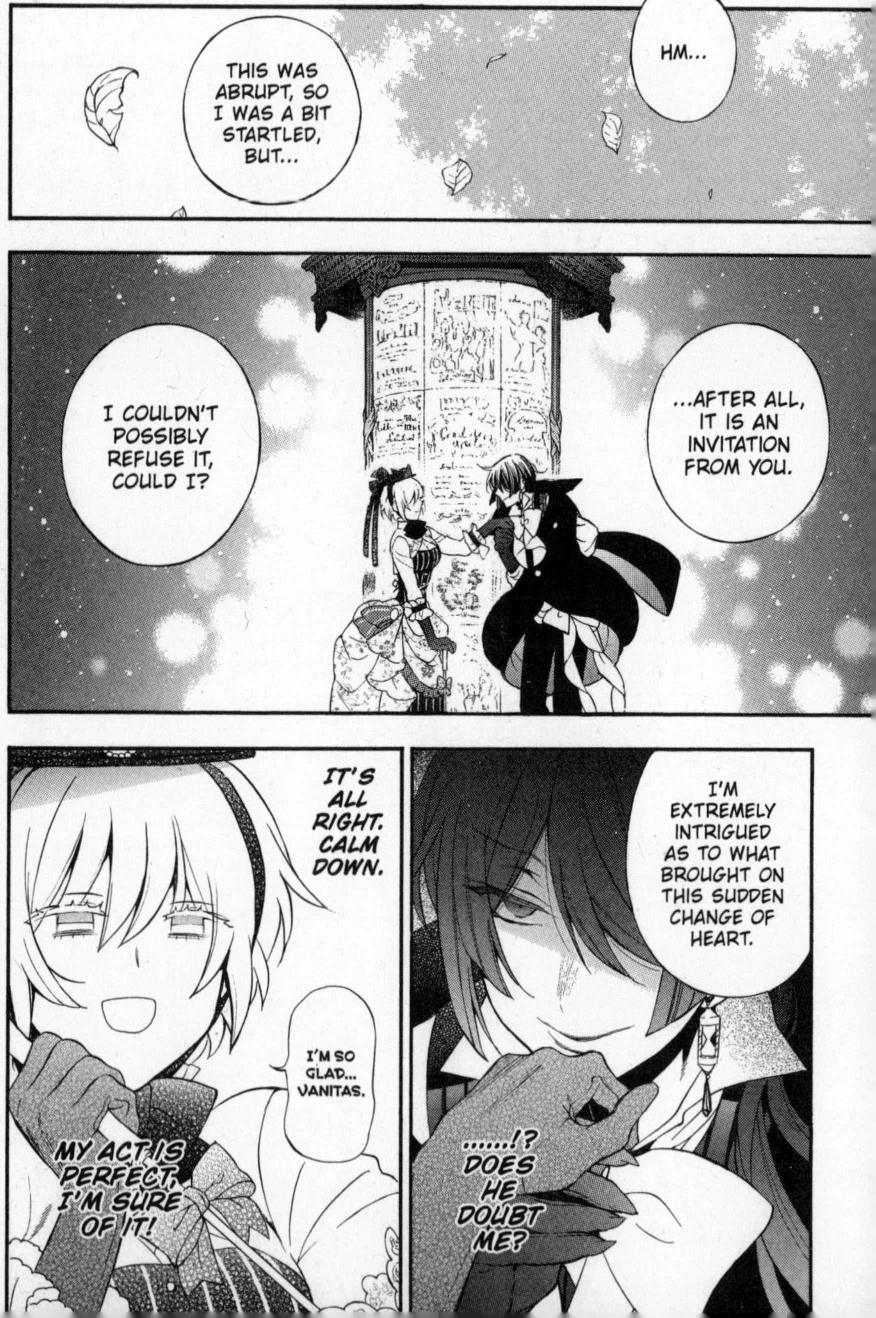
HM...
THIS WAS ABRUPT, SO I WAS A BIT STARTLED, BUT...
...AFTER ALL, IT IS AN INVITATION FROM YOU.
I COULDN'T POSSIBLY REFUSE IT, COULD I?
I'M EXTREMELY INTRIGUED AS TO WHAT BROUGHT ON THIS SUDDEN CHANGE OF HEART.
......!? DOES HE DOUBT ME?
IT'S ALL RIGHT. CALM DOWN.
I'M SO GLAD... VANITAS.
MY ACT IS PERFECT, I'M SURE OF IT!

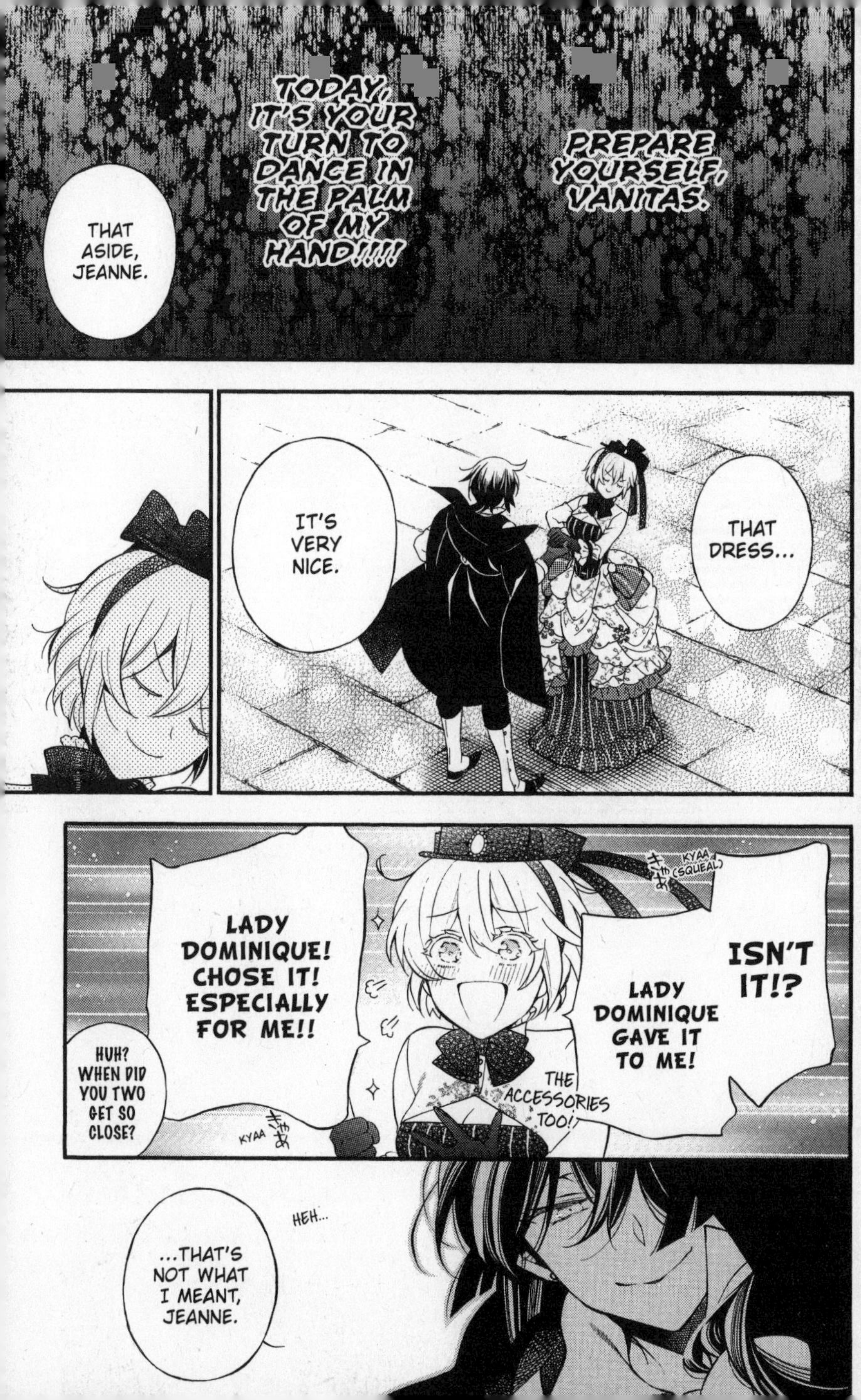
PREPARE YOURSELF, VANITAS.
TODAY, IT'S YOUR TURN TO DANCE IN THE PALM OF MY HAND!!!!
THAT ASIDE, JEANNE.
THAT DRESS...
IT'S VERY NICE.
KYAA (SQUEAL)
ISN'T IT!?
LADY DOMINIQUE GAVE IT TO ME!
THE ACCESSORIES TOO!
LADY DOMINIQUE! CHOSE IT! ESPECIALLY FOR ME!!
HUH? WHEN DID YOU TWO GET SO CLOSE?
KYAA
HEH...
...THAT'S NOT WHAT I MEANT, JEANNE.

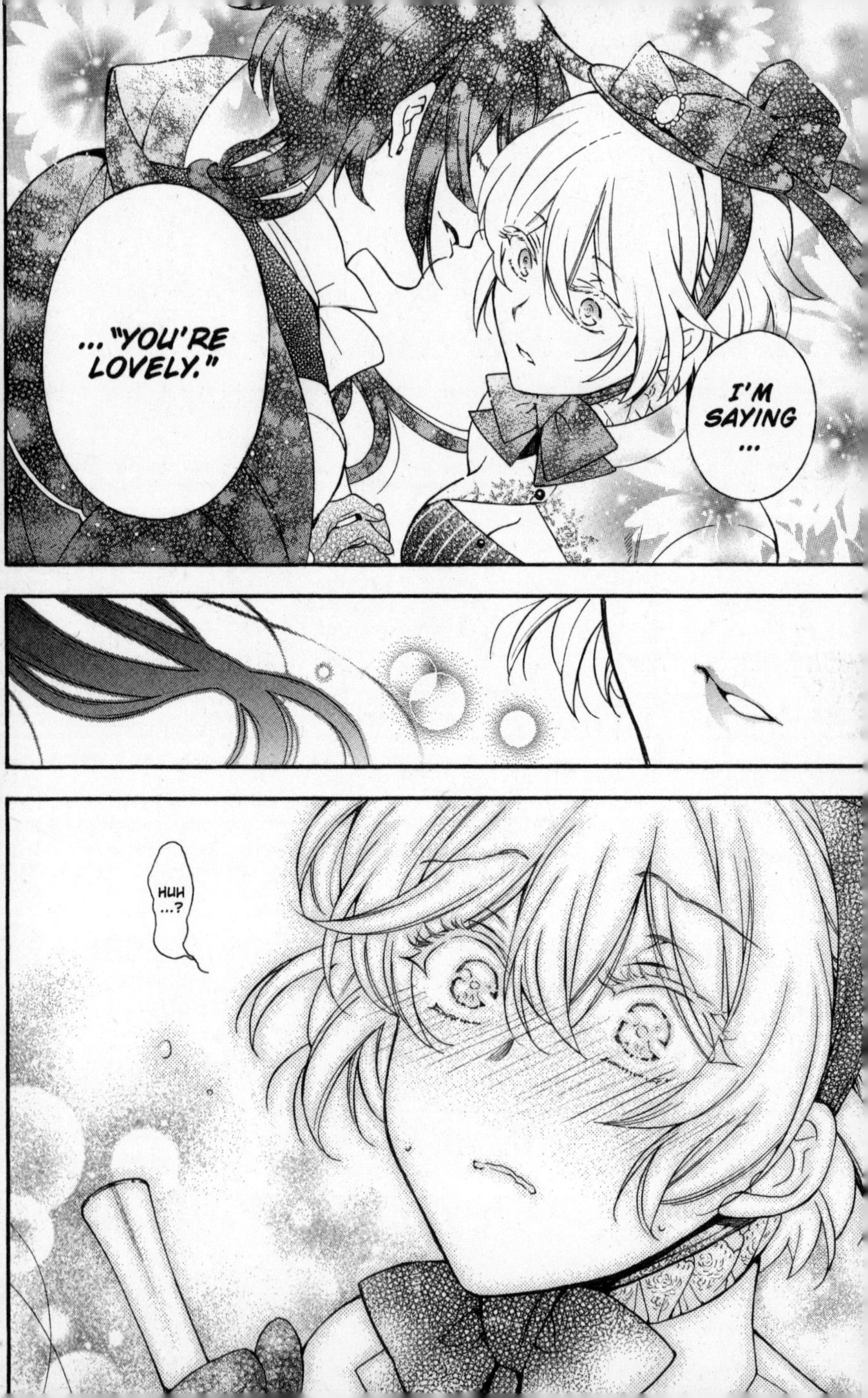
I'M SAYING ...
..."YOU'RE LOVELY."
HUH ...?

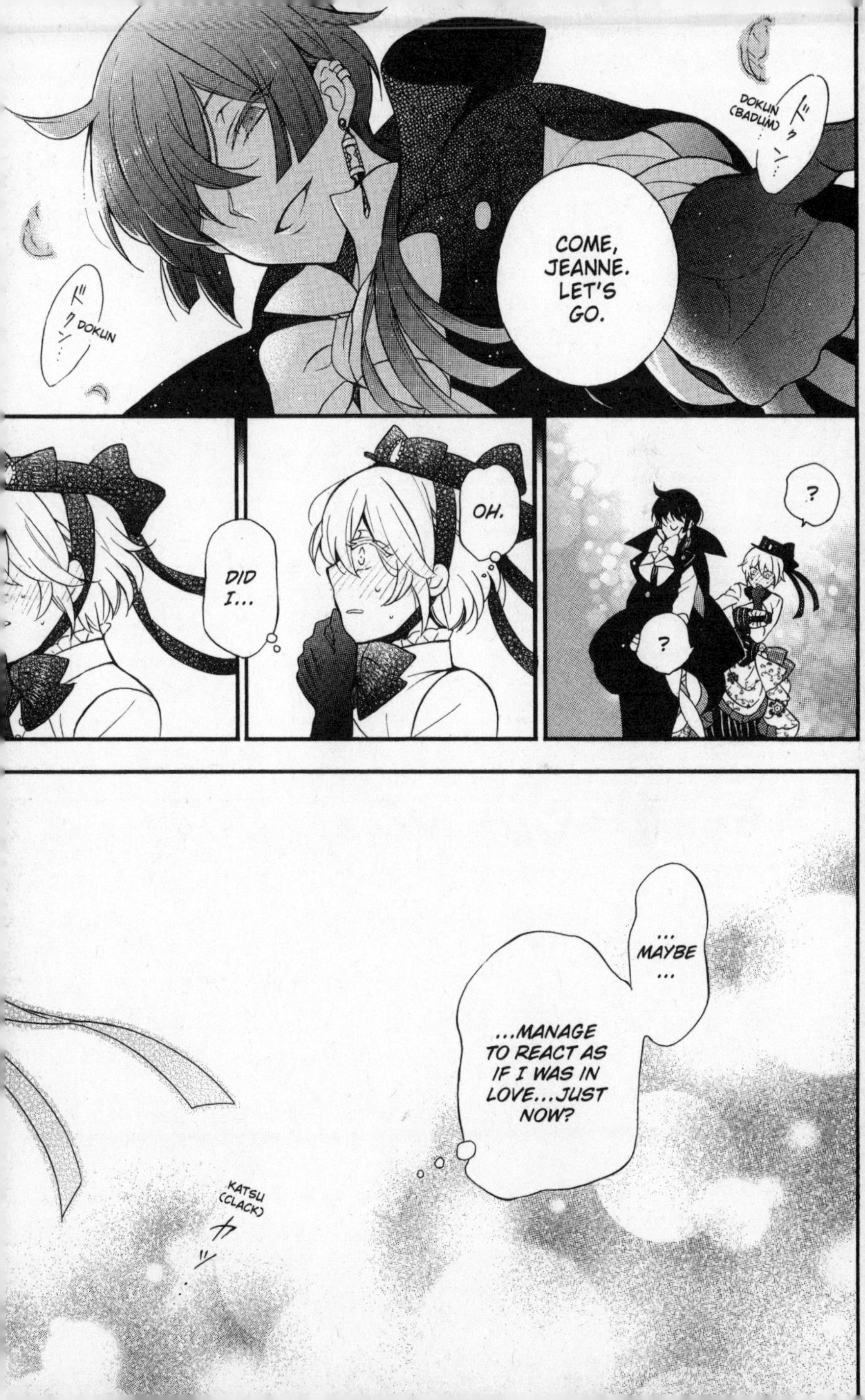
DOKUN (BADUM)
ドクン…
COME, JEANNE. LET'S GO.
ドクン…
DOKUN
?
?
OH.
DID I...
... MAYBE ...
...MANAGE TO REACT AS IF I WAS IN LOVE...JUST NOW?
KATSU (CLACK)
カッ

Mémoire 20 Serment PROMISE (PART I)

# MÉMOIRE 21

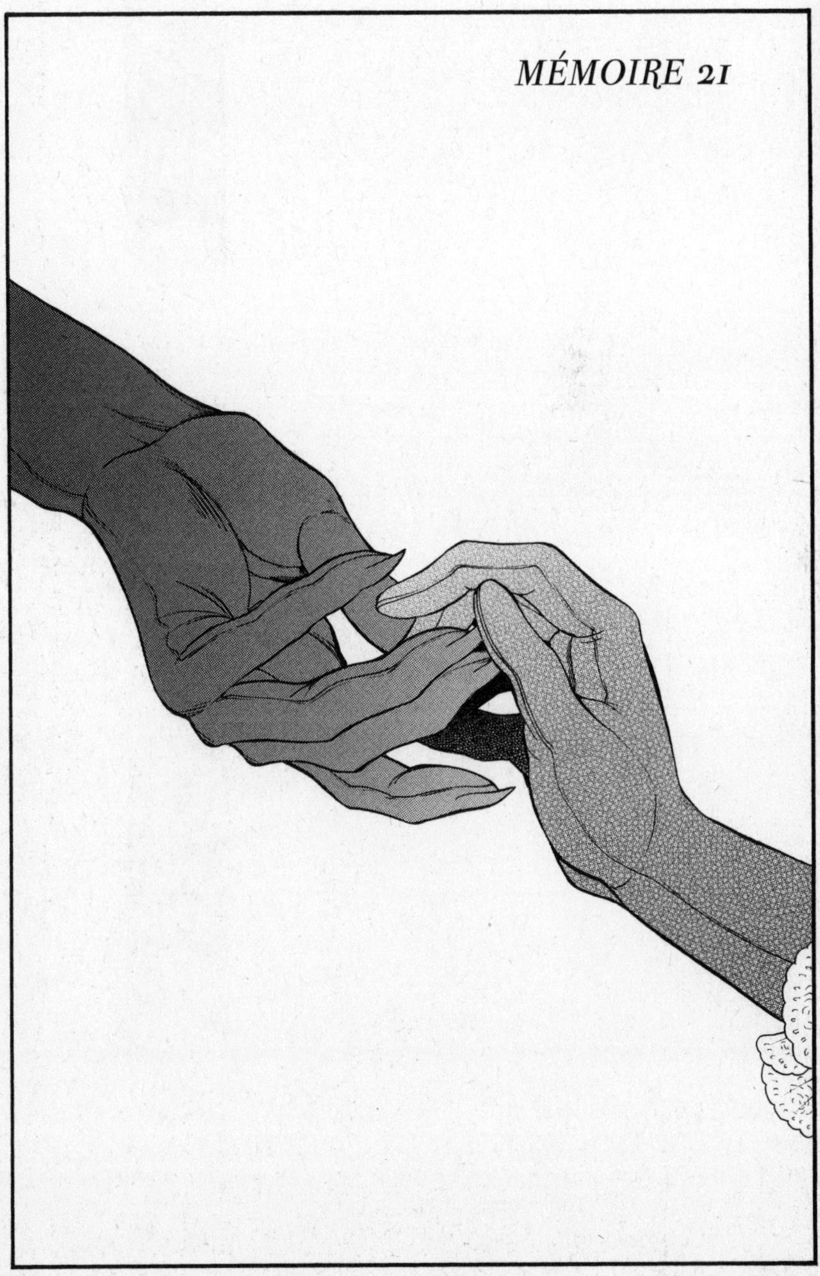

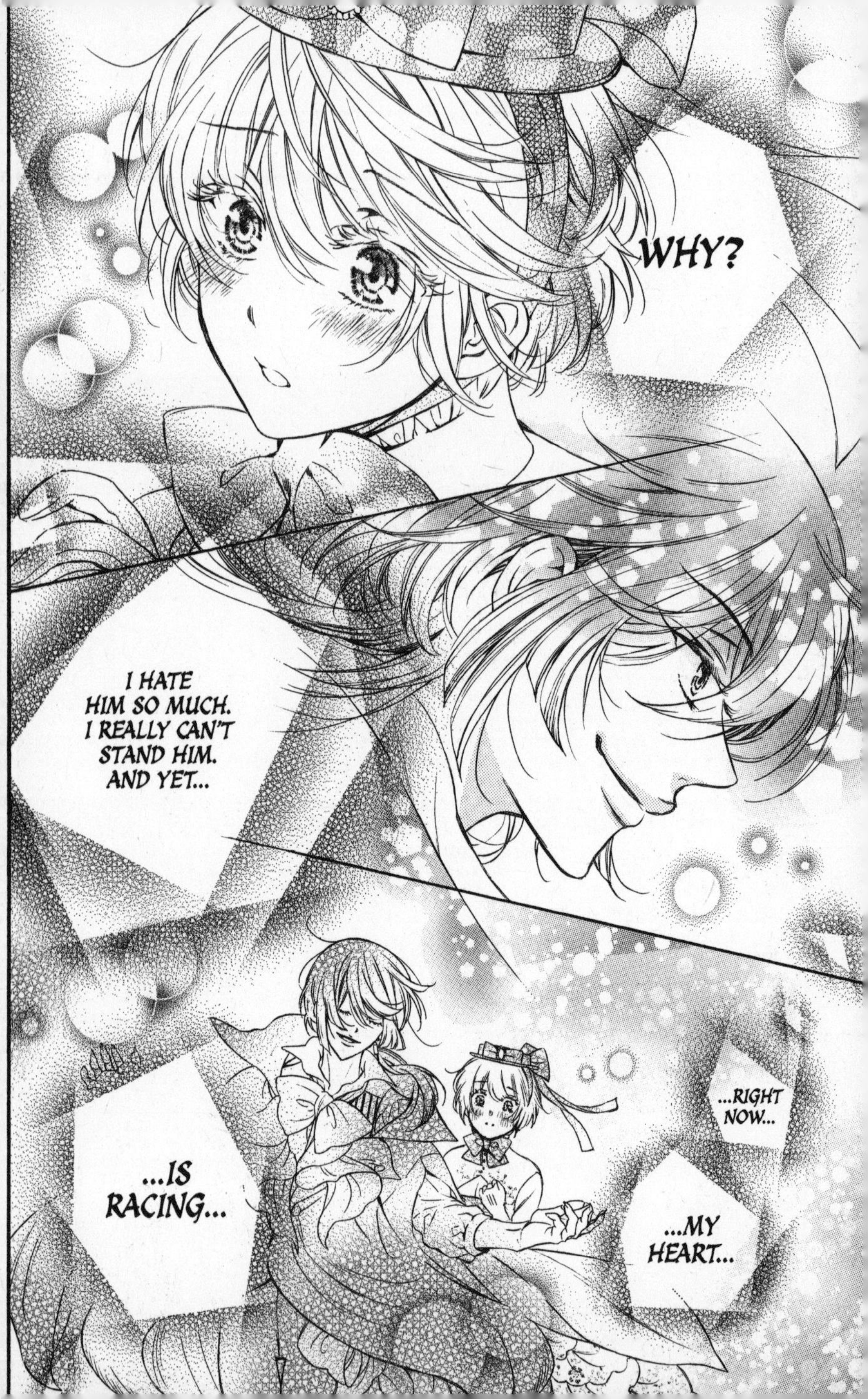
WHY?
I HATE HIM SO MUCH. I REALLY CAN'T STAND HIM. AND YET...
...RIGHT NOW...
...MY HEART...
...IS RACING...

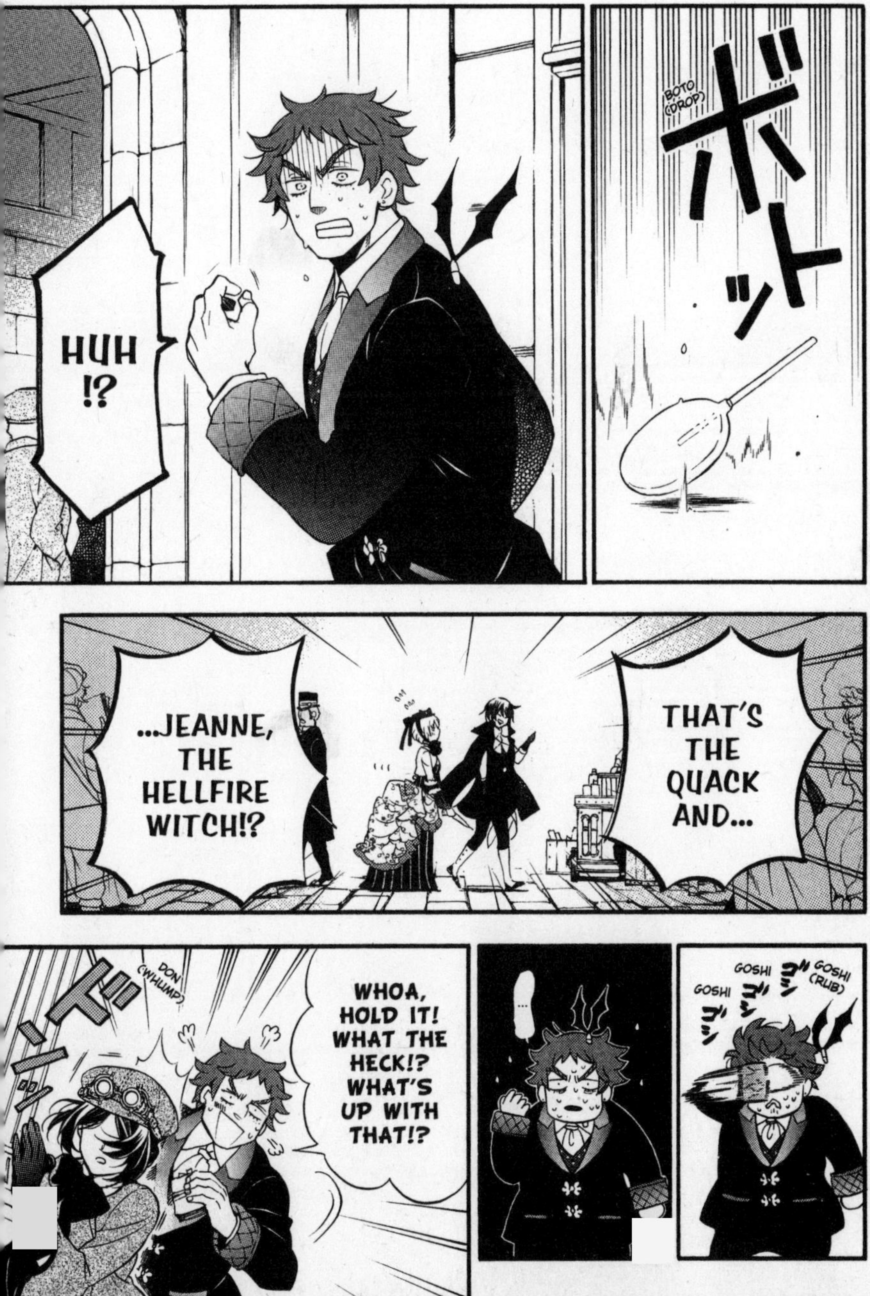

ボトッ
BOTO (DROP)
HUH!?
THAT'S THE QUACK AND...
...JEANNE, THE HELLFIRE WITCH!?
ゴシ ゴシ ゴシ
GOSHI GOSHI (RUB)
GOSHI
...
WHOA, HOLD IT! WHAT THE HECK!? WHAT'S UP WITH THAT!?
ドン
DON (WHUMP)

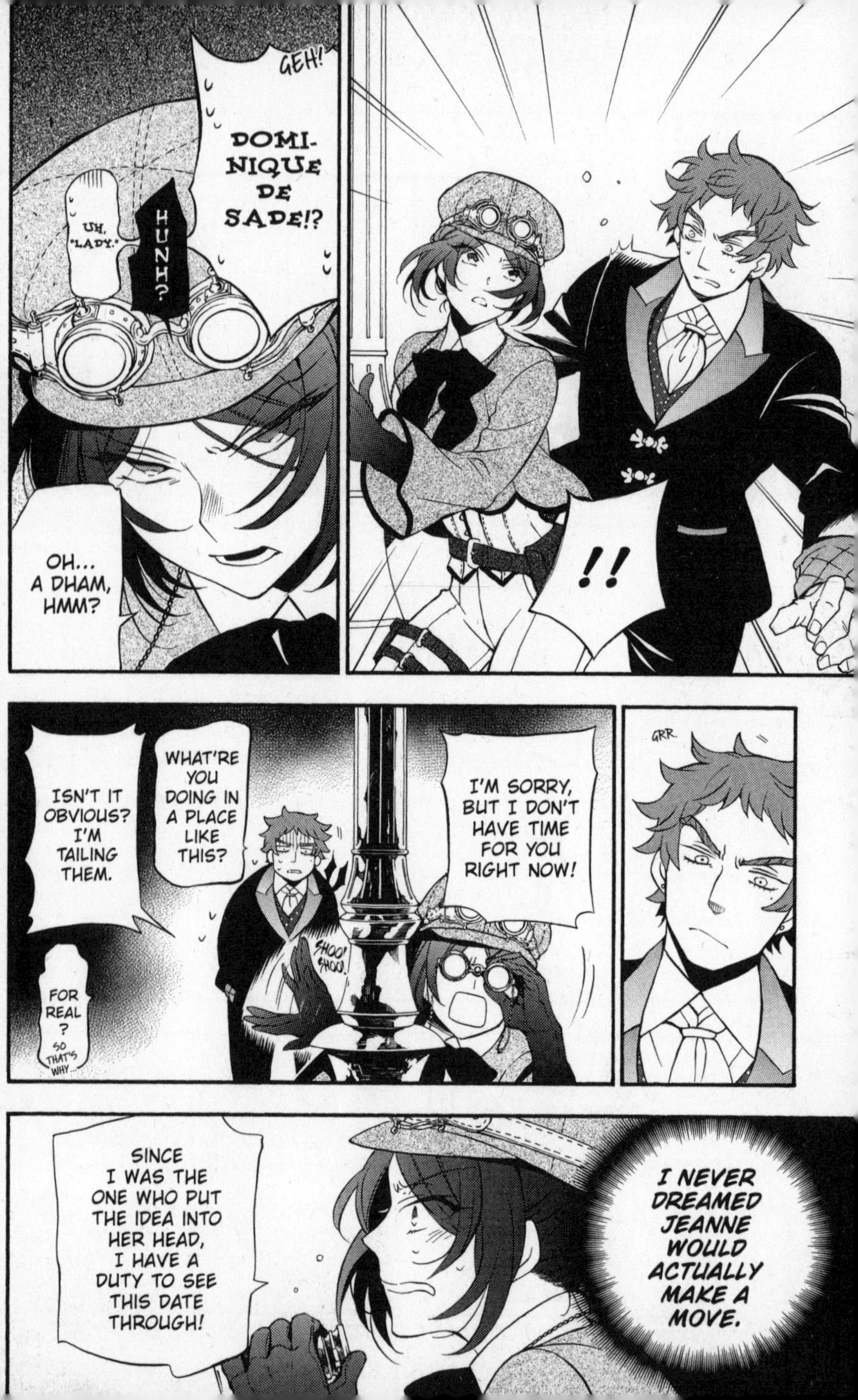
!!
GEH!
DOMINIQUE DE SADE!?
HUNH?
UH, "LADY."
OH... A DHAM, HMM?
GRR.
I'M SORRY, BUT I DON'T HAVE TIME FOR YOU RIGHT NOW!
SHOO! SHOO!
WHAT'RE YOU DOING IN A PLACE LIKE THIS?
ISN'T IT OBVIOUS? I'M TAILING THEM.
FOR REAL?
SO THAT'S WHY...
I NEVER DREAMED JEANNE WOULD ACTUALLY MAKE A MOVE.
SINCE I WAS THE ONE WHO PUT THE IDEA INTO HER HEAD, I HAVE A DUTY TO SEE THIS DATE THROUGH!

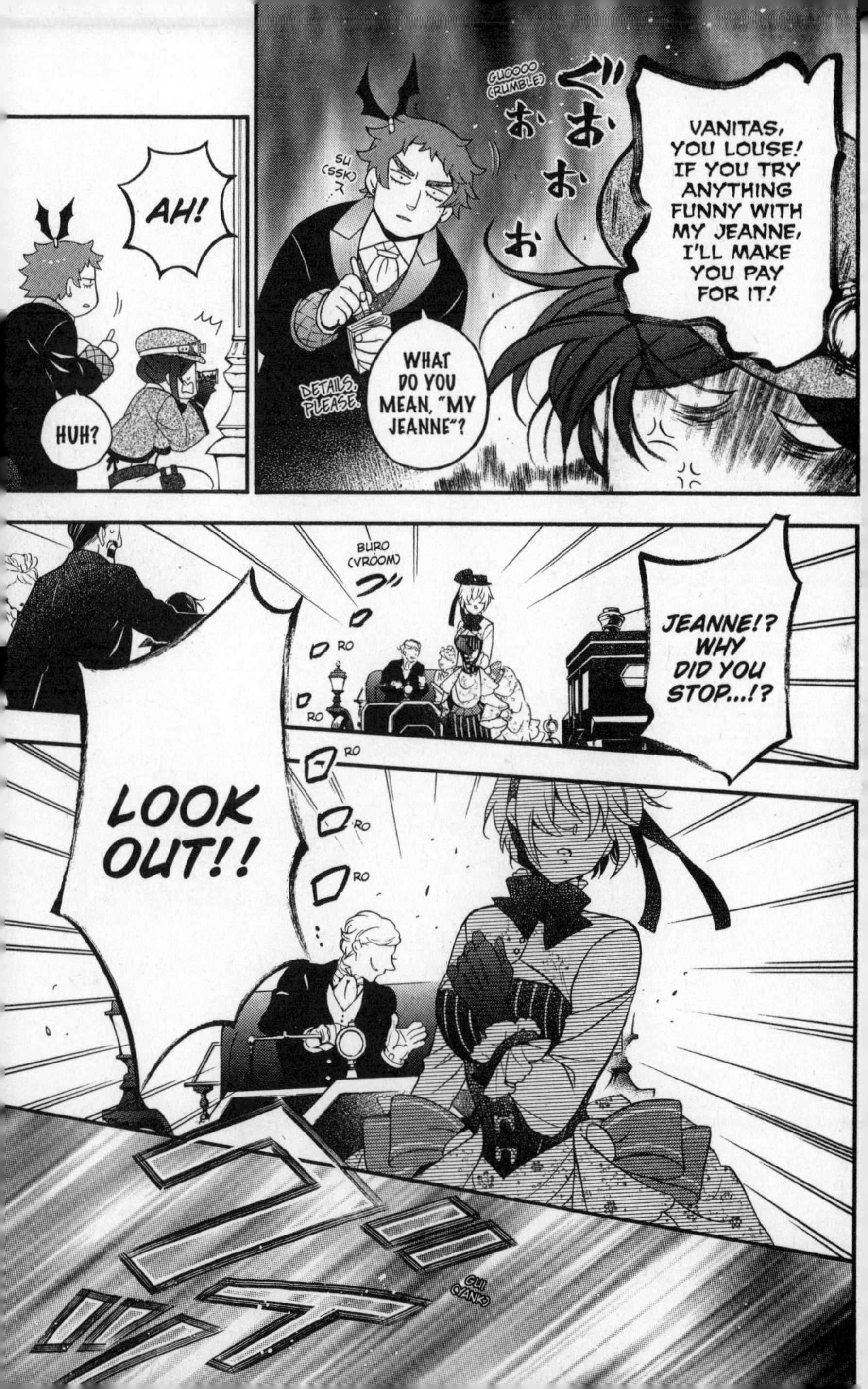
VANITAS, YOU LOUSE! IF YOU TRY ANYTHING FUNNY WITH MY JEANNE, I'LL MAKE YOU PAY FOR IT!
GUOOOO (RUMBLE)
ぐおおおお
SU (SSK)
ス
WHAT DO YOU MEAN, "MY JEANNE"?
DETAILS, PLEASE.
AH!
HUH?
JEANNE!? WHY DID YOU STOP...!?
BURO (VROOM)
RO
RO
RO
RO
RO
LOOK OUT!!
GUI (YANK)

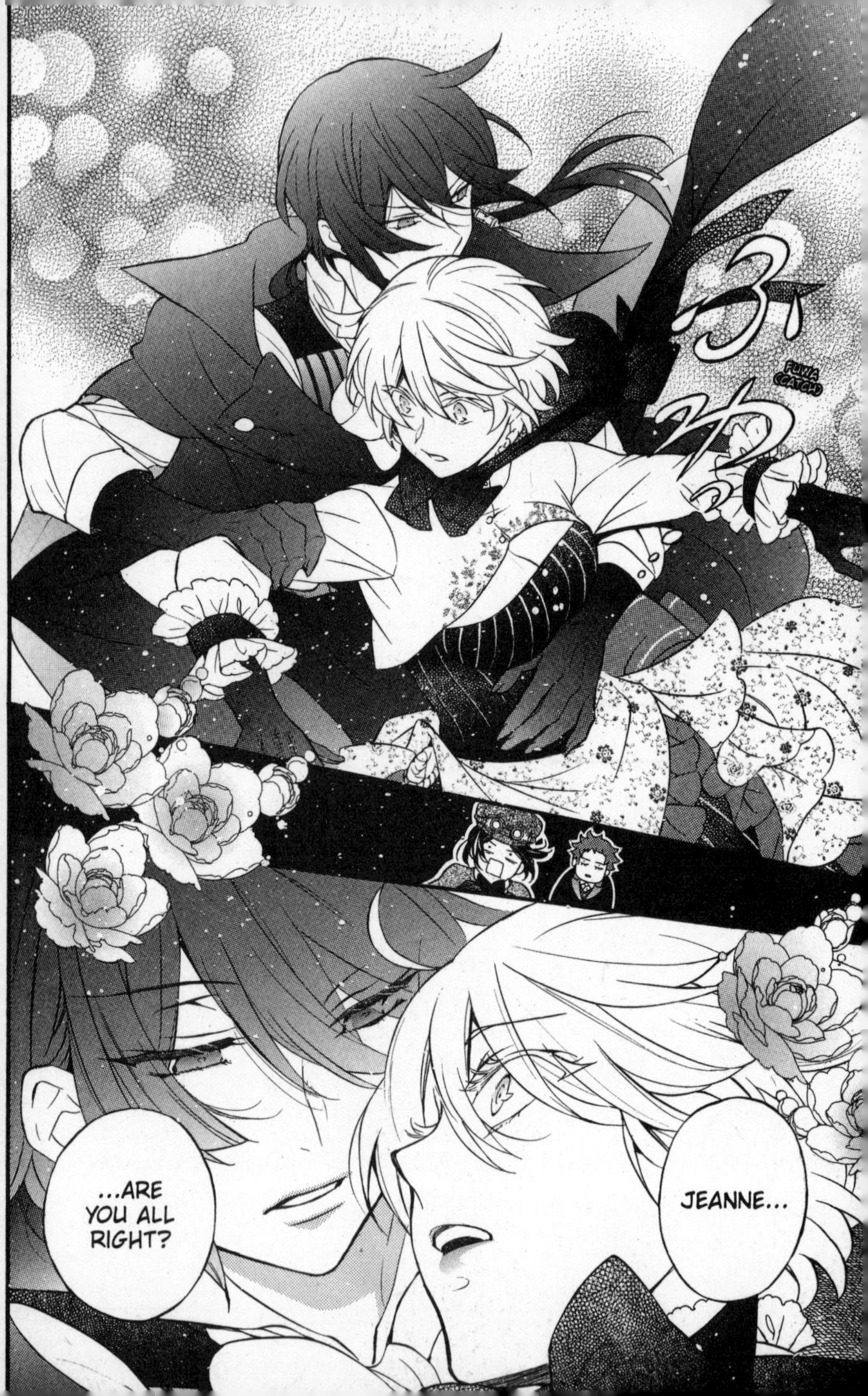
ふわっ
FUWA (CATCH)
JEANNE...
...ARE YOU ALL RIGHT?

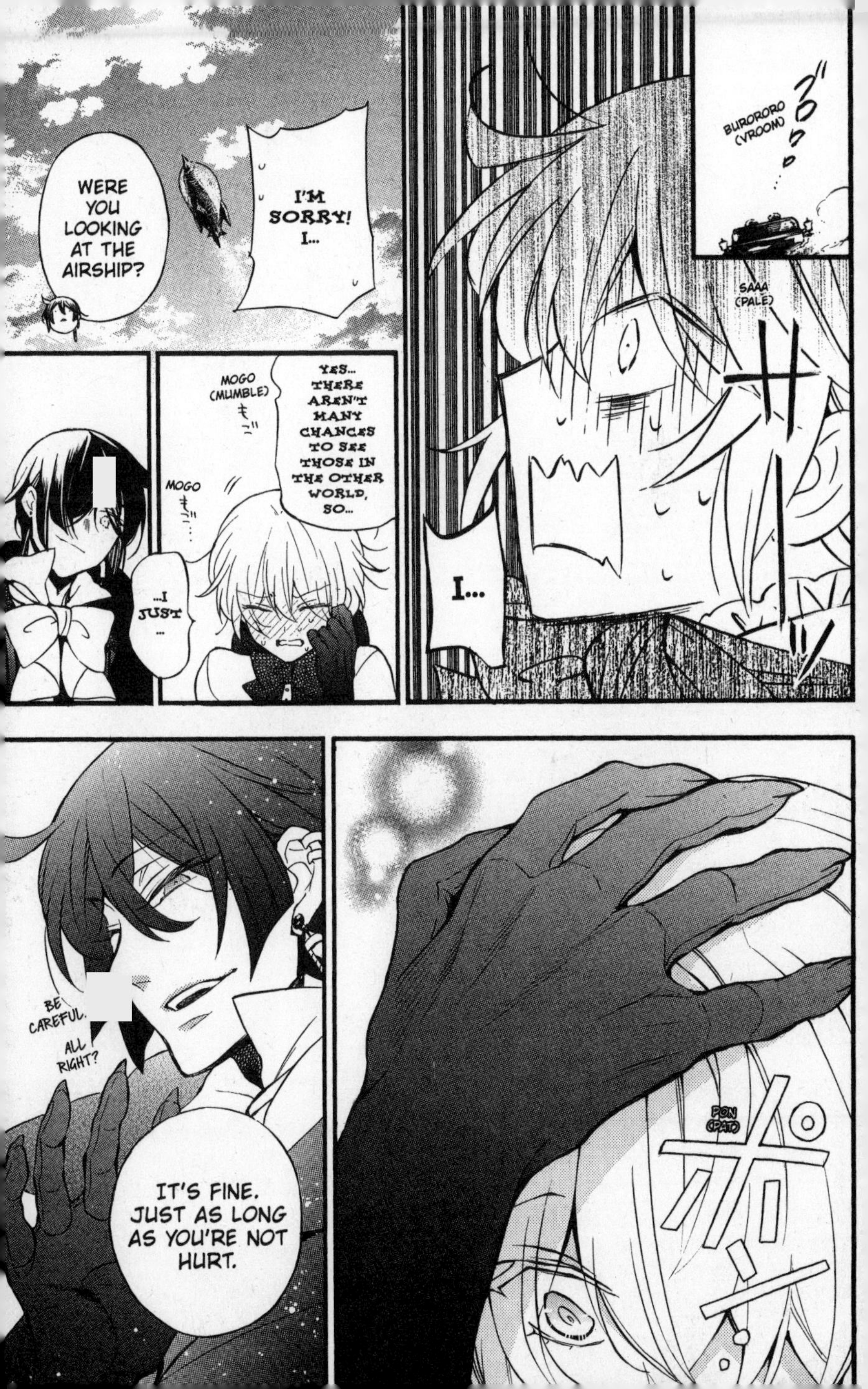
BURORORO (VROOM)
SAAA (PALE)
I...
I'M SORRY! I...
WERE YOU LOOKING AT THE AIRSHIP?
YES... THERE AREN'T MANY CHANCES TO SEE THOSE IN THE OTHER WORLD, SO...
MOGO (MUMBLE)
MOGO
...I JUST ...
PON (PAT)
IT'S FINE. JUST AS LONG AS YOU'RE NOT HURT.
BE CAREFUL.
ALL RIGHT?

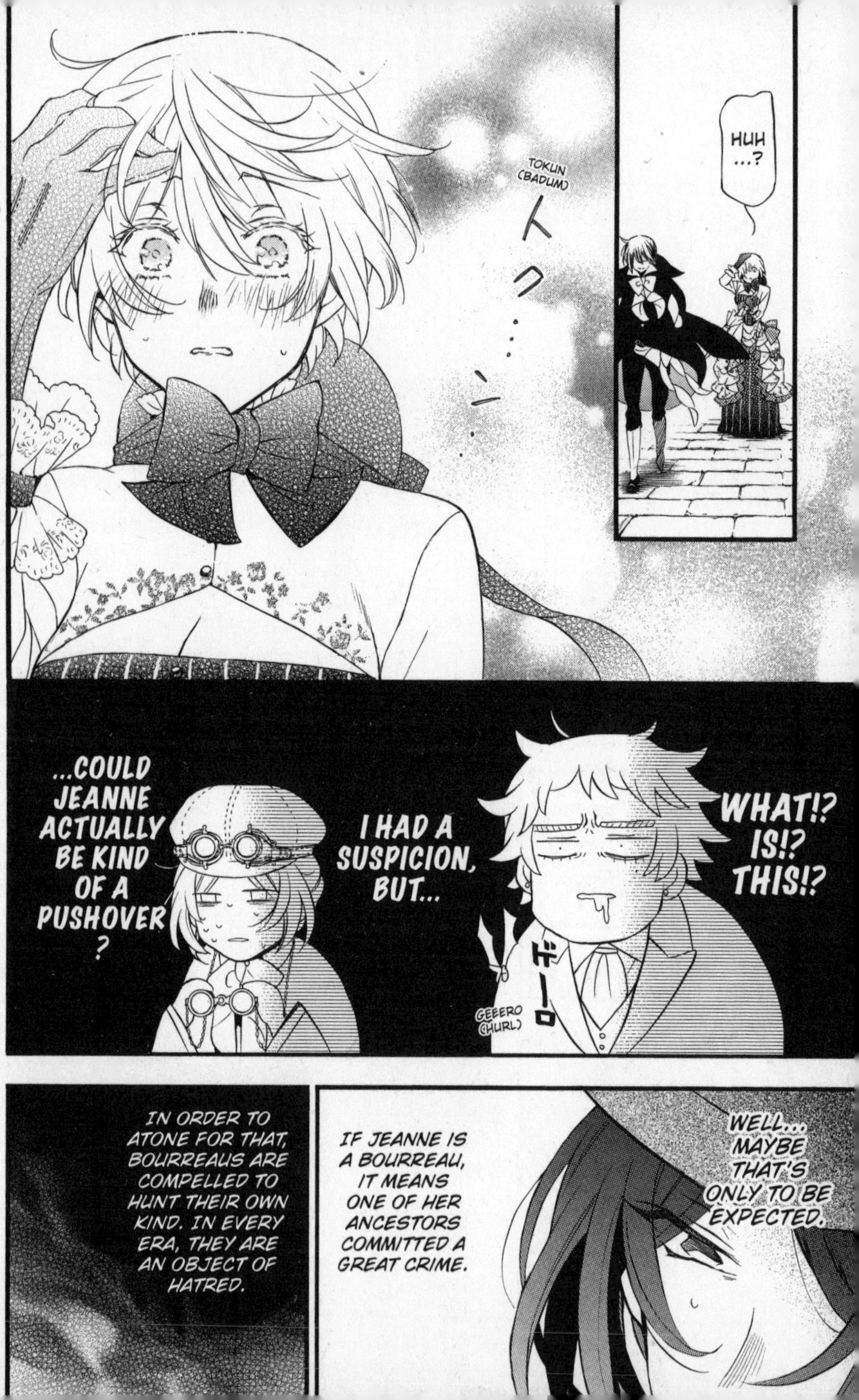
HUH ...?
TOKUN (BADUM)
WHAT!? IS!? THIS!?
GEEERO (HURL)
I HAD A SUSPICION, BUT...
...COULD JEANNE ACTUALLY BE KIND OF A PUSHOVER?
WELL... MAYBE THAT'S ONLY TO BE EXPECTED.
IF JEANNE IS A BOURREAU, IT MEANS ONE OF HER ANCESTORS COMMITTED A GREAT CRIME.
IN ORDER TO ATONE FOR THAT, BOURREAUS ARE COMPELLED TO HUNT THEIR OWN KIND. IN EVERY ERA, THEY ARE AN OBJECT OF HATRED.

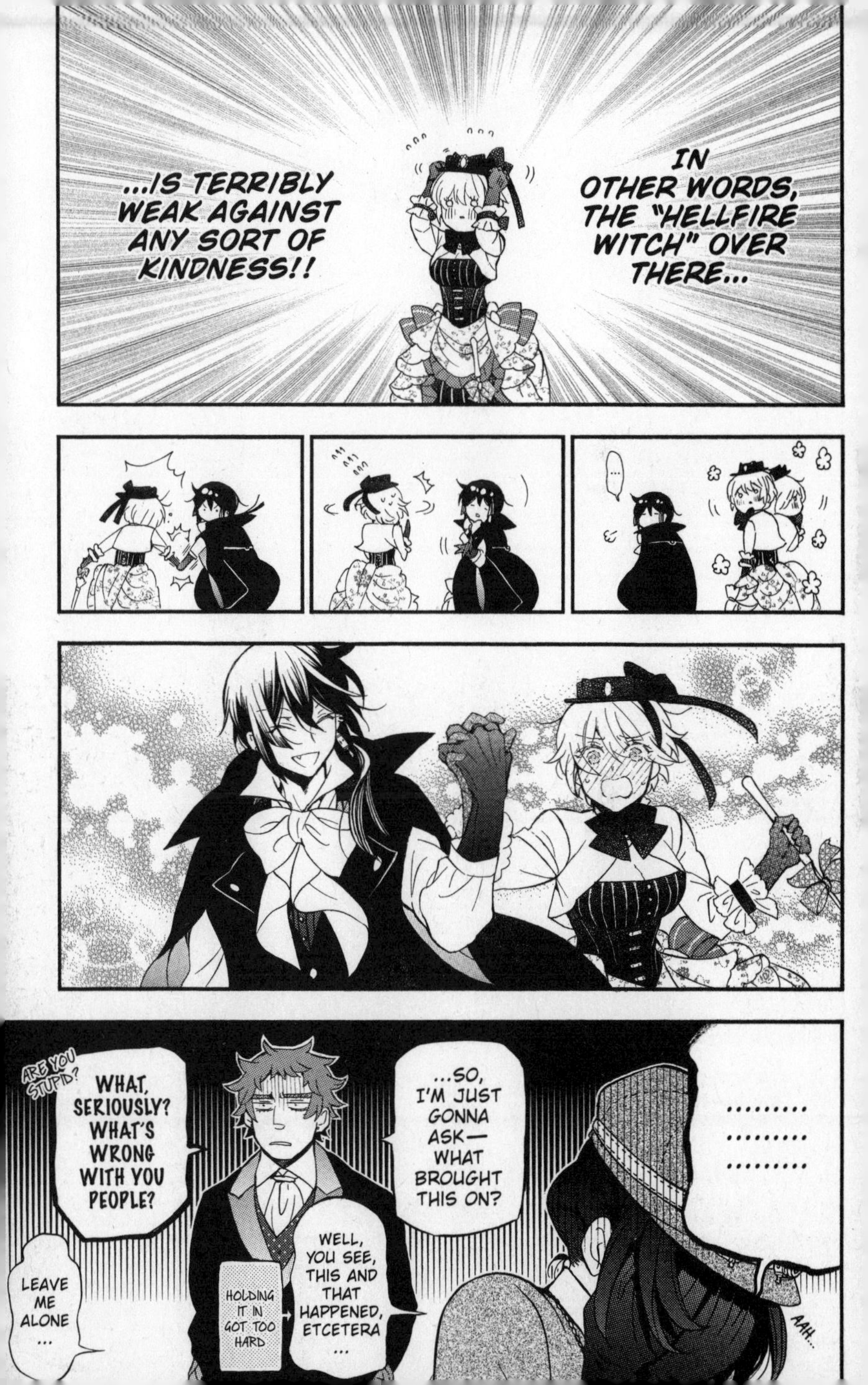
IN OTHER WORDS, THE "HELLFIRE WITCH" OVER THERE...
...IS TERRIBLY WEAK AGAINST ANY SORT OF KINDNESS!!
...
.........
.........
.........
AAH...
...SO, I'M JUST GONNA ASK—WHAT BROUGHT THIS ON?
WHAT, SERIOUSLY? WHAT'S WRONG WITH YOU PEOPLE?
ARE YOU STUPID?
WELL, YOU SEE, THIS AND THAT HAPPENED, ETCETERA...
HOLDING IT IN GOT TOO HARD
LEAVE ME ALONE...

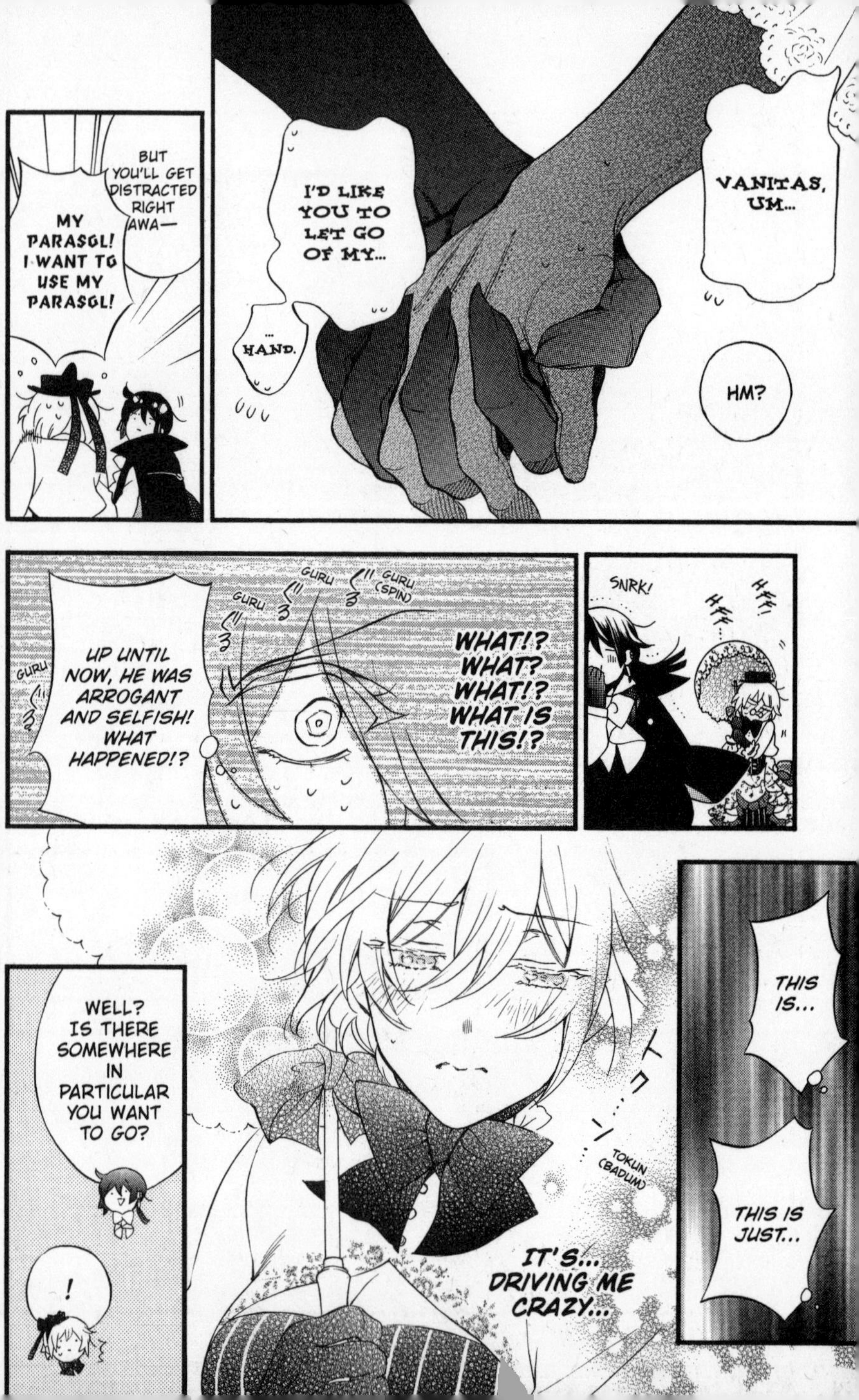
VANITAS, UM...
HM?
I'D LIKE YOU TO LET GO OF MY...
...HAND.
BUT YOU'LL GET DISTRACTED RIGHT AWA—
MY PARASOL! I WANT TO USE MY PARASOL!
SNRK!
HFF HFF
GURU GURU (SPIN)
GURU
GURU
WHAT!? WHAT? WHAT!? WHAT IS THIS!?
UP UNTIL NOW, HE WAS ARROGANT AND SELFISH! WHAT HAPPENED!?
THIS IS...
THIS IS JUST...
TOKUN (BADUM)
IT'S... DRIVING ME CRAZY...
WELL? IS THERE SOMEWHERE IN PARTICULAR YOU WANT TO GO?
!

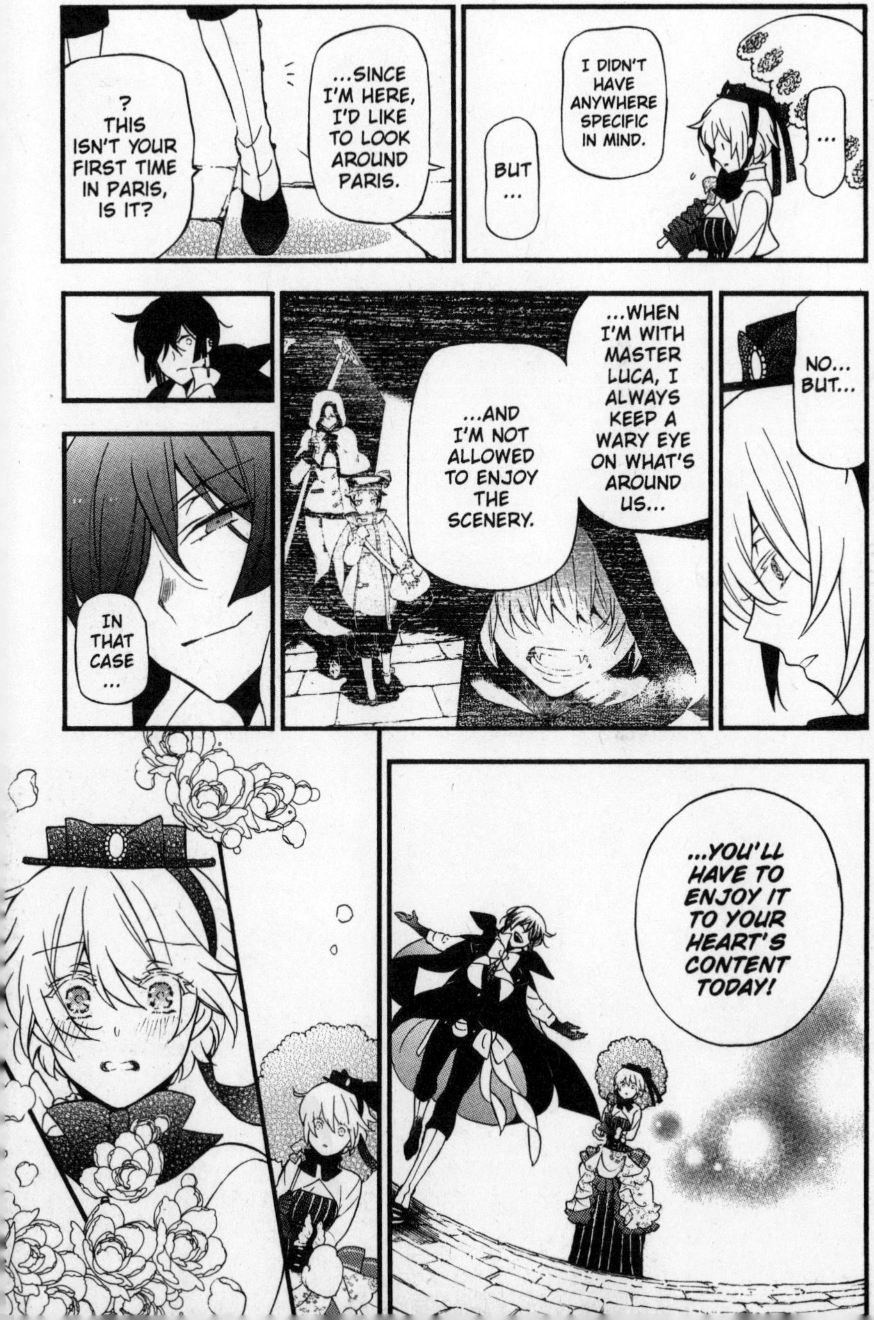
...
I DIDN'T HAVE ANYWHERE SPECIFIC IN MIND.
BUT ...
...SINCE I'M HERE, I'D LIKE TO LOOK AROUND PARIS.
? THIS ISN'T YOUR FIRST TIME IN PARIS, IS IT?
NO... BUT...
...WHEN I'M WITH MASTER LUCA, I ALWAYS KEEP A WARY EYE ON WHAT'S AROUND US...
...AND I'M NOT ALLOWED TO ENJOY THE SCENERY.
IN THAT CASE ...
...YOU'LL HAVE TO ENJOY IT TO YOUR HEART'S CONTENT TODAY!

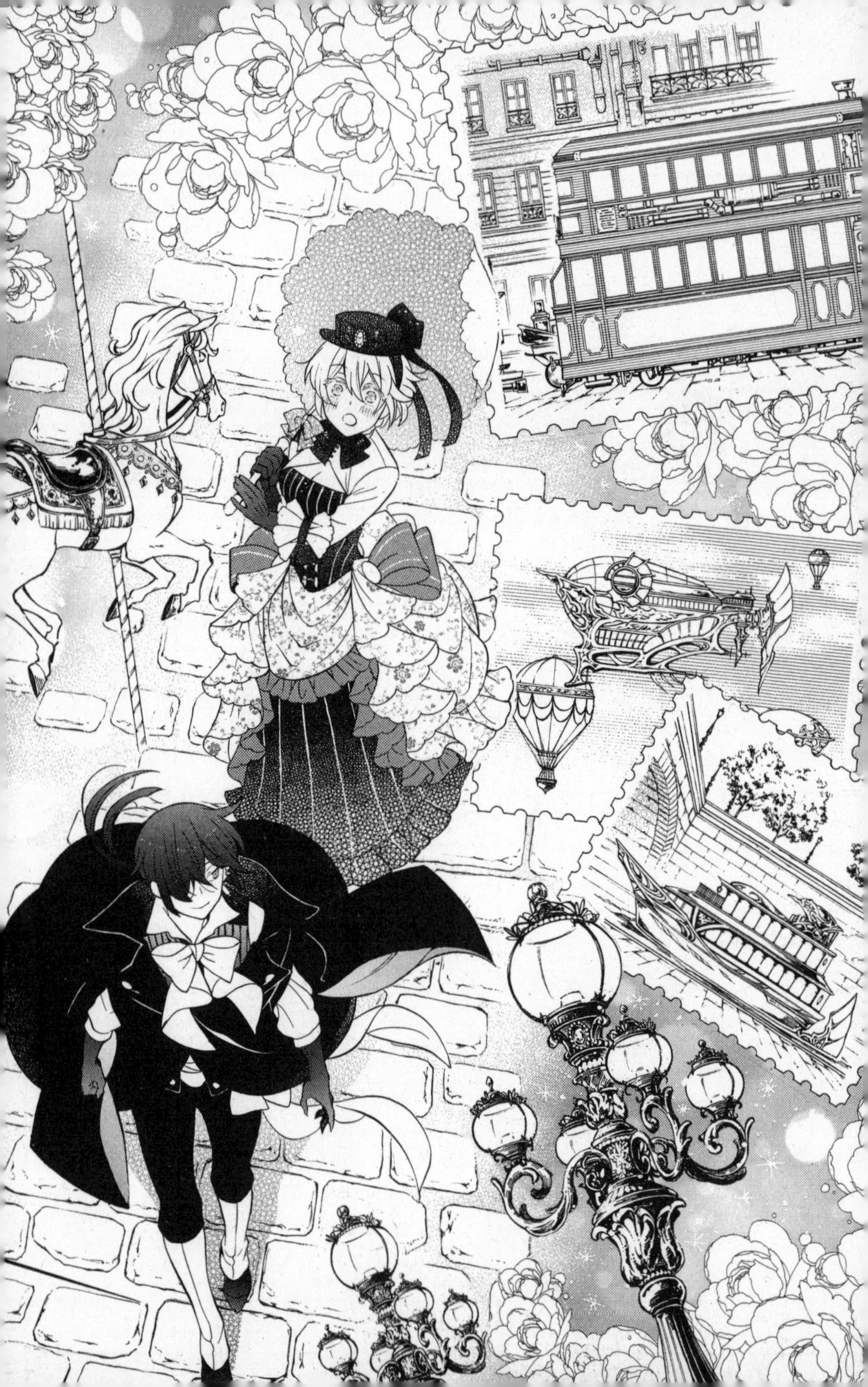

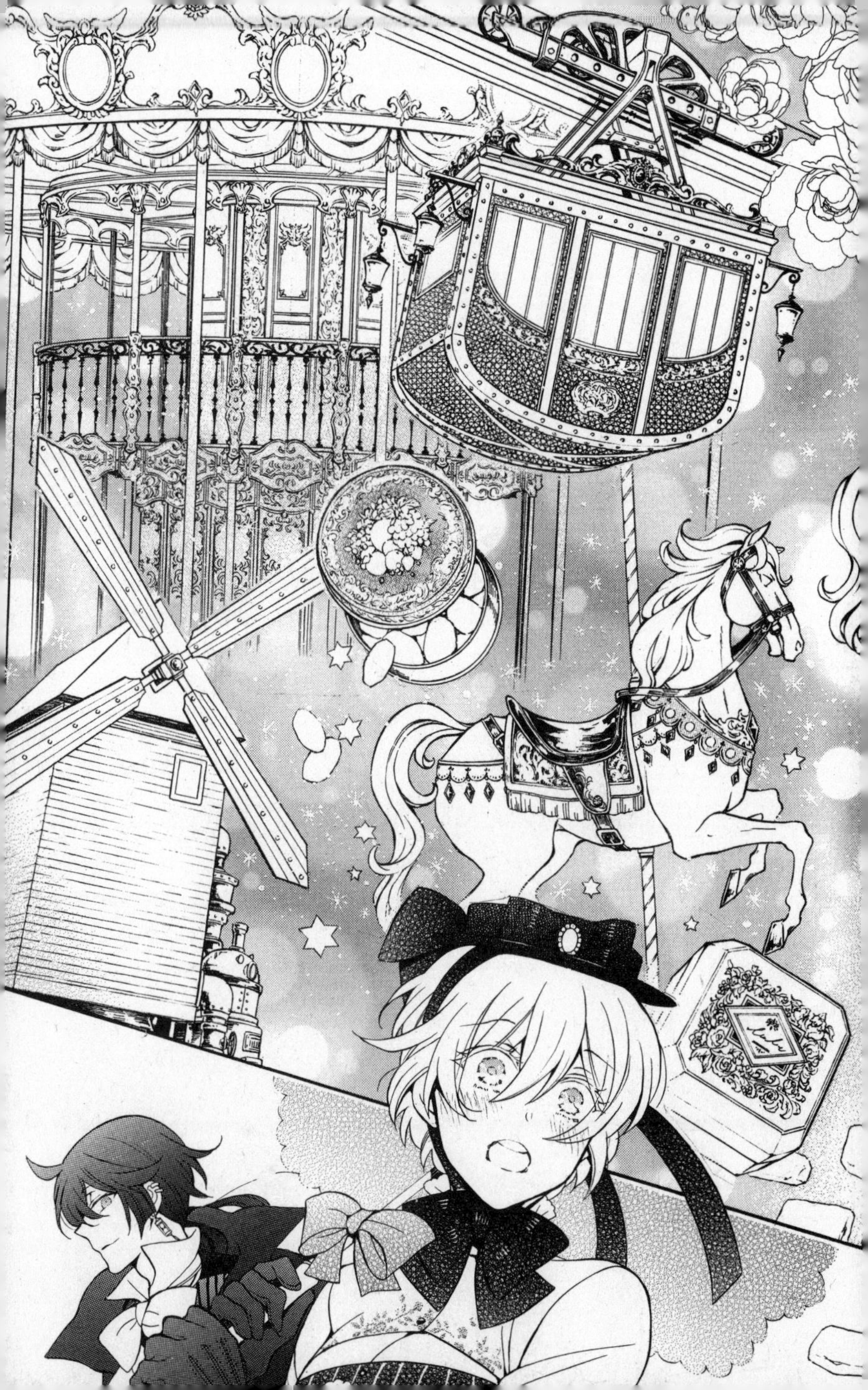

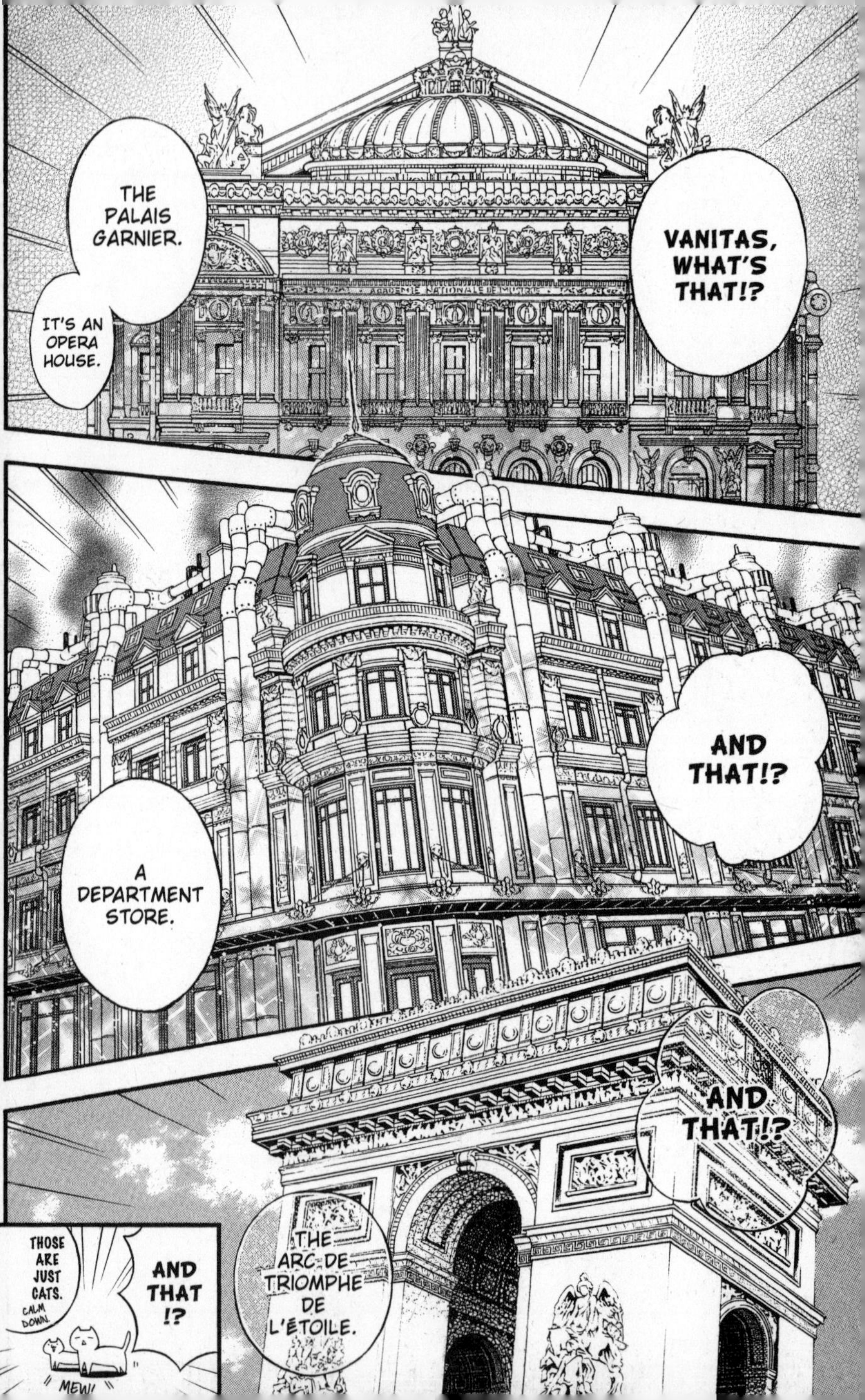
VANITAS, WHAT'S THAT!?
THE PALAIS GARNIER.
IT'S AN OPERA HOUSE.
AND THAT!?
A DEPARTMENT STORE.
AND THAT!?
THE ARC DE TRIOMPHE DE L'ÉTOILE.
AND THAT !?
THOSE ARE JUST CATS.
CALM DOWN.
MEW!

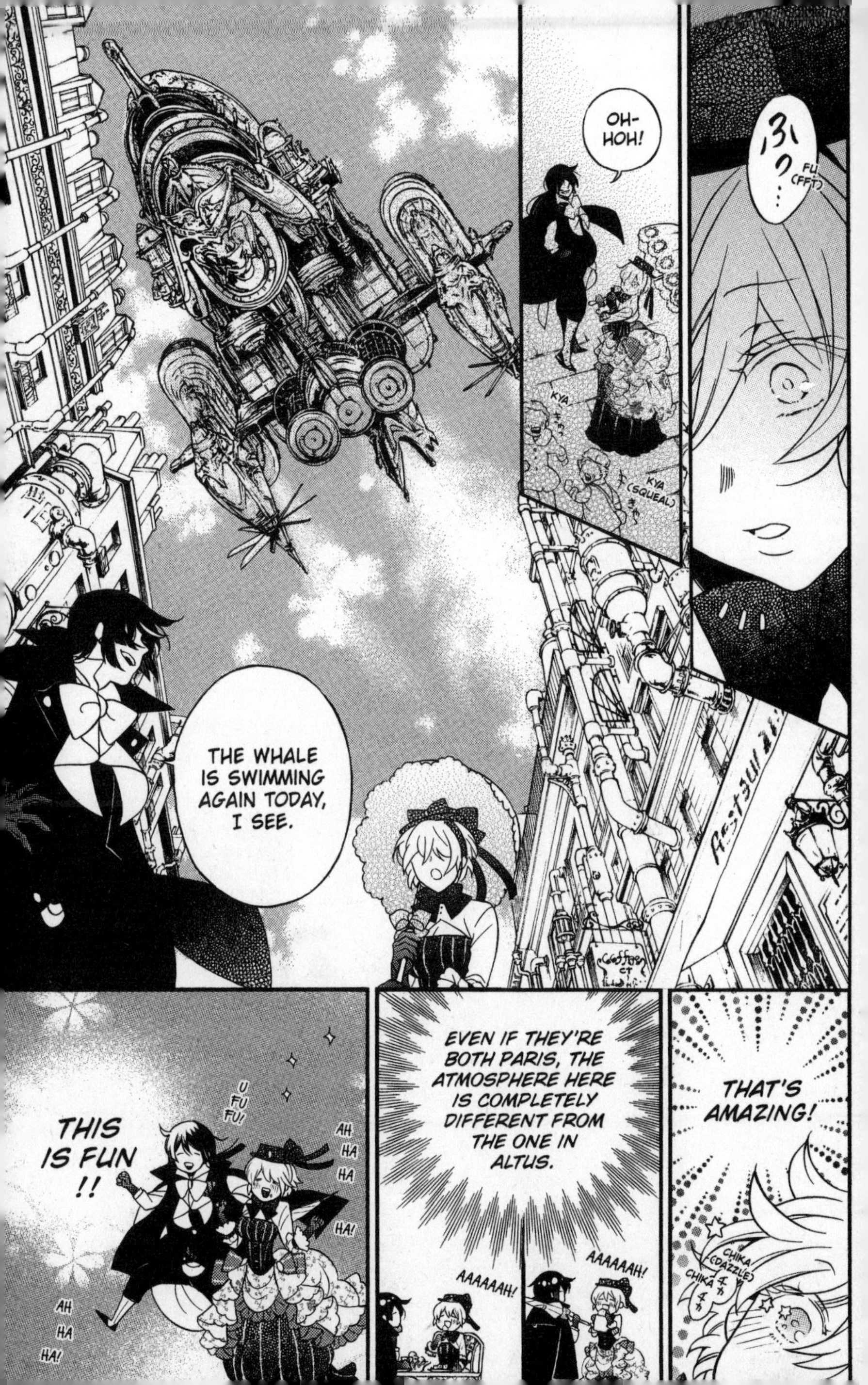
ふっ…
FU (FFT)
OH-HOH!
KYA
KYA (SQUEAL)
THE WHALE IS SWIMMING AGAIN TODAY, I SEE.
THAT'S AMAZING!
CHIKA CHIKA (DAZZLE)
EVEN IF THEY'RE BOTH PARIS, THE ATMOSPHERE HERE IS COMPLETELY DIFFERENT FROM THE ONE IN ALTUS.
AAAAAAH!
AAAAAAH!
THIS IS FUN!!
U FU FU!
AH HA HA HA!
AH HA HA!

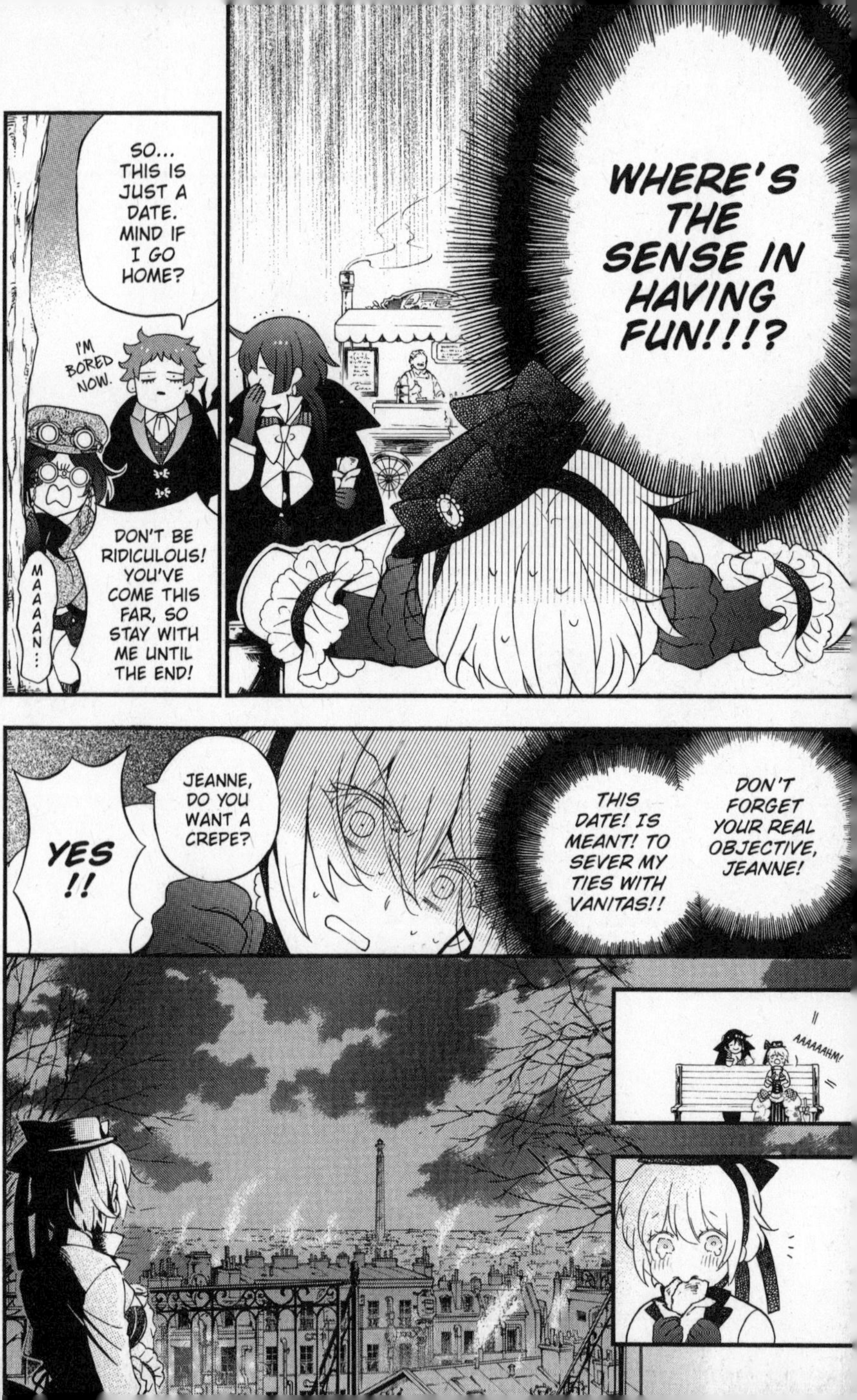
WHERE'S THE SENSE IN HAVING FUN!!!?
SO... THIS IS JUST A DATE. MIND IF I GO HOME?
I'M BORED NOW.
DON'T BE RIDICULOUS! YOU'VE COME THIS FAR, SO STAY WITH ME UNTIL THE END!
MAAAAN...
DON'T FORGET YOUR REAL OBJECTIVE, JEANNE!
THIS DATE! IS MEANT! TO SEVER MY TIES WITH VANITAS!!
JEANNE, DO YOU WANT A CREPE?
YES!!
AAAAAAHM!

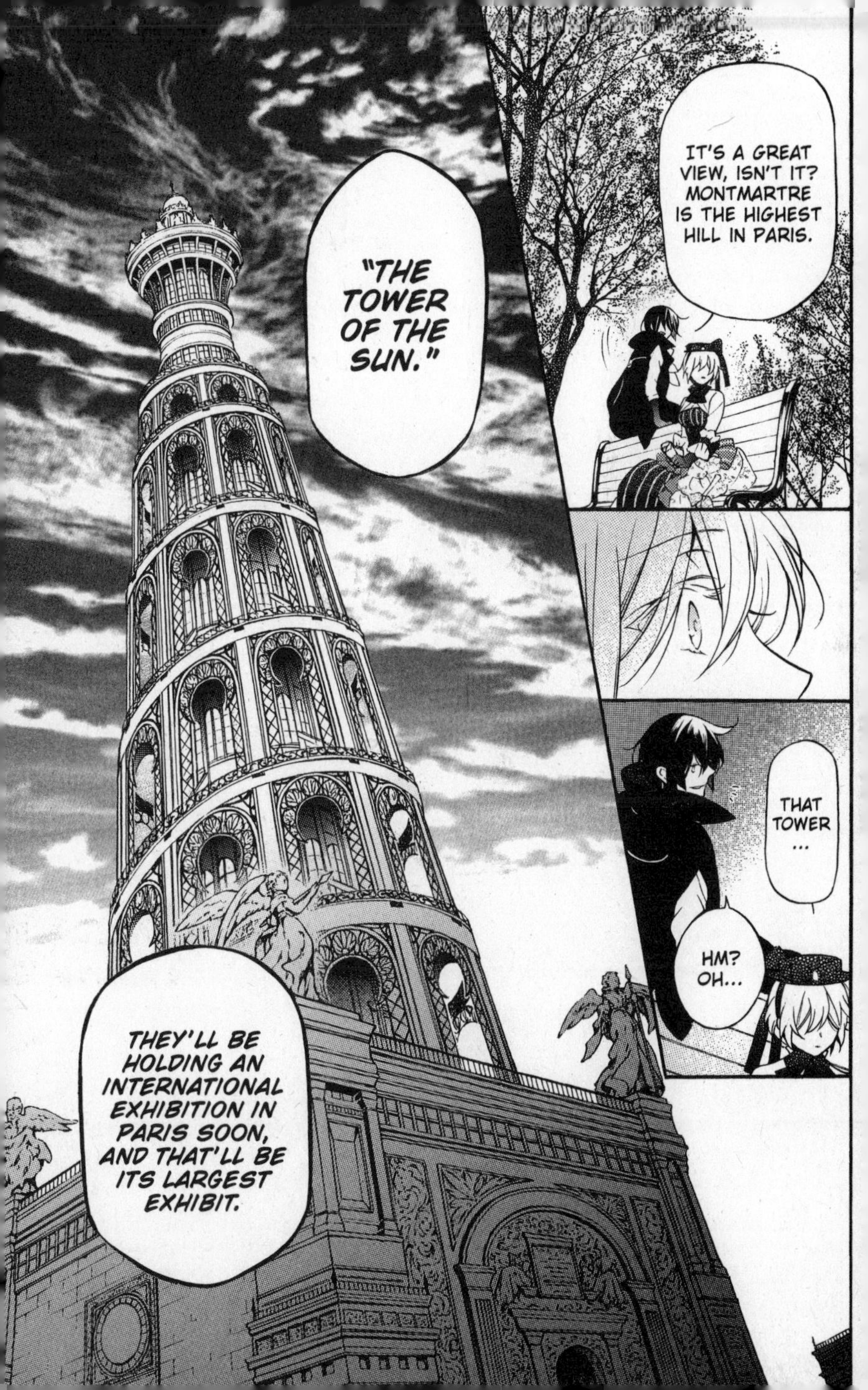
IT'S A GREAT VIEW, ISN'T IT? MONTMARTRE IS THE HIGHEST HILL IN PARIS.
THAT TOWER ...
HM? OH...
"THE TOWER OF THE SUN."
THEY'LL BE HOLDING AN INTERNATIONAL EXHIBITION IN PARIS SOON, AND THAT'LL BE ITS LARGEST EXHIBIT.

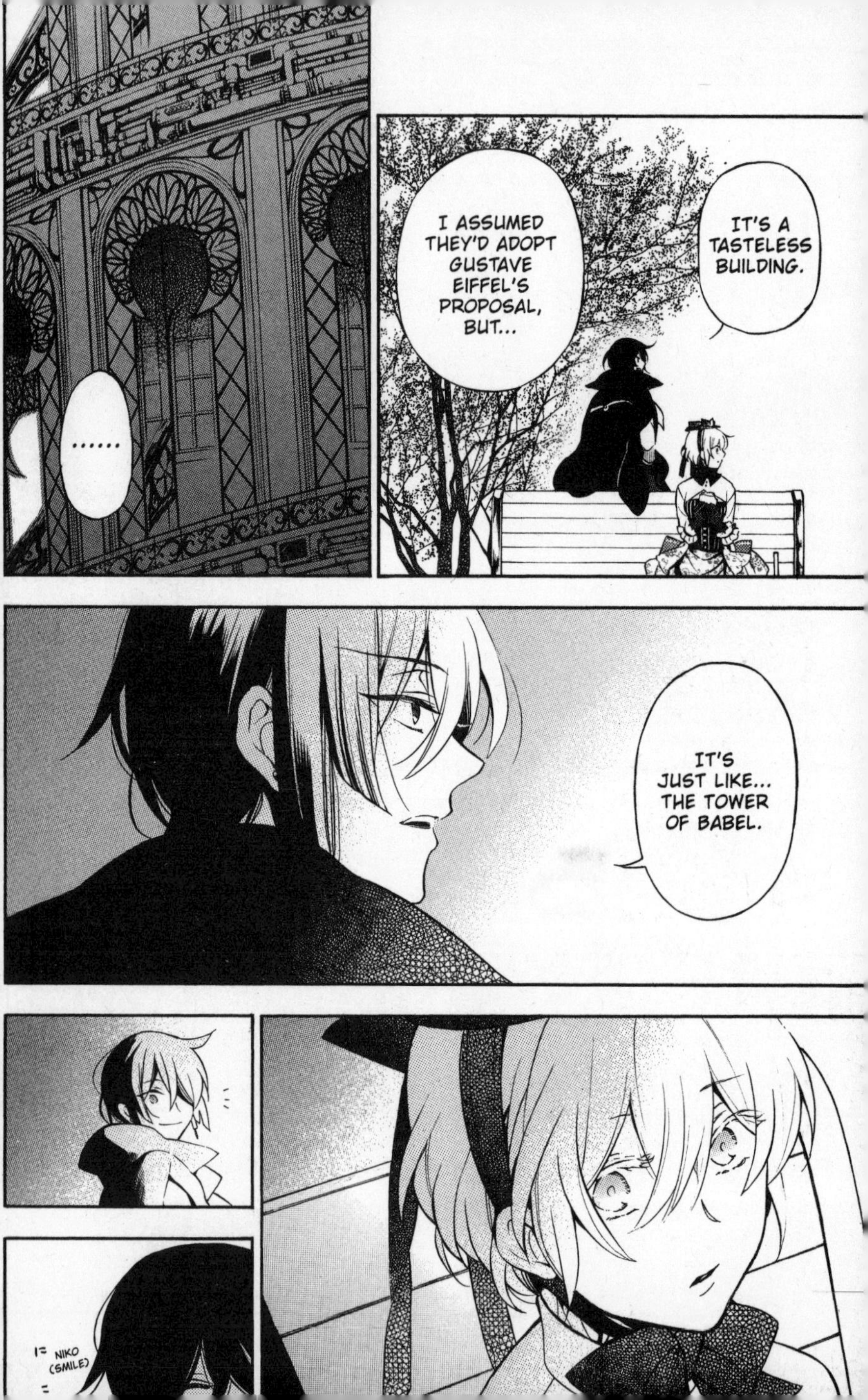
IT'S A TASTELESS BUILDING.
I ASSUMED THEY'D ADOPT GUSTAVE EIFFEL'S PROPOSAL, BUT...
......
IT'S JUST LIKE... THE TOWER OF BABEL.
NIKO (SMILE)

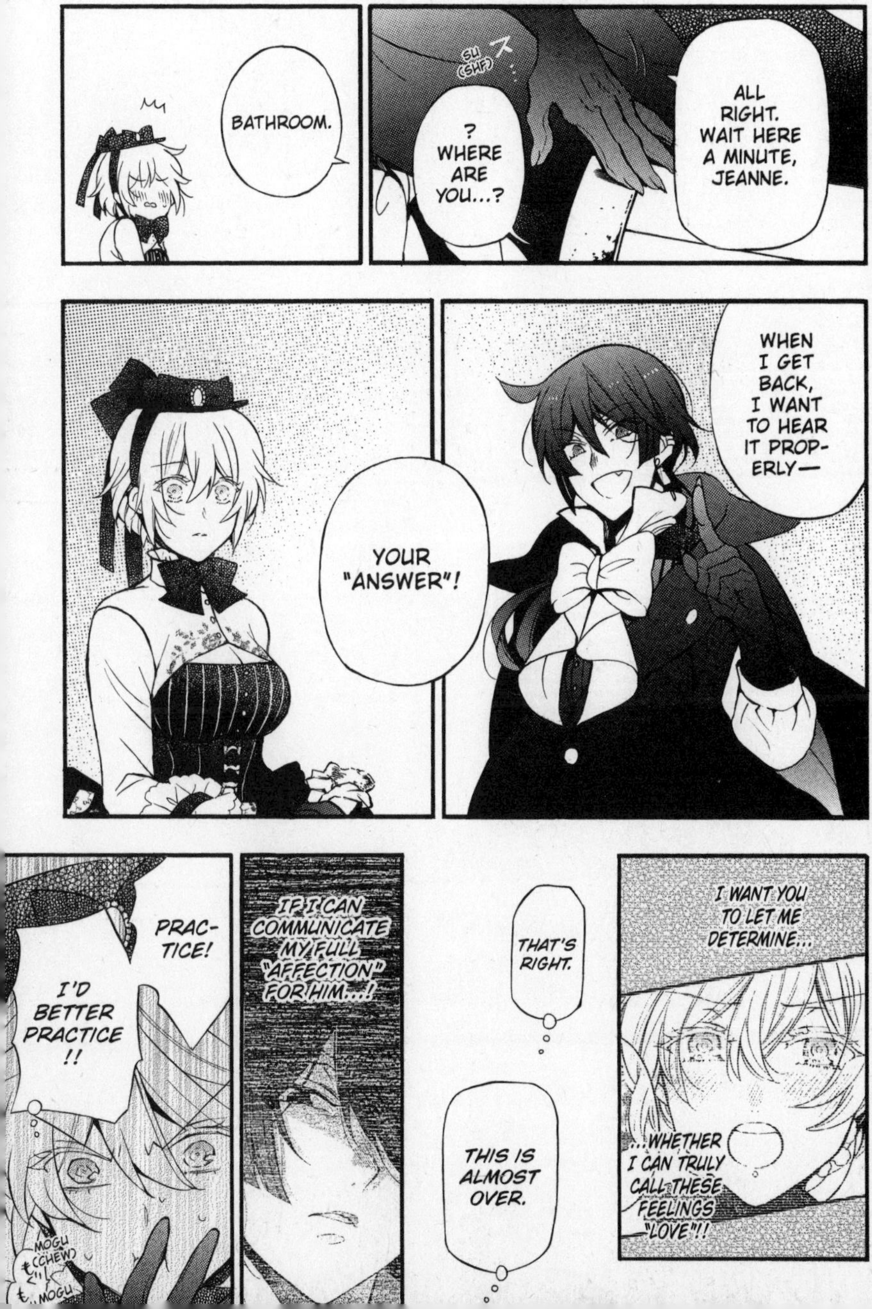
ALL RIGHT. WAIT HERE A MINUTE, JEANNE.
SU (SHF)
? WHERE ARE YOU...?
BATHROOM.
WHEN I GET BACK, I WANT TO HEAR IT PROP-ERLY—
YOUR "ANSWER"!
I WANT YOU TO LET ME DETERMINE...
...WHETHER I CAN TRULY CALL THESE FEELINGS "LOVE"!!
THAT'S RIGHT.
THIS IS ALMOST OVER.
IF I CAN COMMUNICATE MY FULL "AFFECTION" FOR HIM...!
PRAC-TICE!
I'D BETTER PRACTICE!!
MOGU (CHEW) MOGU

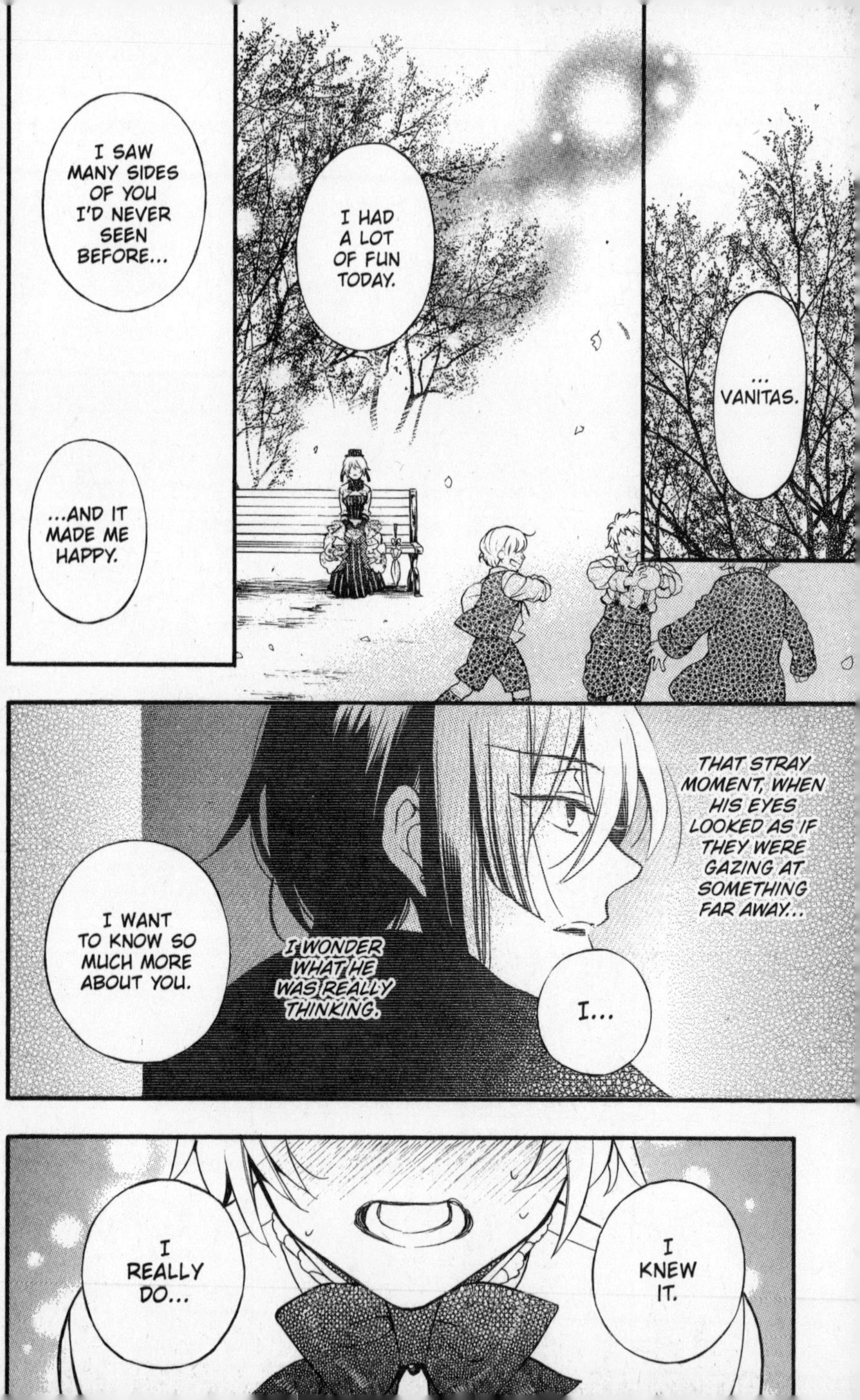
...VANITAS.
I HAD A LOT OF FUN TODAY.
I SAW MANY SIDES OF YOU I'D NEVER SEEN BEFORE...
...AND IT MADE ME HAPPY.
THAT STRAY MOMENT, WHEN HIS EYES LOOKED AS IF THEY WERE GAZING AT SOMETHING FAR AWAY...
I...
I WONDER WHAT HE WAS REALLY THINKING.
I WANT TO KNOW SO MUCH MORE ABOUT YOU.
I KNEW IT.
I REALLY DO...

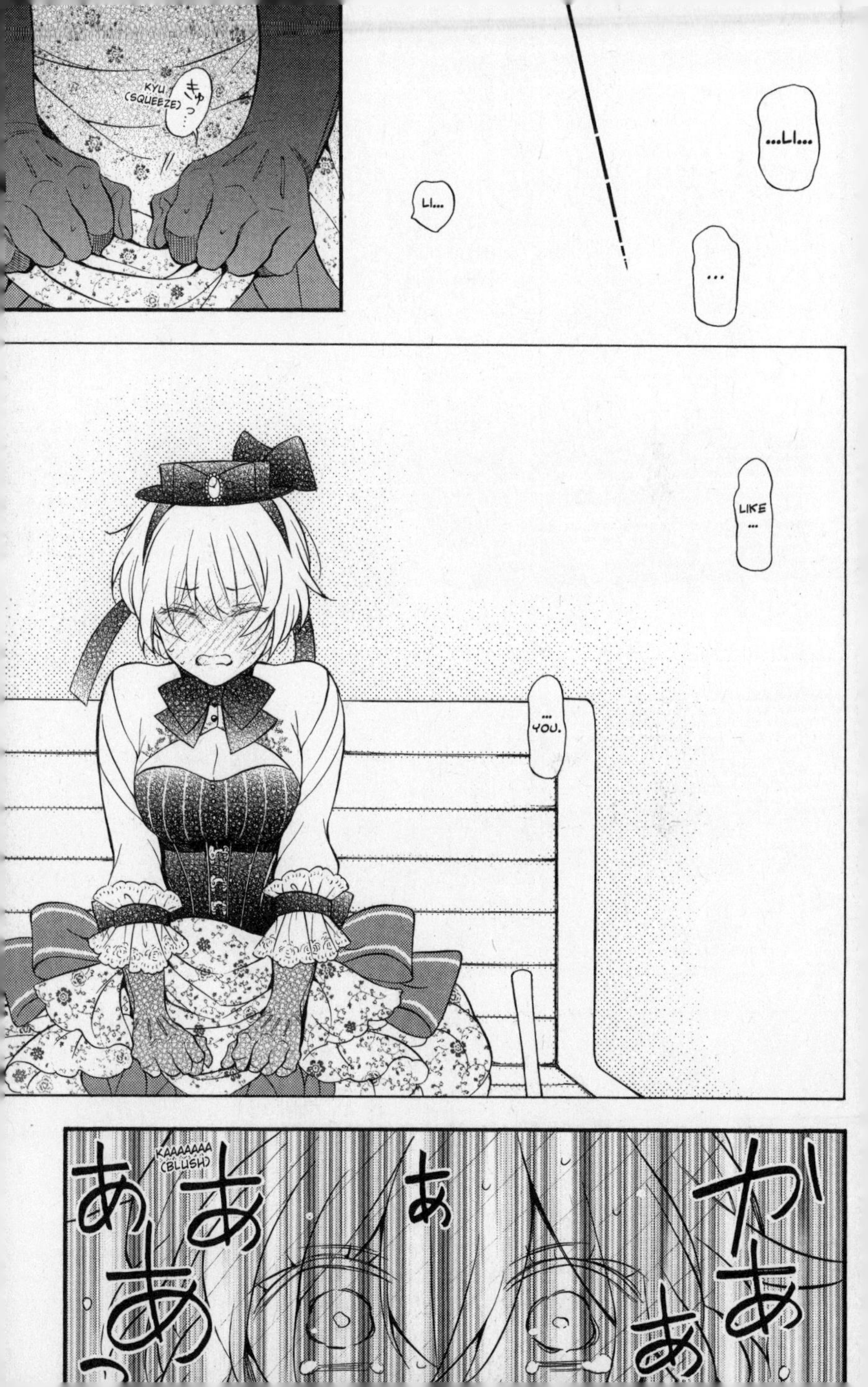

...LI...
...
LI...
きゅっ…
KYU (SQUEEZE)
LIKE ...
... YOU.
やああ あ ああ ああっ
KAAAAAAA (BLUSH)

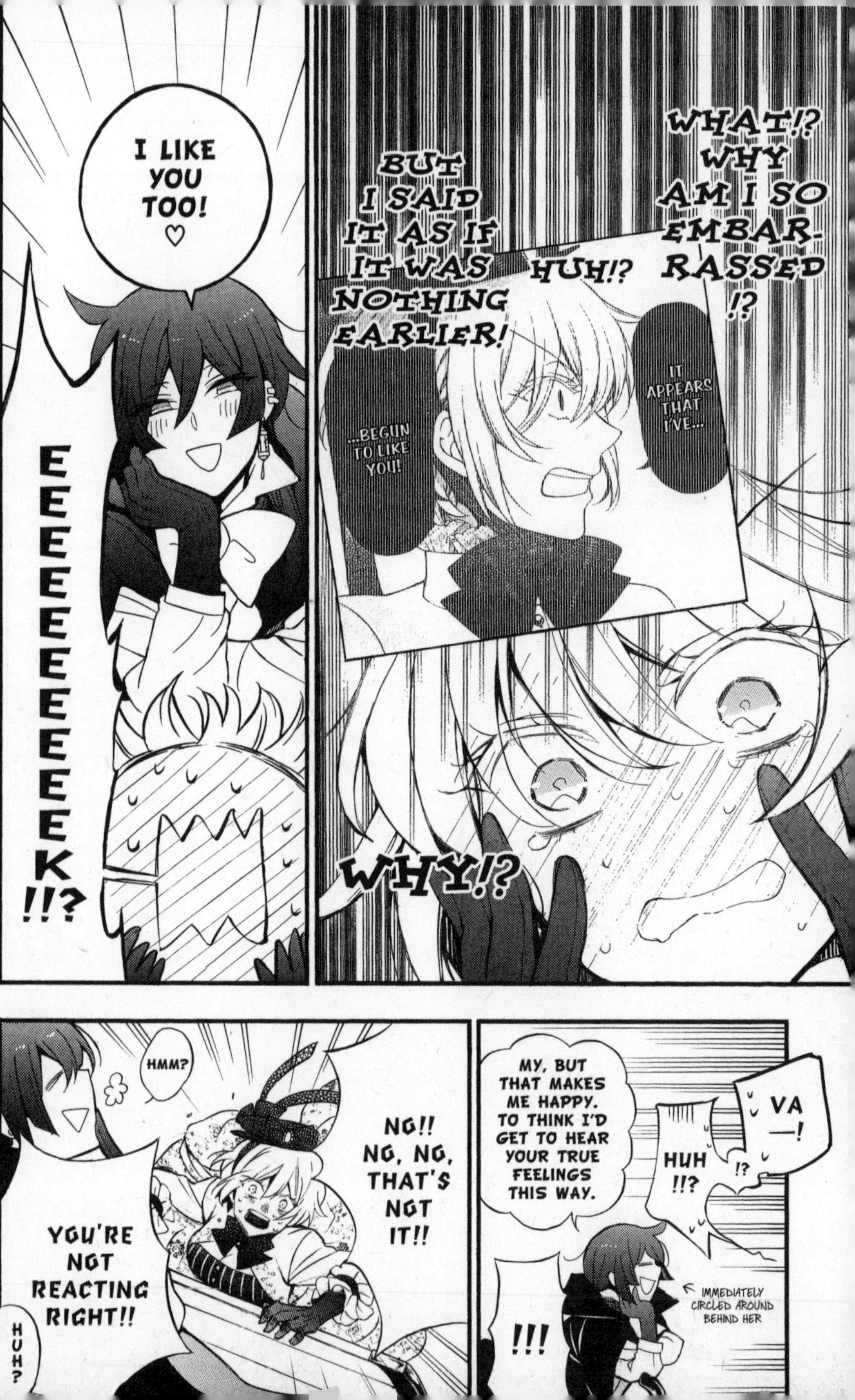
WHAT!? WHY AM I SO EMBARRASSED!?
HUH!?
BUT I SAID IT AS IF IT WAS NOTHING EARLIER!
IT APPEARS THAT I'VE...
...BEGUN TO LIKE YOU!
WHY!?
I LIKE YOU TOO! ♡
EEEEEEEEEEEEEK!!?
VA—!
HUH!?
MY, BUT THAT MAKES ME HAPPY. TO THINK I'D GET TO HEAR YOUR TRUE FEELINGS THIS WAY.
IMMEDIATELY CIRCLED AROUND BEHIND HER
!!!
HMM?
NG!! NG, NG, THAT'S NOT IT!!
YOU'RE NOT REACTING RIGHT!!
HUH?

SFX: KORO (ROLL) KORO KORO KORO

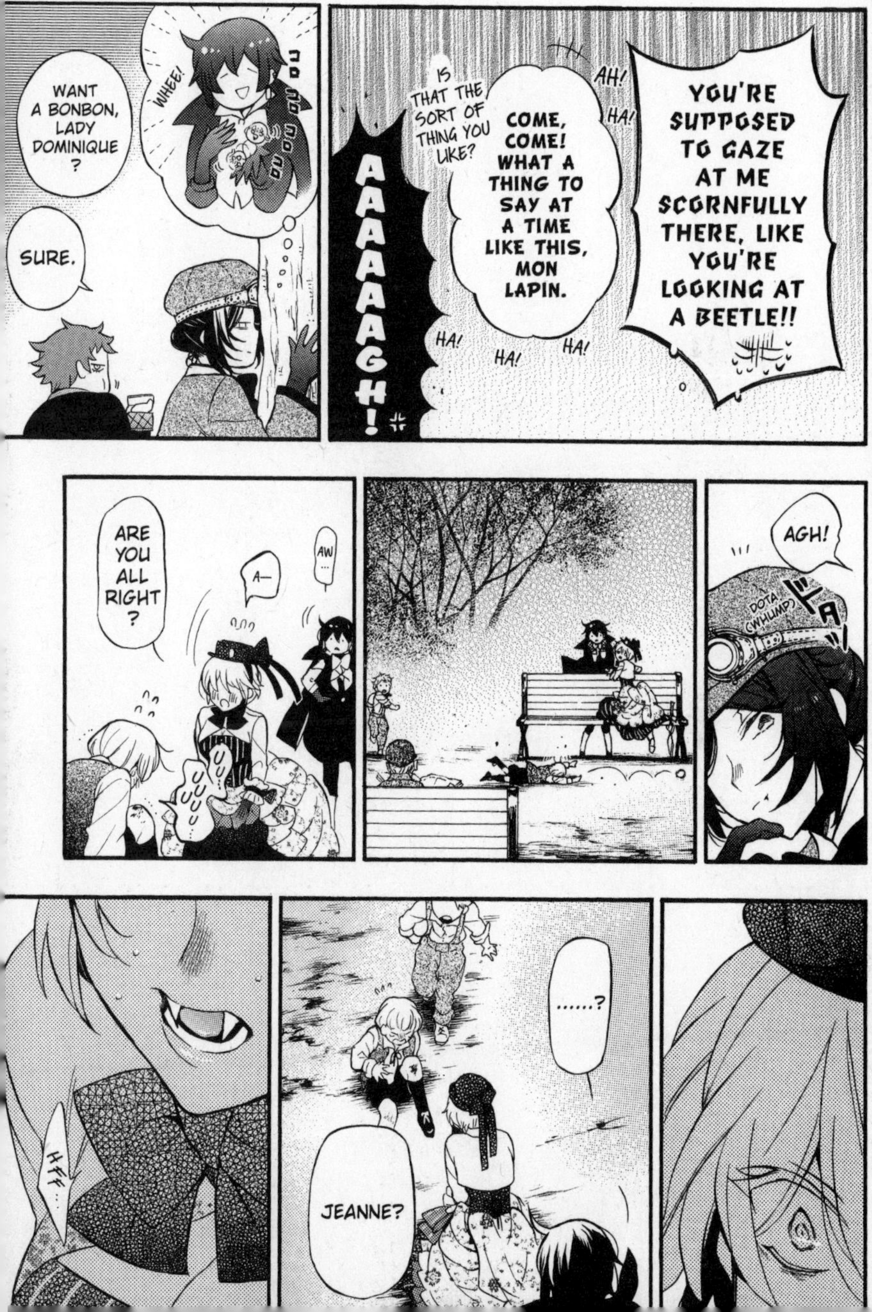
YOU'RE SUPPOSED TO GAZE AT ME SCORNFULLY THERE, LIKE YOU'RE LOOKING AT A BEETLE!!
AH! HA!
COME, COME! WHAT A THING TO SAY AT A TIME LIKE THIS, MON LAPIN.
HA! HA! HA!
IS THAT THE SORT OF THING YOU LIKE?
AAAAAAAAGH!
WHEE!
WANT A BONBON, LADY DOMINIQUE?
SURE.
AGH!
DOTA (WHUMP)
AW...
A—
ARE YOU ALL RIGHT?
......?
JEANNE?
HFF...

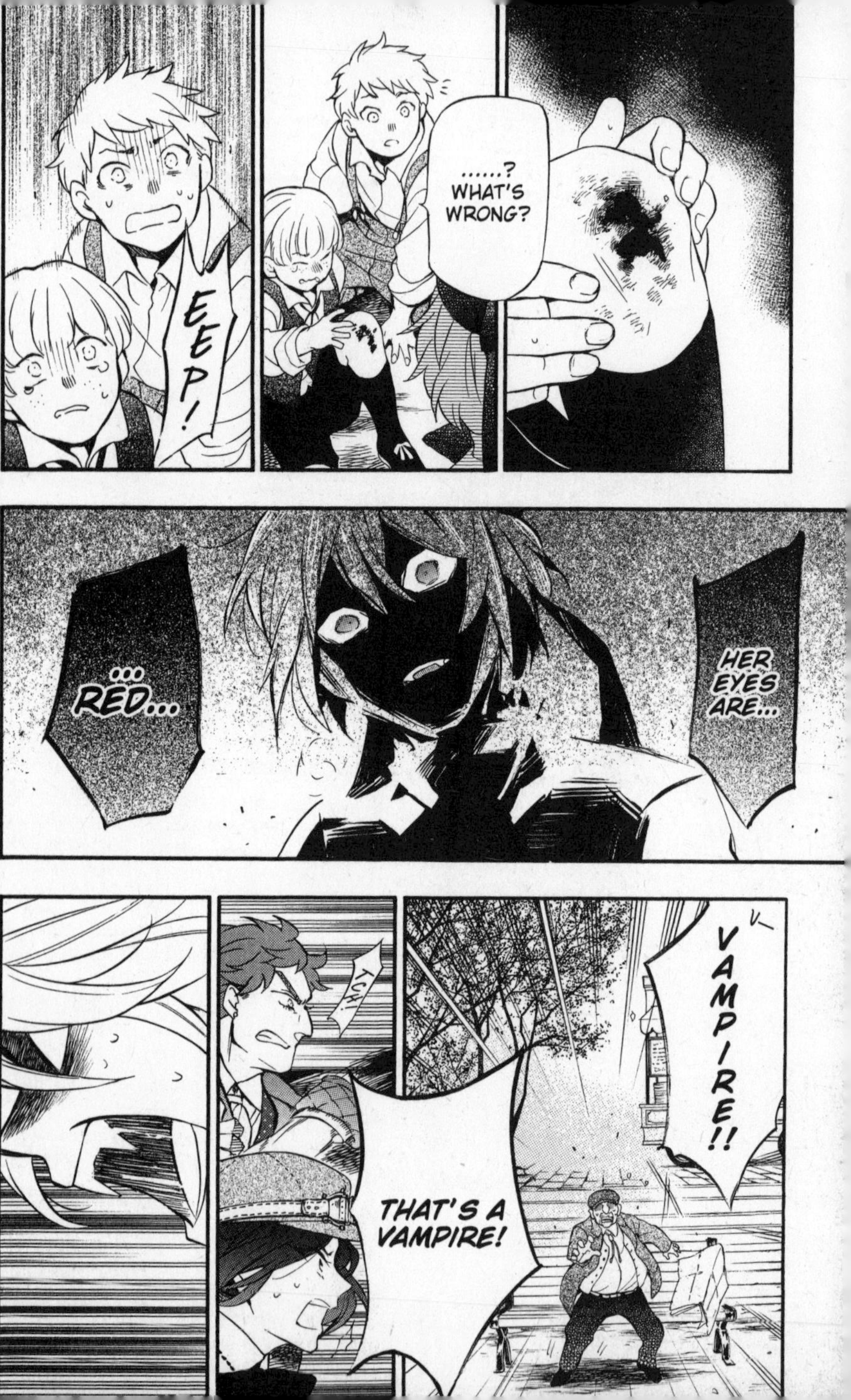
......? WHAT'S WRONG?
EEP!
HER EYES ARE...
...RED...
VAMPIRE!!
THAT'S A VAMPIRE!
TCH!

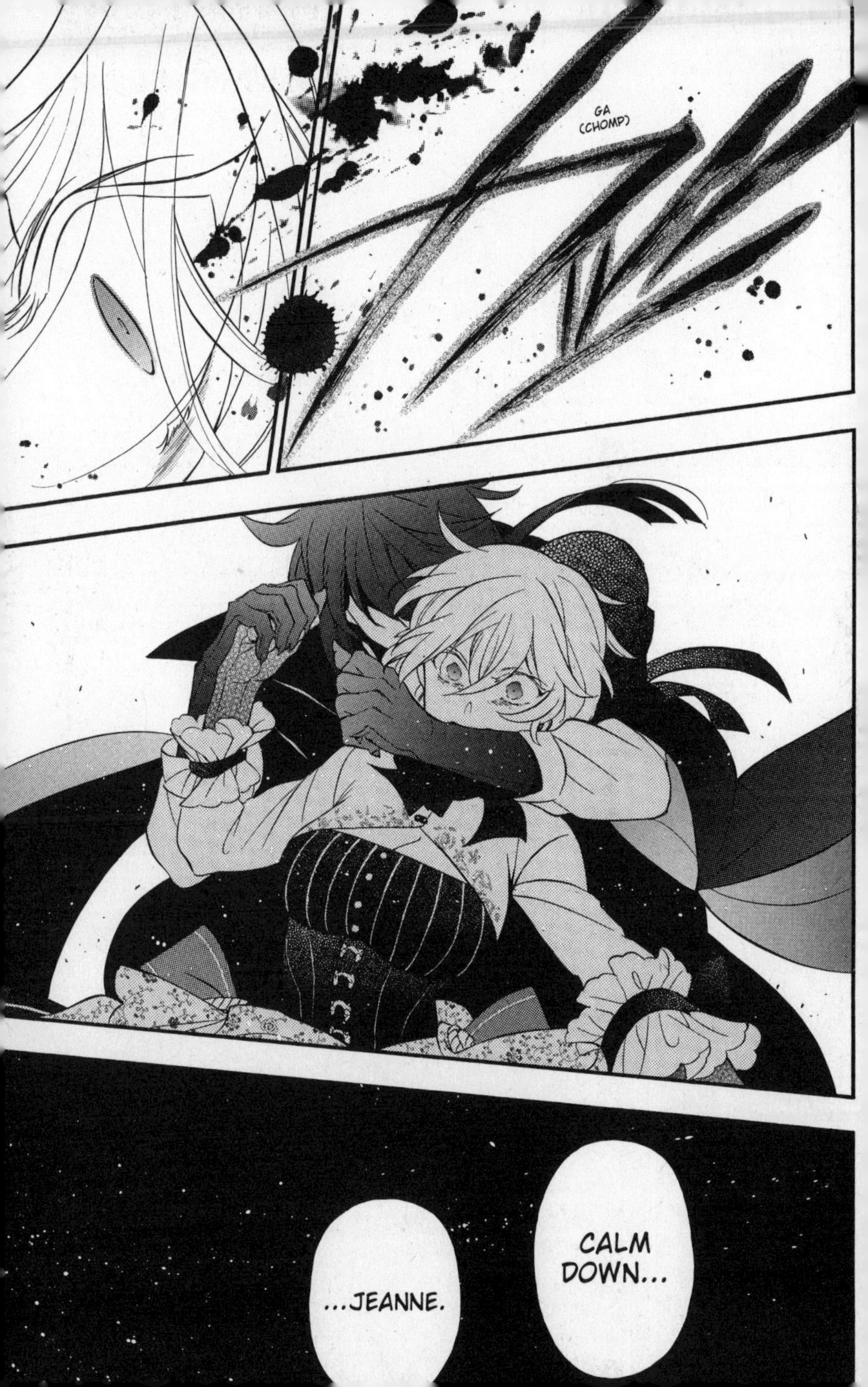
GA
(CHOMP)
CALM DOWN...
...JEANNE.

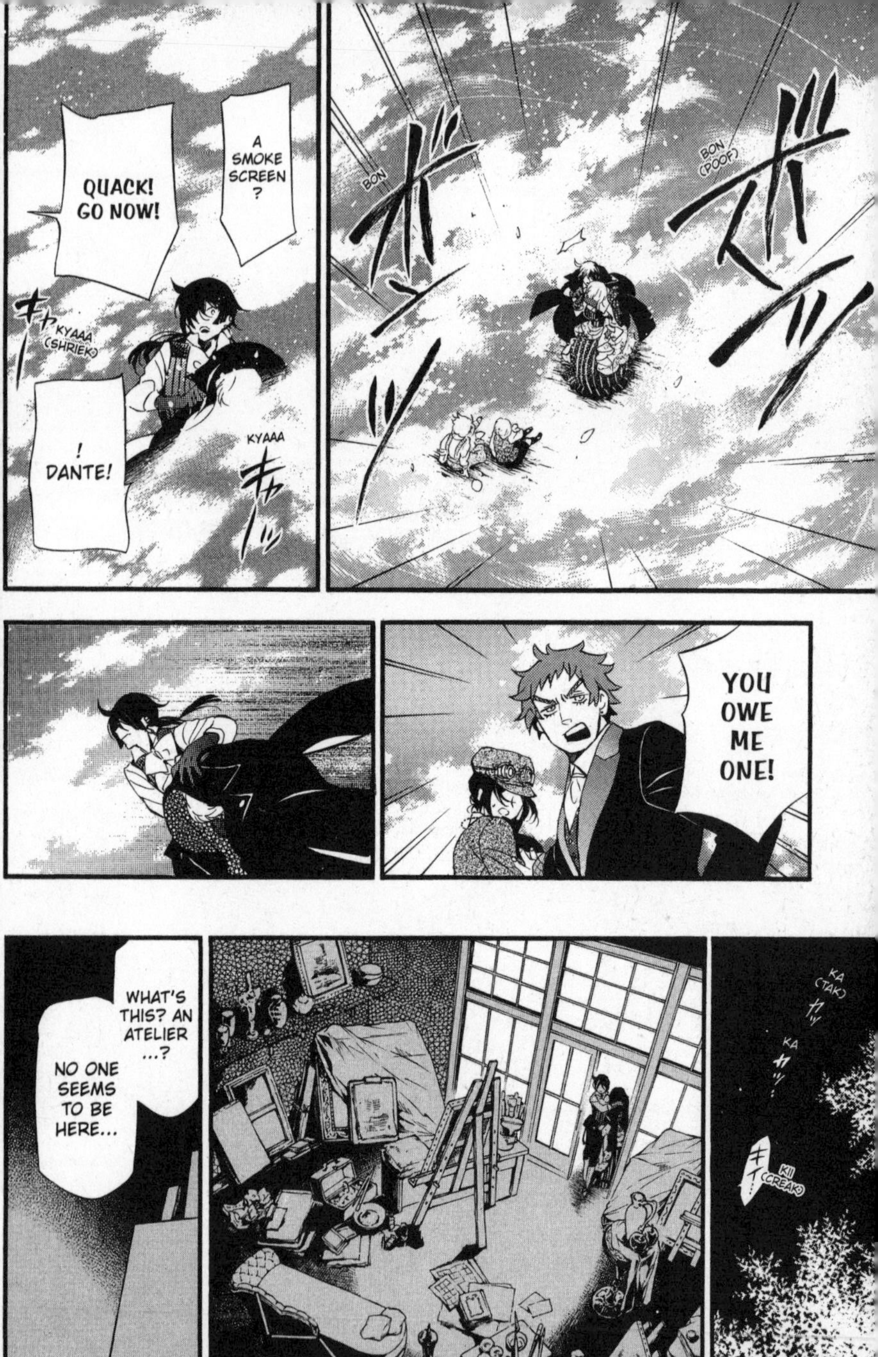
BON
BON (POOF)
A SMOKE SCREEN?
QUACK! GO NOW!
KYAAA (SHRIEK)
! DANTE!
KYAAA
YOU OWE ME ONE!
KA (TAK)
KA
KII (CREAK)
WHAT'S THIS? AN ATELIER ...?
NO ONE SEEMS TO BE HERE...

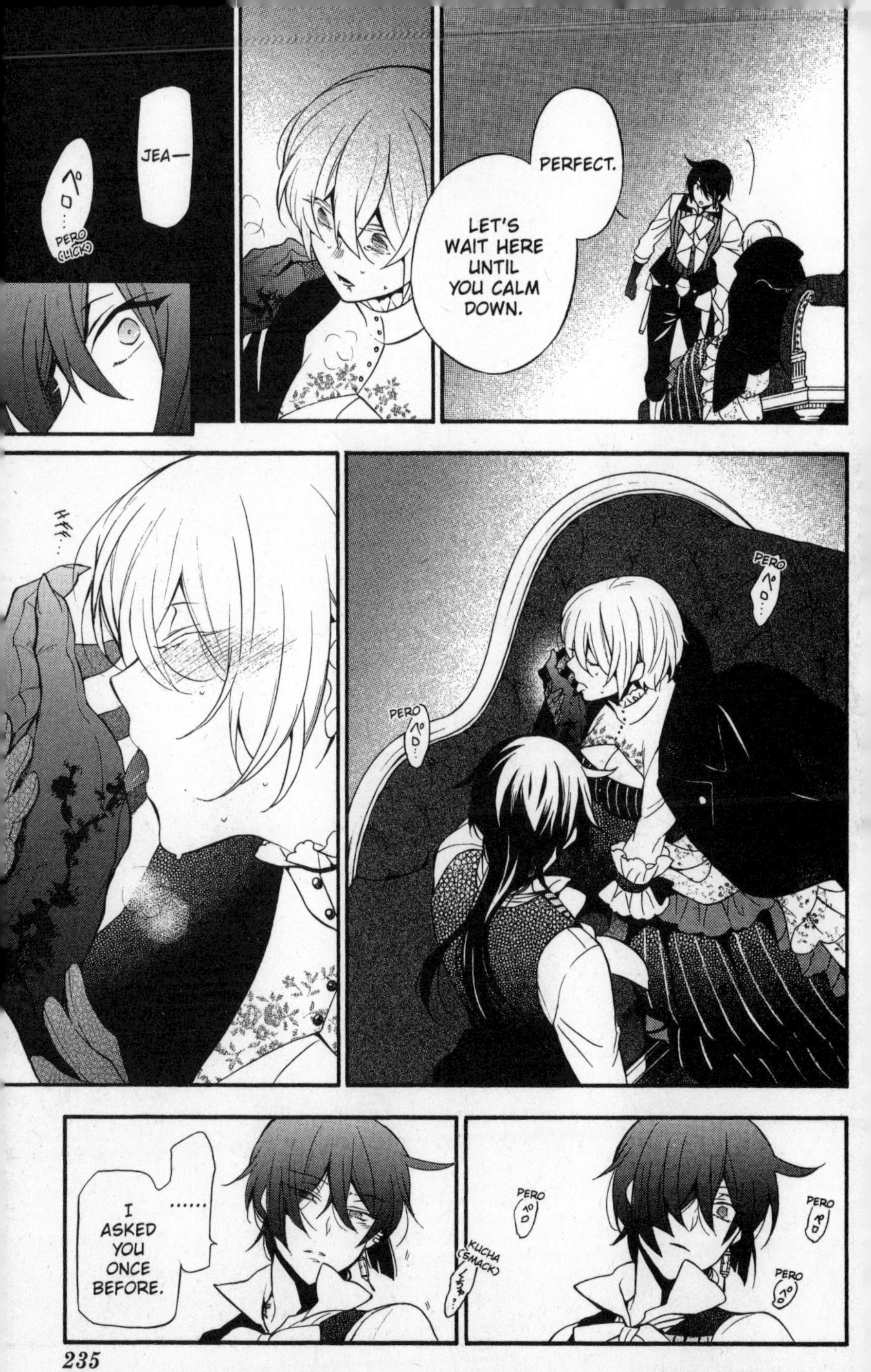
PERFECT.
LET'S WAIT HERE UNTIL YOU CALM DOWN.
JEA—
ペロ… PERO (LICK)
PERO ペロ…
PERO ペロ…
PERO ペロ
PERO ペロ
PERO ペロ
KUCHA (SMACK)
......
I ASKED YOU ONCE BEFORE.

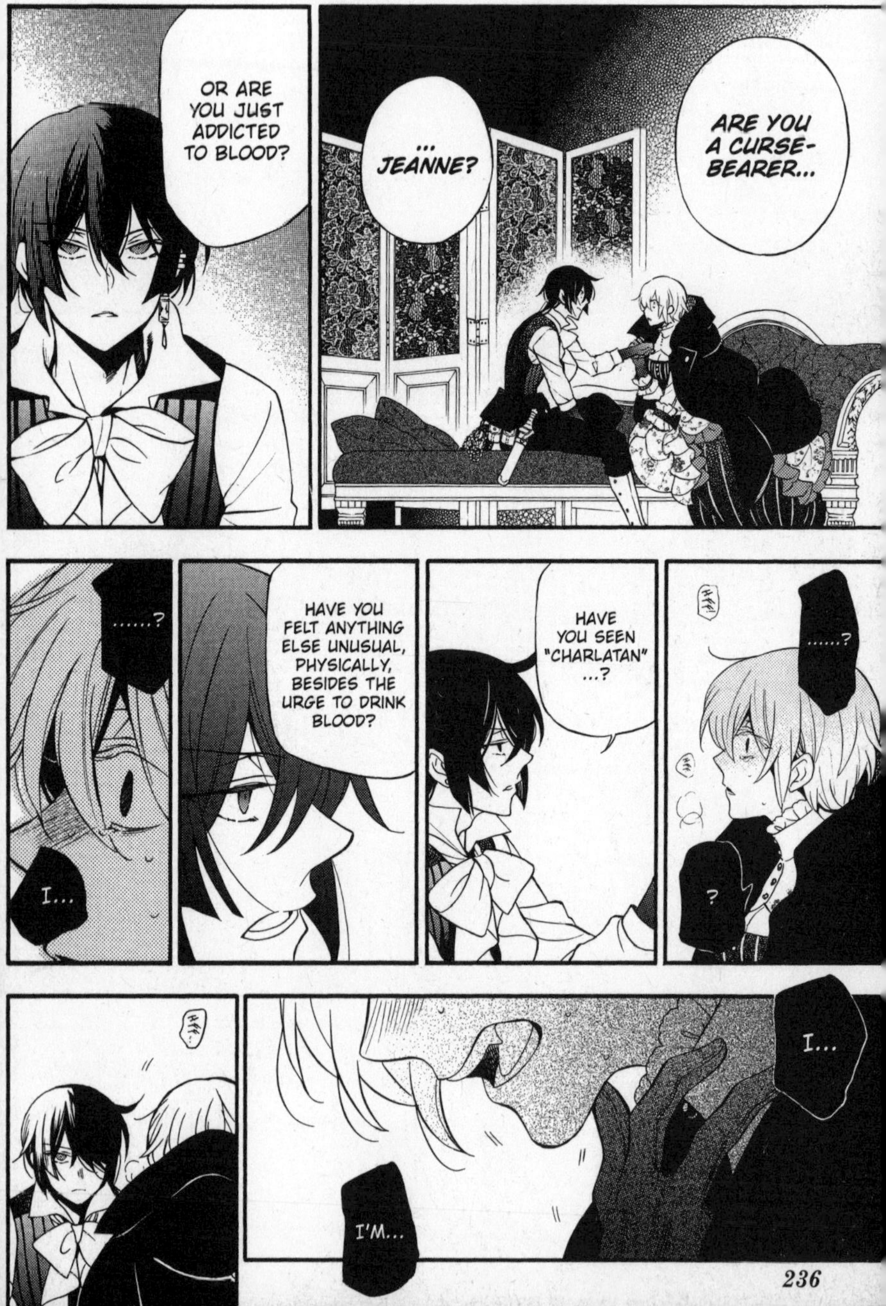
ARE YOU A CURSE-BEARER...
...JEANNE?
OR ARE YOU JUST ADDICTED TO BLOOD?
......?
?
HAVE YOU SEEN "CHARLATAN" ...?
HAVE YOU FELT ANYTHING ELSE UNUSUAL, PHYSICALLY, BESIDES THE URGE TO DRINK BLOOD?
......?
I...
I...
I'M...

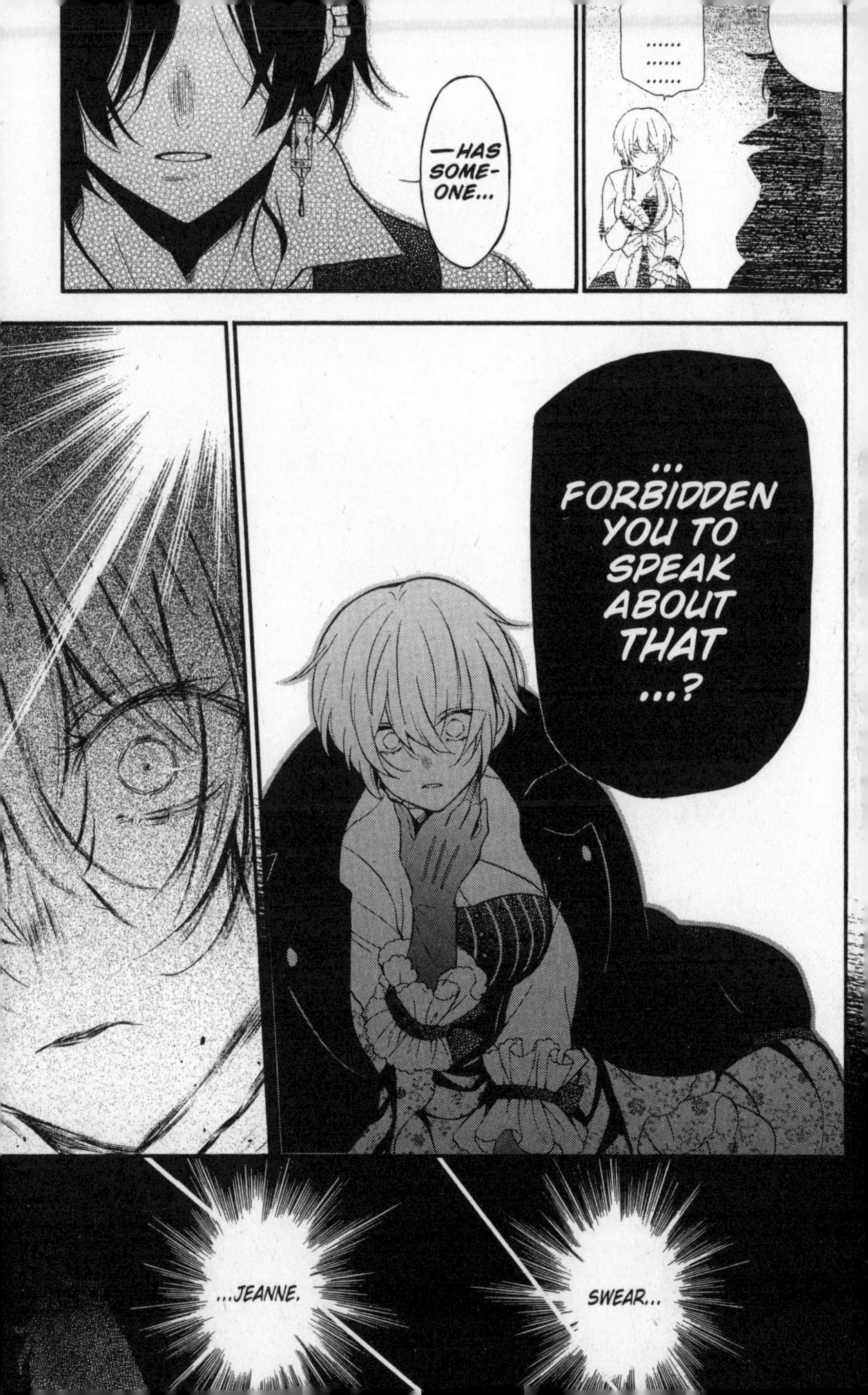
......
......
......
—HAS SOME-ONE...
...FORBIDDEN YOU TO SPEAK ABOUT THAT ...?
SWEAR...
...JEANNE.

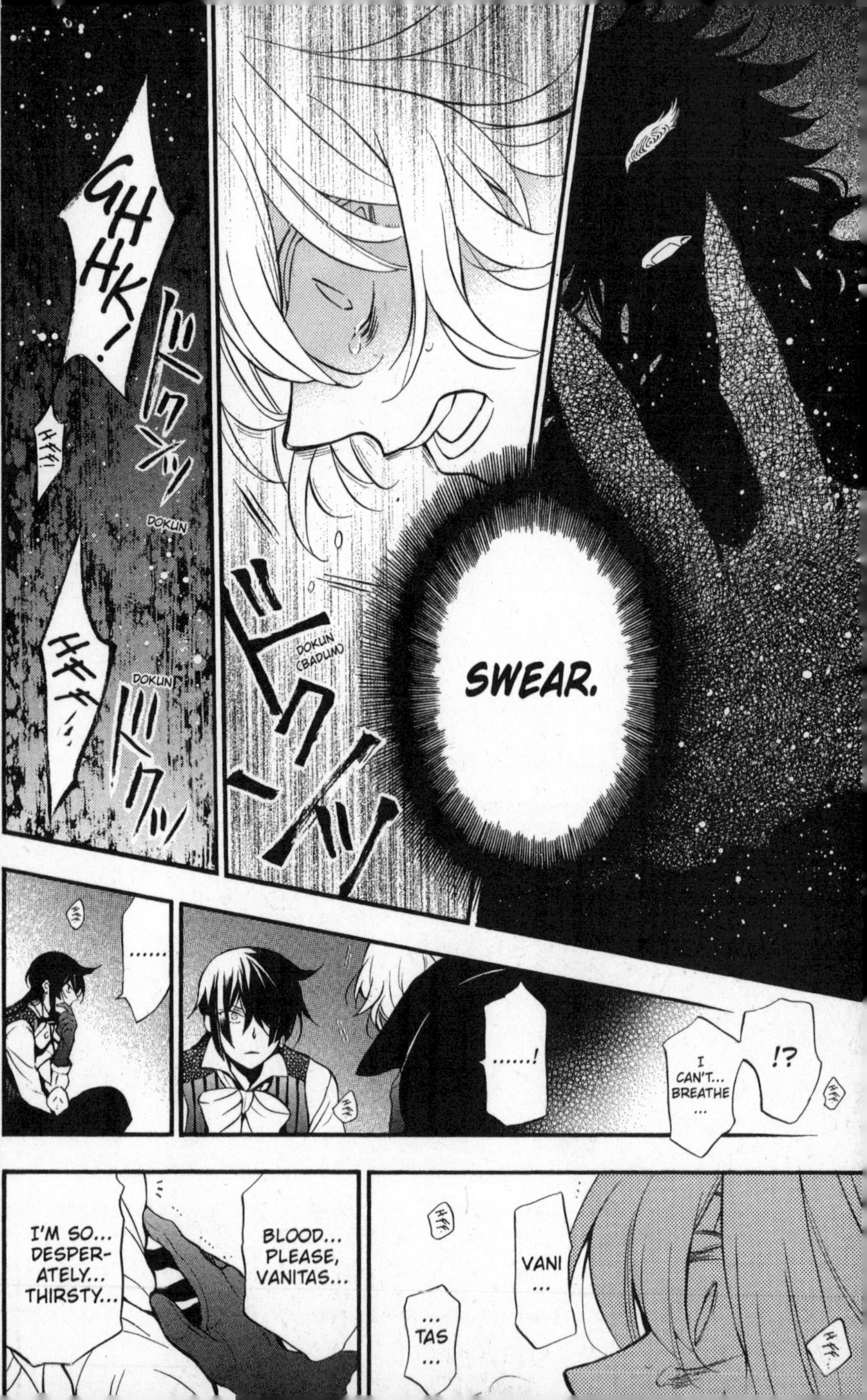
SWEAR.
DOKUN (BADUM)
GHHK!
HFFF!
DOKUN
HFFF...!
DOKUN
!?
I CAN'T... BREATHE ...
HFF
......!
HFF
......
HFF
HFF
VANI ...
... TAS ...
HFF...
BLOOD... PLEASE, VANITAS...
I'M SO... DESPERATELY... THIRSTY...

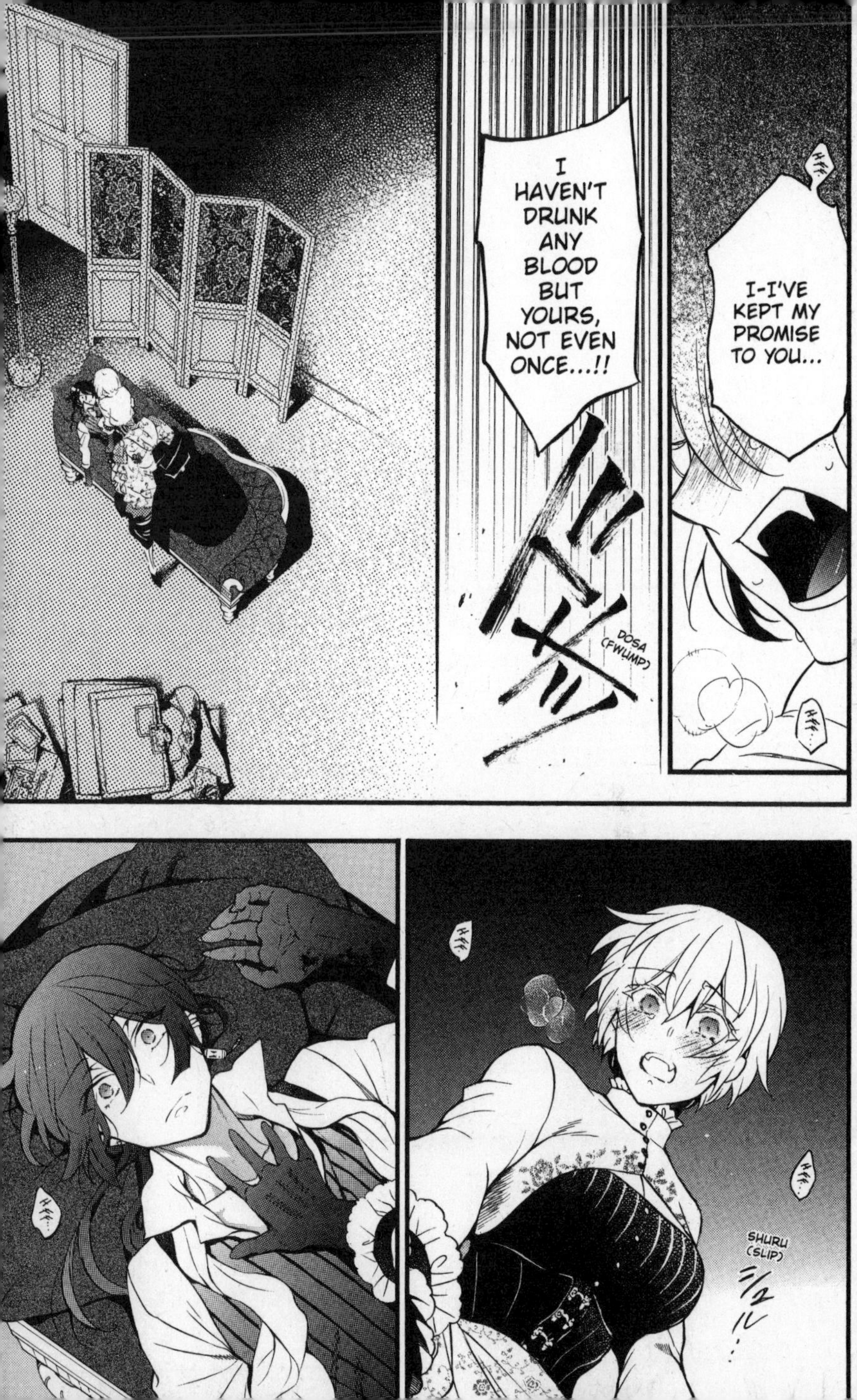
I-I'VE KEPT MY PROMISE TO YOU...
I HAVEN'T DRUNK ANY BLOOD BUT YOURS, NOT EVEN ONCE...!!
DOSA (FWUMP)
SHURU (SLIP)

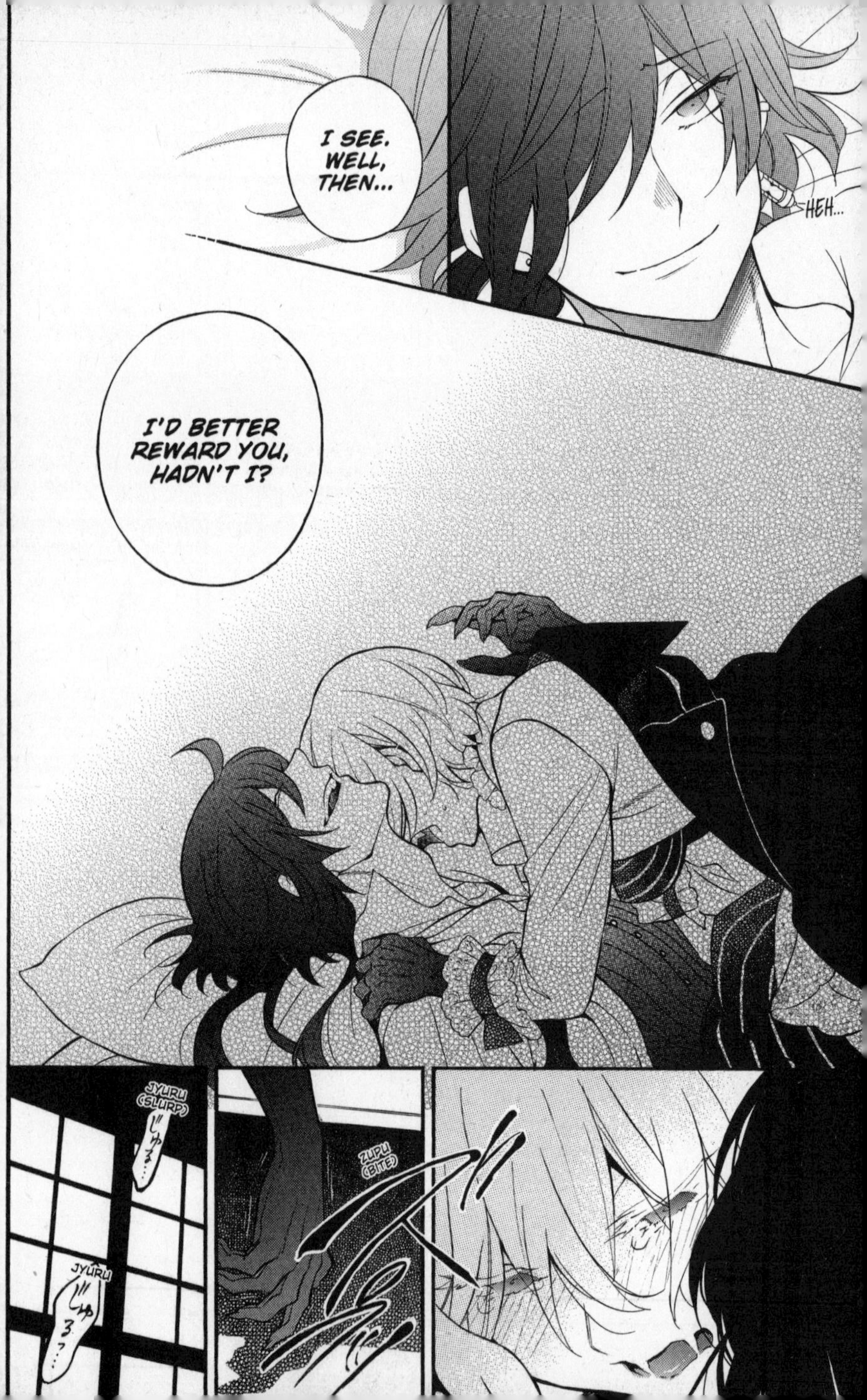
HEH...
I SEE. WELL, THEN...
I'D BETTER REWARD YOU, HADN'T I?
ZUPU (BITE)
JYURU (SLURP)
じゅる…
JYURU
じゅるっ…

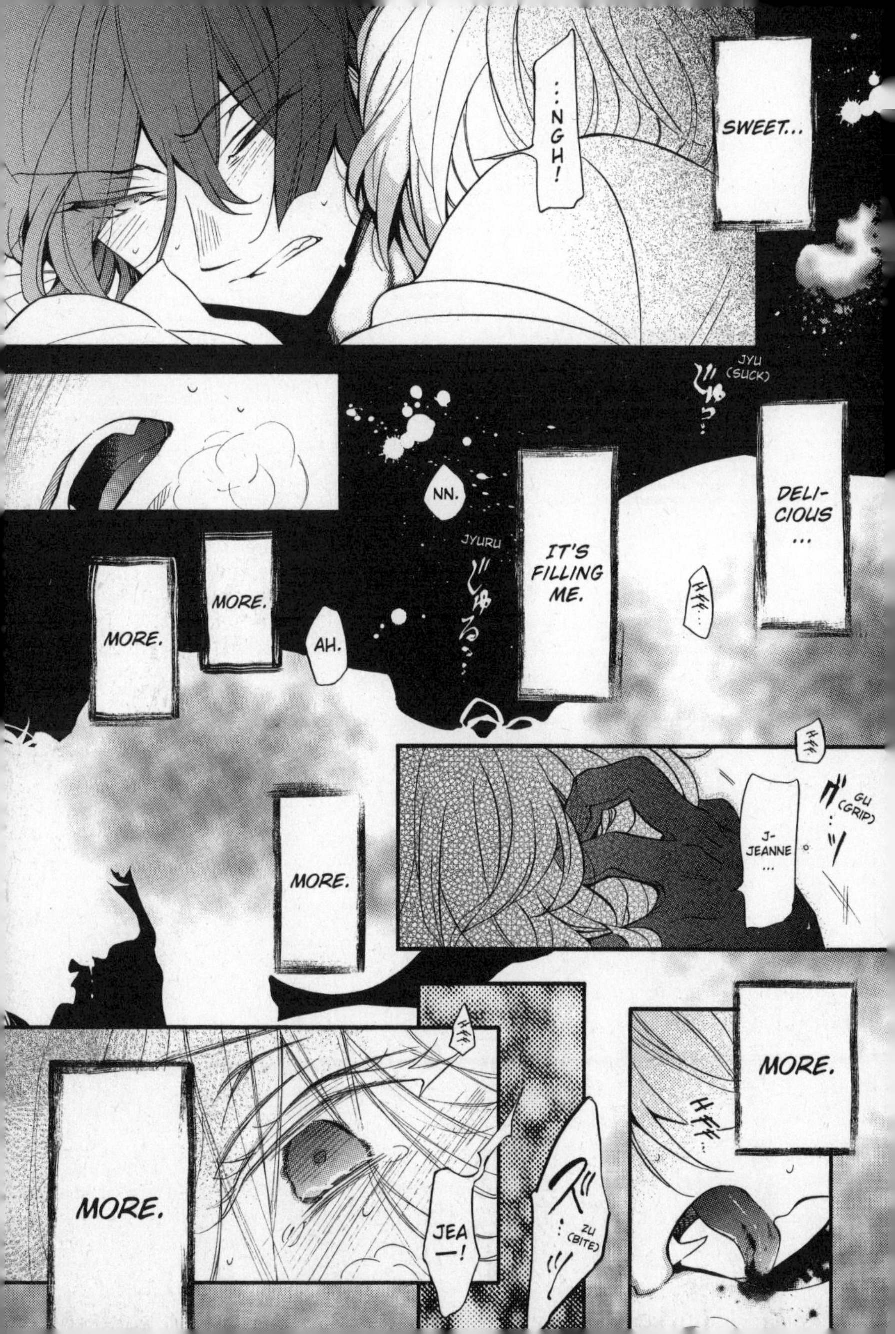
SWEET...
...NGH!
JYU (SUCK)
DELI-CIOUS...
HFF...
IT'S FILLING ME.
NN.
JYURU
AH.
MORE.
MORE.
HFF
GU (GRIP)
J-JEANNE...
MORE.
MORE.
HFF...
ZU (BITE)
JEA—!
HFF
MORE.

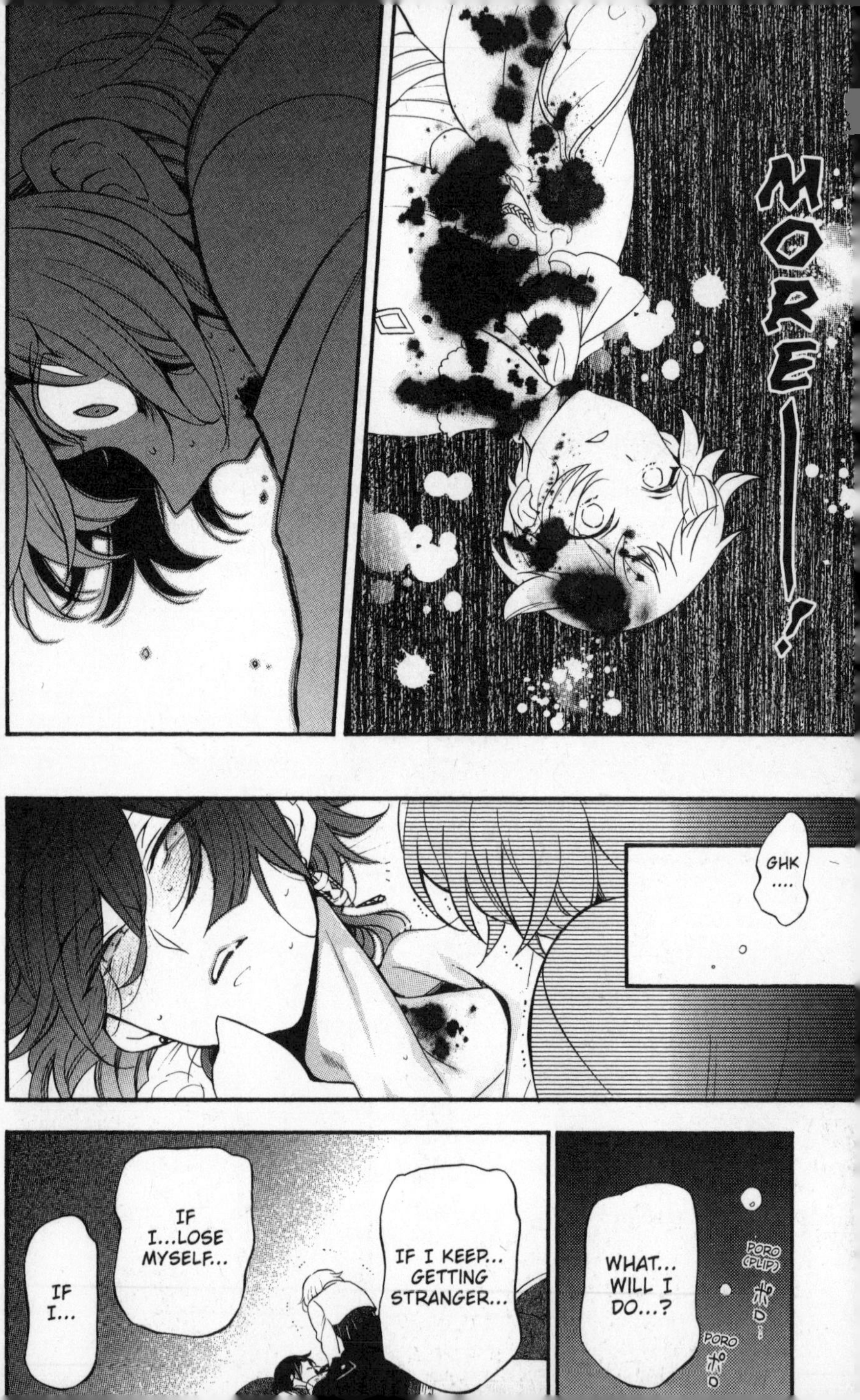
MORE—!?
GHK....
WHAT... WILL I DO...?
PORO (PLIP)
ポロ…
PORO
ポ
IF I KEEP... GETTING STRANGER...
IF I...LOSE MYSELF...
IF I...

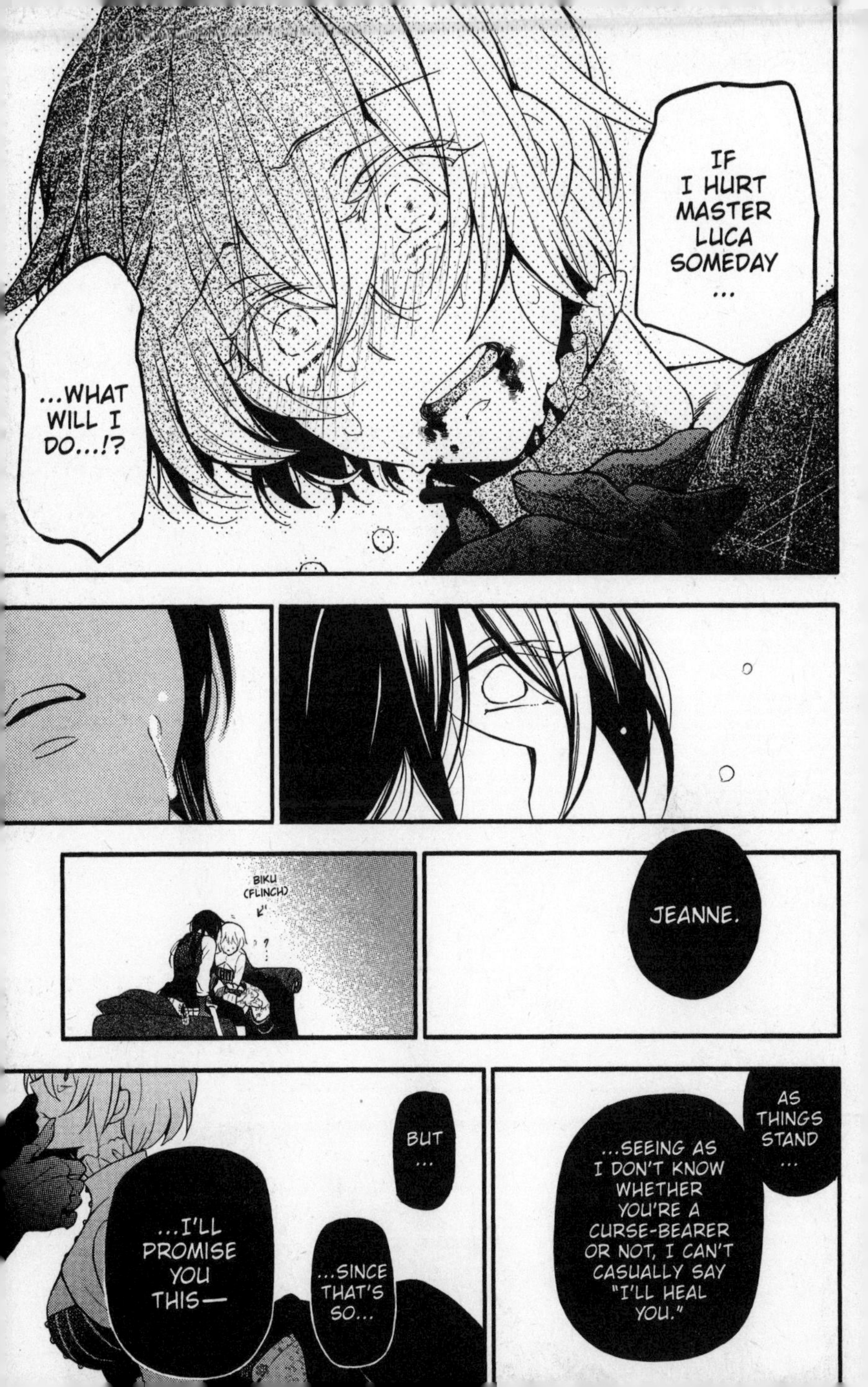

IF I HURT MASTER LUCA SOMEDAY ...
...WHAT WILL I DO...!?
JEANNE.
BIKU (FLINCH)
AS THINGS STAND ...
...SEEING AS I DON'T KNOW WHETHER YOU'RE A CURSE-BEARER OR NOT, I CAN'T CASUALLY SAY "I'LL HEAL YOU."
BUT ...
...SINCE THAT'S SO...
...I'LL PROMISE YOU THIS—

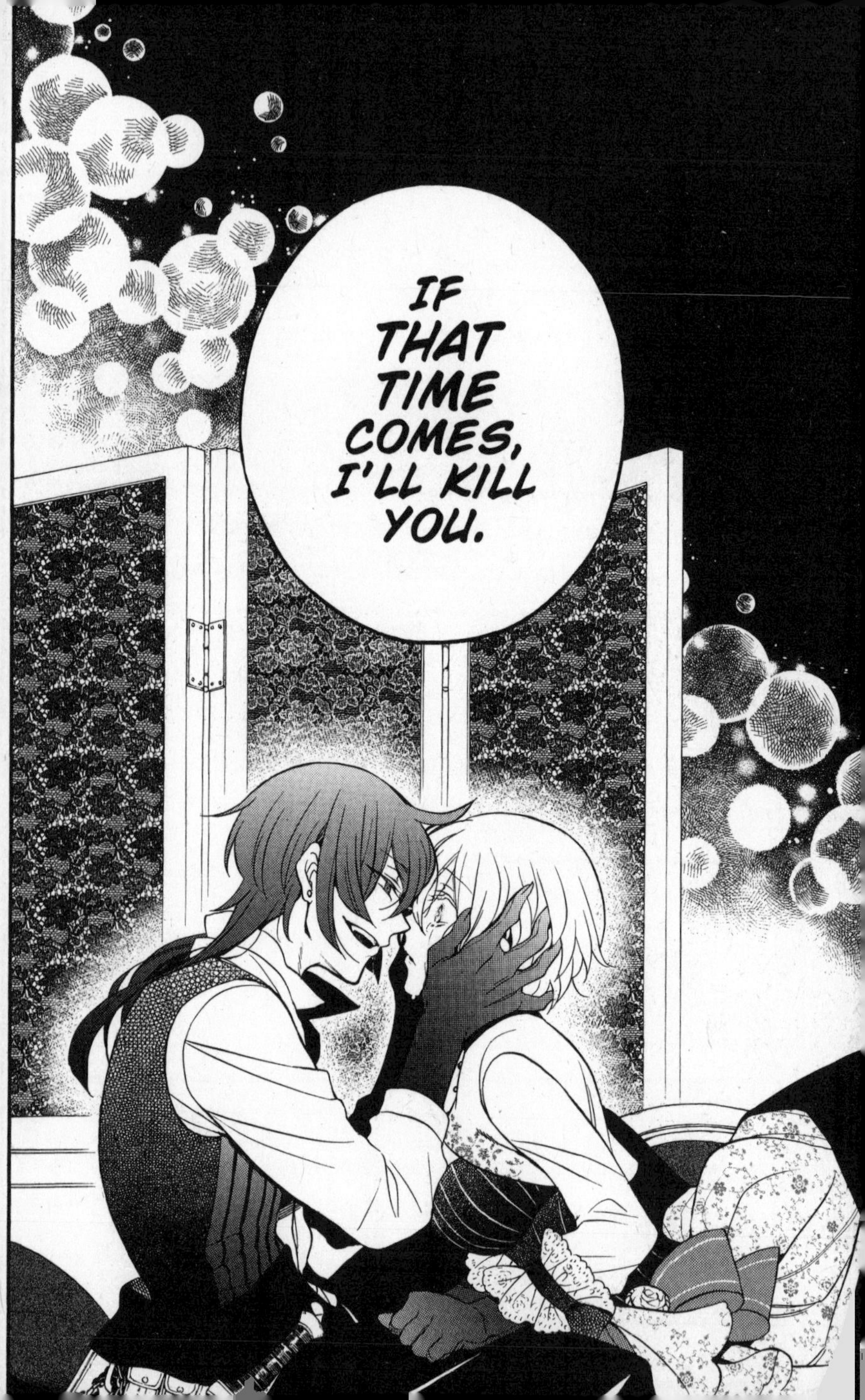
IF THAT TIME COMES, I'LL KILL YOU.

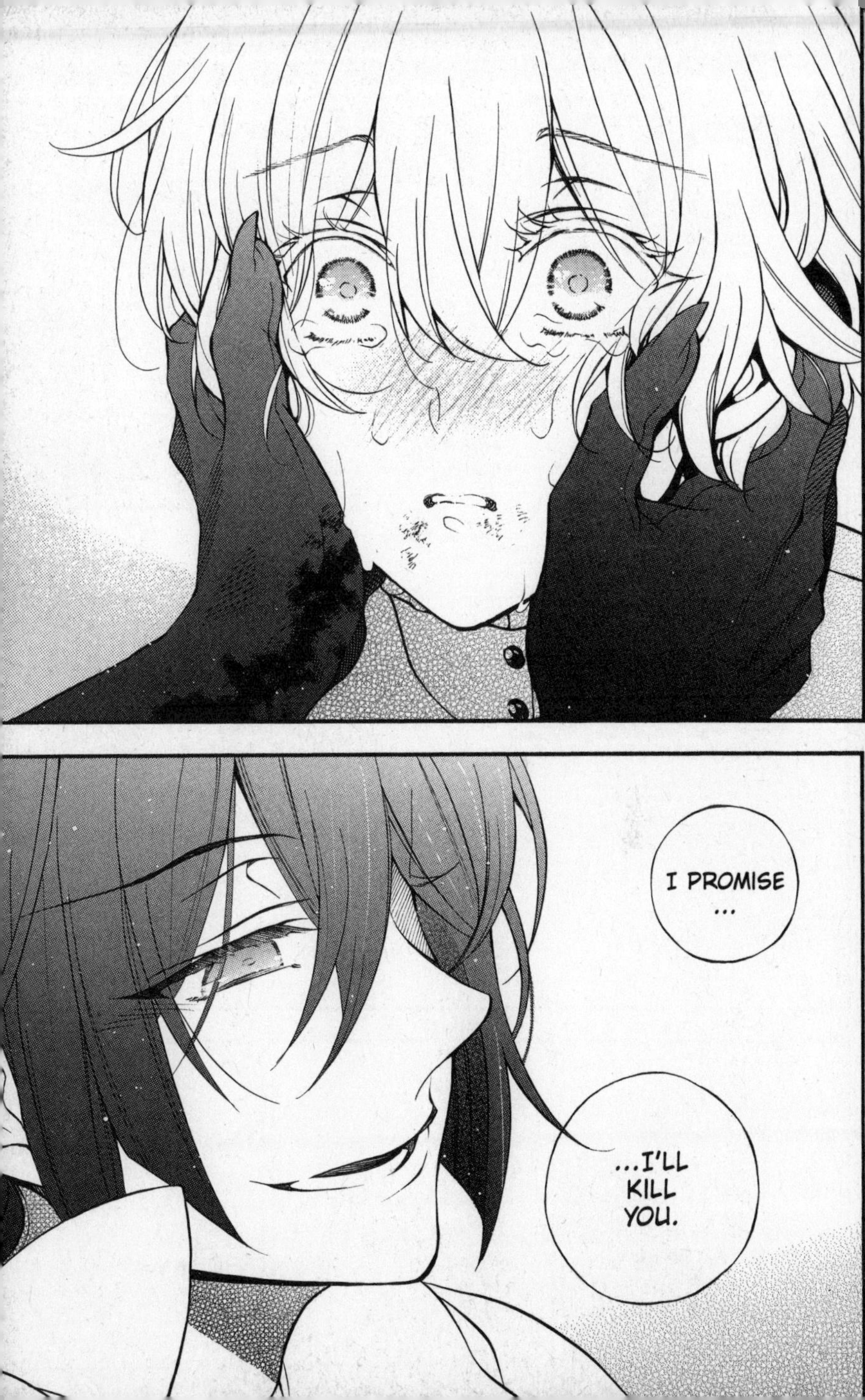
I PROMISE ...
...I'LL KILL YOU.

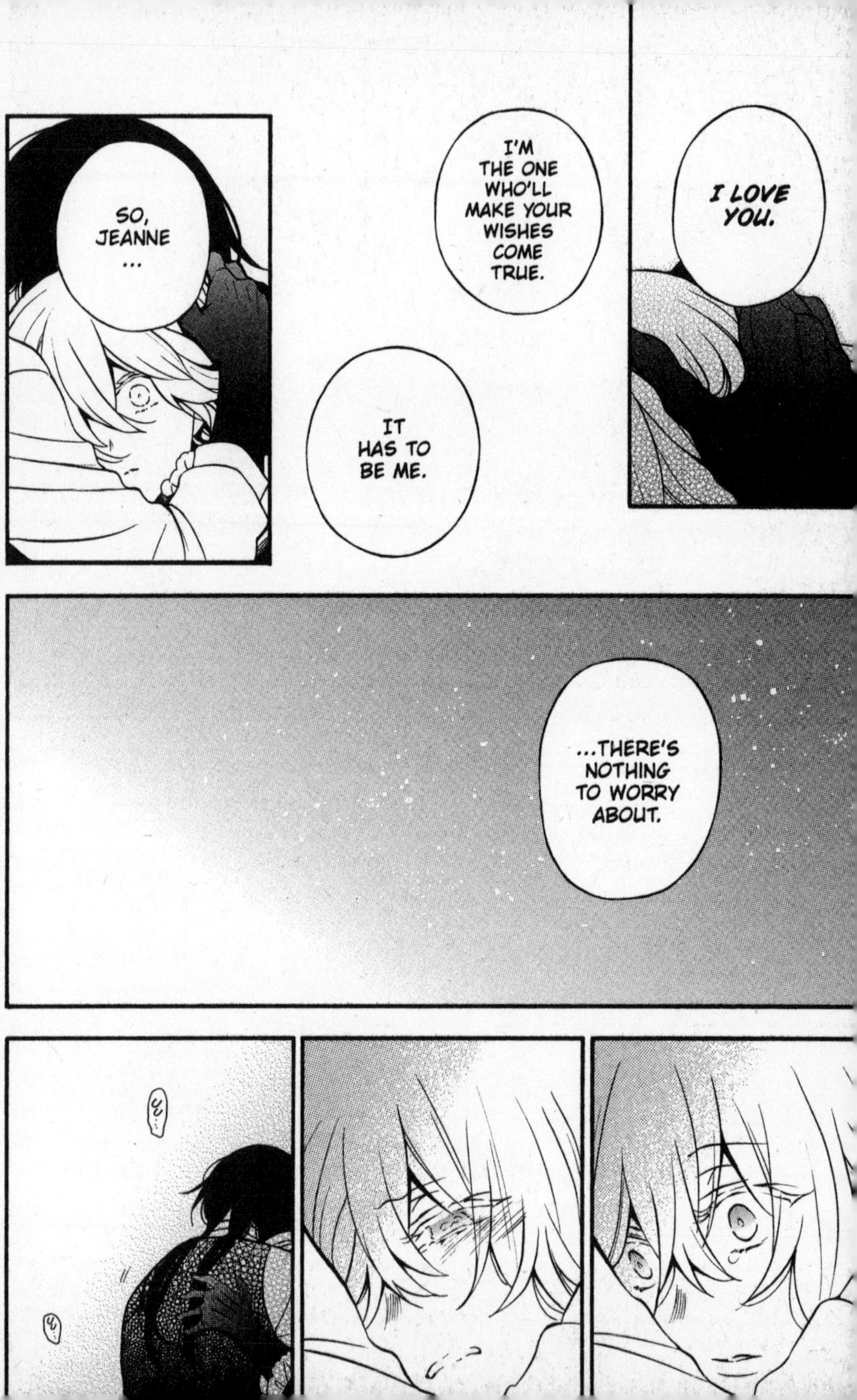
I LOVE YOU.
I'M THE ONE WHO'LL MAKE YOUR WISHES COME TRUE.
IT HAS TO BE ME.
SO, JEANNE ...
...THERE'S NOTHING TO WORRY ABOUT.

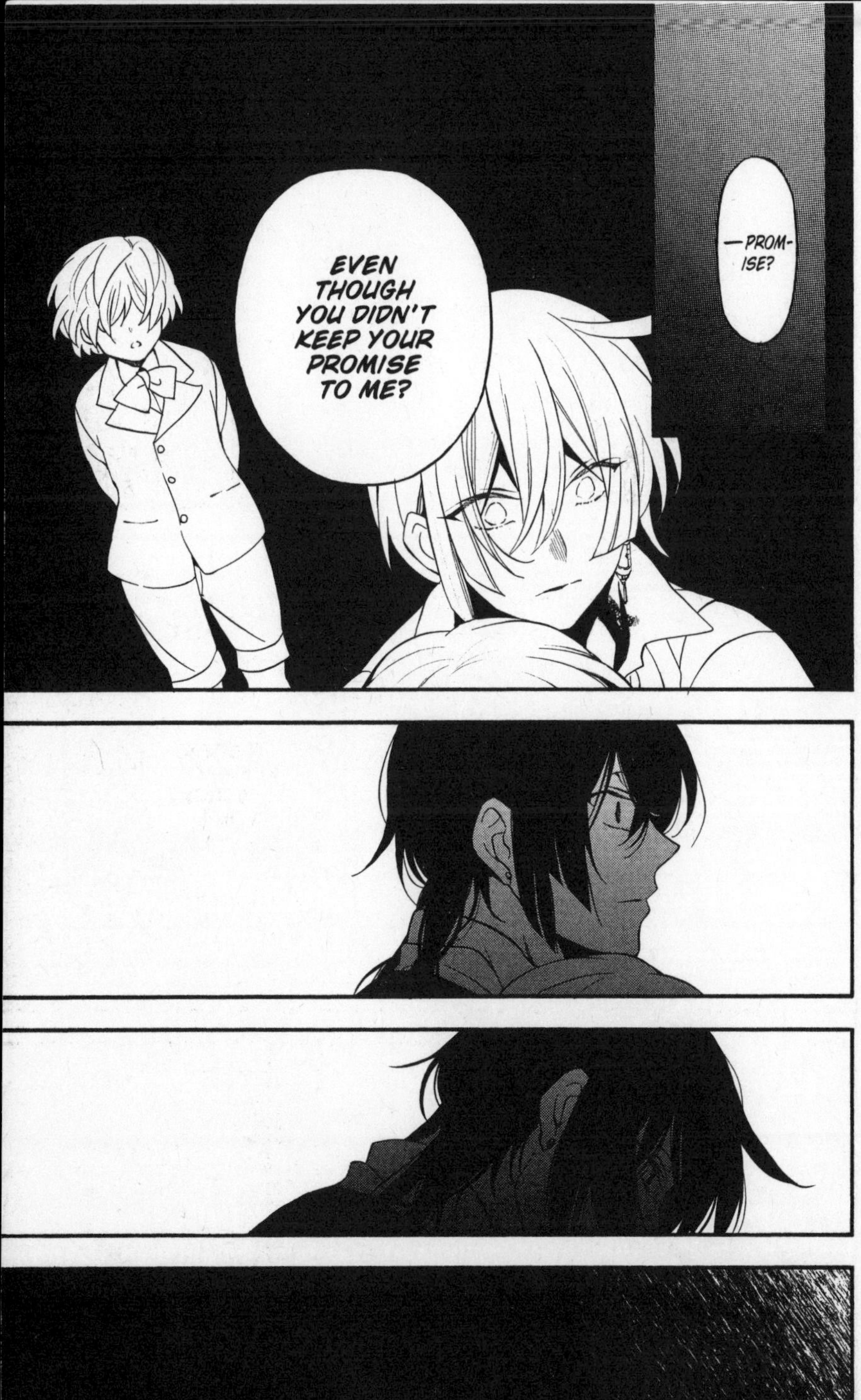
—PROM-ISE?
EVEN THOUGH YOU DIDN'T KEEP YOUR PROMISE TO ME?

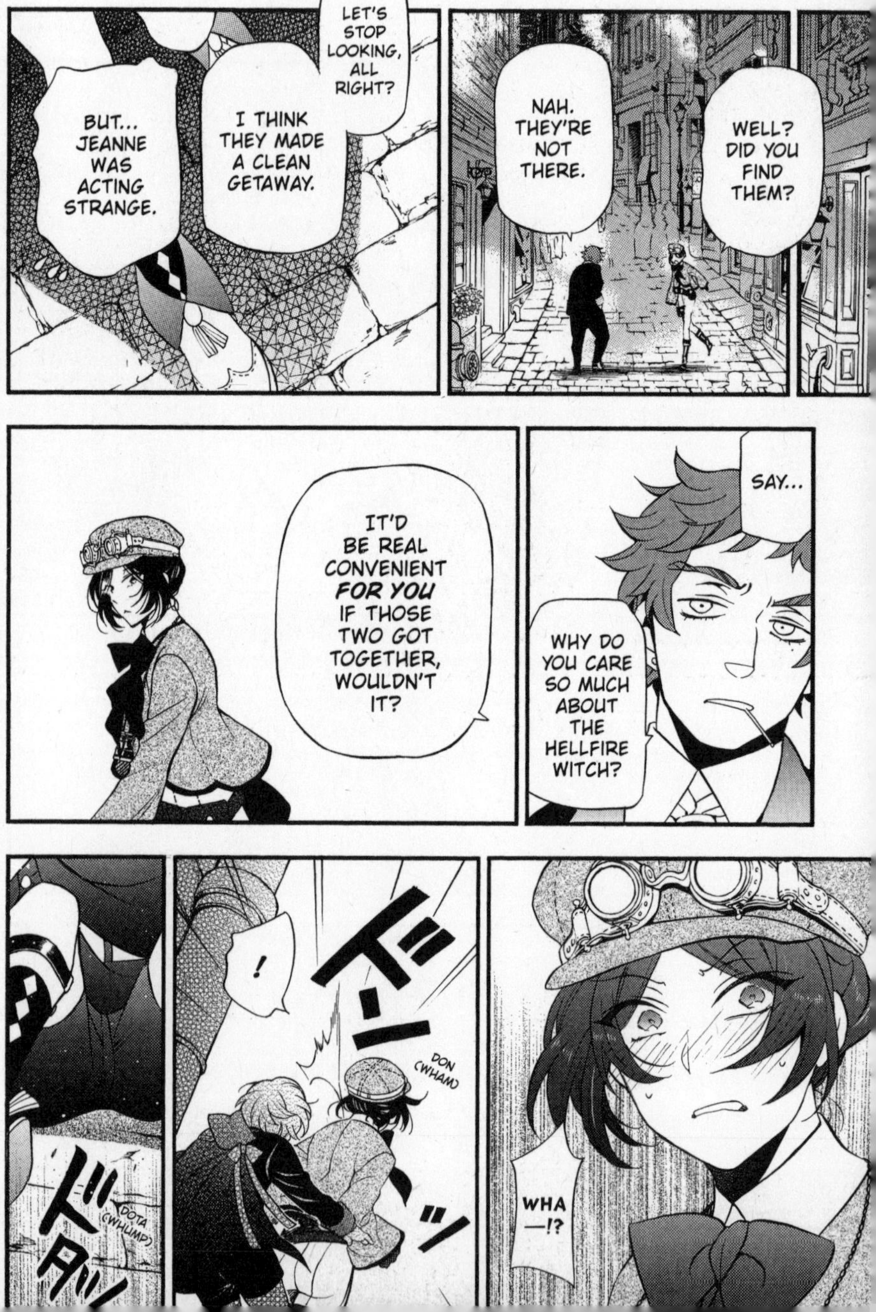
WELL? DID YOU FIND THEM?
NAH. THEY'RE NOT THERE.
LET'S STOP LOOKING, ALL RIGHT?
I THINK THEY MADE A CLEAN GETAWAY.
BUT... JEANNE WAS ACTING STRANGE.
SAY...
WHY DO YOU CARE SO MUCH ABOUT THE HELLFIRE WITCH?
IT'D BE REAL CONVENIENT *FOR YOU* IF THOSE TWO GOT TOGETHER, WOULDN'T IT?
WHA—!?
!
ドン
DON (WHAM)
ドタッ
DOTA (WHUMP)

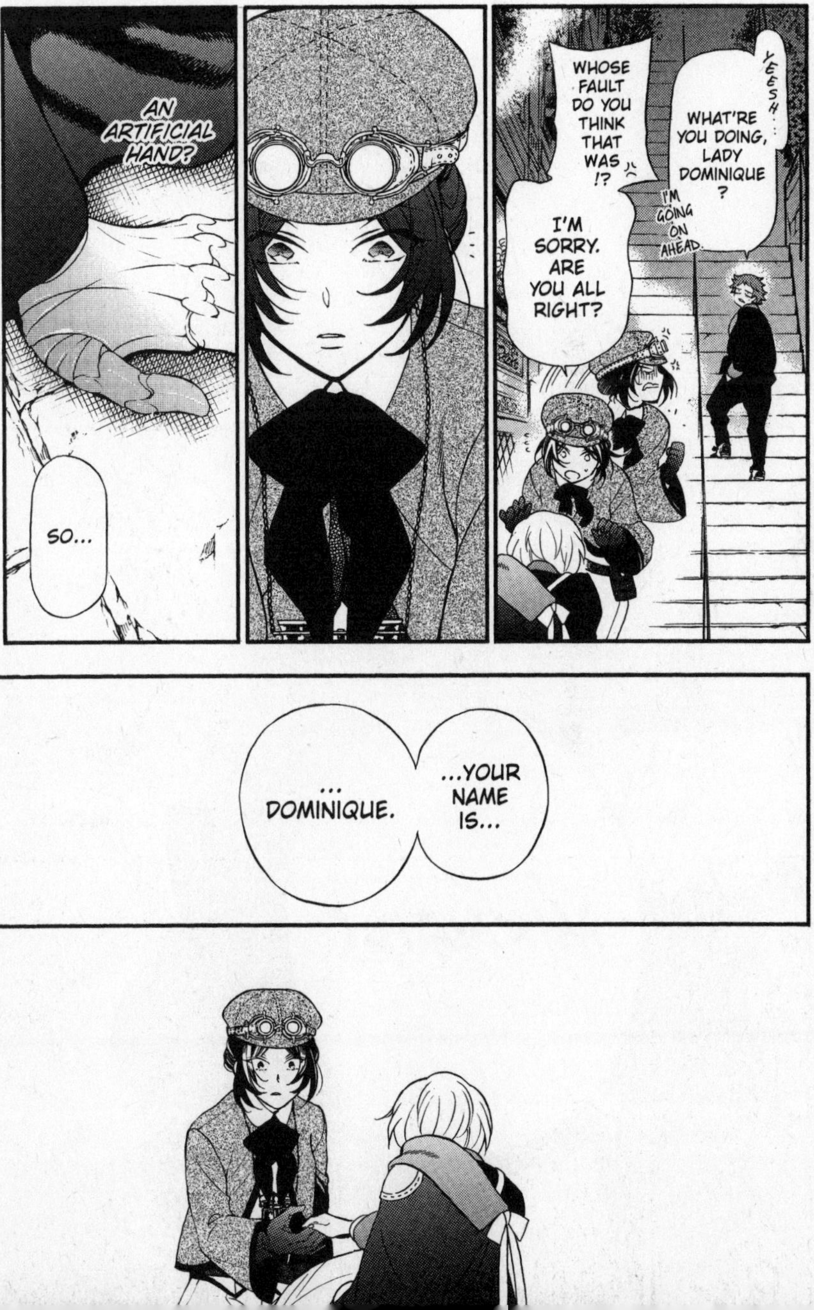
YEESH...
WHAT'RE YOU DOING, LADY DOMINIQUE?
I'M GOING ON AHEAD.
WHOSE FAULT DO YOU THINK THAT WAS!?
I'M SORRY. ARE YOU ALL RIGHT?
AN ARTIFICIAL HAND?
SO...
...YOUR NAME IS...
...DOMINIQUE.

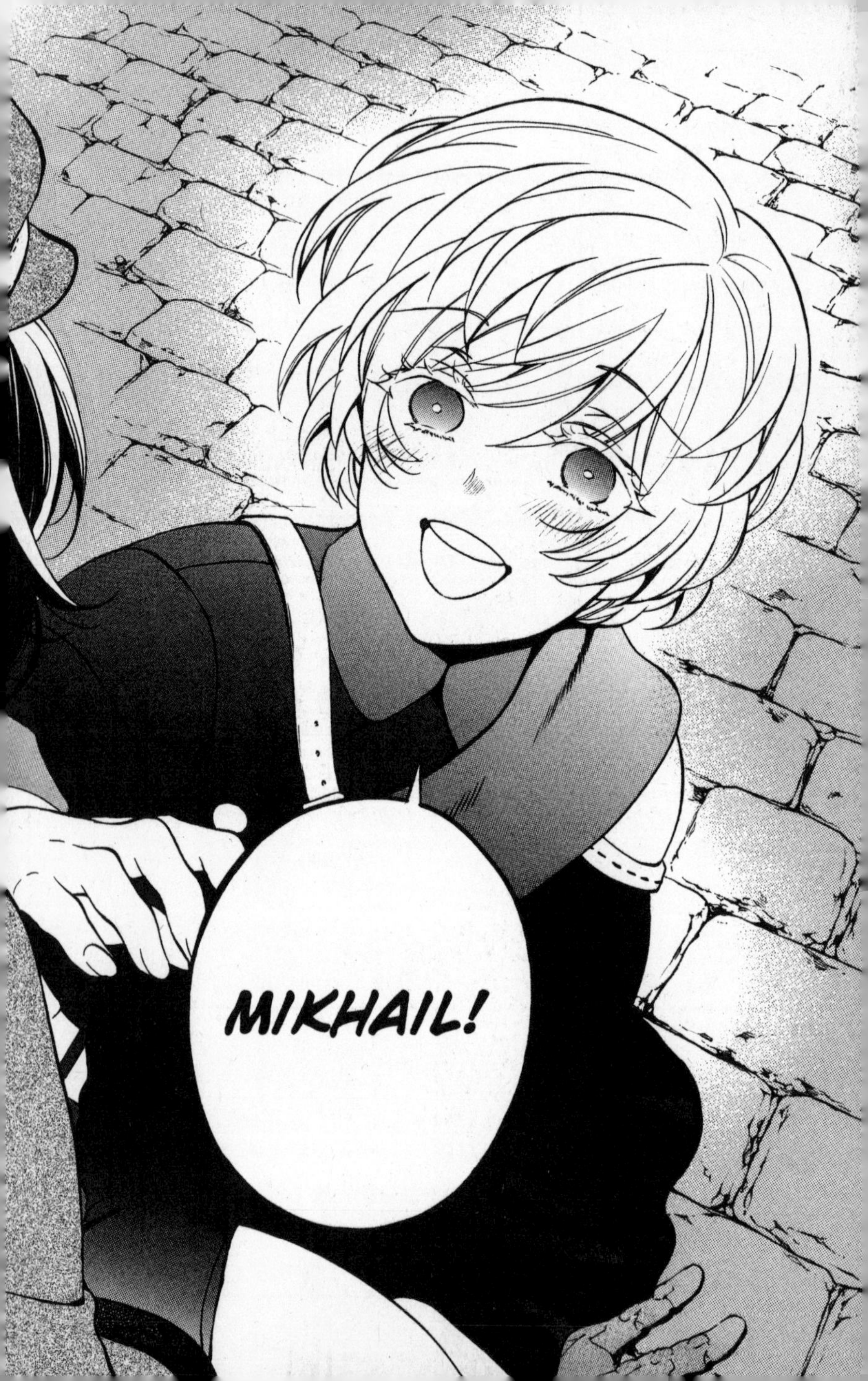
MIKHAIL!

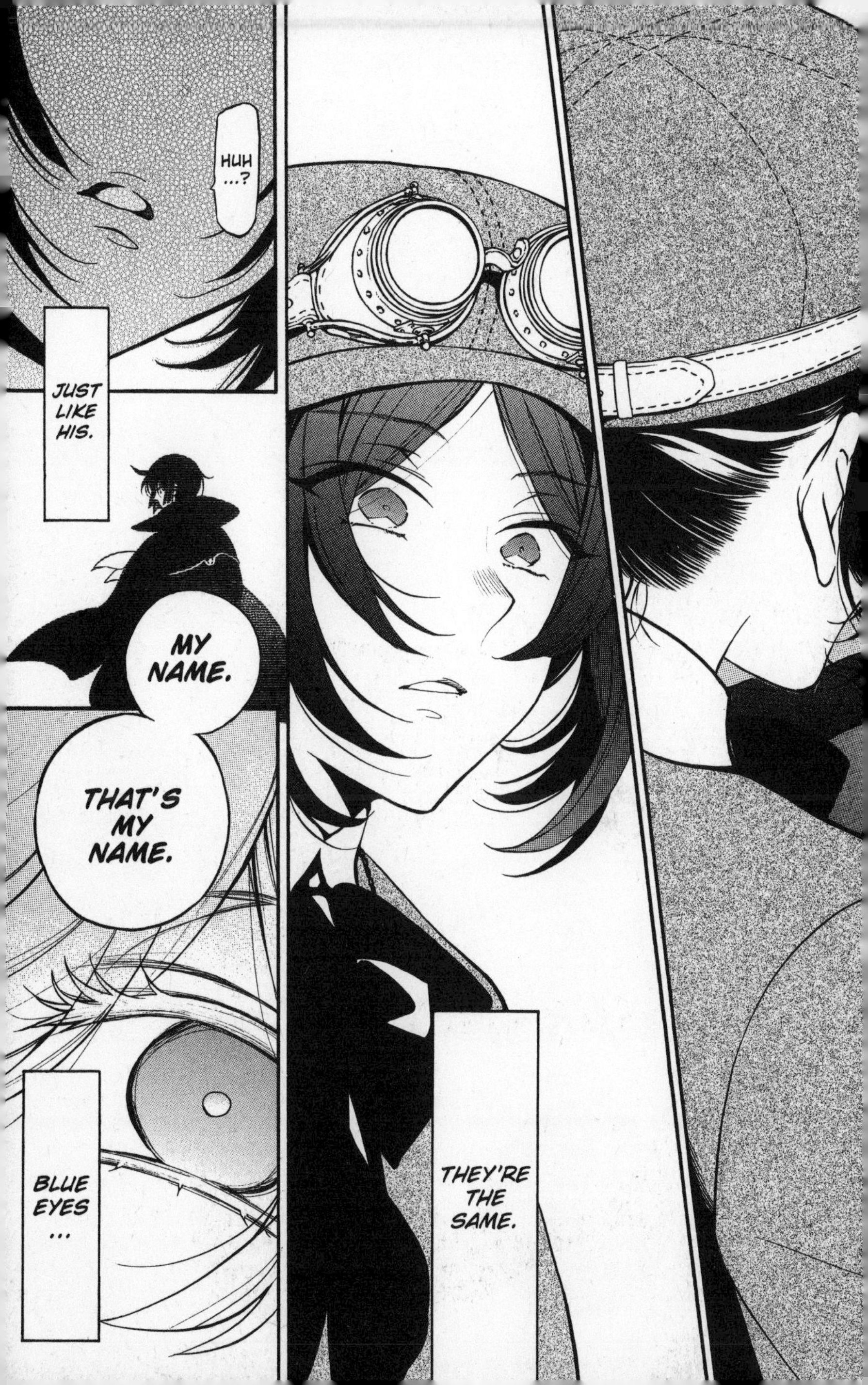
THEY'RE THE SAME.
HUH ...?
JUST LIKE HIS.
MY NAME.
THAT'S MY NAME.
BLUE EYES ...

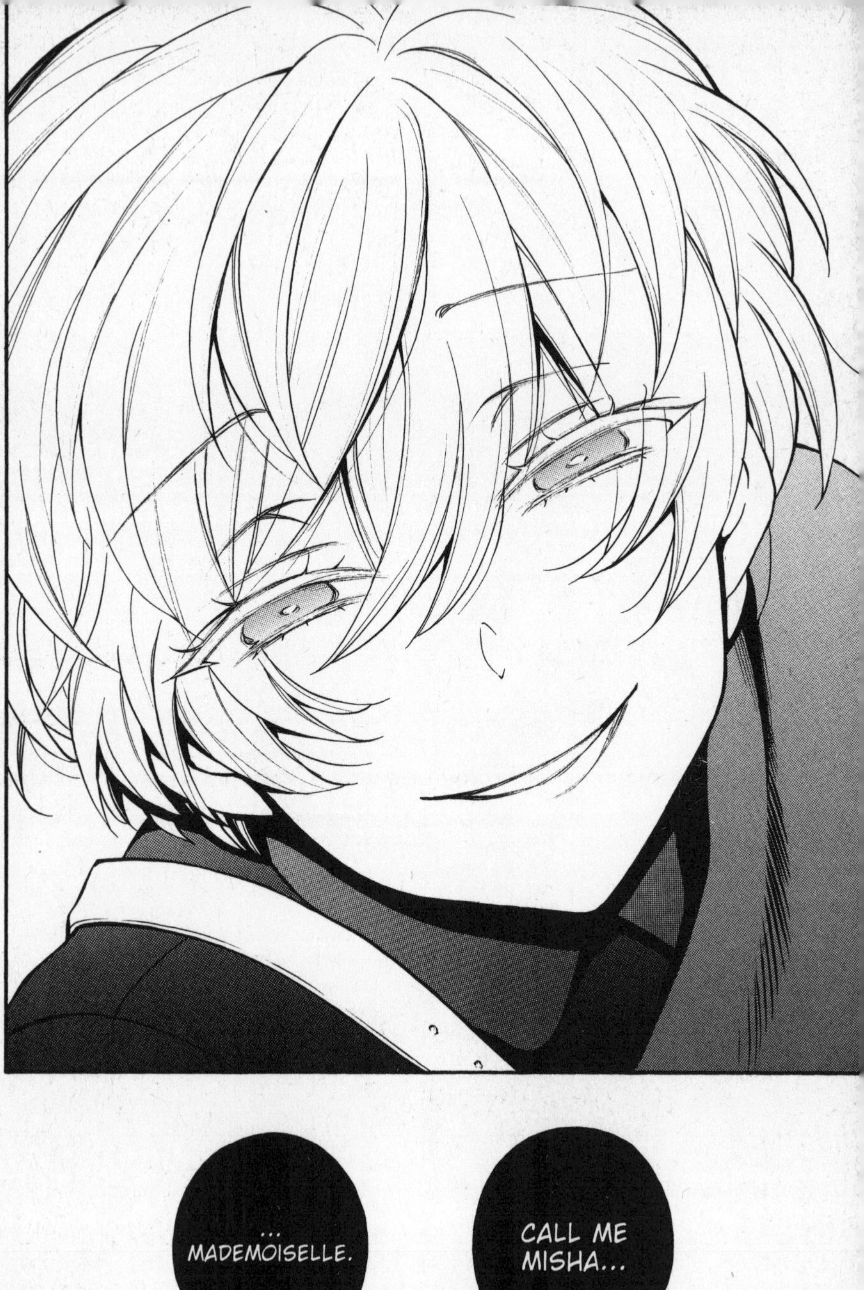
CALL ME MISHA...
... MADEMOISELLE.

THE CASE STUDY OF VANITAS 4 THE END

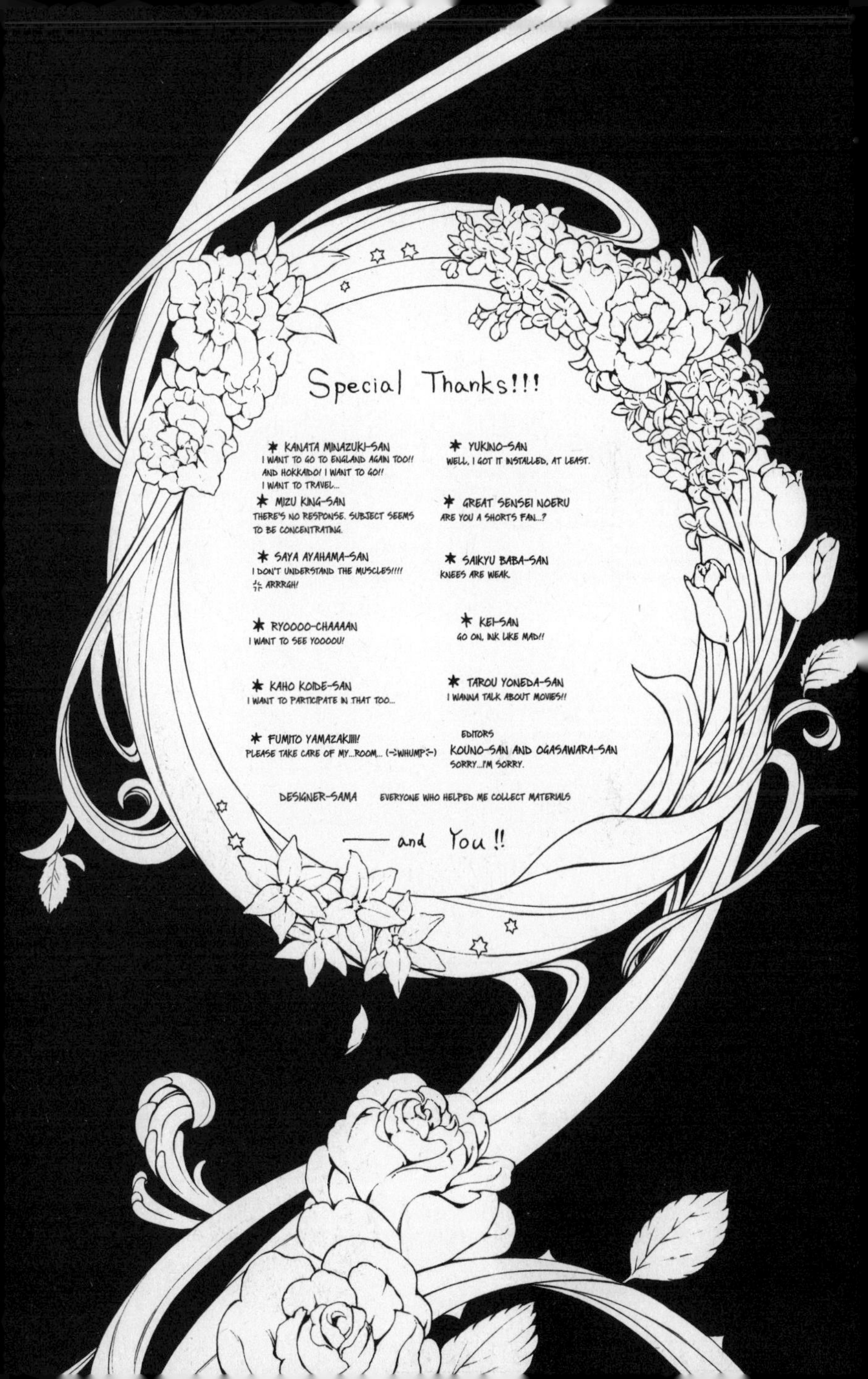
Special Thanks!!!
✱ KANATA MINAZUKI-SAN
I WANT TO GO TO ENGLAND AGAIN TOO!! AND HOKKAIDO! I WANT TO GO!! I WANT TO TRAVEL...
✱ YUKINO-SAN
WELL, I GOT IT INSTALLED, AT LEAST.
✱ MIZU KING-SAN
THERE'S NO RESPONSE. SUBJECT SEEMS TO BE CONCENTRATING.
✱ GREAT SENSEI NOERU
ARE YOU A SHORTS FAN...?
✱ SAYA AYAHAMA-SAN
I DON'T UNDERSTAND THE MUSCLES!!!! ARRRGH!
✱ SAIKYU BABA-SAN
KNEES ARE WEAK.
✱ RYOOOO-CHAAAAN
I WANT TO SEE YOOOOU!
✱ KEI-SAN
GO ON, INK LIKE MAD!!
✱ KAHO KOIDE-SAN
I WANT TO PARTICIPATE IN THAT TOO...
✱ TAROU YONEDA-SAN
I WANNA TALK ABOUT MOVIES!!
✱ FUMITO YAMAZAKIIII!
PLEASE TAKE CARE OF MY...ROOM... (=WHUMP=)
EDITORS
KOUNO-SAN AND OGASAWARA-SAN
SORRY...I'M SORRY.
DESIGNER-SAMA
EVERYONE WHO HELPED ME COLLECT MATERIALS
—and You!!

# Volume Preview

THEY OVERFLOW EQUALLY—

...AND THE LOATHSOME...

PRECIOUS FEELINGS...

...IMPULSE TO DRINK BLOOD...

*The Case Study of Vanitas* VOLUME 5

COMING SOON

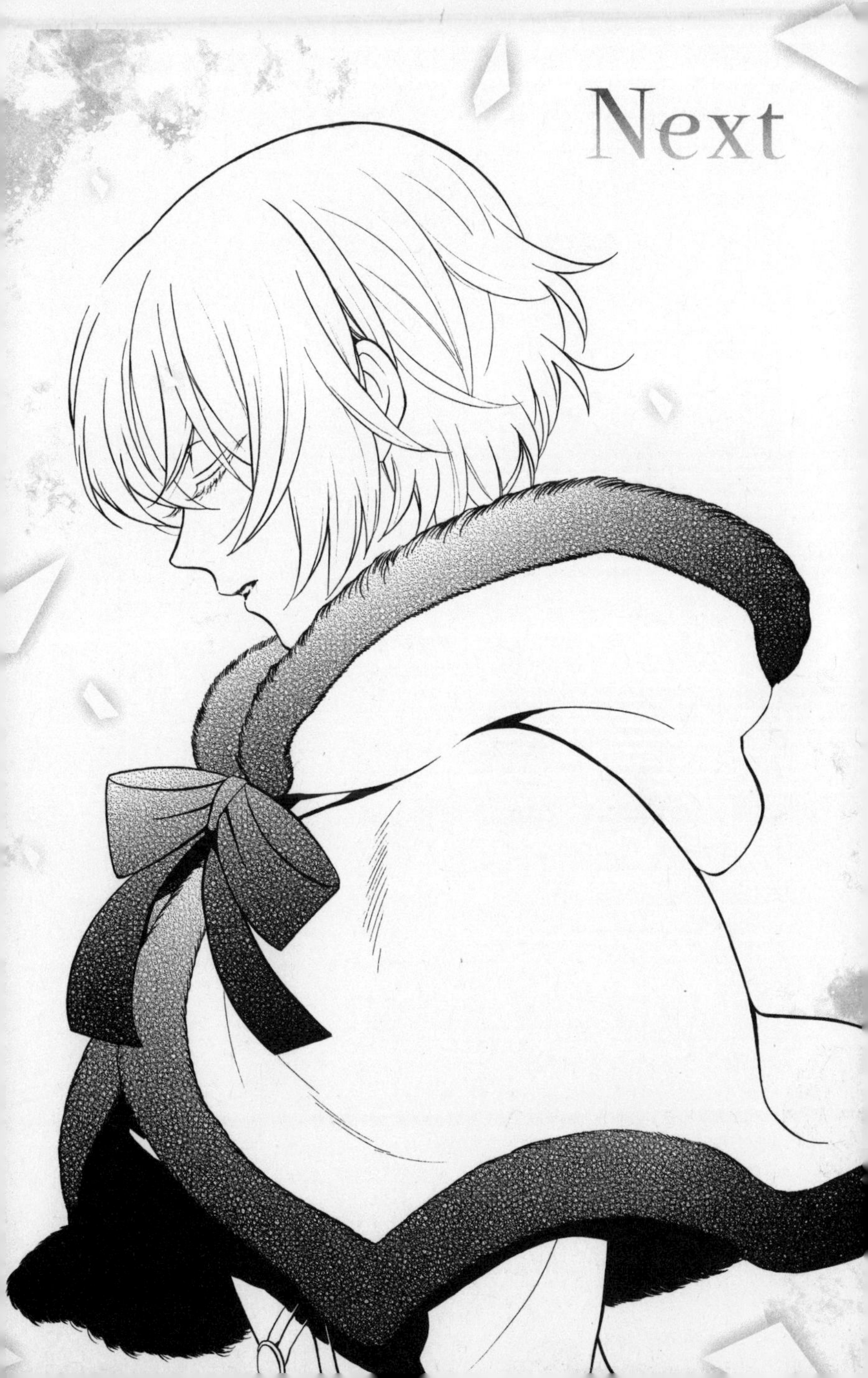
Next

THERE ARE NO BIG SPOILERS HERE, BUT IT MAY BE EASIER TO UNDERSTAND IF YOU READ THE BOOK FIRST.

VANITAS & NOÉ'S ROOM
(A GUEST ROOM AT HÔTEL CHOU CHOU)

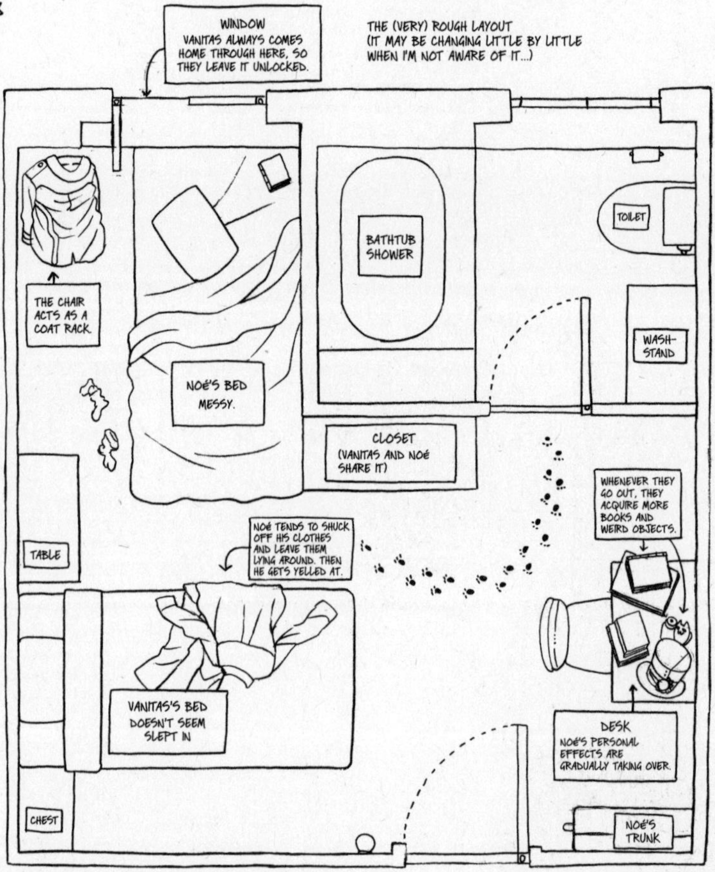

WINDOW
VANITAS ALWAYS COMES HOME THROUGH HERE, SO THEY LEAVE IT UNLOCKED.
THE (VERY) ROUGH LAYOUT
(IT MAY BE CHANGING LITTLE BY LITTLE WHEN I'M NOT AWARE OF IT...)
THE CHAIR ACTS AS A COAT RACK.
NOÉ'S BED
MESSY.
BATHTUB
SHOWER
TOILET
WASH-STAND
CLOSET
(VANITAS AND NOÉ SHARE IT)
TABLE
NOÉ TENDS TO SHUCK OFF HIS CLOTHES AND LEAVE THEM LYING AROUND. THEN HE GETS YELLED AT.
WHENEVER THEY GO OUT, THEY ACQUIRE MORE BOOKS AND WEIRD OBJECTS.
VANITAS'S BED
DOESN'T SEEM SLEPT IN
DESK
NOÉ'S PERSONAL EFFECTS ARE GRADUALLY TAKING OVER.
CHEST
NOÉ'S TRUNK


HÔTEL CHOU CHOU IS MANAGED BY VAMPIRES.

OVER HALF OF ITS GUESTS ARE APPARENTLY VAMPIRES TOO.

MOST VAMPIRES HAVE A SHARPER SENSE OF SMELL THAN HUMANS, SO THEY LIKE TO KEEP THINGS CLEAN AND NEAT AS A RULE.

FOR THAT REASON, MANY OF THE ROOMS AT HÔTEL CHOU CHOU ARE EQUIPPED WITH BATHTUBS/SHOWERS AND TOILETS, EVEN THOUGH IT'S UNUSUAL FOR THE TIME PERIOD.

EVER SINCE THE INCIDENT UNDERGROUND, VANITAS SEEMS TO COME BACK TO THE ROOM MORE OFTEN.

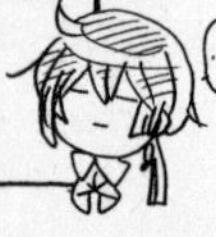

...


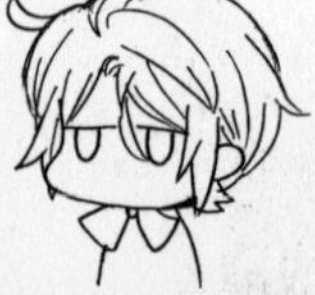

WHETHER HE LIKES THINGS CLEAN OR NOT...
...AND WHETHER HE CAN KEEP HIS ROOM TIDY OR NOT ARE DIFFERENT ISSUES.

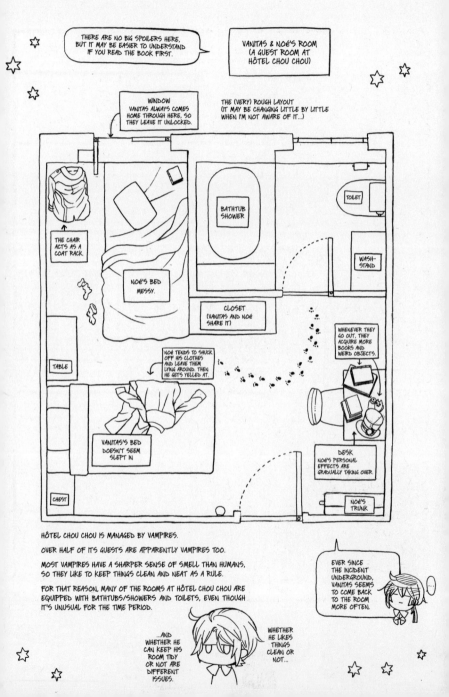

CURIOUS

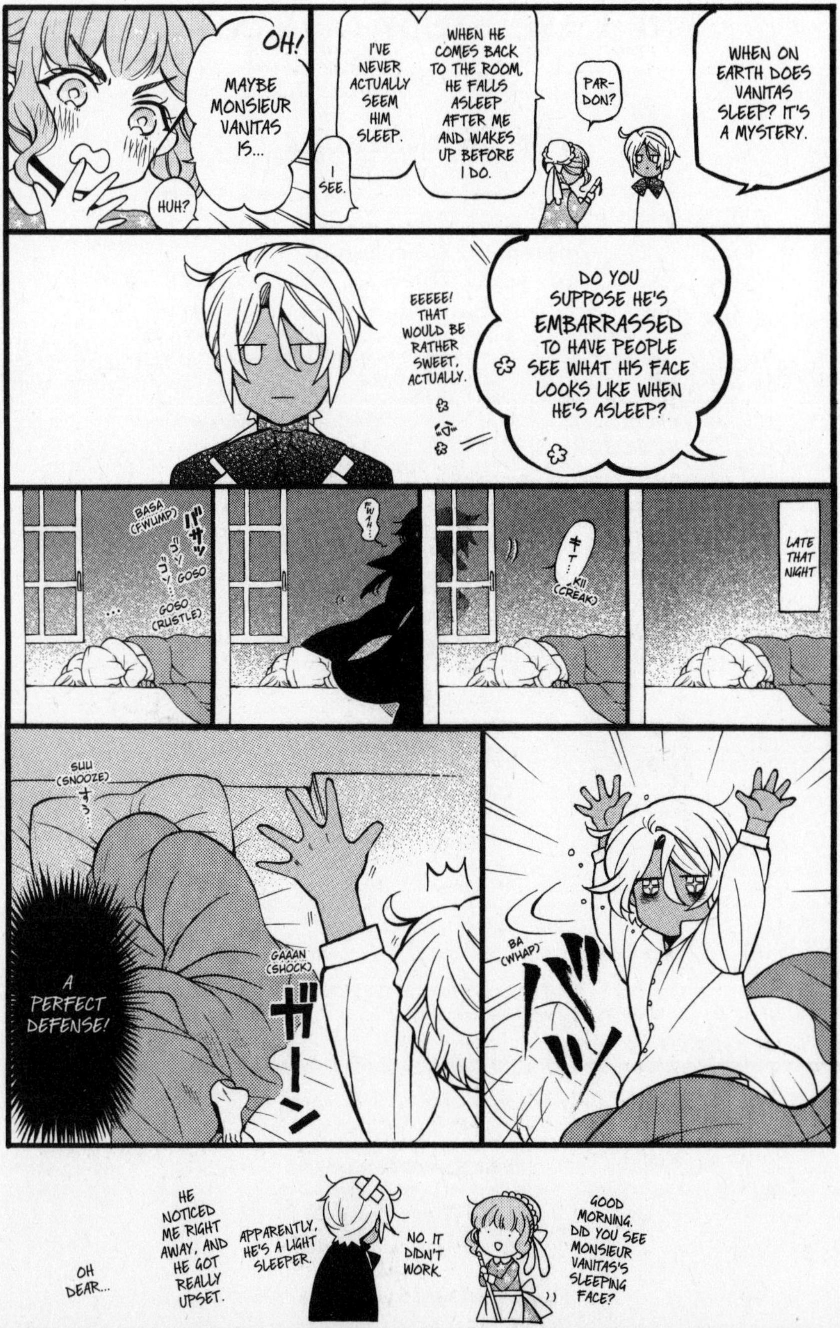
WHEN ON EARTH DOES VANITAS SLEEP? IT'S A MYSTERY.
PAR-DON?
WHEN HE COMES BACK TO THE ROOM, HE FALLS ASLEEP AFTER ME AND WAKES UP BEFORE I DO.
I'VE NEVER ACTUALLY SEEM HIM SLEEP.
I SEE.
OH!
MAYBE MONSIEUR VANITAS IS...
HUH?
DO YOU SUPPOSE HE'S EMBARRASSED TO HAVE PEOPLE SEE WHAT HIS FACE LOOKS LIKE WHEN HE'S ASLEEP?
EEEEE! THAT WOULD BE RATHER SWEET, ACTUALLY.
LATE THAT NIGHT
キ…
KII (CREAK)
FWAH...
BASA (FWUMP)
バサッ
ゴソ ゴソ
GOSO GOSO (RUSTLE)
...
BA (WHAP)
バッ
SUU (SNOOZE)
すう…
GAAAN (SHOCK)
ガーン
A PERFECT DEFENSE!
GOOD MORNING. DID YOU SEE MONSIEUR VANITAS'S SLEEPING FACE?
NO. IT DIDN'T WORK.
APPARENTLY, HE'S A LIGHT SLEEPER.
HE NOTICED ME RIGHT AWAY, AND HE GOT REALLY UPSET.
OH DEAR...

# THE CASE STUDY OF VANITAS
## VOLUME 4

## JUN MOCHIZUKI

### TRANSLATION: TAYLOR ENGEL
### LETTERING: BIANCA PISTILLO

Vanitas no Carte Volume 4 ©2017 Jun Mochizuki/SQUARE ENIX CO., LTD.
First published in Japan in 2017 by SQUARE ENIX CO., LTD. English translation rights arranged with SQUARE ENIX CO., LTD. and Yen Press, LLC through Tuttle-Mori Agency, Inc., Tokyo.

English translation ©2018 by SQUARE ENIX CO., LTD.

Yen Press
1290 Avenue of the Americas
New York, NY 10104

Visit us at yenpress.com
facebook.com/yenpress
twitter.com/yenpress
yenpress.tumblr.com
instagram.com/yenpress

First Yen Press Edition: August 2018
The chapters in this volume were originally published as ebooks by Yen Press.

Yen Press is an imprint of Yen Press, LLC.
The Yen Press name and logo are trademarks of Yen Press, LLC.

The publisher is not responsible for websites (or their content) that are not owned by the publisher.

Library of Congress Control Number: 2016946115

ISBNs: 978-1-9753-8106-6 (paperback)
978-1-9753-8107-3 (ebook)

10 9 8 7 6 5 4 3 2 1

WOR

Printed in the United States of America